Lexicon of Human Rights

Les définitions des droits de l'homme

Lexicon of Human Rights

Les définitions des droits de l'homme

By

Cédric Viale

MARTINUS
NIJHOFF
PUBLISHERS

LEIDEN • BOSTON
2008

This book is printed on acid-free paper.

Library of Congress Cataloging-in-Publication Data

Viale, Cédric, 1972-
Lexicon of human rights = Les définitions des droits de l'homme / by Cédric Viale.
p. cm.
ISBN 978-90-04-16584-7 (hardback : acid-free paper)
1. Human rights—Dictionaries. I. Title. II. Title: Définitions des droits de l'homme.

K3239.6.V53 2008
341.4'803—dc22

2008029424

ISBN 978 90 04 16584 7

PRINTED IN THE NETHERLANDS

Table of Contents

FOREWORD
By Yozo Yokota
Former Member, UN Sub-Commission on the Promotion and Protection of Human Rights vii

INTRODUCTION
By Cédric Viale, Ph.D. ix

ENGLISH

Definitions of human rights terms 1

Human rights themes 200

Relevant documents 250

FRANÇAIS

Les definitions des droits de l'homme 257

Les sujets des droits de l'homme 466

Les documents applicables 513

Foreword

By YOZO YOKOTA

Professor of International Law, Chuo Law School
Former Member, UN Sub-Commission on the Promotion and Protection of Human Rights
Member, ILO Committee of Experts on the Application of Conventions and Recommendations

This volume contains 430 terms often found in international human rights books, articles and instruments together with clear, authentic, objective and easily understandable definitions of them. As the author, Cédric Viale, suggests in his introduction, human rights are so fundamental and so important for everyone that all human rights documents should be understood by anyone, old or young, educated or uneducated, or expert or non-expert. Yet, many human rights conventions, declarations, instruments and volumes and papers are extremely hard to comprehend or are easily misunderstood because certain expressions and terms are not clearly defined, or are written in such a way that only those familiar with UN jargon can understand. This publication is a useful tool for those who face such difficulty in understanding UN human rights documents.

I have known Cédric for almost ten years. I first met him in the late 1990s when he came to the University of Tokyo, where I was teaching, to study the human rights of indigenous peoples, particularly the Ainu people living on the northern island of Hokkaido. He visited the Ainu community and wrote a very deep, analytical paper on the lives and the rights of those people. Later, he expanded his topic to the general study of indigenous people's rights and completed one of the most comprehensive studies of indigenous rights as a doctoral dissertation, submitted to, and accepted by, the University of Paris.

In the early 2000s, Cédric came to Geneva to observe deliberations taking place during the sessions of the Working Group on Indigenous Populations of the UN Sub-Commission on the Promotion and Protection of Human Rights. At that time, I was a member of the Working Group and Cédric assisted me most effectively and efficiently in research as well as in the preparation of my statements in French.

I am happy and honoured to write this foreword for Cédric, my former able student and assistant and now a respected fellow international human rights specialist.

I will certainly put this useful volume on my desk-whenever I am working on international human rights law.

Introduction

The importance of human rights is a fact that one does not need to prove. "Human rights" is a legal tool for some people, an inspiration for others. It represents an inalienable right and a rampart against barbarity for many. Students, diplomats, defendants, barristers, citizens, individuals, NGOs and other organizations – all call on "human rights" when they need to.

The interest and concern for human rights increases all the time. The number of texts and references adopted by countless organizations grows exponentially. But this growth does not necessarily lead to clearer understanding of the meaning of the concepts involved. Instead, human rights terminology is becoming more extended; sometimes more precise but often more complicated to comprehend.

Having attended the meetings of the United Nations, I believe that the number of mistakes used in human rights terminology is huge – whether among experts or interns, diplomats or translators, governments or NGOs, or even among UN officials. Wrong terms are frequently used instead of the correct ones. Lessons I have taught convince me that students, as well as their teachers, often do not fully understand even such simple basic notions as "human", "labour", "culture", etc.

It was for these reasons that I believed it might be constructive to prepare the present book in which I could offer the reader a lexicon of useful human rights definitions. Of course, such books already exist, but they are often incomprehensible for those who are not lawyers. They are usually prepared by scholars and sometimes they are just based on opinion.

Clarity of meaning, along with definitions commonly accepted by the greater part of the world's people: these were my objectives in seeking the correct definitions. I therefore turned to the texts of the United Nations and its agencies, since such documents are the result of agreements between states. These documents are edited by the UN and its various administrations – for instance, the Office of the Secretary General, and that of the High Commissioner of Human Rights.

The paper that I used as the main basis for my work was one of these documents. Its title is "Human Rights, a Compilation of International Instruments." This is a collection of 94 major texts and has more than 1,000 pages. It is a formidable reference to all aspects of international human rights and the UN. Its texts stem from the General Assembly, the Security Council, ECOSOC, UNESCO, ILO, as well as other agencies. The wealth and heterogeneity of the material was of vital assistance in providing clear definitions both in general and in detailed fields such as economic, social, cultural, civil and political rights, as well as terms which are associated with cultural diversity, administration of justice, etc.

I read this book of 94 texts many times. After each reading I extracted the most easily understandable definitions.

Those definitions have been classified here in alphabetical order, in separate English and French lists. In each language there is:

First, an alphabetical list of common terms with the equivalent second language term in square brackets. The list gives the exact detailed meaning followed by the source of each term;

Second, a lexicon of the same terms listed this time under such general themes as "colonialism", "culture", "crime against humanity", etc.

Third, there is a list of relevant UN documents which can be referenced for further information.

This structure should help readers to easily find the correct vocabulary to use in human rights discussions.

Cédric Viale, Ph.D.

Definitions of Human Rights Terms

ACCUSED [Personne accusée]

– "3. The accused shall be presumed innocent until proved guilty according to the provisions of the present Statute."

Art. 21, STATUTE OF THE INTERNATIONAL TRIBUNAL FOR THE PROSECUTION OF PERSONS RESPONSIBLE FOR SERIOUS VIOLATIONS OF INTERNATIONAL HUMANITARIAN LAW COMMITTED IN THE TERRITORY OF FORMER YUGOSLAVIA SINCE 1991.

Art. 20, STATUTE OF INTERNATIONAL CRIMINAL TRIBUNAL FOR THE PROSECUTION OF PERSONS RESPONSIBLE FOR GENOCIDE AND OTHER SERIOUS VIOLATIONS OF INTERNATIONAL HUMANITARIAN LAW COMMITTED IN THE TERRITORY OF RWANDA AND RWANDAN CITIZENS RESPONSIBLE FOR GENOCIDE AND OTHER SUCH VIOLATIONS COMMITTED IN THE TERRITORY OF NEIGHBOURING STATES, BETWEEN 1 JANUARY 1994 AND 31 DECEMBER 1994.

ACHIEVEMENTS OF THE DIFFERENT PEOPLES (DIFFERENCES BETWEEN THE) [Réalisations des différents peuples (les différences entre les)]

– "5. The differences between the achievements of the different peoples are entirely attributable to geographical, historical, political, economic, social and cultural factors. Such differences can in no case serve as a pretext for any rank-ordered classification of nations or peoples."

Art. 1, DECLARATION ON RACE AND RACIAL PREJUDICE.

ACT OF CORRUPTION [Acte de corruption]

– "(*c*) The expression 'act of corruption' referred to above should be understood to encompass attempted corruption."

Art. 7, *Commentary*, CODE OF CONDUCT FOR LAW ENFORCEMENT OFFICIALS.

ACT OF ENFORCED DISAPPEARANCE [Acte conduisant à une disparition forcée]

– "1 Any act of enforced disappearance is an offence to human dignity. [...]"
Article 1, DECLARATION ON THE PROTECTION OF ALL PERSONS FROM ENFORCED DISAPPEARANCE.

ACT OF TORTURE [Acte de torture]

– "55. The World Conference on Human Rights emphasizes that one of the most atrocious violations against human dignity is the act of torture, the result of which destroys the dignity and impairs the capability of victims to continue their lives and their activities."
II, VIENNA DECLARATION AND PROGRAMME OF ACTION.

ACTS, METHODS AND PRACTICES OF TERRORISM [Actes, méthodes et pratiques de terrorisme]

– "17. The acts, methods and practices of terrorism in all its forms and manifestations as well as linkage in some countries to drug trafficking are activities aimed at the destruction of human rights, fundamental freedoms and democracy, threatening territorial integrity, security of States and destabilizing legitimately constituted Governments. The international community should take the necessary steps to enhance cooperation to prevent and combat terrorism."
I, VIENNA DECLARATION AND PROGRAMME OF ACTION.

ACTS HARMFUL TO THE ENEMY (NOT BE CONSIDERED AS) [Actes nuisibles à l'ennemi (ne sont pas considérés comme)]

– "2. The following shall not be considered as acts harmful to the enemy:

(*a*) That civil defence tasks are carried out under the direction or control of military authorities;

(*b*) That civilian civil defence personnel co-operate with military personnel in the performance of civil defence tasks, or that some military personnel are attached to civilian civil defence organizations;

(*c*) That the performance of civil defence tasks may incidentally benefit military victims, particularly those who are hors de combat.

3. It shall also not be considered as an act harmful to the enemy that civilian defence personnel bear light individual weapons for the purpose of maintaining order or for self-defence. However, in areas where land fighting it taking place or is likely to take place, the Parties to the conflict shall undertake the appropriate measures to limit these weapons to handguns, such as pistols or revolvers, in order to assist in distinguishing between civil defence personnel and combatants. Although civil defence personnel bear other light individual weapons in such areas, they shall nevertheless be respected and protected as soon as they have been recognized as such. "

Art. 65, PROTOCOL ADDITIONAL TO THE GENEVA CONVENTIONS OF 12 AUGUST 1949, AND RELATING TO THE PROTECTION OF VICTIMS OF INTERNATIONAL ARMED CONFLICTS (PROTOCOL I).

ADJUDICATING AUTHORITY [Autorité judiciaire]

– "It is difficult to formulate a definition of the competent body or person that would universally describe an adjudicating authority. [...]"

14, *Commentary*, s.p. 1, UNITED NATIONS STANDARD MINIMUM RULES FOR THE ADMINISTRATION OF JUVENILE JUSTICE ("THE BEIJING RULES").

ADOPTION [Parents adoptifs]

– "14. [...] alternative placements including foster care and adoption [...]"[A]

UNITED NATIONS GUIDELINES FOR THE PREVENTION OF JUVENILE DELINQUENCY (THE RIYADH GUIDELINES).

ADVERSE DISTINCTION [Distinction de caractère défavorable]

– "1. This Protocol shall be applied without any adverse distinction founded on race, colour, sex, language, religion or belief, political or other opinion, national or social origin, wealth, birth or other status, or on any other similar criteria [...]"

Art. 2, PROTOCOL ADDITIONAL TO THE GENEVA CONVENTIONS OF 12 AUGUST 1949, AND RELATING TO THE PROTECTION OF VICTIMS OF NON-INTERNATIONAL ARMED CONFLICTS (PROTOCOL II).

[A] « [...] des foyers de substitution (parents nourriciers ou adoptifs) [...] »

AFRICA [Afrique]

– “8. Noting with grave concern that Africa, in particular sub-Saharan Africa, is currently the worst-affected region, where HIV/AIDS is considered a state of emergency which threatens development, social cohesion, political stability, food security and life expectancy and imposes a devastating economic burden, and that the dramatic situation on the continent needs urgent and exceptional national, regional and international action;”

DECLARATION OF COMMITMENT ON HIV/AIDS.

AFTER-CARE (RELEASED PRISONER EFFICIENT) [Aide postpénitentiaire (efficace au détenu libéré)]

– “64. The duty of society does not end with a prisoner’s release. There should, therefore, be governmental or private agencies capable of lending the released prisoner efficient after-care directed towards the lessening of prejudice against him and towards his social rehabilitation.”

STANDARD MINIMUM RULES FOR THE TREATMENT OF PRISONERS.

AGGRESSION, FOREIGN OCCUPATION AND DOMINATION AND INTERFERENCE IN THE INTERNAL AFFAIRS OF STATES (ERADICATION OF) [Agression, d’occupation et de domination étrangères et d’ingérence dans les affaires intérieures des Etats (élimination d’)]

– “*Emphasizing* that the eradication of *apartheid*, all forms of racism, racial discrimination, colonialism, neo-colonialism, aggression, foreign occupation and domination and interference in the internal affairs of States is essential to the full enjoyment of the rights of men and women,”

Pp. 10, CONVENTION ON THE ELIMINATION OF ALL FORMS OF DISCRIMINATION AGAINST WOMEN.

ALCOHOL [Alcool]

– “25. [...] Information on the use and abuse of drugs, including alcohol, should be made available to the student body.”

UNITED NATIONS GUIDELINES FOR THE PREVENTION OF JUVENILE DELINQUENCY (THE RIYADH GUIDELINES).

ALCOHOLISM [Alcoolisme]

– "(*o*) Serious cases of chronic intoxication, for example: lead poisoning, mercury poisoning, morphinism, cocainism, alcoholism; gas or radiation poisoning; etc."

Annex I, 3, GENEVA CONVENTION RELATIVE TO THE TREATMENT OF PRISONERS OF WAR.

ALIEN [Etranger]

– "For the purposes of this Declaration, the term 'alien' shall apply, with due regard to qualifications made in subsequent articles, to any individual who is not a national of the State in which he or she is present."

Art. 1, DECLARATION ON THE HUMAN RIGHTS OF INDIVIDUALS WHO ARE NOT NATIONALS OF THE COUNTRY IN WHICH THEY LIVE.

ALL FORMS OF VIOLENCE AGAINST WOMEN AND GIRLS [Toutes les formes de violence contre les femmes et les filles]

– "61. [...] all forms of violence against women and girls, including harmful traditional and customary practices, abuse, rape and other forms of sexual violence, battering and trafficking in women and girls;"

DECLARATION OF COMMITMENT ON HIV/AIDS.

AMOEBIC OR BACILLARY DYSENTERY WITH GRAVE DISORDERS [Dysenterie amibienne ou bacillaire avec troubles considérables]

– "(s) Serious chronic infectious diseases, persisting for one year after their inception, for example: malaria with decided organic impairment, amoebic or bacillary dysentery with grave disorders; tertiary visceral syphilis resistant to treatment; leprosy; etc."

Annex I, 3, GENEVA CONVENTION RELATIVE TO THE TREATMENT OF PRISONERS OF WAR.

APARTHEID [Apartheid]

– "*Noting* with the gravest concern that racism, racial discrimination, colonialism and *apartheid* continue to afflict the world in ever-changing forms, as a result both of the continuation of legislative provisions and government and administrative practices contrary to the principles of human rights and also of the continued existence of political and social structures, and of relationships and attitudes, characterized by injustice and contempt for human beings and leading to the exclusion, humiliation and exploitation, or to the forced assimilation, of the members of disadvantaged groups,"

Pp. 12, DECLARATION ON RACE AND RACIAL PREJUDICE.

– "2. One of the most serious violations of this principle is represented by *apartheid*, which, like genocide, is a crime against humanity, and gravely disturbs international peace and security."

Art. 4, DECLARATION ON RACE AND RACIAL PREJUDICE.

APARTHEID (ERADICATION OF) [Apartheid (élimination de l')]

– "19. The World Conference on Human Rights considers the elimination of racism and racial discrimination, in particular in their institutionalized forms such as apartheid or resulting from doctrines of racial superiority or exclusivity or contemporary forms and manifestations of racism, as a primary objective for the international community and a worldwide promotion programme in the field of human rights. [...]"

II, VIENNA DECLARATION AND PROGRAM OF ACTION.

– "*Emphasizing* that the eradication of apartheid, all forms of racism, racial discrimination, colonialism, neo-colonialism, aggression, foreign occupation and domination and interference in the internal affairs of States is essential to the full enjoyment of the rights of men and women,"

Pp. 10, CONVENTION ON THE ELIMINATION OF ALL FORMS OF DISCRIMINATION AGAINST WOMEN.

APPROPRIATE AUTHORITIES OR ORGANS VESTED WITH REVIEWING OR REMEDIAL POWER [Autorités ou instances de contrôle ou de recours compétentes]

– "(*c*) The term 'appropriate authorities or organs vested with reviewing or remedial power' refers to any authority or organ existing under national law, whether internal to the law enforcement agency or independent thereof, with statutory, customary or other power to review grievances and complaints arising out of violations within the purview of this Code."

Art. 8, *Commentary*, CODE OF CONDUCT FOR LAW ENFORCEMENT OFFICIALS.

ARMED CONFLICT [Conflit armé]

– "(*c*) In case of an armed conflict not of an international character [...]"
Art. 8, paragraph 2, ROME STATUTE OF THE INTERNATIONAL CRIMINAL COURT.

– "In addition to the provisions which shall be implemented in peace time, the present Convention shall apply to all cases of declared war or of any other armed conflict which may arise between two or more of the High Contracting Parties, even if the state of war is not recognized by one of them."
Art. 2, s.p. 1, GENEVA CONVENTION RELATIVE TO THE TREATMENT OF PRISONERS OF WAR.

– "In the case of armed conflict not of an international character [...]"
Art. 3, s.p. 1, GENEVA CONVENTION RELATIVE TO THE TREATMENT OF PRISONERS OF WAR.

ARMED CONFLICTS [Conflits armés]

– "12. Noting that armed conflicts and natural disasters also exacerbate the spread of the epidemic;"
DECLARATION OF COMMITMENT ON HIV/AIDS.

– "(e) Other serious violations of the laws and customs applicable in armed conflicts not of an international character, within the established framework of international law, namely, any of the following acts:

(i) Intentionally directing attacks against the civilian population as such or against individual civilians not taking direct part in hostilities;

(ii) Intentionally directing attacks against buildings, material, medical units and transport, and personnel using the distinctive emblems of the Geneva Conventions in conformity with international law;

(iii) Intentionally directing attacks against personnel, installations, material, units or vehicles involved in a humanitarian assistance or peacekeeping mission in accordance with the Charter of the United Nations, as long as they are entitled to the protection given to civilians or civilian objects under the international law of armed conflict;

(iv) Intentionally directing attacks against buildings dedicated to religion, education, art, science or charitable purposes, historic monuments, hospitals and places where the sick and wounded are collected, provided they are not military objectives;

(v) Pillaging a town or place, even when taken by assault;

(vi) Committing rape, sexual slavery, enforced prostitution, forced pregnancy, as defined in article 7, paragraph 2 (f)[1], enforced sterilization, and any other form of sexual violence also constituting a serious violation of article 3 common to the four Geneva Conventions[2];

(vii) Conscripting or enlisting children under the age of fifteen years into armed forces or groups or using them to participate actively in hostilities;

(viii) Ordering the displacement of the civilian population for reasons related to the conflict, unless the security of the civilians involved or imperative military reasons so demand;

(ix) Killing or wounding treacherously a combatant adversary;

---

[1] "'Forced pregnancy' means the unlawful confinement of a woman forcibly made pregnant, with the intent of affecting the ethnic composition of any population or carrying out other grave violations of international law. This definition shall not in any way be interpreted as affecting national laws relating to pregnancy;"

[2] "In the case of armed conflict not of an international character occurring in the territory of one of the High Contracting Parties, each Party to the conflict shall be bound to apply, as a minimum, the following provisions:
1. Persons taking no active part in the hostilities, including members of armed forces who have laid down their arms and those placed hors de combat by sickness, wounds, detention, or any other cause, shall in all circumstances be treated humanely, without any adverse distinction founded on race, colour, religion or faith, sex, birth or wealth, or any other similar criteria.
To this end, the following acts are and shall remain prohibited at any time and in any place whatsoever with respect to the above-mentioned persons:
(a) Violence to life and person, in particular murder of all kinds, mutilation, cruel treatment and torture;
(b) Taking of hostages;
(c) Outrages upon personal dignity, in particular humiliating and degrading treatment;
(d) The passing of sentences and the carrying out of executions without previous judgment pronounced by a regularly constituted court, affording all the judicial guarantees which are recognized as indispensable by civilized peoples.
2. The wounded and sick shall be collected and cared for.
An impartial humanitarian body, such as the International Committee of the Red Cross, may offer its services to the Parties to the conflict.
The Parties to the conflict should further endeavour to bring into force, by means of special agreements, all or part of the other provisions of the present Convention.
The application of the preceding provisions shall not affect the legal status of the Parties to the conflict."

(x) Declaring that no quarter will be given;

(xi) Subjecting persons who are in the power of another party to the conflict to physical mutilation or to medical or scientific experiments of any kind which are neither justified by the medical, dental or hospital treatment of the person concerned nor carried out in his or her interest, and which cause death to or seriously endanger the health of such person or persons;

(xii) Destroying or seizing the property of an adversary unless such destruction or seizure be imperatively demanded by the necessities of the conflict;

Art. 8, paragraph 2, ROME STATUTE OF THE INTERNATIONAL CRIMINAL COURT.

ARMED FORCES [Forces armées]

– "1. The armed forces of a Party to a conflict consist of all organized armed forces, groups and units which are under a command responsible to that Party for the conduct of its subordinates, even if that Party is represented by a government or an authority not recognized by an adverse Party. Such armed forces shall be subject to an internal disciplinary system which, inter alia, shall enforce compliance with the rules of international law applicable in armed conflict."

Art. 43, PROTOCOL ADDITIONAL TO THE GENEVA CONVENTIONS OF 12 AUGUST 1949, AND RELATING TO THE PROTECTION OF VICTIMS OF INTERNATIONAL ARMED CONFLICTS (PROTOCOL I).

ARMED FORCES OF A STATE [Forces armées d'un Etat]

– "1. Armed groups that are distinct from the armed forces of a State should not, under any circumstances, recruit or use in hostilities persons under the age of 18 years."

Art. 4, OPTIONAL PROTOCOL TO THE CONVENTION ON THE RIGHTS OF THE CHILD ON THE INVOLVEMENT OF CHILDREN IN ARMED CONFLICT.

ARREST [Arrestation]

– "For the purposes of the Body of Principles:

(*a*) 'Arrest' means the act of apprehending a person for the alleged commission of an offence or by the action of an authority;"

Use of terms, BODY OF PRINCIPLES FOR THE PROTECTION OF ALL PERSONS UNDER ANY FORM OF DETENTION OR IMPRISONMENT.

ARTHRITIS DEFORMANS [Arthroses déformantes]

– "(*p*) Chronic affections of locomotion, with obvious functional disorders, for example: arthritis deformans, primary and secondary progressive chronic polyarthritis; rheumatism with serious clinical symptoms; etc."

Annex I, 3, GENEVA CONVENTION RELATIVE TO THE TREATMENT OF PRISONERS OF WAR.

ASIA-PACIFIC REGION [Asie et du Pacifique (région de l')]

– "10. Recognizing also that other regions are seriously affected and confront similar threats, particularly the Caribbean region, with the second-highest rate of HIV infection after sub-Saharan Africa, the Asia-Pacific region where 7.5 million people living are already living with HIV/AIDS, the Latin American region with 1.5 million people living with HIV/AIDS and the Central and Eastern European region with very rapidly rising infection rates, and that the potential exists for a rapid escalation of the epidemic and its impact throughout the world if no specific measures are taken;"

DECLARATION OF COMMITMENT ON HIV/AIDS.

ATTACK DIRECTED AGAINST ANY CIVILIAN POPULATION [Attaque lancée contre une population civile]

– "2. For the purpose of paragraph 1:

(*a*) 'Attack directed against any civilian population' means a course of conduct involving the multiple commission of acts referred to in paragraph 1[3] against any civilian population, pursuant to or in furtherance of a State or organizational policy to commit such attack;"

---

[3] "1. For the purpose of this Statute, 'crime against humanity' means any of the following acts when committed as part of a widespread or systematic attack directed against any civilian population, with knowledge of the attack:

(a) Murder;
(b) Extermination ;
(c) Enslavement;
(d) Deportation or forcible transfer of population;
(e) Imprisonment or other severe deprivation of physical liberty in violation of fundamental rules of international law;
(f) Torture;
(g) Rape, sexual slavery, enforced prostitution, forced pregnancy, enforced sterilization, or any other form of sexual violence of comparable gravity;
(h) Persecution against any identifiable group or collectivity on political, racial, national, ethnic, cultural, religious, gender, as defined in paragraph 3, or other grounds that are

Art. 7, ROME STATUTE OF THE INTERNATIONAL CRIMINAL COURT.

ATTACKS [Attaques]

– "1. 'Attacks' means acts of violence against the adversary, whether in offence or in defence."

Art. 49, PROTOCOL ADDITIONAL TO THE GENEVA CONVENTIONS OF 12 AUGUST 1949, AND RELATING TO THE PROTECTION OF VICTIMS OF INTERNATIONAL ARMED CONFLICTS (PROTOCOL I).

AUTHORITIES COMPETENT FOR DISPOSITION [Autorités compétentes pour prendre une décision]

– "The authorities competent for disposition may be persons with very different backgrounds (magistrates in the United Kingdom of Great Britain and Northern Ireland and in regions influenced by the common law system; legally trained judges in countries using Roman law and in regions influenced by them; and elsewhere elected or appointed laymen or jurists, members of community-based boards, etc.). For all these authorities, a minimum training in law, sociology, psychology, criminology and behavioural sciences would be required. This is considered as important as the organizational specialization and independence of the competent authority."

22, *Commentary*, s.p. 1, UNITED NATIONS STANDARD MINIMUM RULES FOR THE ADMINISTRATION OF JUVENILE JUSTICE ("THE BEIJING RULES").

AVOID HARM [Eviter de [lui] nuire]

– "Rule 10.3[4] deals with some fundamental aspects of the procedures and behaviour on the part of the police and other law enforcement officials in cases of juvenile crime. To 'avoid harm' admittedly is flexible wording and covers many features of possible interaction (for example the use of harsh language, physical violence or exposure to the environment).

---

universally recognized as impermissible under international law, in connection with any act referred to in this paragraph or any crime within the jurisdiction of the Court;

(i) Enforced disappearance of persons;

(j) The crime of apartheid;

(k) Other inhumane acts of a similar character intentionally causing great suffering, or serious injury to body or to mental or physical health."

[4] "10.3 Contacts between the law enforcement agencies and a juvenile offender shall be managed in such a way as to respect the legal status of the juvenile, promote the well-being of juvenile and avoid harm to her or him, with due regard to the circumstances of case."

Involvement in juvenile justice processes in itself can be 'harmful' to juveniles; the term 'avoid harm' should be broadly interpreted, therefore, as doing the least harm possible to the juvenile in the first instance, as well as any additional or undue harm. This is especially important in the initial contact with law enforcement agencies, which might profoundly influence the juvenile's attitude towards the State and society. Moreover, the success of any further intervention is largely dependent on such initial contacts. Compassion and kind firmness are important in these situations."

10, *Commentary*, s.p. 3, UNITED NATIONS STANDARD MINIMUM RULES FOR THE ADMINISTRATION OF JUVENILE JUSTICE ("THE BEIJING RULES").

BELIEF [Conviction]

– "*Considering* that religion or belief, for anyone who professes either, is one of the fundamental elements in his conception of life and that freedom of religion or belief should be fully respected and guaranteed,"

Pp. 4, DECLARATION ON THE ELIMINATION OF ALL FORMS OF INTOLERANCE AND OF DISCRIMINATION BASED ON RELIGION OR BELIEF.

BLINDNESS OF BOTH EYES OR OF ONE EYE [Cécité des deux yeux ou celle d'un œil]

– "(*i*) Blindness of both eyes, or of one eye when the vision of the other is less than I in spite of the use of corrective glasses; diminution of visual acuity in cases where it is impossible to restore it by correction to an acuity of 1/2 in at least one eye; other grave ocular affections, for example: glaucoma, iritis, choroiditis; trachoma, etc."

Annex I, 3, GENEVA CONVENTION RELATIVE TO THE TREATMENT OF PRISONERS OF WAR.

BRONCHIECTASIS [Bronchectasie]

– "(*c*) Serious diseases of the respiratory organs of non-tubercular etiology, presumed incurable. for example: serious pulmonary emphysema, with or without bronchitis, chronic asthma: chronic bronchitis lasting more than one year in captivity; bronchiectasis, etc."

Annex I, 3, GENEVA CONVENTION RELATIVE TO THE TREATMENT OF PRISONERS OF WAR.

CARIBBEAN REGION [Caraïbes (Région des)]

– "10. Recognizing also that other regions are seriously affected and confront similar threats, particularly the Caribbean region, with the second-highest rate of HIV infection after sub-Saharan Africa, the Asia-Pacific region where 7.5 million people living are already living with HIV/AID, the Latin American region with 1.5 million people living with HIV/AIDS and the Central and Eastern European region with very rapidly rising infection rates, and that the potential exists for a rapid escalation of the epidemic and its impact throughout the world if no specific measures are taken;"

DECLARATION OF COMMITMENT ON HIV/AIDS.

CENTRAL AND EASTERN EUROPEAN REGION [Europe centrale et orientale (Région de l')]

– "10. Recognizing also that other regions are seriously affected and confront similar threats, particularly the Caribbean region, with the second-highest rate of HIV infection after sub-Saharan Africa, the Asia-Pacific region where 7.5 million people living are already living with HIV/AID, the Latin American region with 1.5 million people living with HIV/AIDS and the Central and Eastern European region with very rapidly rising infection rates, and that the potential exists for a rapid escalation of the epidemic and its impact throughout the world if no specific measures are taken;"

DECLARATION OF COMMITMENT ON HIV/AIDS.

CERTAIN CUSTOMS, ANCIENT LAWS AND PRACTICES RELATING TO MARRIAGE AND FAMILY [Certaines coutumes, anciennes lois et pratiques intéressant le mariage et la famille]

– "*Recalling further* that all the General Assembly of the United Nations declared, by resolution 843 (IX) of 17 December 1954, that certain customs, ancient laws and practices relating to marriage and the family were inconsistent with the principles set forth in the Charter of the United Nations and in the Universal Declaration of Human Rights,"

Pp. 3, CONVENTION ON CONSENT TO MARRIAGE, MINIMUM AGE FOR MARRIAGE AND REGISTRATION OF MARRIAGES.

CHILD [Enfant ; Enfants]

– "*Bearing in mind* that, as indicated in the Declaration of the Rights of the Child, 'the child, by reason of his physical and mental immaturity, needs special safeguards and care, including appropriate legal protection, before as well as after birth',"

Pp. 9, CONVENTION ON THE RIGHTS OF THE CHILD.

– "For the purposes of the present Convention, a child means every human being below the age of eighteen years unless under the law applicable to the child, majority is attained earlier."

Art. 1, CONVENTION ON THE RIGHTS OF THE CHILD.

– "*Noting* that article 1 of the Convention on the Rights of the Child specifies that, for the purposes of that Convention, a child means every human being below the age of 18 years unless, under the law applicable to the child, majority is attained earlier;"

Pp. 7, OPTIONAL PROTOCOL TO THE CONVENTION ON THE RIGHTS OF THE CHILD ON THE INVOLVEMENT OF CHILDREN IN ARMED CONFLICT.

– "For the purposes of the Convention, the term 'child' shall apply to all persons under the age of 18."

Art. 2, WORST FORMS OF CHILD LABOUR CONVENTION (N°182).

– "For the purposes of this Protocol:
[...]
(*d*) 'Child' shall mean any person under eighteen years of age."

Art. 3, PROTOCOL TO PREVENT, SUPPRESS AND PUNISH TRAFFICKING IN PERSONS ESPECIALLY WOMEN AND CHILDREN, SUPPLEMENTING THE UNITED NATIONS CONVENTION AGAINST TRANSNATIONAL ORGANIZED CRIME.

CHILD LABOUR [Travail des enfants]

– "*Recognizing* that child labour is to a great extent caused by poverty and that the long-term solution lies in sustained economic growth leading to social progress, in particular poverty alleviation and universal education, [...]"

Pp. 5, WORST FORMS OF CHILD LABOUR CONVENTION (N°182).

CHILD PORNOGRAPHY [Pornographie mettant en scène des enfants]

– "*Believing* that the elimination of the sale of children, child prostitution and child pornography will be facilitated by adopting a holistic approach, addressing the contributing factors, including underdevelopment, poverty, economic disparities, inequitable socio-economic structure, dys-functioning families, lack of education, urban-rural migration, gender discrimination, irresponsible adult sexual behaviour, harmful traditional practices, armed conflicts and trafficking in children,"

Pp. 7, OPTIONAL PROTOCOL TO THE CONVENTION ON THE RIGHTS OF THE CHILD ON THE SALE OF CHILDREN, CHILD PROSTITUTION AND CHILD PORNOGRAPHY.

– "For the purposes of the present Protocol:

[...]

(*c*) Child pornography means any representation, by whatever means, of a child engaged in real or simulated explicit sexual activities or any representation of the sexual parts of a child for primarily sexual purposes."

Art. 2, OPTIONAL PROTOCOL TO THE CONVENTION ON THE RIGHTS OF THE CHILD ON THE SALE OF CHILDREN, CHILD PROSTITUTION AND CHILD PORNOGRAPHY.

CHILD PROSTITUTION [Prostitution des enfants]

– "*Believing* that the elimination of the sale of children, child prostitution and child pornography will be facilitated by adopting a holistic approach, addressing the contributing factors, including underdevelopment, poverty, economic disparities, inequitable socio-economic structure, dysfunctioning families, lack of education, urban-rural migration, gender discrimination, irresponsible adult sexual behaviour, harmful traditional practices, armed conflicts and trafficking in children,"

Pp. 7, OPTIONAL PROTOCOL TO THE CONVENTION ON THE RIGHTS OF THE CHILD ON THE SALE OF CHILDREN, CHILD PROSTITUTION AND CHILD PORNOGRAPHY.

– "For the purposes of the present Protocol:

[...]

(*b*) Child prostitution means the use of a child in sexual activities for remuneration or any other form of consideration;"

Art. 2, OPTIONAL PROTOCOL TO THE CONVENTION ON THE RIGHTS OF THE CHILD ON THE SALE OF CHILDREN, CHILD PROSTITUTION AND CHILD PORNOGRAPHY.

CHOROIDITIS [Chloroïdite]

– "(*i*) Blindness of both eyes, or of one eve when the vision of the other is less than I in spite of the use of corrective glasses; diminution of visual acuity in cases where it is impossible to restore it by correction to an acuity of 1/2 in at least one eye; other grave ocular affections, for example: glaucoma, iritis, choroiditis; trachoma, etc."

Annex I, 3, GENEVA CONVENTION RELATIVE TO THE TREATMENT OF PRISONERS OF WAR.

CHRONIC ASTHMA [Asthme chronique]

– "(*c*) Serious diseases of the respiratory organs of non-tubercular etiology, presumed incurable. for example: serious pulmonary emphysema, with or without bronchitis, chronic asthma: chronic bronchitis lasting more than one year in captivity; bronchiectasis, etc."

Annex I, 3, GENEVA CONVENTION RELATIVE TO THE TREATMENT OF PRISONERS OF WAR.

CHRONIC BRONCHITIS LASTING MORE THAN ONE YEAR IN CAPTIVITY [Bronchite chronique se prolongeant pendant plus d'une année en captivité]

– "(*c*) Serious diseases of the respiratory organs of non-tubercular etiology, presumed incurable, for example: serious pulmonary emphysema, with or without bronchitis, chronic asthma: chronic bronchitis lasting more than one year in captivity; bronchiectasis, etc."

Annex I, 3, GENEVA CONVENTION RELATIVE TO THE TREATMENT OF PRISONERS OF WAR.

CHRONIC CHOLECYSTOPATHY [Cholécystopathie chronique]

– "(*e*) Serious chronic affections of the digestive organs, for example: gastric or duodenal ulcer, sequelae of gastric operations performed in captivity; chronic gastritis, enteritis or colitis, having lasted more than one year and seriously affecting the general condition: cirrhosis of the liver, chronic cholecystopathy; etc."

Annex I, 3, GENEVA CONVENTION RELATIVE TO THE TREATMENT OF PRISONERS OF WAR.

CHRONIC DISEASES OF THE KIDNEY WITH CONSEQUENT DISORDERS [Maladies chroniques du rein avec troubles consécutifs]

– "(*f*) Serious chronic affections of the genito-urinary organs, for example: chronic diseases of the kidney with consequent disorders; nephrectomy because of a tubercular kidney; chronic pyelitis or chronic cystitis: hydronephrosis or pyonephrosis; chronic grave gynaecological conditions, normal pregnancy, and obstetrical disorder, where it is impossible to accommodate in a neutral country; etc."

Annex I, 3, GENEVA CONVENTION RELATIVE TO THE TREATMENT OF PRISONERS OF WAR.

CHRONIC GASTRITIS, ENTERITIS OR COLITIS, HAVING LASTED MORE THAN ONE YEAR AND SERIOUSLY AFFECTING THE GENERAL CONDITION [Gastrite, entérite ou colique chroniques durant plus d'une année et affectant gravement l'état général]

– "(*e*) Serious chronic affections of the digestive organs, for example: gastric or duodenal ulcer, sequelae of gastric operations performed in captivity; chronic gastritis, enteritis or colitis, having lasted more than one year and seriously affecting the general condition: cirrhosis of the liver, chronic cholecystopathy; etc."

Annex I, 3, GENEVA CONVENTION RELATIVE TO THE TREATMENT OF PRISONERS OF WAR.

CHRONIC GRAVE GYNAECOLOGICAL CONDITIONS [Affections gynécologiques chroniques graves]

– "(*f*) Serious chronic affections of the genito-urinary organs, for example: chronic diseases of the kidney with consequent disorders; nephrectomy because of a tubercular kidney; chronic pyelitis or chronic cystitis: hydronephrosis or pyonephrosis; chronic grave gynaecological conditions, normal pregnancy, and obstetrical disorder, where it is impossible to accommodate in a neutral country; etc."

Annex I, 3, GENEVA CONVENTION RELATIVE TO THE TREATMENT OF PRISONERS OF WAR.

CHRONIC PYELITIS OR CHRONIC CYSTITIS [Pyélite chronique ou cystite chronique]

– "(*f*) Serious chronic affections of the genito-urinary organs, for example: chronic diseases of the kidney with consequent disorders; nephrectomy because of a tubercular kidney; chronic pyelitis or chronic cystitis: hydronephrosis or pyonephrosis; chronic grave gynaecological conditions, normal pregnancy, and obstetrical disorder, where it is impossible to accommodate in a neutral country; etc."

Annex I, 3, GENEVA CONVENTION RELATIVE TO THE TREATMENT OF PRISONERS OF WAR.

CIRCUMSTANCES PROPITIOUS TO THE DEVELOPMENT OF A GREAT PART OF MANKIND [Conditions propices au développement pour une grande partie de l'humanité]

– "*Considering* that the elimination of the massive and flagrant violations of the human rights of the peoples and individuals affected by situations such as those resulting from colonialism, neo-colonialism, apartheid, all forms of racism and racial discrimination, foreign domination and occupation, aggression and threats against national sovereignty, national unity and territorial integrity and threats of war would contribute to the establishment of circumstances propitious to the development of a great part of mankind,"

Pp. 9, DECLARATION ON THE RIGHT TO DEVELOPMENT.

CIRRHOSIS OF THE LIVER [Cirrhose hépatique]

– "(*e*) Serious chronic affections of the digestive organs, for example: gastric or duodenal ulcer, sequelae of gastric operations performed in captivity; chronic gastritis, enteritis or colitis, having lasted more than one year and seriously affecting the general condition: cirrhosis of the liver, chronic cholecystopathy; etc."

Annex I, 3, GENEVA CONVENTION RELATIVE TO THE TREATMENT OF PRISONERS OF WAR.

CIVIL, POLITICAL, ECONOMIC, SOCIAL AND CULTURAL RIGHTS [Droits civils, politiques, économiques, sociaux et culturels]

– "2. All human rights and fundamental freedoms are indivisible and interdependent; equal attention and urgent consideration should be given to the implementation, promotion and protection of civil, political, economic, social and cultural rights."

Art.6, DECLARATION ON THE RIGHT TO DEVELOPMENT.

CIVIL DEFENCE [Protection civile]

– "For the purposes of this Protocol:

(*a*) 'Civil defence' means the performance of some or all of the undermentioned humanitarian tasks intended to protect the civilian population against the dangers, and to help it to recover from the immediate effects, of hostilities or disasters and also to provide the conditions necessary for its survival. These tasks are:

(i) Warning;
(ii) Evacuation;
(iii) Management of shelters;
(iv) Management of blackout measures;
(v) Rescue;
(vi) Medical services, including first aid, and religious assistance;
(vii) Fire-fighting;
(viii) Detection and marking of danger areas;
(ix) Decontamination and similar protective measures;
(x) Provision of emergency accommodation and supplies;
(xi) Emergency assistance in the restoration and maintenance of order in distressed areas;
(xii) Emergency repair of indispensable public utilities;
(xiii) Emergency disposal of the dead;
(xiv) Assistance in the preservation of objects essential for survival;
(xv) Complementary activities necessary to carry out any of the tasks mentioned above, including, but not limited to, planning and organization;"

Art. 61, PROTOCOL ADDITIONAL TO THE GENEVA CONVENTIONS OF 12 AUGUST 1949, AND RELATING TO THE PROTECTION OF VICTIMS OF INTERNATIONAL ARMED CONFLICTS (PROTOCOL I).

CIVIL DEFENCE ORGANIZATIONS [Organismes de protection civile]

– "For the purposes of this Protocol:

[...]

(*b*) "Civil defence organizations" means those establishments and other units which are organized or authorized by the competent authorities of a Party to the conflict to perform any of the tasks mentioned under subparagraph (a)[5], and which are assigned and devoted exclusively to such tasks;"

---

[5] "(*a*) "Civil defence" means the performance of some or all of the undermentioned humanitarian tasks intended to protect the civilian population against the dangers, and to help

Art. 61, PROTOCOL ADDITIONAL TO THE GENEVA CONVENTIONS OF 12 AUGUST 1949, AND RELATING TO THE PROTECTION OF VICTIMS OF INTERNATIONAL ARMED CONFLICTS (PROTOCOL I).

CIVILIAN OBJECTS [Biens à caractère civil]

– 1. Civilian objects shall not be the object of attack or of reprisals. Civilian objects are all objects which are not military objectives as defined in paragraph 2.

2. Attacks shall be limited strictly to military objectives. In so far as objects are concerned, military objectives are limited to those objects which by their nature, location, purpose or use make an effective contribution to military action and whose total or partial destruction, capture or neutralization, in the circumstances ruling at the time, offers a definite military of advantage.

3. In case of doubt whether an object which is normally dedicated to civilian purposes, such as a place of worship, a house or other dwelling or a school, is being used to make an effective contribution to military action, it shall be presumed not to be so used."

Art. 52, PROTOCOL ADDITIONAL TO THE GENEVA CONVENTIONS OF 12 AUGUST 1949, AND RELATING TO THE PROTECTION OF VICTIMS OF INTERNATIONAL ARMED CONFLICTS (PROTOCOL I).

---

it to recover from the immediate effects, of hostilities or disasters and also to provide the conditions necessary for its survival. These tasks are:
(i) Warning;
(ii) Evacuation;
(iii) Management of shelters;
(iv) Management of blackout measures;
(v) Rescue;
(vi) Medical services, including first aid, and religious assistance;
(vii) Fire-fighting;
(viii) Detection and marking of danger areas;
(ix) Decontamination and similar protective measures;
(x) Provision of emergency accommodation and supplies;
(xi) Emergency assistance in the restoration and maintenance of order in distressed areas;
(xii) Emergency repair of indispensable public utilities;
(xiii) Emergency disposal of the dead;
(xiv) Assistance in the preservation of objects essential for survival;
(xv) Complementary activities necessary to carry out any of the tasks mentioned above, including, but not limited to, planning and organization;"

CIVILIAN POPULATION [Population civile]

- "2. The civilian population comprises all persons who are civilians.

  3. The presence within the civilian population of individuals who do not come within the definition of civilians does not deprive the population of its civilian character."

Art. 50, PROTOCOL ADDITIONAL TO THE GENEVA CONVENTIONS OF 12 AUGUST 1949, AND RELATING TO THE PROTECTION OF VICTIMS OF INTERNATIONAL ARMED CONFLICTS (PROTOCOL I).

COCAINISM [Cocaïnisme]

- "(*o*) Serious cases of chronic intoxication, for example: lead poisoning, mercury poisoning, morphinism, cocainism, alcoholism; gas or radiation poisoning; etc."

Annex I, 3, GENEVA CONVENTION RELATIVE TO THE TREATMENT OF PRISONERS OF WAR.

COLONIALISM [Colonialisme]

- "*Noting* with the gravest concern that racism, racial discrimination, colonialism and apartheid continue to afflict the world in ever-changing forms, as a result both of the continuation of legislative provisions and government and administrative practices contrary to the principles of human rights and also of the continued existence of political and social structures, and of relationships and attitudes, characterized by injustice and contempt for human beings and leading to the exclusion, humiliation and exploitation, or to the forced assimilation, of the members of disadvantaged groups."

Pp. 12, DECLARATION ON RACE AND RACIAL PREJUDICE.

COLONIALISM (ERADICATION OF ALL FORMS OF) [Colonialisme (élimination de toutes les formes de)]

- "*Emphasizing* that the eradication of *apartheid*, all forms of racism, racial discrimination, colonialism, neo-colonialism, aggression, foreign occupation and domination and interference in the internal affairs of States is essential to the full enjoyment of the rights of men and women."

Pp. 10, CONVENTION ON THE ELIMINATION OF ALL FORMS OF DISCRIMINATION AGAINST WOMEN.

COMMUNITY [Communauté]

– "2. All human beings have a responsibility for development, individually and collectively, taking into account the need for full respect for their human rights and fundamental freedoms as well as their duties to the community, which alone can ensure the free and complete fulfilment of the human being, and they should therefore promote and protect an appropriate political, social and economic order for development."

Art. 2, DECLARATION ON THE RIGHT TO DEVELOPMENT.

– "1. Everyone has duties towards and within the community, in which alone the free and full development of his or her personality is possible."

Art. 18, DECLARATION ON THE RIGHTS AND RESPONSIBILITY OF INDIVIDUALS, GROUPS AND ORGANS OF SOCIETY TO PROMOTE AND PROTECT UNIVERSALLY RECOGNIZED HUMAN RIGHTS AND FUNDAMENTAL FREEDOMS.

COMPETENT AUTHORITY [Autorité compétente ; Autorités compétentes]

– "It is difficult to formulate a definition of the competent body or person that would universally describe an adjudicating authority. 'Competent authority' is meant to include those who preside over courts or tribunals (composed of a single judge or of several members), including professional and lay magistrates as well as administrative boards (for example the Scottish and Scandinavian systems) or other more informal community and conflict resolution agencies of an adjudicatory nature."

14, *Commentary*, s.p. 1, UNITED NATIONS STANDARD MINIMUM RULES FOR THE ADMINIS-TRATION OF JUVENILE JUSTICE ("THE BEIJING RULES").

– "For the purposes of this Convention the term 'competent authority' shall mean either an authority of the metropolitan country or the highest central authority in the territory concerned."

Art. 3, FORCED LABOUR CONVENTION (N° 29).

COMPULSORY OR FORCED LABOUR [Travail forcé ou obligatoire]

– "The High Contracting Parties recognise that recourse to compulsory or forced labour may have grave consequences and undertake, each in respect of the territories placed under its sovereignty, jurisdiction, protection, suzerainty or tutelage, to take all necessary measures to

prevent compulsory or forced labour from developing into conditions analogous to slavery.
It is agreed that:

(1) Subject to the transitional provisions laid down in paragraph(2) below, compulsory or forced labour may only be exacted for public purposes.

(2) In territories in which compulsory or forced labour for other than public purposes still survives, the High Contracting Parties shall endeavour progressively and as soon as possible to put an end to the practice. So long as such forced or compulsory labour exists, this labour shall invariably be of an exceptional character, shall always receive adequate remuneration, and shall not involve the removal of the labourers from their usual place of residence.

(3) In all cases, the responsibility for any recourse to compulsory or forced labour shall rest with the competent central authorities of the territory concerned.

Art. 5, SLAVERY CONVENTION.

CONFLICTS AND DISASTERS [Conflits et catastrophes naturelles]

– "*Conflicts and disasters contribute to the spread of HIV/AIDS*"
HIV/AIDS IN CONFLICT AND DISASTER-AFFECTED REGIONS, DECLARATION OF COMMITMENT ON HIV/AIDS.

CONSTANT PROMOTION AND REALIZATION OF THE RIGHTS OF PERSONS BELONGING TO NATIONAL OR ETHNIC, RELIGIOUS AND LINGUISTIC MINORITIES [Promotion constante et réalisation des droits des personnes appartenant à des minorités nationales ou ethniques, religieuses et linguistiques]

– "*Emphasizing* that the constant promotion and realization of the rights of persons belonging to national or ethnic, religious and linguistic minorities, as an integral part of the development of society as a whole and within a democratic framework based on the rule of law, would contribute to the strengthening of friendship and cooperation among peoples and States,"

Pp. 6, DECLARATION ON THE RIGHTS OF PERSONS BELONGING TO NATIONAL OR ETHNIC, RELIGIOUS AND LINGUISTIC MINORITIES.

CONTACT ZONE [Zone de contact]

– "2. 'Contact zone' means any area on land where the forward elements of opposing forces are in contact with each other, especially where they are exposed to direct fire from the ground."

Art. 26, PROTOCOL ADDITIONAL TO THE GENEVA CONVENTIONS OF 12 AUGUST 1949, AND RELATING TO THE PROTECTION OF VICTIMS OF INTERNATIONAL ARMED CONFLICTS (PROTOCOL I).

CONTINUED EXISTENCE OF COLONIALISM [Maintien du colonialisme]

– "*Convinced* that the continued existence of colonialism prevents the development of international economic co-operation, impedes the social, cultural and economic development of dependent peoples and militates against the United Nations ideal of universal peace,"

Pp. 7, DECLARATION ON THE GRANTING OF INDEPENDENCE TO COLONIAL COUNTRIES AND PEOPLES.

CORPORAL PUNISHMENT [Peines corporelles]

– "The High Contracting Parties specifically agree that each of them is prohibited from taking any measure of such a character as to cause the physical suffering or extermination of protected persons in their hands. This prohibition applies not only to murder, torture, corporal punishment, mutilation and medical or scientific experiments not necessitated by the medical treatment of a protected person but also to any other measures of brutality whether applied by civilian or military agents."

Art. 32, GENEVA CONVENTION RELATIVE TO THE PROTECTION OF CIVILIAN PERSONS IN TIME OF WAR.

– "(*a*) Violence to the life, health, or physical or mental well-being of persons, in particular:
  [...]
  (iii) Corporal punishment; [...]"

Art. 75, PARAGRAPH 2, PROTOCOL ADDITIONAL TO THE GENEVA CONVENTIONS OF 12 AUGUST 1949, AND RELATING TO THE PROTECTION OF VICTIMS OF INTERNATIONAL ARMED CONFLICTS (PROTOCOL I).

CORRUPTION [Corruption]

– "(*b*) While the definition of corruption must be subject to national law, it should be understood to encompass the commission or omission of an act in the performance of or in connection with one's duties, in response to gifts, promises or incentives demanded or accepted, or the wrongful receipt of these once the act has been committed or omitted.

(*c*) The expression 'act of corruption' referred to above should be understood to encompass attempted corruption."

Art. 7, *Commentary*, CODE OF CONDUCT FOR LAW ENFORCEMENT OFFICIALS.

COUNSEL [Conseil]

– "In these Principles:

'Counsel' means a legal or other qualified representative;"

S.p. 1, DEFINITIONS, PRINCIPLES FOR THE PROTECTION OF PERSONS WITH MENTAL ILLNESS AND THE IMPROVEMENT OF MENTAL HEALTH care.[B]

COUNTRY OF HIS NATIONALITY (THE) [Pays dont elle a la nationalité (du)]

– "In the case of a person who has more than one nationality, the term 'the country of his nationality' shall mean each of the countries of which he is a national, and a person shall not be deemed to be lacking the protection of the country of his nationality if, without any valid reason based on well-founded fear, he has not availed himself of the protection of one of the countries of which he is a national."

Art. 1, A, paragraph 2, s.p. 2, CONVENTION RELATING TO THE STATUS OF REFUGEES.

CREATION [Création]

– "Creation draws on the roots of cultural tradition, but flourishes in contact with other cultures. [...]"

Art. 7, UNIVERSAL DECLARATION ON CULTURAL DIVERSITY.

[B] Al. 2, DEFINITIONS, Principes pour la protection des personnes atteintes de maladie mentale et pour l'amélioration des soins de santé mentale.

CREATION AND STRENGTHENING OF THE INALIENABLE SOVEREIGNTY OF STATES OVER THEIR NATURAL WEALTH AND RESOURCES [Exercice et renforcement de la Souveraineté permanente des Etats sur leurs richesses et ressources naturelles]

- "*Noting* that the creation and strengthening of the inalienable sovereignty of States over their natural wealth and resources reinforces their economic independence,"

Pp. 11, General Assembly resolution 1803 (XVII) of 14 December 1962, "Permanent sovereignty over natural resources" .

CRIME [Crime]

- "2.The definition of a crime shall be strictly construed and shall not be extended by analogy. In case of ambiguity, the definition shall be interpreted in favour of the person being investigated, prosecuted or convicted."

Art. 22, Rome Statute of the International Criminal Court.

CRIME OF AGGRESSION [Crime d'agression]

- "2.The Court shall exercise jurisdiction over the crime of aggression once a provision is adopted in accordance with articles 121[6] and 123[7] defining

---

[6] "1. After the expiry of seven years from the entry into force of this Statute, any State Party may propose amendments thereto. The text of any proposed amendment shall be sumitted to the Secretary-General of the United Nations, who shall promptly circulate it to all States Parties.
2. No sooner than there months from the date of notification, the Assembly of States Parties, at its next meetings, shall, by a majority of those present and voting, decide whether to take up the proposal. The Assembly may deal with the proposal directly or convene a Review Conference if the issue involved so warrants.
3. The adoption of an amendment at a meeting of the Assembly of States Parties or at a Review Conference on which consensus cannot be reached shall require a two-thirds majority of States Parties.
4. Except as provided in paragraph 5, an amendment shall enter into force for all States Parties one year after instruments of ratification or acceptance have been deposited with the Secretary-General of the United Nations by seven-eighths of them.
5. Any amendment to articles 5, 6, 7 and 8 of this Statute shall enter into force for those States Parties which have accepted the amendment one year after the deposit of their instruments of ratification or acceptance. In respect of a State Party which has not accepted the amendment, the Court shall not exercise its jurisdiction regarding a crime covered by the amendment when committed by that State Party's nationals or on its territory.

the crime and setting out the conditions under which the Court shall exercise jurisdiction with respect to this crime. Such a provision shall be consistent with the relevant provisions of the Charter of the United Nations."

Art.5, ROME STATUTE OF THE INTERNATIONAL CRIMINAL COURT.

CRIME OF APARTHEID (THE) [Crime d'apartheid]

– "2. For the purpose of paragraph 1[8] :

---

6. If an amendment has been accepted by seven-eighths of States Parties in accordance with paragraph 4, any State Party which has not accepted the amendment may withdraw from this Statute with immediate effect, notwithstanding article 127, paragraph 2, by giving notice no later than one year after the entry into force of such amendment.
7. The Secretary-General of the United Nations shall circulate to all States Parties any amendment adopted at a meeting of the Assembly of States Parties or at a review Conference."

[7] "1. Seven years after the entry into force of this Statute the Secretary-General of the United Nations shall convene a Review Conference to consider any amendments to this Statute. Such review may include, but is not limited to, the list of crimes contained in article 5. The Conference shall be open to those participating in the Assembly of States Parties and on the same conditions.
2. At any time thereafter, at the request of a State Party and for the purposes set out in paragraph 1, the Secretary-General of the United Nations shall, upon approval by a majority of States Parties, convene a Review Conference.
3. The provisions of article 121, paragraphs 3 to 7, shall apply to the adoption and entry into force of any amendment to the Statute considered at a Review Conference."

[8] "1. For the purpose of this Statute, "crime against humanity" means any of the following acts when committed as part of a widespread or systematic attack directed against any civilian population, with knowledge of the attack:
(a) Murder;
(b) Extermination ;
(c) Enslavement;
(d) Deportation or forcible transfer of population;
(e) Imprisonment or other severe deprivation of physical liberty in violation of fundamental rules of international law;
(f) Torture;
(g) Rape, sexual slavery, enforced prostitution, forced pregnancy, enforced sterilization, or any other form of sexual violence of comparable gravity;
(h) Persecution against any identifiable group or collectivity on political, racial, national, ethnic, cultural, religious, gender, as defined in paragraph 3, or other grounds that are universally recognized as impermissible under international law, in connection with any act referred to in this paragraph or any crime within the jurisdiction of the Court;
(i) Enforced disappearance of persons;
(j) The crime of apartheid;
(k) Other inhumane acts of a similar character intentionally causing great suffering, or serious injury to body or to mental or physical health."

[...]

(*h*) 'The crime of apartheid' means inhumane acts of a character similar to those referred to in paragraph 1, committed in the context of an institutionalized regime of systematic oppression and domination by one racial group over any other racial group or groups and committed with the intention of maintaining that regime;"

Art. 7, ROME STATUTE OF THE INTERNATIONAL CRIMINAL COURT.

CRIMES AGAINST HUMANITY [Crimes contre l'humanité]

– "*Recalling* resolutions of the General Assembly of the United Nations 3 (I) of 13 February 1946 and 170 (II) of 31 October 1947 on the extradition and punishment of war criminals, resolution 95 (I) of 11 December 1946 affirming the principles of international law recognized by the Charter of the International Military Tribunal, Nurnberg, and the judgement of the Tribunal, and resolutions 2184(XXI) of 12 December 1966 and 2202(XXI) of 16 December 1966 which expressly condemned as crimes against humanity the violation of the economic and political rights of the indigenous population on the one hand and the policies of apartheid on the other,"

Pp. 1, CONVENTION ON THE NON-APPLICABILITY OF STATUTORY LIMITATIONS TO WAR CRIMES AGAINST HUMANITY.

– "*Considering* that war crimes and crimes against humanity are among the gravest crimes in international law,"

Pp. 4, CONVENTION ON THE NON-APPLICABILITY OF STATUTORY LIMITATIONS TO WAR CRIMES AGAINST HUMANITY.

– "(*b*) Crimes against humanity whether committed in time of war or in time of peace as they are defined in the Charter of the International Military Tribunal, Nurnberg, of 8 August 1945 and confirmed by resolutions 3 (I) of 13 February 1946 and 95 (I) of 11 December 1946 of the General Assembly of the United Nations, eviction by armed attack or occupation and inhuman acts resulting from the policy of apartheid, and the crime of genocide as defined in the 1948 Convention on the Prevention and Punishment of the Crime of Genocide, even if such acts do not constitute a violation of the domestic law of the country in which they were committed."

Art. I, CONVENTION ON THE NON-APPLICABILITY OF STATUTORY LIMITATIONS TO WAR CRIMES AND CRIMES AGAINST HUMANITY.

– “*Crimes against humanity*

The International Tribunal shall have the power to prosecute persons responsible for the following crimes when committed in armed conflict, whether international or internal in character, and directed against any civilian population:

(*a*) murder;

(*b*) extermination;

(*c*) enslavement;

(*d*) deportation;

(*e*) imprisonment;

(*f*) torture;

(*g*) rape;

(*h*) persecutions on political, racial and religious grounds;

(*i*) other inhumane acts.”

Art. 5, STATUTE OF THE INTERNATIONAL TRIBUNAL FOR THE PROSECUTION OF PERSONS RESPONSIBLE FOR SERIOUS VIOLATIONS OF INTERNATIONAL HUMANITARIAN LAW COMMITTED IN THE TERRITORY OF FORMER YUGOSLAVIA SINCE 1991.

– “*Crimes against humanity*

The International Tribunal for Rwanda shall have the power to prosecute persons responsible for the following crimes when committed as part of a widespread or systematic attack against any civilian population on national, political, ethnic, racial or religious grounds:

(*a*) Murder;

(*b*) Extermination;

(*c*) Enslavement;

(*d*) Deportation;

(*e*) Imprisonment;

(*f*) Torture;

(*g*) Rape;

(*h*) Persecutions on political, racial and religious grounds;

(*i*) Other inhumane acts.”

Art.3, STATUTE OF INTERNATIONAL CRIMINAL TRIBUNAL FOR THE PROSECUTION OF PERSONS RESPONSIBLE FOR GENOCIDE AND OTHER SERIOUS VIOLATIONS OF INTERNATIONAL HUMANITARIAN LAW COMMITTED IN THE TERRITORY OF RWANDA AND RWANDAN CITIZENS RESPONSIBLE FOR GENOCIDE AND OTHER SUCH VIOLATIONS COMMITTED IN THE TERRITORY OF NEIGHBOURING STATES, BETWEEN 1 JANUARY 1994 AND 31 DECEMBER 1994.

– "*Crimes against humanity*

1. For the purpose of this Statute, 'crime against humanity' means any of the following acts when committed as part of a widespread or systematic attack directed against any civilian population, with knowledge of the attack:

(*a*) Murder;

(*b*) Extermination;

(*c*) Enslavement;

(*d*) Deportation or forcible transfer of population;

(*e*) Imprisonment or other severe deprivation of physical liberty in violation of fundamental rules of international law;

(*f*) Torture;

(*g*) Rape, sexual slavery, enforced prostitution, forced pregnancy, enforced sterilization, or any other form of sexual violence of comparable gravity;

(*h*) Persecution against any identifiable group or collectivity on political, racial, national, ethnic, cultural, religious, gender as defined in paragraph 3, or other grounds that are universally recognized as impermissible under international law, in connection with any act referred to in this paragraph or any crime within the jurisdiction of the Court;

(*i*) Enforced disappearance of persons;

(*j*) The crime of apartheid;

(*k*) Other inhumane acts of a similar character intentionally causing great suffering, or serious injury to body or to mental or physical health.

2. For the purpose of paragraph 1:

(*a*) 'Attack directed against any civilian population' means a course of conduct involving the multiple commission of acts referred to in paragraph 1 against any civilian population, pursuant to or in furtherance of a State or organizational policy to commit such attack;

(*b*) 'Extermination' includes the intentional infliction of conditions of life, *inter alia* the deprivation of access to food and medicine, calculated to bring about the destruction of part of a population;

(*c*) 'Enslavement' means the exercise of any or all of the powers attaching to the right of ownership over a person and includes the exercise of such power in the course of trafficking in persons, in particular women and children;

(*d*) 'Deportation or forcible transfer of population' means forced displacement of the persons concerned by expulsion or other coercive acts from the area in which they are lawfully present, without grounds permitted under international law;

(*e*) 'Torture' means the intentional infliction of severe pain or suffering, whether physical or mental, upon a person in the custody or under the control of the accused; except that torture shall not include pain or suffering arising only from, inherent in or incidental to, lawful sanctions;

(*f*) 'Forced pregnancy' means the unlawful confinement of a woman forcibly made pregnant, with the intent of affecting the ethnic composition of any population or carrying out other grave violations of international law. This definition shall not in any way be interpreted as affecting national laws relating to pregnancy;

(*g*) 'Persecution' means the intentional and severe deprivation of fundamental rights contrary to international law by reason of the identity of the group or collectivity;

(*h*) 'The crime of apartheid' means inhumane acts of a character similar to those referred to in paragraph 1, committed in the context of an institutionalized regime of systematic oppression and domination by one racial group over any other racial group or groups and committed with the intention of maintaining that regime;

(*i*) 'Enforced disappearance of persons' means the arrest, detention or abduction of persons by, or with the authorization, support or acquiescence of, a State or a political organization, followed by a refusal to acknowledge that deprivation of freedom or to give information on the fate or whereabouts of those persons, with the intention of removing them from the protection of the law for a prolonged period of time.

3. For the purpose of this Statute, it is understood that the term 'gender' refers to the two sexes, male and female, within the context of society. The term 'gender' does not indicate any meaning different from the above.

Art. 7, ROME STATUTE OF THE INTERNATIONAL CRIMINAL COURT.

CRIMINAL RESPONSIBILITY [Responsabilité pénale]

– "1. In addition to other grounds for excluding criminal responsibility provided for in this Statute, a person shall not be criminally responsible if, at the time of that person's conduct:

(*a*) The person suffers from a mental disease or defect that destroys that person's capacity to appreciate the unlawfulness or nature of his or her conduct, or capacity to control his or her conduct to conform to the requirements of law;

(*b*) The person is in a state of intoxication that destroys that person's capacity to appreciate the unlawfulness or nature of his or her conduct, or capacity to control his or her conduct to conform to the requirements of law, unless the person has become voluntarily intoxicated under such circumstances that the person knew, or disregarded the risk, that, as a result of the intoxication, he or she was likely to engage in conduct constituting a crime within the jurisdiction of the Court;

(*c*) The person acts reasonably to defend himself or herself or another person or, in the case of war crimes, property which is essential for the survival of the person or another person or property which is essential for accomplishing a military mission, against an imminent and unlawful use of force in a manner proportionate to the degree of danger to the person or the other person or property protected. The fact that the person was involved in a defensive operation conducted by forces shall not in itself constitute a ground for excluding criminal responsibility under this subparagraph;

(*d*) The conduct which is alleged to constitute a crime within the jurisdiction of the Court has been caused by duress resulting from a threat of imminent death or of continuing or imminent serious bodily harm against that person or another person, and the person acts necessarily and reasonably to avoid this threat, provided that the person does not intend to cause a greater harm than the one sought to be avoided. Such a threat may either be:

(i) Made by other persons; or

(ii) Constituted by other circumstances beyond that person's control.

Art. 31, ROME STATUTE OF THE INTERNATIONAL CRIMINAL COURT.

CRIMINALLY RESPONSIBLE [Pénalement responsable]

– "3. In accordance with this Statute, a person shall be criminally responsible and liable for punishment for a crime within the jurisdiction of the Court if that person:

(*a*) Commits such a crime, whether as an individual, jointly with another or through another person, regardless of whether that other person is criminally responsible;

(*b*) Orders, solicits or induces the commission of such a crime which in fact occurs or is attempted;

(*c*) For the purpose of facilitating the commission of such a crime, aids, abets or otherwise assists in its commission or its attempted commission, including providing the means for its commission;

(*d*) In any other way contributes to the commission or attempted commission of such a crime by a group of persons acting with a common purpose. Such contribution shall be intentional and shall either:

(i) Be made with the aim of furthering the criminal activity or criminal purpose of the group, where such activity or purpose involves the commission of a crime within the jurisdiction of the Court; or

(ii) Be made in the knowledge of the intention of the group to commit the crime;

(*e*) In respect of the crime of genocide, directly and publicly incites others to commit genocide;

(*f*) Attempts to commit such a crime by taking action that commences its execution by means of a substantial step, but the crime does not occur because of circumstances independent of the person's intentions. However, a person who abandons the effort to commit the crime or otherwise prevents the completion of the crime shall not be liable for punishment under this Statute for the attempt to commit that crime if that person completely and voluntarily gave up the criminal purpose."

Art. 25, ROME STATUTE OF INTERNATIONAL CRIMINAL COURT.

– "1. Unless otherwise provided, a person shall be criminally responsible and liable for punishment for a crime within the jurisdiction of the Court only if the material elements are committed with intent and knowledge.
2. For the purposes of this article, a person has intent where:

(*a*) In relation to conduct, that person means to engage in the conduct;

(*b*) In relation to a consequence, that person means to cause that consequence or is aware that it will occur in the ordinary course of events.

3. For the purposes of this article, "knowledge" means awareness that a circumstance exists or a consequence will occur in the ordinary course of events. "Know" and "knowingly" shall be construed accordingly.

Art. 30, ROME STATUTE OF INTERNATIONAL CRIMINAL COURT.

CRUEL, INHUMAN OR DEGRADING TREATMENT OR PUNISHMENT [Peine ou traitement cruel, inhumain ou dégradant]

– "The term 'cruel, inhuman or degrading treatment or punishment' should be interpreted so as to extend the widest possible protection against abuses, whether physical or mental, including the holding of a detained or imprisoned person in conditions which deprive him, temporarily or permanently, of the use of any of his natural senses, such as sight or hearing, or of his awareness of place and the passing of time."

Principle 6, BODY OF PRINCIPLES FOR THE PROTECTION OF ALL PERSONS UNDER ANY FORM OF DETENTION OR IMPRISONMENT.

– "No law enforcement official may inflict, instigate or tolerate any act of torture or other cruel, inhuman or degrading treatment or punishment, nor may any law enforcement official invoke superior orders or exceptional circumstances such as a state of war or a threat of war, a threat to national security, internal political instability or any other public emergency as a justification of torture or other cruel, inhuman or degrading treatment or punishment .

Commentary:

(*a*) This prohibition derives from the Declaration on the Protection of All Persons from Being Subjected to Torture and Other Cruel, Inhuman or Degrading Treatment or Punishment, adopted by the General Assembly, according to which: '[Such an act is] an offence to human dignity and shall be condemned as a denial of the purposes of the Charter of the United Nations and as a violation of the human rights and fundamental freedoms proclaimed in the Universal Declaration of Human Rights [and other international human rights instruments].'
[...]

(*c*) The term 'cruel, inhuman or degrading treatment or punishment' has not been defined by the General Assembly but should be interpreted so as to extend the widest possible protection against abuses, whether physical or mental."

Art. 5, *Commentary*, CODE OF CONDUCT FOR LAW ENFORCEMENT OFFICIALS.

CULTURAL, FAMILY, ETHICAL AND RELIGIOUS FACTORS [Culture, la famille, les valeurs morales et la religion (la)]

– "20. Emphasizing the important role of cultural, family, ethnical and religious factors in the prevention of the epidemic and in treatment, care and support, taking into account the particularities of each country as well as the importance of respecting all human rights and fundamental freedoms;"

DECLARATION OF COMMITMENT ON HIV/AIDS.

CULTURAL DIVERSITY [Diversité culturelle]

– "Culture takes diverse forms across time and space. This diversity embodied in the uniqueness and plurality of the identities of the groups and societies making up humankind. As a source of exchange, innovation and creativity, cultural diversity is as necessary for the humankind as biodiversity is for nature. In this sense, it is the common heritage of humanity and should be recognized and affirmed for the benefit of present and future generations."

Art. 1, UNIVERSAL DECLARATION ON CULTURAL DIVERSITY.

– "Cultural diversity widens the range of options open to everyone; it is one of the roots of development, understood not simply in terms of economic growth, but also as a means to achieve a more satisfactory intellectual, emotional, moral and spiritual existence."

Art. 3, UNIVERSAL DECLARATION ON CULTURAL DIVERSITY.

– "Market forces alone cannot guarantee the preservation and promotion of cultural diversity, which is the key to sustainable human development. [...]"

Art. 11, UNIVERSAL DECLARATION ON CULTURAL DIVERSITY.

CULTURAL GOODS AND SERVICES [Biens et service culturels]

– "In the face of present-day economic and technological change, opening up vast prospects for creation and innovation, particular attention must be paid to the diversity of the supply of creative work, to due recognition of the rights of authors and artists and to the specificity of cultural goods and services which, as vectors of identity, values and meaning, must not be treated as mere commodities or consumer goods."

Art. 8, UNIVERSAL DECLARATION ON CULTURAL DIVERSITY.

CULTURAL PLURALISM [Pluralisme culturel]

– "In our increasingly diverse societies, it is essential to ensure harmonious interaction among people and groups with plural, varied and dynamic cultural identities as well as their willingness to live together. Policies for the inclusion and participation of all citizens are guarantees of social cohesion, the vitality of civil society and peace. Thus defined, cultural pluralism gives policy expression to the reality of cultural diversity. Indissociable from a democratic framework, cultural pluralism is conducive to cultural exchange and to the flourishing of creative capacities that sustain public life."

Art. 2, UNIVERSAL DECLARATION ON CULTURAL DIVERSITY.

CULTURAL POLICIES [Politiques culturelles]

– "Article 9 – Cultural policies as catalysts of creativity." [c]

UNIVERSAL DECLARATION ON CULTURAL DIVERSITY.

CULTURAL RIGHTS [Droits culturels]

– "Cultural rights are an integral part of human rights, which are universal, indivisible and interdependent. [...]"

Art. 5, UNIVERSAL DECLARATION ON CULTURAL DIVERSITY.

CULTURE [Culture]

– "1. Culture, as a product of all human beings and a common heritage of mankind, and education in its broadest sense, offer men and women increasingly effective means of adaptation, enabling them not only to affirm that they are born equal in dignity and rights, but also to recognize that they should respect the right of all groups to their own cultural identity and the development of their distinctive cultural life within the national and international contexts, it being understood that it rests with each group to decide in complete freedom on the maintenance, and, if appropriate, the adaptation or enrichment of the values which it regards as essential to its identity."

Art. 5, DECLARATION ON RACE AND RACIAL PREJUDICE.

– "*Reaffirming* that the culture should be regarded as the set of distinctive spiritual, material, intellectual and emotional features of society or a social group, and that it encompasses, in addition to art and literature, lifestyles, ways of living together, value systems, traditions and beliefs,[2]"

– ["[2] This definition is in line with the conclusion of the World Conference on Cultural Policies (MONDIACULT, Mexico City, 1982), of World Commission on Culture and Development (*Our Creative Diversity*, 1995), and the International Conference on Cultural policies for Development (Stockholm, 1998)."]

Pp. 5, UNIVERSAL DECLARATION ON CULTURAL DIVERSITY.

– "*Noting* that culture is at the heart of contemporary debates about identity, social cohesion, and the development of a knowledge-based economy,"

Pp. 6, UNIVERSAL DECLARATION ON CULTURAL DIVERSITY.

---

[c] "Article 9- Les politiques culturelles, catalyseur de la créativité."

– "Culture takes diverse forms across time and space. This diversity embodied in the uniqueness and plurality of the identities of the groups and societies making up humankind. As a source of exchange, innovation and creativity, cultural diversity is as necessary for the humankind as biodiversity is for nature. In this sense, it is the common heritage of humanity and should be recognized and affirmed for the benefit of present and future generations."

Art. 1, UNIVERSAL DECLARATION ON CULTURAL DIVERSITY.

DEATH PENALTY [Peine de mort]

– "1. No reservation is admissible to the present Protocol, except for a reservation made at the time of ratification or accession that provides for the application of the death penalty in time of war pursuant to a conviction for a most serious crime of a military nature committed during wartime.

Art. 2, SECOND OPTIONAL PROTOCOL TO THE INTERNATIONAL COVENANT ON CIVIL AND POLITICAL RIGHTS, AIMING AT THE ABOLITION OF THE DEATH PENALTY.

DEBT BONDAGE [Servitude pour dettes]

– "Each of States Parties to this Convention shall take all practicable and necessary legislative and other measures to bring about progressively and as soon as possible the complete abolition or abandonment of the following institutions and practices, where they still exist and whether or not they are covered by the definition of slavery contained in article 1[9] of the Slavery Convention signed at Geneva on 25 September 1926:

(*a*) Debt bondage, that is to say, the status or condition arising from a pledge by a debtor of his personal services or of those of a person under his control as security for debt, if the value of those services as reasonably assessed is not applied towards the liquidation of the debt or the length and nature of those services are not respectively limited and defined;"

Art .1, SUPPLEMENTARY CONVENTION ON THE ABOLITION OF SLAVERY, THE SLAVE TRADE AND INSTITUTIONS AND PRACTICES SIMILAR TO SLAVERY.

---

[9] "For the purpose of the present Convention, the following definitions are agreed upon:
(1) Slavery is the status or condition of a person over whom any or all of the powers attaching to the right of ownership are exercised.
(2) The slave trade includes all acts involved in the capture, acquisition or disposal of a person with intent to reduce him to slavery; all acts involved in the acquisition of a slave with a view to selling or exchanging him; all acts of disposal by sale or exchange of a slave acquired with a view to being sold or exchanged, and, in general, every act of trade or transport in slaves."

DEFENCE OF CULTURAL DIVERSITY [Défense de la diversité culturelle]

- "The defence of cultural diversity is an ethical imperative, inseparable from respect for human dignity. It implies a commitment to human rights and fundamental freedoms, in particular the rights of persons belonging to minorities and those of indigenous peoples. [...]"

Art. 4, UNIVERSAL DECLARATION ON CULTURAL DIVERSITY.

DEMILITAREZED ZONE [Zones démilitarisées]

- "3. The subject of such an agreement[10] shall normally be any zone which fulfils the following conditions:

  (*a*) All combatants, as well as mobile weapons and mobile military equipment, must have been evacuated;

  (*b*) No hostile use shall be made of fixed military installations or establishments;

  (*c*) No acts of hostility shall be committed by the authorities or by the population; and

  (*d*) Any activity linked to the military effort must have ceased.

  The Parties to the conflict shall agree upon the interpretation to be given to the condition laid down in sub-paragraph (d) and upon persons to be admitted to the demilitarized zone other than those mentioned in paragraph 4. [11]."

Art. 60- *Demilitarized Zones*, PROTOCOL ADDITIONAL TO THE GENEVA CONVENTIONS OF 12 AUGUST 1949, AND RELATING TO THE PROTECTION OF VICTIMS OF INTERNATIONAL ARMED CONFLICTS (PROTOCOL I).

DEMOCRACY [Démocratie]

- "8. Democracy, development and respect for human rights and fundamental freedoms are interdependent and mutually reinforcing. Democracy is based on the freely expressed will of the people to

---

[10] "Art. 60, 1. It is prohibited for the Parties to the conflict to extend their military operations to zones on which they have conferred by agreement the status of demilitarized zone, if such extension is contrary to the terms of this agreement."

[11] "4. The presence, in this zone, of persons specially protected under the Conventions and this Protocol, and of police forces retained for the sole purpose of maintaining law and order, is not contrary to the conditions laid down in paragraph 3."

determine their own political, economic, social and cultural systems and their full participation in all aspects of their lives.[…]"

I, VIENNA DECLARATION AND PROGRAMME OF ACTION.

DEPORTATION OR FORCIBLE TRANSFER OF POPULATION [Déportation ou transfert forcé de population]

– "2. For the purpose of paragraph 1[12]:

[…]

(*d*) "Deportation or forcible transfer of population" means forced displacement of the persons concerned by expulsion or other coercive acts from the area in which they are lawfully present, without grounds permitted under international law;"

Art.7, ROME STATUTE OF INTERNATIONAL CRIMINAL COURT.

DEPRIVATION OF LIBERTY [Privation de liberté]

– "11. For the purposes of the Rules, the following definitions should apply:

[…]

(*b*) The deprivation of liberty means any form of detention or imprisonment or the placement of a person in a public or private custodial setting, from which this person is not permitted to leave at

[12] "1. For the purpose of this Statute, "crime against humanity" means any of the following acts when committed as part of a widespread or systematic attack directed against any civilian population, with knowledge of the attack:
(a) Murder;
(b) Extermination ;
(c) Enslavement;
(d) Deportation or forcible transfer of population;
(e) Imprisonment or other severe deprivation of physical liberty in violation of fundamental rules of international law;
(f) Torture;
(g) Rape, sexual slavery, enforced prostitution, forced pregnancy, enforced sterilization, or any other form of sexual violence of comparable gravity;
(h) Persecution against any identifiable group or collectivity on political, racial, national, ethnic, cultural, religious, gender, as defined in paragraph 3, or other grounds that are universally recognized as impermissible under international law, in connection with any act referred to in this paragraph or any crime within the jurisdiction of the Court;
(i) Enforced disappearance of persons;
(j) The crime of apartheid;
(k) Other inhumane acts of a similar character intentionally causing great suffering, or serious injury to body or to mental or physical health."

will, by order of any judicial, administrative or other public authority."

UNITED NATIONS RULES FOR THE PROTECTION OF JUVENILES DEPRIVED OF THEIR LIBERTY.

DETAINED PERSON [Personne détenue]

– "For the purposes of the Body of Principles:

[...]

(*b*) 'Detained person' means any person deprived of personal liberty except as a result of conviction for an offence;

Use of terms, BODY OF PRINCIPLES FOR THE PROTECTION OF ALL PERSONS UNDER ANY FORM OF DETENTION OR IMPRISONMENT.

DETENTION [Détention]

– "For the purposes of the Body of Principles:

[...]

(*d*) 'Detention' means the condition of detained persons as defined above[13];"

Use of terms, BODY OF PRINCIPLES FOR THE PROTECTION OF ALL PERSONS UNDER ANY FORM OF DETENTION OR IMPRISONMENT.

DETENTION PENDING TRIAL [Détention préventive]

– "13.1 Detention pending trial shall be used only as a measure of last resort and for the shortest possible period of time"

UNITED NATIONS STANDARD MINIMUM RULES FOR THE ADMINISTRATION OF JUVENILE JUSTICE ("THE BEIJING RULES").

DEVELOPMENT [Développement]

– "*Recognizing* that the primary responsibility for the development of the development countries rests on those countries themselves [...]"

Pp. 10, DECLARATION ON SOCIAL PROGRESS AND DEVELOPMENT.

– "*Recognizing* that development is a comprehensive economic, social, cultural and political process, which aims at the constant improvement of the well-being of the entire population and of all individuals on the basis

---

[13] "Use of Terms, (b) 'Detained person' means any person deprived of personal liberty except as a result of conviction for an offence;"

of their active, free and meaningful participation in development and in the fair distribution of benefits resulting therefrom,"
Pp. 2, DECLARATION ON THE RIGHT TO DEVELOPMENT.

– "*Reaffirming* that there is a close relationship between disarmament and development and that progress in the field of disarmament would considerably promote progress in the field of development and that resources released through disarmament measures should be devoted to the economic and social development and well-being of all peoples and, in particular , those of the developing countries,"
Pp. 12, DECLARATION ON THE RIGHT TO DEVELOPMENT.

DIABETES MELLITUS REQUIRING INSULIN TREATMENT [Diabète sucré nécessitant un traitement à l'insuline]

– "(*l*) Serious affections of metabolism, for example: diabetes mellitus requiring insulin treatment; etc."
Annex I, 3, GENEVA CONVENTION RELATIVE TO THE TREATMENT OF PRISONERS OF WAR.

DIFFERENTIAL RATES BETWEEN WORKERS [Différences de taux]

– "3. Differential rates between workers, which correspond, without regard to sex, to differences, as determined by such objective appraisal, in the work to be performed, shall not be considered as being contrary to the principle of equal remuneration for men and women workers for work of equal value."
Art. 3, EQUAL REMUNERATION CONVENTION (N° 100).

DIGNITY [Dignité]

– "*Whereas* recognition of the inherent dignity and of the equal and inalienable rights of all members of the human family is the foundation of freedom, justice and peace in the world,"
Pp. 1, UNIVERSAL DECLARATION OF HUMAN RIGHTS.

– "*Considering* that, in accordance with the principles proclaimed in the Charter of the United Nations, recognition of the inherent dignity and of the equal and inalienable rights of all members of the human family is the foundation of freedom, justice and peace in the world,"

Pp. 1, INTERNATIONAL COVENANT ON ECONOMIC, SOCIAL AND CULTURAL RIGHTS.
Pp. 1, INTERNATIONAL COVENANT ON CIVIL AND POLITICAL RIGHTS.

– "*Recognizing* that these rights derive from the inherent dignity of the human person,"

Pp. 2, INTERNATIONAL COVENANT ON ECONOMIC, SOCIAL AND CULTURAL RIGHTS.
Pp. 1, INTERNATIONAL COVENANT ON CIVIL AND POLITICAL RIGHTS.

– "1. All persons deprived of their liberty shall be treated with humanity and with respect for the inherent dignity of the human person."

Art. 10, INTERNATIONAL COVENANT ON CIVIL AND POLITICAL RIGHTS.

– "All persons under any form of detention or imprisonment shall be treated in a humane manner and with respect for the inherent dignity of the human person."

Principle 1, BODY OF PRINCIPLES FOR THE PROTECTION OF ALL PERSONS UNDER ANY FORM OF DETENTION OR IMPRISONMENT.

– "*Recognizing* that those rights[14] derive from the inherent dignity of the human person,"

Pp. 2, CONVENTION AGAINST TORTURE AND OTHER CRUEL, INHUMAN OR DEGRADING TREATMENT OR PUNISHMENT.

– "(*b*) That dignity[15] makes it imperative not to reduce individuals to their genetic characteristics and to respect their uniqueness and diversity."

Art. 2, UNIVERSAL DECLARATION ON THE HUMAN GENOME AND HUMAN RIGHTS.

– "*Recalling* that the Preamble to the Constitution of UNESCO affirms 'that the wide diffusion of culture, and the education of humanity for justice and liberty and peace are indispensable to the dignity of man and constitute a sacred duty which all the nations must fulfil in a spirit of mutual assistance and concern',"

Pp. 2, UNIVERSAL DECLARATION ON CULTURAL DIVERSITY.

---

[14] Pp. 1, "Considering that, in accordance with the principles proclaimed in the Charter of the United Nations, recognition of the equal and inalienable rights of all members of the human family is the foundation of freedom, justice and peace in the world,"

[15] Art. 2, "(a) Everyone has a right to respect for their dignity and for their rights regardless of their genetic characteristics."

– "1. Migrant workers and members of their families who are deprived of their liberty shall be treated with humanity and with respect for the inherent dignity of the human person and for their cultural identity."

Art. 17, International Convention on the Protection of the Rights of All Migrant Workers and Members of their Families.

DISABILITY [Incapacité]

– "17. The term 'disability' summarizes a great number of different functional limitations occurring in any population in any country of the world. People may be disabled by physical, intellectual or sensory impairment, medical conditions or mental illness. Such impairments, conditions or illnesses may be permanent or transitory in nature."

INTRODUCTION, Standard Rules on the Equalization of Opportunities for Persons with Disabilities.

– "20. In 1980, the World Health Organization adopted an international classification of impairments, disabilities and handicaps, which suggested a more precise and at the same time relativistic approach. The International Classification of Impairments, Disabilities, and Handicaps makes a clear distinction between 'impairment', 'disability'and 'handicap'. It has been extensively used in areas such as rehabilitation, education, statistics, policy, legislation, demography, sociology, economics and anthropology. Some users have expressed concern that the Classification, in its definition of the term 'handicap', may still be considered too medical and too centred on the individual, and may not adequately clarify the interaction between societal conditions or expectations and the abilities of the individual. Those concerns, and others expressed by users during the 12 years since its publication, will be addressed in forthcoming revisions of the Classification." [D]

[D] « 20. En 1980, l'Organisation mondiale de la santé a adopté une classification internationale des déficiences, incapacités et handicaps qui a défini une approche à la fois plus précise et relativiste. La Classification internationale des handicapés : déficiences, incapacités et désavantages établit des distinctions claires entre la déficience, l'incapacité et handicap. Elle est couramment utilisée dans les domaines suivants : réadaptation, éducation, statistique, prise de décisions, législation, démographique, sociologie, économie et anthropologie. Selon certains des spécialistes à qui elle s'adresse, il se pourrait que la définition du terme « handicap » qui y est donnée revête un caractère trop médical encore, qu'elle soit indûment centrés sur l'individu, et qu'elle ne précise pas assez clairement la manière dont la situation sociale, les attentes de la collectivité et d'autres préoccupations exprimées par les utilisateurs depuis la publication de la Classification, il y a 12 ans, dans les révisions dont celle-ci doit faire l'objet. »

INTRODUCTION, STANDARD RULES ON THE EQUALIZATION OF OPPORTUNITIES FOR PERSONS WITH DISABILITIES.

DISABLED PERSON [Handicapé]

– "1. The term 'disabled person' means any person unable to ensure by himself or herself, wholly or partly, the necessities of a normal individual and/or social life, as a result of deficiency, either congenital or not, in his or her physical or mental capabilities."

DECLARATION ON THE RIGHTS OF DISABLED PERSONS.

DISARMAMENT [Désarmement]

– "*Reaffirming* that there is a close relationship between disarmament and development and that progress in the field of disarmament would considerably promote progress in the field of development and that resources released through disarmament measures should be devoted to the economic and social development and well-being of all peoples and, in particular, those of the developing countries,"

Pp. 12, DECLARATION ON THE RIGHT TO DEVELOPMENT.

DISCRIMINATION [Discrimination ; Discriminations ; Acte de discrimination]

– "1. For the purpose of this Convention the term 'discrimination' includes:

(*a*) Any distinction, exclusion or preference made on the basis of race, colour, sex, religion, political opinion, national extraction or social origin, which has the effect of nullifying or impairing equality of opportunity or treatment in employment or occupation;

(*b*) Such other distinction, exclusion or preference which has the effect of nullifying or impairing equality of opportunity or treatment in employment or occupation as may be determined by the Member concerned after consultation with representative employers' and workers' organisations, where such exist, and with other appropriate bodies.

2. Any distinction, exclusion or preference in respect of a particular job based on the inherent requirements thereof shall not be deemed to be discrimination."

Art. 1, DISCRIMINATION (EMPLOYMENT AND OCCUPATION) CONVENTION (N° 111).

– "Any measures affecting an individual who is justifiably suspected of, or engaged in, activities prejudicial to the security of the State shall not be deemed to be discrimination, provided that the individual concerned shall have the right to appeal to a competent body established in accordance with national practice."

Art. 4, Discrimination (Employment and Occupation) Convention (N° 111).

– "1. Special measures of protection or assistance provided in other Conventions or Recommendations adopted by the International Labour Conference shall not be deemed to be discrimination.

2. Any Member may, after consultation with representative employers' and workers' organisations, where such exist, determine that other special measures designed to meet the particular requirements of persons who, for reasons such as sex, age, disablement, family responsibilities or social or cultural status, are generally recognised to require special protection or assistance, shall not be deemed to be discrimination."

Art.5, Discrimination (Employment and Occupation) Convention (N° 111).

– "*Reaffirming* that discrimination between human beings on the grounds of race, colour or ethnic origin is an obstacle to friendly and peaceful relations among nations and is capable of disturbing peace and security among peoples and the harmony of persons living side by side even within one and the same State,"

Pp. 7, International Convention on the Elimination of All Forms of Racial Discrimination.

– "Any distinction, exclusion, restriction or preference based on race, colour, ethnic or national origin or religious intolerance motivated by racist considerations, which destroys or compromises the sovereign equality of States and the right of peoples to self-determination, or which limits in an arbitrary or discriminatory manner the right of every human being and group to full development is incompatible with the requirements of an international order which is just and guarantees respect for human rights; the right to full development implies equal access to the means of personal and collective advancement and fulfilment in a climate of respect for the values of civilizations and cultures, both national and world-wide."

Art.3, Declaration on Race and Racial Prejudice.

– "1. For the purpose of this Convention, the term 'discrimination' includes any distinction, exclusion, limitation or preference which, being based on race, colour, sex, language, religion, political or other opinion, national or social origin, economic condition or birth, has the purpose or effect of nullifying or impairing equality of treatment in education and in particular:

(*a*) Of depriving any person or group of persons of access to education of any type or at any level;

(*b*) Of limiting any person or group of persons to education of an inferior standard;

(*c*) Subject to the provisions of article 2[16] of this Convention, of establishing or maintaining separate educational systems or institutions for persons or groups of persons; or

(*d*) Of inflicting on any person or group of persons conditions which are incompatible with the dignity of man.

Art. 1, CONVENTION AGAINST DISCRIMINATION IN EDUCATION.

– "When permitted in a State, the following situations shall not be deemed to constitute discrimination, within the meaning of article 1 of this Convention:

(*a*) The establishment or maintenance of separate educational systems or institutions for pupils of the two sexes, if these systems or institutions offer equivalent access to education, provide a teaching

[16] "When permitted in a State, the following situations shall not be deemed to constitute discrimination, within the meaning of article 1 of this Convention:
(a) The establishment or maintenance of separate educational systems or institutions for pupils of the two sexes, if these systems or institutions offer equivalent access to education, provide a teaching staff with qualifications of the same standard as well as school premises and equipment of the same quality, and afford the opportunity to take the same or equivalent courses of study;
(b) The establishment or maintenance, for religious or linguistic reasons, of separate educational systems or institutions offering an education which is in keeping with the wishes of the pupil's parents or legal guardians, if participation in such systems or attendance at such institutions is optional and if the education provided conforms to such standards as may be laid down or approved by the competent authorities, in particular for education of the same level;
(c) The establishment or maintenance of private educational institutions, if the object of the institutions is not to secure the exclusion of any group but to provide educational facilities in addition to those provided by the public authorities, if the institutions are conducted in accordance with that object, and if the education provided conforms with such standards as may be laid down or approved by the competent authorities, in particular for education of the same level."

staff with qualifications of the same standard as well as school premises and equipment of the same quality, and afford the opportunity to take the same or equivalent courses of study;

(*b*) The establishment or maintenance, for religious or linguistic reasons, of separate educational systems or institutions offering an education which is in keeping with the wishes of the pupil's parents or legal guardians, if participation in such systems or attendance at such institutions is optional and if the education provided conforms to such standards as may be laid down or approved by the competent authorities, in particular for education of the same level;

(*c*) The establishment or maintenance of private educational institutions, if the object of the institutions is not to secure the exclusion of any group but to provide educational facilities in addition to those provided by the public authorities, if the institutions are conducted in accordance with that object, and if the education provided conforms with such standards as may be laid down or approved by the competent authorities, in particular for education of the same level."

Art. 2, CONVENTION AGAINST DISCRIMINATION IN EDUCATION.

– "1. Adoption by States Parties of temporary special measures aimed at accelerating de facto equality between men and women shall not be considered discrimination as defined in the present Convention, but shall in no way entail as a consequence the maintenance of unequal or separate standards; these measures shall be discontinued when the objectives of equality of opportunity and treatment have been achieved."

Art. 4, CONVENTION ON THE ELIMINATION OF ALL FORMS OF DISCRIMINATION AGAINST WOMEN.

– "4. There shall be no discrimination on the grounds of mental illness. 'Discrimination' means any distinction, exclusion or preference that has the effect of nullifying or impairing equal enjoyment of rights. Special measures solely to protect the rights, or secure the advancement, of persons with mental illness shall not be deemed to be discriminatory. Discrimination does not include any distinction, exclusion or preference undertaken in accordance with the provisions of these Principles and necessary to protect the human rights of a person with a mental illness or of other individuals."

Principle 1, PRINCIPLES FOR THE PROTECTION OF PERSONS WITH MENTAL ILLNESS AND THE IMPROVEMENT OF MENTAL HEALTH CARE.

DISCRIMINATION AGAINST WOMEN [Discrimination à l'égard des femmes]

– "For the purposes of the present Convention, the term 'discrimination against women' shall mean any distinction, exclusion or restriction made on the basis of sex which has the effect or purpose of impairing or nullifying the recognition, enjoyment or exercise by women, irrespective of their marital status, on a basis of equality of men and women, of human rights and fundamental freedoms in the political, economic, social, cultural, civil or any other field."

Art. 1, CONVENTION ON THE ELIMINATION OF ALL FORMS OF DISCRIMINATION AGAINST WOMEN.

DISREGARD AND CONTEMPT FOR HUMAN RIGHTS [Méconnaissance et mépris des droits de l'homme]

– "*Whereas* disregard and contempt for human rights have resulted in barbarous acts which have outraged the conscience of mankind, [...]"

Pp. 2, UNIVERSAL DECLARATION OF HUMAN RIGHTS.

DISREGARD AND INFRINGEMENT OF HUMAN RIGHTS AND FUNDAMENTAL FREEDOMS [Mépris et violation des droits de l'homme et des libertés fondamentales (le)]

– "*Considering* that the disregard and infringement of human rights and fundamental freedoms, in particular of the right to freedom of thought, conscience, religion or whatever belief, have brought, directly or indirectly, wars and great suffering to mankind, especially where they serve as a means of foreign interference in the internal affairs of other States and amount to kindling hatred between peoples and nations,"

Pp. 3, DECLARATION ON THE ELIMINATION OF ALL FORMS OF INTOLERANCE AND OF DISCRIMINATION BASED ON RELIGION OR BELIEF.

DISTINCTIVE EMBLEM [Signe distinctif]

– "For the purposes of this Protocol:

[...]

(*l*) 'Distinctive emblem' means the distinctive emblem of the red cross, red crescent or red lion and sun on a white ground when used for the protection of medical units and transports, or medical and religious personnel, equipment or supplies;"

Art. 8, PROTOCOL ADDITIONAL TO THE GENEVA CONVENTIONS OF 12 AUGUST 1949, AND RELATING TO THE PROTECTION OF VICTIMS OF INTERNATIONAL ARMED CONFLICTS (PROTOCOL I).

DISTINCTIVE SIGNAL [Signal distinctif]

– "For the purposes of this Protocol:
  [...]

  (*m*) 'Distinctive signal' means any signal or message specified for the identification exclusively of medical units or transports in Chapter III[17] of Annex I to this Protocol."

---

[17] "CHAPTER III. DISTINCTIVE SIGNALS
Article 5. Optional Use
1. Subject to the provisions of Article 6 of these Regulations, the signals specified in this Chapter for exclusive use by medical units and transports shall nol be used for any other purpose. The use of all signals referred to in this Chapter is optional.
2. Temporary medical aircraft which cannot, either for lack of time or because of their characteristics, be marked with the distinctive emblem, may use the distinctive signals authorized in this Chapter. The best method of effective identification and recognition of medical aircraft is, however, the use of a visual signal, either the distinctive emblem or the light signal specified in Article 6, or both, supplemented by the other signals referred to in Articles 7 and 8 of these Regulations .
Article 6. Light signal
1. The light signal, consisting of a flashing blue light. is established for the use of medical aircraft to signal their identity. No other aircraft shall use this signal. The recommended blue colour is obtained by using, as trichromatic co-ordinates:
green boundary y = 0.065 + 0.805x
white boundary y = 0.400 - x
purple boundary x = 0.133 + 0.600y
The recommended flashing rate of the blue light is between sixty and one hundred flashes per minute.
2. Medical aircraft should be equipped with such lights as may be necessary to make the light signal visible in as many directions as possible.
3. In the absence of a special agreement between the Parties to the conflict reserving the use of flashing blue lights for the identification of medical vehicles and ships and craft, the use of such signals for other vehicles or ships is not prohibited.
Article 7. Radio signal
1. The radio signal shall consist of a radiotelephonic or radiotelegraphic message preceded by a distinctive priority signal to be designated and approved by a World Administrative Radio Conference of the International Telecommunication Union. It shall be transmitted three times before the call sign of the medical transport involved. This message shall be transmitted in English at appropriate intervals on a frequency or frequencies specified pursuant to paragraph 3. The use of the priority signal shall be restricted exclusively to medical units and transports.
2. The radio message preceded by the distinctive priority signal mentioned in paragraph I shall convey the following data: *(Continued on next page)*

Art. 8, PROTOCOL ADDITIONAL TO THE GENEVA CONVENTIONS OF 12 AUGUST 1949, AND RELATING TO THE PROTECTION OF VICTIMS OF INTERNATIONAL ARMED CONFLICTS (PROTOCOL I).

DOCTRINE OF SUPERIORITY BASED ON RACIAL DIFFERENTIATION [Doctrine de supériorité fondée sur la différenciation entre les races]

– "*Convinced* that any doctrine of superiority based on racial differentiation is scientifically false, morally condemnable, socially unjust and dangerous, and that there is no justification for racial discrimination, in theory or in practice, anywhere,"

Pp. 6, INTERNATIONAL CONVENTION ON THE ELIMINATION OF ALL FORMS OF RACIAL DISCRIMINATION.

DUE PROCESS OF LAW [Procès « juste et équitable »]

– "The procedure for dealing with juvenile offenders shall in any case follow the minimum standards that are applied almost universally for any

---

(From previous page)(a) Call sign of the medical transport;
(b) Position of the medical transport;
(c) Number and type of medical transports;
(d) Intended route;
(e) Estimated time en route and of departure and arrival, as appropriate;
(f) Any other information such as flight altitude, radio frequencies guarded, languages and secondary surveillance radar modes and codes.

3. In order to facilitate the communications referred to in paragraphs 1 and 2, as well as the communications referred to in Articles 22, 23, 25, 26, 27, 28, 29, 30 and 31 of the Protocol, the High Contracting Parties, the Parties to a conflict, or one of the Parties to a conflict, acting in agreement or alone, may designate, in accordance with the Table of Frequency Allocations in the Radio Regulations annexed to the International Telecommunication Convention, and publish selected national frequencies to be used by them for such communications. These frequencies shall be notified to the International Telecommunication Union in accordance with procedures to be approved by a World Administrative Radio Conference.

Article 8. Electronic identification

1. The Secondary Surveillance Radar (SSR) system, as specified in Annex 10 to the Chicago Convention on International Civil Aviation of 7 December 1944, as amended from time to time, may be used to identify and to follow the course of medical aircraft. The SSR mode and code to be reserved for the exclusive use of medical aircraft shall be established by the High Contracting Parties, the Parties to a conflict, or one of the Parties to a conflict, acting in agreement or alone, in accordance with procedures to be recommended by the International Civil Aviation Organization.

2. Parties to a conflict may, by special agreement between them, establish for their use a similar electronic system for the identification of medical vehicles, and medical ships and craft."

criminal defendant under the procedure known as 'due process of law'. In accordance with due process, a 'fair and just trial' includes such basic safeguards as the presumption of innocence, the presentation and examination of witnesses, the common legal defences, the right to remain silent, the right to have the last word in a hearing, the right to appeal, etc. (See also rule 7.1.) [18 E]"

14, *Commentary*, S.P. 2, UNITED NATIONS STANDARD MINIMUM RULES FOR THE ADMINISTRATION OF JUVENILE JUSTICE ("THE BEIJING RULES").

EDUCATION [Enseignement ; Education]

– "2. For the purposes of this Convention, the term 'education' refers to all types and levels of education, and includes access to education, the standard and quality of education, and the conditions under which it is given."

Art. 1, CONVENTION AGAINST DISCRIMINATION IN EDUCATION.

– "1. The States Parties to this Convention agree that:

(*a*) Education shall be directed to the full development of the human personality an d to the strengthening of respect for human rights and fundamental freedoms; it shall promote understanding, tolerance and friendship among all nations, racial or religious groups, and shall further the activities of the United Nations for the maintenance of peace;"

Art. 5, CONVENTION AGAINST DISCRIMINATION IN EDUCATION.

EDUCATION OF CHILD [Education de l'enfant]

– "1. States Parties agree that the education of the child shall be directed to:

---

[18] "7.1 Basic procedural safeguards such as the presumption of innocence, the right to be notified of the charges, the right to remain silent, the right to counsel, the right to the presence of a parent or guardian, the right to confront and cross-examine witnesses and the right to appeal to a higher authority shall be guaranteed at all stages of proceedings."

[E] « La procédure suivie pour juger les jeunes délinquants doit en tout état de cause se conformer aux normes minima, assurés presque universellement à tout accusé par le respect des formes légales. Dans ces formes, un procès « juste et équitable » comprend des garanties fondamentales telles que la présomption d'innocence, la comparution et la déposition de témoins, les moyens ordinaires de défense, le droit de garder le silence, le droit de répliquer en dernier à l'audience, le droit de faire appel, etc. (Voir également l'article 7.1.) »

(*a*) The development of the child's personality, talents and mental and physical abilities to their fullest potential;

(*b*) The development of respect for human rights and fundamental freedoms, and for the principles enshrined in the Charter of the United Nations;

(*c*) The development of respect for the child's parents, his or her own cultural identity, language and values, for the national values of the country in which the child is living, the country from which he or she may originate, and for civilizations different from his or her own;

(*d*) The preparation of the child for responsible life in a free society, in the spirit of understanding, peace, tolerance, equality of sexes, and friendship among all peoples, ethnic, national and religious groups and persons of indigenous origin;

(*e*) The development of respect for the natural environment."

Art. 29, CONVENTION ON THE RIGHTS OF THE CHILD.

EMPLOYMENT [Emploi]

– "3. For the purpose of this Convention the terms 'employment' and 'occupation' include access to vocational training, access to employment and to particular occupations, and terms and conditions of employment."

Art. 1, DISCRIMINATION (EMPLOYMENT AND OCCUPATION) CONVENTION (N° 111).

ENFORCED DISAPPEARANCE OF PERSONS [Disparitions forcées de personnes]

– "2. For the purpose of paragraph 1[19]:

---

[19] "1. For the purpose of this Statute, 'crime against humanity' means any of the following acts when committed as part of a widespread or systematic attack directed against any civilian population, with knowledge of the attack:

(a) Murder;
(b) Extermination ;
(c) Enslavement;
(d) Deportation or forcible transfer of population;
(e) Imprisonment or other severe deprivation of physical liberty in violation of fundamental rules of international law;
(f) Torture;
(g) Rape, sexual slavery, enforced prostitution, forced pregnancy, enforced sterilization, or any other form of sexual violence of comparable gravity;

[...]

(*i*) 'Enforced disappearance of persons' means the arrest, detention or abduction of persons by, or with the authorization, support or acquiescence of, a State or a political organization, followed by a refusal to acknowledge that deprivation of freedom or to give information on the fate or whereabouts of those persons, with the intention of removing them from the protection of the law for a prolonged period of time."

Art. 7, ROME STATUTE OF THE INTERNATIONAL CRIMINAL COURT.

ENFORCED PROSTITUTION [Prostitution forcée ; Contrainte à la prostitution]

– "(*g*) Rape, sexual slavery, enforced prostitution, forced pregnancy, enforced sterilization, or any other form of sexual violence of comparable gravity;"

Art. 7, Paragraph 1, ROME STATUTE OF THE INTERNATIONAL CRIMINAL COURT.

– "Women shall be especially protected against any attack on their honour, in particular against rape, enforced prostitution, or any form of indecent assault."

Art. 27, s.p. 2, GENEVA CONVENTION RELATIVE TO THE PROTECTION OF CIVILIAN PERSONS IN TIME OF WAR.

– "*b*) Outrages upon personal dignity, in particular humiliating and degrading treatment, enforced prostitution and any form of indecent assault;"

Art. 75, paragraph 2, PROTOCOL ADDITIONAL TO THE GENEVA CONVENTIONS OF 12 AUGUST 1949, AND RELATING TO THE PROTECTION OF VICTIMS OF INTERNATIONAL ARMED CONFLICTS (PROTOCOL I).

(h) Persecution against any identifiable group or collectivity on political, racial, national, ethnic, cultural, religious, gender, as defined in paragraph 3, or other grounds that are universally recognized as impermissible under international law, in connection with any act referred to in this paragraph or any crime within the jurisdiction of the Court;

(i) Enforced disappearance of persons;

(j) The crime of apartheid;

(k) Other inhumane acts of a similar character intentionally causing great suffering, or serious injury to body or to mental or physical health."

– "*e*) Outrages upon personal dignity, in particular humiliating and degrading treatment, rape, enforced prostitution and any form of indecent assault;"

Art. 4, paragraph 2, PROTOCOL ADDITIONAL TO THE GENEVA CONVENTIONS OF 12 AUGUST 1949, AND RELATING TO THE PROTECTION OF VICTIMS OF NON-INTERNATIONAL ARMED CONFLICTS (PROTOCOL II).

ENFORCED STERILIZATION [Stérilisation forcée]

– "(*g*) Rape, sexual slavery, enforced prostitution, forced pregnancy, enforced sterilization, or any other form of sexual violence of comparable gravity;"

Art. 7, Paragraph 1, ROME STATUTE OF THE INTERNATIONAL CRIMINAL COURT.

ENSLAVEMENT [Réduction en esclavage]

– "2. For the purpose of paragraph 1[20]:

[...]

(*c*) 'Enslavement' means the exercise of any or all of the powers attaching to the right of ownership over a person and includes the exercise of such power in the course of trafficking in persons, in particular women and children;"

Art. 7, ROME STATUTE OF THE INTERNATIONAL CRIMINAL COURT.

---

[20] "1. For the purpose of this Statute, 'crime against humanity' means any of the following acts when committed as part of a widespread or systematic attack directed against any civilian population, with knowledge of the attack:

(a) Murder;
(b) Extermination ;
(c) Enslavement;
(d) Deportation or forcible transfer of population;
(e) Imprisonment or other severe deprivation of physical liberty in violation of fundamental rules of international law;
(f) Torture;
(g) Rape, sexual slavery, enforced prostitution, forced pregnancy, enforced sterilization, or any other form of sexual violence of comparable gravity;
(h) Persecution against any identifiable group or collectivity on political, racial, national, ethnic, cultural, religious, gender, as defined in paragraph 3, or other grounds that are universally recognized as impermissible under international law, in connection with any act referred to in this paragraph or any crime within the jurisdiction of the Court;
(i) Enforced disappearance of persons;
(j) The crime of apartheid;
(k) Other inhumane acts of a similar character intentionally causing great suffering, or serious injury to body or to mental or physical health."

EQUAL REMUNERATION FOR MEN AND WOMEN WORKERS FOR WORK OF EQUAL VALUE [Egalité de rémunération entre la main-d'oeuvre féminine pour un travail de valeur égale]

– "For the purpose of this Convention:
 […]

 (*b*) The term 'equal remuneration for men and women workers for work of equal value' refers to rates of remuneration established without discrimination based on sex."

Art. 1, EQUAL REMUNERATION CONVENTION (N° 100).

EQUALITY [Egalité]

– "6. We consider certain fundamental values to be essential to international relations in the twenty-first century. These include:
 […]

 Equality. No individual and no nation must be denied the opportunity to benefit from development. The equal rights and opportunities of women and men must be assured.
 […]"

Second •, UNITED NATIONS MILLENIUM DECLARATION.

EQUALIZATION OF OPPORTUNITIES [Egalisation des chances]

– "24. The term 'equalization of opportunities' means the process through which the various systems of society and the environment, such as services, activities, information and documentation, are made available to all, particularly to persons with disabilities."

INTRODUCTION, STANDARD RULES ON THE EQUALIZATION OF OPPORTUNITIES FOR PERSONS WITH DISABILITIES.

EQUIVALENT TO LOSS OF A HAND OR A FOOT [Equivalents à la perte d'une main ou d'un pied]

– "Without prejudice to a more generous interpretation, the following shall be considered as equivalent to the loss of a hand or a foot:

(*a*) Loss of a hand or of all the fingers, or of the thumb and forefinger of one hand; loss of a foot, or of all the toes and metatarsals of one foot.

(*b*) Ankylosis, loss of osseous tissue, cicatricial contracture preventing the functioning of one of the large articulations or of all the digital joints of one hand.

(*c*) Pseudarthrosis of the long bones.

(*d*) Deformities due to fracture or other injury which seriously interfere with function and weight-bearing power.

Annex I, 1, GENEVA CONVENTION RELATIVE TO THE TREATMENT OF PRISONERS OF WAR.

ESCAPE [Evasion]

– "The escape of a prisoner of war shall be deemed to have succeeded when:

1. He has joined the armed forces of the Power on which he depends, or those of an allied Power;

2. He has left the territory under the control of the Detaining Power, or of an ally of the said Power;

3. He has joined a ship flying the flag of the Power on which he depends, or of an allied Power, in the territorial waters of the Detaining Power, the said ship not being under the control of the last-named Power."

Art. 91, GENEVA CONVENTION RELATIVE TO THE TREATMENT OF PRISONERS OF WAR.

ESPIONAGE [Espionnage]

– "2. A member of the armed forces of a Party to the conflict who, on behalf of that Party and in territory controlled by an adverse Party, gathers or attempts to gather information shall not be considered as engaging in espionage if, while so acting, he is in the uniform of his armed forces.

3. A member of the armed forces of a Party to the conflict who is a resident of territory occupied by an adverse Party and who, on behalf of the Party on which he depends, gathers or attempts to gather information of military value within that territory shall not be considered as engaging in espionage unless he does so through an act of false pretences or deliberately in a clandestine manner. Moreover, such a resident shall not

lose his right to the status of prisoner of war and may not be treated as a spy unless he is captured while engaging in espionage."

Art. 46, PROTOCOL ADDITIONAL TO THE GENEVA CONVENTIONS OF 12 AUGUST 1949, AND RELATING TO THE PROTECTION OF VICTIMS OF INTERNATIONAL ARMED CONFLICTS (PROTOCOL I).

ESTABLISHMENT OF LASTING PEACE ON EARTH [Instauration d'une paix durable sur la Terre]

– "*Aware* that in the nuclear age the establishment of a lasting peace on Earth represents the primary condition for the preservation of human civilization and the survival of mankind,"

Pp. 5, DECLARATION ON THE RIGHT OF PEOPLES TO PEACE.

ETHNIC CLEANSING [Nettoyage ethnique]

– "28. The World Conference on Human Rights expresses its dismay at massive violations of human rights especially in the form of genocide, 'ethnic cleansing' and systematic rape of women in war situations, creating mass exodus of refugees and displaced persons. [...]"

I, VIENNA DECLARATION AND PROGRAM OF ACTION.

EVERYONE [Personne (toute) ; Individu]

– "Everyone, as a member of society, [...]"

Art. 22, UNIVERSAL DECLARATION OF HUMAN RIGHTS.

– "1. Everyone has duties to the community in which in which alone the free and full development of his personality is possible."

Art. 29, UNIVERSAL DECLARATION OF HUMAN RIGHTS.

EXISTING DISEQUILIBRIA IN INTERNATIONAL ECONOMIC RELATIONS [Déséquilibres existant dans les relations économiques internationales]

– "4. Existing disequilibria in international economic relations contribute to the exacerbation of racism and racial prejudice; all States should consequently endeavour to contribute to the restructuring of the international economy on a more equitable basis."

Art. 9, DECLARATION ON RACE AND RACIAL PREJUDICE.

EXPLOITATION [Exploitation]

– "For the purposes of this Protocol:

(*a*) 'Trafficking in persons' shall mean the recruitment, transportation, transfer, harbouring or receipt of persons, by means of the threat or use of force or other forms of coercion, of abduction, of fraud, of deception, of the abuse of power or of position of vulnerability or of the giving or receiving of payments or benefits to achieve the consent of a person having control over another person, for the purpose of exploitation. Exploitation shall include, at minimum, the exploitation of the prostitution of others or other forms of sexual exploitation, forced labour or services, slavery or practices similar to slavery, servitude or removal of organs;"

Art. 3, PROTOCOL TO PREVENT, SUPPRESS AND PUNISH TRAFFICKING IN PERSONS ESPECIALLY WOMEN AND CHILDREN, SUPPLEMENTING THE UNITED NATIONS CONVENTION AGAINST TRANSNATIONAL ORGANIZED CRIME.

EXTENDED FAMILY [Famille élargie]

– "18. It is important to emphasize the socialization function of the family and extended family[...]"

UNITED NATIONS GUIDELINES FOR THE PREVENTION OF JUVENILE DELINQUENCY (THE RIYADH GUIDELINES).

EXTERMINATION [Extermination]

– "2. For the purpose of paragraph 1[21]:

[21] "1. For the purpose of this Statute, 'crime against humanity' means any of the following acts when committed as part of a widespread or systematic attack directed against any civilian population, with knowledge of the attack:

(a) Murder;
(b) Extermination ;
(c) Enslavement;
(d) Deportation or forcible transfer of population;
(e) Imprisonment or other severe deprivation of physical liberty in violation of fundamental rules of international law;
(f) Torture;
(g) Rape, sexual slavery, enforced prostitution, forced pregnancy, enforced sterilization, or any other form of sexual violence of comparable gravity;
(h) Persecution against any identifiable group or collectivity on political, racial, national, ethnic, cultural, religious, gender, as defined in paragraph 3, or other grounds that are

[…]

(*b*) 'Extermination' includes the intentional infliction of conditions of life, *inter alia* the deprivation of access to food and medicine, calculated to bring about the destruction of part of a population;"

Art. 7, ROME STATUTE OF THE INTERNATIONAL CRIMINAL COURT.

EXTRADITION [Extradition]

– "For the purposes of this Statute:

[…]

(*b*) 'extradition' means the delivering up of a person by one State to another as provided by treaty, convention or national legislation."

Art. 102, ROME STATUTE OF THE INTERNATIONAL CRIMINAL COURT.

EXTREME POVERTY [Misère]

– "[…] dehumanizing conditions of extreme poverty, to which more than a billion of them [men, women and children] are currently subjected. […]"[H]

11, UNITED NATIONS MILLENNIUM DECLARATION.

EXTREME POVERTY AND SOCIAL EXCLUSION [Extrême pauvreté et exclusion sociale (l')]

– "25. The World Conference on Human Rights affirms that extreme poverty and social exclusion constitute a violation of human dignity […]"

VIENNA DECLARATION AND PROGRAM OF ACTION.

---

universally recognized as impermissible under international law, in connection with any act referred to in this paragraph or any crime within the jurisdiction of the Court;

(i) Enforced disappearance of persons;

(j) The crime of apartheid;

(k) Other inhumane acts of a similar character intentionally causing great suffering, or serious injury to body or to mental or physical health."

[H] « […] la misère, phénomène abject et déshumanisant qui touche actuellement plus d'un milliard de personnes. […] »

FACTORS THAT MAKES PERSONS [...] VULNERABLE TO TRAFFICKING [Facteurs qui rendent les personnes [...] vulnérables à la traite]

– "4. States Parties shall take or strengthen measures, including through bilateral or multilateral cooperation, to alleviate the factors that makes persons, especially women and children, vulnerable to trafficking, such as poverty, underdevelopment and lack of equal opportunity."

Art. 9, PROTOCOL TO PREVENT, SUPPRESS AND PUNISH TRAFFICKING IN PERSONS ESPECIALLY WOMEN AND CHILDREN, SUPPLEMENTING THE UNITED NATIONS CONVENTION AGAINST TRANSNATIONAL ORGANIZED CRIME.

FAIR AND JUST TRIAL [Procès « juste et équitable »]

– "The procedure for dealing with juvenile offenders shall in any case follow the minimum standards that are applied almost universally for any criminal defendant under the procedure known as 'due process of law'. In accordance with due process, a 'fair and just trial' includes such basic safeguards as the presumption of innocence, the presentation and examination of witnesses, the common legal defences, the right to remain silent, the right to have the last word in a hearing, the right to appeal, etc. (See also rule 7.1.[22])[I]"

14, *Commentary*, s.p. 2, UNITED NATIONS STANDARD MINIMUM RULES FOR THE ADMINISTRATION OF JUVENILE JUSTICE ("THE BEIJING RULES").

FAMILY [Famille]

– "The family is the natural and fundamental group unit of society and is entitled to protection by society and the State."

Art. 16,3, UNIVERSAL DECLARATION OF HUMAN RIGHTS.
Art. 23, 1, INTERNATIONAL COVENANT ON CIVIL AND POLITICAL RIGHTS.

---

[22] "7.1 Basic procedural safeguards such as the presumption of innocence, the right to be notified of the charges, the right to remain silent, the right to counsel, the right to the presence of a parent or guardian, the right to confront and cross-examine witnesses and the right to appeal to a higher authority shall be guaranteed at all stages of proceedings."

[I] « La procédure suivie pour juger les jeunes délinquants doit en tout état de cause se conformer aux normes minima, assurés presque universellement à tout accusé par le respect des formes légales. Dans ces formes, un procès « juste et équitable » comprend des garanties fondamentales telles que la présomption d'innocence, la comparution et la déposition de témoins, les moyens ordinaires de défense, le droit de garder le silence, le droit de répliquer en dernier à l'audience, le droit de faire appel, etc. (Voir également l'article 7.1.) »

– "The States Parties to the present Covenant recognize that:

> 1. The widest possible protection and assistance should be accorded to the family, which is the natural and fundamental group unit of society, [...]."

Art. 10, INTERNATIONAL COVENANT ON ECONOMIC, SOCIAL AND CULTURAL RIGHTS.

– "*Convinced* that the family, as the fundamental group of society and the natural environment for the growth and well-being of all its members and particularly children, should be afforded the necessary protection and assistance so that it can fully assume its responsibilities within the community,"

Pp. 5, CONVENTION ON THE RIGHTS OF THE CHILD.

– "Rule 18.2[23] points to the importance of the family which, according to article 10, paragraph l, of the International Covenant on Economic, Social and Cultural Rights, is 'the natural and fundamental group unit of society'. Within the family, the parents have not only the right but also the responsibility to care for and supervise their children.[...]"

18, *Commentary*, s.p.3, UNITED NATIONS STANDARD MINIMUM RULES FOR THE ADMINISTRATION OF JUVENILE JUSTICE ("THE BEIJING RULES").

– "12. [...] the family is the central unit responsible for the primary socialization of children, [...]"

UNITED NATIONS GUIDELINES FOR THE PREVENTION OF JUVENILE DELINQUENCY (THE RIYADH GUIDELINES).

– "18. It is important to emphasize the socialization function of the family and extended family;[...]"

UNITED NATIONS GUIDELINES FOR THE PREVENTION OF JUVENILE DELINQUENCY (THE RIYADH GUIDELINES).

– "The family as a basic unit of society and the natural environment for the growth and well-being of all its members, particularly children and youth, should be assisted and protected so that it may fully assume its responsibilities within the community. Parents have the exclusive right to determine freely and responsibly the number and spacing of their children."

Art. 4, DECLARATION ON SOCIAL PROGRESS AND DEVELOPMENT.

---

[23] "18.2 No juvenile shall be removed from parental supervision, whether partly or entire l y, unless the circumstances of her or his case make this necessary."

– "(*a*) The development and co-ordination of policies and measures designed to strengthen the essential functions of the family as a basic unit of society;"

Art. 22, DECLARATION ON SOCIAL PROGRESS AND DEVELOPPMENT.

– "*Recognizing* that the family group should be strengthened because it is the basic unit of every society, and that men and women of full age have the right to marry and to found a family, that they are entitled to equal rights as to marriage and that marriage shall be entered into only with the free and full consent of the intending spouses, in accordance with the provisions of article 16[24] of the Universal Declaration of Human Rights,"

Pp. 1, RECOMMENDATION ON CONSENT TO MARRIAGE, MINIMUM AGE FOR MARRIAGE AND REGISTRATION OF MARRIAGES.

– "31. Affirming the key role played by the family in prevention, care, support and treatment of persons affected and infected by HIV/AIDS, bearing in mind that in different cultural , social and political systems various forms of the family exist;"

DECLARATION OF COMMITMENT ON HIV/AIDS.

– "1. States Parties, recognizing that the family is the natural and fundamental group unit of society and is entitled to protection by society and the State, shall take appropriate measures to ensure the protection of the unity of the families of migrant workers."

Art. 44, INTERNATIONAL CONVENTION ON THE PROTECTION OF THE RIGHTS OF ALL MIGRANT WORKERS AND MEMBERS OF THEIR FAMILIES.

FAMILY EDUCATION [Education familiale]

– "States Parties shall take all appropriate measures:

[...]

(*b*) To ensure that family education includes a proper understanding of maternity as a social function and the recognition of the common responsibility of men and women in the upbringing and development

---

[24] "(1) Men and women of full age, without any limitation due to race, nationality or religion, have the right to marry and to found a family. They are entitled to equal rights as to marriage, during marriage and at its dissolution.
(2) Marriage shall be entered into only with the free and full consent of the intending spouses.
(3) The family is the natural and fundamental group unit of society and is entitled to protection by society and the State."

of their children, it being understood that the interest of the children is the primordial consideration in all cases."

Art. 5, CONVENTION ON THE ELIMINATION OF ALL FORMS OF DISCRIMINATION AGAINST WOMEN.

FAMILY GROUP [Structure familiale]

– "*Recognizing* that the family group should be strengthened because it is the basic unit of every society, and that men and women of full age have the right to marry and to found a family, that they are entitled to equal rights as to marriage and that marriage shall be entered into only with the free and full consent of the intending spouses, in accordance with the provisions of article 16[25] of the Universal Declaration of Human Rights,"

Pp. 1, RECOMMENDATION ON CONSENT TO MARRIAGE, MINIMUM AGE FOR MARRIAGE AND REGISTRATION OF MARRIAGES.

FORCED OR COMPULSORY LABOUR [Travail forcé ou obligatoire]

– "(*c*) For the purpose of this paragraph the term 'forced or compulsory labour' shall not include:

(i) Any work or service, not referred to in subparagraph (b), normally required of a person who is under detention in consequence of a lawful order of a court, or of a person during conditional release from such detention;

(ii) Any service of a military character and, in countries where conscientious objection is recognized, any national service required by law of conscientious objectors;

(iii) Any service exacted in cases of emergency or calamity threatening the life or well-being of the community;

(iv) Any work or service which forms part of normal civil obligations."

Art. 8,3, INTERNATIONAL COVENANT ON CIVIL AND POLITICAL RIGHTS.

---

[25] "(1) Men and women of full age, without any limitation due to race, nationality or religion, have the right to marry and to found a family. They are entitled to equal rights as to marriage, during marriage and at its dissolution.
(2) Marriage shall be entered into only with the free and full consent of the intending spouses.
(3) The family is the natural and fundamental group unit of society and is entitled to protection by society and the State."

– "1. For the purposes of this Convention the term 'forced or compulsory labour' shall mean all work or service which is exacted from any person under the menace of any penalty and for which the said person has not offered himself voluntarily.

2. Nevertheless, for the purposes of this Convention the term 'forced or compulsory labour' shall not include:

(*a*) Any work or service exacted in virtue of compulsory military service laws for work of a purely military character;

(*b*) Any work or service which forms part of the normal civic obligations of the citizens of a fully self-governing country;

(*c*) Any work or service exacted from any person as a consequence of a conviction in a court of law, provided that the said work or service is carried out under the supervision and control of a public authority and that the said person is not hired to or placed at the disposal of private individuals, companies or associations;

(*d*) Any work or service exacted in cases of emergency, that is to say, in the event of war or of a calamity or threatened calamity, such as fire, flood, famine, earthquake, violent epidemic or epizootic diseases, invasion by animal, insect or vegetable pests, and in general any circumstances that would endanger the existence or the well-being of the whole or part of the population;

(*e*) Minor communal services of a kind which, being performed by the members of the community in the direct interest of the said community, can therefore be considered as normal civic obligations incumbent upon the members of the community, provided that the members of the community or their direct representatives shall have the right to be consulted in regard to the need for such services."

Art. 2, FORCED LABOUR CONVENTION, (N° 29).

– "4. For the purpose of the present article the term 'forced or compulsory labour' shall not include:

(*a*) Any work or service not referred to in paragraph 3[26] of the present article normally required of a person who is under detention in

[26] "3. Paragraph 2 of the present article shall not be held to preclude, in States where imprisonment with hard labour may be imposed as a punishment for a crime the performance of hard labour in pursuance of a sentence to such punishment by a competent court."

consequence of a lawful order of a court or of a person during conditional release from such detention;

(*b*) Any service exacted in cases of emergency or clamity threatening the life or well-being of the community;

(*c*) Any work or service that forms part of normal civil obligations so far as it is imposed also on citizens of the State concerned.

Art. 11, INTERNATIONAL CONVENTION ON THE PROTECTION OF THE RIGHTS OF ALL MIGRANT WORKERS AND MEMBERS OF THEIR FAMILIES.

FORCED PREGNANCY [Grossesse forcée]

– "(*g*) Rape, sexual slavery, enforced prostitution, forced pregnancy, enforced sterilization, or any other form of sexual violence of comparable gravity;"

Art. 7, Paragraph 1, ROME STATUTE OF THE INTERNATIONAL CRIMINAL COURT.

– "2. For the purpose of paragraph 1[27]:
[...]

(*f*) 'Forced pregnancy' means the unlawful confinement of a woman forcibly made pregnant, with the intent of affecting the ethnic composition of any population or carrying out other grave violations

---

[27] "1. For the purpose of this Statute, 'crime against humanity' means any of the following acts when committed as part of a widespread or systematic attack directed against any civilian population, with knowledge of the attack:

(a) Murder;
(b) Extermination ;
(c) Enslavement;
(d) Deportation or forcible transfer of population;
(e) Imprisonment or other severe deprivation of physical liberty in violation of fundamental rules of international law;
(f) Torture;
(g) Rape, sexual slavery, enforced prostitution, forced pregnancy, enforced sterilization, or any other form of sexual violence of comparable gravity;
(h) Persecution against any identifiable group or collectivity on political, racial, national, ethnic, cultural, religious, gender, as defined in paragraph 3, or other grounds that are universally recognized as impermissible under international law, in connection with any act referred to in this paragraph or any crime within the jurisdiction of the Court;
(i) Enforced disappearance of persons;
(j) The crime of apartheid;
(k) Other inhumane acts of a similar character intentionally causing great suffering, or serious injury to body or to mental or physical health."

of international law. This definition shall not in any way be interpreted as affecting national laws relating to pregnancy;"

Art. 7, ROME STATUTE OF INTERNATIONAL CRIMINAL COURT.

FORCED PROSTITUTION [Contrainte à la prostitution]

– "1. Women shall be the object of special respect and shall be protected in particular against rape, forced prostitution and any other form of indecent assault."

Art. 76, PROTOCOL ADDITIONAL TO THE GENEVA CONVENTIONS OF 12 AUGUST 1949, AND RELATING TO THE PROTECTION OF VICTIMS OF INTERNATIONAL ARMED CONFLICTS (PROTOCOL I).

FORCIBLE TRANSFERS [Transferts forcés]

– "Individual or mass forcible transfers, as well as deportations of protected persons from occupied territory to the territory of the Occupying Power or to that of any other country, occupied or not, are prohibited, regardless of their motive."

Art. 49 s.p. 1, GENEVA CONVENTION RELATIVE TO THE PROTECTION OF CIVILIAN PERSONS IN TIME OF WAR.

FOSTER CARE [Parents nourriciers]

– "14. [...] alternative placements including foster care and adoption [...]"[J]

UNITED NATIONS GUIDELINES FOR THE PREVENTION OF JUVENILE DELINQUENCY (THE RIYADH GUIDELINES).

FOUNDATION OF FREEDOM, JUSTICE AND PEACE IN THE WORLD [Fondement de la liberté, de la justice et de la paix dans le monde]

– "*Considering* that, in accordance with the principles proclaimed in the Charter of the United Nations, recognition of the inherent dignity and of the equal and inalienable rights of all members of the human family is the foundation of freedom, justice and peace in the world,"

Pp. 1, INTERNATIONAL COVENANT ON ECONOMIC, SOCIAL AND CULTURAL RIGHTS.

Pp. 1, INTERNATIONAL COVENANT ON CIVIL AND POLITICAL RIGHTS.

[J] « [...] des foyers de substitution (parents nourriciers ou adoptifs) [...] »

FRAUDULENT TRAVEL OR IDENTITY DOCUMENT [Document de voyage ou d'identité frauduleux]

– "For the purposes of this Protocol:
[...]

(*c*) 'Fraudulent travel or identity document' shall mean any travel or identity document:

(i) That has been falsely made or altered in some material way by anyone other than a person or agency lawfully authorized to make or issue the travel or identity document on behalf of a State; or

(ii) That has been improperly issued or obtained through misrepresentation, corruption or duress or in any other unlawful manner; or

(iii) That being used by a person other than the rightful holder;"

Art. 3, PROTOCOL AGAINST THE SMUGGLING OF MIGRANTS BY LAND, SEA AND AIR, SUPPLEMENTING THE UNITED NATIONS CONVENTION AGAINST TRANSNATIONAL ORGANIZED CRIME.

FREEDOM [Liberté (la)]

– "6. We consider certain fundamental values to be essential to international relations in the twenty-first century. These include:

Freedom. Men and women have the right to live their lives and raise their children in dignity, free from hunger and from the fear of violence, oppression or injustice. Democratic and participatory governance based on the will of the people best assures these rights. [...]"

First footnote (•), UNITED NATIONS MILLENIUM DECLARATION. 6

– "*Considering* that freedom is the birthright of every human being," [K]

Pp. 1, SUPPLEMENTARY CONVENTION ON THE ABOLITION OF SLAVERY, THE SLAVE TRADE AND INSTITUTIONS AND PRACTICES SIMILAR TO SLAVERY.

FREEDOM OF RESEARCH [Liberté de la recherche]

– "(*b*) Freedom of research, which is necessary for the progress of knowledge, is part of freedom of thought.[...]"

[K] « *Considérant* que la liberté est un droit que tout être humain acquiert à sa naissance, »

Art. 12, UNIVERSAL DECLARATION ON THE HUMAN GENOME AND HUMAN RIGHTS.

FRONTIER WORKER [Travailleurs frontaliers]

– "For the purposes of the present Convention:

[…]

(*a*) The term 'frontier worker' refers to a migrant worker who retains his or her habitual residence in a neighbouring State to which he or she normally returns every day or at least once a week;"

Art. 2.2, INTERNATIONAL CONVENTION ON THE PROTECTION OF THE RIGHTS OF ALL MIGRANT WORKERS AND MEMBERS OF THEIR FAMILIES.

FULL UTILIZATION OF HUMAN RESOURCES [Pleine utilisation des ressources humaines]

– "Social progress and development require the full utilization of human resources, including, in particular:

(*a*) The encouragement of creative initiative under conditions of enlightened public opinion;

(*b*) The dissemination of national and international information for the purpose of making individuals aware of changes occurring in society as a whole;

(*c*) The active participation of all elements of society, individually or through associations, in defining and in achieving the common goals of development with full respect for the fundamental freedoms embodied in the Universal Declaration of Human Rights;

(*d*) The assurance to disadvantaged or marginal sectors of the population of equal opportunities for social and economic advancement in order to achieve an effectively integrated society.

Art. 5, DECLARATION ON SOCIAL PROGRESS AND DEVELOPMENT.

FUNDAMENTAL FREEDOMS [Libertés fondamentales]

– "*Recognizing and affirming* that all human rights derive from the dignity and worth inherent in the human person, and that the human person is the central subject of human rights and fundamental freedoms, and consequently should be the principal beneficiary and should participate actively in the realization of these rights and freedoms,"

Pp. 2, VIENNA DECLARATION AND PROGRAMME OF ACTION.

– "1. The World Conference on Human Rights reaffirms the solemn commitment of all States to fulfil their obligations to promote universal respect for, and observance and protection of, all human rights and fundamental freedoms for all in accordance with the Charter of the United Nations, other instruments relating to human rights, and international law. The universal nature of these rights and freedoms is beyond question."

I, VIENNA DECLARATION AND PROGRAMME OF ACTION.

– "Human rights and fundamental freedoms are the birthright[L] of all human beings; their protection and promotion is the first responsibility of Governments."

I, 1, s.p. 3, VIENNA DECLARATION AND PROGRAMME OF ACTION.

– "63. The World Conference on Human Rights reaffirms that all human rights and fundamental freedoms are universal and thus unreservedly include persons with disabilities. [...]"

II, VIENNA DECLARATION AND PROGRAMME OF ACTION.

– "2. All human rights and fundamental freedoms are indivisible and interdependent; equal attention and urgent consideration should be given to the implementation, promotion and protection of civil, political, economic, social and cultural rights."

Art. 6, DECLARATION ON THE RIGHT TO DEVELOPMENT.

– "*Reiterating* that all the human rights and fundamental freedoms are universal, indivisible, interdependent and interrelated and should be promoted and implemented in fair and equitable manner, without prejudice to implementation of each of those rights and freedoms,"

Pp. 6, DECLARATION ON THE RIGHTS AND RESPONSIBILITY OF INDIVIDUALS, GROUPS AND ORGANS OF SOCIETY TO PROMOTE AND PROTECT UNIVERSALLY RECOGNIZED HUMAN RIGHTS AND FUNDAMENTAL FREEDOMS.

[L] « Les droits de l'homme et les libertés fondamentales sont inhérents à tous les êtres humains ; leurs promotion et leur protection incombent au premier chef aux gouvernements. »

GAS OR RADIATION POISONING [Intoxications par les gaz et par les radiations]

– "(*o*) Serious cases of chronic intoxication, for example: lead poisoning, mercury poisoning, morphinism, cocainism, alcoholism; gas or radiation poisoning; etc."

Annex I, 3, GENEVA CONVENTION RELATIVE TO THE TREATMENT OF PRISONERS OF WAR.

GASTRIC OR DUODENAL ULCER [Ulcère de l'estomac ou duodénum]

– "(*e*) Serious chronic affections of the digestive organs, for example: gastric or duodenal ulcer, sequelae of gastric operations performed in captivity; chronic gastritis, enteritis or colitis, having lasted more than one year and seriously affecting the general condition: cirrhosis of the liver, chronic cholecystopathy; etc."

Annex I, 3, GENEVA CONVENTION RELATIVE TO THE TREATMENT OF PRISONERS OF WAR.

GENDER [Sexe]

– "3. For the purpose of this Statute, it is understood that the term 'gender' refers to the two sexes, male and female, within the context of society. The term 'gender' does not indicate any meaning different from the above."

Art. 7, ROME STATUTE OF THE INTERNATIONAL CRIMINAL COURT.

GENDER EQUALITY AND EMPOWERMENT OF WOMEN [Egalité entre les sexes et émancipation des femmes]

– "14. Stressing that gender equality and the empowerment of women are fundamental elements in the reduction of the vulnerability of women and girls to HIV/AIDS;"

DECLARATION OF COMMITMENT ON HIV/AIDS.

GENERAL ASSEMBLY [Assemblée générale]

– "To reaffirm the central position of the General Assembly as the chief deliberative, policy-making and representative organ of the United Nations, and to enable it to play that role effectively."

30, first footnote (•), UNITED NATIONS MILLENIUM DECLARATION.

GENOCIDE [Génocide ; Crime de génocide]

– "28. The World Conference on Human Rights expresses its dismay at massive violations of human rights especially in the form of genocide, 'ethnic cleansing' and systematic rape of women in war situations, creating mass exodus of refugees and displaced persons. [...]"

I, VIENNA DECLARATION AND PROGRAM OF ACTION.

– "2. One of the most serious violations of this principle is represented by apartheid, which, like genocide, is a crime against humanity, and gravely disturbs international peace and security."

Art. 4, DECLARATION ON RACE AND RACIAL PREJUDICE.

– "*Having considered* the declaration made by the General Assembly of the United Nations in its resolution 96(I) dated 11 December 1946 that genocide is a crime under international law, contrary to the spirit and aims of the United Nations and condemned by the civilized world;"

Pp. 1, CONVENTION ON THE PREVENTION AND PUNISHMENT OF THE CRIME OF GENOCIDE.

– "*Recognizing* that at all periods of history genocide has inflicted great losses on humanity;[...]"

Pp. 2, CONVENTION ON THE PREVENTION AND PUNISHMENT OF THE CRIME OF GENOCIDE.

– "In the present Convention, genocide means any of the following acts commited with intent to destroy, in whole or in part, a national, ethical, racial or religious group as such:

(*a*) Killing members of the group;

(*b*) Causing serious bodily or mental harm to members of the group;

(*c*) Deliberately inflicting on the group conditions of life calculated to bring about its physical destruction in whole or in part;

(*d*) Imposing measures intended to prevent births within the group;

(*e*) Forcibly transferring children of the group to another group.

Art. II, CONVENTION ON THE PREVENTION AND PUNISHMENT OF THE CRIME OF GENOCIDE.

– "2. Genocide means any of the following acts committed with intent to destroy, in whole or in part, a national, ethnical, racial or religious group, as such:

(*a*) killing members of the group;

(*b*) causing serious bodily or mental harm to members of the group;

(*c*) deliberately inflicting on the group conditions of life calculated to bring about its physical destruction in whole or in part;

(*d*) imposing measures intended to prevent births within the group;

(*e*) forcibly transferring children of the group to another group."

Art. 4, STATUTE OF THE INTERNATIONAL TRIBUNAL FOR THE PROSECUTION OF PERSONS RESPONSIBLE FOR SERIOUS VIOLATIONS OF INTERNATIONAL HUMANITARIAN LAW COMMITTED IN THE TERRITORY OF FORMER YUGOSLAVIA SINCE 1991.

Art. 2, STATUTE OF INTERNATIONAL CRIMINAL TRIBUNAL FOR THE PROSECUTION OF PERSONS RESPONSIBLE FOR GENOCIDE AND OTHER SERIOUS VIOLATIONS OF INTERNATIONAL HUMANITARIAN LAW COMMITTED IN THE TERRITORY OF RWANDA AND RWANDAN CITIZENS RESPONSIBLE FOR GENOCIDE AND OTHER SUCH VIOLATIONS COMMITTED IN THE TERRITORY OF NEIGHBOURING STATES, BETWEEN 1 JANUARY 1994 AND 31 DECEMBER 1994.

– "For the purpose of this Statute, 'genocide' means any of the following acts committed with intent to destroy, in whole or in part, a national, ethnical, racial or religious group, as such:

(*a*) Killing members of the group;

(*b*) Causing serious bodily or mental harm to members of the group;

(*c*) Deliberately inflicting on the group conditions of life calculated to bring about its physical destruction in whole or in part;

(*d*) Imposing measures intended to prevent births within the group;

(*e*) Forcibly transferring children of the group to another group.

Art. 6, ROME STATUTE OF INTERNATIONAL CRIMINAL COURT.

GIRL CHILDREN [Fillettes]

– "*Recognizing* that a number of particularly vulnerable groups, including girl children, are at greater risk of sexual exploitation, and that girl children are disproportionately represented among the sexually exploited,"

Pp. 5, OPTIONAL PROTOCOL TO CONVENTION ON THE RIGHTS OF THE CHILD ON THE SALE OF CHILDREN, CHILD PROSTITUTION AND CHILD PORNOGRAPHY.

GLAUCOMA [Glaucome]

– "(*i*) Blindness of both eyes, or of one eve when the vision of the other is less than I in spite of the use of corrective glasses; diminution of visual acuity in cases where it is impossible to restore it by correction to an acuity of 1/2 in at least one eye; other grave ocular affections, for example: glaucoma, iritis, choroiditis; trachoma, etc."

Annex I, 3, GENEVA CONVENTION RELATIVE TO THE TREATMENT OF PRISONERS OF WAR.

GLOBAL HIV/AIDS EPIDEMIC [Epidémie mondiale de VIH/sida]

– "2. Deeply concerned that the global HIV/AIDS epidemic, through its devastating scale and impact, constitutes a global emergency and one of the most formidable challenges to human life and dignity, as well as the effective enjoyment of human rights, which undermines social and economic development throughout the world and affects all levels of society – national, community, family and individual;"

DECLARATION OF COMMITMENT ON THE HIV/AIDS.

GLOBALIZATION [Mondialisation]

– "5. We believe that the central challenge we face today is to ensure that globalization becomes a positive force for all the world's people. For while globalization offers great opportunities, at present its benefits are very unevenly shared, while its costs are unevenly distributed. [...]"

I, UNITED NATIONS MILLENIUM DECLARATION.

GRAVE BREACHES [Infractions graves]

– "Grave breaches to which the preceding Article[28] relates shall be those involving any of the following acts, if committed against persons or

[28] "The High Contracting Parties undertake to enact any legislation necessary to provide effective penal sanctions for persons committing, or ordering to be committed, any of the grave breaches of the present Convention defined in the following Article.
Each High Contracting Party shall be under the obligation to search for persons alleged to have committed, or to have ordered to be committed, such grave breaches, and shall bring such persons, regardless of their nationality, before its own courts. It may also, if it prefers, and in accordance with the provisions of its own legislation, hand such persons over for trial to another
High Contracting Party concerned, provided such High Contracting Party has made out a prima facie case.
Each High Contracting Party shall take measures necessary for the suppression of all acts contrary to the provisions of the present Convention other than the grave breaches defined in the following Article.

property protected by the present Convention: wilful killing, torture or inhuman treatment, including biological experiments, wilfully causing great suffering or serious injury to body or health, unlawful deportation or transfer or unlawful confinement of a protected person, compelling a protected person to serve in the forces of a hostile Power, or wilfully depriving a protected person of the rights of fair and regular trial prescribed in the present Convention, taking of hostages and extensive destruction and appropriation of property, not justified by military necessity and carried out unlawfully and wantonly."

Art. 147, GENEVA CONVENTION RELATIVE TO THE PROTECTION OF CIVILIAN PERSONS IN TIME OF WAR.

– "2. Acts described as grave breaches in the Conventions are grave breaches of this Protocol if committed against persons in the power of an adverse Party protected by Articles 44[29], 45[30] and 73[31] of this Protocol, or

---

In all circumstances, the accused persons shall benefit by safeguards of proper trial and defence, which shall not be less favourable than those provided by Article 105 and those following of the Geneva Convention relative to the Treatment of Prisoners of War of August 12, 1949."

[29] "1. Any combatant, as defined in Article 43, who falls into the power of an adverse Party shall be a prisoner of war.

2. While all combatants are obliged to comply with the rules of international law applicable in armed conflict, violations of these rules shall not deprive a combatant of his right to be a combatant or, if he falls into the power of an adverse Party, of his right to be a prisoner of war, except as provided in paragraphs 3 and 4.

3. In order to promote the protection of the civilian population from the effects of hostilities, combatants are obliged to distinguish themselves from the civilian population while they are engaged in an attack or in a military operation preparatory to an attack. Recognizing, however, that there are situations in armed conflicts where, owing to the nature of the hostilities an armed combatant cannot so distinguish himself, he shall retain his status as a combatant, provided that, in such situations, he carries his arms openly:

(*a*) During each military engagement, and

(*b*) During such time as he is visible to the adversary while he is engaged in a military deployment preceding the launching of an attack in which he is to participate.

Acts which comply with the requirements of this paragraph shall not be considered as perfidious within the meaning of Article 37, paragraph 1 (c).

4. A combatant who falls into the power of an adverse Party while failing to meet the requirements set forth in the second sentence of paragraph 3 shall forfeit his right to be a prisoner of war, but he shall, nevertheless, be given protections equivalent in all respects to those accorded to prisoners of war by the Third Convention and by this Protocol. This protection includes protections equivalent to those accorded to prisoners of war by the Third Convention in the case where such a person is tried and punished for any offences he has committed.

against the wounded, sick and shipwrecked of the adverse Party who are protected by this Protocol, or against those medical or religious personnel, medical units or medical transports which are under the control of the adverse Party and are protected by this Protocol.

---

5. Any combatant who falls into the power of an adverse Party while not engaged in an attack or in a military operation preparatory to an attack shall not forfeit his rights to be a combatant and a prisoner of war by virtue of his prior activities.
6. This Article is without prejudice to the right of any person to be a prisoner of war pursuant to Article 4 of the Third Convention.
7. This Article is not intended to change the generally accepted practice of States with respect to the wearing of the uniform by combatants assigned to the regular, uniformed armed units of a Party to the conflict.
8. In addition to the categories of persons mentioned in Article 13 of the First and Second Conventions, all members of the armed forces of a Party to the conflict, as defined in Article 43 of this Protocol, shall be entitled to protection under those Conventions if they are wounded or sick or, in the case of the Second Convention, shipwrecked at sea or in other waters."

[30] 1. A person who takes part in hostilities and falls into the power of an adverse Party shall be presumed to be a prisoner of war, and therefore shall be protected by the Third Convention, if he claims the status of prisoner of war, or if he appears to be entitled to such status, or if the Party on which he depends claims such status on his behalf by notification to the detaining Power or to the Protecting Power. Should any doubt arise as to whether any such person is entitled to the status of prisoner of war, he shall continue to have such status and, therefore, to be protected by the Third Convention and this Protocol until such time as his status has been determined by a competent tribunal.
2. If a person who has fallen into the power of an adverse Party is not held as a prisoner of war and is to be tried by that Party for an offence arising out of the hostilities, he shall have the right to assert his entitlement to prisoner-of-war status before a judicial tribunal and to have that question adjudicated. Whenever possible under the applicable procedure, this adjudication shall occur before the trial for the offence. The representatives of the Protecting Power shall be entitled to attend the proceedings in which that question is adjudicated, unless, exceptionally, the proceedings are held in camera in the interest of State security. In such a case the detaining Power shall advise the Protecting Power accordingly.
3. Any person who has taken part in hostilities, who is not entitled to prisoner-of-war status and who does not benefit from more favourable treatment in accordance with the Fourth Convention shall have the right at all times to the protection of Article 75 of this Protocol. In occupied territory, an such person, unless he is held as a spy, shall also be entitled, notwithstanding Article 5 of the Fourth Convention, to his rights of communication under that Convention.

[31] "Persons who, before the beginning of hostilities, were considered as stateless persons or refugees under the relevant international instruments accepted by the Parties concerned or under the national legislation of the State of refuge or State of residence shall be protected persons within the meaning of Parts I and III of the Fourth Convention, in all circumstances and without any adverse distinction."

3. In addition to the grave breaches defined in Article 11[32], the following acts shall be regarded as grave breaches of this Protocol, when committed wilfully, in violation of the relevant provisions of this Protocol, and causing death or serious injury to body or health:

(*a*) Making the civilian population or individual civilians the object of attack;

(*b*) Launching an indiscriminate attack affecting the civilian population or civilian objects in the knowledge that such attack will

---

[32] "1. The physical or mental health and integrity of persons who are in the power of the adverse Party or who are interned, detained or otherwise deprived of liberty as a result of a situation referred to in Article I shall not be endangered by any unjustified act or omission. Accordingly, it is prohibited to subject the persons described in this Article to any medical procedure which is not indicated by the state of health of the person concerned and which is not consistent with generally accepted medical standards which would be applied under similar medical circumstances to persons who are nationals of the Party conducting the procedure and who are in no way deprived of liberty.

2. It is, in particular, prohibited to carry out on such persons, even with their consent:

(*a*) Physical mutilations;

(*b*) Medical or scientific experiments;

(*c*) Removal of tissue or organs for transplantation,

except where these acts are justified in conformity with the conditions provided for in paragraph 1.

3. Exceptions to the prohibition in paragraph 2 (c) may be made only in the case of donations of blood for transfusion or of skin for grafting, provided that they are given voluntarily and without any coercion or inducement, and then only for therapeutic purposes, under conditions consistent with generally accepted medical standards and controls designed for the benefit of both the donor and the recipient.

4. Any wilful act or omission which seriously endangers the physical or mental health or integrity of any person who is in the power of a Party other than the one on which he depends and which either violates any of the prohibitions in paragraphs 1 and 2 or fails to comply with the requirements of paragraph 3 shall be a grave breach of this Protocol.

5. The persons described in paragraph I have the right to refuse any surgical operation. In case of refusal, medical personnel shall endeavour to obtain a written statement to that effect, signed or acknowledged by the patient.

6. Each Party to the conflict shall keep a medical record for every donation of blood for transfusion or skin for grafting by persons referred to in paragraph 1, if that donation is made under the responsibility of that Party. In addition, each Party to the conflict shall endeavour to keep a record of all medical procedures undertaken with respect to any person who is interned, detained or otherwise deprived of liberty as a result of a situation referred to in Article 1. These records shall be available at all times for inspection by the Protecting Power."

cause excessive loss of life, injury to civilians or damage to civilian objects, as defined in Article 57, paragraph 2 (a) (iii)[33];

(*c*) Launching an attack against works or installations containing dangerous forces in the knowledge that such attack will cause excessive loss of life, injury to civilians or damage to civilian objects, as defined in Article 57, paragraph 2 (a) (iii)[34];

(*d*) Making non-defended localities and demilitarized zones the object of attack;

(*e*) Making a person the object of attack in the knowledge that he is hors de combat;

(*f*) The perfidious use, in violation of Article 37[35], of the distinctive emblem of the red cross, red crescent or red lion and sun or of other protective signs recognized by the Conventions or this Protocol.

4. In addition to the grave breaches defined in the preceding paragraphs and in the Conventions, the following shall be regarded as grave breaches of this Protocol, when committed wilfully and in violation of the Conventions of the Protocol;

(*a*) The transfer by the Occupying Power of parts of its own civilian population into the territory it occupies, or the deportation or transfer of all or parts of the population of the occupied territory within or

---

[33] "(iii) Refrain from deciding to launch any attack which may be expected to cause incidental loss of civilian life, injury to civilians, damage to civilian objects, or a combination thereof, which would be excessive in relation to the concrete and direct military advantage anticipated;"

[34] *Ibid.*

[35] "1. It is prohibited to kill, injure or capture an adversary by resort to perfidy. Acts inviting the confidence of an adversary to lead him to believe that he is entitled to, or is obliged to accord, protection under the rules of international law applicable in armed conflict, with intent to betray that confidence, shall constitute perfidy. The following acts are examples of perfidy:
(*a*) The feigning of an intent to negotiate under a flag of truce or of a surrender;
(*b*) The feigning of an incapacitation by wounds or sickness;
(*c*) The feigning of civilian, non-combatant status; and
(*d*) The feigning of protected status by the use of signs, emblems or uniforms of the United Nations or of neutral or other States not Parties to the conflict.
2. Ruses of war are not prohibited. Such ruses are acts which are intended to mislead an adversary or to induce him to act recklessly but which infringe no rule of international law applicable in armed conflict and which are not perfidious because they do not invite the confidence of an adversary with respect to protection under that law. The following are examples of such ruses: the use of camouflage, decoys, mock operations and misinformation."

outside this territory, in violation of Article 49 of the Fourth Convention[36];

(*b*) Unjustifiable delay in the repatriation of prisoners of war or civilians;

(*c*) Practices of apartheid and other inhuman and degrading practices involving outrages upon personal dignity, based on racial discrimination;

(*d*) Making the clearly-recognized historic monuments, works of art or places of worship which constitute the cultural or spiritual heritage of peoples and to which special protection has been given by special arrangement, for example, within the framework of a competent international organization, the object of attack, causing as a result extensive destruction thereof, where there is no evidence of the violation by the adverse Party of Article 53, sub-paragraph (b)[37], and when such historic monuments, works of art and places of worship are not located in the immediate proximity of military objectives;

(*e*) Depriving a person protected by the Conventions or referred to in paragraph 2 of this Article of the rights of fair and regular trial."

Art. 85, PROTOCOL ADDITIONAL TO THE GENEVA CONVENTIONS OF 12 AUGUST 1949, AND RELATING TO THE PROTECTION OF VICTIMS OF INTERNATIONAL ARMED CONFLICTS (PROTOCOL I).

---

[36] "Individual or mass forcible transfers, as well as deportations of protected persons from occupied territory to the territory of the Occupying Power or to that of any other country, occupied or not, are prohibited, regardless of their motive.
Nevertheless, the Occupying Power may undertake total or partial evacuation of a given area if the security of the population or imperative military reasons so demand. Such evacuations may not involve the displacement of protected persons outside the bounds of the occupied territory except when for material reasons it is impossible to avoid such displacement. Persons thus evacuated shall be transferred back to their homes as soon as hostilities in the area in question have ceased.
The Occupying Power undertaking such transfers or evacuations shall ensure, to the greatest practicable extent, that proper accommodation is provided to receive the protected persons, that the removals are effected in satisfactory conditions of hygiene, health, safety and nutrition, and that members of the same family are not separated.
The Protecting Power shall be informed of any transfers and evacuations as soon as they have taken place.
The Occupying Power shall not detain protected persons in an area particularly exposed to the dangers of war unless the security of the population or imperative military reasons so demand."

[37] "(*b*) To use such objects in support of the military effort;"

HANDICAP [Handicap]

– "6. [...]There also, for the first time, handicap was defined as a function of the relationship between persons with disabilities and their environment."
INTRODUCTION, STANDARD RULES ON THE EQUALIZATION OF OPPORTUNITIES FOR PERSONS WITH DISABILITIES.

– "18. The term 'handicap' means the loss or limitation of opportunities to take part in the life of the community on an equal level with others. It describes the encounter between the person with a disability and the environment. The purpose of this term is to emphasize the focus on the shortcomings in the environment and in many organized activities in society, for example, information, communication and education, which prevent persons with disabilities from participating on equal terms.
INTRODUCTION, STANDARD RULES ON THE EQUALIZATION OF OPPORTUNITIES FOR PERSONS WITH DISABILITIES.

– "20. In 1980, the World Health Organization adopted an international classification of impairments, disabilities and handicaps, which suggested a more precise and at the same time relativistic approach. The International Classification of Impairments, Disabilities, and Handicaps makes a clear distinction between 'impairment', 'disability' and 'handicap'. It has been extensively used in areas such as rehabilitation, education, statistics, policy, legislation, demography, sociology, economics and anthropology. Some users have expressed concern that the Classification, in its definition of the term 'handicap', may still be considered too medical and too centred on the individual, and may not adequately clarify the interaction between societal conditions or expectations and the abilities of the individual. Those concerns, and others expressed by users during the 12 years since its publication, will be addressed in forthcoming revisions of the Classification." [M]

[M] « 20. En 1980, l'Organisation mondiale de la santé a adopté une classification internationale des déficiences, incapacités et handicaps qui a défini une approche à la fois plus précise et relativiste. La Classification internationale des handicapés : déficiences, incapacités et désavantages établit des distinctions claires entre la déficience, l'incapacité et handicap. Elle est couramment utilisée dans les domaines suivants : réadaptation, éducation, statistiques, prise de décisions, législation, démographie, sociologie, économie et anthropologie. Selon certains des spécialistes à qui elle s'adresse, il se pourrait que la définition du terme « handicap » qui est donnée revête un caractère trop médicale encore, qu'elle soit indûment centrée sur l'individu, et qu'elle ne précise pas assez clairement la manière dont la situation sociale, les attentes de la collectivité et d'autres préoccupations exprimées par les utilisateurs depuis la publication de la Classification, il y a 12 ans, dans les révisions dont celle-ci doit faire l'objet. »

INTRODUCTION, STANDARD RULES ON THE EQUALIZATION OF OPPORTUNITIES FOR PERSONS WITH DISABILITIES.

HERITAGE [Patrimoine]

– "Creation draws on the roots of cultural tradition, but flourishes in contact with other cultures For this reason, heritage in all its forms must be preserved, enhanced and handed on to future generations as a record of human experience and aspirations, so as to foster creativity in all its diversity and to inspire genuine dialogue among cultures."

Art. 7, UNIVERSAL DECLARATION ON CULTURAL DIVERSITY.

HIGH COMMISSIONER FOR HUMAN RIGHTS [Haut-Commissaire aux droits de l'homme]

– "18. The World Conference on Human Rights recommends to the General Assembly that when examining the report of the Conference at its forty-eighth session, it begin, as a matter of priority, consideration of the question of the establishment of a High Commissioner for Human Rights for the promotion and protection of all human rights."

II, VIENNA DECLARATION AND PROGRAMME OF ACTION.

HIGHEST ASPIRATION OF THE COMMON PEOPLE (THE) [Plus haute aspiration de l'homme]

– "[...] the advent of a world in which human beings shall enjoy freedom of speech and belief and freedom from fear and want has been proclaimed as the highest aspiration of the common people,"

Pp. 2, UNIVERSAL DECLARATION OF HUMAN RIGHTS.

HIV/AIDS [VIH/sida]

– "To have, by then [2015], halted, and begun to reverse, the spread of HIV/AIDS, the scourge of malaria and other major diseases that afflict humanity."

19, fourth footnote (•), UNITED NATIONS MILLENIUM DECLARATION.

– "2. Deeply concerned that the global HIV/AIDS epidemic, through its devastating scale and impact, constitutes a global emergency and one of the most formidable challenges to human life and dignity, as well as the effective enjoyment of human rights, which undermines social and

economic development throughout the world and affects all levels of society –national, community, family and individual;"
DECLARATION OF COMMITMENT ON HIV/AIDS.

– "3. Noting with profound concern that by the end of 2000, 36.1 million people worldwide were living with HIV/AIDS, 90 per cent in developing countries and 75 per cent in sub-Saharan Africa;"
DECLARATION OF COMMITMENT ON HIV/AIDS.

– "4. Noting with grave concern that all people, rich and poor, without distinction as to age, gender or race, are effected by the HIV/AIDS epidemic, further noting that people in developing countries are the most affected and that women, young adults and children, in particular girls, are the most vulnerable;"
DECLARATION OF COMMITMENT ON THE HIV/AIDS.

HORS DE COMBAT [Hors de combat]

– "2. A person is *hors de combat* if:

(*a*) He is in the power of an adverse Party;

(*b*) He clearly expresses an intention to surrender; or

(*c*) He has been rendered unconscious or is otherwise incapacitated by wounds or sickness, and therefore is incapable of defending himself; provided that in any of these cases he abstains from any hostile act and does not attempt to escape."

Art. 41, PROTOCOL ADDITIONAL TO THE GENEVA CONVENTIONS OF 12 AUGUST 1949, AND RELATING TO THE PROTECTION OF VICTIMS OF INTERNATIONAL ARMED CONFLICTS (PROTOCOL I).

HUMAN BEING [Personne humaine; Etre humain]

– "1. Every human being has the inherent right to life. This right shall be protected by law. No one shall be arbitrarily deprived of his life."
Art. 6, INTERNATIONAL COVENANT ON CIVIL AND POLITICAL RIGHTS.

– "*Recognizing* that the human person is the central subject of the development process and that development policy should therefore make the human being the main participant and beneficiary of development,"[O]

Pp. 13, DECLARATION ON THE RIGHT TO DEVELOPMENT.

HUMAN BEINGS [Etres humains]

– "All human beings are born free and equal in dignity and rights. They are endowed with reason and conscience and should act towards one another in a spirit of brotherhood."

Art. 1 UNIVERSAL DECLARATION OF HUMAN RIGHTS.

– "Human rights and fundamental freedoms are the birthright[N] of all human beings; their protection and promotion is the first responsibility of Governments."

I, 1, s.p. 3, VIENNA DECLARATION AND PROGRAMME OF ACTION.

– "1. All human beings belong to a single species and are descended from a common stock. They are born equal in dignity and rights and all form an integral part of humanity."

Art. 1, DECLARATION ON RACE AND RACIAL PREJUDICE.

HUMAN GENOME [Génome humain]

– "The human genome underlies the fundamental unity of all members of the human family, as well as the recognition of their inherent dignity and diversity. In a symbolic sense, it is the heritage of humanity."

Art. 1, UNIVERSAL DECLARATION ON THE HUMAN GENOME AND HUMAN RIGHTS.

– "The human genome, which by its nature evolves, is subject to mutations. It contains potentialities that are expressed differently according to each individual's natural and social environment including the individual's state of health, living conditions, nutrition and education."

Art. 3, UNIVERSAL DECLARATION ON THE HUMAN GENOME AND HUMAN RIGHTS.

[O] « *Considérant* que l'être humain est le sujet central du processus de développement et qu'en conséquence il devrait être considéré comme le principal participant à ce processus et son principal bénéficiaire par toute politique de développement, »

[N] « Les droits de l'homme et les libertés fondamentales sont inhérents à tous les êtres humains ; leurs promotion et leur protection incombent au premier chef aux gouvernements. »

HUMAN PERSON [Personne humaine ; Etre humain]

– "*Recognizing* that these rights derive from the inherent dignity of the human person, "

Pp. 2, International Covenant on Civil and Political Rights.
Pp. 2, International Covenant on Economic, Social and Cultural Rights.

– "1. All persons deprived of their liberty shall be treated with humanity and with respect for the inherent dignity of the human person."

Art. 10, International Covenant on Civil and Political Rights.

– "As stated in the Declaration on the Right to Development, the human person is the central subject of development."

I, 10, subparagraph 2, Vienna Declaration and Program of Action.

– "All persons under any form of detention or imprisonment shall be treated in a humane manner and with respect for the inherent dignity of the human person."

Principle 1, Body of Principles for the Protection of All Persons under Any Form of Detention or Imprisonment.

– "*Recognizing* that those rights[38] derive from the inherent dignity of human person,"

Pp. 2, Convention against Torture and Other Cruel, Inhuman or Degrading Treatment or Punishment.

– "*Recognizing and affirming* that all human rights derive from the dignity and worth inherent in the human person, and that the human person is the central subject of human rights and fundamental freedoms, and consequently should be the principal beneficiary and should participate actively in the realization of these rights and freedoms,"

Pp. 2, Vienna Declaration and Programme of Action.

– "*Recognizing* that the human person is the central subject of the development process and that development policy should therefore make the human being the main participant and beneficiary of development,"[P]

Pp. 13, Declaration on the Right to Development.

---

[38] Equal and inalienable rights of all members of the human family.

[P] « *Considérant* que l'être humain est le sujet central du processus de développement et qu'en conséquence il devrait être considéré comme le principal participant à ce processus et son principal bénéficiaire par toute politique de développement, »

– "1. The human person is the central subject of development and should be the active participant and beneficiary of the right to development."
Art. 2, DECLARATION ON THE RIGHT TO DEVELOPMENT.

– "*Recalling* that, in cases not covered by the law in force, the human person remains under the protection of the principles of humanity and the dictates of the public conscience,"
Pp. 4, PROTOCOL ADDITIONAL TO THE GENEVA CONVENTIONS OF 12 AUGUST 1949, AND RELATING TO THE PROTECTION OF VICTIMS OF NON-INTERNATIONAL ARMED CONFLICTS (PROTOCOL II).

HUMAN RIGHTS [Droits de l'homme; Droits fondamentaux]

– "*Recognizing and affirming* that all human rights derive from the dignity and worth inherent in the human person, and that the human person is the central subject of human rights and fundamental freedoms, and consequently should be the principal beneficiary and should participate actively in the realization of these rights and freedoms,"
Pp. 2, VIENNA DECLARATION AND PROGRAMME OF ACTION.

– "1. The World Conference on Human Rights reaffirms the solemn commitment of all States to fulfil their obligations to promote universal respect for, and observance and protection of, all human rights and fundamental freedoms for all in accordance with the Charter of the United Nations, other instruments relating to human rights, and international law. The universal nature of these rights and freedoms is beyond question."
I., VIENNA DECLARATION AND PROGRAMME OF ACTION.

– "Human rights and fundamental freedoms are the birthright[Q] of all human beings; their protection and promotion is the first responsibility of Governments."
I, 1, s.p. 3, VIENNA DECLARATION AND PROGRAMME OF ACTION.

– "5. All human rights are universal, indivisible and interdependent and interrelated. The international community must treat human rights globally in a fair and equal manner, on the same footing, and with the same emphasis. While the significance of national and regional particularities and various historical, cultural and religious backgrounds

---

[Q] « Les droits de l'homme et les libertés fondamentales sont inhérents à tous les êtres humains ; leurs promotion et leur protection incombent au premier chef aux gouvernements. »

must be borne in mind, it is the duty of States, regardless of their political, economic and cultural systems, to promote and protect all human rights and fundamental freedoms."

I, VIENNA DECLARATION AND PROGRAMME OF ACTION.

– "63. The World Conference on Human Rights reaffirms that all human rights and fundamental freedoms are universal and thus unreservedly include persons with disabilities."

II, VIENNA DECLARATION AND PROGRAMME OF ACTION.

– "In the performance of their duty, law enforcement officials shall respect and protect human dignity and maintain and uphold the human rights of all persons[R].

Commentary:

(*a*) The human rights in question are identified and protected by national and international law. Among the relevant international instruments are the Universal Declaration of Human Rights, the International Covenant on Civil and Political Rights, the Declaration on the Protection of All Persons from Being Subjected to Torture and Other Cruel, Inhuman or Degrading Treatment or Punishment, the United Nations Declaration on the Elimination of All Forms of Racial Discrimination, the International Convention on the Elimination of All Forms of Racial Discrimination, the International Convention on the Suppression and Punishment of the Crime of *Apartheid*, the Convention on the Prevention and Punishment of the Crime of

---

[R] « Dans l'accomplissement de leur devoir, les responsables de l'application des lois doivent respecter et protéger la dignité humaine et défendre et protéger les droits fondamentaux de toute personne.

Commentaire:

a) Les droits fondamentaux en question sont définis et protégés par le droit national et le droit international. Les instruments internationaux pertinents comprennent notamment la Déclaration universelle des droits de l'homme, le Pacte international relatif aux droits civils et politiques, la Déclaration sur la protection de toutes les personnes contre la torture et autres peines ou traitements cruels, inhumains ou dégradants, la Déclaration des Nations Unies sur l'élimination de toutes les formes de discrimination raciale, la Convention internationale sur l'élimination de toutes les formes de discrimination raciale, la Convention internationale sur l'élimination et la répression du crime d'apartheid, la Convention pour la prévention et la répression du crime de génocide, l'Ensemble de règles minima pour le traitement des détenus et la Convention de Vienne sur les relations consulaires. »

Genocide, the Standard Minimum Rules for the Treatment of Prisoners and the Vienna Convention on Consular Relations."

Art. 2, CODE OF CONDUCT FOR LAW ENFORCEMENT OFFICIALS.

– "2. All human rights and fundamental freedoms are indivisible and interdependent; equal attention and urgent consideration should be given to the implementation, promotion and protection of civil, political, economic, social and cultural rights."

Art. 6, DECLARATION ON THE RIGHT TO DEVELOPMENT.

– "Article 4. Human rights as guarantees of cultural diversity" [S]

UNIVERSAL DECLARATION ON CULTURAL DIVERSITY.

– "Cultural rights are an integral part of human rights, which are universal, indivisible and interdependent. [...]"

Art. 5, UNIVERSAL DECLARATION ON CULTURAL DIVERSITY.

– "*Reiterating* that all the human rights and fundamental freedoms are universal, indivisible, interdependent and interrelated and should be promoted and implemented in a fair and equitable manner, without prejudice to implementation of each of those rights and freedoms,"

Pp. 6, DECLARATION ON THE RIGHTS AND RESPONSIBILITY OF INDIVIDUALS, GROUPS AND ORGANS OF SOCIETY TO PROMOTE AND PROTECT UNIVERSALLY RECOGNIZED HUMAN RIGHTS AND FUNDAMENTAL FREEDOMS.

HUMAN RIGHTS OF WOMEN AND OF THE GIRL-CHILD [Droits fondamentaux des femmes et des fillettes]

– "The human rights of women and of the girl-child are an inalienable, integral and indivisible part of universal human rights. [...]"

I, 18, al.1, VIENNA DECLARATION AND PROGRAM OF ACTION.

HUMILIATING AND DEGRADING TREATMENT [Traitements humiliants et dégradants]

– "(*c*) Outrages upon personal dignity, in particular humiliating and degrading treatment;"

Art. 3, paragraph 1, GENEVA CONVENTION RELATIVE TO THE PROTECTION OF CIVILIAN PERSONS IN TIME OF WAR.

[S] « *Article 4- Les droits de l'homme, garants de la diversité culturelle* »

– “*b*) Outrages upon personal dignity, in particular humiliating and degrading treatment, enforced prostitution and any form of indecent assault;”

ART. 75, PARAGRAPH 2, PROTOCOL ADDITIONAL TO THE GENEVA CONVENTIONS OF 12 AUGUST 1949, AND RELATING TO THE PROTECTION OF VICTIMS OF INTERNATIONAL ARMED CONFLICTS (PROTOCOL I).

– “*e*) Outrages upon personal dignity, in particular humiliating and degrading treatment, rape, enforced prostitution and any form of indecent assault;”

ART. 4, PARAGRAPH 2, PROTOCOL ADDITIONAL TO THE GENEVA CONVENTIONS OF 12 AUGUST 1949, AND RELATING TO THE PROTECTION OF VICTIMS OF NON-INTERNATIONAL ARMED CONFLICTS (PROTOCOL II).

HYDRONEPHROSIS OR PYONEPHROSIS [Hydro ou pyonéphrose]

– “(*f*) Serious chronic affections of the genito-urinary organs, for example: chronic diseases of the kidney with consequent disorders; nephrectomy because of a tubercular kidney; chronic pyelitis or chronic cystitis: hydronephrosis or pyonephrosis; chronic grave gynaecological conditions, normal pregnancy, and obstetrical disorder, where it is impossible to accommodate in a neutral country; etc.”

Annex I, 3, GENEVA CONVENTION RELATIVE TO THE TREATMENT OF PRISONERS OF WAR.

IDENTITY OF ORIGIN [Identité d'origine]

– “3. Identity of origin in no way affects the fact that human beings can and may live differently, nor does it preclude the existence of differences based on cultural, environmental and historical diversity nor the right to maintain cultural identity.”

Art. 1, DECLARATION ON RACE AND RACIAL PREJUDICE.

ILLEGAL ENTRY [Entrée illégale]

– “For the purposes of this Protocol:

[...]

(*b*) ‘Illegal entry’ shall mean crossing borders without complying with the necessary requirements for legal entry into the receiving State;”

Art. 3, PROTOCOL AGAINST THE SMUGGLING OF MIGRANTS BY LAND, SEA AND AIR, SUPPLEMENTING THE UNITED NATIONS CONVENTION AGAINST TRANSNATIONAL ORGANIZED CRIME.

ILLITERACY [Analphabétisme]

– "11. Recognizing that poverty, underdevelopment and illiteracy are among the principal contributing factors to the spread of HIV/AIDS, and noting with grave concern that HIV/AIDS is compounding poverty and is now reversing or impeding development in many countries and should therefore be addressed in an integrated manner;"

DECLARATION OF COMMITMENT ON HIV/AIDS.

IMPAIRMENTS [Déficiences]

– "20. In 1980, the World Health Organization adopted an international classification of impairments, disabilities and handicaps, which suggested a more precise and at the same time relativistic approach. The International Classification of Impairments, Disabilities, and Handicaps makes a clear distinction between 'impairment', 'disability' and 'handicap'. It has been extensively used in areas such as rehabilitation, education, statistics, policy, legislation, demography, sociology, economics and anthropology. Some users have expressed concern that the Classification, in its definition of the term 'handicap', may still be considered too medical and too centred on the individual, and may not adequately clarify the interaction between societal conditions or expectations and the abilities of the individual. Those concerns, and others expressed by users during the 12 years since its publication, will be addressed in forthcoming revisions of the Classification." [T]

INTRODUCTION, STANDARD RULES ON THE EQUALIZATION OF OPPORTUNITIES FOR PERSONS WITH DISABILITIES.

[T] « 20. En 1980, l'Organisation mondiale de la santé a adopté une classification internationale des déficiences, incapacités et handicaps qui a défini une approche à la fois plus précise et relativiste. La Classification internationale des handicapés : déficiences, incapacités et désavantages établit des distinctions claires entre la déficience, l'incapacité et handicap. Elle est couramment utilisée dans les domaines suivants : réadaptation, éducation, statistiques, prise de décisions, législation, démographie, sociologie, économie et anthropologie. Selon certains des spécialistes à qui elle s'adresse, il se pourrait que la définition du terme « handicap » qui est donnée revête un caractère trop médicale encore, qu'elle soit indûment centrée sur l'individu, et qu'elle ne précise pas assez clairement la manière dont la situation sociale, les attentes de la collectivité et d'autres préoccupations exprimées par les utilisateurs depuis la publication de la Classification, il y a 12 ans, dans les révisions dont celle-ci doit faire l'objet. »

IMPRISONED PERSON [Personne emprisonnée]

– "For the purposes of the Body of Principles:
[...]
(*c*) 'Imprisoned person' means any person deprived of personal liberty as a result of conviction for an offence;"

Use of terms, BODY OF PRINCIPLES FOR THE PROTECTION OF ALL PERSONS UNDER ANY FORM OF DETENTION OR IMPRISONMENT.

IMPRISONMENT [Emprisonnement]

– "57. Imprisonment and other measures which result in cutting off an offender from the outside world are afflictive by the very fact of taking from the person the right of self-determination by depriving him of his liberty.[...]"

STANDARD MINIMUM RULES FOR THE TREATMENT OF PRISONERS.

– "For the purposes of the Body of Principles:
[...]
(*e*) 'Imprisonment' means the condition of imprisoned persons as defined above[39];"

Use of terms, BODY OF PRINCIPLES FOR THE PROTECTION OF ALL PERSONS UNDER ANY FORM OF DETENTION OR IMPRISONMENT.

– "[...] internment or imprisonment shall, for such offences, be the only measure adopted for depriving protected persons of liberty[...]".

Art. 68, s.p. 1, GENEVA CONVENTION RELATIVE TO THE PROTECTION OF CIVILIAN PERSONS IN TIME OF WAR.

INCREASE IN JUVENILE CRIME [Accroissement de la délinquance juvénile]

– "While the relationship between urbanization and crime is clearly complex, an increase in juvenile crime has been associated with the growth of large cities, particularly with rapid and unplanned growth.[...]"

12, *Commentary*, s.p. 2, UNITED NATIONS STANDARD MINIMUM RULES FOR THE ADMINISTRATION OF JUVENILE JUSTICE ("THE BEIJING RULES").

---

39 "(c) 'Imprisoned person' means any person deprived of personal liberty as a result of conviction for an offence;"

INDECENT ASSAULT [Attentat à la pudeur]

– "*b*) Outrages upon personal dignity, in particular humiliating and degrading treatment, enforced prostitution and any form of indecent assault;"

Art. 75, paragraph 2, (b) PROTOCOL ADDITIONAL TO THE GENEVA CONVENTIONS OF 12 AUGUST 1949, AND RELATING TO THE PROTECTION OF VICTIMS OF INTERNATIONAL ARMED CONFLICTS (PROTOCOL I).

– "*e*) Outrages upon personal dignity, in particular humiliating and degrading treatment, rape, enforced prostitution and any form of indecent assault;"

ART. 4, PARAGRAPH 2, PROTOCOL ADDITIONAL TO THE GENEVA CONVENTIONS OF 12 AUGUST 1949, AND RELATING TO THE PROTECTION OF VICTIMS OF NON-INTERNATIONAL ARMED CONFLICTS (PROTOCOL II).

INDEPENDENT AUTHORITY [Autorité indépendante]

– "In these Principles:

[...]

'Independent authority' means a competent and independent authority prescribed by domestic law;"

S.p. 2, DEFINITIONS, PRINCIPLES FOR THE PROTECTION OF PERSONS WITH MENTAL ILLNESS AND THE IMPROVEMENT OF MENTAL HEALTH care.[V]

INDIGENOUS PEOPLES [Peuples indigènes]

– "1. This Convention applies to:

[...]

(*b*) Peoples in independent countries who are regarded as indigenous on account of their descent from the populations which inhabited the country, or a geographical region to which the country belongs, at the time of conquest or colonisation or the establishment of present State boundaries and who, irrespective of their legal status, retain some or all of their own social, economic, cultural and political institutions.

2. Self-identification as indigenous or tribal shall be regarded as a fundamental criterion for determining the groups to which the provisions of this Convention apply.

[V] Al. 1, DEFINITIONS, Principes pour la protection des personnes atteintes de maladie mentale et pour l'amélioration des soins de santé mentale.

3. The use of the term 'peoples' in this Convention shall be not be construed as having any implications as regards the rights which may attach to the term under international law."

Art. 1, INDIGENOUS AND TRIBAL PEOPLES CONVENTION (N° 169).

INDISCRIMINATE ATTACKS [Attaques sans discrimination]

– "4. Indiscriminate attacks are prohibited. Indiscriminate attacks are:

(*a*) Those which are not directed at a specific military objective;

(*b*) Those which employ a method or means of combat which cannot be directed at a specific military objective; or

(*c*) Those which employ a method or means of combat the effects of which cannot be limited as required by this Protocol; and consequently, in each such case, are of a nature to strike military objectives and civilians or civilian objects without distinction.

5. Among others, the following types of attacks are to be considered as indiscriminate:

(*a*) An attack by bombardment by any methods or means which treats as a single military objective a number of clearly separated and distinct military objectives located in a city, town, village or other area containing a similar concentration of civilians or civilian objects; and

(*b*) An attack which may be expected to cause incidental loss of civilian life, injury to civilians, damage to civilian objects, or a combination thereof, which would be excessive in relation to the concrete and direct military advantage anticipated.

Art. 51, PROTOCOL ADDITIONAL TO THE GENEVA CONVENTIONS OF 12 AUGUST 1949, AND RELATING TO THE PROTECTION OF VICTIMS OF INTERNATIONAL ARMED CONFLICTS (PROTOCOL I).

INDIVIDUAL [Individu]

– "*Realizing* that the individual, having duties to other individuals and to the community to which he belongs, is under a responsibility to strive for the promotion and observance of the rights recognized in the present Covenant,"

Pp. 5, INTERNATIONAL COVENANT ON CIVIL AND POLITICAL RIGHTS.
Pp. 5, INTERNATIONAL COVENANT ON ECONOMIC, SOCIAL AND CULTURAL RIGHTS.

INDIVIDUALS, GROUPS, INSTITUTIONS AND NON-GOVERNMENTAL ORGANIZATIONS [Individus, groupes, institutions, et organisations non gouvernementales]

– "2. Individuals, groups, institutions and non-governmental organizations also have an important role to play and a responsibility in safeguarding democracy, promoting human rights and fundamental freedoms and contributing to the promotion and advancement of democratic societies, institutions and processes.

  3. Individuals, groups, institutions and non-governmental organizations also have an important role and a responsibility in contributing, as appropriate, to the promotion of the right of everyone to a social and international order in which the rights and freedoms set forth in the Universal Declaration of Human Rights and other human rights instruments can be fully realized."

Art. 18, DECLARATION ON THE RIGHTS AND RESPONSIBILITY OF INDIVIDUALS, GROUPS AND ORGANS OF SOCIETY TO PROMOTE AND PROTECT UNIVERSALLY RECOGNIZED HUMAN RIGHTS AND FUNDAMENTAL FREEDOMS.

INDIVIDUALS, NON-GOVERNEMENTAL ORGANIZATIONS AND RELEVANT INSTITUTIONS [Individus, organisations non gouvernementales et institutions compétentes]

- "Individuals, non-governmental organizations and relevant institutions have an important role to play in contributing to making the public more aware of questions relating to all human rights and fundamental freedoms through activities such as education, training and research in these areas to strengthen further, *inter alia*, understanding, tolerance, peace and friendly relations among nations and among all racial and religious groups, bearing in mind the various backgrounds of societies and communities in which they carry out their activities."

Art. 16, DECLARATION ON THE RIGHTS AND RESPONSIBILITY OF INDIVIDUALS, GROUPS AND ORGANS OF SOCIETY TO PROMOTE AND PROTECT UNIVERSALLY RECOGNIZED HUMAN RIGHTS AND FUNDAMENTAL FREEDOMS.

INFORMED CONSENT [Consentement en connaissance de cause]

– "2. Informed consent is consent obtained freely, without threats or improper inducements, after appropriate disclosure to the patient of adequate and understandable information in a form and language understood by the patient on:

(*a*) The diagnostic assessment;

(*b*) The purpose, method, Likely duration and expected benefit ofthe proposed treatment;

(*c*) Alternative modes oftreatment, including those less intrusive; and

(*d*) Possible pain or discomfort, risks and side-effects ofthe proposed treatment.

Principle 11, CONSENT TO TREATMENT, PRINCIPLES FOR THE PROTECTION OF PERSONS WITH MENTAL ILLNESS AND THE IMPROVEMENT OF MENTAL HEALTH CARE.

INTENT [Intention]

– "2. For the purposes of this article, a person has intent[w] where:

(*a*) In relation to conduct, that person means to engage in the conduct;

(*b*) In relation to a consequence, that person means to cause that consequence or is aware that it will occur in the ordinary course of events."

Art. 30, ROME STATUTE OF INTERNATIONAL CRIMINAL COURT.

INTEREST OF THE CHILDREN (THE) [Intérêt des enfants]

– "(*b*) [...] that family education includes a proper understanding of maternity as a social function and the recognition of the common responsibility of men and women in the upbringing and development of their children, it being understood that the interest of the children is the primordial consideration in all cases."

Art. 5, CONVENTION ON THE ELIMINATION OF ALL FORMS OF DISCRIMINATION AGAINST WOMEN.

---

[w] « 2. Il y a intention au sens du présent article lorsque :
a) Relativement à un comportement, une personne entend adopter ce comportement ;
b) Relativement à une conséquence, une personne entend causer cette conséquence ou est consciente que celle-ci adviendra dans le cours normal des événements. »

– "1. States Parties shall take all appropriate measures to eliminate discrimination against women in all matters relating to marriage and family relations and in particular shall ensure, on a basis of equality of men and women:

[...]

(*f*) The same rights and responsibilities with regard to guardianship, wardship, trusteeship and adoption of children, or similar institutions where these concepts exist in national legislation; in all cases the interests of the children shall be paramount;"

Art. 16, CONVENTION ON THE ELIMINATION OF ALL FORMS OF DISCRIMINATION AGAINST WOMEN.

INTERNATIONAL COMMITTEE OF THE RED CROSS [Comité international de la Croix-Rouge]

– "An impartial humanitarian body, such as the International Committee of the Red Cross, may offer its services to the Parties to the conflict."

Art. 3, paragraph 2, s.p. 1, GENEVA CONVENTION RELATIVE TO THE TREATMENT OF PRISONERS OF WAR.

– "If protection cannot be arranged accordingly, the Detaining Power shall request or shall accept, subject to the provisions of this Article, the offer of the services of a humanitarian organization, such as the International Committee of the Red Cross, to assume the humanitarian functions performed by Protecting Powers under the present Convention."

Art. 10, s.p. 3, GENEVA CONVENTION RELATIVE TO THE TREATMENT OF PRISONERS OF WAR.

– "An impartial humanitarian body, such as the International Committee of the Red Cross, may offer its services to the Parties to the conflict."

Art. 3, paragraph 2, s.p. 2, GENEVA CONVENTION RELATIVE TO THE PROTECTION OF CIVILIAN PERSONS IN TIME OF WAR.

– "The provisions of the present Convention constitute no obstacle to the humanitarian activities which the International Committee of the Red Cross or any other impartial humanitarian organization may, subject to the consent of the Parties to the conflict concerned, undertake for the protection of civilian persons and for their relief."

Art. 10, GENEVA CONVENTION RELATIVE TO THE PROTECTION OF CIVILIAN PERSONS IN TIME OF WAR.

– "If protection cannot be arranged accordingly, the Detaining Power shall request or shall accept, subject to the provisions of this Article, the offer of the services of a humanitarian organization, such as the International

Committee of the Red Cross, to assume the humanitarian functions performed by Protecting Powers under the present Convention."

Art. 11, s.p. 3, GENEVA CONVENTION RELATIVE TO THE PROTECTION OF CIVILIAN PERSONS IN TIME OF WAR.

- "The foregoing provisions shall in no way be interpreted as restricting the humanitarian activities of the International Committee of the Red Cross [...]"

Art. 140, s.p. 4, GENEVA CONVENTION RELATIVE TO THE PROTECTION OF CIVILIAN PERSONS IN TIME OF WAR.

- "1. The Parties to the conflict shall grant to the International Committee of the Red Cross all facilities within their power so as to enable it to carry out the humanitarian functions assigned to it by the Conventions and this Protocol in order to ensure protection and assistance to the victims of conflicts; the International Committee of the Red Cross may also carry out any other humanitarian activities in favour of these victims, subject to the consent of the Parties to the conflict concerned."

Art. 81, PROTOCOL ADDITIONAL TO THE GENEVA CONVENTIONS OF 12 AUGUST 1949, AND RELATING TO THE PROTECTION OF VICTIMS OF INTERNATIONAL ARMED CONFLICTS (PROTOCOL I).

INTERNATIONAL COVENANTS ON HUMAN RIGHTS [Pactes internationaux relatifs aux droits de l'homme]

- "*Reaffirming also* the importance of the Universal Declaration of Human Rights and the International Covenants on Human Rights as basic elements of international efforts to promote universal respect for and observance of human rights and fundamental freedoms and the importance of other human rights instruments adopted within the United Nations system, as well as those at the regional level,"

Pp. 2, DECLARATION ON THE RIGHTS AND RESPONSIBILITY OF INDIVIDUALS, GROUPS AND ORGANS OF SOCIETY TO PROMOTE AND PROTECT UNIVERSALLY RECOGNIZED HUMAN RIGHTS AND FUNDAMENTAL FREEDOMS.

INTERNATIONAL CRIMINAL COURT [Cour pénale internationale]

- "An International Criminal Court ('the Court') is hereby established. It shall be a permanent institution and shall have the power to exercise its jurisdiction over persons for the most serious crimes of international concern, as referred to in this Statute, and shall be complementary to

national criminal jurisdictions. The jurisdiction and functioning of the Court shall be governed by the provisions of this Statute."
Art. 1, ROME STATUTE OF THE INTERNATIONAL CRIMINAL COURT.

INTERNATIONAL CUSTOMARY RULES [Règles [...] caractère coutumier au plan international]

– "14. Although the Rules are not compulsory, they can become international customary rules when they are applied by a great number of States with the intention of respecting a rule in international law. [...]"
INTRODUCTION, STANDARD RULES ON THE EQUALIZATION OF OPPORTUNITIES FOR PERSONS WITH DISABILITIES.

INTERNATIONAL PEACE AND SECURITY [Paix et la sécurité internationales]

– "*Convinced* that international peace and security on the one hand, and social progress and economic development on the other, are closely interdependent and influence each other,"
Pp. 6, DECLARATION ON SOCIAL PROGRESS AND DEVELOPMENT.

– "*Considering* that international peace and security are essential elements for the realization of the right to development,"
Pp. 11, DECLARATION ON THE RIGHT TO DEVELOPMENT.

INTERNMENT [Internement]

– "[...]Furthermore, internment or imprisonment shall, for such offences, be the only measure adopted for depriving protected persons of liberty.[...]"
Art. 68, s.p. 1, GENEVA CONVENTION RELATIVE TO THE PROTECTION OF CIVILIAN PERSONS IN TIME OF WAR.

INTOLERANCE AND DISCRIMINATION BASED ON RELIGION OR BELIEF [Intolérance et discrimination fondées sur la religion ou la conviction]

– "2. For the purposes of the present Declaration, the expression "intolerance and discrimination based on religion or belief" means any distinction, exclusion, restriction or preference based on religion or belief and having as its purpose or as its effect nullification or impairment of the recognition, enjoyment or exercise of human rights and fundamental freedoms on an equal basis."

Art. 2, DECLARATION ON THE ELIMINATION OF ALL FORMS OF INTOLERANCE AND OF DISCRIMINATION BASED ON RELIGION OR BELIEF.

IRITIS [Iritis]

– "(*i*) Blindness of both eyes, or of one eve when the vision of the other is less than I in spite of the use of corrective glasses; diminution of visual acuity in cases where it is impossible to restore it by correction to an acuity of 1/2 in at least one eye; other grave ocular affections, for example: glaucoma, iritis, choroiditis; trachoma, etc."

Annex I, 3, GENEVA CONVENTION RELATIVE TO THE TREATMENT OF PRISONERS OF WAR.

ITINERANT WORKER [Travailleurs itinérants]

– "For the purposes of the present Convention:
[...]

> (e) The term 'itinerant worker' refers to a migrant worker who, having his or her habitual residence in one State, has to travel to another State or States for short periods, owing to the nature of his or her occupation;

Art. 2.2, INTERNATIONAL CONVENTION ON THE PROTECTION OF THE RIGHTS OF ALL MIGRANT WORKERS AND MEMBERS OF THEIR FAMILIES.

JUDGES [Juges]

– "*Whereas* judges are charged with the ultimate decision over life, freedoms, rights, duties and property of citizens,"

Pp. 7, BASIC PRINCIPLES ON THE INDEPENDENCE OF THE JUDICIARY.

JUDICIAL OR OTHER AUTHORITY (A) [Autorité judiciaire ou autre (une)]

– "For the purposes of the Body of Principles:
[...]

> (*f*) The words 'a judicial or other authority' means a judicial or other authority under the law whose status and tenure should afford the strongest possible guarantees of competence, impartiality and independence."

Use of terms, BODY OF PRINCIPLES FOR THE PROTECTION OF ALL PERSONS UNDER ANY FORM OF DETENTION OR IMPRISONMENT.

JUDICIARY [Magistrats]

– "2. The judiciary shall decide matters before them impartially, on the basis of facts and in accordance with the law, without any restrictions, improper influences, inducements, pressures, threats or interferences, direct or indirect, from any quarter or for any reason."

BASIC PRINCIPLES ON THE INDEPENDENCE OF THE JUDICIARY.

– "3. The judiciary shall have jurisdiction over all issues of a judicial nature and shall have exclusive authority to decide whether an issue submitted for its decision is within its competence as defined by law."

BASIC PRINCIPLES ON THE INDEPENDENCE OF THE JUDICIARY.

JUVENILE [Mineur]

– "11. For the purposes of the Rules, the following definitions should apply:

(*a*) A juvenile is every person under the age of 18. The age limit below which it should not be permitted to deprive a child of his or her liberty should be determined by law;"

UNITED NATIONS RULES FOR THE PROTECTION OF JUVENILES DEPRIVED OF THEIR LIBERTY.

– "1.2 Member States shall endeavour to develop conditions that will ensure for the juvenile a meaningful life in the community, which, during that period in life when she or he is most susceptible to deviant behaviour, will foster a process of personal development and education that is as free from crime and delinquency as possible."

UNITED NATIONS STANDARD MINIMUM RULES FOR THE ADMINISTRATION OF JUVENILE JUSTICE ("THE BEIJING RULES").

- "2.2 For purposes of these Rules, the following definitions shall be applied by Member States in a manner which is compatible with their respective legal systems and concepts:

(*a*) A juvenile is a child or young person who, under the respective legal systems, may be dealt with for an offence in a manner which is different from an adult;"

UNITED NATIONS STANDARD MINIMUM RULES FOR THE ADMINISTRATION OF JUVENILE JUSTICE ("THE BEIJING RULES").

JUVENILE JUSTICE [Justice pour mineurs]

– "1.4 Juvenile justice shall be conceived as an integral part of the national development process of each country, within a comprehensive framework of social justice for all juveniles, thus, at the same time, contributing to the protection of the young and the maintenance of a peaceful order in society."

United Nations Standard Minimum Rules for the Administration of Juvenile Justice ("The Beijing Rules").

– "[...].Rule 1.4 defines juvenile justice as an integral part of social justice for juveniles, [...]"

1.6, *Commentary*, s.p. 2, United Nations Standard Minimum Rules for the Administration of Juvenile Justice ("The Beijing Rules").

– "Rule 5 refers to two of the most important objectives of juvenile justice. The first objective is the promotion of the well-being of the juvenile. This is the main focus of those legal systems in which juvenile offenders are dealt with by family courts or administrative authorities, but the well-being of the juvenile should also be emphasized in legal systems that follow the criminal court model, thus contributing to the avoidance of merely punitive sanctions. (See also rule 14.)[40]

---

[40] "14. Competent authority to adjudicate
14.1 Where the case of a juvenile offender has not been diverted (under rule 11), she or he shall be dealt with by the competent authority (court, tribunal, board, council, etc.) according to the principles of a fair and just trial.
14.2 The proceedings shall be conducive to the best interests of the juvenile and shall be conducted in an atmosphere of understanding, which shall allow the juvenile to participate therein and to express herself or himself freely.
Commentary
It is difficult to formulate a definition of the competent body or person that would universally describe an adjudicating authority. "Competent authority" is meant to include those who preside over courts or tribunals (composed of a single judge or of several members), including professional and lay magistrates as well as administrative boards (for example the Scottish and Scandinavian systems) or other more informal community and conflict resolution agencies of an adjudicatory nature.
The procedure for dealing with juvenile offenders shall in any case follow the minimum standards that are applied almost universally for any criminal defendant under the procedure known as "due process of law". In accordance with due process, a "fair and just trial" includes such basic safeguards as the presumption of innocence, the presentation and examination of witnesses, the common legal defences, the right to remain silent, the right to have the last word in a hearing, the right to appeal, etc. (See also rule 7.1.)

The second objective is 'the principle of proportionality'. This principle is well-known as an instrument for curbing punitive sanctions, mostly expressed in terms of just deserts in relation to the gravity of the offence. The response to young offenders should be based on the consideration not only of the gravity of the offence but also of personal circumstances. The individual circumstances of the offender (for example social status, family situation, the harm caused by the offence or other factors affecting personal circumstances) should influence the proportionality of the reactions (for example by having regard to the offender's endeavour to indemnify the victim or to her or his willingness to turn to wholesome and useful life)."

5, *Commentary*, s.p. 1-2, UNITED NATIONS STANDARD MINIMUM RULES FOR THE ADMINISTRATION OF JUVENILE JUSTICE ("THE BEIJING RULES").

JUVENILE JUSTICE SYSTEM [Système de justice pour mineurs]

– "5. 1 The juvenile justice system shall emphasize the well-being of the juvenile and shall ensure that any reaction to juvenile offenders shall always be in proportion to the circumstances of both the offenders and the offence.

UNITED NATIONS STANDARD MINIMUM RULES FOR THE ADMINISTRATION OF JUVENILE JUSTICE ("THE BEIJING RULES").

JUVENILE OFFENDER [Délinquant juvénile]

– "2.2 For purposes of these Rules, the following definitions shall be applied by Member States in a manner which is compatible with their respective legal systems and concepts:

[...]

(*c*) A juvenile offender is a child or young person who is alleged to have committed or who has been found to have committed an offence.

UNITED NATIONS STANDARD MINIMUM RULES FOR THE ADMINISTRATION OF JUVENILE JUSTICE ("THE BEIJING RULES").

– "Rule 2.2 defines 'juvenile' and 'offence' as the components of the notion of the 'juvenile offender', who is the main subject of these Standard

Minimum Rules (see, however, also rules 3[41] and 4[42]). It should be noted that age limits will depend on, and are explicitly made dependent on, each respective legal system, thus fully respecting the economic, social, political, cultural and legal systems of Member States. This makes for a wide variety of ages coming under the definition of 'juvenile', ranging from 7 years to 18 years or above. Such a variety seems inevitable in view of the different national legal systems and does not diminish the impact of these Standard Minimum Rules."

2, Commentary, s.p. 3, UNITED NATIONS STANDARD MINIMUM RULES FOR THE ADMINISTRATION OF JUVENILE JUSTICE ("THE BEIJING RULES").

---

[41] "3. Extension of the Rules

3.1 The relevant provisions of the Rules shall be applied not only to juvenile offenders but also to juveniles who may be proceeded against for any specific behaviour that would not be punishable if committed by an adult.

3.2 Efforts shall be made to extend the principles embodied in the Rules to all juveniles who are dealt with in welfare and care proceedings.

3.3 Efforts shall also be made to extend the principles embodied in the Rules to young adult offenders."

Commentary

Rule 3 extends the protection afforded by the Standard Minimum Rules for the Administration of Juvenile Justice to cover:

(a) The so-called "status offences" prescribed in various national legal systems where the range of behaviour considered to be an offence is wider for juveniles than it is for adults (for example, truancy, school and family disobedience, public drunkenness, etc.) (rule 3.1);

(b) Juvenile welfare and care proceedings (rule 3.2);

(c) Proceedings dealing with young adult offenders, depending of course on each given age limit (rule 3.3).

The extension of the Rules to cover these three areas seems to be justified. Rule 3.1 provides minimum guarantees in those fields, and rule 3.2 is considered a desirable step in the direction of more fair, equitable and humane justice for all juveniles in conflict with the law."

[42] "4. Age of criminal responsibility

4.1 In those legal systems recognizing the concept of the age of criminal responsibility for juveniles, the beginning of that age shall not be fixed at too low an age level, bearing in mind the facts of emotional, mental and intellectual maturity."

Commentary

The minimum age of criminal responsibility differs widely owing to history and culture. The modern approach would be to consider whether a child can live up to the moral and psychological components of criminal responsibility; that is, whether a child, by virtue of her or his individual discernment and understanding, can be held responsible for essentially antisocial be ha vi our. If the age of criminal responsibility is fixed too low or if there is no lower age limit at all, the notion of responsibility would become meaningless. In general, there is a close relationship between the notion of responsibility for delinquent or criminal behaviour and other social rights and responsibilities (such as marital status, civil majority, etc.).

Efforts should therefore be made to agree on a reasonable lowest age limit that is applicable internationally."

KNOWLEDGE [Connaissance]

– "3. For the purposes of this article, 'knowledge' means awareness that a circumstance exists or a consequence will occur in the ordinary course of events. 'Know' and 'knowingly' shall be construed accordingly."

Art. 30, ROME STATUTE OF INTERNATIONAL CRIMINAL COURT.

LABOUR [Travail]

– "67. [...] Labour should always be viewed as an educational tool and a means of promoting the self-respect of the juvenile in preparing him or her for return to the community and should not be imposed as a disciplinary sanction. [...]"

UNITED NATIONS RULES FOR THE PROTECTION OF JUVENILES DEPRIVED OF THEIR LIBERTY.

LANDS [Terres]

– "2. The use of the term 'lands' in Articles 15[43] and 16[44] shall include the concept of territories, which covers the total environment of the areas which the peoples concerned occupy or otherwise use."

---

[43] "1. The rights of the peoples concerned to the natural resources pertaining to their lands shall be specially safeguarded. These rights include the right of these peoples to participate in the use, management and conservation of these resources.
2. In cases in which the State retains the ownership of mineral or sub-surface resources or rights to other resources pertaining to lands, governments shall establish or maintain procedures through which they shall consult these peoples, with a view to ascertaining whether and to what degree their interests would be prejudiced, before undertaking or permitting any programmes for the exploration or exploitation of such resources pertaining to their lands. The peoples concerned shall wherever possible participate in the benefits of such activities, and shall receive fair compensation for any damages which they may sustain as a result of such activities."

[44] "1. Subject to the following paragraphs of this Article, the peoples concerned shall not be removed from the lands which they occupy.
2. Where the relocation of these peoples is considered necessary as an exceptional measure, such relocation shall take place only with their free and informed consent. Where their consent cannot be obtained, such relocation shall take place only following appropriate procedures established by national laws and regulations, including public inquiries where appropriate, which provide the opportunity for effective representation of the peoples concerned.
3. Whenever possible, these peoples shall have the right to return to their traditional lands, as soon as the grounds for relocation cease to exist.
4. When such return is not possible, as determined by agreement or, in the absence of such agreement, through appropriate procedures, these peoples shall be provided in all possible cases with lands of quality and legal status at least equal to that of the lands previously occupied by them, suitable to provide for their present needs and future development. Where the peoples

Art. 13, INDIGENOUS AND TRIBAL PEOPLES CONVENTION (N° 169).

LATIN AMERICAN REGION [Amérique latine (région de l')]

– "10. Recognizing also that other regions are seriously affected and confront similar threats, particularly the Caribbean region, with the second-highest rate of HIV infection after sub-Saharan Africa, the Asia-Pacific region where 7.5 million people living are already living with HIV/AID, the Latin American region with 1.5 million people living with HIV/AIDS and the Central and Eastern European region with very rapidly rising infection rates, and that the potential exists for a rapid escalation of the epidemic and its impact throughout the world if no specific measures are taken;"

DECLARATION OF COMMITMENT ON HIV/AIDS.

LAW ENFORCEMENT OFFICIALS [Responsable de l'application des lois ; Responsables de l'application des lois]

– "(*a*) The term 'law enforcement officials', includes all officers of the law, whether appointed or elected, who exercise police powers, especially the powers of arrest or detention."

Art. 1, *Commentary*, CODE OF CONDUCT FOR LAW ENFORCEMENT OFFICIALS.

– "In accordance with the commentary to article 1 of the Code of Conduct for Law Enforcement Officials, the term 'law enforcement officials' includes all officers of the law, whether appointed or elected, who exercise police powers, especially the powers of arrest or detention. In countries where police powers are exercised by military authorities, whether uniformed or not, or by State security forces, the definition of law enforcement officials shall be regarded as including officers of such services."

Footnote (*), pp. 1, BASIC PRINCIPLES ON THE USE OF FORCE AND FIREARMS BY LAW ENFORCEMENT OFFICIALS.

---

concerned express a preference for compensation in money or in kind, they shall be so compensated under appropriate guarantees.
5. Persons thus relocated shall be fully compensated for any resulting loss or injury."

LAWYERS [Avocats]

– "12. Lawyers shall at all times maintain the honour and dignity of their profession as essential agents of the administration of justice."

BASIC PRINCIPLES ON THE ROLE OF LAWYERS.

LEAD POISONING [Saturnisme]

– "(*o*) Serious cases of chronic intoxication, ffßor example: lead poisoning, mercury poisoning, morphinism, cocainism, alcoholism; gas or radiation poisoning; etc."

Annex I, 3, GENEVA CONVENTION RELATIVE TO THE TREATMENT OF PRISONERS OF WAR.

LEPROSY [Lèpre]

– "(s) Serious chronic infectious diseases, persisting for one year after their inception, for example: malaria with decided organic impairment, amoebic or bacillary dysentery with grave disorders; tertiary visceral syphilis resistant to treatment; leprosy; etc."

Annex I, 3, GENEVA CONVENTION RELATIVE TO THE TREATMENT OF PRISONERS OF WAR.

LIFE WITHOUT WAR [Absence de guerre]

– "*Convinced* that life without war serves as the primary international prerequisite for the material well-being, development and progress of countries, and for the full implementations of the rights and fundamental human freedoms proclaimed by the United Nations,"

Pp. 4, DECLARATION ON THE RIGHT OF PEOPLES TO PEACE.

MALARIA [Paludisme]

– "To have, by then [2015], halted, and begun to reverse, the spread of HIV/AIDS, the scourge of malaria and other major diseases that afflict humanity."

19, fourth footnote, UNITED NATIONS MILLENIUM DECLARATION.

MALARIA WITH DECIDED ORGANIC IMPAIRMENT [Paludisme avec altérations organiques prononcées]

– "(s) Serious chronic infectious diseases, persisting for one year after their inception, for example: malaria with decided organic impairment, amoebic or bacillary dysentery with grave disorders; tertiary visceral syphilis resistant to treatment; leprosy; etc."

Annex I, 3, GENEVA CONVENTION RELATIVE TO THE TREATMENT OF PRISONERS OF WAR.

MAN [Homme]

– "*Convinced* that man can achieve complete fulfilment of his aspirations only within a just social order [...]"

Pp. 5, DECLARATION ON SOCIAL PROGRESS AND DEVELOPMENT.

MARINE AND INLAND WATER RESOURCES [Ressources de la mer et des eaux]

– "5. Marine and inland water resources are today becoming more important than ever as a source of food and economic prosperity. [...]"

UNIVERSAL DECLARATION ON THE ERADICATION OF HUNGER AND MALNUTRITION.

MARKET FORCES [Forces du marché]

– "Market forces alone cannot guarantee the preservation and promotion of cultural diversity, which is the key to sustainable human development. [...]"

Art. 11, UNIVERSAL DECLARATION ON CULTURAL DIVERSITY.

MARRIAGE [Mariage]

– "1. No marriage shall be legally entered into without the full and free consent of both parties, such consent to be expressed by them in person after due publicity and in the presence of the authority competent to solemnize the marriage and of witnesses, as prescribed by law."

Art. 1, CONVENTION ON CONSENT TO MARRIAGE, MINIMUM AGE FOR MARRIAGE AND REGISTRATION OF MARRIAGES.

MASS MEDIA [Communication de masse]

– "(*d*) In some countries, the mass media may be regarded as performing complaint review functions similar to those described in subparagraph (c) above[45]. [...]"

---

[45] "(*c*) The term 'appropriate authorities or organs vested with reviewing or remedial power' refers to any authority or organ existing under national law, whether internal to the law

Art. 8, *Commentary*, CODE OF CONDUCT FOR LAW ENFORCEMENT OFFICIALS.

MATERIEL [Matériel]

– "For the purposes of this Protocol:
[...]
(*d*) 'Matériel' of civil defence organizations means equipment, supplies and transports used by these organizations for the performance of the tasks mentioned under sub-paragraph (a).[46]."

Art. 61, PROTOCOL ADDITIONAL TO THE GENEVA CONVENTIONS OF 12 AUGUST 1949, AND RELATING TO THE PROTECTION OF VICTIMS OF INTERNATIONAL ARMED CONFLICTS (PROTOCOL I).

MATERNITY [Maternité]

– "(*b*) [...] maternity as a social function [...][x] "

Art .5, CONVENTION ON THE ELIMINATION OF ALL FORMS OF DISCRIMINATION AGAINST WOMEN.

---

enforcement agency or independent thereof, with statutory, customary or other power to review grievances and complaints arising out of violations within the purview of this Code."

[46] "(*a*) 'Civil defence' means the performance of some or all of the undermentioned humanitarian tasks intended to protect the civilian population against the dangers, and to help it to recover from the immediate effects, of hostilities or disasters and also to provide the conditions necessary for its survival. These tasks are:
(i) Warning;
(ii) Evacuation;
(iii) Management of shelters;
(iv) Management of blackout measures;
(v) Rescue;
(vi) Medical services, including first aid, and religious assistance;
(vii) Fire-fighting;
(viii) Detection and marking of danger areas;
(ix) Decontamination and similar protective measures;
(x) Provision of emergency accommodation and supplies;
(xi) Emergency assistance in the restoration and maintenance of order in distressed areas;
(xii) Emergency repair of indispensable public utilities;
(xiii) Emergency disposal of the dead;
(xiv) Assistance in the preservation of objects essential for survival;
(xv) Complementary activities necessary to carry out any of the tasks mentioned above, including, but not limited to, planning and organization;"

[x] « *b*) [...] la maternité est une fonction sociale [...] »

MEASURES [...] DISCRIMATORY [Mesures discriminatoires]

– "2. Measures applied under the law and designed solely to protect the rights and special status of women, especially pregnant women and nursing mothers, children and juveniles, aged, sick or handicapped persons shall not be deemed to be discriminatory [...]"

Principle 5, BODY OF PRINCIPLES FOR THE PROTECTION OF ALL PERSONS UNDER ANY FORM OF DETENTION OR IMPRISONMENT.

MEDICAL AIRCRAFT [Aéronef sanitaire]

– "For the purposes of this Protocol:
[...]
(*j*) 'Medical aircraft' means any medical transports by air;"

Art. 8, PROTOCOL ADDITIONAL TO THE GENEVA CONVENTIONS OF 12 AUGUST 1949, AND RELATING TO THE PROTECTION OF VICTIMS OF INTERNATIONAL ARMED CONFLICTS (PROTOCOL I).

MEDICAL ATTENTION [Soins médicaux]

– "(*a*) 'Medical attention', which refers to services rendered by any medical personnel, including certified medical practitioners and paramedics, shall be secured when needed or requested."

Art. 6, *Commentary*, CODE OF CONDUCT FOR LAW ENFORCEMENT OFFICIALS.

MEDICAL OR SCIENTIFIC EXPERIMENTATION [Expérience médicale ou scientifique]

– "No one shall be subjected to torture or to cruel, inhuman or degrading treatment or punishment. In particular, no one shall be subjected without his free consent to medical or scientific experimentation."

Art. 7, INTERNATIONAL COVENANT ON CIVIL AND POLITICAL RIGHTS.

MEDICAL OR SCIENTIFIC EXPERIMENTS NOT NECESSITATED BY THE MEDICAL TREATMENT [Expériences médicales ou scientifiques non nécessitées par le traitement médical]

– "The High Contracting Parties specifically agree that each of them is prohibited from taking any measure of such a character as to cause the physical suffering or extermination of protected persons in their hands.

This prohibition applies not only to murder, torture, corporal punishment, mutilation and medical or scientific experiments not necessitated by the medical treatment of a protected person but also to any other measures of brutality whether applied by civilian or military agents."
Art. 32, GENEVA CONVENTION RELATIVE TO THE PROTECTION OF CIVILIAN PERSONS IN TIME OF WAR.

MEDICAL PERSONNEL [Personnel sanitaire]

– "For the purposes of this Protocol:
[...]

(*c*) 'Medical personnel' means those persons assigned, by a Party to the conflict, exclusively to the medical purposes enumerated under subparagraph (*e*)[47] or to the administration of medical units or to the operation or administration of medical transports. Such assignments may be either permanent or temporary. The term includes:

(i) Medical personnel of a Party to the conflict, whether military or civilian, including those described in the First and Second Conventions, and those assigned to civil defence organizations;

(ii) Medical personnel of national Red Cross (Red Crescent, Red Lion and Sun) Societies and other national voluntary aid societies duly recognized and authorized by a Party to the conflict;

(iii) Medical personnel of medical units or medical transports described in Article 9, paragraph 2[48];"

Art. 8, PROTOCOL ADDITIONAL TO THE GENEVA CONVENTIONS OF 12 AUGUST 1949, AND RELATING TO THE PROTECTION OF VICTIMS OF INTERNATIONAL ARMED CONFLICTS (PROTOCOL I).

---

[47] "(*e*) 'Medical units' means establishments and other units, whether military or civilian, organized for medical purposes, namely the search for, collection, transportation, diagnosis or treatment-including first-aid treatment-of the wounded, sick and shipwrecked, or for the prevention of disease. The term includes, for example, hospitals and other similar units, blood transfusion centres, preventive medicine centres and institutes, medical depots and the medical and pharmaceutical stores of such units. Medical units may be fixed or mobile, permanent or temporary;"

[48] "2. The relevant provisions of Articles 27 and 32 of the First Convention shall apply to permanent medical units and transports (other than hospital ships, to which Article 25 of the Second Convention applies) and their personnel made available to a Party to the conflict for humanitarian purposes:
(*a*) By a neutral or other State which is not a Party to that conflict;
(*b*) By a recognized and authorized aid society of such a State;
(*c*) By an impartial international humanitarian organization."

MEDICAL SHIPS AND CRAFT [Navire et embarcation sanitaires]

– “For the purposes of this Protocol:
[…]

(*i*) ‘Medical ships and craft’ means any medical transports by water;”

Art. 8, PROTOCOL ADDITIONAL TO THE GENEVA CONVENTIONS OF 12 AUGUST 1949, AND RELATING TO THE PROTECTION OF VICTIMS OF INTERNATIONAL ARMED CONFLICTS (PROTOCOL I).

MEDICAL TRANSPORTATION [Transport sanitaire]

– “For the purposes of this Protocol:
[…]

(*f*) ‘Medical transportation’ means the conveyance by land, water or air of the wounded, sick, shipwrecked, medical personnel, religious personnel, medical equipment or medical supplies protected by the Conventions and by this Protocol;”

Art. 8, PROTOCOL ADDITIONAL TO THE GENEVA CONVENTIONS OF 12 AUGUST 1949, AND RELATING TO THE PROTECTION OF VICTIMS OF INTERNATIONAL ARMED CONFLICTS (PROTOCOL I).

MEDICAL TRANSPORTS [Moyen de transport sanitaire]

– “For the purposes of this Protocol:
[…]

(*g*) ‘Medical transports’ means any means of transportation, whether military or civilian, permanent or temporary, as signed exclusively to medical transportation and under the control of a competent authority of a Party to the conflict;”

Art. 8, PROTOCOL ADDITIONAL TO THE GENEVA CONVENTIONS OF 12 AUGUST 1949, AND RELATING TO THE PROTECTION OF VICTIMS OF INTERNATIONAL ARMED CONFLICTS (PROTOCOL I).

MEDICAL UNITS [Unités sanitaires]

– “For the purposes of this Protocol:
[…]

(*e*) ‘Medical units’ means establishments and other units, whether military or civilian, organized for medical purposes, namely the search for, collection, transportation, diagnosis or treatment-including first-aid treatment-of the wounded, sick and shipwrecked, or for the prevention of disease. The term includes, for example, hospitals and other similar units, blood transfusion centres, preventive medicine centres and institutes, medical depots and the medical and pharmaceutical stores of such units. Medical units may be fixed or mobile, permanent or temporary;"

Art. 8, PROTOCOL ADDITIONAL TO THE GENEVA CONVENTIONS OF 12 AUGUST 1949, AND RELATING TO THE PROTECTION OF VICTIMS OF INTERNATIONAL ARMED CONFLICTS (PROTOCOL I).

MEDICAL VEHICLES [Véhicule sanitaire]

- "For the purposes of this Protocol:

[…]

(*h*) 'Medical vehicles' means any medical transports by land;"

Art. 8, PROTOCOL ADDITIONAL TO THE GENEVA CONVENTIONS OF 12 AUGUST 1949, AND RELATING TO THE PROTECTION OF VICTIMS OF INTERNATIONAL ARMED CONFLICTS (PROTOCOL I).

MEMBERS OF THE FAMILY [Membres de la famille]

– "For the purposes of the present Convention the term 'members of the family' refers to persons married to migrant workers or having with them a relationship that, according to applicable law, produces effects equivalent to marriage, as well as their dependent children and other dependent persons who are recognized as members of the family by applicable legislation or applicable bilateral or multilateral agreements between the States concerned."

Art. 4, INTERNATIONAL CONVENTION ON THE PROTECTION OF THE RIGHTS OF ALL MIGRANT WORKERS AND MEMBERS OF THEIR FAMILIES.

MEMBERS OF THE ARMED FORCES [Membres des forces armées]

– "2. Members of the armed forces of a Party to a conflict (other than medical personnel and chaplains covered by Article 33 of the Third Convention[49]) are combatants, that is to say, they have the right to participate directly in hostilities."

[49] "Members of the medical personnel and chaplains while retained by the Detaining Power with a view to assisting prisoners of war, shall not be considered as prisoners of war. They shall, however, receive as a minimum the benefits and protection of the present Convention, and shall also be granted all facilities necessary to provide for the medical care of, and religious ministration to prisoners of war.

Art. 43, PROTOCOL ADDITIONAL TO THE GENEVA CONVENTIONS OF 12 AUGUST 1949, AND RELATING TO THE PROTECTION OF VICTIMS OF INTERNATIONAL ARMED CONFLICTS (PROTOCOL I).

MEMBERS OF THE HUMAN FAMILY [Membres de la famille humaine]

– "*Considering* that, in accordance with the principles proclaimed in the Charter of the United Nations, recognition of the inherent dignity and of the equal and inalienable rights of all members of the human family is the foundation of freedom, justice and peace in the world,"

Pp. 1, INTERNATIONAL COVENANT ON ECONOMIC, SOCIAL AND CULTURAL RIGHTS.
Pp. 1, INTERNATIONAL COVENANT ON CIVIL AND POLITICAL RIGHTS.

MENTAL HEALTH CARE [Soins de santé mentale]

– "In these Principles:

[...]

They shall continue to exercise their medical and spiritual functions for the benefit of prisoners of war, preferably those belonging to the armed forces upon which they depend, within the scope of the military laws and regulations of the Detaining Power and under the control of its competent services, in accordance with their professional etiquette. They shall also benefit by the following facilities in the exercise of their medical or spiritual functions:

(*a*) They shall be authorized to visit periodically prisoners of war situated in working detachments or in hospitals outside the camp. For this purpose, the Detaining Power shall place at their disposal the necessary means of transport.

(*b*) The senior medical officer in each camp shall be responsible to the camp military authorities for everything connected with the activities of retained medical personnel. For this purpose, Parties to the conflict shall agree at the outbreak of hostilities on the subject of the corresponding ranks of the medical personnel, including that of societies mentioned in Article 26 of the Geneva Convention for the Amelioration of the Condition of the Wounded and Sick in Armed Forces in the Field of August 12, 1949. This senior medical officer, as well as chaplains, shall have the right to deal with the competent authorities of the camp on all questions relating to their duties. Such authorities shall afford them all necessary facilities for correspondence relating to these questions.

(*c*) Although they shall be subject to the internal discipline of the camp in which they are retained, such personnel may not be compelled to carry out any work other than that concerned with their medical or religious duties.

During hostilities, the Parties to the conflict shall agree concerning the possible relief of retained personnel and shall settle the procedure to be followed.

None of the preceding provisions shall relieve the Detaining Power of its obligations with regard to prisoners of war from the medical or spiritual point of view."

'Mental health care' includes analysis and diagnosis of a person's mental condition, and treatment, care and rehabilitation for a mental illness or suspected mental illness;"

S.p. 3, DEFINITIONS, PRINCIPLES FOR THE PROTECTION OF PERSONS WITH MENTAL ILLNESS AND THE IMPROVEMENT OF MENTAL HEALTH care.[Y]

MENTAL HEALTH FACILITY [Service de santé mentale]

– "In these Principles:

[...]

'Mental health facility' means any establishment, or any unit of an establishment, which as its primary function provides mental health care;"

S.p. 4, DEFINITIONS, PRINCIPLES FOR THE PROTECTION OF PERSONS WITH MENTAL ILLNESS AND THE IMPROVEMENT OF MENTAL HEALTH CARE.[Z]

MENTAL HEALTH PRACTITIONER [Praticien de santé mentale]

– "In these Principles:

[...]

'Mental health practitioner' means a medical doctor, clinical psychologist, nurse, social worker or other appropriately trained and qualified person with specific skills relevant to mental health care;"

S.p. 5, DEFINITIONS, PRINCIPLES FOR THE PROTECTION OF PERSONS WITH MENTAL ILLNESS AND THE IMPROVEMENT OF MENTAL HEALTH CARE.

MENTAL ILLNESS [Maladie mentale]

– "2. A determination of mental illness shall never be made on the basis of political, economic or social status, or membership of a cultural, racial or religious group, or any other reason not directly relevant to mental health status.

3. Family or professional conflict, or non-conformity with moral, social, cultural or political values or religious beliefs prevailing in a person's

[Y] Al. 8, DEFINITIONS, Principes pour la protection des personnes atteintes de maladie mentale et pour l'amélioration des soins de santé mentale.

[Z] Al. 7, DEFINITIONS, Principes pour la protection des personnes atteintes de maladie mentale et pour l'amélioration des soins de santé mentale.

community, shall never be a determining factor in diagnosing mental illness.

4. A background of past treatment or hospitalization as a patient shall not of itself justify any present or future determination of mental illness."

Principle 4, PRINCIPLES FOR THE PROTECTION OF PERSONS WITH MENTAL ILLNESS AND THE IMPROVEMENT OF MENTAL HEALTH CARE.

MERCENARIES [Mercenaires]

– "*Being aware* of the recruitment, use, financing and training of mercenaries for activities which violate principles of international law, such as those of sovereign equality, political independence, territorial integrity of States and self-determination of peoples,"

Pp. 2, INTERNATIONAL CONVENTION AGAINST THE RECRUITMENT, USE, FINANCING AND TRAINING OF MERCENARIES.

MERCENARY [Mercenaire]

– "For the purposes of the present Convention,

1. A mercenary is any person who:

(*a*) Is specially recruited locally or abroad in order to fight in an armed conflict;

(*b*) Is motivated to take part in the hostilities essentially by the desire for private gain and, in fact, is promised, by or on behalf of a party to the conflict, material compensation substantially in excess of that promised or paid to combatants of similar rank and functions in the armed forces of that party;

(*c*) Is neither a national of a party to the conflict nor a resident of territory controlled by a party to the conflict;

(*d*) Is not a member of the armed forces of a party to the conflict; and

(*e*) Has not been sent by a State which is not a party to the conflict on official duty as a member of its armed forces.

2. A mercenary is also any person who, in any other situation:

(*a*) Is specially recruited locally or abroad for the purpose of participating in a concerted act of violence aimed at :

(i) Overthrowing a Government or otherwise undermining the constitutional order of a State; or

(ii) Undermining the territorial integrity of a State;

(*b*) Is motivated to take part therein essentially by the desire for significant private gain and is prompted by the promise or payment of material compensation;

(*c*) Is neither a national nor a resident of the State against which such an act is directed;

(*d*) Has not been sent by a State on official duty; and

(*e*) Is not a member of the armed forces of the State on whose territory the act is undertaken.

1, INTERNATIONAL CONVENTION AGAINST THE RECRUITMENT, USE, FINANCING AND TRAINING OF MERCENARIES.

– "2. A mercenary is any person who:

(*a*) Is specially recruited locally or abroad in order to fight in an armed conflict;

(*b*) Does, in fact, take a direct part in the hostilities;

(*c*) Is motivated to take part in the hostilities essentially by the desire for private gain and, in fact, is promised, by or on behalf of a Party to the conflict, material compensation substantially in excess of that promised or paid to combatants of similar ranks and functions in the armed forces of that Party;

(*d*) Is neither a national of a Party to the conflict nor a resident of territory controlled by a Party to the conflict;

(*e*) Is not a member of the armed forces of a Party to the conflict; and

(*f*) Has not been sent by a State which is not a Party to the conflict on official duty as a member of its armed forces.

Art. 47, PROTOCOL ADDITIONAL TO THE GENEVA CONVENTIONS OF 12 AUGUST 1949, AND RELATING TO THE PROTECTION OF VICTIMS OF INTERNATIONAL ARMED CONFLICTS (PROTOCOL I).

MERCURY POISONING [Hydragyrisme]

– "(*o*) Serious cases of chronic intoxication, for example: lead poisoning, mercury poisoning, morphinism. cocainism, alcoholism; gas or radiation poisoning; etc."

Annex I, 3, GENEVA CONVENTION RELATIVE TO THE TREATMENT OF PRISONERS OF WAR.

MIGRANT WORKERS [Travailleurs migrants]

– "*Considering* the situation of vulnerability in which migrant workers and members of their families frequently-find themselves owing, among other things, to their absence from their State of origin and to the difficulties they may encounter arising from their presence in the State of employment,"

Pp. 10, INTERNATIONAL CONVENTION ON THE PROTECTION OF THE RIGHTS OF ALL MIGRANT WORKERS AND MEMBERS OF THEIR FAMILIES.

– "For the purposes of the present Convention:

> 1. The term 'migrant worker' refers to a person who is to be engaged, is engaged or has been engaged in a remunerated activity in a State of which he or she is not a national."

Art. 2, INTERNATIONAL CONVENTION ON THE PROTECTION OF THE RIGHTS OF ALL MIGRANT WORKERS AND MEMBERS OF THEIR FAMILIES.

MIGRANT WORKERS AND MEMBERS OF THEIR FAMILIES [Travailleurs migrants et membres de leur famille]

– "The present Convention shall not apply to:

> (*a*) Persons sent or employed by international organizations and agencies or persons sent or employed by a State outside its territory to perform official functions, whose admission and status are regulated by general international law or by specific international agreements or conventions;
>
> (*b*) Persons sent or employed by a State or on its behalf outside its territory who participate in development programmes and other co-operation programmes, whose admission and status are regulated by agreement with the State of employment and who, in accordance with that agreement, are not considered migrant workers;
>
> (*c*) Persons taking up residence in a State different from their State of origin as investors;
>
> (*d*) Refugees and stateless persons, unless such application is provided for in the relevant national legislation of, or international instruments in force for, the State Party concerned;
>
> (*e*) Students and trainees;

(*f*) Seafarers and workers on an offshore installation who have not been admitted to take up residence and engage in a remunerated activity in the State of employment."

Art. 3, International Convention on the Protection of the Rights of All Migrant Workers and Members of their Families.

MIGRANT WORKERS AND MEMBERS OF THEIR FAMILIES (DOCUMENTED OR IN REGULAR SITUATION) [Travailleurs migrants et les membres de leur famille (pourvus de documents ou en situation régulière)]

– "For the purposes of the present Convention, migrant workers and members of their families:

(*a*) Are considered as documented or in a regular situation if they are authorized to enter, to stay and to engage in a remunerated activity in the State of employment pursuant to the law of that State and to international agreements to which that State is a party;"

Art. 5, International Convention on the Protection of the Rights of All Migrant Workers and Members of their Families.

MIGRANT WORKERS AND MEMBERS OF THEIR FAMILIES (NON-DOCUMENTED OR IN IRREGULAR SITUATION) [Travailleurs migrants et les membres de leur famille (dépourvus de documents ou en situation irrégulière)]

– "For the purposes of the present Convention, migrant workers and members of their families:
[…]

(*b*) Are considered as non-documented or in an irregular situation if they do not comply with the conditions provided for in subparagraph (a) [50] of the present article."

Art. 5, International Convention on the Protection of the Rights of All Migrant Workers and Members of their Families.

---

[50] "(*a*) Are considered as documented or in a regular situation if they are authorized to enter, to stay and to engage in a remunerated activity in the State of employment pursuant to the law of that State and to international agreements to which that State is a party;"

MIGRATION [Migrations]

– "*Taking into account* the fact that migration is often the cause of serious problems for the members of the families of migrant workers as well as for the workers themselves, in particular because of the scattering of the family,"

Pp. 12, International Convention on the Protection of the Rights of All Migrant Workers and Members of their Families.

MIGRATION PROCESS OF MIGRANT WORKERS AND MEMBERS OF THEIR FAMILIES [Processus de migration des travailleurs migrants et des membres de leur famille]

– "2. The present Convention shall apply during the entire migration process of migrant workers and members of their families, which comprises preparation for migration, departure, transit and the entire period of stay and remunerated activity in the State of employment as well as return to the State of origin or the State of habitual residence."

Art. 1, International Convention on the Protection of the Rights of All Migrant Workers and Members of their Families.

MINIMUM AGE OF CRIMINAL RESPONSIBILITY [Seuil de responsabilité pénale]

– "The minimum age of criminal responsibility differs widely owing to history and culture. The modern approach would be to consider whether a child can live up to the moral and psychological components of criminal responsibility; that is, whether a child, by virtue of her or his individual discernment and understanding, can be held responsible for essentially antisocial be ha vi our. If the age of criminal responsibility is fixed too low or if there is no lower age limit at all, the notion of responsibility would become meaningless. In general, there is a close relationship between the notion of responsibility for delinquent or criminal behaviour and other social rights and responsibilities (such as marital status, civil majority, etc.)."

4, Commentary, United Nations Standard Minimum Rules for the Administration of Juvenile Justice ("The Beijing Rules").

MISTAKE OF FACT [Erreur de fait]

– "1. A mistake of fact shall be a ground for excluding criminal responsibility only if it negates the mental element required by the crime."

Art. 32, ROME STATUTE OF THE INTERNATIONAL CRIMINAL COURT.

MISTAKE OF LAW [Erreur de droit]

– "2. A mistake of law as to whether a particular type of conduct is a crime within the jurisdiction of the Court shall not be a ground for excluding criminal responsibility. A mistake of law may, however, be a ground for excluding criminal responsibility if it negates the mental element required by such a crime, or as provided for in article 33. [51]."

Art. 32, ROME STATUTE OF THE INTERNATIONAL CRIMINAL COURT.

MORPHINISM [Morphinisme]

– "(*o*) Serious cases of chronic intoxication, for example: lead poisoning, mercury poisoning, morphinism. cocainism, alcoholism; gas or radiation poisoning; etc."

Annex I, 3, GENEVA CONVENTION RELATIVE TO THE TREATMENT OF PRISONERS OF WAR.

MOTHERS [Mères]

– "*Conscious* of its responsibility for the destiny of the rising generation and for the destiny of mothers, who play an important role in society, in the family and particularly in the upbringing of children,"

Pp. 8, DECLARATION ON THE PROTECTION OF WOMEN AND CHILDREN IN EMERGENCY AND ARMED CONFLICT.

---

[51] "1. The fact that a crime within the jurisdiction of the Court has been committed by a person pursuant to an order of a Government or of a superior, whether military or civilian, shall not relieve that person of criminal responsibility unless:
(*a*) The person was under a legal obligation to obey orders of the Government or the superior in question;
(*b*) The person did not manifestly unlawful; and
(*c*) The order was order was not manifestly unlawful.
2. For the purpose of this article, orders to commit genocide or crimes against humanity are manifestly unlawful."

MURDER [Meurtre]

– “The High Contracting Parties specifically agree that each of them is prohibited from taking any measure of such a character as to cause the physical suffering or extermination of protected persons in their hands. This prohibition applies not only to murder, torture, corporal punishment, mutilation and medical or scientific experiments not necessitated by the medical treatment of a protected person but also to any other measures of brutality whether applied by civilian or military agents.”

Art. 32, GENEVA CONVENTION RELATIVE TO THE PROTECTION OF CIVILIAN PERSONS IN TIME OF WAR.

– “(*a*) Violence to the life, health, or physical or mental well-being of persons, in particular:

(i) Murder;”

Art. 75, paragraph 2, PROTOCOL ADDITIONAL TO THE GENEVA CONVENTIONS OF 12 AUGUST 1949, AND RELATING TO THE PROTECTION OF VICTIMS OF INTERNATIONAL ARMED CONFLICTS (PROTOCOL I).

MUTILATION [Mutilations]

– “The High Contracting Parties specifically agree that each of them is prohibited from taking any measure of such a character as to cause the physical suffering or extermination of protected persons in their hands. This prohibition applies not only to murder, torture, corporal punishment, mutilation and medical or scientific experiments not necessitated by the medical treatment of a protected person but also to any other measures of brutality whether applied by civilian or military agents.”

Art. 32, GENEVA CONVENTION RELATIVE TO THE PROTECTION OF CIVILIAN PERSONS IN TIME OF WAR.

– “(*a*) Violence to the life, health, or physical or mental well-being of persons, in particular:

[…]

(iv) Mutilation;”

Art. 75, paragraph 2, PROTOCOL ADDITIONAL TO THE GENEVA CONVENTIONS OF 12 AUGUST 1949, AND RELATING TO THE PROTECTION OF VICTIMS OF INTERNATIONAL ARMED CONFLICTS (PROTOCOL I).

NATIONAL INSTITUTION [Institutions nationales]

– “3. A national institution shall, *inter alia*, have the following responsibilities:

(*a*) To submit to Government, Parliament and any other competent body, on an advisory basis either at the request of the authorities concerned or through the exercise of its power to hear a matter without higher referral, opinions, recommendations, proposals and reports on any matters concerning the promotion and protection of human rights; the national institution may decide to publicize them; these opinions, recommendations, proposals and reports, as well as any prerogative of the national institution, shall relate to the following areas:

(i) Any legislative or administrative provisions, as well as provisions relating to judicial organizations, intended to preserve and extend the protection of human rights; in that connection, the national institution shall examine the legislation and administrative provisions in force, as well as bills and proposals, and shall make such recommendations as it deems appropriate in order to ensure that these provisions conform to the fundamental principles of human rights; it shall, if necessary, recommend the adoption of new legislation, the amendment of legislation in force and the adoption or amendment of administrative measures;

(ii) Any situation of violation of human rights which it decides to take up;

(iii) The preparation of reports on the national situation with regard to human rights in general, and on more specific matters;

(iv) Drawing the attention of the Government to situations in any part of the country where human rights are violated and making proposals to it for initiatives to put an end to such situations and, where necessary, expressing an opinion on the positions and reactions of the Government;

(*b*) To promote and ensure the harmonization of national legislation, regulation ad practices with the international human rights instruments to which the State is a party, and their effective implementation;

(*c*) To encourage ratification of the above-mentioned instruments or accession to those instruments, and to ensure their implementation;

(*d*) To contribute to the reports which States are required to submit to United Nations bodies and committees, and to regional institutions, pursuant to their treaty obligations and, where necessary, to express an opinion on the subject, with due respect for their independence;

(*e*) To cooperate with United Nations and any other organization in the United Nations system, the regional institutions and the national institutions of other countries that are competent in the areas of the protection and promotion of human rights;

(*f*) To assist in the formulation of programmes for the teaching of, and research into, human rights and to take part in their execution in schools, universities and professional circles;

(*g*) To publicize human rights and efforts to combat all forms of discrimination, in particular racial discrimination, by increasing public awareness, especially through information and education and by making use of all press organs."

PRINCIPLES RELATING TO THE STATUS OF NATIONAL INSTITUTIONS (THE PARIS PRINCIPLES).

NATIONAL RED CROSS SOCIETIES [Sociétés nationales de la Croix-Rouge]

– "(*a*) Recognized National Red Cross (Red Crescent, Red Lion and Sun) Societies shall be able to pursue their activities in accordance with Red Cross principles, as defined by the International Red Cross Conferences. Other relief societies shall be permitted to continue their humanitarian activities under similar conditions;"

Art. 63, GENEVA CONVENTION RELATIVE TO THE PROTECTION OF CIVILIAN PERSONS IN TIME OF WAR.

– "1. [...] The civilian population and aid societies, such as national Red Cross (Red Crescent, Red Lion and Sun) Societies, shall be permitted, even on their own initiative, to collect and care for the wounded, sick and shipwrecked, even in invaded or occupied areas.[...]"

Art. 17, PROTOCOL ADDITIONAL TO THE GENEVA CONVENTIONS OF 12 AUGUST 1949, AND RELATING TO THE PROTECTION OF VICTIMS OF INTERNATIONAL ARMED CONFLICTS (PROTOCOL I).

NATURAL DISASTERS [Catastrophes naturelles]

– "12. Noting that armed conflicts and natural disasters also exacerbate the spread of the epidemic;"

DECLARATION OF COMMITMENT ON HIV/AIDS.

NEO-COLONIALISM (ERADICATION OF ALL FORMS OF) [Néocolonialisme (élimination de toutes les formes de)]

– "*Emphasizing* that the eradication of apartheid, all forms of racism, racial discrimination, colonialism, neo-colonialism, aggression, foreign occupation and domination and interference in the internal affairs of States is essential to the full enjoyment of the rights of men and women,"

Pp. 10, CONVENTION ON THE ELIMINATION OF ALL FORMS OF DISCRIMINATION AGAINST WOMEN.

NEPHRECTOMY BECAUSE OF A TUBERCULAR KIDNEY [Néphrectomie pour un rein tuberculeux]

– "(*f*) Serious chronic affections of the genito-urinary organs, for example: chronic diseases of the kidney with consequent disorders; nephrectomy because of a tubercular kidney; chronic pyelitis or chronic cystitis: hydronephrosis or pyonephrosis; chronic grave gynaecological conditions, normal pregnancy, and obstetrical disorder, where it is impossible to accommodate in a neutral country; etc."

Annex I, 3, GENEVA CONVENTION RELATIVE TO THE TREATMENT OF PRISONERS OF WAR.

NEW INTERNATIONAL ECONOMIC ORDER [Nouvel ordre économique mondial]

– "Convinced that the establishment of the new international economic order based on equity and justice will contribute significantly towards the promotion of equality between men and women,"

Pp. 9, CONVENTION ON THE ELIMINATION OF ALL FORMS OF DISCRIMINATION AGAINST WOMEN.

NON-CUSTODIAL MEASURES [Mesures non privatives de liberté]

– "3.8 Non-custodial measures shall not involve medical or psychological experimentation on, or undue risk of physical or mental injury to, the offender."

UNITED NATIONS STANDARD MINIMUM RULES FOR NON-CUSTODIAL MEASURES (THE TOKYO RULES).

NON-CUSTODIAL MEASURES (THE INTRODUCTION, DEFINITION AND APPLICATION OF) [Mesures non privatives de liberté (L'adoption, le définition et l'application de)]

– "3.1 The introduction, definition and application of non-custodial measures shall be prescribed by law."

UNITED NATIONS STANDARD MINIMUM RULES FOR NON-CUSTODIAL MEASURES (THE TOKYO RULES).

NON-DEFENDED LOCALITY [Localité non défendue]

– "2. The appropriate authorities of a Party to the conflict may declare as a non-defended locality any inhabited place near or in a zone where armed forces are in contact which is open for occupation by an adverse Party. Such a locality shall fulfil the following conditions:

(*a*) All combatants, as well as mobile weapons and mobile military equipment must have been evacuated;

(*b*) No hostile use shall be made of fixed military installations or establishments;

(*c*) No acts of hostility shall be committed by the authorities or by the population; and

(*d*) No activities in support of military operations shall be undertaken."

Art. 59, PROTOCOL ADDITIONAL TO THE GENEVA CONVENTIONS OF 12 AUGUST 1949, AND RELATING TO THE PROTECTION OF VICTIMS OF INTERNATIONAL ARMED CONFLICTS (PROTOCOL I).

NORMAL PREGNANCY, AND OBSTETRICAL DISORDER, WHERE IT IS IMPOSSIBLE TO ACCOMMODATE IN A NEUTRAL COUNTRY [Grossesses et affections obstétricales, lorsque l'hospitalisation en pays neutre est impossible]

– "(*f*) Serious chronic affections of the genito-urinary organs, for example: chronic diseases of the kidney with consequent disorders; nephrectomy because of a tubercular kidney; chronic pyelitis or chronic cystitis: hydronephrosis or pyonephrosis; chronic grave gynaecological conditions, normal pregnancy, and obstetrical disorder, where it is impossible to accommodate in a neutral country; etc."

Annex I, 3, GENEVA CONVENTION RELATIVE TO THE TREATMENT OF PRISONERS OF WAR.

OCCUPATION [Profession ; Occupation]

- "3. For the purpose of this Convention the terms 'employment' and 'occupation' include access to vocational training, access to employment and to particular occupations, and terms and conditions of employment."

Art. 1, DISCRIMINATION (EMPLOYMENT AND OCCUPATION) CONVENTION (N° 111).

- "The Convention shall also apply to all cases of partial or total occupation of the territory of a High Contracting Party, even if the said occupation meets with no armed resistance."

Art. 2, s.p. 2, GENEVA CONVENTION RELATIVE TO THE TREATMENT OF PRISONERS OF WAR.

- "The Convention shall also apply to all cases of partial or total occupation of the territory of a High Contracting Party, even if the said occupation meets with no armed resistance."

Art. 2, s.p. 2, GENEVA CONVENTION RELATIVE TO THE PROTECTION OF CIVILIAN PERSONS IN TIME OF WAR.

OFFENCE [Délit]

- "2.2 For purposes of these Rules, the following definitions shall be applied by Member States in a manner which is compatible with their respective legal systems and concepts:

  [...]

  (*b*) An offence is any behaviour (act or omission) that is punishable by law under the respective legal systems;"

UNITED NATIONS STANDARD MINIMUM RULES FOR THE ADMINISTRATION OF JUVENILE JUSTICE ("THE BEIJING RULES").

OFFENDERS [Délinquants]

- "2.1 The relevant provisions of the present Rules shall be applied to all persons subject to prosecution, trial or the execution of a sentence, at all stages of the administration of criminal justice. For the purposes of the Rules, these persons are referred to as "offenders", irrespective of whether they are suspected, accused or sentenced."

UNITED NATIONS STANDARD MINIMUM RULES FOR NON-CUSTODIAL MEASURES (THE TOKYO RULES).

OLDER PERSONS [Personnes âgées]

– "*Appreciating* the contribution that older persons make to their societies,"
Pp. 1, UNITED NATIONS PRINCIPLES FOR OLDER PERSONS.

– "*Appreciating* the tremendous diversity in the situation of older persons, not only between countries but within countries and between individuals, which requires a variety of policy responses,"
Pp. 5, UNITED NATIONS PRINCIPLES FOR OLDER PERSONS.

OPEN DETENTION FACILITIES [Etablissements ouverts]

– "30. [...] Open detention facilities are those with no or minimal security measures. The population in such detention facilities should be as small as possible. [...][az]"
UNITED NATIONS RULES FOR THE PROTECTION OF JUVENILES DEPRIVED OF THEIR LIBERTY.

OPEN INSTITUTIONS [Etablissements ouverts]

– "(2) [...] Open institutions, by the very fact that they provide no physical security against escape but rely on the self-discipline of the inmates, provide the conditions most favourable to rehabilitation for carefully selected prisoners."
63, STANDARD MINIMUM RULES FOR THE TREATMENT OF PRISONERS.

ORGANISATION [Organisation]

– "In this Convention the term 'organisation' means any organisation of workers or of employers for furthering and defending the interests of workers or of employers."
Art. 10, FREEDOM OF ASSOCIATION AND PROTECTION OF THE RIGHT TO ORGANIZE CONVENTION (N° 87).

PATIENT [Patient]

– " In these Principles:

[az] « 30. [...] Les établissements ouverts sont des établissements dans lesquels les mesures matérielles de sécurité sont aussi réduites que possible. Dans de tels établissements, la population doit être assez restreinte pour permettre un traitement individualisé. [...] »

[...]'Patient' means a person receiving mental health care and includes all persons who are admitted to a mental health facility;"

S.p. 6, DEFINITIONS, PRINCIPLES FOR THE PROTECTION OF PERSONS WITH MENTAL ILLNESS AND THE IMPROVEMENT OF MENTAL HEALTH CARE.[AA]

PEOPLES [Peuples]

– "All peoples have the right of self-determination. By virtue of that right they freely determine their political status and freely pursue their economic, social and cultural development."

Art. 1, 1, INTERNATIONAL COVENANT ON CIVIL AND POLITICAL RIGHTS[1].

Art. 1, 1, INTERNATIONAL COVENANT ON ECONOMIC, SOCIAL AND CULTURAL RIGHTS[32].

I, 2, s.p.1, VIENNA DECLARATION AND PROGRAMME OF ACTION[2].

2, UNITED NATIONS DECLARATION ON THE GRANTING OF INDEPENDENCE TO COLONIAL COUNTRIES AND PEOPLES[3?].

– "4. All peoples of the world possess equal faculties for attaining the highest level in intellectual, technical, social, economic, cultural and political development."

Art. 1, DECLARATION ON RACE AND RACIAL PREJUDICE.

PERFIDY [Perfidie]

– "1. It is prohibited to kill, injure or capture an adversary by resort to perfidy. Acts inviting the confidence of an adversary to lead him to believe that he is entitled to, or is obliged to accord, protection under the rules of international law applicable in armed conflict, with intent to betray that confidence, shall constitute perfidy. The following acts are examples of perfidy:

[AA] Al. 4, DEFINITIONS, Principes pour la protection des personnes atteintes de maladie mentale et pour l'amélioration des soins de santé mentale.

[1] « Tous les peuples ont le droit de disposer d'eux-mêmes. En vertu de ce droit, ils déterminent librement leur statut politique et *assurent* librement leur développement économique, social et culturel. ». *Italics added.*

[2] « Tous les peuples ont le droit de disposer d'eux-mêmes. En vertu de ce droit, ils déterminent librement leur statut politique et *poursuivent* librement leur développement économique, social et culturel. ». *Italics added.*

[3] « Tous les peuples ont le *droit de libre détermination* ; en vertu de ce droit, ils déterminent librement leur statut politique et poursuivent librement leur développement économique, sociale et culturel. ». *Italics added.*

[?] "[...] to self-determination; by virtue [...]" . *Italics added.*

(*a*) The feigning of an intent to negotiate under a flag of truce or of a surrender;

(*b*) The feigning of an incapacitation by wounds or sickness;

(*c*) The feigning of civilian, non-combatant status; and

(*d*) The feigning of protected status by the use of signs, emblems or uniforms of the United Nations or of neutral or other States not Parties to the conflict.

Art. 37, Protocol Additional to the Geneva Conventions of 12 August 1949, and relating to the Protection of Victims of International Armed Conflicts (Protocol I).

PERMANENT MEDICAL PERSONNEL [Personnel sanitaire permanent]

– "For the purposes of this Protocol:
  [...]

  (*k*) 'Permanent medical personnel', 'permanent medical units' and 'permanent medical transports' mean those assigned exclusively to medical purposes for an indeterminate period. 'Temporary medical personnel', 'temporary medical units' and 'temporary medical transports' mean those devoted exclusively to medical purposes for limited periods during the whole of such periods. Unless otherwise specified, the terms 'medical personnel', 'medical units' and 'medical transports' cover both permanent and temporary categories;"

Art. 8, Protocol Additional to the Geneva Conventions of 12 August 1949, and relating to the Protection of Victims of International Armed Conflicts (Protocol I).

PERMANENT MEDICAL TRANSPORTS [Moyens de transport sanitaire Permanents]

– "For the purposes of this Protocol:
  [...]

  (*k*) 'Permanent medical personnel', 'permanent medical units' and 'permanent medical transports' mean those assigned exclusively to medical purposes for an indeterminate period. 'Temporary medical personnel', 'temporary medical units' and 'temporary medical transports' mean those devoted exclusively to medical purposes for limited periods during the whole of such periods. Unless otherwise specified, the terms 'medical personnel','medical units'and 'medical transports' cover both permanent and temporary categories;"

Art. 8, PROTOCOL ADDITIONAL TO THE GENEVA CONVENTIONS OF 12 AUGUST 1949, AND RELATING TO THE PROTECTION OF VICTIMS OF INTERNATIONAL ARMED CONFLICTS (PROTOCOL I).

PERMANENT MEDICAL UNITS [Unités sanitaires permanentes]

– "For the purposes of this Protocol:

[...]

(*k*) 'Permanent medical personnel', 'permanent medical units' and 'permanent medical transports' mean those assigned exclusively to medical purposes for an indeterminate period. 'Temporary medical personnel', 'temporary medical units' and 'temporary medical transports' mean those devoted exclusively to medical purposes for limited periods during the whole of such periods. Unless otherwise specified, the terms 'medical personnel', 'medical units' and 'medical transports' cover both permanent and temporary categories;"

Art. 8, PROTOCOL ADDITIONAL TO THE GENEVA CONVENTIONS OF 12 AUGUST 1949, AND RELATING TO THE PROTECTION OF VICTIMS OF INTERNATIONAL ARMED CONFLICTS (PROTOCOL I).

PERSECUTION [Persécution]

– "2. For the purpose of paragraph 1[4]:

[4] "1. For the purpose of this Statute, 'crime against humanity' means any of the following acts when committed as part of a widespread or systematic attack directed against any civilian population, with knowledge of the attack:

(a) Murder;
(b) Extermination ;
(c) Enslavement;
(d) Deportation or forcible transfer of population;
(e) Imprisonment or other severe deprivation of physical liberty in violation of fundamental rules of international law;
(f) Torture;
(g) Rape, sexual slavery, enforced prostitution, forced pregnancy, enforced sterilization, or any other form of sexual violence of comparable gravity;
(h) Persecution against any identifiable group or collectivity on political, racial, national, ethnic, cultural, religious, gender, as defined in paragraph 3, or other grounds that are universally recognized as impermissible under international law, in connection with any act referred to in this paragraph or any crime within the jurisdiction of the Court;
(i) Enforced disappearance of persons;
(j) The crime of apartheid;
(k) Other inhumane acts of a similar character intentionally causing great suffering, or serious injury to body or to mental or physical health."

[…]

(*g*) 'Persecution' means the intentional and severe deprivation of fundamental rights contrary to international law by reason of the identity of the group or collectivity;"

Art. 7, ROME STATUTE OF THE INTERNATIONAL CRIMINAL COURT.

PERSON [Etres humains]

– "63. […] Every person is born equal and has the same rights to life and welfare, education and work, living independently and active participation in all aspects of society. […]"

II, VIENNA DECLARATION AND PROGRAMME OF ACTION.

PERSON OF SERVILE STATUS (A) [Personne de condition servile]

– "For the purpose of the present Convention:

[…]

(*b*) 'A person of servile status' means a person in the condition or status resulting from any of the institutions or practices mentioned in article 1[5] of this Convention;"

[5] "Each of States Parties to this Convention shall take all practicable and necessary legislative and other measures to bring about progressively and as soon as possible the complete abolition or abandonment of the following institutions and practices, where they still exist and whether or not they are covered by the definition of slavery contained in article 1 of the Slavery Convention signed at Geneva on 25 September 1926:

(*a*) Debt bondage, that is to say, the status or condition arising from a pledge by a debtor of his personal services or of those of a person under his control as security for debt, if the value of those services as reasonably assessed is not applied towards the liquidation of the debt or the length and nature of those services are not respectively limited and defined;

(*b*) Serfdom, that is to say, the condition or status of a tenant who is by law, custom or agreement bound to live and labour on land belonging to another person and to render some determinate service to such other person, whether for reward or not, and is not free to change his status;

c) Any institution or practice whereby:

(i) A woman, without the right to refuse, is promised or given in marriage on payment of a consideration in money or in kind to her parents, guardian, family or any other person or group; or

(ii) The husband of a woman, his family, or his clan, has the right to transfer her to another person for value received or otherwise; or

(iii) A woman on the death of her husband is liable to be inherited by another person;

Art. 7, SUPPLEMENTARY CONVENTION ON THE ABOLITION OF SLAVERY, THE SLAVE TRADE AND INSTITUTIONS AND PRACTICES SIMILAR TO SLAVERY.

PERSONAL REPRESENTATIVE [Représentant personnel]

– "In these Principles:

[...]

'Personal representative' means a person charged by law with the duty of representing a patient's interests in any specified respect or of exercising specified rights on the patient's behalf, and includes the parent or legal guardian of a minor unless otherwise provided by domestic law;"

S.p. 7, DEFINITIONS, PRINCIPLES FOR THE PROTECTION OF PERSONS WITH MENTAL ILLNESS AND THE IMPROVEMENT OF MENTAL HEALTH CARE.[AB]

PERSONNEL [Personnel]

– "For the purposes of this Protocol:

[...]

(*c*) 'Personnel' of civil defence organizations means those persons assigned by a Party to the conflict exclusively to the performance of the tasks mentioned under sub-paragraph (a)[6], including personnel

---

(*d*) Any institution or practice whereby a child or young person under the age of 18 years, is delivered by either or both of his natural parents or by his guardian to another person, whether for reward or not, with a view to the exploitation of the child or young person or of his labour."

[AB] Al. 6, DEFINITIONS, Principes pour la protection des personnes atteintes de maladie mentale et pour l'amélioration des soins de santé mentale.

[6] "(*a*) "Civil defence" means the performance of some or all of the undermentioned humanitarian tasks intended to protect the civilian population against the dangers, and to help it to recover from the immediate effects, of hostilities or disasters and also to provide the conditions necessary for its survival. These tasks are:

(i) Warning;

(ii) Evacuation;

(iii) Management of shelters;

(iv) Management of blackout measures;

(v) Rescue;

(vi) Medical services, including first aid, and religious assistance;

(vii) Fire-fighting;

(viii) Detection and marking of danger areas;

(ix) Decontamination and similar protective measures;

(x) Provision of emergency accommodation and supplies;

(xi) Emergency assistance in the restoration and maintenance of order in distressed areas;

assigned by the competent authority of that Party exclusively to the administration of these organizations;"

Art. 61, PROTOCOL ADDITIONAL TO THE GENEVA CONVENTIONS OF 12 AUGUST 1949, AND RELATING TO THE PROTECTION OF VICTIMS OF INTERNATIONAL ARMED CONFLICTS (PROTOCOL I).

PERSONS [Personnes]

– "All persons are equal before the law and are entitled without any discrimination to the equal protection of the law.[...]"

Art. 26, INTERNATIONAL COVENANT ON CIVIL AND POLITICAL RIGHTS.

PERSONS WITH DISABILITIES [Personnes souffrant d'incapacités ; Handicapés]

– "63. The World Conference on Human Rights reaffirms that all human rights and fundamental freedoms are universal and thus unreservedly include persons with disabilities. Every person is born equal and has the same rights to life and welfare, education and work, living independently and active participation in all aspects of society. [...]"

II, VIENNA DECLARATION AND PROGRAMME OF ACTION.

– "1. There are persons with disabilities in all parts of the world and at all levels in every society. The number of persons with disabilities in the world is large and is growing."

INTRODUCTION, STANDARD RULES ON THE EQUALIZATION OF OPPORTUNITIES FOR PERSONS WITH DISABILITIES.

– "26. Persons with disabilities are members of society and have the right to remain within their local communities. They should receive the support they need within the ordinary structures of education, health, employment and social services."

INTRODUCTION, STANDARD RULES ON THE EQUALIZATION OF OPPORTUNITIES FOR PERSONS WITH DISABILITIES.

(xii) Emergency repair of indispensable public utilities;
(xiii) Emergency disposal of the dead;
(xiv) Assistance in the preservation of objects essential for survival;
(xv) Complementary activities necessary to carry out any of the tasks mentioned above, including, but not limited to, planning and organization;"

– "3. All persons with disabilities, including persons with severe and/or multiple disabilities, who require rehabilitation should have access to it [Support services]."

I., Rule 3, STANDARD RULES ON THE EQUALIZATION OF OPPORTUNITIES FOR PERSONS WITH DISABILITIES.

PISTOLS [Pistolets]

– 3. It shall also not be considered as an act harmful to the enemy that civilian defence personnel bear light individual weapons for the purpose of maintaining order or for self-defence. However, in areas where land fighting it taking place or is likely to take place, the Parties to the conflict shall undertake the appropriate measures to limit these weapons to handguns, such as pistols or revolvers, in order to assist in distinguishing between civil defence personnel and combatants. Although civil defence personnel bear other light individual weapons in such areas, they shall nevertheless be respected and protected as soon as they have been recognized as such. "

Art. 65, PROTOCOL ADDITIONAL TO THE GENEVA CONVENTIONS OF 12 AUGUST 1949, AND RELATING TO THE PROTECTION OF VICTIMS OF INTERNATIONAL ARMED CONFLICTS (PROTOCOL I).

POLITICAL CRIMES [Crimes politiques]

– "Genocide and the other acts enumerated in Article III[7] shall not be considered as political crimes for the purpose of extradition."

Art. VII, s.p. 1, CONVENTION ON THE PREVENTION AND PUNISHMENT OF THE CRIME OF GENOCIDE.

POPULAR PARTICIPATION [Participation populaire]

– "2. States should encourage popular participation in all spheres as an important factor in development and in the full realization of all human rights."

Art. 8, DECLARATION ON THE RIGHT TO DEVELOPMENT.

---

[7] "The following acts shall be punishable:
(*a*) Genocide;
(*b*) Conspiracy to commit genocide;
(*c*) Direct and public incitement to commit genocide;
(*d*) Attempt to commit genocide;
(*e*) Complicity in genocide."

POPULATIONS DESTABILIZED BY ARMED CONFLICT, HUMARITARIAN EMERGENCIES AND NATURAL DISASTERS [Populations déstabilisées par les conflits armés, les situations d'urgence humanitaire et les catastrophes naturelles]

– "75. [...] populations destabilized by armed conflict, humanitarian emergencies and natural disasters, including refugees, internally displaced persons, and in particular women and children, are at increased risk of exposure to HIV infection; and, where appropriate, factor HIV/AIDS components into international assistance programmes;"

Declaration of Commitment on HIV/AIDS.

POSSESSION OF PERSONAL EFFECTS [Possession d'effets personnels]

– "35. The possession of personal effects is a basic element of the right to privacy and essential to the psychological well-being of the juvenile.[...]"

United Nations Rules for the Protection of Juveniles Deprived of their Liberty.

POVERTY [Pauvreté]

– "11. Recognizing that poverty, underdevelopment and illiteracy are among the principal contributing factors to the spread of HIV/AIDS, and noting with grave concern that HIV/AIDS is compounding poverty and is now reversing or impeding development in many countries and should therefore be addressed in an integrated manner;"

Declaration of Commitment on HIV/AIDS.

PRACTICES OF APARTHEID [Pratiques de l'Apartheid]

– "(*c*) Practices of apartheid and other inhuman and degrading practices involving outrages upon personal dignity, based on racial discrimination;"

Art. 85, paragraph 4, Protocol Additional to the Geneva Conventions of 12 August 1949, and relating to the Protection of Victims of International Armed Conflicts (Protocol I).

PRE-TRIAL DETENTION [Détention provisoire]

– "6.1 Pre-trial detention shall be used as a means of last resort in criminal proceedings, with due regard for the investigation of the alleged offence and for the protection of society and the victim."

United Nations Standard Minimum Rules for Non-custodial Measures (The Tokyo Rules).

PRESENT DISABILITY POLICY [Politique actuellement adoptée en faveur des handicapés]

– "3. Present disability policy is the result of developments over the past 200 years. In many ways it reflects the general living conditions and social and economic policies of different times. In the disability field, however, there are also many specific circumstances that have influenced the living conditions of persons with disabilities. [...]"

INTRODUCTION, Standard Rules on the Equalization of Opportunities for Persons with Disabilities.

PRESUMED INNOCENT [Présumée innocente]

– "1. Everyone charged with a penal offence has the right to be presumed innocent until proved guilty according to law in a public trial at which he has had all the guarantees necessary for his defence."

Art. 11, Universal Declaration of Human Rights.

– "2. Everyone charged with a criminal offence shall have the right to be presumed innocent until proved guilty according to law."

Art. 14, International Covenant on Civil and Political Rights.

PREVENTION [Prévention]

– "22. The term 'prevention' means action aimed at preventing the occurrence of physical, intellectual, psychiatric or sensory impairments (primary prevention) or at preventing impairments from causing a permanent functional limitation or disability (secondary prevention). Prevention may include many different types of action, such as primary health care, prenatal and postnatal care, education in nutrition, immunization campaigns against communicable diseases, measures to control endemic diseases, safety regulations, programmes for the prevention of accidents in different environments, including adaptation of workplaces to prevent occupational disabilities and diseases, and prevention of disability resulting from pollution of the environment or armed conflict."

INTRODUCTION, STANDARD RULES ON THE EQUALIZATION OF OPPORTUNITIES FOR PERSONS WITH DISABILITIES.

PRIMARY AND SECONDARY PROGRESSIVE CHRONIC POLYARTHRITIS [Polyarthrite chronique évolutive primaire et secondaire]

– "(*p*) Chronic affections of locomotion, with obvious functional disorders, for example: arthritis deformans, primary and secondary progressive chronic polyarthritis; rheumatism with serious clinical symptoms; etc."

Annex I, 3, GENEVA CONVENTION RELATIVE TO THE TREATMENT OF PRISONERS OF WAR.

PRIMARY CONDITIONS OF SOCIAL PROGRESS AND DEVELOPMENT [Conditions primordiales du progrès et du développement]

– "The following are considered primary conditions of social progress and development:

(*a*) National independence based on the right of peoples to self-determination;

(*b*) The principle of non-interference in the internal affairs of States;

(*c*) Respect for the sovereignty and territorial integrity of States;

(*d*) Permanent sovereignty of each nation over its natural wealth and resources;

(*e*) The right and responsibility of each State and, as &r as they are concerned, each nation and people to determine freely its own objectives of social development, to set its own priorities and to decide in conformity with the principles of the Charter of the United Nations the means and methods of their achievement without any external interference;

(*f*) Peaceful coexistence, peace, friendly relations and co-operation among States irrespective of differences in their social, economic or political systems.

Art. 3, DECLARATION ON SOCIAL PROGRESS AND DEVELOPMENT.

PRIMARY TASK OF ALL STATES AND INTERNATIONAL ORGANIZATIONS [Tâche primordiale de tous les Etats et de toutes les organisations internationales]

– "*Believing* that the primary task of all States and international organizations is to eliminate from the life of society all evils and obstacles to social progress, particularly such evils as inequality, exploitation, war, colonialism and racism,"

Pp. 13, DECLARATION ON SOCIAL PROGRESS AND DEVELOPMENT.

PRINCIPLE OF EQUAL RIGHTS [Principe de l'égalité des droits]

– "25. The principle of equal rights implies that the needs of each and every individual are of equal importance, that those needs must be made the basis for the planning of societies and that all resources must be employed in such a way as to ensure that every individual has equal opportunity for participation."

Introduction, STANDARD RULES ON THE EQUALIZATION OF OPPORTUNITIES FOR PERSONS WITH DISABILITIES.

PRINCIPLE OF EQUALITY IN DIGNITY AND RIGHTS [Principe de l'égalité en dignité et en droits]

– "1. The principle of the equality in dignity and rights of all human beings and all peoples, irrespective of race, colour and origin, is a generally accepted and recognized principle of international law. [...]."

Art. 9, DECLARATION ON RACE AND RACIAL PREJUDICE.

PRINCIPLE OF PROPORTIONALITY [Principe de proportionnalité]

– "The second objective is 'the principle of proportionality'. This principle is well-known as an instrument for curbing punitive sanctions, mostly expressed in terms of just deserts in relation to the gravity of the offence. The response to young offenders should be based on the consideration not only of the gravity of the offence but also of personal circumstances. The individual circumstances of the offender (for example social status, family situation, the harm caused by the offence or other factors affecting personal circumstances) should influence the proportionality of the reactions (for example by having regard to the offender's endeavour to indemnify the victim or to her or his willingness to turn to wholesome and useful life)."

5, al.2, *Commentary*, s.p. 1-2, UNITED NATIONS STANDARD MINIMUM RULES FOR THE ADMINISTRATION OF JUVENILE JUSTICE ("THE BEIJING RULES").

PRINCIPLE OF THE INADMINISSIBILITY OF DISCRIMINATION [Principe de la non-discrimination]

– "*Noting* that the Universal Declaration of Human Rights affirms the principle of the inadmissibility of discrimination[U] and proclaims that all human beings are born free and equal in dignity and rights and that everyone is entitled to all the rights and freedoms set forth therein, without distinction of any kind, including distinction based on sex,"

Pp. 2, CONVENTION ON THE ELIMINATION OF ALL FORMS OF DISCRIMINATION AGAINST WOMEN.

PRISONERS OF WAR [Prisonniers de guerre]

– "A. Prisoners of war, in the sense of the present Convention, are persons belonging to one of the following categories, who have fallen into the power of the enemy:

1. Members of the armed forces of a Party to the conflict as well as members of militias or volunteer corps forming part of such armed forces.

2. Members of other militias and members of other volunteer corps, including those of organized resistance movements, belonging to a Party to the conflict and operating in or outside their own territory, even if this territory is occupied, provided that such militias or volunteer corps, including such organized resistance movements, fulfil the following conditions:

(*a*) That of being commanded by a person responsible for his subordinates;

(*b*) That of having a fixed distinctive sign recognizable at a distance;

[U] « *Notant* que la Déclaration universelle des droits de l'homme affirme le principe de la non-discrimination et proclame que tous les êtres humains naissent libres et égaux en dignité et en droits et que chacun peut se prévaloir de tous les droits et de toutes les libertés qui y sont énoncés, sans distinction aucune, notamment de sexe, »

(*c*) That of carrying arms openly;

(*d*) That of conducting their operations in accordance with the laws and customs of war.

3. Members of regular armed forces who profess allegiance to a government or an authority not recongized by Detaining Power.

4. Persons who accompany the armed forces without actually being members thereof, such as civilian members of military aircraft crews, war correspondents, supply contractors, members of labour units or of services responsible for the welfare of the armed forces, provided that they have received authorization from the armed forces which they accompany, who shall provide them for that purpose with an identity card similar to the annexed model.

5. Members of crews, including masters, pilots and apprentices, of the merchant marine and the crews of civil aircraft of the Parties to the conflict, who do not benefit by more favourable treatment under any other provisions of international law.

6. Inhabitants of non-occupied territory, who on the approach of the enemy spontaneously take up arms to resist the invading forces, without having had time to form themselves into regular armed units, provided they carry arms openly and respect the laws and customs of war.

B. The following shall likewise be treated as prisoners of war under the present Convention:

1. Persons belonging, or having belonged, to the armed forces of the occupied country, if the occupying Power considers it necessary by reason of such allegiance to intern them, even though it has originally liberated them while hostilities were going on outside the territory it occupies, in particular where such persons have made an unsuccessful attempts to rejoin the armed forces to which they belong and which are engaged in combat, or where they fail to comply with a summons made them with a view to internment.

2.The persons belonging to one of the categories enumerated in the present Article, who have been received by neutral or non-belligerent Powers on their territory and whom these Powers are required to intern under international law, without prejudice to any more favourable treatment which these Powers may choose to give and with the exception of Articles 8[8], 10[9], 15[10], 30, fifth paragraph[11], 58-67[12], 92[13], 126[14] and where diplomatic relations exist between the Parties to the

---

[8] "The present Convention shall be applied with the cooperation and under the scrutiny of the Protecting Powers whose duty it is to safeguard the interests of the Parties to the conflict. For this purpose, the Protecting Powers may appoint, apart from their diplomatic or consular staff, delegates shall be subject to the approval of the Power with they are to carry out their duties. The parties to the conflict shall facilitate to the greatest extent possible the task of the representatives or delegates of the Protecting Powers.
The representatives or delegates of the Protecting Powers shall not in any case exceed their mission under the present Convention. They shall, in particular, take account of the imperative necessities of security of the State wherein they carry out their duties."

[9] "The High Contracting Parties may at any time agree to entrust to an organization which offers all guarantees of impartiality and efficacy the duties incumbent on the Protecting Powers by virtue of the present Convention.
When prisoners of war do not benefit or cease to benefit, no matter for what reason, by the activities of a Protecting Power or of an organization provided for in the first paragraph above, the Detaining Power shall request a neutral State, or such an organization, to undertake the functions performed under the present Convention by a Protecting Power designated by the Parties to a conflict.
If protection cannot be arranged accordingly, the Detaining Power shall request or shall accept, subject to the provisions of this Article, the offer of the services of a humanitarian organization, such as the International Committee of the Red Cross, to assume the humanitarian functions performed by Protecting Powers under the present Convention.
Any neutral or any organization invited by the Power concerned or offering itself for these purposes, shall be required to act with a sense of responsibility towards the Party to the conflict on which persons protected by the present Convention depend, and shall be required to furnish sufficient assurances that it is in a position to undertake the appropriate functions and to discharge them impartially.
No derogation from the preceding provisions shall be made by special agreements between Powers one of which is restricted, even temporarily, in its freedom to negotiate with the other Power or its allies by reason of military events, more particularly where the whole, or a substantial part, of the territory of the said Power is occupied.
Whenever in the present Convention mention is made of a Protecting Power, such mention applies to substitute organizations in the sense of the present Article."

[10] "The Power detaining prisoners of war shall be bound to provide free of charge for their maintenance and for the medical attention required by their state of health."

[11] "The costs of treatment, including those of any apparatus necessary for the maintenance of prisoners of war in good health, particularly dentures and other artificial appliances, and spectacles, shall be borne by Detaining Power."

[12] *Art. 58* : "Upon the outbreak of hostilities, and pending an arrangement on this matter with the Protecting Power, the Detaining Power may determine the maximum amount of money in cash or in any similar form, that prisoners may have in their possession. Any amount in excess, which was properly in their possession and which has been taken or withheld from them, shall be placed to their account, together with any monies deposited by them, and shall not be converted into any other without their consent.

If prisoners of war are permitted to purchase services or commodities outside the camp against payment in cash, such payments shall be made by the prisoner himself or by camp administration who will charge them to the accounts of the prisoners concerned. The Detaining Power will establish the necessary rules in this respect."

Art. 59: "Cash which was taken from prisoners of war, in accordance with article 18, at the time of their capture, and which is in the currency of the Detaining Power, shall be placed to their separate accounts, in accordance with the provisions of Article 64 of the present Section.

The amounts, in the currency of the Detaining Power, due to the conversion of sums also be credited to their separate accounts."

Art. 60: The Detaining Power shall grant all prisoners of war a monthly advance of pay, the amount of which shall be fixed by conversion, into the currency of the said power, of the following amounts:

Category I: Prisoners ranking below sergeant: eight Swiss francs.

Category II: Sergeants and other non-commissioned officers, or prisoners of equivalent rank: twelve Swiss francs.

Category III: Warrant officers and commissioned officers below the rank of major or prisoners of equivalent rank : fifty Swiss francs;

Category IV: Majors, lieutenant-colonels, colonels or prisoners of equivalent rank: sixty Swiss francs.

Category V: General officers or prisoners of equivalent rank: seventy-five Swiss francs.

However, the Parties to the conflict concerned may by special agreement modify the amount of advances of pay due to prisoners of the preceding categories.

Furthermore, if the amounts indicated in the first paragraph above would be unduly high compared with the pay of the Detaining Power's armed forces or would, for any reason, seriously embarrass the Detaining Power, then, pending the conclusion of a special agreement with the Power on which the prisoners depend to vary the amounts indicated above, the Detaining power:

(*a*) Shall continue to credit the accounts of the prisoners with the amounts indicated in the first paragraph above;

(*b*) may temporarily limit the amount made available from these advances of pay to prisoners of war for their own use, to sums which are reasonable, but which for Category I, shall never be inferior to the amount that the Detaining Power gives to the members of its own armed forces. The reasons for any limitations will be given without delay to the Protecting Power."

Art. 61: "The Detaining Power shall accept for distribution as supplementary pay to prisoners of war sums which the Power on which the prisoners depend may forward to them, on condition that the sums to be paid shall be the same for each prisoner of the same category, shall be payable to all prisoners of that category depending on that Power, and shall be placed in their separate accounts, at the earliest opportunity, in accordance with the provisions of Article 64. Such supplementary pay shall not relieve the Detaining Power of any obligation under this Convention."

Art. 62: "Prisoners of war shall be paid a fair working rate of pay by the detaining authorities direct. The rate shall be fixed by the said authorities, but shall at no time be less than one-fourth of one Swiss franc for a full working day. The Detaining Power shall inform prisoners of war, as well as the Power on which they depend, through the intermediary of the Protecting Power, of the rate of daily working pay that it has fixed.

Working pay shall likewise be paid by the detaining authorities to prisoners of war permanently detailed to duties or to a skilled or semi-skilled occupation in connection with the admin-

istration, installation or maintenance of camps, and to the prisoners who are required to carry out spiritual or medical duties on behalf of their comrades.
The working pay of the prisoners' representative, of his advisers, if any, and of his assistants, shall be paid out of the fund maintained by canteen profits. The scale of this working pay shall be fixed by the prisoners' representative and approved by the camp commander. If there is no such fund, the detaining authorities shall pay these prisoners a fair working rate of pay."
Art. 63: "Prisoners of war shall be permitted to receive remittances of money addressed to them individually or collectively.
Every prisoner of war shall have at his disposal the credit balance of his account as provided for in the following Article, within the limits fixed by the Detaining Power, which shall make such payments as are requested. Subject to financial or monetary restrictions which the Detaining Power regards as essential, prisoners of war may also have payments made abroad. In this case payments addressed by prisoners of war to dependants shall be given priority.
In any event, and subject to the consent of the Power on which they depend, prisoners may have payments made in their own country, as follows: the Detaining Power shall send to the aforesaid Power through the Protecting Power a notification giving all the necessary particulars concerning the prisoners of war, the beneficiaries of the payments, and the amount of the sums to be paid, expressed in the Detaining Power's currency. The said notification shall be signed by the prisoners and countersigned by the camp commander. The Detaining Power shall debit the prisoners' account by a corresponding amount; the sums thus debited shall be placed by it to the credit of the Power on which the prisoners depend.
To apply the foregoing provisions, the Detaining Power may usefully consult the Model Regulations in Annex V of the present Convention."
Art. 64: "The Detaining Power shall hold an account for each prisoner of war, showing at least the following: 1. The amounts due to the prisoner or received by him as advances of pay, as working pay or derived from any other source; the sums in the currency of the Detaining Power which were taken from him; the sums taken from him and converted at his request into the currency of the said Power.
2. The payments made to the prisoner in cash, or in any other similar form; the payments made on his behalf and at his request; the sums transferred under Article 63, third paragraph."
Art. 65: "Every item entered in the account of a prisoner of war shall be countersigned or initialled by him, or by the prisoners' representative acting on his behalf.
Prisoners of war shall at all times be afforded reasonable facilities for consulting and obtaining copies of their accounts, which may likewise be inspected by the representatives of the Protecting Powers at the time of visits to the camp.
When prisoners of war are transferred from one camp to another, their personal accounts will follow them. In case of transfer from one Detaining Power to another, the monies which are their property and are not in the currency of the Detaining Power will follow them. They shall be given certificates for any other monies standing to the credit of their accounts.
The Parties to the conflict concerned may agree to notify to each other at specific intervals through the Protecting Power, the amount of the accounts of the prisoners of war."
Art. 66: "On the termination of captivity, through the release of a prisoner of war or his repatriation, the Detaining Power shall give him a statement, signed by an authorized officer of that Power, showing the credit balance then due to him. The Detaining Power shall also send through the Protecting Power to the government upon which the prisoner of war depends, lists giving all appropriate particulars of all prisoners of war whose captivity has been terminated by repatriation, release, escape, death or any other means, and showing the amount of their credit

conflict and the neutral or non-belligerent power concerned, those Articles concerning the Protecting Power; Where such diplomatic relations exists, the Parties to a conflict on whom these persons depend shall be allowed to perform towards them the functions of a Protecting Power as provided in the present Convention, without prejudice to the functions which these Parties normally exercise in conformity with diplomatic and consular usage and treaties."

C. This Article shall in no way affect the status of medical personnel

---

balances. Such lists shall be certified on each sheet by an authorized representative of the Detaining Power.
Any of the above provisions of this Article may be varied by mutual agreement between any two Parties to the conflict.
The Power on which the prisoner of war depends shall be responsible for settling with him any credit balance due to him from the Detaining Power on the termination of his captivity."
Art.67 : "Advances of pay, issued to prisoners of war in conformity with Article 60, shall be considered as made on behalf of the Power on which they depend. Such advances of pay, as well as all payments made by the said Power under Article 63, third paragraph, and Article 68, shall form the subject of arrangements between the Powers concerned, at the close of hostilities." .

[13] A prisoner of war who attempts to escape and is recaptured before having made good his escape in the sense of Article 91 shall be liable only to a disciplinary punishment in respect of this act, even if it is a repeated offence.
A prisoner of war who is recaptured shall be handed over without delay to the competent military authority.
Article 88, fourth paragraph, notwithstanding, prisoners of war punished as a result of an unsuccessful escape may be subjected to special surveillance. Such surveillance must not affect the state of their health, must be undergone in a prisoner of war camp, and must not entail the suppression of any of the safeguards granted them by the present Convention."

[14] "Representatives or delegates of the Protecting Powers shall have permission to go to all places where prisoners of war may be, particularly to places of internment, imprisonment and labour, and shall have access to all premises occupied by prisoners of war; they shall also be allowed to go to the places of departure, passage and arrival of prisoners who are being transferred. They shall be able to interview the prisoners, and in particular the prisoners' representatives, without witnesses, either personally or through an interpreter.
Representatives and delegates of the Protecting Powers shall have full liberty to select the places they wish to visit. The duration and frequency of these visits shall not be restricted. Visits may not be prohibited except for reasons of imperative military necessity, and then only as an exceptional and temporary measure.
The Detaining Power and the Power on which the said prisoners of war depend may agree, if necessary, that compatriots of these prisoners of war be permitted to participate in the visits. The delegates of the International Committee of the Red Cross shall enjoy the same prerogatives. The appointment of such delegates shall be submitted to the approval of the Power detaining the prisoners of war to be visited."

and chaplains as provided for in Article 33[15] of the present Convention."

Art. 4, GENEVA CONVENTION RELATIVE TO THE TREATMENT OF PRISONERS OF WAR.

PROCESS OF GLOBALIZATION [Processus de mondialisation]

– "*Considering* that the process of globalization, facilitated by the rapid development of new information and communication technologies, though representing a challenge for cultural for cultural diversity, creates the conditions for renewed dialogue among cultures and civilizations,"

Pp. 9, UNIVERSAL DECLARATION ON CULTURAL DIVERSITY.

---

[15] "Members of the medical personnel and chaplains while retained by the Detaining Power with a view to assisting prisoners of war, shall not be considered as prisoners of war. They shall, however, receive as a minimum the benefits and protection of the present Convention, and shall also be granted all facilities necessary to provide for the medical care of, and religious ministration to, prisoners of war.

They shall continue to exercise their medical and spiritual functions for the benefit of prisoners of war, preferably those belonging to the armed forces upon which they depend, within the scope of the military laws and regulations of the Detaining Power and under the control of its competent services, in accordance with their professional etiquette. They shall also benefit by the following facilities in the exercise of their medical or spiritual functions:

(*a*) They shall be authorized to visit periodically prisoners of war situated in working detachments or in hospitals outside the camp. For this purpose, the Detaining Power shall place at their disposal the necessary means of transport.

(*b*) The senior medical officer in each camp shall be responsible to camp military authorities for everything connected with the activities of retained medical personnel. For this purpose, Parties to the conflict shall agree at the outbreak of hostilities on the subject of the corresponding ranks of the medical personnel, including that of societies mentioned in Articles of the Geneva Convention for the Amelioration of the Condition of the Wounded and Sick in Armed Forces in the Field of August 12, 1949. This senior medical officer, as well chaplains, shall have the right to deal with the competent authorities of the camp on all questions relating to their duties. Such authorities shall afford them all necessary facilities for correspondence relating to these questions.

(*c*) Although they shall be subject to the internal discipline of the camp in which they are retained, such personnel may not be compelled to carry our any work other than that concerned with their medical or religious duties.

During hostilities, the Parties to the conflict shall agree concerning the possible relief of retained personnel and shall settle the procedure to be followed.

None of the preceding provisions shall relieve the Detaining Power of its obligations with regard to prisoners of war from the medical or spiritual point of view."

PROJECT-TIED WORKER [Travailleurs employés au titre de projets]

– "For the purposes of the present Convention:

[...]

(*f*) The term 'project-tied worker' refers to a migrant worker admitted to a State of employment for a defined period to work solely on a specific project being carried out in that State by his or her employer;"

Art. 2.2, INTERNATIONAL CONVENTION ON THE PROTECTION OF THE RIGHTS OF ALL MIGRANT WORKERS AND MEMBERS OF THEIR FAMILIES.

PROMOTION AND PROTECTION OF ALL HUMAN RIGHTS AND FUNDAMENTAL FREEDOMS [Promotion et protection de tous les droits de l'homme et de toutes les libertés fondamentales]

– "4. The promotion and protection of all human rights and fundamental freedoms must be considered as a priority objective of the United Nations in accordance with its purposes and principles, in particular the purpose of international cooperation. In the framework of these purposes and principles, the promotion and protection of all human rights is a legitimate concern of the international community. The organs and specialized agencies related to human rights should therefore further enhance the coordination of their activities based on the consistent and objective application of international human rights instruments."

I, VIENNA DECLARATION AND PROGRAMME OF ACTION.

PROMOTION AND PROTECTION OF THE RIGHTS OF PERSONS BELONGING TO NATIONAL OR ETHNIC, RELIGIOUS AND LINGUISTIC MINORITIES [Promotion et protection des droits des personnes appartenant à des minorités nationales ou ethniques, religieuses et linguistiques]

– "*Considering* that the promotion and protection of the rights of persons belonging to national or ethnic, religious and linguistic minorities contribute to the political and social stability of States in which they live,

Pp. 5, DECLARATION ON THE RIGHTS OF PERSONS BELONGING TO NATIONAL OR ETHNIC, RELIGIOUS AND LINGUISTIC MINORITIES.

PROSECUTORS [Magistrats du parquet]

- "3. Prosecutors, as essential agents of the administration of justice, shall at all times maintain the honour and dignity of their profession."

GUIDELINES ON THE ROLE OF PROSECUTORS.

PROSTITUTION [Prostitution]

- "*Whereas* prostitution and the accompanying evil of the traffic in persons for the purpose of prostitution are incompatible with the dignity and worth of the human person and endanger the welfare of the individual, the family and the community,"

Pp. 1, CONVENTION FOR THE SUPPRESSION OF THE TRAFFIC IN PERSONS AND OF THE EXPLOITATION OF THE PROSTITUTION OF OTHERS.

PROTECTING POWER [Puissance protectrice]

- "(*c*) 'Protecting Power' means a neutral or other State not a Party to the conflict which has been designated by a Party to the conflict and accepted by the adverse Party and has agreed to carry out the functions assigned to a Protecting Power under the Conventions and this Protocol;"

Art. 2, PROTOCOL ADDITIONAL TO THE GENEVA CONVENTIONS OF 12 AUGUST 1949, AND RELATING TO THE PROTECTION OF VICTIMS OF INTERNATIONAL ARMED CONFLICTS (PROTOCOL I).

PROVINCIAL AND LOCAL GOVERNMENTS [Pouvoirs intermédiaires et pouvoirs locaux]

- "(*g*) Close interdisciplinary co-operation between national, State, provincial and local governments, [...]" [AC]

9, UNITED NATIONS GUIDELINES FOR THE PREVENTION OF JUVENILE DELINQUENCY (THE RIYADH GUIDELINES).

PURPOSE AND JUSTIFICATION OF A SENTENCE OF IMPRISONMENT OR A SIMILAR MEASURE DEPRIVATIVE OF LIBERTY [But et la justification des peines et des mesures privatives de liberté (le)]

- "58. The purpose and justification of a sentence of imprisonment or a similar measure deprivative of liberty is ultimately to protect society

[AC] « Une étroite coopération interdisciplinaire entre pouvoir central, pouvoirs intermédiaires (province, Etat, département) et pouvoirs locaux, [...] »

against crime. This end can only be achieved if the period of imprisonment is used to ensure, so far as possible, that upon his return to society the offender is not only willing but able to lead a law-abiding and self-supporting life."

STANDARD MINIMUM RULES FOR THE TREATMENT OF PRISONERS.

PURPOSES AND PRINCIPLES OF CHARTER OF THE UNITED NATIONS [Buts et principes énoncés dans la Charte des Nations Unies]

– "3. We reaffirm our commitment to the purposes and principles of the Charter of the United Nations, which have proved timeless and universal. Indeed, their relevance and capacity to inspire have increased, as nations and peoples have become increasingly interconnected and interdependent."

UNITED NATIONS MILLENIUM DECLARATION.

RACIAL BARRIERS [Barrières raciales]

– "Convinced that the existence of racial barriers is repugnant to the ideals of any human society,"

Pp. 8, INTERNATIONAL CONVENTION ON THE ELIMINATION OF ALL FORMS OF RACIAL DISCRIMINATION.

RACIAL DISCRIMINATION [Discrimination raciale]

– "1. In this Convention, the term 'racial discrimination' shall mean any distinction, exclusion, restriction or preference based on race, colour, descent, or national or ethnic origin which has the purpose or effect of nullifying or impairing the recognition, enjoyment or exercise, on an equal footing, of human rights and fundamental freedoms in the political, economic, social, cultural or any other field of public life.

2. This Convention shall not apply to distinctions, exclusions, restrictions or preferences made by a State Party to this Convention between citizens and non-citizens.

3. Nothing in this Convention may be interpreted as affecting in any way the legal provisions of States Parties concerning nationality, citizenship or naturalization, provided that such provisions do not discriminate against any particular nationality.

4. Special measures taken for the sole purpose of securing adequate advancement of certain racial or ethnic groups or individuals requiring such protection as may be necessary in order to ensure such groups or individuals equal enjoyment or exercise of human rights and fundamental freedoms shall not be deemed racial discrimination, provided, however, that such measures do not, as a consequence, lead to the maintenance of separate rights for different racial groups and that they shall not be continued after the objectives for which they were taken have been achieved.

Art. 1, INTERNATIONAL CONVENTION ON THE ELIMINATION OF ALL FORMS OF RACIAL DISCRIMINATION.

– "*Noting* with the gravest concern that racism, racial discrimination, colonialism and apartheid continue to afflict the world in ever-changing forms, as a result both of the continuation of legislative provisions and government and administrative practices contrary to the principles of human rights and also of the continued existence of political and social structures, and of relationships and attitudes, characterized by injustice and contempt for human beings and leading to the exclusion, humiliation and exploitation, or to the forced assimilation, of the members of disadvantaged groups."

Pp. 12, DECLARATION ON RACE AND RACIAL PREJUDICE.

RACIAL DISCRIMINATION (ERADICATION OF) [Discrimination raciale (élimination de)]

– "*Emphasizing* that the eradication of apartheid, all forms of racism, racial discrimination, colonialism, neo-colonialism, aggression, foreign occupation and domination and interference in the internal affairs of States is essential to the full enjoyment of the rights of men and women."

Pp. 10, CONVENTION ON THE ELIMINATION OF ALL FORMS OF DISCRIMINATION AGAINST WOMEN.

RACIAL OR ETHNIC SUPERIORITY/INFERIORITY (THEORY) [Supériorité/infériorité raciale ou ethnique (théorie)]

– "1. Any theory which involves the claim that racial or ethnic groups are inherently superior or inferior, thus implying that some would be entitled to dominate or eliminate others, presumed to be inferior, or which bases value judgements on racial differentiation, has no scientific foundation and is contrary to the moral and ethical principles of humanity."

Art. 2, DECLARATION ON RACE AND RACIAL PREJUDICE.

RACIAL PREJUDICE [Préjugé racial]

- "3. Racial prejudice, historically linked with inequalities in power, reinforced by economic and social differences between individuals and groups, and still seeking today to justify such inequalities, is totally without justification."

Art. 2, DECLARATION ON RACE AND RACIAL PREJUDICE.

RACISM [Racisme]

- "*Noting* with the gravest concern that racism, racial discrimination, colonialism and apartheid continue to afflict the world in ever-changing forms, as a result both of the continuation of legislative provisions and government and administrative practices contrary to the principles of human rights and also of the continued existence of political and social structures, and of relationships and attitudes, characterized by injustice and contempt for human beings and leading to the exclusion, humiliation and exploitation, or to the forced assimilation, of the members of disadvantaged groups,"

Pp. 12, DECLARATION ON RACE AND RACIAL PREJUDICE.

- "2. Racism includes racist ideologies, prejudiced attitudes, discriminatory behaviour, structural arrangements and institutionalized practices resulting in racial inequality as well as the fallacious notion that discriminatory relations between groups are morally and scientifically justifiable; it is reflected in discriminatory provisions in legislation or regulations and discriminatory practices as well as in anti-social beliefs and acts; it hinders the development of its victims, perverts those who practise it, divides nations internally, impedes international co-operation and gives rise to political tensions between peoples; it is contrary to the fundamental principles of international law and, consequently, seriously disturbs international peace and security."

Art. 2, DECLARATION ON RACE AND RACIAL PREJUDICE.

RACISM (ERADICATION OF ALL FORMS) [Racisme (élimination de toutes les formes de)]

- "*Emphasizing* that the eradication of apartheid, all forms of racism, racial discrimination, colonialism, neo-colonialism, aggression, foreign

occupation and domination and interference in the internal affairs of States is essential to the full enjoyment of the rights of men and women,"
Pp. 10, CONVENTION ON THE ELIMINATION OF ALL FORMS OF DISCRIMINATION AGAINST WOMEN.

RAPE [Viol]

– "(*g*) Rape, sexual slavery, enforced prostitution, forced pregnancy, enforced sterilization, or any other form of sexual violence of comparable gravity;"
Art. 7, Paragraph 1, ROME STATUTE OF THE INTERNATIONAL CRIMINAL COURT.

– "Women shall be especially protected against any attack on their honour, in particular against rape, enforced prostitution, or any form of indecent assault."
Art. 27, s.p. 2, GENEVA CONVENTION RELATIVE TO THE PROTECTION OF CIVILIAN PERSONS IN TIME OF WAR.

– "1. Women shall be the object of special respect and shall be protected in particular against rape, forced prostitution and any other form of indecent assault."
Art. 76, PROTOCOL ADDITIONAL TO THE GENEVA CONVENTIONS OF 12 AUGUST 1949, AND RELATING TO THE PROTECTION OF VICTIMS OF INTERNATIONAL ARMED CONFLICTS (PROTOCOL I).

– "*e*) Outrages upon personal dignity, in particular humiliating and degrading treatment, rape, enforced prostitution and any form of indecent assault;"
Art.4, paragraph 2, PROTOCOL ADDITIONAL TO THE GENEVA CONVENTIONS OF 12 AUGUST 1949, AND RELATING TO THE PROTECTION OF VICTIMS OF NON-INTERNATIONAL ARMED CONFLICTS (PROTOCOL II).

REALIZATION OF HUMAN RIGHTS AND FUNDAMENTAL FREEDOMS FOR ALL [Réalisation universelle des droits de la personne et des libertés fondamentales]

– "*Realization of human rights and fundamental freedoms for all is essential to reduce vulnerability to HIV/AIDS*"
HIV/AIDS AND HUMAN RIGHTS, DECLARATION OF COMMITMENT ON HIV/AIDS.

REBELLION AGAINST TYRANNY AND OPPRESSION [Révolte contre la tyrannie et l'oppression]

– "*Whereas* it is essential, if man is not to be compelled to have recourse, as a last resort, to rebellion against tyranny and oppression, that human rights should be protected by the rule of law,"

Pp. 3, UNIVERSAL DECLARATION OF HUMAN RIGHTS.

REFUGEE [Réfugié]

– "Article 1. – Definition of the term 'refugee'

A. For the purposes of the present Convention, the term 'refugee' shall apply to any person who:

(1) Has been considered a refugee under the Arrangements of 12 May 1926 and 30 June 1928 or under the Conventions of 28 October 1933 and 10 February 1938, the Protocol of 14 September 1939 or the Constitution of the International Refugee Organization; Decisions of non-eligibility taken by the International Refugee Organization during the period of its activities shall not prevent the status of refugee being accorded to persons who fulfil the conditions of paragraph 2 of this section;

(2) As a result of events occurring before 1 January 1951 and owing to well-founded fear of being persecuted for reasons of race, religion, nationality, membership of a particular social group or political opinion, is outside the country of his nationality and is unable, or owing to such fear, is unwilling to avail himself of the protection of that country; or who, not having a nationality and being outside the country of his former habitual residence as a result of such events, is unable or, owing to such fear, is unwilling to return to it.

In the case of a person who has more than one nationality, the term 'the country of his nationality' shall mean each of the countries of which he is a national, and a person shall not be deemed to be lacking the protection of the country of his nationality if, without any valid reason based on well-founded fear, he has not availed himself of the protection of one of the countries of which he is a national.

B. (1) For the purposes of this Convention, the words 'events occurring before 1 January 1951' in article 1, section A, shall be understood to mean either (a) 'events occurring in Europe before 1 January 1951'; or (b)'events occurring in Europe or elsewhere before 1 January 1951'; and each Contracting State shall make a declaration at the time of signature, ratification or accession, specifying which of these meanings it applies for the purpose of its obligations under this Convention.

(2) Any Contracting State which has adopted alternative (a) may at any time extend its obligations by adopting alternative (b) by means of a notification addressed to the Secretary-General of the United Nations.

C. This Convention shall cease to apply to any person falling under the terms of section A if:

(1) He has voluntarily re-availed himself of the protection of the country of his nationality; or

(2) Having lost his nationality, he has voluntarily reacquired it; or

(3) He has acquired a new nationality, and enjoys the protection of the country of his new nationality; or

(4) He has voluntarily re-established himself in the country which he left or outside which he remained owing to fear of persecution; or

(5) He can no longer, because the circumstances in connection with which he has been recognized as a refugee have ceased to exist, continue to refuse to avail himself of the protection of the country of his nationality; Provided that this paragraph shall not apply to a refugee falling under section A (1) of this article who is able to invoke compelling reasons arising out of previous persecution for refusing to avail himself of the protection of the country of nationality;

(6) Being a person who has no nationality he is, because the circumstances in connection with which he has been recognized as a refugee have ceased to exist, able to return to the country of his former habitual residence; Provided that this paragraph shall not apply to a refugee falling under section A (1) of this article who is able to invoke compelling reasons arising out of previous persecution for refusing to return to the country of his former habitual residence.

D. This Convention shall not apply to persons who are at present receiving from organs or agencies of the United Nations other than the United Nations High Commissioner for Refugees protection or assistance. When such protection or assistance has ceased for any reason, without the position of such persons being definitively settled in accordance with the relevant resolutions adopted by the General Assembly of the United Nations, these persons shall ipso facto be entitled to the benefits of this Convention.

E. This Convention shall not apply to a person who is recognized by the competent authorities of the country in which he has taken residence as having the rights and obligations which are attached to the possession of the nationality of that country.

F. The provisions of this Convention shall not apply to any person with respect to whom there are serious reasons for considering that:

(*a*) He has committed a crime against peace, a war crime, or a crime against humanity, as defined in the international instruments drawn up to make provision in respect of such crimes;

(*b*) He has committed a serious non-political crime outside the country of refuge prior to his admission to that country as a refugee;

(*c*) He has been guilty of acts contrary to the purposes and principles of the United Nations.

Art. 1, CONVENTION RELATING TO THE STATUS OF REFUGEES.

– "2. For the purpose of the present Protocol, the term 'refugee' shall, except as regards the application of paragraph 3[16] of this article, mean any person within the definition of article 1[17] of the Convention[18] as if the words 'As a result of events occurring before 1 January 1951 and ...' and the words '... as a result of such events', in article 1 A (2) were omitted."

Art. 1, PROTOCOL RELATING TO THE STATUS OF REFUGEES.

[16] "3. The present Protocol shall be applied by the States Parties hereto without any geographic limitation, save that existing declarations made by States already Parties to the Convention in accordance with article 1 B (1) (a) of the Convention, shall, unless extended under article 1 B (2) thereof, apply also under the present Protocol."

[17] See above, same term.

[18] Convention relating to the Status of Refugees.

REHABILITATION [Réadaptation]

– "23. The term 'rehabilitation' refers to a process aimed at enabling persons with disabilities to reach and maintain their optimal physical, sensory, intellectual, psychiatric and/or social functional levels, thus providing them with the tools to change their lives towards a higher level of independence. Rehabilitation may include measures to provide and/or restore functions, or compensate for the loss or absence of a function or for a functional limitation. The rehabilitation process does not involve initial medical care. It includes a wide range of measures and activities from more basic and general rehabilitation to goal-oriented activities, for instance vocational rehabilitation."

INTRODUCTION, STANDARD RULES ON THE EQUALIZATION OF OPPORTUNITIES FOR PERSONS WITH DISABILITIES.

RELIGION [Religion]

– "*Considering* that religion or belief, for anyone who professes either, is one of the fundamental elements in his conception of life and that freedom of religion or belief should be fully respected and guaranteed,"

Pp. 4, DECLARATION ON THE ELIMINATION OF ALL FORMS OF INTOLERANCE AND OF DISCRIMINATION BASED ON RELIGION OR BELIEF.

RELIGIOUS PERSONNEL [Personnel religieux]

– "For the purposes of this Protocol:

[…]

(*d*) 'Religious personnel' means military or civilian persons, such as chaplains, who are exclusively engaged in the work of their ministry and attached:

(i) To the armed forces of a Party to the conflict;

(ii) To medical units or medical transports of a Party to the conflict;

(iii) To medical units or medical transports described in Article 9, paragraph 2[19]; or

---

[19] "2. The relevant provisions of Articles 27 and 32 of the First Convention shall apply to permanent medical units and transports (other than hospital ships, to which Article 25 of the Second Convention applies) and their personnel made available to a Party to the conflict for humanitarian purposes:

(a) By a neutral or other State which is not a Party to that conflict;

(iv) To civil defence organizations of a Party to the conflict.

The attachment of religious personnel may be either permanent or temporary, and the relevant provisions mentioned under sub-paragraph (k)[20] apply to them;"

Art. 8, PROTOCOL ADDITIONAL TO THE GENEVA CONVENTIONS OF 12 AUGUST 1949, AND RELATING TO THE PROTECTION OF VICTIMS OF INTERNATIONAL ARMED CONFLICTS (PROTOCOL I).

REMOVAL OF MINES [Enlèvement des mines]

– "The removal of mines or similar devices shall be considered as dangerous labour."

Art. 52, s.p. 3, GENEVA CONVENTION RELATIVE TO THE TREATMENT OF PRISONERS OF WAR.

REMUNERATION [Rémunération]

– "For the purpose of this Convention:

(*a*) The term 'remuneration' includes the ordinary, basic or minimum wage or salary and any additional emoluments whatsoever payable directly or indirectly, whether in cash or in kind, by the employer to the worker and arising out of the worker's employment;"

Art. 1, EQUAL REMUNERATION CONVENTION (N° 100).

REPRODUCTIVE CLONING OF HUMAN BEINGS [Clonage à des fins de reproduction d'êtres humains]

– "Practices which are contrary to human dignity, such as reproductive cloning of human beings, shall not be permitted.[...]"

Art. 11, UNIVERSAL DECLARATION ON THE HUMAN GENOME AND HUMAN RIGHTS.

(b) By a recognized and authorized aid society of such a State;

(c) By an impartial international humanitarian organization."

[20] "(k) 'Permanent medical personnel', 'permanent medical units' and 'permanent medical transports' mean those assigned exclusively to medical purposes for an indeterminate period. 'Temporary medical personnel', 'temporary medical units' and 'temporary medical transports' mean those devoted exclusively to medical purposes for limited periods during the whole of such periods. Unless otherwise specified, the terms 'medical personnel', 'medical units' and 'medical transports' cover both permanent and temporary categories;'

RESEARCH ON THE HUMAN GENOME AND RESULTING APPLICATIONS [Recherches sur le génome humain et leurs applications]

– "*Recognizing* that research on the human genome and the resulting applications open up vast prospects for progress in improving the health of individuals and of humankind as a whole, but emphasizing that such research should fully respect human dignity, freedom and human rights, as well as the prohibition of all forms of discrimination based on genetic characteristics,"

Pp. 6, UNIVERSAL DECLARATION ON THE HUMAN GENOME AND HUMAN RIGHTS.

RESPECT FOR NATURE [Respect de la nature (le)]

– "6. We consider certain fundamental values to be essential to international relations in the twenty-first century. These include:

  [...]

  > *Respect for nature.* Prudence must be shown in the management of all living species and natural resources, in accordance with the precepts of sustainable development. Only in this way can the immeasurable riches provided to us by nature be preserved and passed on to our descendants. The current unsustainable patterns of production and consumption must be changed in the interest of our future welfare and that of our descendants.

  [...]"

Fifth footnote (•), UNITED NATIONS MILLENIUM DECLARATION.

RESPECT FOR THE DIVERSITY OF CULTURES, TOLERANCE, DIALOGUE AND COOPERATION [Respect de la diversité des cultures, tolérance, dialogue et coopération]

– "*Affirming* that respect for the diversity of cultures, tolerance, dialogue and cooperation, in a climate of mutual trust and understanding are among the best guarantees of international peace and security,"

Pp. 7, UNIVERSAL DECLARATION ON CULTURAL DIVERSITY.

RESPONSIBILITIES INHERENT IN THE ACTIVITIES OF RESEARCHERS [Responsabilités inhérentes aux activités des chercheurs]

– "The responsibilities inherent in the activities of researchers, including meticulousness, caution, intellectual honesty and integrity in carrying out their research as well as in the presentation and utilization of their findings, should be the subject of particular attention in the framework of research on the human genome, because of its ethical and social implications. Public and private science policy-makers also have particular responsibilities in this respect."

Art. 13, UNIVERSAL DECLARATION ON THE HUMAN GENOME AND HUMAN RIGHTS.

RESTITUTION [Réparation ; Restitution]

– "8. Offenders or third parties responsible for their behaviour should, where appropriate, make fair restitution to victims, their families or dependants. Such restitution should include the return of property or payment for the harm or loss suffered, reimbursement of expenses incurred as a result of the victimization, the provision of services and the restoration of rights."

DECLARATION OF BASIC PRINCIPLES OF JUSTICE VICTIMS OF CRIME AND ABUSE OF POWER.

– "10. In cases of substantial harm to the environment, restitution, if ordered, should include, as far as possible, restoration of the environment, reconstruction of the infrastructure, replacement of community facilities and reimbursement of the expenses of relocation, whenever such harm results in the dislocation of a community.

DECLARATION OF BASIC PRINCIPLES OF JUSTICE VICTIMS OF CRIME AND ABUSE OF POWER.

REVIEW BODY (THE) [Organe de révision]

– " In these Principles:

[...]

'The review body' means the body established in accordance with Principle 17[21] to review the involuntary admission or retention of a patient in a mental health facility."

---

[21] "Review body

1. The review body shall be a judicial or other independent and impartial body established by domestic law and functioning in accordance with procedures laid down by domestic law. It shall, in formulating its decisions, have the assistance of one or more qualified and independent mental health practitioners and take their advice into account.

2. The review body's initial review, as required by paragraph 2 of Principle 16, of a decision to admit or retain a person as an involuntary patient shall take place as soon as possible after that

s.p. 8, DEFINITIONS, PRINCIPLES FOR THE PROTECTION OF PERSONS WITH MENTAL ILLNESS AND THE IMPROVEMENT OF MENTAL HEALTH CARE.[AD]

REVOLVERS [Revolvers]

– 3. It shall also not be considered as an act harmful to the enemy that civilian defence personnel bear light individual weapons for the purpose of maintaining order or for self-defence. However, in areas where land fighting it taking place or is likely to take place, the Parties to the conflict shall undertake the appropriate measures to limit these weapons to handguns, such as pistols or revolvers, in order to assist in distinguishing between civil defence personnel and combatants. Although civil defence personnel bear other light individual weapons in such areas, they shall nevertheless be respected and protected as soon as they have been recognized as such."

Art. 65, PROTOCOL ADDITIONAL TO THE GENEVA CONVENTIONS OF 12 AUGUST 1949, AND RELATING TO THE PROTECTION OF VICTIMS OF INTERNATIONAL ARMED CONFLICTS (PROTOCOL I).

RHEUMATISM WITH SERIOUS CLINICAL SYMPTOMS [Rhumatisme avec manifestations cliniques graves]

– "(*p*) Chronic affections of locomotion, with obvious functional disorders, for example: arthritis deformans, primary and secondary progressive chronic polyarthritis; rheumatism with serious clinical symptoms; etc."

Annex I, 3, GENEVA CONVENTION RELATIVE TO THE TREATMENT OF PRISONERS OF WAR.

---

decision and shall be conducted in accordance with simple and expeditious procedures as specified by domestic law.

3. The review body shall periodically review the cases of involuntary patients at reasonable intervals as specified by domestic law.

4. An involuntary patient may apply to the review body for release or voluntary status, at reasonable intervals as specified by domestic law.

5. At each review, the review body shall consider whether the criteria for involuntary admission set out in paragraph 1 of Principle 16 are still satisfied, and, if not, the patient shall be discharged as an involuntary patient.

6. If at any time the mental health practitioner responsible for the case is satisfied that the conditions for the retention of a person as an involuntary patient are no longer satisfied, he or she shall order the discharge of that person as such a patient.

7. A patient or his personal representative or any interested person shall have the right to appeal to a higher court against a decision that the patient be admitted to, or be retained in, a mental health facility."

[AD] Al. 3, DEFINITIONS, Principes pour la protection des personnes atteintes de maladie mentale et pour l'amélioration des soins de santé mentale.

RIGHT OF EVERYONE TO AN ADEQUATE STANDARD OF LIVING [Droit de toute personne à un niveau de vie suffisant]

– "1. The States Parties to the present Covenant recognize the right of everyone to an adequate standard of living for himself and his family, including adequate food, clothing and housing, and to the continuous improvement of living conditions.[...]"

Art. 11, INTERNATIONAL COVENANT ON ECONOMIC, SOCIAL AND CULTURAL RIGHTS.

RIGHT OF EVERYONE TO THE ENJOYMENT OF JUST AND FAVOURABLE CONDITIONS OF WORK [Droit qu'a toute personne de jouir de conditions de travail justes et favorables]

– "The States Parties to the present Covenant recognize the right of everyone to the enjoyment of just and favourable conditions of work which ensure, in particular:

(a) Remuneration which provides all workers, as a minimum, with:

(i) Fair wages and equal remuneration for work of equal value without distinction of any kind, in particular women being guaranteed conditions of work not inferior to those enjoyed by men, with equal pay for equal work;

(ii) A decent living for themselves and their families in accordance with the provisions of the present Covenant;

(b) Safe and healthy working conditions;

(c) Equal opportunity for everyone to be promoted in his employment to an appropriate higher level, subject to no considerations other than those of seniority and competence;

(d) Rest, leisure and reasonable limitation of working hours and periodic holidays with pay, as well as remuneration for public holidays."

Art. 7, INTERNATIONAL COVENANT ON ECONOMIC, SOCIAL AND CULTURAL RIGHTS.

RIGHT OF PEOPLES TO SELF-DETERMINATION [Droit des peuples à disposer d'eux-mêmes]

– "*Recalling* the right of peoples to self-determination, by virtue of which they have the right freely to determine their political status and to pursue their economic, social and cultural development,"

Pp. 6, DECLARATION ON THE RIGHT TO DEVELOPMENT.

RIGHT TO DEVELOPMENT [Droit au développement]

– "The World Conference on Human Rights reaffirms the right to development, as established in the Declaration on the Right to Development, as a universal and inalienable right and an integral part of fundamental human rights."

I, 10, subparagraph, VIENNA DECLARATION AND PROGRAM OF ACTION.

– "1. All the aspects of the right to development set forth in the present Declaration are indivisible and interdependent and each of them should be considered in the context of the whole."

Art. 9, DECLARATION ON THE RIGHT TO DEVELOPMENT.

RIGHT TO FREEDOM OF EXPRESSION [Droit à la liberté d'expression]

– "2. Everyone shall have the right to freedom of expression; this right shall include freedom to seek, receive and impart information and ideas of all kinds, regardless of frontiers, either orally, in writing or in print, in the form of art, or through any other media of his choice."

Art. 19, INTERNATIONAL COVENANT ON CIVIL AND POLITICAL RIGHTS.

RIGHT TO FREEDOM OF OPINION AND EXPRESSION [Droit à la liberté d'opinion et d'expression]

– "Everyone has the right to freedom of opinion and expression; this right includes freedom to hold opinions without interference and to seek, receive and impart information and ideas through any media and regardless of frontiers."

Art. 19, UNIVERSAL DECLARATION OF HUMAN RIGHTS.

RIGHT TO FREEDOM OF THOUGHT, CONSCIENCE, RELIGION OR BELIEF [Droit à la liberté de pensée, de conscience, de religion ou de conviction]

– "In accordance with article I[22] of the present Declaration, and subject to the provisions of article 1, paragraph 3, the right to freedom of thought, conscience, religion or belief shall include, *inter alia*, the following freedoms:

(*a*) To worship or assemble in connection with a religion or belief, and to establish and maintain places for these purposes;

(*b*) To establish and maintain appropriate charitable or humanitarian institutions;

(*c*) To make, acquire and use to an adequate extent the necessary articles and materials related to the rites or customs of a religion or belief;

(*d*) To write, issue and disseminate relevant publications in these areas;

(*e*) To teach a religion or belief in places suitable for these purposes;

(*f*) To solicit and receive voluntary financial and other contributions from individuals and institutions;

(*g*) To train, appoint, elect or designate by succession appropriate leaders called for by the requirements and standards of any religion or belief;

(*h*) To observe days of rest and to celebrate holidays and ceremonies in accordance with the precepts of one's religion or belief;

(*i*) To establish and maintain communications with individuals and communities in matters of religion and belief at the national and international levels.

Art. 6, Declaration on the Elimination of All Forms of Intolerance and of Discrimination Based on Religion or Belief.

---

[22] "1. Everyone shall have the right to freedom of thought, conscience and religion. This right shall include freedom to have a religion or whatever belief of his choice, and freedom, either individually or in community with others and in public or private, to manifest his religion or belief in worship, observance, practice and teaching.
2. No one shall be subject to coercion which would impair his freedom to have a religion or belief of his choice.
3. Freedom to manifest one's religion or belief may be subject only to such limitations as are prescribed by law and are necessary to protect public safety, order, health or morals or the fundamental rights and freedoms of others."

RIGHT TO FREEDOM OF THOUGHT, CONSCIENCE AND RELIGION [Droit à la liberté de pensée, de conscience et de religion]

- "Everyone has the right to freedom of thought, conscience and religion; this right includes freedom to change his religion or belief, and freedom, either alone or in community with others and in public or private, to manifest his religion or belief in teaching, practice, worship and observance."

Art. 18, UNIVERSAL DECLARATION OF HUMAN RIGHTS.

- "1. Everyone shall have the right to freedom of thought, conscience and religion. This right shall include freedom to have or to adopt a religion or belief of his choice, and freedom, either individually or in community with others and in public or private, to manifest his religion or belief in worship, observance, practice and teaching."

Art. 18, INTERNATIONAL COVENANT ON CIVIL AND POLITICAL RIGHTS.

RIGHT TO WORK [Droit au travail]

- "1. The States Parties to the present Covenant recognize the right to work, which includes the right of everyone to the opportunity to gain his living by work which he freely chooses or accepts, and will take appropriate steps to safeguard this right."

Art. 6, INTERNATIONAL COVENANT ON ECONOMIC, SOCIAL AND CULTURAL RIGHTS.

RIGHTS OF CHILD [Droits de l'enfant]

- "10. The importance of a comprehensive and consistent national approach in the area of juvenile should be recognized, with respect for the interdependence and indivisibility of all rights of the child."

GUIDELINES FOR ACTION ON CHILDREN IN THE CRIMINAL JUSTICE SYSTEM.

RIOTS [Emeutes]

- "2. This Protocol shall not apply to situations of internal disturbances and tensions, such as riots, isolated and sporadic acts of violence and other acts of a similar nature, as not being armed conflicts."

ART. 1, PROTOCOL ADDITIONAL TO THE GENEVA CONVENTIONS OF 12 AUGUST 1949, AND RELATING TO THE PROTECTION OF VICTIMS OF NON-INTERNATIONAL ARMED CONFLICTS (PROTOCOL II).

ROOT SOCIO-ECONOMIC CAUSES OF THE SMUGGLING OF MIGRANTS [Causes économiques profondes du trafic illicite de migrants]

– "3. Each State Party shall promote or strengthen, as appropriate, development programmes and cooperation at the national, regional and international levels, taking into account the socio-economic realities of migration and paying special attention to economically and socially depressed areas, in order to combat the root socio-economic causes of the smuggling of migrants, such as poverty and underdevelopment."

Art. 15, PROTOCOL AGAINST THE SMUGGLING OF MIGRANTS BY LAND, SEA AND AIR, SUPPLEMENTING THE UNITED NATIONS CONVENTION AGAINST TRANSNATIONAL ORGANIZED CRIME.

RULES OF INTERNATIONAL LAW APPLICABLE IN ARMED CONFLICT [Règles du droit international applicable dans les conflits armés]

– "(*b*) 'Rules of international law applicable in armed conflict' means the rules applicable in armed conflict set forth in international agreements to which the Parties to the conflict are Parties and the generally recognized principles and rules of international law which are applicable to armed conflict; »

Art. 2, PROTOCOL ADDITIONAL TO THE GENEVA CONVENTIONS OF 12 AUGUST 1949, AND RELATING TO THE PROTECTION OF VICTIMS OF INTERNATIONAL ARMED CONFLICTS (PROTOCOL I).

RURAL WOMEN [Femmes rurales]

– "1. States Parties shall take into account the particular problems faced by rural women and the significant roles which rural women play in the economic survival of their families, including their work in the non-monetized sectors of the economy, and shall take all appropriate measures to ensure the application of the provisions of the present Convention to women in rural areas."

Art. 14, CONVENTION ON THE ELIMINATION OF ALL FORMS OF DISCRIMINATION AGAINST WOMEN.

RUSES OF WAR [Ruses de guerre]

– "2. Ruses of war are not prohibited. Such ruses are acts which are intended to mislead an adversary or to induce him to act recklessly but which infringe no rule of international law applicable in armed conflict and which are not perfidious because they do not invite the confidence of an adversary with respect to protection under that law. The following are examples of such ruses: the use of camouflage, decoys, mock operations and misinformation."

Art. 37, PROTOCOL ADDITIONAL TO THE GENEVA CONVENTIONS OF 12 AUGUST 1949, AND RELATING TO THE PROTECTION OF VICTIMS OF INTERNATIONAL ARMED CONFLICTS (PROTOCOL I).

SALE OF CHILDREN [Vente d'enfants]

– "*Believing* that the elimination of the sale of children, child prostitution and child pornography will be facilitated by adopting a holistic approach, addressing the contributing factors, including underdevelopment, poverty, economic disparities, inequitable socio-economic structure, dysfunctioning families, lack of education, urban-rural migration, gender discrimination, irresponsible adult sexual behaviour, harmful traditional practices, armed conflicts and trafficking in children,"

Pp. 7, OPTIONAL PROTOCOL TO THE CONVENTION ON THE RIGHTS OF THE CHILD ON THE SALE OF CHILDREN, CHILD PROSTITUTION AND CHILD PORNOGRAPHY.

– "For the purposes of the present Protocol:

(*a*) Sale of children means any act or transaction whereby a child is transferred by any person or group of persons to another for remuneration or any other consideration;"

Art. 2, OPTIONAL PROTOCOL TO THE CONVENTION ON THE RIGHTS OF THE CHILD ON THE SALE OF CHILDREN, CHILD PROSTITUTION AND CHILD PORNOGRAPHY.

SCIENTIFIC AND TECHNOLOGICAL ACHIEVEMENTS [Réalisations de la science et de la technique]

– "*Noting with concern* that scientific and technological achievements can be used to intensify the arms race, suppress national liberation movements and deprive individuals and peoples of their human rights and fundamental freedoms,"

Pp. 3, DECLARATION ON THE USE OF SCIENTIFIC AND TECHNOLOGICAL PROGRESS IN THE INTERESTS OF PEACE FOR THE BENEFIT OF MANKIND.

– "*Also noting with concern* that scientific and technological achievements can entail dangers for the civil and political rights of the individual or of the group and for human dignity,"

Pp. 4, DECLARATION ON THE USE OF SCIENTIFIC AND TECHNOLOGICAL PROGRESS IN THE INTERESTS OF PEACE FOR THE BENEFIT OF MANKIND.

SEAFARER [Gens de mer]

– "For the purposes of the present Convention:

[…]

(*c*) The term 'seafarer', which includes a fisherman, refers to a migrant worker employed on board a vessel registered in a State of which he or she is not a national;"

Art. 2.2, INTERNATIONAL CONVENTION ON THE PROTECTION OF THE RIGHTS OF ALL MIGRANT WORKERS AND MEMBERS OF THEIR FAMILIES.

SEASONAL WORKER [Travailleurs saisonniers]

– "For the purposes of the present Convention:

[…]

(*b*) The term 'seasonal worker' refers to a migrant worker whose work by its character is dependent on seasonal conditions and is performed only during part of the year;"

Art. 2.2, INTERNATIONAL CONVENTION ON THE PROTECTION OF THE RIGHTS OF ALL MIGRANT WORKERS AND MEMBERS OF THEIR FAMILIES.

SELF-EMPLOYED WORKER [Travailleurs indépendants]

– "For the purposes of the present Convention:

[…]

(*h*) The term 'self-employed worker' refers to a migrant worker who is engaged in a remunerated activity otherwise than under acontract of employment and who earns his or her living through this activity normally working alone or together with members of his or her family, and to any other migrant worker recognized as self-employed by applicable legislation of the State of employment or bilateral or multilateral agreements."

Art. 2.2, INTERNATIONAL CONVENTION ON THE PROTECTION OF THE RIGHTS OF ALL MIGRANT WORKERS AND MEMBERS OF THEIR FAMILIES.

SEQUELAE OF GASTRIC OPERATIONS PERFORMED IN CAPTIVITY [Suite d'intervention chirurgicale sur l'estomac faite en captivité]

– "(*e*) Serious chronic affections of the digestive organs, for example: gastric or duodenal ulcer, sequelae of gastric operations performed in captivity;

chronic gastritis, enteritis or colitis, having lasted more than one year and seriously affecting the general condition: cirrhosis of the liver, chronic cholecystopathy; etc."

Annex I, 3, GENEVA CONVENTION RELATIVE TO THE TREATMENT OF PRISONERS OF WAR.

SERFDOM [Servage]

– "Each of States Parties to this Convention shall take all practicable and necessary legislative and other measures to bring about progressively and as soon as possible the complete abolition or abandonment of the following institutions and practices, where they still exist and whether or not they are covered by the definition of slavery contained in article 1 of the Slavery Convention signed at Geneva on 25 September 1926:
[…]

(*b*) Serfdom, that is to say, the condition or status of a tenant who is by law, custom or agreement bound to live and labour on land belonging to another person and to render some determinate service to such other person, whether for reward or not, and is not free to change his status;"

Art. 1, SUPPLEMENTARY CONVENTION ON THE ABOLITION OF SLAVERY, THE SLAVE TRADE AND INSTITUTIONS AND PRACTICES SIMILAR TO SLAVERY.

SERIOUS PULMONARY EMPHYSEMA, WITH OR WITHOUT BRONCHITIS [Emphysème pulmonaire grave (avec ou sans bronchite)]

– "(*c*) Serious diseases of the respiratory organs of non-tubercular etiology, presumed incurable. for example: serious pulmonary emphysema, with or without bronchitis, chronic asthma: chronic bronchitis lasting more than one year in captivity; bronchiectasis, etc."

Annex I, 3, GENEVA CONVENTION RELATIVE TO THE TREATMENT OF PRISONERS OF WAR.

SEX TOURISM [Tourisme sexuel]

– "Deeply concerned at the widespread and continuing practice of sex tourism, to which children are especially vulnerable, as it directly promotes the sale of children, child prostitution and child pornography,"

Pp. 4, OPTIONAL PROTOCOL TO CONVENTION ON THE RIGHTS OF THE CHILD ON THE SALE OF CHILDREN, CHILD PROSTITUTION AND CHILD PORNOGRAPHY.

SEXUAL SLAVERY [Esclavage sexuel]

– "(*g*) Rape, sexual slavery, enforced prostitution, forced pregnancy, enforced sterilization, or any other form of sexual violence of comparable gravity;"

Art. 7, Paragraph 1, ROME STATUTE OF THE INTERNATIONAL CRIMINAL COURT.

SEXUAL VIOLENCE [Violence sexuelle]

– "(xxii) Committing rape, sexual slavery, enforced prostitution, forced pregnancy, as defined in article 7, paragraph 2 (f) [23], enforced sterilization, or any other form of sexual violence also constituting a grave breach of the Geneva Conventions;"

Art. 8, 2, (b), ROME STATUTE OF THE INTERNATIONAL CRIMINAL COURT.

SHARED RESPONSIBILITY [Partage des responsabilités (le)]

– "6. We consider certain fundamental values to be essential to international relations in the twenty-first century. These include:

[...]

Shared responsibility. Responsibility for managing worldwide economic and social development, as well as threats to international peace and security, must be shared among the nations of the world and should be exercised multilaterally. As the most universal and most representative organization in the world, the United Nations must play the central role."

Sixth footnote (•), UNITED NATIONS MILLENIUM DECLARATION.

SHIPWRECKED [Naufragés]

– "For the purposes of this Protocol:

[...]

(*b*) 'Shipwrecked' means persons, whether military or civilian, who are in peril at sea or in other waters as a result of misfortune affecting them or the vessel or aircraft carrying them and who refrain from any

[23] "(*f*) 'Forced pregnancy' means the unlawful confinement of a woman forcibly made pregnant, with the intent of affecting the ethnic composition of any population or carrying out other grave violations of international law. This definition shall not in any way be interpreted as affecting national laws relating to pregnancy;"

act of hostility. These persons, provided that they continue to refrain from any act of hostility, shall continue to be considered shipwrecked during their rescue until they acquire another status under the Conventions or this Protocol;"

Art. 8, Protocol Additional to the Geneva Conventions of 12 August 1949, and relating to the Protection of Victims of International Armed Conflicts (Protocol I).

SICK [Malades]

– "For the purposes of this Protocol:

(*a*) 'Wounded' and 'sick' mean persons, whether military or civilian, who, because of trauma, disease or other physical or mental disorder or disability, are in need of medical assistance or care and who refrain from any act of hostility. These terms also cover maternity cases, new-born babies and other persons who may be in need of immediate medical assistance or care, such as the infirm or expectant mothers, and who refrain from any act of hostility;"

Art. 8, Protocol Additional to the Geneva Conventions of 12 August 1949, and relating to the Protection of Victims of International Armed Conflicts (Protocol I).

SITUATION OF THE PEOPLES AFFLICTED BY HUNGER AND MALNUTRITION [Situation des peuples qui souffrent de la faim et de la sous-alimentation]

– "(*c*) The situation of the peoples afflicted by hunger and malnutrition arises from their historical circumstances, especially social inequalities, including in many cases alien and colonial domination, foreign occupation, racial discrimination, apartheid and neo-colonialism in all its forms, which continue to be among the greatest obstacles to the full emancipation and progress of the developing countries and all the peoples involved;"

Universal Declaration on the Eradication of Hunger and Malnutrition.

SLAVE [Esclave]

– "For the purposes of the present Convention:

(*a*) 'Slavery' means, as defined in the Slavery Convention of 1926[24], the status or condition of a person over whom any or all of the powers attaching to the right of ownership are exercised, and 'slave' means a person in such condition or status;"

Art. 7, SUPPLEMENTARY CONVENTION ON THE ABOLITION OF SLAVERY, THE SLAVE TRADE AND INSTITUTIONS AND PRACTICES SIMILAR TO SLAVERY.

SLAVE TRADE [Traite des esclaves]

– "For the purpose of the present Convention, the following definitions are agreed upon:

[...]

(2) The slave trade includes all acts involved in the capture, acquisition or disposal of a person with intent to reduce him to slavery; all acts involved in the acquisition of a slave with a view to selling or exchanging him; all acts of disposal by sale or exchange of a slave acquired with a view to being sold or exchanged, and, in general, every act of trade or transport in slaves."

Art. 1, SLAVERY CONVENTION.

– "For the purposes of the present Convention:

[...]

(*c*) 'Slave trade' means and includes all acts involved in the capture, acquisition or disposal of a person with intent to reduce him to slavery; all acts involved in the acquisition of a slave with a view to selling or exchanging him; all acts of disposal by sale or exchange of a person acquired with a view to being sold or exchanged; and, in general, every act of trade or transport in slaves by whatever means of conveyance."

Art. 7, SUPPLEMENTARY CONVENTION ON THE ABOLITION OF SLAVERY, THE SLAVE TRADE AND INSTITUTIONS AND PRACTICES SIMILAR TO SLAVERY.

SLAVERY [Esclavage]

– "For the purpose of the present Convention, the following definitions are agreed upon:

[24] Art.1 "(1) Slavery is the status or condition of a person over whom any or all of the powers attaching to the right of ownership are exercised."

(1) Slavery is the status or condition of a person over whom any or all of the powers attaching to the right of ownership are exercised."

Art. 1, SLAVERY CONVENTION.

– "Each of States Parties to this Convention shall take all practicable and necessary legislative and other measures to bring about progressively and as soon as possible the complete abolition or abandonment of the following institutions and practices, where they still exist and whether or not they are covered by the definition of slavery contained in article 1[25] of the Slavery Convention signed at Geneva on 25 September 1926:

(*a*) Debt bondage, that is to say, the status or condition arising from a pledge by a debtor of his personal services or of those of a person under his control as security for debt, if the value of those services as reasonably assessed is not applied towards the liquidation of the debt or the length and nature of those services are not respectively limited and defined;

(*b*) Serfdom, that is to say, the condition or status of a tenant who is by law, custom or agreement bound to live and labour on land belonging to another person and to render some determinate service to such other person, whether for reward or not, and is not free to change his status;

(*c*) Any institution or practice whereby:

(i) A woman, without the right to refuse, is promised or given in marriage on payment of a consideration in money or in kind to her parents, guardian, family or any other person or group; or

(ii) The husband of a woman, his family, or his clan, has the right to transfer her to another person for value received or otherwise; or

(iii) A woman on the death of her husband is liable to be inherited by another person;

(*d*) Any institution or practice whereby a child or young person under the age of 18 years, is delivered by either or both of his natural parents

---

[25] "(1) Slavery is the status or condition of a person over whom any or all of the powers attaching to the right of ownership are exercised.
(2) The slave trade includes all acts involved in the capture, acquisition or disposal of a person with intent to reduce him to slavery; all acts involved in the acquisition of a slave with a view to selling or exchanging him; all acts of disposal by sale or exchange of a slave acquired with a view to being sold or exchanged, and, in general, every act of trade or transport in slaves."

or by his guardian to another person, whether for reward or not, with a view to the exploitation of the child or young person or of his labour."

Art. 1, SUPPLEMENTARY CONVENTION ON THE ABOLITION OF SLAVERY, THE SLAVE TRADE AND INSTITUTIONS AND PRACTICES SIMILAR TO SLAVERY.

– "For the purposes of the present Convention:

(*a*) 'Slavery' means, as defined in the Slavery Convention of 1926[26], the status or condition of a person over whom any or all of the powers attaching to the right of ownership are exercised, [...]"

Art. 7, SUPPLEMENTARY CONVENTION ON THE ABOLITION OF SLAVERY, THE SLAVE TRADE AND INSTITUTIONS AND PRACTICES SIMILAR TO SLAVERY.

SMUGGLING OF MIGRANTS [Trafic illicite de migrants]

– "For the purposes of this Protocol:

(*a*) 'Smuggling of migrants' shall mean the procurement, in order to obtain, directly or indirectly, a financial or other material benefit, of the illegal entry of a person into a State Party of which the person is not a national or a permanent resident;"

Art. 3, PROTOCOL AGAINST THE SMUGGLING OF MIGRANTS BY LAND, SEA AND AIR, SUPPLEMENTING THE UNITED NATIONS CONVENTION AGAINST TRANSNATIONAL ORGANIZED CRIME.

SOCIAL PROGRESS [Progrès social]

– "*Convinced* that international peace and security on the one hand, and social progress and economic development on the other, are closely interdependent and influence each other,"

Pp. 6, DECLARATION ON SOCIAL PROGRESS AND DEVELOPMENT.

– "The rapid expansion of national income and wealth and their equitable distribution among all members of society are fundamental to all social progress, and they should therefore be in the forefront of the preoccupations of every State and Government."

Art. 7, s.p. 1, DECLARATION ON SOCIAL PROGRESS AND DEVELOPMENT.

---

[26] "(1) Slavery is the status or condition of a person over whom any or all of the powers attaching to the right of ownership are exercised."

SOCIAL PROGRESS AND DEVELOPMENT [Développement et progrès dans le domaine social]

– "Social progress and development shall be founded on respect for the dignity and value of the human person and shall ensure the promotion of human rights and social justice, which requires:

  (*a*) The immediate and final elimination of all forms of inequality, exploitation of peoples and individuals, colonialism and racism, including nazism and apartheid, and all other policies and ideologies opposed to the purposes and principles of the United Nations;

  (*b*) The recognition and effective implementation of civil and political rights as well as of economic, social and cultural rights without any discrimination."

Art. 2, DECLARATION ON SOCIAL PROGRESS AND DEVELOPMENT.

SOCIAL SECURITY [Sécurité sociale]

– "(*b*) Social security (legal provisions in respect of employment injury, occupational diseases, maternity, sickness, disability, old age, death, unemployment, family responsibilities and any other contingency which, according to national laws or regulations, is covered by a social security scheme), [...]"

Art. 24, CONVENTION RELATING TO THE STATUS OF STATELESS PERSONS.
Art. 24, CONVENTION RELATING TO THE STATUS OF REFUGEES.

SOCIETAL AND JUSTICE RESPONSES TO JUVENILE CRIME AND DELINQUENCY [Réactions de la société et de la justice à la criminalité et à la délinquance juvéniles]

– "[...].With rapid and often drastic changes in the life-styles of the young and in the forms and dimensions of juvenile crime, the societal and justice responses to juvenile crime and delinquency quickly become outmoded and inadequate."

30, *Commentary*, s.p. 1, UNITED NATIONS STANDARD MINIMUM RULES FOR THE ADMINISTRATION OF JUVENILE JUSTICE ("THE BEIJING RULES").

SOLIDARITY [Solidarité (la)]

– "6. We consider certain fundamental values to be essential to international relations in the twenty-first century. These include:

[...]

Solidarity. Global challenges must be managed in a way that distributes the costs and burdens fairly in accordance with basic principles of equity and soßcial justice. Those who suffer or who benefit least deserve help from those who benefit most.[...]"

Third footnote (•), UNITED NATIONS MILLENIUM DECLARATION.

SPECIFIC MANDATE WHICH HAS BEEN ENTRUSTED TO UNESCO [Mandat spécifique qui a été confié à l'UNESCO]

– "*Aware* of the specific mandate which has been entrusted to UNESCO, within the United Nations system, to ensure the preservation and promotion of the fruitful diversity of cultures,"

Pp. 10, UNIVERSAL DECLARATION ON CULTURAL DIVERSITY.

SPECIFIED-EMPLOYMENT WORKER [Travailleurs admis pour un emploi spécifique]

– "For the purposes of the present Convention:

[...]

(*g*) The term 'specified-employment worker' refers to a migrant worker:

(i) Who has been sent by his or her employer for a restricted and defined period of time to a State of employment to undertake a specific assignment or duty; or

(ii) Who engages for a restricted and defined period of time in work that requires professional, commercial, technical or other highly specialized skill; or

(iii) Who, upon the request of his or her employer in the State of employment, engages for a restricted and defined period of time in work whose nature is transitory or brief; and who is required to depart from the State of employment either at the expiration of his or her authorized period of stay, or earlier if he or she no longer undertakes that specific assignment or duty or engages in that work;"

Art. 2.2, INTERNATIONAL CONVENTION ON THE PROTECTION OF THE RIGHTS OF ALL MIGRANT WORKERS AND MEMBERS OF THEIR FAMILIES.

STATE OF EMPLOYMENT [Etat d'emploi]

– "For the purposes of the present Convention:
[...]

(*b*) The term 'State of employment' means a State where the migrant worker is to be engaged, is engaged or has been engaged in a remunerated activity, as the case may be;"

Art. 6, INTERNATIONAL CONVENTION ON THE PROTECTION OF THE RIGHTS OF ALL MIGRANT WORKERS AND MEMBERS OF THEIR FAMILIES.

STATE OF ORIGIN [Etat d'origine]

– "For the purposes of the present Convention:

(*a*) The term 'State of origin' means the State of which the person concerned is a national;"

Art. 6, INTERNATIONAL CONVENTION ON THE PROTECTION OF THE RIGHTS OF ALL MIGRANT WORKERS AND MEMBERS OF THEIR FAMILIES.

STATE OF TRANSIT [Etat de transit]

– "For the purposes of the present Convention:
[...]

(*c*) The term 'State of transit' means any State through which the person concerned passes on any journey to the State of employment or from the State of employment to the State of origin or the State of habitual residence."

Art. 6, INTERNATIONAL CONVENTION ON THE PROTECTION OF THE RIGHTS OF ALL MIGRANT WORKERS AND MEMBERS OF THEIR FAMILIES.

STATELESS [Apatride]

– "3. Notwithstanding the provisions of paragraphs 1 (b) and 2 of this article[27], a child born in wedlock in the territory of a Contracting State,

---

[27] "(b) Upon an application being lodged with the appropriate authority, by or on behalf of the person concerned, in the manner prescribed by the national law. Subject to the provisions of paragraph 2 of this article, no such application may be rejected.
A Contracting State which provides for the grant of its nationality in accordance with subparagraph (b) of this paragraph may also provide for the grant of its nationality by operation of law at such age and subject to such conditions as may be prescribed by the national law.

whose mother has the nationality of that State, shall acquire at birth that nationality if it otherwise would be stateless."

Art. 1, CONVENTION ON THE REDUCTION OF STATELESS.

STATELESS PERSON [Apatride]

– "Article 1. – Definition of the term 'stateless person'

1. For the purpose of this Convention, the term 'stateless person' means a person who is not considered as a national by any State under the operation of its law.

2. This Convention shall not apply:

(i) To persons who are at present receiving from organs or agencies of the United Nations other than the United Nations High Commissioner for Refugees protection or assistance so long as they are receiving such protection or assistance;

(ii) To persons who are recognized by the competent authorities of the country in which they have taken residence as having the rights and obligations which are attached to the possession of the nationality of that country;

(iii) To persons with respect to whom there are serious reasons for considering that:

(*a*) They have committed a crime against peace, a war crime, or a crime against humanity, as defined in the international instruments drawn up to make provisions in respect of such crimes;

---

2. A Contracting State may make the grant of its nationality in accordance with subparagraph (b) -of paragraph 1 of this article subject to one or more of the following conditions:
(a) That the application is lodged during a period, fixed by the Contracting State, beginning not later than at the age of eighteen years and ending not earlier than at the age of twenty-one years, so, however, that the person concerned shall be allowed at least one year during which he may himself make the application without having to obtain legal authorization to do so;
(b) That the person concerned has habitually resided in the territory of the Contracting State for such period as may be fixed by that State, not exceeding five years immediately preceding the lodging of the application nor ten years in all;
(c) That the person concerned has neither been convicted of an offence against national security nor has been sentenced to imprisonment for a term of five years or more on a criminal charge;
(d) That the person concerned has always been stateless."

(*b*) They have committed a serious non-political crime outside the country of their residence prior to their admission to that country;

(*c*) They have been guilty of acts contrary to the purposes and principles of the United Nations.

CONVENTION RELATING TO THE STATUS OF STATELESS PERSONS.

STIGMA, SILENCE, DISCRIMINATION AND DENIAL, AS WELL AS A LACK OF CONFIDENTIALITY [Opprobre, le silence, la discrimination et la dénégation ainsi que l'absence de confidentialité (l')]

– "13. Noting further that stigma, silence, discrimination and denial, as well as a lack of confidentiality, undermine prevention, care and treatment efforts and increase the impact of the epidemic on individuals, families, communities and nations and must also be addressed;"

DECLARATION OF COMMITMENT ON HIV/AIDS.

SUB-SAHARAN AFRICA [Afrique subsaharienne]

– "8. Noting with grave concern that Africa, in particular sub-Saharan Africa, is currently the worst-affected region, where HIV/AIDS is considered a state of emergency which threatens development, social cohesion, political stability, food security and life expectancy and imposes a devastating economic burden, and that the dramatic situation on the continent needs urgent and exceptional national, regional and international action;"

DECLARATION OF COMMITMENT ON HIV/AIDS.

– "10. Recognizing also that other regions are seriously affected and confront similar threats, particularly the Caribbean region, with the second-highest rate of HIV infection after sub-Saharan Africa, the Asia-Pacific region where 7.5 million people living are already living with HIV/AID, the Latin American region with 1.5 million people living with HIV/AIDS and the Central and Eastern European region with very rapidly rising infection rates, and that the potential exists for a rapid escalation of the epidemic and its impact throughout the world if no specific measures are taken;"

DECLARATION OF COMMITMENT ON HIV/AIDS.

SUBJECTION OF PEOPLE [Sujétion des peuples]

- "1. The subjection of peoples to alien subjugation, domination and exploitation constitutes a denial of fundamental human rights, is contrary to the Charter of the United Nations and is an impediment to the promotion of world peace and co-operation."

UNITED NATIONS DECLARATION ON THE GRANTING OF INDEPENDENCE TO COLONIAL COUNTRIES AND PEOPLES.

SUBSTITUTE [Substitut]

- "(*d*) 'Substitute' means an organization acting in place of a Protecting Power in accordance with Article 5[28]."

[28] 1. It is the duty of the Parties to a conflict from the beginning of that conflict to secure the supervision and implementation of the Conventions and of this Protocol by the application of the system of Protecting Powers, including inter alia the designation and acceptance of those Powers, in accordance with the following paragraphs. Protecting Powers shall have the duty of safeguarding the interests of the Parties to the conflict.
2. From the beginning of a situation referred to in Article each Party to the conflict shall without delay designate a Protecting Power for the purpose of applying the Conventions and this Protocol and shall, likewise without delay and for the same purpose, permit the activities of a Protecting Power which has been accepted by it as such after designation by the adverse Party.
3. If a Protecting Power has not been designated or accepted from the beginning of a situation referred to in Article 1, the International Committee
of the Red Cross, without prejudice to the right of any other impartial humanitarian organization to do likewise, shall offer its good offices to the Parties to the conflict with a view to the designation without delay of a Protecting Power to which the Parties to the conflict consent. For that purpose it may, inter alia, ask each Party to provide it with a list of at least five States which that Party considers acceptable to act as Protecting Power on its behalf in relation to an adverse Party, and ask each adverse Party to provide a list of at least five States which it would accept as the Protecting Power of the first Party; these lists shall be communicated to the Committee within two weeks after the receipt of the request; it shall compare them and seek the agreement of any proposed State named on both lists.
4. If, despite the foregoing, there is no Protecting Power, the Parties to the conflict shall accept without delay an offer which may be made by the International Committee of the Red Cross or by any other organization which offers all guarantees of impartiality and efficacy, after due consultations with the said Parties and taking into account the result of these consultations, to act as a substitute. The functioning of such a substitute is subject to the consent of the Parties to the conflict; every effort shall be made by the Parties to the conflict to facilitate the operations of the substitute in the performance of its tasks under the Conventions and this Protocol.

Art. 2, PROTOCOL ADDITIONAL TO THE GENEVA CONVENTIONS OF 12 AUGUST 1949, AND RELATING TO THE PROTECTION OF VICTIMS OF INTERNATIONAL ARMED CONFLICTS (PROTOCOL I).

SURRENDER [Remise]

– "For the purposes of this Statute:

(*a*) 'surrender' means the delivering up of a person by a State to the Court, pursuant to this Statute."

Art.102, ROME STATUTE OF THE INTERNATIONAL CRIMINAL COURT.

SYSTEMATIC RAPE OF WOMEN IN WAR SITUATIONS [Viol systématique des femmes en temps de guerre]

- "28. The World Conference on Human Rights expresses its dismay at massive violations of human rights especially in the form of genocide, 'ethnic cleansing' and systematic rape of women in war situations, creating mass exodus of refugees and displaced persons. [...]"

I, VIENNA DECLARATION AND PROGRAM OF ACTION.

TEMPORARY MEDICAL PERSONNEL [Personnel sanitaire temporaire]

– "For the purposes of this Protocol:

[...]

(*k*) [...] 'Temporary medical personnel', 'temporary medical units' and 'temporary medical transports' mean those devoted exclusively to medical purposes for limited periods during the whole of such periods. Unless otherwise specified, the terms 'medical personnel', 'medical units' and 'medical transports' cover both permanent and temporary categories;"

Art. 8, PROTOCOL ADDITIONAL TO THE GENEVA CONVENTIONS OF 12 AUGUST 1949, AND RELATING TO THE PROTECTION OF VICTIMS OF INTERNATIONAL ARMED CONFLICTS (PROTOCOL I).

---

5. In accordance with Article 4, the designation and acceptance of Protecting Powers for the purpose of applying the Conventions and this Protocol shall not affect the legal status of the Parties to the conflict or of any territory, including occupied territory.
6. The maintenance of diplomatic relations between Parties to the conflict or the entrusting of the protection of a Party's interests and those of its nationals to a third State in accordance with the rules of international law relating to diplomatic relations is no obstacle to the designation of Protecting Powers for the purpose of applying the Conventions and this Protocol.
7. Any subsequent mention in this Protocol of a Protecting Power includes also a substitute."

TEMPORARY MEDICAL TRANSPORTS [Moyen de transport sanitaire temporaire]

– "For the purposes of this Protocol:

[…]

(*k*) […]. 'Temporary medical personnel', 'temporary medical units' and 'temporary medical transports' mean those devoted exclusively to medical purposes for limited periods during the whole of such periods. Unless otherwise specified, the terms 'medical personnel', 'medical units' and 'medical transports' cover both permanent and temporary categories;"

Art. 8, Protocol Additional to the Geneva Conventions of 12 August 1949, and relating to the Protection of Victims of International Armed Conflicts (Protocol I).

TEMPORARY MEDICAL UNITS [Unités sanitaires temporaires]

– "For the purposes of this Protocol:

[…]

(*k*) […]. 'Temporary medical personnel', 'temporary medical units' and 'temporary medical transports' mean those devoted exclusively to medical purposes for limited periods during the whole of such periods. Unless otherwise specified, the terms 'medical personnel', 'medical units' and 'medical transports' cover both permanent and temporary categories;"

Art. 8, Protocol Additional to the Geneva Conventions of 12 August 1949, and relating to the Protection of Victims of International Armed Conflicts (Protocol I)

TERTIARY VISCERAL SYPHILIS RESISTANT TO TREATMENT [Syphilis viscérale tertiaire, résistant au traitement]

– "(s) Serious chronic infectious diseases, persisting for one year after their inception, for example: malaria with decided organic impairment, amoebic or bacillary dysentery with grave disorders; tertiary visceral syphilis resistant to treatment; leprosy; etc."

Annex I, 3, Geneva Convention relative to the Treatment of Prisoners of War.

THREAT TO THE LIFE AND SAFETY OF LAW ENFORCEMENT OFFICIALS [Menace à la vie et à la sécurité des responsables de l'application des lois]

– "*Whereas* a threat to the life and safety of law enforcement officials must be seen as a threat to the stability of society as a whole,"

Pp. 2, BASIC PRINCIPLES ON THE USE OF FORCE AND FIREARMS BY LAW ENFORCEMENT OFFICIALS.

TOLERANCE [Tolérance (la)]

– "6. We consider certain fundamental values to be essential to international relations in the twenty-first century. These include:

[...]

Tolerance. Human beings must respect one other, in all their diversity of belief, culture and language. Differences within and between societies should be neither feared nor repressed, but cherished as a precious asset of humanity. A culture of peace and dialogue among all civilizations should be actively promoted.

[...]"

Fourth footnote (•), UNITED NATIONS MILLENIUM DECLARATION.

TORTURE [Torture]

– "1. For the purpose of this Declaration, torture means any act by which severe pain or suffering, whether physical or mental, is intentionally inflicted by or at the instigation of a public official on a person for such purposes as obtaining from him or a third person information or confession, punishing him for an act he has committed or is suspected of having committed, or intimidating him or other persons. It does not include pain or suffering arising only from, inherent in or incidental to, lawful sanctions to the extent consistent with the Standard Minimum Rules for the Treatment of Prisoners.

2. Torture constitutes an aggravated and deliberate form of cruel, inhuman or degrading treatment or punishment.

Art. 1, DECLARATION ON THE PROTECTION OF ALL PERSONS FROM BEING SUBJECTED TO TORTURE AND OTHER CRUEL, INHUMAN OR DEGRADING TREATMENT OR PUNISHMENT.

– "1. For the purposes of this Convention, the term 'torture' means any act by which severe pain or suffering, whether physical or mental, is intentionally inflicted on a person for such purposes as obtaining from him or a third person information or a confession, punishing him for an act he or a third person has committed or is suspected of having committed, or intimidating or coercing him or a third person, or for any reason based on discrimination of any kind, when such pain or suffering is inflicted by or at the instigation of or with the consent or acquiescence of a public official or other person acting in an official capacity. It does not include pain or suffering arising only from, inherent in or incidental to lawful sanctions.

2. This article is without prejudice to any international instrument or national legislation which does or may contain provisions of wider applications"

Art. 1, CONVENTION AGAINST TORTURE AND OTHER CRUEL, INHUMAN OR DEGRADING TREATMENT OR PUNISHMENT.

– "No law enforcement official may inflict, instigate or tolerate any act of torture or other cruel, inhuman or degrading treatment or punishment, nor may any law enforcement official invoke superior orders or exceptional circumstances such as a state of war or a threat of war, a threat to national security, internal political instability or any other public emergency as a justification of torture or other cruel, inhuman or degrading treatment or punishment.

Commentary:

(*a*) This prohibition derives from the Declaration on the Protection of All Persons from Being Subjected to Torture and Other Cruel, Inhuman or Degrading Treatment or Punishment, adopted by the General Assembly, according to which: '[Such an act is] an offence to human dignity and shall be condemned as a denial of the purposes of the Charter of the United Nations and as a violation of the human rights and fundamental freedoms proclaimed in the Universal Declaration of Human Rights [and other international human rights instruments].'

(*b*) The Declaration defines torture as follows:
'. . . torture means any act by which severe pain or suffering, whether physical or mental, is intentionally inflicted by or at the instigation of a public official on a person for such purposes as obtaining from him or a third person information or confession, punishing him for an act he has committed or is suspected of having committed, or intimidating him or

other persons. It does not include pain or suffering arising only from, inherent in or incidental to, lawful sanctions to the extent consistent with the Standard Minimum Rules for the Treatment of Prisoners.'

Art. 5, CODE OF CONDUCT FOR LAW ENFORCEMENT OFFICIALS.

– "2. For the purpose of paragraph 1[29]:
[…]

(*e*) 'Torture' means the intentional infliction of severe pain or suffering, whether physical or mental, upon a person in the custody or under the control of the accused; except that torture shall not include pain or suffering arising only from, inherent in or incidental to, lawful sanctions;"

Art. 7, ROME STATUTE OF THE INTERNATIONAL CRIMINAL COURT.

– "No physical or mental torture, nor any other form of coercion, may be inflicted on prisoners of war to secure from them information of any kind whatever. Prisoners of war who refuse to answer may not be threatened, insulted, or exposed to any unpleasant or disadvantageous treatment of any kind. ." [AE]

---

[29] "1. For the purpose of this Statute, 'crime against humanity' means any of the following acts when committed as part of a widespread or systematic attack directed against any civilian population, with knowledge of the attack:
(a) Murder;
(b) Extermination ;
(c) Enslavement;
(d) Deportation or forcible transfer of population;
(e) Imprisonment or other severe deprivation of physical liberty in violation of fundamental rules of international law;
(f) Torture;
(g) Rape, sexual slavery, enforced prostitution, forced pregnancy, enforced sterilization, or any other form of sexual violence of comparable gravity;
(h) Persecution against any identifiable group or collectivity on political, racial, national, ethnic, cultural, religious, gender, as defined in paragraph 3, or other grounds that are universally recognized as impermissible under international law, in connection with any act referred to in this paragraph or any crime within the jurisdiction of the Court;
(i) Enforced disappearance of persons;
(j) The crime of apartheid;
(k) Other inhumane acts of a similar character intentionally causing great suffering, or serious injury to body or to mental or physical health."

[AE] « Aucune torture physique ou morale ni aucune contrainte ne pourra être exercée sur les prisonniers de guerre pour obtenir d'eux des renseignements de quelque sorte que ce soit. Les prisonniers qui refuseront de répondre ne pourront être ni menacés, ni insultés, ni exposés à des désagréments ou désavantages de quelque nature que ce soit. »

Art. 17 s.p. 4, GENEVA CONVENTION RELATIVE TO THE TREATMENT OF PRISONERS OF WAR.

- "The High Contracting Parties specifically agree that each of them is prohibited from taking any measure of such a character as to cause the physical suffering or extermination of protected persons in their hands. This prohibition applies not only to murder, torture, corporal punishment, mutilation and medical or scientific experiments not necessitated by the medical treatment of a protected person but also to any other measures of brutality whether applied by civilian or military agents."

Art. 32, GENEVA CONVENTION RELATIVE TO THE PROTECTION OF CIVILIAN PERSONS IN TIME OF WAR.

- "(*a*) Violence to the life, health, or physical or mental well-being of persons, in particular:

  [...]

  (ii) Torture of all kinds, whether physical or mental;

  [...]"

Art. 75, paragraph 2, PROTOCOL ADDITIONAL TO THE GENEVA CONVENTIONS OF 12 AUGUST 1949, AND RELATING TO THE PROTECTION OF VICTIMS OF INTERNATIONAL ARMED CONFLICTS (PROTOCOL 1).

TRACHOMA [Trachome]

- "(*i*) Blindness of both eyes, or of one eve when the vision of the other is less than I in spite of the use of corrective glasses; diminution of visual acuity in cases where it is impossible to restore it by correction to an acuity of 1/2 in at least one eye; other grave ocular affections, for example: glaucoma, iritis, choroiditis; trachoma, etc."

Annex I, 3, GENEVA CONVENTION RELATIVE TO THE TREATMENT OF PRISONERS OF WAR.

TRAFFIC IN PERSONS AND THE EXPLOITATION OF PROSTITUTION OF OTHERS (THE) [Traite des êtres humains et de l'exploitation de la prostitution d'autrui (la)]

- "The Parties to the present Convention agree to punish any person who, to gratify the passions of another:

  (1) Procures, entices or leads away, for purposes of prostitution, another person, even with the consent of that person;

  (2) Exploits the prostitution of another person, even with the consent of that person."

Art. 1, Convention for the Suppression of the Traffic in Persons and of the Exploitation of the Prostitution of Others.

– "The Parties to the present Convention further agree to punish any person who:

(1) Keeps or manages, or knowingly finances or takes part in the financing of a brothel;

(2) Knowingly lets or rents a building or other place or any part thereof for the purpose of the prostitution of others."

Art. 2, Convention for the Suppression of the Traffic in Persons and of the Exploitation of the Prostitution of Others.

TRAFFIC IN PERSONS FOR THE PURPOSE OF PROSTITUTION [Traite des êtres humains en vue de la prostitution]

– "*Whereas* prostitution and the accompanying evil of the traffic in persons for the purpose of prostitution are incompatible with the dignity and worth of the human person and endanger the welfare of the individual, the family and the community,"

Pp. 1, Convention for the Suppression of the Traffic in Persons and of the Exploitation of the Prostitution of Others.

TRAFFICKING IN PERSONS [Traite des personnes]

– "For the purposes of this Protocol:

(*a*) 'Trafficking in persons' shall mean the recruitment, transportation, transfer, harbouring or receipt of persons, by means of the threat or use of force or other forms of coercion, of abduction, of fraud, of deception, of the abuse of power or of position of vulnerability or of the giving or receiving of payments or benefits to achieve the consent of a person having control over another person, for the purpose of exploitation. Exploitation shall include, at minimum, the exploitation of the prostitution of others or other forms of sexual exploitation, forced labour or services, slavery or practices similar to slavery, servitude or removal of organs;

(*b*) The consent of a victim of trafficking in persons to intended exploitation set forth in subparagraph (*a*) of this article shall be irrelevant where any of the means set forth in subparagraph (*a*) have been used;

(*c*) The recruitment, transportation, transfer, harbouring or receipt of a child for the purpose of exploitation shall be considered 'trafficking in persons' even if this does not involve any of the means set forth in subparagraph (*a*) of this article;"

Art. 3, PROTOCOL TO PREVENT, SUPPRESS AND PUNISH TRAFFICKING IN PERSONS ESPECIALLY WOMEN AND CHILDREN, SUPPLEMENTING THE UNITED NATIONS CONVENTION AGAINST TRANSNATIONAL ORGANIZED CRIME.

TRANSFER OF SCIENCE AND TECHNOLOGY [Transfert de la science et de la technique]

– "*Aware* that the transfer of science and technology is one of the principal ways of accelerating the economic development of developing countries,"

Pp. 7, DECLARATION ON THE USE OF SCIENTIFIC AND TECHNOLOGICAL PROGRESS IN THE INTERESTS OF PEACE FOR THE BENEFIT OF MANKIND.

TRIBAL PEOPLES [Peuples tribaux]

– "1. This Convention applies to:

(*a*) Tribal peoples in independent countries whose social, cultural and economic conditions distinguish them from other sections of the national community, and whose status is regulated wholly or partially by their own customs or traditions or by special laws or regulations;
[...]

2. Self-identification as indigenous or tribal shall be regarded as a fundamental criterion for determining the groups to which the provisions of this Convention apply.
3. The use of the term 'peoples' in this Convention shall be not be construed as having any implications as regards the rights which may attach to the term under international law."

Art. 1, INDIGENOUS AND TRIBAL PEOPLES CONVENTION (N° 169).

UNDERDEVELOPMENT [Sous-développement]

– "11. Recognizing that poverty, underdevelopment and illiteracy are among the principal contributing factors to the spread of HIV/AIDS, and noting with grave concern that HIV/AIDS is compounding poverty and is now reversing or impeding development in many countries and should therefore be addressed in an integrated manner;"

DECLARATION OF COMMITMENT ON HIV/AIDS.

UNITED NATIONS [Organisation des Nations Unies]

– "[...] As the most universal and most representative organization in the world, the United Nations [...]"

6, Sixth footnote (•), UNITED NATIONS MILLENIUM DECLARATION.

– "32. We solemnly reaffirm, on this historic occasion, that the United Nations is the indispensable common house of the entire human family, through which we will seek to realize our universal aspirations for peace, cooperation and development. [...]"

UNITED NATIONS MILLENIUM DECLARATION.

UNIVERSAL DECLARATION OF HUMAN RIGHTS [Déclaration universelle des droits de l'homme]

– "*Proclaims* this Universal Declaration of Human Rights as a common standard of achievement for all peoples and all nations [...]"

Pp. 8, UNIVERSAL DECLARATION OF HUMAN RIGHTS.

– "*Emphasizing* that the Universal Declaration of Human Rights, which constitutes a common standard of achievement for all peoples and all nations, is the source of inspiration and has been the basis for the United Nations in making advances in standard setting as contained in the existing international human rights instruments, in particular the International Covenant on Civil and Political Rights and the International Covenant on Economic, Social and Cultural Rights."

Pp. 8, VIENNA DECLARATION AND PROGRAMME OF ACTION.

– "*Reaffirming also* the importance of the Universal Declaration of Human Rights and the International Covenants on Human Rights as basic elements of international efforts to promote universal respect for and observance of human rights and fundamental freedoms and the importance of other human rights instruments adopted within the United Nations system, as well as those at the regional level,"

Pp. 2, DECLARATION ON THE RIGHTS AND RESPONSIBILITY OF INDIVIDUALS, GROUPS AND ORGANS OF SOCIETY TO PROMOTE AND PROTECT UNIVERSALLY RECOGNIZED HUMAN RIGHTS AND FUNDAMENTAL FREEDOMS.

UNTRIED PRISONERS [Prévenu]

– "84. (1) Persons arrested or imprisoned by reason of a criminal charge against them, who are detained either in police custody or in prison custody (jail) but have not yet been tried and sentenced, will be referred to as 'untried prisoners' , hereinafter in these rules."

STANDARD MINIMUM RULES FOR THE TREATMENT OF PRISONERS.

VESSEL [Navire]

– "For the purposes of this Protocol:

[...]

(*d*) 'Vessel' shall mean any type of water craft, including non-displacement craft and seaplanes, used or capable of being used as a means of transportation on water, except a warship, naval auxiliary or other vessel owned or operated by a Government and used, for the time being, only on government non-commercial service."

Art. 3, PROTOCOL AGAINST THE SMUGGLING OF MIGRANTS BY LAND, SEA AND AIR, SUPPLEMENTING THE UNITED NATIONS CONVENTION AGAINST TRANSNATIONAL ORGANIZED CRIME.

VICTIM [Victime]

– "2. A person may be considered a victim, under this Declaration, regardless of whether the perpetrator is identified, apprehended, prosecuted or convicted and regardless of the familial relationship between the perpetrator and the victim. The term 'victim' also includes, where appropriate, the immediate family or dependants of the direct victim and persons who have suffered harm in intervening to assist victims in distress or to prevent victimization."

DECLARATION OF BASIC PRINCIPLES OF JUSTICE VICTIMS OF CRIME AND ABUSE OF POWER.

VICTIMS [Victimes]

– "1. 'Victims' means persons who, individually or collectively, have suffered harm, including physical or mental injury, emotional suffering, economic loss or substantial impairment of their fundamental rights, through acts or omissions that are in violation of criminal laws operative within Member States, including those laws proscribing criminal abuse of power."

DECLARATION OF BASIC PRINCIPLES OF JUSTICE VICTIMS OF CRIME AND ABUSE OF POWER.

– "18. 'Victims' means persons who, individually or collectively, have suffered harm, including physical or mental injury, emotional suffering, economic loss or substantial impairment of their fundamental rights, through acts or omissions that do not yet constitute violations of national criminal laws but of internationally recognized norms relating to human rights."

DECLARATION OF BASIC PRINCIPLES OF JUSTICE VICTIMS OF CRIME AND ABUSE OF POWER.

VIOLATIONS OF LAWS OR CUSTOMS OF WAR [Violations des lois ou coutumes de la guerre]

– "*Violations of the laws or customs of war*

The International Tribunal shall have the power to prosecute persons violating the laws or customs of war. Such violations shall include, but not be limited to:

(*a*) employment of poisonous weapons or other weapons calculated to cause unnecessary suffering;

(*b*) wanton destruction of cities, towns or villages, or devastation not justified by military necessity;

(*c*) attack, or bombardment, by whatever means, of undefended towns, villages, dwellings, or buildings;

(*d*) seizure of, destruction or wilful damage done to institutions dedicated to religion, charity and education, the arts and sciences, historic monuments and works of art and science;

(*e*) plunder of public or private property.

Art. 3, STATUTE OF THE INTERNATIONAL TRIBUNAL FOR THE PROSECUTION OF PERSONS RESPONSIBLE FOR SERIOUS VIOLATIONS OF INTERNATIONAL HUMANITARIAN LAW COMMITTED IN THE TERRITORY OF FORMER YUGOSLAVIA SINCE 1991.

VIOLENCE [Violence]

– "*Alarmed* that opportunities for women to achieve legal, social, political and economic equality in society are limited, inter alia, by continuing and endemic violence"

Pp. 11, DECLARATION ON THE ELIMINATION OF VIOLENCE AGAINST WOMEN.

VIOLENCE AGAINST WOMEN [Violence à l'égard des femmes]

– "*Recognizing* that violence against women is a manifestation of historically unequal power relations between men and women, which have led to domination over and discrimination against women by men and to the prevention of the full advancement of women, and that violence against women is one of the crucial social mechanisms by which women are forced into a subordinate position compared with men."

Pp. 6, DECLARATION ON THE ELIMINATION OF VIOLENCE AGAINST WOMEN.

– "For the purpose of this Declaration, the term 'Violence against women' means any act of gender-based violence that results in, or is likely to result in, physical, sexual or psychological harm or suffering to women, including threats of such acts, coercion or arbitrary depravation of liberty, whether occurring in public or in private live."

Art. 1, DECLARATION ON THE ELIMINATION OF VIOLENCE AGAINST WOMEN.

– "Violence against women shall be understood to encompass, but not be limited to, the following:

(*a*) Physical, sexual and psychological violence occurring in the family, including battering, sexual abuse of female children in household, dowry-related violence, marital rape, female genital mutilation and other traditional practices harmful to women, non-spousal violence and violence related to exploitation;

(*b*) Physical, sexual and psychological violence occurring within the general community, including rape, sexual abuse, sexual harassment and intimidation at work, in educational institutions and elsewhere, trafficking in women and forced prostitution;

(*c*) Physical, sexual and psychological violence perpetrated or condoned by the State, wherever it occurs."

Art. 2, DECLARATION ON THE ELIMINATION OF VIOLENCE AGAINST WOMEN.

WAR [Guerre]

– "[…] war, whether within or between States, […]"
8, United Nations Millennium Declaration.

WAR CRIMES [Crimes de guerre]

– "*Considering* that war crimes and crimes against humanity are among the gravest crimes in international law,"
Pp. 4, Convention on the Non-Applicability of Statutory limitations to War Crimes Against Humanity.

– "(*a*) War crimes as they are defined in the Charter of the International Military Tribunal, Nurnberg, of 8 August 1945 and confirmed by resolutions 3 (1) of 13 February 1946 and 95 (I) of 11 December 1946 of the General Assembly of the United Nations, particularly the 'grave breaches' enumerated in the Geneva Conventions of 12 August 1949 for the protection of war victims;"
Art. I, Convention on the Non-Applicability of Statutory Limitations to War Crimes and Crimes Against Humanity.

– "2. For the purpose of this Statute, 'war crimes' means:

(*a*) Grave breaches of the Geneva Conventions of 12 August 1949, namely, any of the following acts against persons or property protected under the provisions of the relevant Geneva Convention:

(i) Wilful killing;

(ii) Torture or inhuman treatment, including biological experiments;

(iii) Wilfully causing great suffering, or serious injury to body or health;

(iv) Extensive destruction and appropriation of property, not justified by military necessity and carried out unlawfully and wantonly;

(v) Compelling a prisoner of war or other protected person to serve in the forces of a hostile Power;

(vi) Wilfully depriving a prisoner of war or other protected person of the rights of fair and regular trial;

(vii) Unlawful deportation or transfer or unlawful confinement;

(viii) Taking of hostages.

(*b*) Other serious violations of the laws and customs applicable in international armed conflict, within the established framework of international law, namely, any of the following acts:

(i) Intentionally directing attacks against the civilian population as such or against individual civilians not taking direct part in hostilities;

(ii) Intentionally directing attacks against civilian objects, that is, objects which are not military objectives;

(iii) Intentionally directing attacks against personnel, installations, material, units or vehicles involved in a humanitarian assistance or peacekeeping mission in accordance with the Charter of the United Nations, as long as they are entitled to the protection given to civilians or civilian objects under the international law of armed conflict;

(iv) Intentionally launching an attack in the knowledge that such attack will cause incidental loss of life or injury to civilians or damage to civilian objects or widespread, long-term and severe damage to the natural environment which would be clearly excessive in relation to the concrete and direct overall military advantage anticipated;

(v) Attacking or bombarding, by whatever means, towns, villages, dwellings or buildings which are undefended and which are not military objectives;

(vi) Killing or wounding a combatant who, having laid down his arms or having no longer means of defence, has surrendered at discretion;

(vii) Making improper use of a flag of truce, of the flag or of the military insignia and uniform of the enemy or of the United Nations, as well as of the distinctive emblems of the Geneva Conventions, resulting in death or serious personal injury;

(viii) The transfer, directly or indirectly, by the Occupying Power of parts of its own civilian population into the territory it occupies, or the deportation or transfer of all or parts of the population of the occupied territory within or outside this territory;

(ix) Intentionally directing attacks against buildings dedicated to religion, education, art, science or charitable purposes, historic monuments, hospitals and places where the sick and wounded are collected, provided they are not military objectives;

(x) Subjecting persons who are in the power of an adverse party to physical mutilation or to medical or scientific experiments of any kind which are neither justified by the medical, dental or hospital treatment of the person concerned nor carried out in his or her interest, and which cause death to or seriously endanger the health of such person or persons;

(xi) Killing or wounding treacherously individuals belonging to the hostile nation or army;

(xii) Declaring that no quarter will be given;

(xiii) Destroying or seizing the enemy's property unless such destruction or seizure be imperatively demanded by the necessities of war;

(xiv) Declaring abolished, suspended or inadmissible in a court of law the rights and actions of the nationals of the hostile party;

(xv) Compelling the nationals of the hostile party to take part in the operations of war directed against their own country, even if they were in the belligerent's service before the commencement of the war;

(xvi) Pillaging a town or place, even when taken by assault;

(xvii) Employing poison or poisoned weapons;

(xviii) Employing asphyxiating, poisonous or other gases, and all analogous liquids, materials or devices;

(xix) Employing bullets which expand or flatten easily in the human body, such as bullets with a hard envelope which does not entirely cover the core or is pierced with incisions;

(xx) Employing weapons, projectiles and material and methods of warfare which are of a nature to cause superfluous injury or unnecessary suffering or which are inherently indiscriminate in violation of the international law of armed conflict, provided that such weapons, projectiles and material and methods of warfare are the subject of a comprehensive prohibition and are included in an annex to this Statute, by an amendment in accordance with the relevant provisions set forth in articles 121[30] and 123[31];

---

[30] "1. After the expiry of seven years from the entry into force of this Statute, any State Party may propose amendments thereto. The text of any proposed amendment shall be sumitted to the Secretary-General of the United Nations, who shall promptly circulate it to all States Parties.

(xxi) Committing outrages upon personal dignity, in particular humiliating and degrading treatment;

(xxii) Committing rape, sexual slavery, enforced prostitution, forced pregnancy, as defined in article 7, paragraph 2 (*f*)[32], enforced sterilization, or any other form of sexual violence also constituting a grave breach of the Geneva Conventions;

---

2. No sooner than there months from the date of notification, the Assembly of States Parties, t its next meetings, shall, by a majority of those present and voting, decide whether to take up the proposal. The Assembly may deal with the proposal directly or convene a Review Conference if the issue involved so warrants.
3. The adoption of an amendment at a meeting of the Assembly of States Parties or at a Review Conference on which consensus cannot be reached shall require a two-thirds majority of States Parties.
4. Except as provided in paragraph 5, an amendment shall enter into force for all States Parties one year after instruments of ratification or acceptance have been deposited with the Secretary-General of the United Nations by seven-eighths of them.
5. Any amendment to articles 5, 6, 7 and 8 of this Statute shall enter into force for those States Parties which have accepted the amendment one year after the deposit of their instruments of ratification or acceptance. In respect of a State Party which has not accepted the amendment, the Court shall not exercise its jurisdiction regarding a crime covered by the amendment when committed by that State Party's nationals or on its territory.
6. If an amendment has been accepted by seven-eighths of States Parties in accordance with paragraph, any State Party which has not accepted the amendment may withdraw from this Statute with immediate effect, notwithstanding article 127, paragraph 2, by giving notice no later than one year after the entry into force of such amendment.
7. The Secretary-General of the United Nations shall circulate to all States Parties any amendment adopted at a meeting of the Assembly of States Parties or at a review Conference."

[31] "1. Seven years after the entry into force of this Statute the Secretary-General of the United Nations shall convene a Review Conference to consider any amendments to this Statute . Such review may include, but is not limited to, the list of crimes contained in article 5. The Conference shall be open to those participating in the Assembly of States Parties and on the same conditions.
2. At any time thereafter, at the request of a State Party and for the purposes set out in paragraph 1, the Secretary-General of the United Nations shall, upon approval by a majority of States Parties, convene a Review Conference.
3. The provisions of article 121, paragraphs 3 to 7, shall apply to the adoption and entry into force of any amendment to the Statute considered at a Review Conference."

[32] "(*f*) 'Forced pregnancy' means the unlawful confinement of a woman forcibly made pregnant, with the intent of affecting the ethnic composition of any population or carrying out grave violations of international law. This definition shall not in any way be interpreted as affecting national laws relating to pregnancy;"

(xxiii) Utilizing the presence of a civilian or other protected person to render certain points, areas or military forces immune from military operations;

(xxiv) Intentionally directing attacks against buildings, material, medical units and transport, and personnel using the distinctive emblems of the Geneva Conventions in conformity with international law;

(xxv) Intentionally using starvation of civilians as a method of warfare by depriving them of objects indispensable to their survival, including wilfully impeding relief supplies as provided for under the Geneva Conventions;

(xxvi) Conscripting or enlisting children under the age of fifteen years into the national armed forces or using them to participate actively in hostilities.

(*c*) In the case of an armed conflict not of an international character, serious violations of article 3 common to the four Geneva Conventions of 12 August 1949[33], namely, any of the following acts committed against

---

[33] "In the case of armed conflict not of an international character occurring in the territory of one of the High Contracting Parties, each Party to the conflict shall be bound to apply, as a minimum, the following provisions:
1. Persons taking no active part in the hostilities, including members of armed forces who have laid down their arms and those placed *hors de combat* by sickness, wounds, detention, or any other cause, shall in all circumstances be treated humanely, without any adverse distinction founded on race, colour, religion or faith, sex, birth or wealth, or any other similar criteria.
To this end, the following acts are and shall remain prohibited at any time and in any place whatsoever with respect to the above-mentioned persons:
(a) Violence to life and person, in particular murder of all kinds, mutilation, cruel treatment and torture;
(b) Taking of hostages;
(c) Outrages upon personal dignity, in particular humiliating and degrading treatment;
(d) The passing of sentences and the carrying out of executions without previous judgment pronounced by a regularly constituted court, affording all the judicial guarantees which are recognized as indispensable by civilized peoples.
2. The wounded and sick shall be collected and cared for.
An impartial humanitarian body, such as the International Committee of the Red Cross, may offer its services to the Parties to the conflict.
The Parties to the conflict should further endeavour to bring into force, by means of special agreements, all or part of the other provisions of the present Convention.
The application of the preceding provisions shall not affect the legal status of the Parties to the conflict."

persons taking no active part in the hostilities, including members of armed forces who have laid down their arms and those placed *hors de combat* by sickness, wounds, detention or any other cause:

(i) Violence to life and person, in particular murder of all kinds, mutilation, cruel treatment and torture;

(ii) Committing outrages upon personal dignity, in particular humiliating and degrading treatment;

(iii) Taking of hostages;

(iv) The passing of sentences and the carrying out of executions without previous judgement pronounced by a regularly constituted court, affording all judicial guarantees which are generally recognized as indispensable.

(*d*) Paragraph 2 (c) applies to armed conflicts not of an international character and thus does not apply to situations of internal disturbances and tensions, such as riots, isolated and sporadic acts of violence or other acts of a similar nature.

(*e*) Other serious violations of the laws and customs applicable in armed conflicts not of an international character, within the established framework of international law, namely, any of the following acts:

(i) Intentionally directing attacks against the civilian population as such or against individual civilians not taking direct part in hostilities;

(ii) Intentionally directing attacks against buildings, material, medical units and transport, and personnel using the distinctive emblems of the Geneva Conventions in conformity with international law;

(iii) Intentionally directing attacks against personnel, installations, material, units or vehicles involved in a humanitarian assistance or peacekeeping mission in accordance with the Charter of the United Nations, as long as they are entitled to the protection given to civilians or civilian objects under the international law of armed conflict;

(iv) Intentionally directing attacks against buildings dedicated to religion, education, art, science or charitable purposes, historic monuments, hospitals and places where the sick and wounded are collected, provided they are not military objectives;

(v) Pillaging a town or place, even when taken by assault;

(vi) Committing rape, sexual slavery, enforced prostitution, forced pregnancy, as defined in article 7, paragraph 2 (*f*)[34], enforced sterilization, and any other form of sexual violence also constituting a serious violation of article 3 common to the four Geneva Conventions[35];

(vii) Conscripting or enlisting children under the age of fifteen years into armed forces or groups or using them to participate actively in hostilities;

(viii) Ordering the displacement of the civilian population for reasons related to the conflict, unless the security of the civilians involved or imperative military reasons so demand;

(ix) Killing or wounding treacherously a combatant adversary;

(x) Declaring that no quarter will be given;

---

[34] "(*f*) 'Forced pregnancy' means the unlawful confinement of a woman forcibly made pregnant, with the intent of affecting the ethnic composition of any population or carrying out grave violations of international law. This definition shall not in any way be interpreted as affecting national laws relating to pregnancy;"

[35] "In the case of armed conflict not of an international character occurring in the territory of one of the High Contracting Parties, each Party to the conflict shall be bound to apply, as a minimum, the following provisions:
1. Persons taking no active part in the hostilities, including members of armed forces who have laid down their arms and those placed hors de combat by sickness, wounds, detention, or any other cause, shall in all circumstances be treated humanely, without any adverse distinction founded on race, colour, religion or faith, sex, birth or wealth, or any other similar criteria.
To this end, the following acts are and shall remain prohibited at any time and in any place whatsoever with respect to the above-mentioned persons:
(a) Violence to life and person, in particular murder of all kinds, mutilation, cruel treatment and torture;
(b) Taking of hostages;
(c) Outrages upon personal dignity, in particular humiliating and degrading treatment;
(d) The passing of sentences and the carrying out of executions without previous judgment pronounced by a regularly constituted court, affording all the judicial guarantees which are recognized as indispensable by civilized peoples.
2. The wounded and sick shall be collected and cared for.
An impartial humanitarian body, such as the International Committee of the Red Cross, may offer its services to the Parties to the conflict.
The Parties to the conflict should further endeavour to bring into force, by means of special agreements, all or part of the other provisions of the present Convention.
The application of the preceding provisions shall not affect the legal status of the Parties to the conflict."

(xi) Subjecting persons who are in the power of another party to the conflict to physical mutilation or to medical or scientific experiments of any kind which are neither justified by the medical, dental or hospital treatment of the person concerned nor carried out in his or her interest, and which cause death to or seriously endanger the health of such person or persons;

(xii) Destroying or seizing the property of an adversary unless such destruction or seizure be imperatively demanded by the necessities of the conflict;

– (*f*) Paragraph 2 (e) applies to armed conflicts not of an international character and thus does not apply to situations of internal disturbances and tensions, such as riots, isolated and sporadic acts of violence or other acts of a similar nature. It applies to armed conflicts that take place in the territory of a State when there is protracted armed conflict between governmental authorities and organized armed groups or between such groups."

Art. 8, ROME STATUTE OF INTERNATIONAL CRIMINAL COURT.

WELL-BEING OF THE PEOPLES OF THE WORLD [Bien-être des peuples du monde]

– "(*g*) The well-being of the peoples of the world largely depends on the adequate production and distribution of food as well as the establishment of a world food security system which would ensure adequate availability of, and reasonable prices for, food at all times, irrespective of periodic fluctuations and vagaries of weather and free of political and economic pressures, and should thus facilitate, amongst other things, the development process of developing countries;"

UNIVERSAL DECLARATION ON THE ERADICATION OF HUNGER AND MALNUTRITION.

WOMEN [Femmes]

– "Concerned, however, that despite these various instruments extensive discrimination against women continues to exist,"

Pp. 6, CONVENTION ON THE ELIMINATION OF ALL FORMS OF DISCRIMINATION AGAINST WOMEN.

– "4. [...] Moreover, it is necessary to recognize the key role of women in agricultural production and rural economy in many countries, [...]."

UNIVERSAL DECLARATION ON THE ERADICATION OF HUNGER AND MALNUTRITION.

WORK [Travail]

– "2. In order to prevent discrimination against women on the grounds of marriage or maternity and to ensure their effective right to work, States Parties shall take appropriate measures:
[...]

(*d*) To provide special protection to women during pregnancy in types of work proved to be harmful to them.[AF]"

Art. 11, CONVENTION ON THE ELIMINATION OF ALL FORMS OF DISCRIMINATION AGAINST WOMEN.

WORKER ON AN OFFSHORE INSTALLATION [Travailleurs d'une installation en mer]

– "For the purposes of the present Convention:
[...]

(*d*) The term 'worker on an offshore installation' refers to a migrant worker employed on an offshore installation that is under the jurisdiction of a State of which he or she is not a national;"

Art. 2.2, INTERNATIONAL CONVENTION ON THE PROTECTION OF THE RIGHTS OF ALL MIGRANT WORKERS AND MEMBERS OF THEIR FAMILIES.

WORST FORMS OF CHILD LABOUR (THE) [Pires formes de travail des enfants (les)]

– "For the purposes of this Convention, the term 'the worst forms of child labour'comprises:

(*a*) all forms of slavery or practices similar to slavery, such as the sale and trafficking of children, debt bondage and serfdom and forced or compulsory labour, including forced or compulsory recruitment of children for use in armed conflict;

(*b*) the use, procuring or offering of a child for prostitution, for the production of pornography or for pornographic performances;

[AF] « 2 Afin de prévenir la discrimination à l'égard des femmes en raison de leur mariage ou de leur maternité et de garantir leur droit effectif au travail les Etats Parties s'engagent à prendre des mesures appropriés ayant pour objet :
[...]
(*d*) D'assurer une protection spéciale aux femmes enceintes dont il est prouvé que le travail est nocif. »

(*c*) the use, procuring or offering of a child for illicit activities, in particular for the production and trafficking of drugs as defined in the relevant international treaties;

(*d*) work which, by its nature or the circumstances in which it is carried out, is likely to harm the health, safety or morals of children."

Art. 3, WORST FORMS OF CHILD LABOUR CONVENTION (N°182).

WOUNDED [Blessés]

– "For the purposes of this Protocol:

(*a*) 'Wounded' and 'sick' mean persons, whether military or civilian, who, because of trauma, disease or other physical or mental disorder or disability, are in need of medical assistance or care and who refrain from any act of hostility. These terms also cover maternity cases, new-born babies and other persons who may be in need of immediate medical assistance or care, such as the infirm or expectant mothers, and who refrain from any act of hostility;"

Art. 8, PROTOCOL ADDITIONAL TO THE GENEVA CONVENTIONS OF 12 AUGUST 1949, AND RELATING TO THE PROTECTION OF VICTIMS OF INTERNATIONAL ARMED CONFLICTS (PROTOCOL I).

YOUNG PRISONERS [Jeunes détenus]

– "(2) The category of young prisoners should include at least all young persons who come within the jurisdiction of juvenile courts. As a rule, such young persons should not be sentenced to imprisonment."

5, STANDARD MINIMUM RULES FOR THE TREATMENT OF PRISONERS.

YOUTHFUL BEHAVIOUR OR CONDUCT THAT DOES NOT CONFORM TO OVERALL SOCIAL NORMS AND VALUES [Comportement ou la conduite d'un jeune qui n'est pas conforme aux normes et valeurs sociales (le)]

– (e) Consideration that youthful behaviour or conduct that does not conform to overall social norms and values is often part of the maturation and growth process and tends to disappear spontaneously in most individuals with the transition to adulthood;"

5, UNITED NATIONS GUIDELINES FOR THE PREVENTION OF JUVENILE DELINQUENCY (THE RIYADH GUIDELINES).

Human Rights Themes

Child

- Adoption
- All forms of violence against women and girls
- Armed forces of a State
- Avoid harm
- Child
- Child pornography
- Child labour
- Consideration that youthful behaviour or conduct that does not conform to overall social norms and values
- Crimes against humanity
- Due process of law
- Education of the child
- Enslavement
- Factors that make persons [...] vulnerable to trafficking
- Fair and just trial
- Family
- Family education
- Family group
- Foster care
- Freedom
- Gender equality and the empowerment of women
- Girl children
- HIV/AIDS
- Human rights of women and of the girl-child
- Increase in juvenile crime
- Interest of the children (the)
- Juvenile
- Juvenile justice
- Juvenile justice system

- Juvenile offender
- Maternity
- Measures [...] Discriminatory
- Members of the family
- Minimum age of criminal responsibility
- Mothers
- Person of servile status (a)
- Personal representative
- Populations destabilized by armed conflict, humanitarian emergencies and natural disasters
- Possession of personal effects
- Principle of proportionality
- Rights of the child
- Sex tourism
- Sick
- Slavery
- Societal and justice responses to juvenile crime and delinquency
- Stateless
- Traffic in persons and the exploitation of prostitution of others (the)
- Violence against women
- War crimes
- Worst forms of child labour (The)
- Wounded
- Young prisoners

Colonialism

- Aggression, foreign occupation and domination and interference in the internal affairs of States (eradication of)
- Apartheid
- Apartheid (eradication of)
- Circumstances propitious to the development of a great part of mankind
- Colonialism
- Colonialism (eradication of all forms)
- Competent authority
- Continued existence of colonialism
- Crime of apartheid (the)
- Discrimination
- Forced or compulsory labour
- Indigenous peoples

- Mercenaries
- Neo-colonialism (eradication of all forms)
- Primary task of all States and international organizations
- Racial discrimination
- Racial discrimination (eradication of)
- Racism
- Racism (eradication of all forms)
- Right of peoples to self-determination
- Situation of the peoples afflicted by hunger and malnutrition
- Social progress and development
- Subjection of peoples

Corruption
- Fraudulent travel or identity document

Crime against Humanity
- Apartheid
- Crime of apartheid (the)
- Crimes against humanity
- Genocide
- Mistake of law
- Refugee
- Stateless person
-

Culture
- Achievements of the different of the different peoples (differences between)
- Attack directed against any civilian population
- Civil, political, economic, social and cultural rights
- Continued existence of colonialism
- Creation
- Cultural, family, ethnical and religious factors
- Cultural diversity
- Cultural goods and services
- Cultural pluralism
- Cultural policies
- Cultural rights
- Culture
- Defence of cultural diversity

- Democracy
- Development
- Dignity
- Discrimination
- Discrimination against women
- Education of the child
- Enslavement
- Establishment of a lasting peace on Earth
- Family
- Fundamental freedoms
- Globalization
- Grave breaches
- Heritage
- Human rights
- Identity of origin
- Indigenous peoples
- Juvenile justice
- Juvenile offender
- Market forces
- Mental illness
- Peoples
- Process of globalization
- Racial discrimination
- Respect for the diversity of cultures, tolerance, dialogue and cooperation
- Right of peoples to self-determination
- Right to freedom of expression
- Social progress and development
- Specific mandate which has been entrusted to UNESCO
- Tolerance
- War crimes

Democracy
- Acts, methods and practices of terrorism
- Democracy
- Individuals, groups, institutions and non-governmental organizations

Deprivation of liberty
- Act of enforced disappearance
- After care (released prisoner efficient)

- Armed conflicts
- Attack directed against any civilian population
- Crimes against humanity
- Cruel, inhuman or degrading treatment or punishment
- Deportation or forcible transfer of population
- Deprivation of liberty
- Detained person
- Detention
- Detention pending trial
- Dignity
- Enforced disappearance of persons
- Enslavement
- Escape
- Espionage
- Grave breaches
- Human being
- Human person
- Imprisoned person
- Imprisonment
- Internment
- Juvenile
- Members of the armed forces
- Open detention facilities
- Open institutions
- Pre-trial detention
- Prisoners of war
- Purpose and justification of a sentence of imprisonment or a similar measure deprivative of liberty
- Torture
- Untried prisoners
- Violence against women
- War crimes
- Young prisoners

Development
- Africa
- Child labour
- Child pornography
- Child prostitution

- Circumstances propitious to the development of a great part of mankind
- Community
- Continued existence of colonialism
- Cultural diversity
- Culture
- Democracy
- Development
- Disarmament
- Discrimination
- Equality
- Factors that make Persons [...] vulnerable to trafficking
- Full utilization of human resources
- Global HIV/AIDS epidemic
- HIV/AIDS
- Human being
- Human person
- Illiteracy
- International peace and security
- Juvenile justice
- Market forces
- Peoples
- Popular participation
- Poverty
- Primary conditions of social progress and development
- Respect for nature
- Right of peoples to self-determination
- Right to development
- Root socio-economic causes of the smuggling of migrants
- Sale of children
- Shared responsibility
- Social progress
- Social progress and development
- Sub-Saharan Africa
- Transfer of science and technology
- Underdevelopment
- United nations
- Well-being of the peoples of the world

Dignity

- Act of enforced disappearance
- Act of torture
- Armed conflicts
- Cruel, inhuman or degrading treatment or punishment
- Culture
- Defence of cultural diversity
- Dignity
- Discrimination
- Enforced prostitution
- Extreme poverty and social exclusion
- Foundation of freedom, justice and peace in the world
- Freedom
- Fundamental freedoms
- Global HIV/AIDS epidemic
- Grave breaches
- HIV/AIDS
- Human Genome
- Human person
- Human rights
- Humiliating and degrading treatment
- Indecent assault
- Lawyers
- Members of the human family
- Practices of apartheid
- Principle of equality in dignity and rights
- Prosecutors
- Prostitution
- Rape
- Reproductive cloning of human beings
- Research on the human genome and the resulting applications
- Right of everyone to the enjoyment of just and favourable conditions of work
- Scientific and technological achievements
- Social progress and development
- Torture
- War crimes

Disabled

- Counsel
- Disability
- Disabled person
- Discrimination
- Equalization of opportunities
- Handicap
- Impairment
- Independent authority
- Informed consent
- International customary rules
- Measures [...] Discriminatory
- Persons with disabilities
- Present disability policy
- Rehabilitation

Discrimination

- Adverse distinction
- Aggression, foreign occupation and domination and interference in the internal affairs of States (eradication of)
- Apartheid
- Apartheid (eradication of)
- Attack directed against any civilian population
- Child pornography
- Child prostitution
- Circumstances propitious to the development of a great part of mankind
- Colonialism
- Colonialism (eradication of all forms)
- Crime of apartheid (the)
- Crimes against humanity
- Differential rates between workers
- Discrimination
- Discrimination against women
- Doctrine of superiority based on racial differentiation
- Enslavement
- Equal remuneration for men and women workers for work of equal value
- Equalization of opportunities
- Existing disequilibria in international economic relations
- Genocide

- Grave breaches
- Human rights
- Interest of the children (the)
- Intolerance and discrimination based on religion or belief
- National institutions
- Neo-colonialism (eradication of all forms)
- Persecution
- Practices of apartheid
- Principle of the inadmissibility of discrimination
- Racial barriers
- Racial discrimination
- Racial discrimination (eradication of)
- Racism
- Racism (eradication of all forms)
- Research on the human genome and the resulting applications
- Right of everyone to the enjoyment of just and favourable conditions of work
- Sale of children
- Situation of the peoples afflicted by hunger and malnutrition
- Stigma, silence, discrimination and denial, as well as a lack of confidentiality
- Torture
- Violence against women
- Women
- Work

Economy

- Achievements of the different of the different peoples (differences between)
- Africa
- Child labour
- Child pornography
- Child prostitution
- Civil, political, economic, social and cultural rights
- Continued existence of colonialism
- Community
- Creation and strengthening of inalienable sovereignty of states over their natural wealth and resources
- Crimes against humanity

- Cultural diversity
- Cultural goods and services
- Culture
- Debt bondage
- Democracy
- Development
- Differential rates between workers
- Disability
- Disarmament
- Discrimination
- Discrimination against women
- Existing disequilibria in international economic relations
- Extreme poverty
- Extreme poverty and social exclusion
- Factors that make Persons [...] vulnerable to trafficking
- Family
- Freedom of research
- Full utilization of human resources
- Fundamental freedoms
- Global HIV/AIDS epidemic
- Globalization
- Handicap
- Highest aspiration of the common people (the)
- HIV/AIDS
- Human rights
- Impairment
- International peace and security
- Illiteracy
- Indigenous peoples
- Juvenile justice
- Juvenile offender
- Lands
- Marine and inland water resources
- Market forces
- Mental illness
- New international economic order
- Peoples
- Person of servile status (a)
- Poverty

- Present disability policy
- Primary conditions of social progress and development
- Prisoners of war
- Process of globalization
- Racial discrimination
- Racial prejudice
- Respect for nature
- Right of everyone to an adequate standard of living
- Right of peoples to self-determination
- Right to freedom of thought, conscience, religion or belief
- Root socio-economic causes of the smuggling of migrants
- Rural women
- Sale of children
- Shared responsibility
- Slavery
- Social progress
- Social progress and development
- Solidarity
- Sub-Saharan Africa
- Transfer of science and technology
- Tribal peoples
- Underdevelopment
- Violence
- Well-being of the peoples of the world
- Women

Education
- Alcohol
- Armed conflicts
- Child labour
- Child pornography
- Child prostitution
- Civilian objects
- Culture
- Dignity
- Disability
- Discrimination
- Education
- Education of the child

- Family education
- Handicap
- Human Genome
- Illiteracy
- Impairment
- Individuals, non-governmental organizations and relevant institutions
- Interest of the children (the)
- Juvenile
- Labour
- Migrant workers and members of their families
- National institutions
- Person
- Persons with disabilities
- Poverty
- Present disability policy
- Racism
- Right to freedom of thought, conscience, religion or belief
- Right to freedom of thought, conscience and religion
- Sale of children
- Underdevelopment
- Violations of the laws or customs of war
- Violence against women
- War crimes

Environment

- Armed conflicts
- Conflicts and disasters
- Crimes against humanity
- Cultural diversity
- Culture
- Education of the child
- Lands
- Marine and inland water resources
- Natural disasters
- Populations destabilized by armed conflict, humanitarian emergencies and natural disasters
- Prevention
- Respect for nature
- Restitution

Equality

- Culture
- Differential rates between workers
- Discrimination
- Discrimination against women
- Education of the child
- Equal remuneration for men and women workers for work of equal value
- Equalization of opportunities
- Equality
- Foundation of freedom, justice and peace in the world
- Full utilization of human resources
- Gender equality and the empowerment of women
- Handicap
- Human beings
- Human rights
- Interest of the children (the)
- Intolerance and discrimination based on religion or belief
- Mercenaries
- Person
- Persons
- Persons with disabilities
- Primary task of all States and international organizations
- Principle of equal rights
- Principle of equality in dignity and rights
- Principle of the inadmissibility of discrimination
- Racial discrimination
- Right of everyone to the enjoyment of just and favourable conditions of work
- Social progress and development
- Violence

Enforced disappearance

- Enforced disappearance of persons

Family

- Adoption
- Child pornography
- Child prostitution
- Cultural, family, ethnical and religious factors

- Dignity
- Discrimination
- Extended family
- Fair and just trial
- Family
- Family education
- Family group
- Foster care
- Global HIV/AIDS epidemic
- Grave breaches
- HIV/AIDS
- Interest of the children (the)
- Mental illness
- Migrant workers and members of their families
- Migrant workers and members of their families (non-documented or in irregular situation)
- Migrant workers and members of their families (documented or in regular situation)
- Migration
- Migration process of migrant workers and members of their families
- Mothers
- Person of servile status (a)
- Personal representative
- Principle of proportionality
- Prostitution
- Restitution
- Right of everyone to an adequate standard of living
- Right of everyone to the enjoyment of just and favourable conditions of work
- Rural women
- Sale of children
- Self-employed worker
- Slavery
- Social security
- Stigma, silence, discrimination and denial, as well as a lack of confidentiality
- Traffic in persons for the purpose of prostitution
- Violence against women

Freedom

- Informed consent
- Cultural diversity
- Culture
- Democracy
- Detained person
- Dignity
- Education of the child
- Family group
- Foundation of freedom, justice and peace in the world
- Freedom
- Freedom of research
- Fundamental freedoms
- Highest aspiration of the common people (the)
- Human beings
- Judges
- Juvenile
- Members of the human family
- Peoples
- Principle of the inadmissibility of discrimination
- Research on the human genome and the resulting applications
- Religion
- Right to freedom of expression
- Right to freedom of opinion and expression
- Right to freedom of thought, conscience, religion or belief
- Right to freedom of thought, conscience and religion

Gender

- Apartheid (eradication of)
- Adverse distinction
- Armed conflicts
- Attack directed against any civilian population
- Child pornography
- Child prostitution
- Crimes against humanity
- Differential rates between workers
- Discrimination
- Discrimination against women
- Education of the child

- Equal remuneration for men and women workers for work of equal value
- Gender
- Gender equality and the empowerment of women
- HIV/AIDS
- Neo-colonialism (eradication of all forms)
- New international economic order
- Persecution
- Principle of the inadmissibility of discrimination
- Right of everyone to the enjoyment of just and favourable conditions of work
- Sale of children
- Violence against women

Gene
- Dignity
- Human Genome
- Reproductive cloning of human beings
- Research on the human genome and the resulting applications
- Responsibilities inherent in the activities of researchers

Genocide
- Apartheid
- Crimes against humanity
- Criminally responsible
- Disregard and contempt for human rights
- Ethnic cleansing
- Extermination
- Forced pregnancy
- Genocide
- Human rights
- Political crimes
- Systematic rape of women in war situations
- Violence against women

Geography
- Africa
- Asia-Pacific region
- Authorities competent for disposition
- Caribbean region

- Central and Eastern Europe region
- Crimes against humanity
- Deportation or forcible transfer of population
- HIV/AIDS
- Indigenous peoples
- Juvenile justice
- Latin American region
- Persons with disabilities
- Refugee
- Sub-Saharan Africa

Health
- Alcohol
- Alcoholism
- Amoebic or bacillary dysentery with grave disorders
- Armed conflicts
- Arthritis deformans
- Blindness of both eyes, or of one eye
- Bronchiectasis
- Caribbean region
- Central and Eastern Europe region
- Choroiditis
- Chronic asthma
- Chronic bronchitis lasting more than one year in captivity
- Chronic cholecystopathy
- Chronic diseases of the kidney with consequent disorders
- Chronic gastritis, enteritis or colitis, having lasted more than one year and seriously affecting the general condition
- Chronic grave gynaecological conditions
- Chronic pyelitis or chronic cystitis
- Cirrhosis of the liver
- Civil defence
- Civil defence organizations
- Cocainism
- Corporal punishment
- Crimes against humanity
- Cultural, family, ethnical and religious factors
- Diabetes mellitus requiring insulin treatment
- Disability

- Disabled person
- Distinctive emblem
- Enslavement
- Equivalent to the loss of a hand or a foot
- Extermination
- Family
- Forced or compulsory labour
- Gas or radiation poisoning
- Gastric or duodenal ulcer
- Glaucoma
- Global HIV/AIDS epidemic
- Grave breaches
- Handicap
- HIV/AIDS
- Hors de combat
- Human Genome
- Hydronephrosis or pyonephrosis
- Impairment
- Informed consent
- Iritis
- Lead poisoning
- Latin American region
- Leprosy
- Malaria
- Malaria with decided organic impairment
- Matériel
- Measures […] Discriminatory
- Medical aircraft
- Medical attention
- Medical or scientific experimentation
- Medical or scientific experiments not necessitated by the medical treatment
- Medical personnel
- Medical ships and craft
- Medical transportation
- Medical units
- Medical vehicles
- Members of the armed forces
- Mental health care

- Mental health facility
- Mental illness
- Mental health practitioner
- Mercury poisoning
- Morphinism
- Murder
- Mutilation
- Nephrectomy because of a tubercular kidney
- Non-custodial measures
- Non-custodial measures (the introduction, definition and application of)
- Normal pregnancy, and obstetrical disorder, where it is impossible to accommodate in a neutral country
- Patient
- Permanent medical personnel
- Permanent medical transports
- Permanent medical units
- Personnel
- Persons with disabilities
- Prevention
- Primary and secondary progressive chronic polyarthritis
- Prisoners of war
- Rehabilitation
- Religious personnel
- Responsibilities inherent in the activities of researchers
- Review body (the)
- Rheumatism with serious clinical symptoms
- Right of everyone to the enjoyment of just and favourable conditions of work
- Right to freedom of thought, conscience, religion or belief
- Sequelae of gastric operations performed in captivity
- Serious pulmonary emphysema, with or without bronchitis
- Sick
- Social security
- Stigma, silence, discrimination and denial, as well as a lack of confidentiality
- Temporary medical personnel
- Temporary medical transports
- Temporary medical units
- Tertiary visceral syphilis resistant to treatment
- Torture

- Trachoma
- War crimes
- Worst forms of child labour (The)
- Wounded

HIV/AIDS

- Africa
- All forms of violence against women and girls
- Armed conflicts
- Asia-Pacific region
- Caribbean region
- Central and Eastern Europe region
- Conflicts and disasters
- Cultural, family, ethnical and religious factors
- Family
- Gender equality and the empowerment of women
- Global HIV/AIDS epidemic
- HIV/AIDS
- Illiteracy
- Latin American region
- Malaria
- Natural disasters
- Populations destabilized by armed conflict, humanitarian emergencies and natural disasters
- Poverty
- Realization of human rights and fundamental freedoms for all
- Stigma, silence, discrimination and denial, as well as a lack of confidentiality
- Sub-Saharan Africa
- Underdevelopment

Housing

- Civilian objects
- Matériel
- Right of everyone to an adequate standard of living

Human being

- Act of enforced disappearance

- Act of torture
- Apartheid
- Child
- Colonialism
- Community
- Cruel, inhuman or degrading treatment or punishment
- Culture
- Defence of cultural diversity
- Dignity
- Disability
- Discrimination
- Education
- Equality
- Everyone
- Extreme poverty
- Extreme poverty and social exclusion
- Factors that make Persons [...] vulnerable to trafficking
- Foundation of freedom, justice and peace in the world
- Freedom
- Fundamental freedoms
- Handicap
- Highest aspiration of the common people (the)
- HIV/AIDS
- Humiliating and degrading treatment
- Human being
- Human beings
- Human Genome
- Human person
- Human rights
- Human rights of women and of the girl-child
- Identity of Origin
- Individual
- Individuals, groups, institutions and non-governmental organizations
- Individuals, non-governmental organizations and relevant institutions
- Man
- Medical or scientific experimentation
- Neo-colonialism (eradication of all forms)
- Person
- Principle of equality in dignity and rights

- Principle of the inadmissibility of discrimination
- Prostitution
- Racial discrimination
- Racial discrimination (eradication of)
- Racism
- Racism (eradication of all forms)
- Reproductive cloning of human beings
- Research on the human genome and the resulting applications
- Right to freedom of expression
- Right to development
- Scientific and technological achievements
- Social progress and development
- Tolerance
- Torture
- Traffic in persons for the purpose of prostitution

Humanitarian

- Armed conflicts
- Civil defence
- Civil defence organizations
- Crimes against humanity
- Distinctive emblem
- Distinctive signal
- Grave breaches
- International Committee of the Red Cross
- Matériel
- Medical personnel
- Medical ships and craft
- Medical transportation
- Medical units
- Medical vehicles
- Members of the armed forces
- National Red Cross
- Permanent medical personnel
- Permanent medical transports
- Permanent medical units
- Personnel
- Populations destabilized by armed conflict, humanitarian emergencies and natural disasters

- Prisoners of war
- Religious personnel
- Right to freedom of thought, conscience, religion or belief
- Substitute
- Temporary medical personnel
- Temporary medical transports
- Temporary medical units

Humanity
- Circumstances propitious to the development of a great part of mankind
- Cultural diversity
- Culture
- Dignity
- Disregard and infringement of human rights and fundamental freedoms
- Establishment of a lasting peace on Earth
- Foundation of freedom, justice and peace in the world
- Genocide
- Globalization
- Heritage
- HIV/AIDS
- Human beings
- Human Genome
- Human person
- Malaria
- Members of the human family
- Personnel
- Racial or ethnic superiority/inferiority (theory)
- Research on the human genome and the resulting applications
- Tolerance
- United nations

Identity
- Cultural diversity
- Cultural pluralism
- Culture
- Dignity
- Education of the child
- Identity of Origin

Justice

- Accused
- Adjudicating authority
- Appropriate authorities or organs vested with reviewing or remedial power
- Authorities competent for disposition
- Child
- Competent authority
- Counsel
- Crime of agression
- Crimes against humanity
- Criminal responsibility
- Cruel, inhuman or degrading treatment or punishment
- Death penalty
- Deprivation of liberty
- Detained person
- Detention
- Detention pending trial
- Dignity
- Due process of law
- Fair and just trial
- Forced or compulsory labour
- Foundation of freedom, justice and peace in the world
- Grave breaches
- Imprisoned person
- Imprisonment
- International criminal court
- Judicial or other authority (a)
- Judges
- Judiciary
- Juvenile
- Juvenile justice
- Juvenile justice system
- Juvenile offender
- Knowledge
- Law enforcement officials
- Lawyers
- Mass media
- Measures [...] Discriminatory

- Members of the human family
- Mistake of fact
- Mistake of law
- Mutilation
- National institutions
- New international economic order
- Offence
- Offenders
- Political crimes
- Presumed innocent
- Pre-trial detention
- Prosecutors
- Purpose and justification of a sentence of imprisonment or a similar measure deprivative of liberty
- Rights of the child
- Review body (the)
- Social progress and development
- Societal and justice responses to juvenile crime and delinquency
- Surrender
- Threat to the life and safety of law enforcement officials
- Victim
- Victims
- Violence
- War crimes
- Young prisoners

Labour
- Child labour
- Dignity
- Discrimination
- Employment
- Equal remuneration for men and women workers for work of equal value
- Exploitation
- Forced or compulsory labour
- Frontier worker
- Itinerant worker
- Labour
- Members of the family
- Mental illness

- Migrant workers
- Migrant workers and members of their families
- Migrant workers and members of their families (documented or in regular situation)
- Migrant workers and members of their families (non-documented or in irregular situation)
- Occupation
- Organisation
- Person
- Person of servile status (a)
- Persons with disabilities
- Prisoners of war
- Project-tied worker
- Rehabilitation
- Removal of mines
- Remuneration
- Right of everyone to the enjoyment of just and favourable conditions of work
- Right to freedom of thought, conscience, religion or belief
- Right to work
- Rural women
- Seafarer
- Seasonal worker
- Self-employed worker
- Serfdom
- Slavery
- Social security
- Specified-employment worker
- State of employment
- State of origin
- State of transit
- Violence against women
- Women
- Work
- Worker on an offshore installation
- Worst forms of child labour (The)

Language

- Adverse distinction

- Civil, political, economic, social and cultural rights
- Constant promotion and realization of the rights of persons belonging to national or ethnic, religious and linguistic minorities
- Discrimination
- Education of the child
- Informed consent
- Promotion and protection of all Human rights and fundamental freedoms
- Promotion and protection of the rights of persons belonging to national or ethnic, religious and linguistic minorities
- Tolerance

Marriage
- Certain customs, ancient laws and practices relating to marriage and the family
- Discrimination against women
- Family
- Family group
- Interest of the children (the)
- Marriage
- Members of the family
- Person of servile status (a)
- Slavery
- Work

Mental integrity
- Attack directed against any civilian population
- Corporal punishment
- Criminal responsibility
- Crimes against humanity
- Cruel, inhuman or degrading treatment or punishment
- Disability
- Disabled person
- Discrimination
- Education of the child
- Enslavement
- Genocide
- Grave breaches
- Handicap
- Informed consent

- Mental health care
- Mental health facility
- Mental health practitioner
- Mental illness
- Minimum age of criminal responsibility
- Mistake of fact
- Mistake of law
- Murder
- Mutilation
- Non-custodial measures
- Non-custodial measures (the introduction, definition and application of)
- Patient
- Persons with disabilities
- Prevention
- Rehabilitation
- Review body (the)
- Sick
- Social security
- Torture
- Victims
- Violence against women
- Wounded

Migrant

- Dignity
- Exploitation
- Family
- Forced or compulsory labour
- Fraudulent travel or identity document
- Frontier worker
- Illegal entry
- Itinerant worker
- Members of the family
- Migrant workers
- Migrant workers and members of their families
- Migrant workers and members of their families (documented or in regular situation)
- Migrant workers and members of their families (non-documented or in irregular situation)

- Migration
- Migration process of migrant workers and members of their families
- Project-tied worker
- Root socio-economic causes of the smuggling of migrants
- Seafarer
- Seasonal worker
- Self-employed worker
- Smuggling of migrants
- Specified-employment worker
- State of employment
- State of origin
- State of transit
- Worker on an offshore installation

Minority
- Apartheid
- Apartheid (eradication of)
- Colonialism
- Constant promotion and realization of the rights of persons belonging to national or ethnic, religious and linguistic minorities
- Crimes against humanity
- Defence of cultural diversity
- Discrimination
- Education of the child
- Forced or compulsory labour
- Indigenous peoples
- Lands
- Promotion and protection of all Human rights and fundamental freedoms
- Promotion and protection of the rights of persons belonging to national or ethnic, religious and linguistic minorities
- Racial discrimination
- Racism
- Restitution

Nation
- Achievements of the different of the different peoples (differences between)
- Attack directed against any civilian population
- Circumstances propitious to the development of a great part of mankind

- Dignity
- Discrimination
- Disregard and infringement of human rights and fundamental freedoms
- Education
- Education of the child
- Equality
- Global HIV/AIDS epidemic
- Human rights
- Individuals, non-governmental organizations and relevant institutions
- Persecution
- Primary conditions of social progress and development
- Promotion and protection of all Human rights and fundamental freedoms
- Promotion and protection of the rights of persons belonging to national or ethnic, religious and linguistic minorities
- Constant promotion and realization of the rights of persons belonging to national or ethnic, religious and linguistic minorities
- Purposes and principles of Charter of the United Nations
- Racism
- Rights of the child
- Scientific and technological achievements
- Shared responsibility
- Stigma, silence, discrimination and denial, as well as a lack of confidentiality
- Tribal peoples
- Universal declaration of human rights
- War crimes
-

Nationality

- Alien
- Country of his nationality (the)
- Discrimination
- Enslavement
- Family group
- Grave breaches
- Migrant workers and members of their families
- Persecution
- Populations destabilized by armed conflict, humanitarian emergencies and natural disasters
- Racial discrimination

- Refugee
- Seafarer
- Smuggling of migrants
- Stateless
- Stateless person
- Systematic rape of women in war situations
- War crimes
- Worker on an offshore installation

Norm

- Act of torture
- Armed conflicts
- Authorities competent for disposition
- Certain customs, ancient laws and practices relating to marriage and the family
- Child
- Consideration that youthful behaviour or conduct that does not conform to overall social norms and values
- Crime of agression
- Crimes against humanity
- Cruel, inhuman or degrading treatment or punishment
- Cultural, family, ethnical and religious factors
- Culture
- Debt bondage
- Defence of cultural diversity
- Demilitarezed Zones
- Dignity
- Distinctive signal
- Education of the child
- Enslavement
- Ethnic cleansing
- Extreme poverty and social exclusion
- Family
- Foundation of freedom, justice and peace in the world
- Full utilization of human resources
- Fundamental freedoms
- Genocide
- Grave breaches
- High commissioner for human rights

- Human rights
- Individual
- Individuals, groups, institutions and non-governmental organizations
- International Covenants on Human Rights
- International customary rules
- Life without war
- Medical transportation
- Members of the human family
- Person of servile status (a)
- Primary conditions of social progress and development
- Prisoners of war
- Protecting power
- Purposes and principles of Charter of the United Nations
- Rebellion against and oppression
- Rules of international law applicable in armed conflict
- Rural women
- Self-employed worker
- Serfdom
- Shipwrecked
- Slavery
- Slave
- Subjection of peoples
- Torture
- Universal declaration of human rights
- Violence
- War crimes

Older people

- Consideration that youthful behaviour or conduct that does not conform to overall social norms and values
- Discrimination
- Measures [...] Discriminatory
- Older persons

Peace

- Apartheid
- Armed conflicts
- Continued existence of colonialism
- Crimes against humanity
- Cultural pluralism

- Dignity
- Discrimination
- Education
- Education of the child
- Establishment of a lasting peace on Earth
- Foundation of freedom, justice and peace in the world
- Genocide
- Individuals, non-governmental organizations and relevant institutions
- International peace and security
- Juvenile justice
- Members of the human family
- Racism
- Refugee
- Respect for the diversity of cultures, tolerance, dialogue and cooperation
- Shared responsibility
- Social progress
- Stateless person
- Subjection of peoples
- Tolerance
- United nations
- War crimes
-

Penal

- Accused
- Act of corruption
- After care (released prisoner efficient)
- Arrest
- Attack directed against any civilian population
- Avoid harm
- Child pornography
- Corporal punishment
- Corruption
- Crime
- Crimes against humanity
- Criminally responsible
- Death penalty
- Deportation or forcible transfer of population
- Deprivation of liberty
- Detained person
- Detention
- Detention pending trial

- Disregard and contempt for human rights
- Due process of law
- Enforced disappearance of persons
- Fair and just trial
- Fraudulent travel or identity document
- Genocide
- Grave breaches
- Human rights
- Imprisoned person
- Imprisonment
- Increase in juvenile crime
- Intent
- International criminal court
- Judges
- Juvenile
- Juvenile justice
- Juvenile justice system
- Juvenile offender
- Knowledge
- Law enforcement officials
- Minimum age of criminal responsibility
- Mistake of law
- Murder
- Offenders
- Persecution
- Political crimes
- Presumed innocent
- Pre-trial detention
- Principle of proportionality
- Purpose and justification of a sentence of imprisonment or a similar measure deprivative of liberty
- Restitution
- Riots
- Societal and justice responses to juvenile crime and delinquency
- Surrender
- Sexual slavery
- Torture
- Untried prisoners
- Victims
- Young prisoners

Peoples

- Achievements of the different of the different peoples (differences between)
- Continued existence of colonialism
- Criminal responsibility
- Democracy
- Development
- Disarmament
- Discrimination
- Disregard and infringement of human rights and fundamental freedoms
- Education of the child
- Indigenous peoples
- Lands
- Peoples
- Primary conditions of social progress and development
- Principle of equal rights
- Promotion and protection of all Human rights and fundamental freedoms
- Purposes and principles of Charter of the United Nations
- Racism
- Right of peoples to self-determination
- Situation of the peoples afflicted by hunger and malnutrition
- Social progress and development
- Subjection of peoples
- Tribal peoples
- Universal declaration of human rights
- Well-being of the peoples of the world

Physical integrity

- Amoebic or bacillary dysentery with grave disorders
- Armed conflicts
- Attack directed against any civilian population
- Bronchiectasis
- Chronic asthma
- Chronic bronchitis lasting more than one year in captivity
- Corporal punishment
- Crimes against humanity
- Criminal responsibility
- Cruel, inhuman or degrading treatment or punishment
- Diabetes mellitus requiring insulin treatment
- Disability
- Disabled person

- Education of the child
- Enforced sterilization
- Enslavement
- Equivalent to the loss of a hand or a foot
- Forced pregnancy
- Genocide
- Glaucoma
- Grave breaches
- Handicap
- Indiscriminate attacks
- Leprosy
- Malaria with decided organic impairment
- Medical or scientific experiments not necessitated by the medical treatment
- Murder
- Mutilation
- Non-custodial measures
- Non-custodial measures (the introduction, definition and application of)
- Persons with disabilities
- Prevention
- Rehabilitation
- Serious pulmonary emphysema, with or without bronchitis
- Sexual violence
- Social security
- Tertiary visceral syphilis resistant to treatment
- Torture
- Trachoma
- Victims
- Violence against women
- War crimes
- Wounded

Politics

- Adverse distinction
- Africa
- Attack directed against any civilian population
- Civil, political, economic, social and cultural rights
- Community
- Crimes against humanity
- Cultural pluralism
- Cultural policies

- Democracy
- Development
- Discrimination
- Discrimination against women
- Enforced disappearance of persons
- Family
- Human rights
- Indigenous peoples
- International Covenants on Human Rights
- Mental illness
- Mercenaries
- Peoples
- Political crimes
- Present disability policy
- Primary conditions of social progress and development
- Racial discrimination
- Right of peoples to self-determination
- Right to freedom of opinion and expression
- Social progress and development
- Sub-Saharan Africa
- Well-being of the peoples of the world

Poor country
- Africa
- Disarmament
- Development
- HIV/AIDS
- Root socio-economic causes of the smuggling of migrants
- Situation of the peoples afflicted by hunger and malnutrition
- Sub-Saharan Africa
- Transfer of science and technology
- Underdevelopment
- Well-being of the peoples of the world

Positive action
- Indiscriminate attacks
- Discrimination
- Grave breaches
- Measures […] Discriminatory
- Racial discrimination
- War crimes

Race

- Adverse distinction
- Aggression, foreign occupation and domination and interference in the internal affairs of States (eradication of)
- Apartheid
- Armed conflicts
- Attack directed against any civilian population
- Circumstances propitious to the development of a great part of mankind
- Civil, political, economic, social and cultural rights
- Colonialism
- Colonialism (eradication of all forms)
- Constant promotion and realization of the rights of persons belonging to national or ethnic, religious and linguistic minorities
- Crimes against humanity
- Crime of apartheid (the)
- Discrimination
- Doctrine of superiority based on racial differentiation
- Education
- Enslavement
- Eradication of apartheid
- Ethnic cleansing
- Existing disequilibria in international economic relations
- Family
- Family group
- Genocide
- HIV/AIDS
- Individuals, non-governmental organizations and relevant institutions
- Mental illness
- National institutions
- Neo-colonialism (eradication of all forms)
- Persecution
- Practices of apartheid
- Principle of equality in dignity and rights
- Primary task of all States and international organizations
- Promotion and protection of all Human rights and fundamental freedoms
- Promotion and protection of the rights of persons belonging to national or ethnic, religious and linguistic minorities
- Racial barriers
- Racial discrimination
- Racial discrimination (eradication of)

- Racial or ethnic superiority/inferiority (theory)
- Racial prejudice
- Racism
- Racism (eradication of all forms)
- Refugee
- Sexual violence
- Situation of the peoples afflicted by hunger and malnutrition
- Social progress and development
- Systematic rape of women in war situations

Red Cross
- Armed conflicts
- Distinctive emblem
- Distinctive signal
- Graves breaches
- International committee of the Red Cross
- Medical personnel
- Medical transports
- National Red Cross
- Prisoners of war
- Substitute
- War crimes

Relativism
- Achievements of the different of the different peoples (differences between)
- Child
- Cultural, family, ethnical and religious factors
- Cultural diversity
- Cultural pluralism
- Culture
- Defence of cultural diversity
- Dignity
- Family
- Gender
- Handicap
- Heritage
- Human rights
- Identity of Origin
- Individuals, non-governmental organizations and relevant institutions

- Juvenile offender
- Offence
- Older persons
- Minimum age of criminal responsibility
- Tolerance
- Universal declaration of human rights
-

Sex

- All forms of violence against women and girls
- Armed conflicts
- Attack directed against any civilian population
- Child pornography
- Child prostitution
- Crimes against humanity
- Enforced prostitution
- Enforced sterilization
- Enslavement
- Ethnic cleansing
- Exploitation
- Forced pregnancy
- Genocide
- Girl children
- Humiliating and degrading treatment
- Indecent assault
- Prostitution
- Rape
- Sale of children
- Sex tourism
- Sexual slavery
- Sexual violence
- Systematic rape of women in war situations
- Torture
- Traffic in persons and the exploitation of prostitution of others (the)
- Traffic in persons for the purpose of prostitution
- Violence against women
- War crimes
- Worst forms of child labour (The)

Slavery

- All forms of violence against women and girls
- Attack directed against any civilian population
- Child prostitution
- Crimes against humanity
- Debt bondage
- Deportation or forcible transfer of population
- Enforced prostitution
- Enslavement
- Exploitation
- Factors that make Persons [...] vulnerable to trafficking
- Forced or compulsory labour
- Forced pregnancy
- Girl children
- Person of servile status (a)
- Primary task of all States and international organizations
- Prostitution
- Racial discrimination
- Rape
- Sale of children
- Slave trade
- Serfdom
- Sexual slavery
- Sexual violence
- Slavery
- Torture
- Traffic in persons for the purpose of prostitution
- Traffic in persons and the exploitation of prostitution of others (the)
- Violence against women
- War crimes
- Worst forms of child labour (The)

Social

- Achievements of the different of the different peoples (differences between)
- Africa
- Child pornography
- Child prostitution
- Civil, political, economic, social and cultural rights

- Community
- Consideration that youthful behaviour or conduct that does not conform to overall social norms and values
- Continued existence of colonialism
- Cultural pluralism
- Culture
- Democracy
- Development
- Disability
- Disarmament
- Discrimination
- Discrimination against women
- Doctrine of superiority based on racial differentiation
- Everyone
- Extreme poverty
- Extreme poverty and social exclusion
- Family
- Family education
- Full utilization of human resources
- Fundamental freedoms
- Global HIV/AIDS epidemic
- HIV/AIDS
- Human Genome
- Human rights
- Indigenous peoples
- Individuals, groups, institutions and non-governmental organizations
- Interest of the children (the)
- International peace and security
- Juvenile justice
- Juvenile offender
- Man
- Mental health practitioner
- Mental illness
- Minimum age of criminal responsibility
- Peoples
- Persons with disabilities
- Present disability policy
- Primary conditions of social progress and development
- Primary task of all States and international organizations

- Principle of proportionality
- Process of globalization
- Racial discrimination
- Racial prejudice
- Refugee
- Rehabilitation
- Responsibilities inherent in the activities of researchers
- Right of peoples to self-determination
- Root socio-economic causes of the smuggling of migrants
- Sale of children
- Shared responsibility
- Situation of the peoples afflicted by hunger and malnutrition
- Social progress
- Social progress and development
- Social security
- Solidarity
- Sub-Saharan Africa
- Tribal peoples
- Violence
- Violence against women

Spirituality
- Adverse distinction
- Armed conflicts
- Attack directed against any civilian population
- Belief
- Civil, political, economic, social and cultural rights
- Civil defence
- Civil defence organizations
- Constant promotion and realization of the rights of persons belonging to national or ethnic, religious and linguistic minorities
- Crimes against humanity
- Cultural diversity
- Cultural, family, ethnical and religious factors
- Culture
- Discrimination
- Disregard and infringement of human rights and fundamental freedoms
- Distinctive emblem
- Education

- Education of the child
- Enslavement
- Family
- Family group
- Genocide
- Grave breaches
- Human rights
- Individuals, non-governmental organizations and relevant institutions
- Intolerance and discrimination based on religion or belief
- Matériel
- Medical transportation
- Members of the armed forces
- Persecution
- Personnel
- Prisoners of war
- Promotion and protection of all Human rights and fundamental freedoms
- Promotion and protection of the rights of persons belonging to national or ethnic, religious and linguistic minorities
- Refugee
- Religion
- Religious personnel
- Right to freedom of thought, conscience, religion or belief
- Right to freedom of thought, conscience and religion
- Tolerance
- Violations of the laws or customs of war
- War crimes

Sustenance
- Africa
- Crimes against humanity
- Extermination
- Freedom
- Grave breaches
- Human Genome
- Marine and inland water resources
- Prevention
- Right of everyone to an adequate standard of living
- Situation of the peoples afflicted by hunger and malnutrition
- Sub-Saharan Africa

- Well-being of the peoples of the world

Tolerance
- Education
- Education of the child
- Individuals, non-governmental organizations and relevant institutions
- Respect for the diversity of cultures, tolerance, dialogue and cooperation
- Tolerance

Torture
- Act of torture
- Armed conflicts
- Attack directed against any civilian population
- Corporal punishment
- Crimes against humanity
- Cruel, inhuman or degrading treatment or punishment
- Enforced prostitution
- Enslavement
- Forced pregnancy
- Grave breaches
- Human rights
- Humiliating and degrading treatment
- Indecent assault
- Medical or scientific experimentation
- Medical or scientific experiments not necessitated by the medical treatment
- Murder
- Mutilation
- Torture

United Nations Organisations
- Armed conflicts
- Certain customs, ancient laws and practices relating to marriage and the family
- Constant promotion and realization of the rights of persons belonging to national or ethnic, religious and linguistic minorities
- Continued existence of colonialism
- Crime of agression
- Crimes against humanity
- Cruel, inhuman or degrading treatment or punishment

- Dignity
- Disability
- Discrimination
- Education
- Education of the child
- Family
- Foundation of freedom, justice and peace in the world
- Full utilization of human resources
- Fundamental freedoms
- General assembly
- Genocide
- Handicap
- High commissioner for human rights
- Human rights
- Impairment
- Individuals, groups, institutions and non-governmental organizations
- International Covenants on Human Rights
- International criminal court
- Life without war
- Migrant workers and members of their families
- Members of the human family
- National institutions
- Primary conditions of social progress and development
- Primary task of all States and international organizations
- Purposes and principles of Charter of the United Nation
- Refugee
- Shared responsibility
- Social progress and development
- Specific mandate which has been entrusted to UNESCO
- Stateless person
- Subjection of peoples
- Torture
- Universal declaration of human rights

War

- Acts harmful to the enemy (not be considered)
- Aggression, foreign occupation and domination and interference in the internal affairs of States (eradication of)
- Armed conflict

- Armed conflicts
- Armed forces
- Armed forces of a State
- Attack directed against any civilian population
- Attacks
- Child pornography
- Child prostitution
- Civil defence
- Civil defence organizations
- Civilian objects
- Civilian population
- Conflicts and disasters
- Contact zone
- Corporal punishment
- Crime of agression
- Crimes against humanity
- Criminal responsibility
- Cruel, inhuman or degrading treatment or punishment
- Death penalty
- Demilitarezed Zones
- Disarmament
- Disregard and infringement of human rights and fundamental freedoms
- Escape
- Espionage
- Establishment of a lasting peace on Earth
- Ethnic cleansing
- Forced or compulsory labour
- Forcible transfers
- Genocide
- Grave breaches
- Hors de combat
- Human person
- International Committee of the Red Cross
- Indiscriminate attacks
- Life without war
- Matériel
- Medical or scientific experiments not necessitated by the medical treatment
- Medical personnel

- Medical transports
- Medical vehicles
- Members of the armed forces
- Mercenaries
- Mercenary
- Mutilation
- Murder
- National Red Cross
- Non-defended locality
- Occupation
- Perfidy
- Permanent medical personnel
- Permanent medical transports
- Permanent medical units
- Personnel
- Populations destabilized by armed conflict, humanitarian emergencies and natural disasters
- Prevention
- Primary task of all States and international organizations
- Prisoners of war
- Protecting power
- Refugee
- Religious personnel
- Removal of mines
- Riots
- Rules of international law applicable in armed conflict
- Ruses of war
- Sale of children
- Scientific and technological achievements
- Shipwrecked
- Sick
- Stateless person
- Substitute
- Systematic rape of women in war situations
- Temporary medical personnel
- Temporary medical transports
- Temporary medical units
- Torture
- Violations of the laws or customs of war

- War
- War crimes
- Worst forms of child labour (The)
- Wounded

Woman

- All forms of violence against women and girls
- Chronic grave gynaecological conditions
- Crimes against humanity
- Discrimination against women
- Enslavement
- Equal remuneration for men and women workers for work of equal value
- Equality
- Factors that make Persons […] vulnerable to trafficking
- Family education
- Forced pregnancy
- Gender
- Gender equality and the empowerment of women
- Genocide
- Girl children
- HIV/AIDS
- Human rights of women and of the girl-child
- Interest of the children (the)
- Maternity
- Measures […] Discriminatory
- Mothers
- Normal pregnancy, and obstetrical disorder, where it is impossible to accommodate in a neutral country
- Person of servile status (a)
- Populations destabilized by armed conflict, humanitarian emergencies and natural disasters
- Rape
- Right of everyone to the enjoyment of just and favourable conditions of work
- Rural women
- Sick
- Slavery
- Systematic rape of women in war situations
- Violence

- Violence against women
- Women
- Work
- Wounded

Relevant Documents

Abolition of Forced Labour Convention, N° 105 (25 June 1957)

Basic Principles for the Treatment of Prisoners (14 December 1990)

Basic Principles on the Independence of the Judiciary (29 November 1985, 13 December 1985)

Basic Principles on the Role of Lawyers (27 August-7 September 1990)

Basic Principles on the Use of Force and Firearms by Law Enforcement Officials (27 August-7 September 1990)

Body of Principles for the Protection of All Persons under Any Form of Detention or Imprisonment (9 December 1988)

Code of Conduct for Law Enforcement Officials (17 December 1979)

Convention against Discrimination in Education (14 December 1960)

Convention against Torture and Other Cruel, Inhuman or Degrading Treatment or Punishment (10 December 1984)

Convention for the Suppression of the Traffic in Persons and of the Exploitation of the Prostitution of Others (2 December 1949)

Convention on Consent to Marriage, Minimum Age for Marriage and Registration of Marriages (7 November 1962)

Convention on the Elimination of All Forms of Discrimination against Women (18 December 1979)

Convention on the Non-Applicability of Statutory Limitations to War Crimes and Crimes against Humanity (26 November 1968)

Convention on the Prevention and Punishment of the Crime of Genocide (9 December 1948)

Convention on the Reduction of Statelessness (4 December 1954)

Convention on the Rights of the Child (20 November 1989)

Convention relating to the Status of Refugees (14 December 1950)

Convention relating to the Status of Stateless Persons (26 April 1954)

Declaration of Basic Principles of Justice for Victims of Crime and Abuse of Power (29 November 1985)

Declaration of Commitment on HIV/AIDS (27 June 2001)

Declaration on Race and Racial Prejudice (27 November 1978)

Declaration on Social Progress and Development (11 December 1969)

Declaration on the Elimination of All Forms of Intolerance and of Discrimination Based on Religion or Belief (25 November 1981)

Declaration on the Elimination of Violence against Women (20 December 1993)

Declaration on the Human Rights of Individuals Who are not Nationals of the Country in which They Live (13 December 1985)

Declaration on the Protection of All Persons from Being Subjected to Torture and Other Cruel, Inhuman or Degrading Treatment or Punishment (9 December 1975)

Declaration on the Protection of All Persons from Enforced Disappearance (18 December 1992)

Declaration on the Protection of Women and Children in Emergency and Armed Conflict (14 December 1974)

Declaration on the Right and Responsibility of Individuals, Groups and Organs of Society to Promote and Project Universally Recognized Human Rights and Fundamental Freedoms (9 December 1998)

Declaration on the Right of Peoples to Peace (12 November 1984)

Declaration on the Right to Development (4 December 1986)

Declaration on the Rights of Disabled Persons (9 December 1975)

Declaration on the Rights of Mentally Retarded Persons (20 December 1971)

Declaration on the Rights of Persons Belonging to National or Ethnic, Religious and Linguistic Minorities (18 December 1992)

Declaration on the Use of Scientific and Technological Progress in the Interests of Peace and for the Benefit of Mankind (6 November 1975)

Discrimination (Employment and Occupation) Convention N° 111 (25 June 1958)

Employment Policy Convention, N° 122 (9 July 1964)

Equal Remuneration Convention, N° 100 (29 June 1951)

Forced Labour Convention, N°29 (28 June 1930)

Freedom of Association and Protection of the Right to Organise Convention, N° 87 (9 July 1948)

General Assembly resolution 1803 (XVII) of 14 December 1962, "Permanent sovereignty over natural resources" (14 December 1962)

Geneva Convention relative to the Protection of Civilian Persons in Time of War (21 April-12 August 1949)

Geneva Convention relative to the Treatment of Prisoners of War (22 September 1949)

Guidelines for Action on Children in the Criminal Justice System (21 July 1997)

Guidelines on the Role of Prosecutors (27 August-7 September 1990)

Indigenous and Tribal Peoples, N° 169, (27 June 1989)

International Covenant on Civil and Political Rights (16 December 1966)

International Covenant on Economic, Social and Cultural Rights (16 December 1966)

International Convention against the Recruitment, Use, Financing and Training of Mercenaries (4 December 1989)

International Convention on the Elimination of all Forms of Racial Discrimination (21 November 1965)

International Convention on the Protection of the Rights of All Migrant Workers and Members of Their Families (18 December 1990)

Minimum Age Convention, N° 138 (26 June 1973)

Optional Protocol to the Convention against Torture and Other Cruel, Inhuman or Degrading Treatment or Punishment (18 December 2002)

Optional Protocol to the Convention on the Elimination of All Forms of Discrimination against Women (10 December 1999)

Optional Protocol to the Convention on the Rights of the Child on the involvement of children in armed conflict (25 May 2000)

Optional Protocol to the Convention on the Rights of the Child on the sale of children, child prostitution and child pornography (25 May 2000)

Optional Protocol to the International Covenant on Civil and Political Rights (16 December 1966)

Principles for the protection of persons with mental illness and the improvement of mental health care (17 December 1991)

Principles of international co-operation in the detection, arrest, extradition and punishment of persons guilty of war crimes and crimes against humanity (3 December 1973)

Principles of Medical Ethics relevant to the Role of Health Personnel, particularly Physicians, in the Protection of Prisoners and Detainees against Torture and Other Cruel, Inhuman or Degrading Treatment or Punishment (18 December 1982)

Principles on the Effective Investigation and Documentation of Torture and Other Cruel, Inhuman or Degrading Treatment or Punishment (4 December 2000)

Principles on the Effective Prevention and Investigation of Extra-legal, Arbitrary and Summary Executions (24 May 1989)

Principles relating to the status of national institutions (The Paris Principles) (20 December 1993)

Protocol Additional to the Geneva Conventions of 12 August 1949, and relating to the Protection of Victims of International Armed Conflicts (Protocol I)(8 June 1977)

Protocol Additional to the Geneva Conventions of 12 August 1949, and relating to the Protection of Victims of Non-International Armed Conflicts (Protocol I)(8 June 1977)

Protocol against the Smuggling of Migrants by Land, Sea and Air, supplementing the United Nations Convention against Transnational Organized Crime (15 November 2000)

Protocol amending the Slavery Convention signed at Geneva on 25 September 1926 (25 September 1953)

Protocol Instituting a Conciliation and Good Offices Commission to be responsible for seeking a settlement of any disputes which may arise between States Parties to the Convention against Discrimination in Education (10 December 1962)

Protocol relating to the Status of Refugees (18 November 1966)

Protocol to Prevent, Suppress and Punish Trafficking in Persons, Especially Women and Children, supplementing the United Nations Convention against Transnational Organized Crime (15 December 2000)

Recommendation on Consent to Marriage, Minimum Age for Marriage and Registration of Marriages (1 November 1965)

Right to Organise and Collective Bargaining Convention, N° 98 (1 July 1949)

Rome Statute of the International Criminal Court (17 June 1998)

Safeguards guaranteeing protection of the right of those facing the death penalty (25 May 1984)

Second Optional Protocol to the international Covenant on Civil and Political Rights, aiming at the abolition of the death penalty (15 December 1989)

Slavery Convention (25 September 1926)

Standard Rules on the Equalization of Opportunities for Persons with Disabilities (20 December 1993)

Standard Minimum Rules for the Treatment of Prisoners (31 July 1957, 13 May 1977)

Statute of International Criminal Tribunal for the Prosecution of Persons Responsible for Genocide and Other Serious Violations of International Humanitarian Law Committed in the Territory of Rwanda and Rwandan Citizens Responsible for Genocide and Other Such Violations Committed in the Territory of Neighbouring States, between 1 January 1994 and 31 December 1994. (8 November 1994)

Statute of the International Tribunal for the Prosecution of Persons Responsible for Serious Violations of International Humanitarian law Committed in the Territory of Former Yugoslavia since 1991. (25 May 1993)

Supplementary Convention on the Abolition of Slavery, the Slave Trade, and Institutions and Practices Similar to Slavery (30 April 1956)

United Nations Declaration on the Granting of Independence to Colonial Countries and Peoples (14 December 1960)

United Nations Guidelines for the Prevention of Juvenile Delinquency (The Riyadh Guidelines) (14 December 1990)

United Nations Millennium Declaration (8 September 2000)

United Nations Principles for Older Persons (16 December 1991)

United Nations Rules for the Protection of Juveniles Deprived of their Liberty (14 December 1990)

United Nations Standard Minimum Rules for Non-custodial Measures (The Tokyo Rules) (14 December 1990)

United Nations Standard Minimum Rules for the Administration of Juvenile Justice (The Beijing Rules) (29 November 1985)

Universal Declaration of Human Rights (10 December 1948)

Universal Declaration on Cultural Diversity (2 November 2001)

Universal Declaration on the Eradication of Hunger and Malnutrition (16 November 1974)

Universal Declaration on the Human Genome and Human Rights (11 November 1997)

Vienna Declaration and Programme of Action (25 June 1993)

Worst Forms of Child Labour Convention, N° 182 (17 June 1999)

Les Definitions des Droits de l'Homme

ABSENCE DE GUERRE [Life without war]

– « *Convaincue* que l'absence de guerre est, au niveau international, une condition primordiale du bien-être, de la prospérité matérielle et du progrès des Etats, ainsi que de la réalisation complète des droits et des libertés fondamentales de l'homme proclamés par l'Organisation des Nations Unies, »

Pp. 4, DÉCLARATION SUR LE DROIT DES PEUPLES À LA PAIX.

ACCROISSEMENT DE LA DELINQUANCE JUVENILE [Increase in juvenile crime]

– « Même si le rapport entre l'urbanisation et la criminalité est très complexe, on associe souvent l'accroissement de la délinquance juvénile au développement des grandes villes, surtout s'il est rapide et anarchique. [...] »

12, *Commentaire*, ENSEMBLE DE RÈGLES MINIMA DES NATIONS UNIES CONCERNANT L'ADMINISTRATION DE LA JUSTICE POUR LES MINEURS (RÈGLES DE BEIJING).

ACTE CONDUISANT A UNE DISPARITION FORCEE [Act of enforced disappearance]

– « 1. Tout acte conduisant à une disparition forcée constitue un outrage à la dignité humaine. [...] »

Art. 1er, DÉCLARATION SUR LA PROTECTION DE TOUTES LES PERSONNES CONTRE LES DISPARITIONS FORCÉES.

ACTE DE CORRUPTION [Act of corruption]

– « *c*) L'expression "acte de corruption" mentionné ci-dessus comprend la tentative de corruption. »

Art.7, *Commentaire*, Art. 1, CODE DE CONDUITE POUR LES RESPONSABLE DE L'APPLICATION DES LOIS.

ACTE DE TORTURE [Act of torture]

– « 55. La Conférence mondiale sur les droits de l'homme souligne que l'une des violations les plus atroces de la dignité humaine est l'acte de torture, qui a pour conséquence d'ôter sa dignité à la victime et de porter atteinte à sa capacité de vivre et de poursuivre ses activités normalement. »

II, DÉCLARATION ET PROGRAMMATION D'ACTION DE VIENNE.

ACTES, METHODES ET PRATIQUES DE TERRORISME [Acts, methods and practices of terrorism]

– « 17. Les actes, méthodes et pratiques de terrorisme sous quelque forme que ce soit et dans toutes ses manifestations et leur lien, dans certains pays, avec le trafic de stupéfiants, visent l'anéantissement des droits de l'homme, des libertés fondamentales et de la démocratie, menacent l'intégrité territoriale et la sécurité des Etats et déstabilisent des gouvernements légitimement constitués. La communauté internationale doit prendre les mesures qui s'imposent pour renforcer la coopération en vue d'empêcher et de combattre le terrorisme. »

I, DÉCLARATION ET PROGRAMMATION D'ACTION DE VIENNE.

ACTES NUISIBLES A L'ENNEMI (NE SONT PAS CONSIDERES COMME) [Acts harmful to the enemy (not be considered)]

– « 2. Ne seront pas considérés comme actes nuisibles à l'ennemi :

a) le fait d'exécuter des tâches de protection civile sous la direction ou la surveillance d'autorités militaires;

b) le fait que le personnel civil de protection civile coopère avec du personnel militaire dans l'accomplissement de tâches de protection civile, ou que des militaires soient attachés à des organismes civils de protection civile;

c) le fait que l'accomplissement des tâches de protection civile puisse incidemment profiter à des victimes militaires, en particulier à celles qui sont hors de combat.

3. Ne sera pas considéré non plus comme acte nuisible à l'ennemi le port d'armes légères individuelles par le personnel civil de protection civile, en vue du maintien de l'ordre ou pour sa propre protection. Toutefois, dans les zones où des combats terrestres se déroulent ou semblent devoir se dérouler, les Parties au conflit prendront les dispositions appropriées pour limiter ces armes aux armes de poing, telles que les pistolets ou revolvers, afin de faciliter la distinction entre le personnel de protection civile et les combattants. Même si le personnel de protection civile porte d'autres armes légères individuelles dans ces zones, il doit être respecté et protégé dès qu'il aura été reconnu comme tel. »

Art. 65, PROTOCOLE ADDITIONNEL AUX CONVENTIONS DE GENÈVE DU 12 AOÛT 1949 RELATIF À LA PROTECTION DES VICTIMES DES CONFLITS ARMÉS INTERNATIONAUX (PROTOCOLE I).

AERONEF SANITAIRE [Medical aircraft]

– « Aux fins du présent Protocole :

[...]

j) l'expression "aéronef sanitaire" s'entend de tout moyen de transport sanitaire par air; »

Art. 8, PROTOCOLE ADDITIONNEL AUX CONVENTIONS DE GENÈVE DU 12 AOÛT 1949 RELATIF À LA PROTECTION DES VICTIMES DES CONFLITS ARMÉS INTERNATIONAUX (PROTOCOLE I).

AFFECTIONS GYNECOLOGIQUES CHRONIQUES GRAVES [Chronic grave gynaecological conditions]

– « *f)* Les affections chroniques graves des organes génito-urinaires, par exemple : maladies chroniques du rein avec troubles consécutifs; néphrectomie pour un rein tuberculeux; pyélite chronique ou cystite chronique; hydro ou pyonéphrose; affections gynécologiques chroniques graves; grossesses et affections obstétricales, lorsque l'hospitalisation en pays neutre est impossible ; etc. »

Annexe I, 3, CONVENTION DE GENÈVE RELATIVE AU TRAITEMENT DES PRISONNIERS DE GUERRE.

AFRIQUE [Africa]

– « 8. Constatant avec une grave préoccupation que l'Afrique, en particulier l'Afrique subsaharienne, est actuellement la région la plus touchée, que le VIH/sida y est considéré comme créant un état d'urgence qui menace le développement, la cohésion sociale, la stabilité politique, la sécurité alimentaire et l'espérance de vie et constitue un fardeau dévastateur pour l'économie, et que la situation dramatique du continent exige que des mesures exceptionnelles soient prises d'urgence aux niveaux national, régional et international; »

DÉCLARATION D'ENGAGEMENT SUR LE VIH/SIDA.

AFRIQUE SUBSAHARIENNE [Sub-Saharan Africa]

– « 8. Constatant avec une grave préoccupation que l'Afrique, en particulier l'Afrique subsaharienne, est actuellement la région la plus touchée, que le VIH/sida y est considéré comme créant un état d'urgence qui menace le développement, la cohésion sociale, la stabilité politique, la sécurité alimentaire et l'espérance de vie et constitue un fardeau dévastateur pour l'économie, et que la situation dramatique du continent exige que des mesures exceptionnelles soient prises d'urgence aux niveaux national, régional et international; »

DÉCLARATION D'ENGAGEMENT SUR LE VIH/SIDA.

– « 10. Constatant également que d'autres régions sont gravement touchées et courent des risques du même ordre, notamment la région des Caraïbes, où le taux de contamination par le VIH est le plus élevé après l'Afrique subsaharienne, la région de l'Asie et du Pacifique où 7,5 millions de personnes sont déjà atteintes du VIH/sida, la région de l'Amérique latine où 1,5 million de personnes sont séropositives ou atteintes du sida et la région de l'Europe centrale et orientale où les taux de contamination sont en augmentation très rapide, et qu'en l'absence de mesures concrètes l'épidémie pourrait se propager rapidement et avoir des répercussions dans le monde entier; »

DÉCLARATION D'ENGAGEMENT SUR LE VIH/SIDA.

AGRESSION, D'OCCUPATION ET DE DOMINATION ETRANGERES ET D'INGERENCE DANS LES AFFAIRES INTERIEURES DES ETATS (ELIMINATION D') [Aggression, foreign occupation and domination and interference in the internal affairs of States (eradication of)]

– « *Soulignant* que l'élimination de l'apartheid, de toutes les formes de racisme, de discrimination raciale, de colonialisme, de néocolonialisme, d'agression, d'occupation et de domination étrangères et d'ingérence dans les affaires intérieures des Etats est indispensable à la pleine jouissance par l'homme et la femme de leurs droits. »

Pp. 10, CONVENTION SUR L'ÉLIMINATION DE TOUTES LES FORMES DE DISCRIMINATION À L'ÉGARD DES FEMMES.

AIDE POSTPENITENTIAIRE (EFFICACE AU DETENU LIBERE) [After-care (released prisoner efficient)]

– « 64. Le devoir de la société ne cesse pas à la libération d'un détenu. Il faudrait donc disposer d'organismes gouvernementaux ou privés capables d'apporter au détenu libéré une aide postpénitentiaire efficace, tendant à diminuer les préjugés à son égard et lui permettant de se reclasser dans la communauté. »

ENSEMBLE DE RÈGLES MINIMA POUR LE TRAITEMENT DES DÉTENUS.

ALCOOL [Alcohol]

– « 25. [...] Des informations sur la consommation et l'abus des drogues, y compris l'alcool, doivent être fournies à la population scolaire et universitaire. »

PRINCIPES DIRECTEURS DES NATIONS UNIES POUR LA PRÉVENTION DE LA DÉLINQUANCE JUVÉNILE (PRINCIPES DIRECTEURS DE RIYAD).

ALCOOLISME [Alcoholism]

– « *o)* Les intoxications chroniques graves, par exemple : saturnisme, hydrargyrisme; morphinisme, cocaïnisme, alcoolisme; intoxications par les gaz et par les radiations; etc. »

Annexe I, 3, CONVENTION DE GENÈVE RELATIVE AU TRAITEMENT DES PRISONNIERS DE GUERRE.

AMERIQUE LATINE (REGION DE L') [Latin American region]

– « 10. Constatant également que d'autres régions sont gravement touchées et courent des risques du même ordre, notamment la région des Caraïbes, où le taux de contamination par le VIH est le plus élevé après l'Afrique subsaharienne, la région de l'Asie et du Pacifique où 7,5 millions de personnes sont déjà atteintes du VIH/sida, la région de l'Amérique latine où 1,5 million de personnes sont séropositives ou atteintes du sida et la région de l'Europe centrale et orientale où les taux de contamination sont en augmentation très rapide, et qu'en l'absence de mesures concrètes l'épidémie pourrait se propager rapidement et avoir des répercussions dans le monde entier; »

DÉCLARATION D'ENGAGEMENT SUR LE VIH/SIDA.

ANALPHABETISME [Illiteracy]

– « 11. Estimant que la pauvreté, le sous-développement et l'analphabétisme figurent parmi les principaux facteurs contribuant à la propagation du VIH/sida, et notant avec une vive préoccupation que l'épidémie aggrave la pauvreté et entrave ou enraye désormais le développement dans un grand nombre de pays et qu'il faudrait donc y remédier dans une optique intégrée; »

DÉCLARATION D'ENGAGEMENT SUR LE VIH/SIDA.

APARTHEID [Apartheid]

– « 19. La Conférence mondiale sur les droits de l'homme considère que l'élimination du racisme et de la discrimination raciale, en particulier sous une forme institutionnalisée comme l'apartheid ou résultant de doctrines fondées sur la supériorité raciale ou sur l'exclusion, ainsi que d'autres formes et manifestations contemporaines de racisme, constitue un objectif primordial de la communauté internationale et d'un programme mondial de promotion des droits de l'homme. [...] »

II, DÉCLARATION ET PROGRAMME D'ACTION DE VIENNE.

– « *Constatant* avec la préoccupation la plus vive que le racisme, la discrimination raciale, le colonialisme et l'apartheid continuent à sévir dans le monde sous ses formes toujours renouvelées, tant par le maintien de dispositions législatives et de pratiques de gouvernements et d'administration contraires aux principes des droits de l'homme, que la permanence de structures marquées par l'injuste et le mépris de la personne humaine et engendrant l'exclusion, l'humiliation et l'exploitation, ou l'assimilation forcée, des membres de groupes défavorisés, »

Pp. 12, DÉCLARATION SUR LA RACE ET LES PRÉJUGÉES RACIAUX.

– « 2. Une des violations les plus graves de ce principe est constituée par l'apartheid qui, comme le génocide, est un crime contre l'humanité et qui trouble gravement la paix et la sécurité internationales. »

Art. 4, DÉCLARATION SUR LA RACE ET LES PRÉJUGÉS RACIAUX.

APARTHEID (ELIMINATION DE L') [Apartheid (eradication of)]

– « *Soulignant* que l'élimination de l'apartheid, de toutes les formes de racisme, de discrimination raciale, de colonialisme, de néocolonialisme, d'agression, d'occupation et domination étrangères et d'ingérence dans les affaires intérieures des Etats est indispensable à la pleine jouissance par l'homme et la femme de leurs droits, »

Pp. 10, CONVENTION SUR L'ÉLIMINATION DE TOUTES LES FORMES DE DISCRIMINATION À L'ÉGARD DES FEMMES.

APATRIDE [Stateless; Stateless person]

– « 3. Nonobstant les dispositions de l'alinéa *b* du paragraphe 1 et le paragraphe 2[1] du présent article, l'enfant légitime qui est né sur le territoire

[1] « *b*) Sur demande souscrite, suivant les modalités prévues par la législation de l'Etat en cause, auprès de l'autorité compétente par l'intéressé ou en son nom; sous réserve des dispositions du paragraphe 2 du présent article, la demande ne peut être rejetée.
L'Etat contractant dont la législation prévoit l'octroi de sa nationalité sur demande conformément à l'alinéa b du présent paragraphe peut également accorder sa nationalité de plein droit à l'âge et dans les conditions fixées par sa loi.
2. L'Etat contractant peut subordonner l'acquisition de sa nationalité en vertu de l'alinéa b du paragraphe 1 du présent article, à une ou plusieurs des conditions suivantes :
a) Que la demande soit souscrite pendant une période fixée par l'Etat contractant, période commençant au plus tard à l'âge de 18 ans et ne pouvant se terminer avant 21 ans, étant entendu toutefois que l'intéressé doit disposer d'au moins une année pour souscrire sa demande personnellement et sans habilitation;
b) Que l'intéressé ait résidé habituellement sur le territoire de l'Etat contractant, sans toutefois que la durée de résidence fixée par ce dernier puisse excéder 10 ans au total, dont 5 ans au plus précédant immédiatement le dépôt de la demande;
c) Que l'intéressé n'ait pas été déclaré coupable d'une infraction contre la sécurité nationale ou qu'il n'ait pas été condamné à une peine d'emprisonnement d'au moins cinq années pour fait criminel;

d'un Etat contractant et dont la mère possède la nationalité de cet Etat acquiert cette nationalité à la naissance si, autrement, il serait apatride. »

Art. 1, CONVENTION SUR LA RÉDUCTION DES CAS D'APATRIDIE.

– « Article premier – Définition du terme "apatride"

1. Aux fins de la présente Convention, le terme "apatride" désigne une personne qu'aucun Etat ne considère comme son ressortissant par application de sa législation.

2. Cette Convention ne sera pas applicable :

i)Aux personnes qui bénéficient actuellement d'une protection ou d'une assistance de la part d'un organisme ou d'une institution des Nations Unies autre que le Haut Commissariat des Nations Unies pour les réfugiés, tant qu'elles bénéficieront de ladite protection ou de ladite assistance;

ii)Aux personnes considérées par les autorités compétentes du pays dans lequel ces personnes ont établi leur résidence comme ayant les droits et les obligations attachés à la possession de la nationalité de ce pays;

iii)Aux personnes dont on aura des raisons sérieuses de penser :

a) Qu'elles ont commis un crime contre la paix, un crime de guerre ou un crime contre l'humanité, au sens des instruments internationaux élaborés pour prévoir des dispositions relatives à ces crimes;

b) Qu'elles ont commis un crime grave de droit commun en dehors du pays de leur résidence avant d'y être admises;

c) Qu'elles se sont rendues coupables d'agissements contraires aux buts et aux principes des Nations Unies. »

CONVENTION RELATIVE AU STATUT DES APATRIDES.

ARRESTATION [Arrest]

– « Aux fins de l'Ensemble de principes:

---

d) Que l'intéressé n'ait pas acquis à la naissance ou postérieurement une nationalité. »

a) Le terme "arrestation" s'entend de l'acte qui consiste à appréhender une personne du chef d'une prétendue infraction ou par le fait d'une autorité quelconque; »

Emploi des termes, ENSEMBLE DE PRINCIPES POUR LA PROTECTION DE TOUTES LES PERSONNES SOUMISES À UNE FORME QUELCONQUE DE DÉTENTION OU D'EMPRISONNEMENT.

ARTHROSES DEFORMANTES [Arthritis deformans]

– «*p)* Les affections chroniques des organes locomoteurs avec troubles fonctionnels manifestes, par exemple: arthroses déformantes; polyarthrite chronique évolutive primaire et secondaire; rhumatisme avec manifestations cliniques graves; etc. »

Annexe I, 3, CONVENTION DE GENÈVE RELATIVE AU TRAITEMENT DES PRISONNIERS DE GUERRE.

ASIE ET DU PACIFIQUE (REGION DE L') [Asia-Pacific region]

– « 10. Constatant également que d'autres régions sont gravement touchées et courent des risques du même ordre, notamment la région des Caraïbes, où le taux de contamination par le VIH est le plus élevé après l'Afrique subsaharienne, la région de l'Asie et du Pacifique où 7,5 millions de personnes sont déjà atteintes du VIH/sida, la région de l'Amérique latine où 1,5 million de personnes sont séropositives ou atteintes du sida et la région de l'Europe centrale et orientale où les taux de contamination sont en augmentation très rapide, et qu'en l'absence de mesures concrètes l'épidémie pourrait se propager rapidement et avoir des répercussions dans le monde entier; »

DÉCLARATION D'ENGAGEMENT SUR LE VIH/SIDA.

ASSEMBLEE GENERALE [General assembly]

– « De réaffirmer le rôle central de l'Assemblée générale en tant que principal organe délibérant et représentatif et représentatif de l'Organ-isation des Nations, et lui permettre de s'en acquitter efficacement .»

30, premier note (•), DÉCLARATION DU MILLÉNAIRE.

ASTHME CHRONIQUE [Chronic asthma]

– «*c)* Les maladies graves des organes respiratoires, d'étiologie non tuberculeuse, présumées incurables, par exemple : emphysème pulmonaire grave (avec ou sans bronchite); asthme chronique; bronchite chronique se prolongeant pendant plus d'une année en captivité; bronchectasie"; etc. »

Annexe I, 3, CONVENTION DE GENÈVE RELATIVE AU TRAITEMENT DES PRISONNIERS DE GUERRE.

ATTAQUE LANCEE CONTRE UNE POPULATION CIVILE [Attack directed against any civilian population]

– « 2. Aux fins du paragraphe 1[2]:

a) Par «attaque lancée contre une population civile», on entend le comportement qui consiste en la commission multiple d'actes visés au paragraphe 1[2] à l'encontre d'une population civile quelconque, en application ou dans la poursuite de la politique d'un État ou d'une organisation ayant pour but une telle attaque; »

Art. 7, STATUT DE ROME DE LA COUR PÉNALE INTERNATIONALE.

ATTAQUES [Attacks]

– « 1. L'expression "attaques" s'entend des actes de violence contre l'adversaire, que ces actes soient offensifs ou défensifs. »

---

[2] « 1. Aux fins du présent Statut, on entend par crime contre l'humanité l'un quelconque des actes ci-après lorsqu'il est commis dans le cadre d'une attaque généralisée ou systématique lancée contre toute population civile et en connaissance de cette attaque:
a) Meurtre;
b) Extermination;
c) Réduction en esclavage;
d) Déportation ou transfert forcé de population;
e) Emprisonnement ou autre forme de privation grave de liberté physique en violation des dispositions fondamentales du droit international;
f) Torture;
g) Viol, esclavage sexuel, prostitution forcée, grossesse forcée, stérilisation forcée ou toute autre forme de violence sexuelle de gravité comparable;
h) Persécution de tout groupe ou de toute collectivité identifiable pour des motifs d'ordre politique, racial, national, ethnique, culturel, religieux ou sexiste au sens du paragraphe 3, ou en fonction d'autres critères universellement reconnus comme inadmissibles en droit international, en corrélation avec tout acte visé dans le présent paragraphe ou tout crime relevant de la compétence de la Cour;
i) Disparitions forcées de personnes;
j) Crime d'apartheid;
k) Autres actes inhumains de caractère analogue causant intentionnellement de grandes souffrances ou des atteintes graves à l'intégrité physique ou à la santé physique ou mentale. »

Art. 49, PROTOCOLE ADDITIONNEL AUX CONVENTIONS DE GENÈVE DU 12 AOÛT 1949 RELATIF À LA PROTECTION DES VICTIMES DES CONFLITS ARMÉS INTERNATIONAUX (PROTOCOLE I).

ATTAQUES SANS DISCRIMINATION [Indiscriminate attacks]

– « 4. Les attaques sans discrimination sont interdites. L'expression "attaques sans discrimination" s'entend :

a) des attaques qui ne sont pas dirigées contre un objectif militaire déterminé;

b) des attaques dans lesquelles on utilise des méthodes ou moyens de combat qui ne peuvent pas être dirigés contre un objectif militaire déterminé; ou

c) des attaques dans lesquelles on utilise des méthodes ou moyens de combat dont les effets ne peuvent pas être limités comme le prescrit le présent Protocole;

et qui sont, en conséquence, dans chacun de ces cas, propres à frapper indistinctement des objectifs militaires et des personnes civiles ou des biens de caractère civil.

5. Seront, entre autres, considérés comme effectués sans discrimination les types d'attaques suivants:

a) les attaques par bombardement, quels que soient les méthodes ou moyens utilisés, qui traitent comme un objectif militaire unique un certain nombre d'objectifs militaires nettement espacés et distincts situés dans une ville, un village ou toute autre zone contenant une concentration analogue de personnes civiles ou de biens de caractère civil;

b) les attaques dont on peut attendre qu'elles causent incidemment des pertes en vies humaines dans la population civile, des blessures aux personnes civiles, des dommages aux biens de caractère civil, ou une combinaison de ces pertes et dommages, qui seraient excessifs par rapport à l'avantage militaire concret et direct attendu.»

Art. 51, PROTOCOLE ADDITIONNEL AUX CONVENTIONS DE GENÈVE DU 12 AOÛT 1949 RELATIF À LA PROTECTION DES VICTIMES DES CONFLITS ARMÉS INTERNATIONAUX (PROTOCOLE I).

ATTENTAT A LA PUDEUR [Indecent assault]

– « les atteintes à la dignité de la personne, notamment les traitements humiliants et dégradants, la prostitution forcée et toute forme d'attentat à la pudeur; »

Art. 75, *b*), PROTOCOLE ADDITIONNEL AUX CONVENTIONS DE GENEVE DU 12 AOUT 1949 RELATIF A LA PROTECTION DES VICTIMES DES CONFLITS ARMES INTERNATIONAUX (PROTOCOLE I).

AUTORITE COMPETENTE [Competent authority]

– « Il est difficile de donner de l'organisme compétent ou de la personne compétente une définition qui décrirait de façon universellement acceptable l'autorité juridictionnelle. L'expression "autorité compétente" est censée comprendre les présidents de cours ou de tribunaux (composés d'un juge unique ou de plusieurs membres), à savoir les magistrats professionnels et non professionnels, ainsi que les commissions administratives (systèmes écossais et scandinave, par exemple) ou d'autres organismes communautaires moins officiels, spécialisés dans la solution des conflits et de caractère juridictionnel. »

14, *Commentaire*, al. 1, ENSEMBLE DE RÈGLES MINIMA DES NATIONS UNIES CONCERNANT L'ADMINISTRATION DE LA JUSTICE POUR LES MINEURS (RÈGLES DE BEIJING).

AUTORITE INDEPENDANT [Independent authority]

– « Dans les présents Principes :

L'expression "autorité indépendante" désigne une autorité compétente et indépendante prévue par la législation nationale; »

Al. 1, DEFINITIONS, PRINCIPES POUR LA PROTECTION DES PERSONNES ATTEINTES DE MALADIE MENTALE ET POUR L'AMELIORATION DES SOINS DE SANTE MENTALE [a].

AUTORITE JURIDICIAIRE [Adjudicating authority]

– « Il est difficile de donner de l'organisme compétent ou de la personne compétente une définition qui décrirait de façon universellement acceptable l'autorité juridictionnelle. [...] »

14, *Commentaire*, al. 1, ENSEMBLE DE RÈGLES MINIMA DES NATIONS UNIES CONCERNANT L'ADMINISTRATION DE LA JUSTICE POUR LES MINEURS (RÈGLES DE BEIJING).

[A] Sp 2, DEFINITIONS, Principles for the protection of persons with mental illness and the improvement of mental health care.

AUTORITE JUDICIAIRE OU AUTRE (UNE) [Judicial or other authority (a)]

– « Aux fins de l'ensemble de principes :

[...]

f) L'expression "une autorité judiciaire ou autre" s'entend d'une autorité judiciaire ou autre habilitée par la loi et dont le statut et la durée du mandat offrent les garanties les plus solides possibles de compétence, d'impartialité et d'indépendance. »

Emploi des termes, ENSEMBLE DE PRINCIPES POUR LA PROTECTION DE TOUTES LES PERSONNES SOUMISES À UNE FORME QUELCONQUE DE DÉTENTION OU D'EMPRISONNEMENT.

AUTORITES COMPETENTES [Competent authority]

– « Aux fins de la présente convention, le terme « autorités compétentes » désignera soit les autorités métropolitaines, soit les autorités centrales supérieures du territoire intéressé. »

Art. 3, CONVENTION SUR LE TRAVAIL FORCE (N° 29).

AUTORITES COMPETENTES POUR PRENDRE UNE DECISION [Authorities competent for disposition]

– « Les autorités compétentes pour prendre une décision peuvent être de formation très différente (magistrats au Royaume-Uni de Grande-Bretagne et d'Irlande du Nord et dans les régions qui s'inspirent du système de la common law, juges ayant reçu une formation juridique dans les pays de droit romain et dans les régions qui s'en inspirent; ailleurs, profanes ou juristes, élus ou désignés, membres de commissions communautaires, etc.). Pour toutes ces autorités, une connaissance minimale du droit, de la sociologie et de la psychologie, de la criminologie et des sciences du comportement est nécessaire, car elle est jugée aussi importante que la spécialisation ou l'indépendance de l'autorité compétente. »

22, *Commentaire*, ENSEMBLE DE REGLES MINIMA DES NATIONS UNIES CONCERNANT L'ADMINISTRATION DE LA JUSTICE POUR LES MINEURS (REGLES DE BEIJING).

AUTORITES OU INSTANCES DE CONTROLE OU DE RECOURS COMPETENTES [Appropriate authorities or organs vested with reviewing or remedial power]

– « *c*) L'expression "autorités ou instances de contrôle ou de recours compétentes" désigne toute autorité ou toute instance créée conformément à la législation nationale, qu'elle relève du service responsable de l'application des lois ou en soit indépendante, et dotée du pouvoir statutaire, coutumier ou autre de connaître des plaintes et griefs relatifs à une violation des règles visées dans le présent Code. »

Art. 8, *Commentaire*, CODE DE CONDUITE POUR LES RESPONSABLE DE L'APPLICATION DES LOIS.

AVOCATS [Lawyers]

– « 12. Les avocats, en tant qu'agents essentiels de l'administration de la justice, préservent à tous moments l'honneur et la dignité de leur profession. »

PRINCIPES DE BASE RELATIFS AU RÔLE DU BARREAU.

BARRIERES RACIALES [Racial barriers]

– « *Convaincus* que l'existence de barrières raciales est incompatibles avec les idéals de toute société humaine, »

Pp. 8, CONVENTION INTERNATIONALE SUR L'ÉLIMINATION DE TOUTES LES FORMES DE DISCRIMINATION RACIALE.

BIEN-ETRE DES PEUPLES DU MONDE [Well-being of the peoples of the world]

– « *g*) Le bien-être des peuples du monde dépend en grande partie de la production et de la distribution de denrées alimentaires en quantités suffisantes ainsi que de l'établissement d'un système de sécurité alimentaire mondiale qui assure à tout moment des disponibilités alimentaires adéquates à des prix raisonnables, quels que soient les fluctuations périodiques et les caprices du temps et en l'absence de toute pression politique et économique, facilitant ainsi, entre autres choses, le processus de développement des pays du tiers monde; »

DÉCLARATION UNIVERSELLE POU L'ÉLIMINATION DÉFINITIVE DE LA FAIM ET DE LA MALNUTRITION.

BIENS A CARACTERE CIVIL [Civilian objects]

– « 1. Les biens de caractère civil ne doivent être l'objet ni d'attaques ni de représailles. Sont biens de caractère civil tous les biens qui ne sont pas des objectifs militaires au sens du paragraphe 2.

2. Les attaques doivent être strictement limitées aux objectifs militaires. En ce qui concerne les biens, les objectifs militaires sont limités aux biens qui, par leur nature, leur emplacement, leur destination ou leur utilisation apportent une contribution effective à l'action militaire et dont la destruction totale ou partielle, la capture ou la neutralisation offre en l'occurrence un avantage militaire précis.

3. En cas de doute, un bien qui est normalement affecté à un usage civil, tel qu'un lieu de culte, une maison, un autre type d'habitation ou une école, est présumé ne pas être utilisé en vue d'apporter une contribution effective à l'action militaire. »

Art. 52, Protocole additionnel aux Conventions de Genève du 12 août 1949 relatif à la protection des victimes des conflits armés internationaux (Protocole I).

BIENS ET SERVICES CULTURELS [Cultural goods and services]

– « Face aux mutations économiques et technologiques actuelles, qui ouvrent de vastes perspectives pour la création et l'innovation, une attention particulière doit être accordée à la diversité de l'offre créatrice, à la juste prise en compte des culturels qui parce qu'ils sont porteurs d'identité, de valeurs et de sens, ne doivent pas être considérés comme des marchandises ou des biens de consommation comme les autres. »

Art. 8, Déclaration universelle sur la diversité culturelle.

BLESSES [Wounded]

– « Aux fins du présent Protocole :

a) les termes "blessés" et "malades" s'entendent des personnes, militaires ou civiles, qui, en raison d'un traumatisme, d'une maladie ou d'autres incapacités ou troubles physiques ou mentaux, ont besoin de soins médicaux et qui s'abstiennent de tout acte d'hostilité. Ces termes visent aussi les femmes en couches, les nouveau-nés, et les autres personnes qui pourraient avoir besoin de soins immédiats, telles que les infirmes et les femmes enceintes, et qui s'abstiennent de tout acte d'hostilité; »

Art. 8, Protocole additionnel aux Conventions de Genève du 12 août 1949 relatif à la protection des victimes des conflits armés internationaux (Protocole I).

BRONCHECTASIE [Bronchiectasis]

– « *c)* Les maladies graves des organes respiratoires, d'étiologie non tuberculeuse, présumées incurables, par exemple : emphysème pulmonaire grave (avec ou sans bronchite); asthme chronique*; bronchite chronique se prolongeant pendant plus d'une année en captivité; bronchectasie"; etc. »

Annexe I, 3, CONVENTION DE GENÈVE RELATIVE AU TRAITEMENT DES PRISONNIERS DE GUERRE.

BRONCHITE CHRONIQUE SE PROLONGEANT PENDANT PLUS D'UNE ANNEE EN CAPTIVITE [Chronic bronchitis lasting more than one year in captivity]

– « *c)* Les maladies graves des organes respiratoires, d'étiologie non tuberculeuse, présumées incurables, par exemple : emphysème pulmonaire grave (avec ou sans bronchite); asthme chronique*; bronchite chronique se prolongeant pendant plus d'une année en captivité; bronchectasie"; etc. »

Annexe I, 3, CONVENTION DE GENEVE RELATIVE AU TRAITEMENT DES PRISONNIERS DE GUERRE.

BUT ET LA JUSTIFICATION DES PEINES ET MESURES PRIVATIVES DE LIBERTE (LE) [Purpose and justification of a sentence of imprisonment or a similar measure deprivative of liberty]

– « 58. Le but et la justification des peines et mesures privatives de liberté sont en définitive de protéger la société contre le crime. Un tel but ne sera atteint que si la période de privation de liberté est mise à profit pour obtenir, dans toute la mesure du possible, que le délinquant, une fois libéré, soit non seulement désireux, mais aussi capable de vivre en respectant la loi et de subvenir à ses besoins. »

ENSEMBLE DE RÈGLES MINIMA POUR LE TRAITEMENT DES DÉTENUS.

BUTS ET PRINCIPES ENONCES DANS LA CHARTE DES NATIONS UNIES [Purposes and principles of Charter of the United Nations]

– « 3. Nous affirmons notre attachement aux buts et principes énoncés dans la Charte des Nations, qui ont une valeur éternelle et universelle. En fait, leur pertinence et leur importance en tant que source d'inspiration se sont

accrues avec la multiplication des liens et le renforcement de l'interdépendance entre les nations et les peuples. »
DÉCLARATION DU MILLÉNAIRE.

CARAIBES (REGION DES) [Caribbean region]

– « 10. Constatant également que d'autres régions sont gravement touchées et courent des risques du même ordre, notamment la région des Caraïbes, où le taux de contamination par le VIH est le plus élevé après l'Afrique subsaharienne, la région de l'Asie et du Pacifique où 7,5 millions de personnes sont déjà atteintes du VIH/sida, la région de l'Amérique latine où 1,5 million de personnes sont séropositives ou atteintes du sida et la région de l'Europe centrale et orientale où les taux de contamination sont en augmentation très rapide, et qu'en l'absence de mesures concrètes l'épidémie pourrait se propager rapidement et avoir des répercussions dans le monde entier; »
DÉCLARATION D'ENGAGEMENT SUR LE VIH/SIDA.

CATASTROPHES NATURELLES [Natural disasters]

– « 12. Notant que les conflits armés et les catastrophes naturelles aggravent eux aussi la propagation de l'épidémie; »
DÉCLARATION D'ENGAGEMENT SUR LE VIH/SIDA.

CAUSES SOCIOECONOMIQUES PROFONDES DU TRAFIC ILLICITE DE MIGRANTS [Root socio-economic causes of the smuggling of migrants]

– « 3. Chaque État Partie promeut ou renforce, selon qu'il convient, des programmes de développement et une coopération aux niveaux national, régional et international, en tenant compte des réalités socioéconomiques des migrations, et en accordant une attention particulière aux zones économiquement et socialement défavorisées, afin de s'attaquer aux causes socioéconomiques profondes du trafic illicite de migrants, telles que la pauvreté et le sous-développement. »
Art. 15, PROTOCOLE CONTRE LE TRAFIC ILLICITE DE MIGRANTS PAR TERRE, AIR ET MER, ADDITIONNEL À LA CONVENTION DES NATIONS UNIES CONTRE LA CRIMINALITÉ TRANSNATIONALE ORGANISÉE.

CECITE DES YEUX OU CELLE D'UN ŒIL [Blindness of both eyes, or of one eye]

- « *i)* La cécité des deux yeux ou celle d'un œil lorsque la vue de l'autre œil est moins de 1, malgré l'emploi de verres correcteurs; la diminution de l'acuité visuelle ne pouvant être corrigée à 1/2 pour un œil au moins*; les autres affections oculaires graves, par exemple: glaucome; iritis; chloroïdite; trachome; etc. »

Annexe I, 3, CONVENTION DE GENÈVE RELATIVE AU TRAITEMENT DES PRISONNIERS DE GUERRE.

CERTAINES COUTUMES, ANCIENNES LOIS ET PRATIQUES INTERESSANT LE MARIAGE ET LA FAMILLE [Certain customs, ancient laws and practices relating to marriage and the family]

- « *Rappelant en outre* que, dans sa résolution 843 (IX) du 17 décembre 1954, l'assemblée générale de l'Organisation des Nations Unies a déclaré que certaines coutumes, anciennes lois et pratiques intéressant le mariage et la famille étaient incompatibles avec les principes énoncés dans la Charte des Nations Unies et la Déclaration universelle des droits de l'homme, »

Pp. 2, CONVENTION SUR LE CONSENTEMENT AU MARIAGE, L'ÂGE MINIMUM DU MARIAGE ET L'ENREGISTREMENT DES MARIAGES.

CHLOROIDITE [Choroiditis]

- « *i)* La cécité des deux yeux ou celle d'un œil lorsque la vue de l'autre œil est moins de 1, malgré l'emploi de verres correcteurs; la diminution de l'acuité visuelle ne pouvant être corrigée à 1/2 pour un œil au moins*; les autres affections oculaires graves, par exemple : glaucome; iritis; chloroïdite; trachome; etc. »

Annexe I, 3, CONVENTION DE GENÈVE RELATIVE AU TRAITEMENT DES PRISONNIERS DE GUERRE.

CHOLECYSTOPATHIE CHRONIQUE [Chronic cholecystopathy]

- « *e)* Les affections chroniques graves des organes digestifs, par exemple : ulcère de l'estomac ou du duodénum; suite d'intervention chirurgicale sur l'estomac faite en captivité; gastrite, entérite ou colique chroniques durant plus d'une année et affectant gravement l'état général; cirrhose hépatique; cholécystopathie chronique*; etc. »

Annexe I, 3, CONVENTION DE GENÈVE RELATIVE AU TRAITEMENT DES PRISONNIERS DE GUERRE.

CIRRHOSE HEPATIQUE [Cirrhosis of the liver]

– « *e)* Les affections chroniques graves des organes digestifs, par exemple : ulcère de l'estomac ou du duodénum; suite d'intervention chirurgicale sur l'estomac faite en captivité; gastrite, entérite ou colique chroniques durant plus d'une année et affectant gravement l'état général; cirrhose hépatique; cholécystopathie chronique*; etc. »

Annexe I, 3, CONVENTION DE GENEVE RELATIVE AU TRAITEMENT DES PRISONNIERS DE GUERRE.

CLONAGE A DES FINS DE REPRODUCTION D'ETRES HUMAINS [Reproductive cloning of human beings]

– « Des pratiques qui sont contraires à la dignité humaine, telles que le clonage à des fins de reproduction d'êtres humains, ne doivent pas être permises. [...]. »

Art. 11, DÉCLARATION UNIVERSELLE SUR LE GÉNOME HUMAIN ET LES DROITS DE L'HOMME.

COCAINISME [Cocainism]

– « *o)* Les intoxications chroniques graves, par exemple : saturnisme, hydrargyrisme; morphinisme, cocaïnisme, alcoolisme; intoxications par les gaz et par les radiations; etc. »

Annexe I, 3, CONVENTION DE GENÈVE RELATIVE AU TRAITEMENT DES PRISONNIERS DE GUERRE.

COLONIALISME [Colonialism]

– « *Constatant* avec la préoccupation la plus vive que le racisme, la discrimination raciale, le colonialisme et l'apartheid continuent à sévir dans le monde sous ses formes toujours renouvelées, tant par le maintien de dispositions législatives et de pratiques de gouvernements et d'administration contraires aux principes des droits de l'homme, que la permanence de structures marquées par l'injuste et le mépris de la personne humaine et engendrant l'exclusion, l'humiliation et l'exploitation, ou l'assimilation forcée, des membres de groupes défavorisés, »

Pp. 12, DÉCLARATION SUR LA RACE ET LES PRÉJUGÉES RACIAUX.

COLONIALISME (ELIMINATION DE TOUTES LES FORMES DE) [Colonialism (eradication of all forms)]

– « *Soulignant* que l'élimination de l'apartheid, de toutes les formes de racisme, de discrimination raciale, de colonialisme, de néocolonialisme, d'agression, d'occupation et domination étrangères et d'ingérence dans les affaires intérieures des Etats est indispensable à la pleine jouissance par l'homme et la femme de leurs droits, »

Pp. 10, CONVENTION SUR L'ÉLIMINATION DE TOUTES LES FORMES DE DISCRIMINATION À L'ÉGARD DES FEMMES.

COMITE INTERNATIONAL DE LA CROIX-ROUGE [International Committee of the Red Cross]

– « Un organisme humanitaire impartial, tel que le Comité international de la Croix-Rouge, pourra offrir ses services aux Parties au conflit. »

Art. 3, § 2, al. 1, CONVENTION DE GENÈVE RELATIVE AU TRAITEMENT DES PRISONNIERS DE GUERRE.

– « Si une protection ne peut être ainsi assurée, la Puissance détentrice devra demander à un organisme humanitaire, tel que le Comité international de la Croix-Rouge, d'assumer les tâches humanitaires dévolues par la présente Convention aux Puissances protectrices ou devra accepter, sous réserve des dispositions du présent article, les offres de services émanant d'un tel organisme. »

Art. 10, Al. 3, CONVENTION DE GENÈVE RELATIVE AU TRAITEMENT DES PRISONNIERS DE GUERRE.

– « Un organisme humanitaire impartial, tel que le Comité international de la Croix- Rouge, pourra offrir ses services aux Parties au conflit. »

Art. 2, § 2, CONVENTION DE GENÈVE RELATIVE À LA PROTECTION DES PERSONNES CIVILES EN TEMPS DE GUERRE DU 12 AOÛT 1949.

– « Les dispositions de la présente Convention ne font pas obstacle aux activités humanitaires que le Comité international de la Croix-Rouge, ainsi que tout autre organisme humanitaire impartial, entreprendra pour la protection des personnes civiles et pour les secours à leur apporter, moyennant l'agrément des Parties au conflit intéressées. »

Art. 10, CONVENTION DE GENÈVE RELATIVE À LA PROTECTION DES PERSONNES CIVILES EN TEMPS DE GUERRE DU 12 AOÛT 1949.

– « Si une protection ne peut être ainsi assurée, la Puissance détentrice devra demander à un organisme humanitaire, tel que le Comité international de la Croix-Rouge, d'assumer les tâches humanitaires dévolues par la présente Convention aux Puissances protectrices ou devra accepter, sous réserve des dispositions du présent article, les offres de services émanant d'un tel organisme. »

Art. 11, al. 3, CONVENTION DE GENÈVE RELATIVE À LA PROTECTION DES PERSONNES CIVILES EN TEMPS DE GUERRE DU 12 AOÛT 1949.

– « Les dispositions qui précèdent ne devront pas être interprétées comme restreignant l'activité humanitaire du Comité international de la Croix-Rouge [...] »

Art. 140, al. 4, CONVENTION DE GENÈVE RELATIVE À LA PROTECTION DES PERSONNES CIVILES EN TEMPS DE GUERRE DU 12 AOÛT 1949.

– « 1. Les Parties au conflit accorderont au Comité international de la Croix-Rouge toutes les facilités en leur pouvoir pour lui permettre d'assumer les tâches humanitaires qui lui sont attribuées par les Conventions et le présent Protocole afin d'assurer protection et assistance aux victimes des conflits; le Comité international de la Croix-Rouge pourra également exercer toutes autres activités humanitaires en faveur de ces victimes, avec le consentement des Parties au conflit. »

Art. 81, PROTOCOLE ADDITIONNEL AUX CONVENTIONS DE GENÈVE DU 12 AOÛT 1949 RELATIF À LA PROTECTION DES VICTIMES DES CONFLITS ARMÉS INTERNATIONAUX (PROTOCOLE I).

COMMUNAUTE [Community]

– « 2. Tous les êtres humains ont la responsabilité du développement individuellement et collectivement, compte tenu des exigences du plein respect de leurs droits de l'homme et de leurs libertés fondamentales et eu égard à leurs devoirs envers la communauté, qui seule peut assurer l'entier et libre épanouissement de l'être humain et qui doit donc promouvoir et protéger un ordre politique, social et économique propre à favoriser le développement. »

Art. 2, DÉCLARATION SUR LE DROIT AU DÉVELOPPEMENT.

– « 1. Chacun a des devoirs envers la communauté et au sein de celle-ci, seul cadre permettant le libre et plein épanouissement de sa personnalité. »

Art. 18, DÉCLARATION SUR LE DROIT ET LA RESPONSABILITÉ DES INDIVIDUS, GROUPES ET ORGANES DE LA SOCIÉTÉ DE PROMOUVOIR ET PROTÉGER LES DROITS DE L'HOMME ET LES LIBERTÉS FONDAMENTALES UNIVERSELLEMENT RECONNUS.

COMMUNICATION DE MASSE [Mass media]

– « *d*) Dans certains pays, les moyens de communication de masse peuvent être considérés comme remplissant des fonctions de contrôle analogues à celles qui sont décrites à l'alinéa c ci-dessus.[...] [3]»

Art. 8, *Commentaire*, CODE DE CONDUITE POUR LES RESPONSABLES DE L'APPLICATION DES LOIS.

COMPORTEMENT OU LA CONDUITE D'UN JEUNE QUI N'EST PAS CONFORME AUX NORMES ET VALEURS SOCIALES (LE) [Youthful behaviour or conduct that does not conform to overall social norms and values]

– « *e*) Conscience que le comportement ou la conduite d'un jeune qui n'est pas conforme aux normes et valeurs sociales générales relève souvent du processus de maturation et de croissance et tend à disparaître spontanément chez la plupart des individus avec le passage à l'âge adulte; »

5, PRINCIPES DIRECTEURS DES NATIONS UNIES POUR LA PRÉVENTION DE LA DÉLINQUANCE JUVÉNILE (PRINCIPES DIRECTEURS DE RIYAD).

CONDITIONS PRIMORDIALES DU PROGRES ET DU DEVELOPPEMENT [Primary conditions of social progress and development]

– « Sont considérés comme des conditions primordiales du progrès et du développement dans le domaine social :

a) L'indépendance nationale fondée sur le droit des peuples à l'autodétermination;

b) Le principe de la non-ingérence dans les affaires intérieures des Etats;

c) Le respect de la souveraineté et de l'intégralité territoriale des Etats;

d) La souveraineté permanente de chaque nation sur ses richesses et ressources naturelles;

---

[3] « c) L'expression "autorités ou instances de contrôle ou de recours compétentes" désigne toute autorité ou toute instance créée conformément à la législation nationale, qu'elle relève du service responsable de l'application des lois ou en soit indépendante, et dotée du pouvoir statutaire, coutumier ou autre de connaître des plaintes et griefs relatifs à une violation des règles visées dans le présent Code. »

e) Le droit et la responsabilité de chaque Etat et, en ce qui les concerne, de chaque nation et de chaque peuple, de déterminer en toute liberté ses propres objectifs de développement social, de fixer ses propres priorités et de choisir, conformément aux principes de la Charte des Nations Unies, les moyens et méthodes permettant de les atteindre, à l'abri de toute ingérence extérieure;

f) La coexistence pacifique, la paix, les relations amicales et la coopération entre les Etats, quelles que soient les différences existant entre leurs systèmes sociaux, économiques ou politiques. »

Art. 3, DÉCLARATION SUR LE PROGRÈS ET LE DÉVELOPPEMENT DANS LE DOMAINE SOCIALE.

CONDITIONS PROPICES AU DEVELOPPEMENT POUR UNE GRANDE PARTIE DE L'HUMANITE [Circumstances propitious to the development of a great part of mankind]

– « *Considérant* que l'élimination des violations massives et flagrantes des droits fondamentaux des peuples et des individus qui se ressentent de situations telles que celles qui résultent du colonialisme et du néocolonialisme, de l'apartheid, du racisme et de la discrimination raciale sous toutes leurs formes, de la domination et de l'occupation étrangère, de l'agression et des menaces contre la souveraineté nationale, l'unité nationale et l'intégrité territoriale, ainsi que des menaces de guerre, contribuerait à créer des conditions propices au développement pour une grande partie de l'humanité, »

Pp. 9, DÉCLARATION SUR LE DROIT AU DÉVELOPPEMENT.

CONFLIT ARME [Armed conflict]

– « *c*) En cas de conflit armé ne présentant pas un caractère international, [...] »

Art. 8, § 2, STATUT DE ROME DE LA COUR PÉNALE INTERNATIONALE.

– « En dehors des dispositions qui doivent entrer en vigueur dès le temps de paix, la présente Convention s'appliquera en cas de guerre déclarée ou de tout autre conflit armé surgissant entre deux ou plusieurs des Hautes Parties contractantes, même si l'état de guerre n'est pas reconnu par l'une d'elles. »

Art. 2, al. 1, CONVENTION DE GENÈVE RELATIVE AU TRAITEMENT DES PRISONNIERS DE GUERRE.

– « [...] conflit armé ne présentant pas de un caractère international [...] »

Art. 3, al. 1, CONVENTION DE GENÈVE RELATIVE AU TRAITEMENT DES PRISONNIERS DE GUERRE.

CONFLITS ARMES [Armed conflicts]

– « 12. Notant que les conflits armés et les catastrophes naturelles aggravent eux aussi la propagation de l'épidémie; »

DÉCLARATION D'ENGAGEMENT SUR LE VIH/SIDA.

– « *e*) Les autres violations graves des lois et coutumes applicables aux conflits armés ne présentant pas un caractère international, dans le cadre établi du droit international, à savoir l'un quelconque des actes ci-après:

i) Le fait de diriger intentionnellement des attaques contre la population civile en tant que telle ou contre des personnes civils qui ne participent pas directement aux hostilités;

ii) Le fait de diriger intentionnellement des attaques contre les bâtiments, le matériel, les unités et les moyens de transport sanitaires, et le personnel utilisant, conformément au droit international, les signes distinctifs des Conventions de Genève;

iii) Le fait de diriger intentionnellement des attaques contre le personnel, les installations, le matériel, les unités ou les véhicules employés dans le cadre d'une mission d'aide humanitaire ou de maintien de la paix conformément à la Charte des Nations Unies, pour autant qu'ils aient droit à la protection que le droit international des conflits armés garantit aux civils et aux biens de caractère civil;

iv) Le fait de diriger intentionnellement des attaques contre des bâtiments consacrés à la religion, à l'enseignement, à l'art, à la science ou à l'action caritative, des monuments historiques, des hôpitaux et des lieux où des malades et des blessés sont rassemblés, pour autant que ces bâtiments ne soient pas des objectifs militaires;

v) Le pillage d'une ville ou d'une localité, même prise d'assaut;

vi) Le viol, l'esclavage sexuel, la prostitution forcée, la grossesse forcée, telle que définie à l'article 7, paragraphe 2, alinéa f)[4], la stérilisation forcée, ou toute autre forme de violence sexuelle

[4] « Par «grossesse forcée», on entend la détention illégale d'une femme mise enceinte de force, dans l'intention de modifier la composition ethnique d'une population ou de commettre d'autres violations graves du droit international. Cette définition ne peut en aucune manière s'interpréter comme ayant une incidence sur les lois nationales relatives à la grossesse; »

constituant une violation grave de l'article 3 commun aux quatre Conventions de Genève[5];

vii) Le fait de procéder à la conscription ou à l'enrôlement d'enfants de moins de 15 ans dans les forces armées ou dans des groupes armés ou de les faire participer activement à des hostilités;

viii) Le fait d'ordonner le déplacement de la population civile pour des raisons ayant trait au conflit, sauf dans les cas où la sécurité des civils ou des impératifs militaires l'exigent;

ix) Le fait de tuer ou de blesser par traîtrise un adversaire combattant;

x) Le fait de déclarer qu'il ne sera pas fait de quartier;

xi) Le fait de soumettre des personnes d'une autre partie au conflit tombées en son pouvoir à des mutilations ou à des expériences médicales ou scientifiques quelles qu'elles soient qui ne sont ni motivées par un traitement médical, dentaire ou hospitalier, ni effectuées dans l'intérêt de ces personnes, et qui entraînent la mort de celles-ci ou mettent sérieusement en danger leur santé;

---

[5] « En cas de conflit armé ne présentant pas un caractère international et surgissant sur le territoire de l'une des Hautes Parties contractantes, chacune des Parties au conflit sera tenue d'appliquer au moins les dispositions suivantes:
1) Les personnes qui ne participent pas directement aux hostilités, y compris les membres de forces armées qui ont déposé les armes et les personnes qui ont été mises hors de combat par maladie, blessure, détention, ou pour toute autre cause, seront, en toutes circonstances, traitées avec humanité, sans aucune distinction de caractère défavorable basée sur la race, la couleur, la religion ou la croyance, le sexe, la naissance ou la fortune, ou tout autre critère analogue.
A cet effet, sont et demeurent prohibés, en tout temps et en tout lieu, à l'égard des personnes mentionnées ci-dessus:
a) les atteintes portées à la vie et à l'intégrité corporelle, notamment le meurtre sous toutes ses formes, les mutilations, les traitements cruels, tortures et supplices;
b) les prises d'otages;
c) les atteintes à la dignité des personnes, notamment les traitements humiliants et dégradants;
d) les condamnations prononcées et les exécutions effectuées sans un jugement préalable, rendu par un tribunal régulièrement constitué, assorti des garanties judiciaires reconnues comme indispensables par les peuples civilisés.
2) Les blessés et les malades seront recueillis et soignés.
Un organisme humanitaire impartial, tel que le Comité international de la Croix- Rouge, pourra offrir ses services aux Parties au conflit.
Les Parties au conflit s'efforceront, d'autre part, de mettre en vigueur par voie d'accords spéciaux tout ou partie des autres dispositions de la présente Convention.
L'application des dispositions qui précèdent n'aura pas d'effet sur le statut juridique des Parties au conflit. »

xii) Le fait de détruire ou de saisir les biens d'un adversaire, sauf si ces destructions ou saisies sont impérieusement commandées par les nécessités du conflit; »

Art. 8, § 2, STATUT DE ROME DE LA COUR PÉNALE INTERNATIONALE.

CONFLITS ET CATASTROPHES NATURELLES [Conflicts and disasters]

– « Les conflits et les catastrophes naturelles contribuent à la propagation du VIH/sida »

LE VIH/SIDA DANS LES REGIONS TOUCHEES PAR LES CONFLITS ET LES CATASTROPHES NATURELLES, DÉCLARATION D'ENGAGEMENT SUR LE VIH/SIDA.

CONNAISSANCE [Knowledge]

– « 3. Il y a connaissance, au sens du présent article, lorsqu'une personne est consciente qu'une circonstance existe ou qu'une conséquence adviendra dans le cours normal des événements. «Connaître» et «en connaissance de cause» s'interprètent en conséquence. »

Art. 30, STATUT DE ROME DE LA COUR PÉNALE INTERNATIONALE.

CONSEIL [Counsel]

– « Dans les présents Principes :

[...]

Le terme « conseil » désigne un représentant qualifié, légal ou autre; »

Al. 2, DEFINITIONS, PRINCIPES POUR LA PROTECTION DES PERSONNES ATTEINTES DE MALADIE MENTALE ET POUR L'AMÉLIORATION DES SOINS DE SANTÉ MENTALE[b].

CONSENTEMENT EN CONNAISSANCE DE CAUSE [Informed consent]

– «2. Par consentement en connaissance de cause, on entend le consentement librement donné, en l'absence de toute menace ou manœuvre, et après des explications suffisantes et compréhensibles données au patient, sous une forme et dans un langage qui lui sont accessibles, sur :

a) Le processus de diagnostic;

---

[b] Sp. 1, DEFINITIONS, Principles for the protection of persons with mental illness and the improvement of mental health care.

b) Le but, les méthodes, la durée probable et les bénéfices escomptés du traitement proposé;

c) Les autres modes de traitement possibles, y compris les modes de traitement portant moins atteinte à l'intégrité du patient;

d) Les douleurs et désagréments pouvant résulter du traitement, ses risques éventuels et ses effets secondaires. »

Principe 11, PRINCIPES POUR LA PROTECTION DES PERSONNES ATTEINTES DE MALADIE MENTALE ET POUR L'AMÉLIORATION DES SOINS DE SANTÉ MENTALE.

CONTRAINTE A LA PROSTITUTION [Enforced prostitution; Forced prostitution]

– « Les femmes seront spécialement protégées contre toute atteinte à leur honneur, et notamment contre le viol, la contrainte à la prostitution et tout attentat à leur pudeur. »

Art. 27, al. 2, CONVENTION DE GENÈVE RELATIVE À LA PROTECTION DES PERSONNES CIVILES EN TEMPS DE GUERRE DU 12 AOÛT 1949.

– « Les femmes doivent faire l'objet d'un respect particulier et seront protégées, notamment contre le viol, la contrainte à la prostitution et toute autre forme d'attentat à la pudeur. »

Art. 76, PROTOCOLE ADDITIONNEL AUX CONVENTIONS DE GENÈVE DU 12 AOÛT 1949 RELATIF À LA PROTECTION DES VICTIMES DES CONFLITS ARMÉS INTERNATIONAUX (PROTOCOLE I).

– « *e*) les atteintes à la dignité de la personne, notamment les traitements humiliants et dégradants, le viol, la contrainte à la prostitution et tout attentat à la pudeur; »

Art. 4, 2., PROTOCOLE ADDITIONNEL AUX CONVENTION DE GENÈVE DU 12 AOÛT 1949 RELATIF À LA PROTECTION DES VICTIMES DES CONFLITS ARMÉS NON INTERNATIONAUX (PROTOCOLE II).

CONVICTION [Belief]

– « *Considérant* que la religion ou la conviction constitue pour celui qui la professe un des éléments fondamentaux de sa conception de la vie et que la liberté de religion ou de conviction doit être intégralement respectée et garantie, »

Pp. 4, DÉCLARATION SUR L'ÉLIMINATION DE TOUTES LES FORMES D'INTOLÉRANCE ET DE DISCRIMINATION FONDÉES SUR LA RELIGION OU LA CONVICTION.

CORRUPTION [Corruption]

– « *b*) Bien que la définition de la corruption doive être du ressort du droit interne, elle devrait s'entendre comme englobant tout acte de commission ou d'omission accompli par le responsable dans l'exercice ou à l'occasion de ses fonctions en échange de dons, de promesses ou d'avantages exigés ou acceptés, ou le fait de recevoir ceux-ci indûment, une fois l'acte considéré accompli. »

Art. 7, *Commentaire*, CODE DE CONDUITE POUR LES RESPONSABLE DE L'APPLICATION DES LOIS.

COUR PENALE INTERNATIONALE [International criminal court]

– « Il est créé une Cour pénale internationale («la Cour») en tant qu'institution permanente, qui peut exercer sa compétence à l'égard des personnes pour les crimes les plus graves ayant une portée internationale, au sens du présent Statut. Elle est complémentaire des juridictions pénales nationales. Sa compétence et son fonctionnement sont régis par les dispositions du présent Statut. »

Art. 1, STATUT DE ROME DE LA COUR PÉNALE INTERNATIONALE.

CREATION [Creation]

– « Chaque création puise aux racines des traditions culturelles, mais s'épanouissent au contact des autres cultures. [...] »

Art. 7, DÉCLARATION UNIVERSELLE SUR LA DIVERSITÉ CULTURELLE.

CRIME [Crime]

– « 2. La définition d'un crime est d'interprétation stricte et ne peut être étendue par analogie. En cas d'ambiguïté, elle est interprétée en faveur de la personne qui fait l'objet d'une enquête, de poursuites ou d'une condamnation. »

Art. 22, STATUT DE ROME DE LA COUR PÉNALE INTERNATIONALE.

CRIME D'AGRESSION [Crime of agression]

– « 2. La Cour exercera sa compétence à l'égard du crime d'agression quand une disposition aura été adoptée conformément aux articles 121[6] et 123[7], qui définira ce crime et fixera les conditions de l'exercice de la compétence de la Cour à son égard. Cette disposition devra être compatible avec les dispositions pertinentes de la Charte des Nations Unies. »

Art. 5, STATUT DE ROME DE LA COUR PÉNALE INTERNATIONALE.

---

[6] «1. À l'expiration d'une période de sept ans commençant à la date d'entrée en vigueur du présent Statut, tout État Partie peut proposer des amendements à celui-ci. Le texte des propositions d'amendement est soumis au Secrétaire général de l'Organisation des Nations Unies, qui le communique sans retard à tous les États Parties.

2. Trois mois au plus tôt après la date de cette communication, l'Assemblée des États Parties, à la réunion suivante, décide, à la majorité de ses membres présents et votants, de se saisir ou non de la proposition. L'Assemblée peut traiter cette proposition elle-même ou convoquer une conférence de révision si la question soulevée le justifie.

3. L'adoption d'un amendement lors d'une réunion de l'Assemblée des États Parties ou d'une conférence de révision requiert, s'il n'est pas possible de parvenir à un consensus, la majorité des deux tiers des États Parties.

4. Sous réserve des dispositions du paragraphe 5, un amendement entre en vigueur à l'égard de tous les États Parties un an après que les sept huitièmes d'entre eux ont déposé leurs instruments de ratification ou d'acceptation auprès du Secrétaire général de l'Organisation des Nations Unies.

5. Un amendement aux articles 5, 6, 7 et 8 du présent Statut entre en vigueur à l'égard des États Parties qui l'ont accepté unan après le dépôt de leurs instruments de ratification ou d'acceptation. La Cour n'exerce pas sa compétence à l'égard d'un crime faisant l'objet de cet amendement lorsque ce crime a été commis par un ressortissant d'un État Partie qui n'a pas accepté l'amendement ou sur le territoire de cet État.

6. Si un amendement a été accepté par les sept huitièmes des États Parties conformément au paragraphe 4, tout État Partie qui ne l'a pas accepté peut se retirer du présent Statut avec effet immédiat, nonobstant l'article 127, paragraphe 1, mais sous réserve de l'article 127, paragraphe 2, en donnant notification de son retrait au plus tard un an après l'entrée en vigueur de cet amendement.

7. Le Secrétaire général de l'Organisation des Nations Unies communique à tous les États Parties les amendements adoptés lors d'une réunion de l'Assemblée des États Parties ou d'une conférence de révision.»

[7] « 1. Sept ans après l'entrée en vigueur du présent Statut, le Secrétaire général de l'Organisation des Nations Unies convoquera une conférence de révision pour examiner tout amendement au présent Statut. L'examen pourra porter notamment, mais pas exclusivement, sur la liste des crimes figurant à l'article 5. La conférence sera ouverte aux participants à l'Assemblée des États Parties, selon les mêmes conditions.

2. À tout moment par la suite, à la demande d'un État Partie et aux fins énoncées au paragraphe 1, le Secrétaire général de l'Organisation des Nations Unies, avec l'approbation de la majorité des États Parties, convoque une conférence de révision.

3. L'adoption et l'entrée en vigueur de tout amendement au Statut examiné lors d'une conférence de révision sont régies parles dispositions de l'article 121, paragraphes 3 à 7. »

CRIME D'APARTHEID [Crime of apartheid (the)]

– « 2. Aux fins du paragraphe 1[8]:

[…]

h) Par «crime d'apartheid», on entend des actes inhumains analogues à ceux que vise le paragraphe 1, commis dans le cadre d'un régime institutionnalisé d'oppression systématique et de domination d'un groupe racial sur tout autre groupe racial ou tous autres groupes raciaux et dans l'intention de maintenir ce régime; »

Art. 7, STATUT DE ROME DE LA COUR PÉNALE INTERNATIONALE.

CRIMES CONTRE L'HUMANITE [Crimes against humanity]

– « *Rappelant* les résolutions 3 (I) et 170 (II) de l'Assemblée générale de l'Organisation des Nations Unies, en date des 13 février 1946 et 31 octobre 1947, portant sur l'extradition et le châtiment des criminels de guerre, et la résolution 95 (I) du 11 décembre 1946, confirmant les principes de droit international reconnus par le Statut du Tribunal militaire international de Nuremberg et par le jugement de ce tribunal, ainsi que les résolutions 2184 (XXI) du 12 décembre 1966 et 2202 (XXI) du 16 décembre 1966, par lesquelles l'Assemblée générale a expressément condamné en tant que

---

[8] « 1. Aux fins du présent Statut, on entend par crime contre l'humanité l'un quelconque des actes ci-après lorsqu'il est commis dans le cadre d'une attaque généralisée ou systématique lancée contre toute population civile et en connaissance de cette attaque:

a) Meurtre;

b) Extermination;

c) Réduction en esclavage;

d) Déportation ou transfert forcé de population;

e) Emprisonnement ou autre forme de privation grave de liberté physique en violation des dispositions fondamentales du droit international;

f) Torture;

g) Viol, esclavage sexuel, prostitution forcée, grossesse forcée, stérilisation forcée ou toute autre forme de violence sexuelle de gravité comparable;

h) Persécution de tout groupe ou de toute collectivité identifiable pour des motifs d'ordre politique, racial, national, ethnique, culturel, religieux ou sexiste au sens du paragraphe 3, ou en fonction d'autres critères universellement reconnus comme inadmissibles en droit international, en corrélation avec tout acte visé dans le présent paragraphe ou tout crime relevant de la compétence de la Cour;

i) Disparitions forcées de personnes;

j) Crime d'apartheid;

k) Autres actes inhumains de caractère analogue causant intentionnellement de grandes souffrances ou des atteintes graves à l'intégrité physique ou à la santé physique ou mentale. »

crimes contre l'humanité, d'une part, la violation des droits économiques et politiques des populations autochtones et, d'autre part, la politique d'*apartheid*, »

Pp. 1, CONVENTION SUR L'IMPRESCRIPTIBILITÉ DES CRIMES DE GUERRE ET DES CRIMES CONTRE L'HUMANITÉ.

– « *Considérant* que les crimes de guerre et les crimes contre l'humanité comptent au nombre des crimes de droit international les plus graves, »

Pp. 4, CONVENTION SUR L'IMPRESCRIPTIBILITÉ DES CRIMES DE GUERRE ET DES CRIMES CONTRE L'HUMANITÉ.

– « Les crimes suivants sont imprescriptibles, quelle que soit la date à laquelle ils ont été commis :

[...]

b) Les crimes contre l'humanité, qu'ils soient commis en temps de guerre ou en temps de paix, tels qu'ils sont définis dans le Statut du Tribunal militaire international de Nuremberg du 8 août 1945 et confirmés par les résolutions 3 (I) et 95 (I) de l'Assemblée générale l'Organisation des Nations, en date des 13 février 1946 et 11 décembre 1946, l'éviction par une attaque armée ou l'occupation et les actes inhumains découlant de la politique d'*apartheid*, ainsi que le crime de génocide, tel qu'il est défini dans la Convention de 1948 pour la prévention et la répression du crime de génocide, même si ces actes ne constituent pas une violation du droit interne du pays où ils ont été commis. »

Art. 1, CONVENTION SUR L'IMPRESCRIPTIBILITÉ DES CRIMES DE GUERRE ET DES CRIMES CONTRE L'HUMANITÉ.

– « Crimes contre l'humanité

Le Tribunal international est habilité à juger les personnes présumées responsables des crimes suivants lorsqu'ils ont été commis au cours d'un conflit armé, de caractère international ou interne, et dirigés contre une population civile quelle qu'elle soit :

a) Assassinat ;

b) Extermination ;

c) Réduction en esclavage ;

d) Expulsion ;

e) Emprisonnement ;

f) Torture ;

g) Viol ;

h) Persécutions pour des raisons politiques, raciales et religieuses ;

i) Autres actes inhumains. »

Art. 5, STATUT DU TRIBUNAL INTERNATIONAL CHARGÉ DE POURSUIVRE LES PERSONNES PRÉSUMÉES RESPONSABLE DE VIOLATIONS GRAVES DU DROIT INTERNATIONAL HUMANITAIRE COMMISES SUR LE TERITOIRE DE L'EX-YOUGOSLAVIE DEPUIS 1991.

– « Crimes contre l'humanité

Le Tribunal international pour le Rwanda est habilité à juger les personnes présumées responsables des crimes suivants lorsqu'ils ont été commis dans le cadre d'une attaque généralisée et systématique dirigée contre une population civile quelle qu'elle soit, en raison de son appartenance nationale, politique, ethnique, raciale ou religieuse ;

a) Assassinat ;

b) Extermination ;

c) Réduction en esclavage ;

d) Expulsion ;

e) Emprisonnement ;

f) Torture ;

g) Viol ;

h) Persécutions pour des raisons politique, raciales et religieuses ;

i) Autres actes inhumains. »

Art. 3, STATUT DU TRIBUNAL PÉNAL INTERNATIONAL CHARGÉ DE JUGER LES PERSONNES PRÉSUMÉES RESPONSABLES D'ACTES DE GÉNOCIDE OU D'AUTRES VIOLATIONS GRAVES DU DROIT INTERNATIONAL HUMANITAIRE COMMIS SUR LE TERRITOIRE DU RWANDA ET LES CITOYENS RWANDAIS PRÉSUMÉS RESPONSABLES DE TELS ACTES OU VIOLATIONS COMMIS SUR LE TERRITOIRE D'ETATS VOISINS ENTRE LE 1ER JANVIER 1994 ET LE 31 DÉCEMBRE 1994.

– « Crimes contre l'humanité

1. Aux fins du présent Statut, on entend par crime contre l'humanité l'un quelconque des actes ci-après lorsqu'il est commis dans le cadre d'une attaque généralisée ou systématique lancée contre toute population civile et en connaissance de cette attaque:

a) Meurtre;

b) Extermination;

c) Réduction en esclavage;

d) Déportation ou transfert forcé de population;

e) Emprisonnement ou autre forme de privation grave de liberté physique en violation des dispositions fondamentales du droit international;

f) Torture;

g) Viol, esclavage sexuel, prostitution forcée, grossesse forcée, stérilisation forcée ou toute autre forme de violence sexuelle de gravité comparable;

h) Persécution de tout groupe ou de toute collectivité identifiable pour des motifs d'ordre politique, racial, national, ethnique, culturel, religieux ou sexiste au sens du paragraphe 3, ou en fonction d'autres critères universellement reconnus comme inadmissibles en droit international, en corrélation avec tout acte visé dans le présent paragraphe ou tout crime relevant de la compétence de la Cour;

i) Disparitions forcées de personnes;

j) Crime d'apartheid;

k) Autres actes inhumains de caractère analogue causant intentionnellement de grandes souffrances ou des atteintes graves à l'intégrité physique ou à la santé physique ou mentale.

2. Aux fins du paragraphe 1:

a) Par «attaque lancée contre une population civile», on entend le comportement qui consiste en la commission multiple d'actes visés au paragraphe 1 à l'encontre d'une population civile quelconque, en application ou dans la poursuite de la politique d'un État ou d'une organisation ayant pour but une telle attaque;

b) Par «extermination», on entend notamment le fait d'imposer intentionnellement des conditions de vie, telles que la privation d'accès à la nourriture et aux médicaments, calculées pour entraîner la destruction d'une partie de la population;

c) Par «réduction en esclavage», on entend le fait d'exercer sur une personne l'un quelconque ou l'ensemble des pouvoirs liés au droit de propriété, y compris dans le cadre de la traite des être humains, en particulier des femmes et des enfants;

d) Par «déportation ou transfert forcé de population», on entend le fait de déplacer de force des personnes, en les expulsant ou par d'autres moyens coercitifs, de la région où elles se trouvent légalement, sans motifs admis en droit international;

e) Par «torture», on entend le fait d'infliger intentionnellement une douleur ou des souffrances aiguës, physiques ou mentales, à une personne se trouvant sous sa garde ou sous son contrôle; l'acception de ce terme ne s'étend pas à la douleur ou aux souffrances résultant uniquement de sanctions légales, inhérentes à ces sanctions ou occasionnées par elles;

f) Par «grossesse forcée», on entend la détention illégale d'une femme mise enceinte de force, dans l'intention de modifier la composition ethnique d'une population ou de commettre d'autres violations graves du droit international. Cette définition ne peut en aucune manière s'interpréter comme ayant une incidence sur les lois nationales relatives à la grossesse;

g) Par «persécution», on entend le déni intentionnel et grave de droits fondamentaux en violation du droit international, pour des motifs liés à l'identité du groupe ou de la collectivité qui en fait l'objet;

h) Par «crime d'apartheid», on entend des actes inhumains analogues à ceux que vise le paragraphe 1, commis dans le cadre d'un régime institutionnalisé d'oppression systématique et de domination d'un groupe racial sur tout autre groupe racial ou tous autres groupes raciaux et dans l'intention de maintenir ce régime;

i) Par «disparitions forcées de personnes», on entend les cas où des personnes sont arrêtées, détenues ou enlevées par un État ou une organisation politique ou avec l'autorisation, l'appui ou l'assentiment de cet État ou de cette organisation, qui refuse ensuite d'admettre que ces personnes sont privées de liberté ou de révéler le sort qui leur est réservé ou l'endroit où elles se trouvent, dans l'intention de les soustraire à la protection de la loi pendant une période prolongée.

3. Aux fins du présent Statut, le terme «sexe» s'entend de l'un et l'autre sexes, masculin et féminin, suivant le contexte de la société. Il n'implique aucun autre sens. »

Art. 7, Statut de Rome de la Cour pénale internationale.

CRIMES DE GUERRE [War crimes]

– « *Considérant* que les crimes de guerre et les crimes contre l'humanité comptent au nombre des crimes de droit international les plus graves, »

Pp. 4, CONVENTION SUR L'IMPRESCRIPTIBILITÉ DES CRIMES DE GUERRE ET DES CRIMES CONTRE L'HUMANITÉ.

– « Les crimes suivants sont imprescriptibles, quelle que soit la date à laquelle ils ont été commis :

a) Les crimes de guerre, tels qu'ils sont définis dans le Statut du Tribunal militaire international de Nuremberg du 8 août 1945 et confirmés par les résolutions 3 (I) et 95 (I) de l'Assemblée générale de l'Organisation des Nations Unies, en date des 13 février 1946 et 11 décembre 1946, notamment les "infractions graves" énumérées dans les Conventions de Genève du 12 août 1949 pour la protection des victimes de la guerre; »

Art. 1, CONVENTION SUR L'IMPRESCRIPTIBILITÉ DES CRIMES DE GUERRE ET DES CRIMES CONTRE L'HUMANITÉ.

– « 2. Aux fins du Statut, on entend par «crimes de guerre»:

a) Les infractions graves aux Conventions de Genève du 12 août 1949, à savoir l'un quelconque des actes ci-après lorsqu'ils visent des personnes ou des biens protégés par les dispositions des Conventions de Genève:

i) L'homicide intentionnel;

ii) La torture ou les traitements inhumains, y compris les expériences biologiques;

iii) Le fait de causer intentionnellement de grandes souffrances ou de porter gravement atteinte à l'intégrité physique ou à la santé;

iv) La destruction et l'appropriation de biens, non justifiées par des nécessités militaires et exécutées sur une grande échelle de façon illicite et arbitraire;

v) Le fait de contraindre un prisonnier de guerre ou une personne protégée à servir dans les forces d'une puissance ennemie;

vi) Le fait de priver intentionnellement un prisonnier de guerre ou toute autre personne protégée de son droit d'être jugé régulièrement et impartialement;

vii) La déportation ou le transfert illégal ou la détention illégale;

viii) La prise d'otages;

b) Les autres violations graves des lois et coutumes applicables aux conflits armés internationaux dans le cadre établi du droit international, à savoir, l'un quelconque des actes ci-après:

i) Le fait de diriger intentionnellement des attaques délibérées contre la population civile en tant que telle ou contre des civils qui ne participent pas directement aux hostilités;

ii) Le fait de diriger intentionnellement des attaques délibérées contre des biens de caractère civil, c'est-à-dire des biens qui ne sont pas des objectifs militaires;

iii) Le fait de diriger intentionnellement des attaques contre le personnel, les installations, le matériel, les unités ou les véhicules employés dans le cadre d'une mission d'aide humanitaire ou de maintien de la paix conformément à la Charte des Nations Unies, pour autant qu'ils aient droit à la protection que le droit international des conflits armés garantit aux civils et aux biens de caractère civil;

iv) Le fait de diriger intentionnellement une attaque en sachant qu'elle causera incidemment des pertes en vies humaines dans la population civile, des blessures aux personnes civiles, des dommages aux biens de caractère civil ou des dommages étendus, durables et graves à l'environnement naturel qui seraient manifestement excessifs par rapport à l'ensemble de l'avantage militaire concret et direct attendu;

v) Le fait d'attaquer ou de bombarder, par quelque moyen que ce soit, des villes, villages, habitations ou bâtiments qui ne sont pas défendus et qui ne sont pas des objectifs militaires;

vi) Le fait de tuer ou de blesser un combattant qui, ayant déposé les armes ou n'ayant plus de moyens de se défendre, s'est rendu à discrétion;

vii) Le fait d'utiliser indûment le pavillon parlementaire, le drapeau ou les insignes militaires et l'uniforme de l'ennemi ou de l'Organisation des Nations Unies, ainsi que les signes distinctifs prévus par les Conventions de Genève, et, ce faisant, de causer la perte de vies humaines ou des blessures graves;

viii) Le transfert, direct ou indirect, par une puissance occupante d'une partie de sa population civile, dans le territoire qu'elle occupe, ou la déportation ou le transfert à l'intérieur ou hors du territoire occupé de la totalité ou d'une partie de la population de ce territoire;

ix) Le fait de diriger intentionnellement des attaques contre des bâtiments consacrés à la religion, à l'enseignement, à l'art, à la science ou à l'action caritative, des monuments historiques, des hôpitaux et des lieux où des malades ou des blessés sont rassemblés, à condition qu'ils ne soient pas des objectifs militaires;

x) Le fait de soumettre des personnes d'une partie adverse tombées en son pouvoir à des mutilations ou à des expériences médicales ou scientifiques quelles qu'elles soient qui ne sont ni motivées par un traitement médical, dentaire ou hospitalier, ni effectuées dans l'intérêt de ces personnes, et qui entraînent la mort de celles-ci ou mettent sérieusement en danger leur santé;

xi) Le fait de tuer ou de blesser par traîtrise des individus appartenant à la nation ou à l'armée ennemie;

xii) Le fait de déclarer qu'il ne sera pas fait de quartier;

xiii) Le fait de détruire ou de saisir les biens de l'ennemi, sauf dans les cas où ces destructions ou saisies seraient impérieusement commandées par les nécessités de la guerre;

xiv) Le fait de déclarer éteints, suspendus ou non recevables en justice les droits et actions des nationaux de la partie adverse;

xv) Le fait pour un belligérant de contraindre les nationaux de la partie adverse à prendre part aux opérations de guerre dirigées contre leur pays, même s'ils étaient au service de ce belligérant avant le commencement de la guerre;

xvi) Le pillage d'une ville ou d'une localité, même prise d'assaut;

xvii) Le fait d'employer du poison ou des armes empoisonnées;

xviii) Le fait d'employer des gaz asphyxiants, toxiques ou similaires, ainsi que tous liquides, matières ou procédés analogues;

xix) Le fait d'utiliser des balles qui s'épanouissent ou s'aplatissent facilement dans le corps humain, telles que des balles dont l'enveloppe dure ne recouvre pas entièrement le centre ou est percée d'entailles;

xx) Le fait d'employer les armes, projectiles, matières et méthodes de guerre de nature à causer des maux superflus ou des souffrances inutiles ou à frapper sans discrimination en violation du droit international des conflits armés, à condition que ces armes, projectiles, matières et méthodes de guerre fassent l'objet d'une interdiction générale et qu'ils soient inscrits dans une annexe au présent Statut, par voie d'amendement adopté selon les dispositions des articles 121[9] et 123[10];

---

[9] « 1. À l'expiration d'une période de sept ans commençant à la date d'entrée en vigueur du présent Statut, tout État Partie peut proposer des amendements à celui-ci. Le texte des propositions d'amendement est soumis au Secrétaire général de l'Organisation des Nations Unies, qui le communique sans retard à tous les États Parties.

2. Trois mois au plus tôt après la date de cette communication, l'Assemblée des États Parties, à la réunion suivante, décide, à la majorité de ses membres présents et votants, de se saisir ou non de la proposition. L'Assemblée peut traiter cette proposition elle-même ou convoquer une conférence de révision si la question soulevée le justifie.

3. L'adoption d'un amendement lors d'une réunion de l'Assemblée des États Parties ou d'une conférence de révision requiert, s'il n'est pas possible de parvenir à un consensus, la majorité des deux tiers des États Parties.

4. Sous réserve des dispositions du paragraphe 5, un amendement entre en vigueur à l'égard de tous les États Parties un an après que les sept huitièmes d'entre eux ont déposé leurs instruments de ratification ou d'acceptation auprès du Secrétaire général de l'Organisation des Nations Unies.

5. Un amendement aux articles 5, 6, 7 et 8 du présent Statut entre en vigueur à l'égard des États Parties qui l'ont accepté unan après le dépôt de leurs instruments de ratification ou d'acceptation. La Cour n'exerce pas sa compétence à l'égard d'un crime faisant l'objet de cet amendement lorsque ce crime a été commis par un ressortissant d'un État Partie qui n'a pas accepté l'amendement ou sur le territoire de cet État.

6. Si un amendement a été accepté par les sept huitièmes des États Parties conformément au paragraphe 4, tout État Partie qui ne l'a pas accepté peut se retirer du présent Statut avec effet immédiat, nonobstant l'article 127, paragraphe 1, mais sous réserve de l'article 127, paragraphe 2, en donnant notification de son retrait au plus tard un an après l'entrée en vigueur de cet amendement.

7. Le Secrétaire général de l'Organisation des Nations Unies communique à tous les États Parties les amendements adoptés lors d'une réunion de l'Assemblée des États Parties ou d'une conférence de révision. »

xxi) Les atteintes à la dignité de la personne, notamment les traitements humiliants et dégradants;

xxii) Le viol, l'esclavage sexuel, la prostitution forcée, la grossesse forcée, telle que définie à l'article 7, paragraphe 2, alinéa f)[11], la stérilisation forcée ou toute autre forme de violence sexuelle constituant une infraction grave aux Conventions de Genève;

xxiii) Le fait d'utiliser la présence d'un civil ou d'une autre personne protégée pour éviter que certains points, zones ou forces militaires ne soient la cible d'opérations militaires;

xxiv) Le fait de diriger intentionnellement des attaques contre les bâtiments, le matériel, les unités et les moyens de transport sanitaires, et le personnel utilisant, conformément au droit international, les signes distinctifs prévus par les Conventions de Genève;

xxv) Le fait d'affamer délibérément des civils comme méthode de guerre, en les privant de biens indispensables à leur survie, y compris en empêchant intentionnellement l'envoi des secours prévus par les Conventions de Genève;

xxvi) Le fait de procéder à la conscription ou à l'enrôlement d'enfants de moins de 15 ans dans les forces armées nationales ou de les faire participer activement à des hostilités;

c) En cas de conflit armé ne présentant pas un caractère international, les violations graves de l'article 3 commun aux quatre Conventions de

---

[10] « 1. Sept ans après l'entrée en vigueur du présent Statut, le Secrétaire général de l'Organisation des Nations Unies convoquera une conférence de révision pour examiner tout amendement au présent Statut. L'examen pourra porter notamment, mais pas exclusivement, sur la liste des crimes figurant à l'article 5. La conférence sera ouverte aux participants à l'Assemblée des États Parties, selon les mêmes conditions.
2. À tout moment par la suite, à la demande d'un État Partie et aux fins énoncées au paragraphe 1, le Secrétaire général de l'Organisation des Nations Unies, avec l'approbation de la majorité des États Parties, convoque une conférence de révision.
3. L'adoption et l'entrée en vigueur de tout amendement au Statut examiné lors d'une conférence de révision sont régies parles dispositions de l'article 121, paragraphes 3 à 7. »

[11] « *f*) Par «grossesse forcée», on entend la détention illégale d'une femme mise enceinte de force, dans l'intention de modifier la composition ethnique d'une population ou de commettre d'autres violations graves du droit international. Cette définition ne peut en aucune manière s'interpréter comme ayant une incidence sur les lois nationales relatives à la grossesse; »

Genève du 12 août 1949[12], à savoir l'un quelconque des actes ci-après commis à l'encontre de personnes qui ne participent pas directement aux hostilités, y compris les membres de forces armées qui ont déposé les armes et les personnes qui ont été mises hors de combat par maladie, blessure, détention ou par toute autre cause:

i) Les atteintes à la vie et à l'intégrité corporelle, notamment le meurtre sous toutes ses formes, les mutilations, les traitements cruels et la torture;

ii) Les atteintes à la dignité de la personne, notamment les traitements humiliants et dégradants;

iii) Les prises d'otages;

iv) Les condamnations prononcées et les exécutions effectuées sans un jugement préalable, rendu par un tribunal régulièrement constitué, assorti des garanties judiciaires généralement reconnues comme indispensables;

d) L'alinéa c) du paragraphe 2 s'applique aux conflits armés ne présentant pas un caractère international et ne s'applique donc pas

---

[12] « En cas de conflit armé ne présentant pas un caractère international et surgissant sur le territoire de l'une des Hautes Parties contractantes, chacune des Parties au conflit sera tenue d'appliquer au moins les dispositions suivantes :
1) Les personnes qui ne participent pas directement aux hostilités, y compris les membres de forces armées qui ont déposé les armes et les personnes qui ont été mises hors de combat par maladie, blessure, détention, ou pour toute autre cause, seront, en toutes circonstances, traitées avec humanité, sans aucune distinction de caractère défavorable basée sur la race, la couleur, la religion ou la croyance, le sexe, la naissance ou la fortune, ou tout autre critère analogue.
A cet effet, sont et demeurent prohibés, en tout temps et en tout lieu, à l'égard des personnes mentionnées ci-dessus :
a) les atteintes portées à la vie et à l'intégrité corporelle, notamment le meurtre sous toutes ses formes, les mutilations, les traitements cruels, tortures et supplices;
b) les prises d'otages;
c) les atteintes à la dignité des personnes, notamment les traitements humiliants et dégradants;
d) les condamnations prononcées et les exécutions effectuées sans un jugement préalable, rendu par un tribunal régulièrement constitué, assorti des garanties judiciaires reconnues comme indispensables par les peuples civilisés.
2) Les blessés et malades seront recueillis et soignés.
Un organisme humanitaire impartial, tel que le Comité international de la Croix-Rouge, pourra offrir ses services aux Parties au conflit.
Les Parties au conflit s'efforceront, d'autre part, de mettre en vigueur par voie d'accords spéciaux tout ou partie des autres dispositions de la présente Convention.
L'application des dispositions qui précèdent n'aura pas d'effet sur le statut juridique des Parties au conflit. »

aux situations de troubles et tensions internes telles que les émeutes, les actes isolés et sporadiques de violence ou les actes de nature similaire;

e) Les autres violations graves des lois et coutumes applicables aux conflits armés ne présentant pas un caractère international, dans le cadre établi du droit international, à savoir l'un quelconque des actes ci-après:

i) Le fait de diriger intentionnellement des attaques contre la population civile en tant que telle ou contre des personnes civils qui ne participent pas directement aux hostilités;

ii) Le fait de diriger intentionnellement des attaques contre les bâtiments, le matériel, les unités et les moyens de transport sanitaires, et le personnel utilisant, conformément au droit international, les signes distinctifs des Conventions de Genève;

iii) Le fait de diriger intentionnellement des attaques contre le personnel, les installations, le matériel, les unités ou les véhicules employés dans le cadre d'une mission d'aide humanitaire ou de maintien de la paix conformément à la Charte des Nations Unies, pour autant qu'ils aient droit à la protection que le droit international des conflits armés garantit aux civils et aux biens de caractère civil;

iv) Le fait de diriger intentionnellement des attaques contre des bâtiments consacrés à la religion, à l'enseignement, à l'art, à la science ou à l'action caritative, des monuments historiques, des hôpitaux et des lieux où des malades et des blessés sont rassemblés, pour autant que ces bâtiments ne soient pas des objectifs militaires;

v) Le pillage d'une ville ou d'une localité, même prise d'assaut;

vi) Le viol, l'esclavage sexuel, la prostitution forcée, la grossesse forcée, telle que définie à l'article 7, paragraphe 2, alinéa f)[13], la stérilisation forcée, ou toute autre forme de violence sexuelle

[13] « *f*) Par «grossesse forcée», on entend la détention illégale d'une femme mise enceinte de force, dans l'intention de modifier la composition ethnique d'une population ou de commettre d'autres violations graves du droit international. Cette définition ne peut en aucune manière s'interpréter comme ayant une incidence sur les lois nationales relatives à la grossesse; »

constituant une violation grave de l'article 3 commun aux quatre Conventions de Genève[14];

vii) Le fait de procéder à la conscription ou à l'enrôlement d'enfants de moins de 15 ans dans les forces armées ou dans des groupes armés ou de les faire participer activement à des hostilités;

viii) Le fait d'ordonner le déplacement de la population civile pour des raisons ayant trait au conflit, sauf dans les cas où la sécurité des civils ou des impératifs militaires l'exigent;

ix) Le fait de tuer ou de blesser par traîtrise un adversaire combattant;

x) Le fait de déclarer qu'il ne sera pas fait de quartier;

xi) Le fait de soumettre des personnes d'une autre partie au conflit tombées en son pouvoir à des mutilations ou à des expériences médicales ou scientifiques quelles qu'elles soient qui ne sont ni motivées par un traitement médical, dentaire ou hospitalier, ni effectuées dans l'intérêt de ces personnes, et qui

---

[14] « En cas de conflit armé ne présentant pas un caractère international et surgissant sur le territoire de l'une des Hautes Parties contractantes, chacune des Parties au conflit sera tenue d'appliquer au moins les dispositions suivantes:

1) Les personnes qui ne participent pas directement aux hostilités, y compris les membres de forces armées qui ont déposé les armes et les personnes qui ont été mises hors de combat par maladie, blessure, détention, ou pour toute autre cause, seront, en toutes circonstances, traitées avec humanité, sans aucune distinction de caractère défavorable basée sur la race, la couleur, la religion ou la croyance, le sexe, la naissance ou la fortune, ou tout autre critère analogue.

A cet effet, sont et demeurent prohibés, en tout temps et en tout lieu, à l'égard des personnes mentionnées ci-dessus:

a) les atteintes portées à la vie et à l'intégrité corporelle, notamment le meurtre sous toutes ses formes, les mutilations, les traitements cruels, tortures et supplices;

b) les prises d'otages;

c) les atteintes à la dignité des personnes, notamment les traitements humiliants et dégradants;

d) les condamnations prononcées et les exécutions effectuées sans un jugement préalable, rendu par un tribunal régulièrement constitué, assorti des garanties judiciaires reconnues comme indispensables par les peuples civilisés.

2) Les blessés et les malades seront recueillis et soignés.

Un organisme humanitaire impartial, tel que le Comité international de la Croix-Rouge, pourra offrir ses services aux Parties au conflit.

Les Parties au conflit s'efforceront, d'autre part, de mettre en vigueur par voie d'accords spéciaux tout ou partie des autres dispositions de la présente Convention.

L'application des dispositions qui précèdent n'aura pas d'effet sur le statut juridique des Parties au conflit. »

entraînent la mort de celles-ci ou mettent sérieusement en danger leur santé;

xii) Le fait de détruire ou de saisir les biens d'un adversaire, sauf si ces destructions ou saisies sont impérieusement commandées par les nécessités du conflit;

f) L'alinéa e) du paragraphe 2 s'applique aux conflits armés ne présentant pas un caractère international et ne s'applique donc pas aux situations de troubles et tensions internes telles que les émeutes, les actes isolés et sporadiques de violence ou les actes de nature similaire. Il s'applique aux conflits armés qui opposent de manière prolongée sur le territoire d'un État les autorités du gouvernement de cet État et des groupes armés organisés ou des groupes armés organisés entre eux. »

Art. 8, STATUT DE ROME DE LA COUR PÉNALE INTERNATIONALE.

CRIMES POLITIQUES [Political crimes]

– « Le génocide et les autres actes énumérés à l'article III[15] ne seront pas considérés comme des crimes politiques pour ce qui est de l'extradition. »

Art. VII, al. 1, CONVENTION POUR LA PRÉVENTION ET LA RÉPRESSION DU CRIME DE GÉNOCIDE.

CULTURE [Culture]

– « 1. La culture, œuvre de tous les humains et patrimoine commun de l'humanité, et l'éducation, au sens le plus large, offrent aux hommes et aux femmes des moyens sans cesse plus efficaces d'adaptation, leur permettant non seulement d'affirmer qu'ils naissent égaux en dignité et en droits, mais aussi de reconnaître qu'ils doivent respecter le droit de tous les groupes humains à l'identité culturelle et au développement de leur vie culturelle propre dans le cadre national et international, étant entendu qu'il appartient à chaque groupe de décider en toute liberté du maintien et, le cas échéant, de l'adaptation ou de l'enrichissement des valeurs qu'il considère comme essentielles à son identité. »

Art. 5, DÉCLARATION SUR LA RACE ET LES PRÉJUGÉS RACIAUX.

---

[15] « Seront punis les actes suivants :

a) Le génocide;

b) L'entente en vue de commettre le génocide;

c) L'incitation directe et publique à commettre le génocide;

d) La tentative de génocide;

e) La complicité dans le génocide. »

- « *Réaffirmant* que la culture doit être considérée comme l'ensemble des traits distinctifs spirituels et matériels, intellectuels et affectifs qui caractérisent une société ou un groupe social et qu'elle englobe, outre les arts et les lettres, les modes de vie, les façons de vivre ensemble, les systèmes de valeurs, les traditions et les croyances[2], »

Pp. 5, DÉCLARATION UNIVERSELLE SUR LA DIVERSITÉ CULTURELLE.

- « *Constatant* que la culture se trouve au cœur des débats contemporains sur l'identité, la cohésion sociale et le développement d'une économie fondée sur le savoir, »

Pp. 6, DÉCLARATION UNIVERSELLE SUR LA DIVERSITÉ CULTURELLE.

- « La culture prend des formes diverses à travers le temps et l'espace. Cette diversité s'incarne dans l'originalité et la pluralité des identités qui caractérisent les groupes et les sociétés composant l'humanité. Source d'échanges, d'innovation et de créativité, la diversité culturelle est, pour le genre humain, aussi nécessaire que l'est la biodiversité dans l'ordre du vivant. En ce sens, elle constitue le patrimoine commun de l'humanité et elle doit être reconnue et affirmée au bénéfice des générations présentes et des générations futures. »

Art. 1, DÉCLARATION UNIVERSELLE SUR LA DIVERSITÉ CULTURELLE.

CULTURE, LA FAMILLE, LES VALEURS MORALES ET LA RELIGION (LA) [Cultural, family, ethnical and religious factors]

- « 20. Soulignant le rôle important que peuvent jouer la culture, la famille, les valeurs morales et la religion dans la prévention de l'épidémie et dans les activités de traitement, de soins et d'appui, compte tenu des particularités de chaque pays et de la nécessité de respecter tous les droits de l'homme et les libertés fondamentales; »

DÉCLARATION D'ENGAGEMENT SUR LE VIH/SIDA.

DECLARATION UNVERSELLE DES DROITS DE L'HOMME [Universal declaration of human rights]

[« [2] Définition conforme aux conclusions de la Conférence mondiale sur les politiques culturelles (MONDIACULT, Mexico, 1982), de la Commission mondiale de la culture et du développement (*Notre diversité créatrice*, 1995) et de la Conférence intergouvernementale sur les politiques culturelles pour le développement (Stockholm, 1998). »]

– « *Proclame* la présente Déclaration universelle des droits de l'homme comme l'idéal commun à atteindre par tous les peuples et toutes les nations [...] »

Pp. 8, DÉCLARATION UNIVERSELLE DES DROITS DE L'HOMME.

– « *Soulignant* que la Déclaration universelle des droits de l'homme, qui constitue un modèle *commun* à suivre pour tous les peuples et toutes les nations, est la source d'inspiration de l'Organisation des Nations Unies et l'assise à partir de laquelle elle a progressivement élaboré les normes énoncées dans les instruments internationaux en vigueur dans le domaine considéré, en particulier dans le Pacte international relatif aux droits civils et politiques et le Pacte international relatif aux droits économiques, sociaux et culturels, »

Pp. 8, DÉCLARATION ET PROGRAMMATION D'ACTION DE VIENNE.

– « *Réaffirmant* également l'importance de la Déclaration universelle des droits de l'homme et des Pactes internationaux relatifs aux droits de l'homme en tant qu'éléments fondamentaux des efforts internationaux visant à promouvoir le respect universel effectif des droits de l'homme et des libertés fondamentales, ainsi que l'importance des autres instruments relatifs aux droits de l'homme adoptés par les organes et organismes des Nations Unies, et de ceux adoptés au niveau régional, »[16]

Pp. 2, DÉCLARATION SUR LE DROIT ET LA RESPONSABILITÉ DES INDIVIDUS, GROUPES ET ORGANES DE LA SOCIÉTÉ DE PROMOUVOIR ET PROTÉGER LES DROITS DE L'HOMME ET LES LIBERTÉS FONDAMENTALES UNIVERSELLEMENT RECONNUS.

DEFENSE DE LA DIVERSITE CULTURELLE [Defence of cultural diversity]

– « La défense de la diversité culturelle est un impératif éthique, inséparable du respect de la dignité de la personne humaine. Elle implique l'engagement de respecter les droits de l'homme et les libertés fondamentales, en particulier les droits des personnes appartenant à des

---

[16] Face à la version papier sur laquelle nous travaillons existe une version electronique dont le texte diffère et dont voici la version : « *Réaffirmant également* l'importance de la Déclaration universelle des droits de l'homme[2] et des Pactes internationaux relatifs aux droits de l'homme Résolution 2200 A (XXI), annexe. en tant qu'éléments fondamentaux des efforts internationaux visant à promouvoir le respect universel et effectif des droits de l'homme et des libertés fondamentales, ainsi que l'importance des autres instruments relatifs aux droits de l'homme adoptés par les organes et organismes des Nations Unies, et de ceux adoptés au niveau régional, »

minorités et ceux des peuples autochtones. Nul ne peut invoquer la diversité culturelle pour porter atteinte aux droits de l'homme garantis par le droit international, ni pour en limiter la portée. »

Art. 4, DÉCLARATION UNIVERSELLE SUR LA DIVERSITÉ CULTURELLE.

DEFICIENCES [Impairments]

– « 20. En 1980, l'Organisation mondiale de la santé a adopté une classification internationale des déficiences, incapacités et handicaps qui a défini une approche à la fois plus précise et relativiste. La Classification internationale des handicapés : déficiences, incapacités et désavantages établit des distinctions claires entre la déficience, l'incapacité et handicap. Elle est couramment utilisée dans les domaines suivants : réadaptation, éducation, statistiques, prise de décisions, législation, démographie, sociologie, économie et anthropologie. Selon certains des spécialistes à qui elle s'adresse, il se pourrait que la définition du terme « handicap » qui est donnée revête un caractère trop médicale encore, qu'elle soit indûment centrée sur l'individu, et qu'elle ne précise pas assez clairement la manière dont la situation sociale, les attentes de la collectivité et d'autres préoccupations exprimées par les utilisateurs depuis la publication de la Classification, il y a 12 ans, dans les révisions dont celle-ci doit faire l'objet. »[c]

INTRODUCTION, RÈGLES POUR L'ÉGALISATION DES CHANCES DES PERSONNES HANDICAPÉES.

DELINQUANT JUVENILE [Juvenile offender]

– « .2 Aux fins du présent Ensemble de règles, chaque Etat Membre applique les définitions ci-après de manière compatible avec son système et ses concepts juridiques propres :

[...]

---

[c] "20. In 1980, the World Health Organization adopted an international classification of impairments, disabilities and handicaps, which suggested a more precise and at the same time relativistic approach. The International Classification of Impairments, Disabilities, and Handicaps makes a clear distinction between 'impairment', 'disability' and 'handicap'. It has been extensively used in areas such as rehabilitation, education, statistics, policy, legislation, demography, sociology, economics and anthropology. Some users have expressed concern that the Classification, in its definition of the term 'handicap', may still be considered too medical and too centred on the individual, and may not adequately clarify the interaction between societal conditions or expectations and the abilities of the individual. Those concerns, and others expressed by users during the 12 years since its publication, will be addressed in forthcoming revisions of the Classification."

c) Un délinquant juvénile est un enfant ou un jeune, accusé ou déclaré coupable d'avoir commis un délit. »

ENSEMBLE DE RÈGLES MINIMA DES NATIONS UNIES CONCERNANT L'ADMINISTRATION DE LA JUSTICE POUR LES MINEURS (RÈGLES DE BEIJING).

– « L'article 2.2 définit les termes "mineur" et "délit" en tant qu'éléments de la notion de "délinquant juvénile", qui fait l'objet principal du présent Ensemble de règles minima (voir aussi les articles 3[17] et 4[18]). Il faut noter que les limites d'âge dépendent expressément de chaque système juridique et

---

[17] « 3. Extension des règles
3.1 Les dispositions pertinentes du présent Ensemble de règles seront appliquées non seulement aux délinquants juvéniles mais aussi aux mineurs contre qui des poursuites pourraient être engagées pour tout comportement qui ne serait pas punissable s'il était commis par un adulte.
3.2 On s'efforcera d'étendre les principes incorporés dans le présent Ensemble de règles à tous les mineurs auxquels s'appliquent des mesures de protection et d'aide sociale.
3.3 On s'efforcera également d'étendre aux jeunes adultes délinquants les principes incorporés dans le présent Ensemble de règles.
Commentaire :
L'article 3 étend la protection assurée par l'Ensemble de règles minima concernant l'administration de la justice pour mineurs :
a) Aux "délits d'état" prévus par les systèmes juridiques nationaux où des comportements plus nombreux que pour les adultes sont considérés comme délictueux chez les jeunes (par exemple l'absentéisme scolaire, l'indiscipline à l'école et en famille, l'ivresse publique, etc.) [art. 3.1];
b) Aux mesures de protection et d'aide sociale à l'intention des jeunes (art. 3.2);
c) Au traitement des jeunes délinquants adultes, selon la limite d'âge fixée dans chaque cas, bien entendu (art. 3.3).
L'extension de l'Ensemble de règles à ces trois domaines semble se justifier. L'article 3.1 prévoit des garanties minima dans ces domaines et l'article 3.2 est considéré comme une étape souhaitable sur la voie d'une justice pénale plus juste, plus équitable et plus humaine pour les mineurs entrés en conflit avec la loi. »

[18] « 4. Age de la responsabilité pénale
4.1 Dans les systèmes juridiques qui reconnaissent la notion de seuil de responsabilité pénale, celui-ci ne doit pas être fixé trop bas eu égard aux problèmes de maturité affective, psychologique et intellectuelle.
Commentaire :
Le seuil de responsabilité pénale varie largement selon les époques et les cultures. L'attitude moderne serait de se demander si un enfant peut supporter les conséquences morales et psychologiques de la responsabilité pénale, c'est-à-dire si un enfant, compte tenu de sa capacité de discernement et de compréhension, peut être tenu responsable d'un comportement essentiellement antisocial. Si l'âge de la responsabilité pénale est fixé trop bas ou s'il n'y a pas d'âge limite du tout, la notion n'a plus de sens. En général, il existe une relation étroite entre la notion de responsabilité pour un comportement délictueux ou criminel et les autres droits et responsabilités sociales (par exemple la situation matrimoniale, la majorité civile, etc.).
Il faudrait donc chercher à convenir d'un seuil raisonnablement bas applicable dans tous les pays. »

tiennent pleinement compte des systèmes économiques, sociaux, politiques et culturels des Etats Membres. Il s'ensuit que toute une gamme d'âges relève de la catégorie des jeunes qui va donc de 7 ans à 18 ans ou plus. Cette disparité est inévitable eu égard à la diversité des systèmes juridiques nationaux et ne diminue en rien l'impact du présent Ensemble de règles minima. »

Art. 2, *Commentaire*, ENSEMBLE DE RÈGLES MINIMA DES NATIONS UNIES CONCERNANT L'ADMINISTRATION DE LA JUSTICE POUR LES MINEURS (RÈGLES DE BEIJING).

DELINQUANTS [Offenders]

– « 2.1 Les dispositions pertinentes des présentßes Règles s'appliquent à toutes personnes faisant l'objet de poursuites judiciaires, d'un procès ou de l'exécution d'une sentence, à tous les stades de l'administration de la justice pénale. Aux fins des présentes Règles, ces personnes sont dénommées "délinquants" – qu'il s'agisse de suspects, d'accusés ou de condamnés. »

RÈGLES MINIMA DES NATIONS UNIES POUR L'ÉLABORATION DE MESURES NON PRIVATIVES DE LIBERTÉ (RÈGLES DE TOKYO).

DELIT [Offence]

– - « 2.2 Aux fins du présent Ensemble de règles, chaque Etat Membre applique les définitions ci-après de manière compatible avec son système et ses concepts juridiques propres :

[…]

b) Un délit désigne tout comportement (acte ou omission) punissable par la loi en vertu du système juridique considéré; »

ENSEMBLE DE RÈGLES MINIMA DES NATIONS UNIES CONCERNANT L'ADMINISTRATION DE LA JUSTICE POUR LES MINEURS (RÈGLES DE BEIJING).

DEMOCRATIE [Democracy]

– « 8. La démocratie, le développement et le respect des droits de l'homme et des libertés fondamentales sont interdépendants et se renforcent mutuellement. La démocratie est fondée sur la volonté, librement exprimée, du peuple qui détermine le système politique, économique, social et culturel qui sera le sien et sur sa pleine participation à tous les aspects de la vie de la société. […] »

I, DÉCLARATION ET PROGRAMMATION D'ACTION DE VIENNE.

DEPORTATION OU TRANSFERT FORCE DE POPULATION [Deportation or forcible transfer of population]

– « 2. Aux fins du paragraphe 1[19]:

[...]

d) Par «déportation ou transfert forcé de population», on entend le fait de déplacer de force des personnes, en les expulsant ou par d'autres moyens coercitifs, de la région où elles se trouvent légalement, sans motifs admis en droit international; »

Art. 7, STATUT DE ROME DE LA COUR PÉNALE INTERNATIONALE.

DESARMEMENT [Disarmament]

– « *Réaffirmant* qu'il existe une relation étroite entre le désarmement et le développement, que des progrès dans le domaine du désarmement contribueraient dans une mesure considérable à des progrès dans le domaine du développement et que les ressources libérées grâce à des mesures de désarmement devraient être consacrées au développement économique et social et au bien-être de tous les peuples, en particulier ceux des pays en développement, »

Pp. 12, DÉCLARATION SUR LE DROIT AU DÉVELOPPEMENT.

---

[19] « 1. Aux fins du présent Statut, on entend par crime contre l'humanité l'un quelconque des actes ci-après lorsqu'il est commis dans le cadre d'une attaque généralisée ou systématique lancée contre toute population civile et en connaissance de cette attaque:

a) Meurtre;

b) Extermination;

c) Réduction en esclavage;

d) Déportation ou transfert forcé de population;

e) Emprisonnement ou autre forme de privation grave de liberté physique en violation des dispositions fondamentales du droit international;

f) Torture;

g) Viol, esclavage sexuel, prostitution forcée, grossesse forcée, stérilisation forcée ou toute autre forme de violence sexuelle de gravité comparable;

h) Persécution de tout groupe ou de toute collectivité identifiable pour des motifs d'ordre politique, racial, national, ethnique, culturel, religieux ou sexiste au sens du paragraphe 3, ou en fonction d'autres critères universellement reconnus comme inadmissibles en droit international, en corrélation avec tout acte visé dans le présent paragraphe ou tout crime relevant de la compétence de la Cour;

i) Disparitions forcées de personnes;

j) Crime d'apartheid;

k) Autres actes inhumains de caractère analogue causant intentionnellement de grandes souffrances ou des atteintes graves à l'intégrité physique ou à la santé physique ou mentale. »

DESEQUILIBRES EXISTANT DANS LES RELATIONS ECONOMIQUES INTERNATIONALES [Existing disequilibria in international economic relations]

– « 4. Les déséquilibres existant dans les relations économiques internationales contribuent à exacerber le racisme et les préjugés raciaux; en conséquence, tous les Etats devraient s'efforcer de contribuer à restructurer l'économie internationale sur la base d'une plus grande équité. »

Art. 9, DÉCLARATION SUR LA RACE ET LES PRÉJUGÉS RACIAUX.

DETENTION [Detention]

– « Aux fins de l'Ensemble de principes:
[...]
d) Le terme "détention" s'entend de la condition des personnes détenues telle qu'elle est définie ci-dessus[20]; »

Emploi des termes, ENSEMBLE DE PRINCIPES POUR LA PROTECTION DE TOUTES LES PERSONNES SOUMISES À UNE FORME QUELCONQUE DE DÉTENTION OU D'EMPRISONNEMENT.

DETENTION PROVISOIRE [Pre-trial detention; Detention pending trial]

– « 6.1 La détention provisoire ne peut être qu'une mesure de dernier ressort dans les procédures pénales, compte dûment tenu de l'enquête sur le délit présumé et de la protection de la société et de la victime. »

RÈGLES MINIMA DES NATIONS UNIES POUR L'ÉLABORATION DE MESURES NON-PIVATIVES DE LIBERTÉ (RÈGLES DE TOKYO).

– « 13.1 La détention préventive ne peut être qu'une mesure de dernier ressort et sa durée doit être aussi courte que possible. »

ENSEMBLE DE RÈGLES MINIMA DES NATIONS UNIES CONCERNANT L'ADMINISTRATION DE LA JUSTICE POUR LES MINEURS (RÈGLES DE BEIJING).

DEVELOPPEMENT [Development]

– « *Reconnaissant* que la responsabilité du développement des pays en voie de développement incombe au premier chef à ces pays eux-mêmes [...] »

Pp. 10, DÉCLARATION SUR LE PROGRÈS ET LE DÉVELOPPEMENT DANS LE DOMAINE SOCIALE.

---

[20] Emploi des termes, « *b*) Le terme "personne détenue" s'entend de toute personne privée de la liberté individuelle sauf à la suite d'une condamnation pour infraction; »

– « *Consciente* que le développement est un processus global, économique, social, culturel et politique, qui vise à améliorer sans cesse le bien-être de l'ensemble de la population et de tous les individus, sur la base de leur participation active, libre et significative au développement et au partage équitable des bienfaits qui en découlent, »

Pp. 2, DÉCLARATION SUR LE DROIT AU DÉVELOPPEMENT.

– « *Réaffirmant* qu'il existe une relation étroite entre le désarmement et le développement, que des progrès dans le domaine du désarmement contribueraient dans une mesure considérable à des progrès dans le domaine du développement et que les ressources libérées grâce à des mesures de désarmement devraient être consacrées au développement économique et social et au bien-être de tous les peuples, en particulier ceux des pays en développement, »

Pp. 12, DÉCLARATION SUR LE DROIT AU DÉVELOPPEMENT.

DEVELOPPEMENT ET LE PROGRES DANS LE DOMAINE SOCIAL (LE) [Social progress and development]

– « Le développement et le progrès dans le domaine social sont fondés sur le respect de la dignité et de la valeur de la personne humaine et doivent assurer la promotion des droits de l'homme ainsi que la justice sociale, ce qui exige :

a) L'élimination immédiate et définitive de toutes les formes d'inégalité, d'exploitation des peuples et des individus, de colonialisme, de racisme, y compris le nazisme et l'apartheid, et de toute autre politique et idéologie contraires aux buts et aux principes des Nations Unies;

b) La reconnaissance et la mise en œuvre effective des droits civils et politiques ainsi que des droits économiques, sociaux et culturels sans aucune discrimination. »

Art. 2 , DÉCLARATION SUR LE PROGRÈS ET LE DÉVELOPPEMENT DANS LE DOMAINE SOCIALE.

DIABETE SUCRE NECESSITANT UN TRAITEMENT A L'INSULINE [Diabetes mellitus requiring insulin treatment]

– « *l)* Les maladies graves du métabolisme, par exemple : diabète sucré nécessitant un traitement à l'insuline; etc. »

Annexe I, 3, CONVENTION DE GENÈVE RELATIVE AU TRAITEMENT DES PRISONNIERS DE GUERRE.

DIFFERENCE ENTRE LES TAUX DE REMUNERATION [Differential rates between workers]

– « 3. Les différences entre les taux de rémunération qui correspondent, sans considération de sexe, à des différences résultant d'une telle évaluation objective dans les travaux à effectuer ne devront pas être considérées comme contraires au principe de l'égalité de rémunération entre la main-d'œuvre pour un travail de valeur égale. »

Art. 3, CONVENTION SUR L'ÉGALITÉ DE RÉMUNÉRATION, (N° 100).

DIGNITE [Dignity]

– « *Considérant* que la reconnaissance de la dignité inhérente à tous les membres de la famille humaine et de leurs droits égaux et inaliénables constitue le fondement de la liberté, de la justice et de la paix dans le monde, »

Pp. 1 DÉCLARATION UNIVERSELLE DES DROITS DE L'HOMME.

– « *Considérant* que, conformément aux principes énoncés dans la Charte des Nations Unies, la reconnaissance de la dignité inhérente à tous les membres de la famille humaine et de leurs droits égaux et inaliénables constitue le fondement de la liberté, de la justice et de la paix dans le monde, »

Pp. 1, PACTE INTERNATIONAL RELATIF AUX DROITS ÉCONOMIQUES SOCIAUX ET CULTURELS.
Pp. 1, PACTE INTERNATIONAL RELATIF AUX DROITS CIVILS ET POLITIQUES.

– « *Reconnaissant* que ces droits découlent de la dignité humaine inhérente à la personne humaine, »

Pp. 2, PACTE INTERNATIONAL RELATIF AUX DROITS ÉCONOMIQUES SOCIAUX ET CULTURELS.
Pp. 2, PACTE INTERNATIONAL RELATIF AUX DROITS CIVILS ET POLITIQUES.

– « 1. Toute personne privée de sa liberté est traitée avec humanité et avec le respect de la dignité inhérente à la personne humaine.

Art. 10, PACTE INTERNATIONAL RELATIF AUX DROITS CIVILS ET POLITIQUES.

– « Toute personne soumise à une forme quelconque de détention ou d'emprisonnement est traitée avec humanité et avec le respect de la dignité inhérente à la personne humaine. »

Principe 1, ENSEMBLE DE PRINCIPES POUR LA PROTECTION DE TOUTES LES PERSONNES SOUMISES À UNE FORME QUELCONQUE DE DÉTENTION OU D'EMPRISONNEMENT.

– « *Reconnaissant* que ces droits[21] procèdent de la dignité inhérente à la personne humaine, »

Pp.2, CONVENTION CONTRE LA TORTURE ET AUTRES PEINES OU TRAITEMENT CRUELS, INHUMAINS OU DÉGRADANTS.

– « (*b*) Cette dignité[22] impose de ne pas réduire les individus à leurs caractéristiques génétiques et de respecter le caractère unique de chacun et leur diversité. »

Art. 2, DÉCLARATION UNIVERSELLE SUR LE GÉNOME HUMAIN ET LES DROITS DE L'HOMME.

– « *Rappelant* que le Préambule de l'Acte constitutif de l'UNESCO affirme « (...) que la dignité de l'homme exigeant la diffusion de la culture et l'éducation de tous en vue de la justice, de la liberté et de la paix, il y a là, pour toutes les nations, des devoirs sacrés à remplir dans un esprit de mutuelle assistance. »

Pp. 2, DÉCLARATION UNIVERSELLE SUR LA DIVERSITÉ CULTURELLE.

– « 1. Les travailleurs migrants et les membres de leur famille qui sont privés de leur liberté sont traités avec humanité et avec le respect de la dignité inhérente à la personne humaine et de leur identité culturelle. »

Art. 17, CONVENTION INTERNATIONALE SUR LA PROTECTION DES DROITS DE TOUS LES TRAVAILLEURS MIGRANTS ET DES MEMBRES DE LEUR FAMILLE.

DISCRIMINATION [Discrimination]

– « 1. Aux fins de la présente Convention, le terme "discrimination" comprend:

Toute distinction, exclusion ou préférence fondée sur la race, la couleur, le sexe, la religion, l'opinion politique, l'ascendance nationale ou l'origine sociale, qui a pour effet de détruire ou d'altérer l'égalité de chances ou de traitement en matière d'emploi ou de profession;

Toute autre distinction, exclusion ou préférence ayant pour effet de détruire ou d'altérer l'égalité de chances ou de traitement en matière d'emploi ou de profession, qui pourra être spécifiée par le Membre

---

[21] Pp.1,« *Considérant* que, conformément aux principes proclamés dans la Charte des Nations Unies, la reconnaissance des droits égaux et inaliénables de tous les membres de la famille humaine est le fondement de la liberté, de la justice et de la paix dans le monde, »

[22] Art. 2 « (a) Chaque individu a droit au respect de sa dignité et de ses droits, quelles que soient ses caractéristiques génétiques. »

intéressé après consultation des organisations représentatives d'employeurs et de travailleurs, s'il en existe, et d'autres organismes appropriés.

2. Les distinctions, exclusions ou préférences fondées sur les qualifications exigées pour un emploi déterminé ne sont pas considérées comme des discriminations. »

Art. 1, CONVENTION CONCERNANT LA DISCRIMINATION (EMPLOI ET PROFESSION) (N° 111).

– « *Réaffirmant* que la discrimination entre les être humains pour des motifs fondés sur la race, la couleur ou l'origine ethnique est un obstacle aux relations amicales et pacifiques entre les nations et est susceptible de troubler la paix et la sécurité entre les peuples ainsi que la coexistence harmonieuse des personnes au sein d'un même Etat, »

Pp. 7, CONVENTION INTERNATIONALE SUR L'ÉLIMINATION DE TOUTES LES FORMES DE DISCRIMINATION RACIALE.

– « Est incompatible avec les exigences d'un ordre international juste et garantissant le respect des droits de l'homme toute distinction, exclusion, restriction ou préférence fondée sur la race, la couleur, l'origine ethnique ou nationale ou sur l'intolérance religieuse motivée par des considérations racistes, qui détruit ou compromet l'égalité souveraine des Etats et le droit des peuples à l'autodétermination ou qui limite d'une manière arbitraire ou discriminatoire le droit au développement intégral de tout être et groupe humains; ce droit implique un accès en pleine égalité aux moyens de progrès et d'épanouissement collectif et individuel dans un climat qui respecte les valeurs de civilisation et les cultures nationales et universelles. »

Art. 3, DÉCLARATION SUR LA RACE ET LES PRÉJUGÉS RACIAUX.

– « 1.Aux fins de la présente Convention, le terme "discrimination" comprend toute distinction, exclusion, limitation ou préférence qui, fondée sur la race, la couleur, le sexe, la langue, la religion, l'opinion politique ou toute autre opinion, l'origine nationale ou sociale, la condition économique ou la naissance, a pour objet de détruire ou d'altérer l'égalité de traitement en matière d'enseignement et, notamment:

a) D'écarter une personne ou un groupe de l'accès aux divers types ou degrés d'enseignement;

b) De limiter à un niveau inférieur l'éducation d'une personne ou d'un groupe;

c) Sous réserve de ce qui est dit à l'article 2[23] de la présente Convention, d'instituer ou de maintenir des systèmes ou des établissements d'enseignement séparés pour des personnes ou des groupes; ou

d) De placer une personne ou un groupe dans une situation incompatible avec la dignité de l'homme. »

Art. 1, CONVENTION CONCERNANT LA LUTTE CONTRE LA DISCRIMINATION DANS LE DOMAINE DE L'ENSEIGNEMENT.

DISCRIMINATION A L'EGARD DES FEMMES [Discrimination against women]

– « Aux fins de la présente Convention, l'expression "discrimination à l'égard des femmes" vise toute distinction, exclusion ou restriction fondée sur le sexe qui a pour effet ou pour but de compromettre ou de détruire la reconnaissance, la jouissance ou l'exercice par les femmes, quel que soit leur état matrimonial, sur la base de l'égalité de l'homme et de la femme, des droits de l'homme et des libertés fondamentales dans les domaines politique, économique, social, culturel et civil ou dans tout autre domaine. »

Art. 1, CONVENTION SUR L'ÉLIMINATION DE TOUTES LES FORMES DE DISCRIMINATION À L'ÉGARD DES FEMMES.

---

[23] « Lorsqu'elles sont admises par l'Etat, les situations suivantes ne sont pas considérées comme constituant des discriminations au sens de l'article premier de la présente Convention:
a) La création ou le maintien de systèmes ou d'établissements d'enseignement séparés pour les élèves des deux sexes, lorsque ces systèmes ou établissements présentent des facilités d'accès à l'enseignement équivalentes, disposent d'un personnel enseignant possédant des qualifications de même ordre, ainsi que de locaux scolaires et d'un équipement de même qualité, et permettent de suivre les mêmes programmes d'études ou des programmes d'études équivalents;
b) La création ou le maintien, pour des motifs d'ordre religieux ou linguistique, de systèmes ou d'établissements séparés dispensant un enseignement qui correspond au choix des parents ou tuteurs légaux des élèves, si l'adhésion à ces systèmes ou la fréquentation de ces établissements demeure facultative et si l'enseignement dispensé est conforme aux normes qui peuvent avoir été prescrites ou approuvées par les autorités compétentes, en particulier pour l'enseignement du même degré;
c) La création ou le maintien d'établissements d'enseignement privés, si ces établissements ont pour objet non d'assurer l'exclusion d'un groupe quelconque, mais d'ajouter aux possibilités d'enseignement qu'offrent les pouvoirs publics, si leur fonctionnement répond à cet objet et si l'enseignement dispensé est conforme aux normes qui peuvent avoir été prescrites ou approuvées par les autorités compétentes, en particulier pour l'enseignement du même degré. »

DISCRIMINATION RACIALE [Racial discrimination]

– 1. Dans la présente Convention, l'expression « discrimination raciale » vise toute distinction, exclusion, restriction ou préférence fondée sur la race, la couleur, l'ascendance ou l'origine nationale ou ethnique, qui a pour but ou pour effet de détruire ou de compromettre la reconnaissance, la jouissance ou l'exercice, dans des conditions d'égalité, des droits de l'homme et des libertés fondamentales dans les domaines politiques, économiques, social et culturel ou dans tout autre domaine de la vie publique.

2. La présente Convention ne s'applique pas aux distinctions, exclusions, restrictions ou préférences établies par un Etat partie à la Convention selon qu'il s'agit de ses ressortissants ou non-ressortissants.

3. Aucune disposition de la présente Convention ne peut être interprétée comme affectant de quelque manière que ce soit les dispositions législatives des Etats parties à la Convention concernant la nationalité, la citoyenneté ou la naturalisation, à la condition que ces dispositions ne soient pas discriminatoires à l'égard d'une nationalité particulière. »

4. Les mesures spéciales prises à seule fin d'assurer comme il convient le progrès de certains groupes raciaux ou ethniques ou d'individus ayant besoin de la protection qui peut être nécessaire pour leur garantir la jouissance et l'exercice des droits de l'homme et des libertés fondamentales dans des conditions d'égalité ne sont pas considérées comme des mesures de discrimination raciale, à condition toutefois qu'elles n'aient pas pour effet le maintien de droits distincts pour des groupes raciaux différents et qu'elles ne soient pas maintenues en vigueur une fois atteints les objectifs auxquelles elles répondaient. »

Art,1 CONVENTION INTERNATIONALE SUR L'ÉLIMINATION DE TOUTES LES FORMES DE DISCRIMINATION RACIALE.

– « *Constatant* avec la préoccupation la plus vive que le racisme, la discrimination raciale, le colonialisme et l'apartheid continuent à sévir dans le monde sous ses formes toujours renouvelées, tant par le maintien de dispositions législatives et de pratiques de gouvernements et d'administration contraires aux principes des droits de l'homme, que la permanence de structures marquées par l'injuste et le mépris de la personne humaine et engendrant l'exclusion, l'humiliation et l'exploitation, ou l'assimilation forcée, des membres de groupes défavorisés, »

Pp. 12, DÉCLARATION SUR LA RACE ET LES PRÉJUGÉES RACIAUX.

DISCRIMINATION RACIALE (ELIMINATION DE LA) [Racial discrimination (eradication of)]

– « *Soulignant* que l'élimination de l'apartheid, de toutes les formes de racisme, de discrimination raciale, de colonialisme, de néocolonialisme, d'agression, d'occupation et domination étrangère et d'ingérence dans les affaires intérieures des Etats indispensable à la pleine jouissance par l'homme et la femme de leurs droits, »

Pp. 10, CONVENTION SUR L'ÉLIMINATION DE TOUTES LES FORMES DE DISCRIMINATION À L'ÉGARD DES FEMMES.

DISCRIMINATIONS [Discrimination]

– « Ne sont pas considérés comme des discriminations toutes mesures affectant une personne qui fait individuellement l'objet d'une suspicion légitime de se livrer à une activité préjudiciable à la sécurité de l'Etat ou dont il est établi qu'elle se livre en fait à cette activité, pour autant que ladite personne ait le droit de recourir à une instance compétente établie suivant la pratique nationale. »

Art. 4, CONVENTION CONCERNANT LA DISCRIMINATION (EMPLOI ET PROFESSION) (N° 111).

– « 1. Les mesures spéciales de protection ou d'assistance prévues dans d'autres conventions ou recommandations adoptées par la Conférence internationale du Travail ne sont pas considérées comme des discriminations.

2. Tout Membre peut, après consultation, là où elles existent, des organisations représentatives d'employeurs et de travailleurs, définir comme non discriminatoires toutes autres mesures spéciales destinées à tenir compte des besoins particuliers de personnes à l'égard desquelles une protection ou une assistance spéciale est, d'une façon générale, reconnue nécessaire pour des raisons telles que le sexe, l'âge, l'invalidité, les charges de famille ou le niveau social ou culturel. »

Art. 5, CONVENTION CONCERNANT LA DISCRIMINATION (EMPLOI ET PROFESSION) (N° 111).

– « Lorsqu'elles sont admises par l'Etat, les situations suivantes ne sont pas considérées comme constituant des discriminations au sens de l'article premier de la présente Convention:

> La création ou le maintien de systèmes ou d'établissements d'enseignement séparés pour les élèves des deux sexes, lorsque ces systèmes ou établissements présentent des facilités d'accès à l'enseignement équivalentes, disposent d'un personnel enseignant possédant des qualifications de même ordre, ainsi que de locaux scolaires et d'un équipement de même qualité, et permettent de suivre les mêmes programmes d'études ou des programmes d'études équivalents;
>
> La création ou le maintien, pour des motifs d'ordre religieux ou linguistique, de systèmes ou d'établissements séparés dispensant un enseignement qui correspond au choix des parents ou tuteurs légaux des élèves, si l'adhésion à ces systèmes ou la fréquentation de ces établissements demeure facultative et si l'enseignement dispensé est conforme aux normes qui peuvent avoir été prescrites ou approuvées par les autorités compétentes, en particulier pour l'enseignement du même degré;
>
> La création ou le maintien d'établissements d'enseignement privés, si ces établissements ont pour objet non d'assurer l'exclusion d'un groupe quelconque, mais d'ajouter aux possibilités d'enseignement qu'offrent les pouvoirs publics, si leur fonctionnement répond à cet objet et si l'enseignement dispensé est conforme aux normes qui peuvent avoir été prescrites ou approuvées par les autorités compétentes, en particulier pour l'enseignement du même degré.

Art. 2, CONVENTION CONCERNANT LA LUTTE CONTRE LA DISCRIMINATION DANS LE DOMAINE DE L'ENSEIGNEMENT.

– « 1. L'adoption par les Etats parties de mesures temporaires spéciales visant à accélérer l'instauration d'une égalité de fait entre les hommes et les femmes n'est pas considérée comme un acte de discrimination tel qu'il est défini dans la présente Convention, mais ne doit en aucune façon avoir pour conséquence le maintien de normes inégales ou distinctes; ces mesures doivent être abrogées dès que les objectifs en matière d'égalité de chances et de traitement ont été atteints. »

Art.4, CONVENTION SUR L'ÉLIMINATION DE TOUTES LES FORMES DE DISCRIMINATION À L'ÉGARD DES FEMMES.

– « 4. Aucune discrimination fondée sur la maladie mentale n'est admise. Le mot "discrimination" s'entend de tout traitement différent, exclusif ou préférentiel ayant pour effet de supprimer l'égalité de droits ou d'y faire obstacle. Les mesures spéciales visant uniquement à protéger les droits des personnes atteintes de maladie mentale ou à améliorer leur état ne doivent pas être considérées comme ayant un caractère discriminatoire. Il n'y a pas discrimination en cas de traitement différent, exclusif ou préférentiel conforme aux dispositions des présents Principes et nécessaire pour protéger les droits de l'homme d'une personne atteinte de maladie mentale ou de toute autre personne. »

Principe 1, PRINCIPE POUR LA PROTECTION DES PERSONNES ATTEINTES DE MALADIE MENTALE ET POUR L'AMÉLIORATION DES SOINS DE SANTÉ MENTALE.

DISPARITIONS FORCEES DE PERSONNES [Enforced disappearance of persons]

« 2. Aux fins du paragraphe 1[24]:

[...]

i) Par «disparitions forcées de personnes», on entend les cas où des personnes sont arrêtées, détenues ou enlevées par un État ou une organisation politique ou avec l'autorisation, l'appui ou l'assentiment de cet État ou de cette organisation, qui refuse ensuite d'admettre que

---

[24] « 1. Aux fins du présent Statut, on entend par crime contre l'humanité l'un quelconque des actes ci-après lorsqu'il est commis dans le cadre d'une attaque généralisée ou systématique lancée contre toute population civile et en connaissance de cette attaque:

a) Meurtre;

b) Extermination;

c) Réduction en esclavage;

d) Déportation ou transfert forcé de population;

e) Emprisonnement ou autre forme de privation grave de liberté physique en violation des dispositions fondamentales du droit international;

f) Torture;

g) Viol, esclavage sexuel, prostitution forcée, grossesse forcée, stérilisation forcée ou toute autre forme de violence sexuelle de gravité comparable;

h) Persécution de tout groupe ou de toute collectivité identifiable pour des motifs d'ordre politique, racial, national, ethnique, culturel, religieux ou sexiste au sens du paragraphe 3, ou en fonction d'autres critères universellement reconnus comme inadmissibles en droit international, en corrélation avec tout acte visé dans le présent paragraphe ou tout crime relevant de la compétence de la Cour;

i) Disparitions forcées de personnes;

j) Crime d'apartheid;

k) Autres actes inhumains de caractère analogue causant intentionnellement de grandes souffrances ou des atteintes graves à l'intégrité physique ou à la santé physique ou mentale. »

ces personnes sont privées de liberté ou de révéler le sort qui leur est réservé ou l'endroit où elles se trouvent, dans l'intention de les soustraire à la protection de la loi pendant une période prolongée. »

Art. 7, STATUT DE ROME DE LA COUR PÉNALE INTERNATIONALE.

DISTINCTION DE CARACTERE DEFAVORABLE [Adverse distinction]

– « 1. Le présent Protocole s'applique sans aucune distinction de caractère défavorable fondée sur la race, la couleur, le sexe, la langue, la religion ou la croyance, les opinions politiques ou autres, l'origine nationale ou sociale, la fortune, la naissance ou une autre situation, ou tous autres critères analogues [...] »

Art. 2, PROTOCOLE ADDITIONNEL AUX CONVENTION DE GENÈVE DU 12 AOÛT 1949 RELATIF À LA PROTECTION DES VICTIMES DES CONFLITS ARMÉS NON INTERNATIONAUX (PROTOCOLE II).

DIVERSITE CULTURELLE [Cultural diversity]

– « La culture prend des formes diverses à travers le temps et l'espace. Cette diversité s'incarne dans l'originalité et la pluralité des identités qui caractérisent les groupes et les sociétés composant l'humanité. Source d'échanges, d'innovation et de créativité, la diversité culturelle est, pour le genre humain, aussi nécessaire que l'est la biodiversité dans l'ordre du vivant. En ce sens, elle constitue le patrimoine commun de l'humanité et elle doit être reconnue et affirmée au bénéfice des générations présentes et des générations futures. »

Art. 1, DÉCLARATION UNIVERSELLE SUR LA DIVERSITÉ CULTURELLE.

– « La diversité culturelle élargit les possibilités de choix offertes à chacun ; elle est l'une des sources du développement, entendu non seulement en termes de croissance économique, mais aussi comme moyen d'accéder à une existence intellectuelle, affective, morale et spirituelle suffisante. »

Art.3, DÉCLARATION UNIVERSELLE SUR LA DIVERSITÉ CULTURELLE.

– « Les forces du marché ne peuvent garantir la préservation et la promotion de la diversité culturelle, gage d'un développement humain durable. [...] »

Art. 11, DÉCLARATION UNIVERSELLE SUR LA DIVERSITÉ CULTURELLE.

DOCTRINE DE SUPERIORITE FONDEE SUR LA DIFFERENCIATION ENTRE LES RACES [Doctrine of superiority based on racial differentiation]

– « *Convaincus* que toute doctrine de supérioritéfondée sur la différenciation entre les races est scientifiquement fausse, moralement condamnable et socialement injuste et dangereuse et que rien ne saurait justifier, où que ce soit, la discrimination raciale, ni en théorie ni en pratique, »

Pp.6, CONVENTION INTERNATIONALE SUR L'ÉLIMINATION DE TOUTES LES FORMES DE DISCRIMINATION RACIALE.

DOCUMENT DE VOYAGE OU D'IDENTITE FRAUDULEUX [Fraudulent travel or identity document]

– - « Aux fins du présent Protocole :

[...]

c) L'expression « document de voyage ou d'identité frauduleux » désigne tout document de voyage ou d'identité :

i) Qui a été contrefait ou modifié de manière substantielle par quiconque autre qu'une personne ou une autorité légalement habilitée à établir ou à délivrer le document de voyage ou d'identité au nom d'un État; ou

ii) Qui a été délivré ou obtenu de manière irrégulière moyennant fausse déclaration, corruption ou contrainte, ou de toute autre manière illégale; ou

iii) Qui est utilisé par une personne autre que le titulaire légitime; »

Art. 3, PROTOCOLE CONTRE LE TRAFIC ILLICITE DE MIGRANTS PAR TERRE, AIR ET MER, ADDITIONNEL À LA CONVENTION DES NATIONS UNIES CONTRE LA CRIMINALITÉ TRANSNATIONALE ORGANISÉE.

DROIT A LA LIBERTE D'EXPRESSION [Right to freedom of expression]

– « 2. Toute personne a droit à la liberté d'expression; ce droit comprend la liberté de rechercher, de recevoir et de répandre des informations et des idées de toute espèce, sans considération de frontières, sous une forme orale, écrite, imprimée ou artistique, ou par tout autre moyen de son choix. »

Art. 19, PACTE INTERNATIONAL RELATIF AUX DROITS CIVILS ET POLITIQUES.

DROIT A LA LIBERTE D'OPINION ET D'EXPRESSION [Right to freedom of opinion and expression]

– « Tout individu a droit à la liberté d'opinion et d'expression, ce qui implique le droit de ne pas être inquiété pour ses opinions et celui de chercher, de recevoir et de répondre, sans considérations de frontières, les informations et les idées par quelque moyen d'expression que ce soit. »

Art. 19, DECLARATION UNIVERSELLE DES DROITS DE L'HOMME.

DROIT A LA LIBERTE DE PENSEE, DE CONSCIENCE, DE RELIGION OU DE CONVICTION [Right to freedom of thought, conscience, religion or belief]

– « Conformément à l'article premier[25] de la présente Déclaration et sous réserve des dispositions du paragraphe 3 dudit article, le droit à la liberté de pensée, de conscience, de religion ou de conviction implique, entre autres, les libertés suivantes:

a) La liberté de pratiquer un culte et de tenir des réunions se rapportant à une religion ou à une conviction et d'établir et d'entretenir des lieux à ces fins;

b) La liberté de fonder et d'entretenir des institutions charitables ou humanitaires appropriées;

c) La liberté de confectionner, d'acquérir et d'utiliser, en quantité adéquate, les objets et le matériel requis par les rites ou les usages d'une religion ou d'une conviction;

d) La liberté d'écrire, d'imprimer et de diffuser des publications sur ces sujets;

e) La liberté d'enseigner une religion ou une conviction dans les lieux convenant à cette fin;

---

[25] « 1. Toute personne a droit à la liberté de pensée, de conscience et de religion. Ce droit implique la liberté d'avoir une religion ou n'importe quelle conviction de son choix, ainsi que la liberté de manifester sa religion ou sa conviction, individuellement ou en commun, tant en public qu'en privé, par le culte et l'accomplissement des rites, les pratiques et l'enseignement.
2. Nul ne subira de contrainte pouvant porter atteinte à sa liberté d'avoir une religion ou une conviction de son choix.
3. La liberté de manifester sa religion ou sa conviction ne peut faire l'objet que des seules restrictions qui sont prévues par la loi et qui sont nécessaires à la protection de la sécurité publique, de l'ordre public, de la santé ou de la morale ou des libertés et droits fondamentaux d'autrui. »

f) La liberté de solliciter et de recevoir des contributions volontaires, financières et autres, de particuliers et d'institutions;

g) La liberté de former, de nommer, d'élire ou de désigner par succession les dirigeants appropriés, conformément aux besoins et aux normes de toute religion ou conviction;

h) La liberté d'observer les jours de repos et de célébrer les fêtes et cérémonies conformément aux préceptes de sa religion ou de sa conviction;

i) La liberté d'établir et de maintenir des communications avec des individus et des communautés en matière de religion ou de conviction aux niveaux national et international. »

Art.6, DÉCLARATION SUR L'ÉLIMINATION DE TOUTES LES FORMES D'INTOLÉRANCE ET DE DISCRIMINATION FONDÉES SUR LA RELIGION OU LA CONVICTION.

DROIT A LA LIBERTE DE PENSEE, DE CONSCIENCE ET DE RELIGION [Right to freedom of thought, conscience and religion]

– « Toute personne a droit à la liberté de pensée, de conscience et de religion ; ce droit implique la liberté de changer de religion ou de conviction ainsi que la liberté de manifester sa religion ou sa conviction, seule ou en commun, tant en public qu'en privé, par l'enseignement, les pratiques, le culte et l'accomplissement »

Art. 18, DÉCLARATION UNIVERSELLE DES DROITS DE L'HOMME.

– « 1. Toute personne a droit à la liberté de pensée, de conscience et de religion; ce droit implique la liberté d'avoir ou d'adopter une religion ou une conviction de son choix, ainsi que la liberté de manifester sa religion ou sa conviction, individuellement ou en commun, tant en public qu'en privé, par le culte et l'accomplissement des rites, les pratiques et l'enseignement. »

Art. 18, PACTE INTERNATIONAL RELATIF AUX DROITS CIVILS ET POLITIQUES.

DROIT AU DEVELOPPEMENT [Right to development]

– « 10. La Conférence mondiale sur les droits de l'homme réaffirme que le droit au développement, tel qu'il est établi dans la Déclaration sur le droit au développement, est un droit universel et inaliénable qui fait partie intégrante des droits fondamentaux de la personne humaine. »

I, 10, al. 1, DÉCLARATION ET PROGRAMME D'ACTION DE VIENNE.

– « 1. Tous les aspects du droit au développement énoncés dans la présente Déclaration sont indivisibles et interdépendants et chacun d'eux doit être considéré compte tenu de l'ensemble. »

Art. 9, DÉCLARATION SUR LE DROIT AU DÉVELOPPEMENT.

DROIT AU TRAVAIL [Right to work]

– « 1. Les Etats parties au présent Pacte reconnaissent le droit au travail, qui comprend le droit qu'a toute personne d'obtenir la possibilité de gagner sa vie par un travail librement choisi ou accepté, et prendront des mesures appropriés pour sauvegarder ce droit. »

Art. 6, PACTE INTERNATIONAL RELATIF AUX DROITS ÉCONOMIQUES, SOCIAUX ET CULTURELS.

DROIT DE TOUTE PERSONNE A UN NIVEAU DE VIE SUFFISANT [Right of everyone to an adequate standard of living]

– « 1. Les Etats Parties au présent Pacte reconnaissent le droit de toute personne à un niveau de vie suffisant pour elle-même et sa famille, y compris une nourriture, un vêtement et un logement suffisants, ainsi qu'à une amélioration constante de ses conditions d'existence. [...] »

Art. 11, PACTE INTERNATIONAL RELATIF AUX DROITS ÉCONOMIQUES, SOCIAUX ET CULTURELS.

DROIT DES PEUPLES A DISPOSER D'EUX-MEMES [Right of peoples to self-determination]

– « *Rappelant* le droit des peuples à disposer d'eux-mêmes, en vertu duquel ils ont le droit de déterminer librement leur statut politique et d'assurer librement leur développement économique, social et culturel, »

Pp. 6, DÉCLARATION SUR LE DROIT AU DÉVELOPPEMENT.

DROIT QU'A TOUTE PERSONNE DE JOUIR DE CONDITIONS DE TRAVAIL JUSTES ET FAVORABLES [Right of everyone to the enjoyment of just and favourable conditions of work]

– « Les Etats parties au présent Pacte reconnaissent le droit qu'a toute personne de jouir de conditions de travail justes et favorables, qui assurent notamment :

a) La rémunération qui procure, au minimum, à tous les travailleurs :

i) Un salaire équitable et une rémunération égale pour un travail de valeur égale sans distinction aucune ; en particulier, les femmes doivent avoir la garantie que les conditions de travail qui leur sont accordées ne sont pas inférieures à celles dont bénéficient les hommes et recevoir la même rémunération qu'eux pour un même travail ;

ii) Une existence décente pour eux et leur famille conformément aux dispositions du présent Pacte ;

b) La sécurité et l'hygiène du travail ;

c) La même possibilité pour tous d'être promus, dans leur travail, à la catégorie supérieure appropriée, sans autre considération que la durée des services accomplis et les aptitudes ;

d) Le repos, les loisirs, la limitation raisonnable de la durée du travail et les congés payés périodiques, ainsi que la rémunération des jours fériés. »

Art. 7, PACTE INTERNATIONAL RELATIF AUX DROITS ÉCONOMIQUES, SOCIAUX ET CULTURELS.

DROITS CIVILS, POLITIQUES, ECONOMIQUES, SOCIAUX ET CULTURELS [Civil, political, economic, social and cultural rights]

– « 2. Tous les droits de l'homme et toutes les libertés fondamentales sont indivisibles et interdépendantes; la réalisation, la promotion et la protection des droits civils, politiques, économiques, sociaux et culturels doivent bénéficier d'une attention égale et être envisagées avec une égale urgence.»

Art. 6, DÉCLARATION SUR LE DROIT AU DÉVELOPPEMENT.

DROITS CULTURELS [Cultural rights]

– « Les droits culturels sont partie intégrante des droits de l'homme, qui sont universels, indissociables et interdépendants.[...] »

Art. 5, DÉCLARATION UNIVERSELLE SUR LA DIVERSITÉ CULTURELLE.

DROITS DE L'ENFANT [Rights of the child]

– « 10. Il convient de reconnaître l'importance d'une approche nationale globale et cohérente en matière de justice pour mineurs, compte tenu de l'interdépendance et de l'indivisibilité des droits de l'enfant. »

DIRECTIVES RELATIVES AUX DROITS AUX ENFANTS DANS LE SYSTÈME DE JUSTICE PÉNALE.

DROITS DE L'HOMME [Human rights]

– « *Reconnaissant* et *affirmant* que tous les droits de l'homme découlent de la dignité et de la valeur inhérentes à la personne humaine, que la personne humaine est le sujet même des droits de l'homme et des libertés fondamentales et que, par conséquent, elle doit en être le principal bénéficiaire et participer activement à leur réalisation, »

Pp. 2, DÉCLARATION ET PROGRAMME D'ACTION DE VIENNE.

– « 1. La Conférence mondiale sur les droits de l'homme réaffirme l'engagement solennel pris par tous les Etats de s'acquitter de l'obligation de promouvoir le respect universel, l'observation et la protection de l'ensemble des droits de l'homme et des libertés fondamentales pour tous, conformément à la Charte des Nations Unies, aux autres instruments relatifs aux droits de l'homme et au droit international. Le caractère universel de ces droits et libertés est incontestable. »

I, DÉCLARATION ET PROGRAMME D'ACTION DE VIENNE.

– « Les droits de l'homme et les libertés fondamentales sont inhérents[d] à tous les êtres humains; leur promotion et leur protection incombent au premier chef aux gouvernements. »

I, 1, al. 3, DÉCLARATION ET PROGRAMME D'ACTION DE VIENNE.

– « 5. Tous les droits de l'homme sont universels, indissociables, interdépendants et intimement liés. La communauté internationale doit traiter des droits de l'homme globalement, de manière équitable et équilibrée, sur un pied d'égalité et en leur accordant la même importance. S'il convient de ne pas perdre de vue l'importance des particularismes nationaux et régionaux et la diversité historique, culturelle et religieuse, il est du devoir des Etats, quel qu'en soit le système politique, économique et culturel, de promouvoir et de protéger tous les droits de l'homme et toutes les libertés fondamentales. »

I, DÉCLARATION ET PROGRAMME D'ACTION DE VIENNE.

– « 2. Tous les droits de l'homme et toutes les libertés fondamentales sont indivisibles et interdépendantes; la réalisation, la promotion et la protection des droits civils, politiques, économiques, sociaux et culturels

[D] " Human rights and fundamental freedoms are the birthright of all human beings; their protection and promotion is the first responsibility of Governments."

doivent bénéficier d'une attention égale et être envisagées avec une égale urgence. »

Art. 6, DÉCLARATION SUR LE DROIT AU DÉVELOPPEMENT.

– « Article 4 – Les droits de l'homme, garants de la diversité culturelle »[26]

DÉCLARATION UNIVERSELLE SUR LA DIVERSITÉ CULTURELLE.

– « Les droits culturels sont partie intégrante des droits de l'homme, qui sont universels, indissociables et interdépendants. [...] »

Art. 5, DÉCLARATION UNIVERSELLE SUR LA DIVERSITÉ CULTURELLE.

– « *Réaffirmant* que tous les droits de l'homme et toutes les libertés fondamentales sont universels, indivisibles, interdépendants et indissociables, et qu'il faut les promouvoir et les rendre effectifs en toute équité, sans préjudice de leur mise en œuvre individuelle, »

Pp. 6, DÉCLARATION SUR LE DROIT ET LA RESPONSABILITÉ DES INDIVIDUS, GROUPES ET ORGANES DE LA SOCIÉTÉ DE PROMOUVOIR ET PROTÉGER LES DROITS DE L'HOMME ET LES LIBERTÉS FONDAMENTALES UNIVERSELLEMENT RECONNUS.

DROITS FONDAMENTAUX [Human rights]

– « Dans l'accomplissement de leur devoir, les responsables de l'application des lois doivent respecter et protéger la dignité humaine et défendre et protéger les droits fondamentaux de toute personne[e].

Commentaire:

a) Les droits fondamentaux en question sont définis et protégés par le droit national et le droit international. Les instruments internationaux pertinents comprennent notamment la Déclaration universelle des

---

[26] « Article 4- Human rights as guarantees of cultural diversity »

[e] " In the performance of their duty, law enforcement officials shall respect and protect human dignity and maintain and uphold the human rights of all persons.
Commentary:
(a) The human rights in question are identified and protected by national and international law. Among the relevant international instruments are the Universal Declaration of Human Rights, the International Covenant on Civil and Political Rights, the Declaration on the Protection of All Persons from Being Subjected to Torture and Other Cruel, Inhuman or Degrading Treatment or Punishment, the United Nations Declaration on the Elimination of All Forms of Racial Discrimination, the International Convention on the Elimination of All Forms of Racial Discrimination, the International Convention on the Suppression and Punishment of the Crime of Apartheid, the Convention on the Prevention and Punishment of the Crime of Genocide, the Standard Minimum Rules for the Treatment of Prisoners and the Vienna Convention on Consular Relations."

droits de l'homme, le Pacte international relatif aux droits civils et politiques, la Déclaration sur la protection de toutes les personnes contre la torture et autres peines ou traitements cruels, inhumains ou dégradants, la Déclaration des Nations Unies sur l'élimination de toutes les formes de discrimination raciale, la Convention internationale sur l'élimination de toutes les formes de discrimination raciale, la Convention internationale sur l'élimination et la répression du crime d'apartheid, la Convention pour la prévention et la répression du crime de génocide, l'Ensemble de règles minima pour le traitement des détenus et la Convention de Vienne sur les relations consulaires. »

Art. 2, CODE DE CONDUITE POUR LES RESPONSABLE DE L'APPLICATION DES LOIS.

DROITS FONDAMENTAUX DES FEMMES ET DES FILLETTES [Human rights of women and of the girl-child]

– « Les droits fondamentaux des femmes et des fillettes font inaliénablement, intégralement et indissociablement partie des droits universels de la personne. [...] »

I, 18, al.1, DÉCLARATION ET PROGRAMME D'ACTION DE VIENNE.

DYSSENTRIE AMIBIENNE OU BACILLAIRE AVEC TROUBLES CONSIDERABLES [Amoebic or bacillary dysentery with grave disorders]

– « *s)* Les maladies infectieuses chroniques graves persistant une année après le début, par exemple : paludisme avec altérations organiques prononcées; dysenterie amibienne ou bacillaire avec troubles considérables; syphilis viscérale tertiaire, résistant au traitement; lèpre; etc. »

Annexe I, 3, CONVENTION DE GENÈVE RELATIVE AU TRAITEMENT DES PRISONNIERS DE GUERRE.

EDUCATION [Education]

– « 1. Les Etats parties à la présente Convention conviennent:

a) Que l'éducation doit viser au plein épanouissement de la personnalité humaine et au renforcement du respect des droits de l'homme et des libertés fondamentales et qu'elle doit favoriser la compréhension, la tolérance et l'amitié entre toutes les nations et tous les groupes raciaux ou religieux, ainsi que le développement des activités des Nations Unies pour le maintien de la paix; »

Art. 5, Convention concernant la lutte contre la discrimination dans le domaine de l'enseignement.

EDUCATION DE L'ENFANT [Education of the child]

– « 1. Les Etats Parties conviennent que l'éducation de l'enfant doit viser à :

a) Favoriser l'épanouissement de la personnalité de l'enfant et le développement de ses dons et de ses aptitudes mentales et physiques, dans toute la mesure de leurs potentialités ;

b) Inculquer à l'enfant le respect des droits de l'homme et des libertés fondamentales, et des principes consacrés dans la Charte des Nations Unies ;

c) Inculquer à l'enfant le respect de ses parents, de son identité, de sa langue et de ses valeurs culturelles, ainsi que le respect des valeurs nationales du pays dans lequel il vit, du pays duquel il peut être originaire et des civilisations différentes de la sienne ;

d) Préparer l'enfant à assumer les responsabilités de la vie dans une société libre, dans un esprit de compréhension, de paix, de tolérance, d'égalité entre les sexes et d'amitié entre tous les peuples et groupes ethniques, nationaux et religieux, et avec les personnes d'origine autochtone ;

e) Inculquer à l'enfant le respect du milieu naturel.»

Art. 29, Convention relative aux droits de l'enfant.

EDUCATION FAMILIALE [Family education]

– « Les Etats parties prennent toutes les mesures appropriées pour :

[...]

b) Faire en sorte que l'éducation familiale contribue à faire bien comprendre que la maternité est une fonction sociale et à faire reconnaître la responsabilité commune de l'homme et de la femme dans le soin d'élever leurs enfants et d'assurer leur développement, étant entendu que l'intérêt des enfants est la condition primordiale dans tous les cas. »

Art.4, Convention sur l'élimination de toutes les formes de discrimination à l'égard des femmes.

EGALISATION DES CHANCES [Equalization of opportunities]

– « 24. L'« égalisation » des chances désigne le processus par lequel les divers systèmes de la société, le cadre matériel, les services, les activités et l'information sont rendus accessibles à tous , et en particulier aux handicapés. »

INTRODUCTION, RÈGLE POUR L'ÉGALISATION DES CHANCES DES PERSONNES HANDICAPÉES.

EGALITE (L') [Equality]

– « 6. Nous estimons que certaines valeurs fondamentales doivent sous-tendre les relations internationales au XXe siècle, à savoir :
[…]

L'égalité. Aucune personne, aucune nation ne doit être privée des bienfaits du développement. L'égalité des droits et des chances des femmes et des hommes doit être assurée.
[…] »

Deuxième note (•), DÉCLARATION DU MILLÉNAIRE.

EGALITE DE REMUNERATION ENTRE LA MAIN-D'ŒUVRE MASCULINE ET LA MAIN-D'ŒUVRE FEMININE POUR UN TRAVAIL DE VALEUR EGALE [Equal remuneration for men and women workers for work of equal value]

– « Aux fins de la présente Convention:
[…]

b) L'expression "égalité de rémunération entre la main-d'œuvre masculine et la main-d'œuvre féminine pour un travail de valeur égale" se réfère aux taux de rémunération fixés sans discrimination fondée sur le sexe. »

Art. 1, CONVENTION SUR L'ÉGALITÉ DE RÉMUNÉRATION (N° 100).

EGALITE ENTRE LES SEXES ET EMANCIPATION DES FEMMES [Gender equality and the empowerment of women]

– « 14. Soulignant que l'égalité entre les sexes et l'émancipation des femmes sont des conditions essentielles pour réduire la vulnérabilité des femmes et des filles au VIH/sida; »

DÉCLARATION D'ENGAGEMENT SUR LE VIH/SIDA.

EMEUTES [Riots]

– « 2. Le présent Protocole ne s'applique pas aux situations de tensions internes, de troubles intérieurs, comme les émeutes, les actes isolés et sporadiques de violence et autres actes analogues, qui ne sont pas considérés comme des conflits armés. »

Art. 1, PROTOCOLE ADDITIONNEL AUX CONVENTION DE GENÈVE DU 12 AOÛT 1949 RELATIF À LA PROTECTION DES VICTIMES DES CONFLITS ARMÉS NON INTERNATIONAUX (PROTOCOLE II).

EMPHYSEME PULMONAIRE GRAVE (AVEC OU SANS BRONCHITE) [Serious pulmonary emphysema, with or without bronchitis]

– « *c)* Les maladies graves des organes respiratoires, d'étiologie non tuberculeuse, présumées incurables, par exemple : emphysème pulmonaire grave (avec ou sans bronchite); asthme chronique*; bronchite chronique se prolongeant pendant plus d'une année en captivité; bronchectasie"; etc. »

Annexe I, 3, CONVENTION DE GENÈVE RELATIVE AU TRAITEMENT DES PRISONNIERS DE GUERRE.

EMPLOI [Employment]

– « 3. Aux fins de la présente Convention, les mots "emploi" et "profession" recouvrent l'accès à la formation professionnelle, l'accès à l'emploi et aux différentes professions, ainsi que les conditions d'emploi. »

Art. 1, CONVENTION CONCERNANT LA DISCRIMINATION (EMPLOI ET PROFESSION) (N° 111).

EMPRISONNEMENT [Imprisonment]

– « 57. L'emprisonnement et les autres mesures qui ont pour effet de retrancher un délinquant du monde extérieur sont afflictives par le fait même qu'elles dépouillent l'individu du droit de dispose de sa personne en le privant de sa liberté. [...] »

ENSEMBLES DE RÈGLES MINIMA POUR LE TRAITEMENT DES DÉTENUS.

– « Aux fins de l'ensemble de principes :
[...]

e) Le terme "emprisonnement" s'entend de la condition des personnes emprisonnées telle qu'elle est définie ci-dessus[27]; »

Emploi des termes, ENSEMBLE DE PRINCIPES POUR LA PROTECTION DE TOUTES LES PERSONNES SOUMISES À UNE FORME QUELCONQUE DE DÉTENTION OU D'EMPRISONNEMENT.

– « [...] l'internement ou l'emprisonnement sera pour de telles infractions la seule mesure privative de liberté [...] »

Art. 68, al. 1, CONVENTION DE GENÈVE RELATIVE À LA PROTECTION DES PERSONNES CIVILES EN TEMPS DE GUERRE DU 12 AOÛT 1949.

ENFANT [Child]

– « *Ayant à l'esprit* que, comme indiqué dans la Déclaration des droits de l'enfant, « l'enfant, en raison de son manque de maturité physique et intellectuelle, a besoin d'une protection spéciale et de soins spéciaux notamment d'une protection juridique appropriée, avant comme après la naissance », »

Pp. 9, CONVENTION RELATIVE AUX DROITS DE L'ENFANT.

– « Au sens de la présente Convention, un enfant s'entend de tout être humain âgé de moins de dix-huit ans, sauf si la majorité est atteinte plus tôt en vertu de la législation qui lui est applicable »

Art. 1, CONVENTION RELATIVE AUX DROITS DE L'ENFANT.

– « *Notant* que l'article premier de la Convention relative aux droits de l'enfant spécifie qu'au sens de ladite Convention, un enfant s'entend de tout être humain âgé de moins de 18 ans, sauf si la majorité est atteinte plus tôt en vertu de la législation qui lui est applicable, »

Pp. 7, PROTOCOLE FACULTATIF À LA CONVENTION RELATIVE AUX DROITS DE L'ENFANT, CONCERNANT L'IMPLICATION D'ENFANTS DANS LES CONFLITS ARMÉS.

– « Aux fins du présent Protocole :
[...]

d) Le termes « enfant » désigne toute personnes âgée de moins de 18 ans. »

Art. 3, PROTOCOLE ADDITIONNEL À LA CONVENTION DES NATIONS UNIES CONTRE LA CRIMINALITÉ TRANSNATIONALE ORGANISÉE, VISANT À PRÉVENIR, RÉPRIMER ET PUNIR LA TRAITE DES PERSONNES EN PARTICULIER DES FEMMES ET DES ENFANTS.

---

[27] *c*) Le terme "personne emprisonnée" s'entend de toute personne privée de la liberté individuelle à la suite d'une condamnation pour infraction;

ENFANTS [Child]

– « Aux fins de la présente convention, le terme « enfants » s'applique à l'ensemble des personnes de moins de 18 ans. »

Art. 2, Convention sur les pires formes de travail des enfants (n° 182).

ENLEVEMENT DES MINES [Removal of mines]

– « L'enlèvement des mines ou d'autres engins analogues sera considéré comme un travail dangereux. »

Art. 52, al. 3, Convention de Genève relative au traitement des prisonniers de guerre.

ENSEIGNEMENT [Education]

– « 2. Aux fins de la présente Convention, le mot "enseignement" vise les divers types et les différents degrés de l'enseignement et recouvre l'accès à l'enseignement, son niveau et sa qualité, de même que les conditions dans lesquelles il est dispensé. »

Art. 1, Convention concernant la lutte contre la discrimination dans le domaine de l'enseignement.

ENTREE ILLEGALE [Illegal entry]

– « Aux fins du présent Protocole :
[...]
b) L'expression « entrée illégale » désigne le franchissement de frontières alors que les conditions nécessaires à l'entrée légale dans l'État d'accueil ne sont pas satisfaites; »

Art. 3, Protocole contre le trafic illicite de migrants par terre, air et mer, additionnel à la Convention des Nations Unies contre la criminalité transnationale organisée.

EPIDEMIE MONDIALE DE VIH/SIDA [Global HIV/AIDS epidemic]

– « 2. Profondément préoccupés par le fait que l'épidémie mondiale de VIH/sida, en raison de son ampleur et de son incidence dévastatrices, constitue une crise mondiale et l'un des défis les plus redoutables pour la vie et la dignité humaines ainsi que pour l'exercice effectif des droits de l'homme, compromet le développement social et économique dans le monde entier et affecte la société à tous les niveaux – national, local, familial et individuel; »

DÉCLARATION D'ENGAGEMENT SUR LE VIH/SIDA.

EQUIVALENTS A LA PERTE D'UNE MAIN OU D'UN PIED [Equivalent to the loss of a hand or a foot]

– « Sans qu'il soit, pour autant, porté préjudice à une interprétation plus large, les cas suivants seront considérés comme équivalents à la perte d'une main ou d'un pied :

  a) Perte de la main, de tous les doigts ou du pouce et de l'index d'une main; perte du pied ou de tous les orteils et des métatarsiens d'un pied.

  b) Ankylose, perte de tissu osseux, rétrécissement cicatriciel abolissant la fonction d'une des grandes articulations ou de toutes les articulations digitales d'une main.

  c) Pseudarthrose des os longs.

  d) Difformités résultant de fractures ou autre accident et comportant un sérieux amoindrissement de l'activité et de l'aptitude à porter des poids. »

Annexe I, 1, CONVENTION DE GENÈVE RELATIVE AU TRAITEMENT DES PRISONNIERS DE GUERRE.

ERREUR DE DROIT [Mistake of law]

– « 2. Une erreur de droit portant sur la question de savoir si un comportement donné constitue un crime relevant de la compétence de la Cour n'est pas un motif d'exonération de la responsabilité pénale. Toutefois, une erreur de droit peut être un motif d'exonération de la responsabilité pénale si elle fait disparaître l'élément psychologique du crime ou si elle relève de l'article 33[28]. »

Art. 32, STATUT DE ROME DE LA COUR PÉNALE INTERNATIONALE.

---

[28] « 1. Le fait qu'un crime relevant de la compétence de la Cour a été commis sur ordre d'un gouvernement ou d'un supérieur, militaire ou civil, n'exonère pas la personne qui l'a commis de sa responsabilité pénale, à moins que:

a) Cette personne n'ait eu l'obligation légale d'obéir aux ordres du gouvernement ou du supérieur en question;

b) Cette personne n'ait pas su que l'ordre était illégal; et

c) L'ordre n'ait pas été manifestement illégal.

2. Aux fins du présent article, l'ordre de commettre un génocide ou un crime contre l'humanité est manifestement illégal. »

ERREUR DE FAIT [Mistake of fact]

– « 1. Une erreur de fait n'est un motif d'exonération de la responsabilité pénale que si elle fait disparaître l'élément psychologique du crime. »

Art. 32, STATUT DE ROME DE LA COUR PÉNALE INTERNATIONALE.

ESCLAVAGE [Slavery]

– « Aux fins de la présente Convention, il est entendu que :

1. L'esclavage est l'état ou condition d'un individu sur lequel s'exercent les attributs du droit de propriété ou certains d'entre eux; »

Art. 1, CONVENTION RELATIVE À L'ESCLAVAGE.

– « Chacun des Etats parties à la présente Convention prendra toutes les mesures, législatives et autres, qui seront réalisables et nécessaires pour obtenir progressivement et aussitôt que possible l'abolition complète ou l'abandon des institutions et pratiques suivantes, là où elles subsistent encore, qu'elles rentrent ou non dans la définition de l'esclavage qui figure à l'article premier de la Convention[29] relative à l'esclavage signée à Genève le 25 septembre 1926:

a) La servitude pour dettes, c'est-à-dire l'état ou la condition résultant du fait qu'un débiteur s'est engagé à fournir en garantie d'une dette ses services personnels ou ceux de quelqu'un sur lequel il a autorité, si la valeur équitable ce ces services n'est pas affectée à la liquidation de la dette ou si la durée de ces services n'est pas limitée ni leur caractère défini;

b) Le servage, c'est-à-dire la condition de quiconque est tenu par la loi, la coutume ou un accord, de vivre et de travailler sur une terre appartenant à une autre personne et de fournir à cette autre personne, contre rémunération ou gratuitement, certains services déterminés, sans pouvoir changer sa condition;

c) Toute institution ou pratique en vertu de laquelle :

---

[29] « 1.L'esclavage est l'état ou condition d'un individu sur lequel s'exercent les attributs du droit de propriété ou certains d'entre eux ;
2. La traite des esclaves comprend tout acte de capture, d'acquisition ou de cession d'un individu en vue de le réduire en esclavage ; tout acte d'acquisition d'un esclave en vue de le vendre ou de l'échanger ; tout acte de cession par vente ou échange d'un esclave acquis en vue d'être vendu ou échangé, ainsi que, en général, tout acte de commerce ou de transport d'esclaves.»

i) Une femme est, sans qu'elle ait le droit de refuser, promise ou donnée en mariage moyennant une contrepartie en espèces ou en nature versée à ses parents, à son tuteur, à sa famille ou à toute autre personne ou tout autre groupe de personnes;

ii) Le mari d'une femme, la famille ou le clan de celui-ci ont le droit de la céder à un tiers, à titre onéreux ou autrement;

iii) La femme peut, à la mort de son mari, être transmise par succession à une autre personne;

e) Toute institution ou pratique en vertu de laquelle un enfant ou un adolescent de moins de dix-huit ans est remis, soit par ses parents ou par l'un d'eux, soit par son tuteur, à un tiers, contre paiement ou non, en vue de l'exploitation de la personne, ou du travail dudit enfant ou adolescent. »

Art. 1, CONVENTION SUPPLÉMENTAIRE RELATIVE À L'ABOLITION DE L'ESCLAVAGE, DE LA TRAITE DES ESCLAVES ET DES INSTITUTIONS ET PRATIQUES ANALOGUES À L'ESCLAVAGE.

– « Aux fins de la présente Convention :

a) L'«esclavage», tel qu'il est défini dans la Convention de 1926[30] relative à l'esclavage, est l'état ou la condition d'un individu sur lequel s'exercent les attributs du droit de propriété ou certains d'entre eux [...] »

Art. 7, CONVENTION SUPPLÉMENTAIRE RELATIVE À L'ABOLITION DE L'ESCLAVAGE, DE LA TRAITE DES ESCLAVES ET DES INSTITUTIONS ET PRATIQUES ANALOGUES À L'ESCLAVAGE.

ESCLAVAGE SEXUEL [Sexual slavery]

– «*g*) Viol, esclavage sexuel, prostitution forcée, grossesse forcée, stérilisation forcée ou toute autre forme de violence sexuelle de gravité comparable; »

Art. 7, § 1, STATUT DE ROME DE LA COUR PÉNALE INTERNATIONALE.

ESCLAVE [Slave]

– « Aux fins de la présente Convention :

[30] Art. 1 « 1.L'esclavage est l'état ou condition d'un individu sur lequel s'exercent les attributs du droit de propriété ou certains d'entre eux ; »

a) L'«esclavage», tel qu'il est défini dans la Convention de 1926[31] relative à l'esclavage, est l'état ou la condition d'un individu sur lequel s'exercent les attributs du droit de propriété ou certains d'entre eux et l'«esclave» est l'individu qui a ce statut ou cette condition; »

Art. 7, CONVENTION SUPPLÉMENTAIRE RELATIVE À L'ABOLITION DE L'ESCLAVAGE, DE LA TRAITE DES ESCLAVES ET DES INSTITUTIONS ET PRATIQUES ANALOGUES À L'ESCLAVAGE.

ESPIONNAGE [Espionage]

– « 2. Un membre des forces armées d'une Partie au conflit qui recueille ou cherche à recueillir, pour le compte de cette Partie, des renseignements dans un territoire contrôlé par une Partie adverse ne sera pas considéré comme se livrant à des activités d'espionnage si, ce faisant, il est revêtu de l'uniforme de ses forces armées.

3. Un membre des forces armées d'une Partie au conflit qui est résident d'un territoire occupé par une Partie adverse, et qui recueille ou cherche à recueillir, pour le compte de la Partie dont il dépend, des renseignements d'intérêt militaire dans ce territoire, ne sera pas considéré comme se livrant à des activités d'espionnage, à moins que, ce faisant, il n'agisse sous de fallacieux prétextes ou de façon délibérément clandestine. De plus, ce résident ne perd son droit au statut de prisonnier de guerre et ne peut être traité en espion qu'au seul cas où il est capturé alors qu'il se livre à des activités d'espionnage. »

Art. 46, PROTOCOLE ADDITIONNEL AUX CONVENTIONS DE GENÈVE DU 12 AOÛT 1949 RELATIF À LA PROTECTION DES VICTIMES DES CONFLITS ARMÉS INTERNATIONAUX (PROTOCOLE I).

ETABLISSEMENTS OUVERTS [Open institutions; Open detention facilities]

– «2) [...] Les établissements ouverts, par le fait même qu'ils ne prévoient pas de mesures de sécurité physique contre les évasions mais s'en remettent à cet égard à l'autodiscipline des détenus, fournissent à des détenus soigneusement choisis les conditions les plus favorables à leur reclassement. »

63, ENSEMBLE DE RÈGLES MINIMA POUR LE TRAITEMENT DES DÉTENUS.

---

[31] Art. 1 « 1.L'esclavage est l'état ou condition d'un individu sur lequel s'exercent les attributs du droit de propriété ou certains d'entre eux ; »

– « 30. [...] Les établissements ouverts sont des établissements dans lesquels les mesures matérielles de sécurité sont aussi réduites que possible. Dans de tels établissements, la population doit être assez restreinte pour permettre un traitement individualisé. [...] [f] »

RÈGLES DES NATIONS UNIES POUR LA PROTECTION DES MINEURS PRIVÉS DE LIBERTÉ.

ETAT D'EMPLOI [State of employment]

– « Aux fins de la présente Convention:

[...]

b) L'expression "Etat d'emploi" s'entend de l'Etat où le travailleur migrant va exercer, exerce ou a exercé une activité rémunérée, selon le cas; »

Art. 6, CONVENTION INTERNATIONALE SUR LA PROTECTION DES DROITS DE TOUS LES TRAVAILLEURS MIGRANTS ET DES MEMBRES DE LEUR FAMILLE.

ETAT D'ORIGINE [State of origin]

– « Aux fins de la présente Convention:

a) L'expression "Etat d'origine" s'entend de l'Etat dont la personne intéressée est ressortissante; »

Art. 6, CONVENTION INTERNATIONALE SUR LA PROTECTION DES DROITS DE TOUS LES TRAVAILLEURS MIGRANTS ET DES MEMBRES DE LEUR FAMILLE.

ETAT DE TRANSIT [State of transit]

– « Aux fins de la présente Convention:

[...]

c) L'expression "Etat de transit" s'entend de tout Etat par lequel la personne intéressée passe pour se rendre dans l'Etat d'emploi ou de l'Etat d'emploi à l'Etat d'origine ou à l'Etat de résidence habituelle. »

ART. 6, CONVENTION INTERNATIONALE SUR LA PROTECTION DES DROITS DE TOUS LES TRAVAILLEURS MIGRANTS ET DES MEMBRES DE LEUR FAMILLE.

ETRANGER [Alien]

– « Aux fins de la présente Déclaration le terme « étranger » s'applique compte dûment tenu des précisions apportées dans les articles suivants, à

[f] "30. [...]Open detention facilities are those with no or minimal security measures. The population in such detention facilities should be as small as possible. [...]"

tout individu qui ne possède pas la nationalité de l'Etat dans lequel il se trouve. »

ART. 1, DÉCLARATION SUR LES DROITS DE L'HOMME DES PERSONNES QUI NE POSSÈDENT PAS LA NATIONALITÉ DU PAYS DANS LEQUEL ELLES VIVENT.

ETRE HUMAIN [Human person; Human being]

– « *Considérant* que l'être humain est le sujet central du processus de développement et qu'en conséquence il devrait être considéré comme le principal participant à ce processus et son principal bénéficiaire par toute politique de développement, »[g]

Pp. 13, DÉCLARATION SUR LE DROIT AU DÉVELOPPEMENT.

– « 1. L'être humain est le sujet central du développement et doit donc être le participant actif et le bénéficiaire du droit au développement. »

Art. 2, DÉCLARATION SUR LE DROIT AU DÉVELOPPEMENT.

ETRES HUMAINS [Person, Human beings]

– « Tous les êtres humains naissent libres et égaux en dignité et en droits[h]. Ils sont doués de raison et de conscience et doivent agir les uns envers les autres dans un esprit de fraternité. »

Art. 1, DÉCLARATION UNIVERSELLE DES DROITS DE L'HOMME.

– « Les droits de l'homme et les libertés fondamentales sont inhérents à tous les êtres humains; leur promotion et leur protection incombent au premier chef aux gouvernements. »

I, 1, al. 3, DÉCLARATION ET PROGRAMME D'ACTION DE VIENNE.

– « 63. [...] Tous les êtres humains naissent égaux et ont les mêmes droits à la vie et au bien-être, à l'éducation et au travail, à une vie indépendante et à une participation active à tous les aspects de la vie en société. [...] »

II, DÉCLARATION ET PROGRAMME D'ACTION DE VIENNE.

G "*RECOGNIZING* THAT THE HUMAN PERSON IS THE CENTRAL SUBJECT OF THE DEVELOPMENT PROCESS AND THAT DEVELOPMENT POLICY SHOULD THEREFORE MAKE THE HUMAN BEING THE MAIN PARTICIPANT AND BENEFICIARY OF DEVELOPMENT."

H "HUMAN RIGHTS AND FUNDAMENTAL FREEDOMS ARE THE BIRTHRIGHT OF ALL HUMAN BEINGS; THEIR PROTECTION AND PROMOTION IS THE FIRST RESPONSIBILITY OF GOVERNMENTS."

– « 1. Tous les êtres humains appartiennent à la même espèce et proviennent de la même souche. Ils naissent égaux en dignité et en droits et font tous partie intégrante de l'humanité. »

Art. 1, DÉCLARATION SUR LA RACE ET LES PRÉJUGÉS RACIAUX.

EUROPE CENTRALE ET ORIENTALE (REGION DE L') [Central and Eastern Europe region]

– « 10. Constatant également que d'autres régions sont gravement touchées et courent des risques du même ordre, notamment la région des Caraïbes, où le taux de contamination par le VIH est le plus élevé après l'Afrique subsaharienne, la région de l'Asie et du Pacifique où 7,5 millions de personnes sont déjà atteintes du VIH/sida, la région de l'Amérique latine où 1,5 million de personnes sont séropositives ou atteintes du sida et la région de l'Europe centrale et orientale où les taux de contamination sont en augmentation très rapide, et qu'en l'absence de mesures concrètes l'épidémie pourrait se propager rapidement et avoir des répercussions dans le monde entier; »

DÉCLARATION D'ENGAGEMENT SUR LE VIH/SIDA.

EVASION [Escape]

– « L'évasion d'un prisonnier de guerre sera considérée comme réussie lorsque :

1) il aura rejoint les forces armées de la Puissance dont il dépend ou celles d'une Puissance alliée;

2) il aura quitté le territoire placé sous le pouvoir de la Puissance détentrice ou d'une Puissance alliée à celle-ci;

3) il aura rejoint un navire battant pavillon de la Puissance dont il dépend ou d'une Puissance alliée et qui se trouverait dans les eaux territoriales de la Puissance détentrice, à condition que ce navire ne soit pas placé sous l'autorité de cette dernière.

Les prisonniers de guerre qui, après avoir réussi leur évasion au sens du présent article, seraient de nouveau faits prisonniers, ne seront passibles d'aucune peine pour leur évasion antérieure. »

Art. 91, CONVENTION DE GENÈVE RELATIVE AU TRAITEMENT DES PRISONNIERS DE GUERRE.

EVITER DE [LUI] NUIRE [Avoid harm]

– « L'article 10.3[32] traite d'aspects fondamentaux relatifs aux procédures et au comportement des policiers ou autres agents des services de répression dans les cas de délinquance juvénile. L'expression "éviter de [lui] nuire" est assurément vague et recouvre maints aspects de l'interaction possible (paroles, violence physique, risques dus au milieu). Avoir affaire à la justice pour mineurs peut en soi être "nocif" pour les jeunes, il faut donc interpréter l'expression "éviter de [lui] nuire" comme signifiant tout d'abord qu'il faut faire le moins de mal possible aux mineurs et éviter tout tort supplémentaire ou indu. Cela est particulièrement important dans le premier contact avec les services de répression, car ce contact peut influencer profondément l'attitude du mineur à l'égard de l'Etat et de la société. En outre, le succès de toute autre intervention dépend largement de ces premiers contacts. Bienveillance et fermeté sont essentielles en pareilles situations. »

ENSEMBLE DE RÈGLES MINIMA DES NATIONS UNIES CONCERNANT L'ADMINISTRATION DE LA JUSTICE POUR LES MINEURS (RÈGLES DE BEIJING).

EXERCICE ET LE RENFORCEMENT DE LA SOUVERAINETE PERMANENTE DES ETATS SUR LEURS RICHESSES ET RESSOURCES NATURELLES [Creation and strengthening of inalienable sovereignty of states over their natural wealth and resources]

– « *Notant* que l'exercice et le renforcement de la souveraineté permanente des Etats sur leurs richesses et ressources naturelles favorisent l'affermissement de leur indépendance économique, »

Pp. 11, RÉSOLUTION 1803 (XVII) DE L'ASSEMBLÉE GÉNÉRALE EN DATE DU 14 DÉCEMBRE 1962 : « SOUVERAINETÉ PERMANENTE SUR LES RESSOURCES NATURELLES ».

EXPERIENCE MEDICALE OU SCIENTIFIQUE [Medical or scientific experimentation]

– « Nul ne sera soumis à la torture ni à des peines ou traitements cruels, inhumains ou dégradants. En particulier, il est interdit de soumettre une

---

[32] « 10.3 Les contacts entre les services de répression et le jeune délinquant sont établis de manière à respecter le statut juridique du mineur, à favoriser son bien-être et à éviter de lui nuire, compte dûment tenu des circonstances de l'affaire. »

personne sans son libre consentement à une expérience médicale ou scientifique. »

Art. 7, PACTE INTERNATIONAL RELATIF AUX DROITS CIVILS ET POLITIQUES.

EXPERIENCES MEDICALES OU SCIENTIFIQUES NON NECESSITEES PAR LE TRAITEMENT MEDICAL [Medical or scientific experiments not necessitated by the medical treatment]

– « Les Hautes Parties contractantes s'interdisent expressément toute mesure de nature à causer soit des souffrances physiques, soit l'extermination des personnes protégées en leur pouvoir. Cette interdiction vise non seulement le meurtre, la torture, les peines corporelles, les mutilations et les expériences médicales ou scientifiques non nécessitées par le traitement médical d'une personne protégée, mais également toutes autres brutalités, qu'elles soient le fait d'agents civils ou d'agents militaires. »

Art. 32, CONVENTION DE GENÈVE RELATIVE À LA PROTECTION DES PERSONNES CIVILES EN TEMPS DE GUERRE DU 12 AOÛT 1949.

EXPLOITATION [Exploitation]

– « Aux fins du présent Protocole :

a) L'expression « traite des personnes » désigne le recrutement, le transport, le transfert, l'hébergement ou l'accueil de personnes, par la menace de recours ou le recours à la force ou à d'autres formes de contrainte, par enlèvement, fraude, tromperie, abus d'autorité ou d'une situation de vulnérabilité ou par l'offre ou l'acceptation de paiements ou d'avantages pour obtenir le consentement d'une personne ayant autorité sur une autre aux fins d'exploitation. l'exploitation comprend au minimum, l'exploitation sexuelle, le travail ou les services forcés, l'esclavage ou les pratiques analogues à l'esclavage, la servitude ou le prélèvement d'organes ; »

Art. 3, PROTOCOLE ADDITIONNEL À LA CONVENTION DES NATIONS UNIES CONTRE LA CRIMINALITÉ TRANSNATIONALE ORGANISÉE, VISANT À PRÉVENIR, RÉPRIMER ET PUNIR LA TRAITE DES PERSONNES EN PARTICULIER DES FEMMES ET DES ENFANTS.

EXTERMINATION [Extermination]

– « 2. Aux fins du paragraphe 1[33]:

[33] « 1. Aux fins du présent Statut, on entend par crime contre l'humanité l'un quelconque des actes ci-après lorsqu'il est commis dans le cadre d'une attaque généralisée ou systématique lancée contre toute population civile et en connaissance de cette attaque:

b) Par «extermination», on entend notamment le fait d'imposer intentionnellement des conditions de vie, telles que la privation d'accès à la nourriture et aux médicaments, calculées pour entraîner la destruction d'une partie de la population; »

Art. 7, STATUT DE ROME DE LA COUR PÉNALE INTERNATIONALE.

EXTRADITION [Extradition]

– « Aux fins du présent Statut:

[...]

b) On entend par «extradition» le fait pour un État de livrer une personne à un autre État en application d'un traité, d'une convention ou de la législation nationale. »

Art. 102, STATUT DE ROME DE LA COUR PÉNALE INTERNATIONALE.

EXTREME PAUVRETE ET L'EXCLUSION SOCIALE (L') [Extreme poverty and social exclusion]

– « 25. La Conférence mondiale sur les droits de l'homme affirme que l'extrême pauvreté et l'exclusion sociale constituent une violation de la dignité humaine [...] »

DÉCLARATION ET PROGRAMME D'ACTION DE VIENNE.

---

a) Meurtre;

b) Extermination;

c) Réduction en esclavage;

d) Déportation ou transfert forcé de population;

e) Emprisonnement ou autre forme de privation grave de liberté physique en violation des dispositions fondamentales du droit international;

f) Torture;

g) Viol, esclavage sexuel, prostitution forcée, grossesse forcée, stérilisation forcée ou toute autre forme de violence sexuelle de gravité comparable;

h) Persécution de tout groupe ou de toute collectivité identifiable pour des motifs d'ordre politique, racial, national, ethnique, culturel, religieux ou sexiste au sens du paragraphe 3, ou en fonction d'autres critères universellement reconnus comme inadmissibles en droit international, en corrélation avec tout acte visé dans le présent paragraphe ou tout crime relevant de la compétence de la Cour;

i) Disparitions forcées de personnes;

j) Crime d'apartheid;

k) Autres actes inhumains de caractère analogue causant intentionnellement de grandes souffrances ou des atteintes graves à l'intégrité physique ou à la santé physique ou mentale. »

FACTEURS QUI RENDENT LES PERSONNES [...] VULNERABLES A LA TRAITE [Factors that make Persons [...] vulnerable to trafficking]

– « 4. Les Etats Parties prennent ou renforcent des mesures, notamment par le biais d'une coopération bilatérale ou multilatérale, pour remédier aux facteurs qui rendent les personne, en particulier les femmes et les enfants vulnérables à la traite, tels que la pauvreté , le sous-développement et l'inégalité des chances. »

Art. 9, PROTOCOLE ADDITIONNEL À LA CONVENTION DES NATIONS UNIES CONTRE LA CRIMINALITÉ TRANSNATIONALE ORGANISÉE, VISANT À PRÉVENIR, RÉPRIMER ET PUNIR LA TRAITE DES PERSONNES EN PARTICULIER DES FEMMES ET DES ENFANTS.

FAMILLE [Family]

– « La famille est l'élément naturel et fondamental de la société et a droit à la protection de la société et de l'Etat. »

Art. 16.3, DÉCLARATION UNIVERSELLE DES DROITS DE L'HOMME.
Art. 23.1, PACTES INTERNATIONAL RELATIF AUX DROITS CIVILS ET POLITIQUES.

– « Les Etats parties au présent Pacte reconnaissent que :

1. Une protection et une assistance aussi larges que possibles doivent être accordées à la famille, qui est l'élément naturel et fondamental de la société,[...] »

Art. 10, PACTE INTERNATIONAL RELATIF AUX DROITS ÉCONOMIQUES, SOCIAUX ET CULTURELS.

– « *Convaincus* que la famille, unité fondamentale de la société et milieu naturel pour la croissance et le bien-être de tous ses membres et en particulier des enfants, doit recevoir la protection et l'assistance dont elle a besoin pour pouvoir jouer pleinement son rôle dans la communauté.»

Pp. 5, CONVENTION RELATIVE AUX DROITS DE L'ENFANT.

– « L'article 18.2[34] souligne l'importance de la famille qui, selon le paragraphe 1 de l'article 10 du Pacte international relatif aux droits économiques, sociaux et culturels, est "l'élément naturel et fondamental de la société". A l'intérieur de la famille, les parents ont non seulement le droit mais aussi le devoir d'entretenir et de surveiller leurs enfants. [...]»

---

[34] « 18.2 Aucun mineur ne sera soustrait à la surveillance de ses parents, que ce soit partiellement ou totalement, à moins que les circonstances ne rendent cette séparation nécessaire. »

18, *Commentaire*, ENSEMBLE DE RÈGLES MINIMA DES NATIONS UNIES CONCERNANT L'ADMINISTRATION DE LA JUSTICE POUR LES MINEURS (RÈGLES DE BEIJING).

– « 12. [...] la famille est l'unité centrale responsable de la socialisation primaire de l'enfant, [...] »

PRINCIPES DIRECTEURS DES NATIONS UNIES POUR LA PRÉVENTION DE LA DÉLINQUANCE JUVÉNILE (PRINCIPES DIRECTEURS DE RIYAD).

– « 18. Il est important d'insister sur la fonction de socialisation de la famille et de la famille élargie [...] »

PRINCIPES DIRECTEURS DES NATIONS UNIES POUR LA PRÉVENTION DE LA DÉLINQUANCE JUVÉNILE (PRINCIPES DIRECTEURS DE RIYAD).

– « La famille, en tant qu'élément de base de la société et que milieu naturel pour la croissance et le bien-être de tous ses membres, et en particulier des enfants et des jeunes, doit être aidée et protégée afin qu'elle puisse assumer pleinement ses responsabilités au sein de la communauté. Les parents ont le droit exclusif de déterminer librement et en toute responsabilité le nombre et l'échelonnement des naissances .»

Art. 4, DÉCLARATION SUR LE PROGRÈS ET LE DÉVELOPPEMENT DANS LE DOMAINE SOCIALE.

– « a) L'élaboration et la coordination de politiques et des mesures visant à renforcer les fonctions essentielles de la famille en tant que cellule de base de la société; »

Art. 22, DÉCLARATION SUR LE PROGRÈS ET LE DÉVELOPPEMENT DANS LE DOMAINE SOCIALE.

– « *Reconnaissant* qu'il importe d'encourager le renforcement de la structure familiale de manière à en faire la cellule fondamentale de toute société et que les hommes et les femmes ont, à partir de l'âge nubile, le droit de se marier et de fonder une famille, qu'ils ont des droits égaux au regard du mariage et que le mariage ne peut être conclu qu'avec le libre et plein consentement des futurs époux, conformément aux dispositions de l'article 16[35] de la Déclaration universelle des droits de l'homme, »

Pp. 1, RECOMMANDATION SUR LE CONSENTEMENT AU MARIAGE, L'ÂGE MINIMUM DU MARIAGE ET L'ENREGISTREMENT DES MARIAGES.

---

[35] « 1. A partir de l'âge nubile, l'homme et la femme, sans aucune restriction quant à la race, la nationalité ou la religion, ont le droit de se marier et de fonder une famille. Ils ont des droits égaux au regard du mariage, durant le mariage et lors de sa dissolution.
2. Le mariage ne peut être conclu qu'avec le libre et plein consentement des futurs époux.
3. La famille est l'élément naturel et fondamental de la société et a droit à la protection de la société et de l'Etat. »

– « 31. Affirmant le rôle déterminant joué par la famille dans les activités de prévention, de soins, d'appui et de traitement à l'intention des personnes contaminées ou touchées par le VIH/sida, en tenant compte du fait que la famille revêt des formes diverses selon les différents systèmes culturels, sociaux et politiques; »

DÉCLARATION D'ENGAGEMENT SUR LE VIH/SIDA.

– « 1. Les Etats parties, reconnaissant que la famille est l'élément naturel et fondamental de la société et qu'elle a droit à la protection de la société et de l'Etat, prennent les mesures appropriées pour assurer la protection de l'unité de la famille du travailleur migrant. »

Art. 44, CONVENTION INTERNATIONALE SUR LA PROTECTION DES DROITS DE TOUS LES TRAVAILLEURS MIGRANTS ET DES MEMBRES DE LEUR FAMILLE.

FAMILLE ELARGIE [Extended family]

– « Il est important d'insister sur la fonction de socialisation de la famille et de la famille élargie [...] »

ART. 18, PRINCIPES DIRECTEURS DES NATIONS UNIES POUR LA PRÉVENTION DE LA DÉLINQUANCE JUVÉNILE (PRINCIPES DIRECTEURS DE RIYAD).

FEMMES [Women]

– « *Préoccupés* toutefois de constater qu'en dépit de ces divers instruments les femmes continuent de faire l'objet d'importantes discriminations, »

Pp. 6, CONVENTION SUR L'ÉLIMINATION DE TOUTES LES FORMES DE DISCRIMINATION À L'ÉGARD DES FEMMES.

– « 4. [...]le rôle clé des femmes dans la production agricole et l'économie rurale de nombreux pays [...] »

DÉCLARATION UNIVERSELLE POUR L'ÉLIMINATION DÉFINITIVE DE LA FAIM ET DE LA MALNUTRITION.

FEMMES RURALES [Rural women]

– « 1. Les Etats parties tiennent compte des problèmes particuliers qui se posent aux femmes rurales et du rôle important que ces femmes jouent dans la survie économique de leurs familles, notamment par leur travail dans les secteurs non monétaires de l'économie, et prennent toutes les mesures appropriées pour assurer l'application des dispositions de la présente Convention aux femmes des zones rurales. »

Art. 14, CONVENTION SUR L'ÉLIMINATION DE TOUTES LES FORMES DE DISCRIMINATION À L'ÉGARD DES FEMMES.

FILLETTES [Girl children]

- « *Conscients* qu'un certain nombre de groupes particulièrement vulnérables, notamment les fillettes, sont davantage exposés au risque d'exploitation sexuelle, et qu'on recense un nombre anormalement élevé de fillettes parmi les victimes de l'exploitation sexuelle »

Pp. 5, PROTOCOLE FACULTATIF À LA CONVENTION RELATIVE AUX DROITS DE L'ENFANT, CONCERNANT LA VENTE D'ENFANTS, LA PROSTITUTION DES ENFANTS ET LA PORNOGRAPHIE METTANT EN SCÈNE DES ENFANTS.

FONDEMENT DE LA LIBERTE, DE LA JUSTICE ET DE LA PAIX DANS LE MONDE [Foundation of freedom, justice and peace in the world]

- « *Considérant* que, conformément aux principes énoncés dans la Charte des Nations Unies, la reconnaissance de la dignité inhérente à tous les membres de la famille humaine et de leurs droits égaux et inaliénables constitue le fondement de la liberté, de la justice et de la paix dans le monde, »

Pp. 1, PACTE INTERNATIONAL RELATIF AUX DROITS ÉCONOMIQUES SOCIAUX ET CULTURELS.

FORCES ARMEES [Armed forces]

- « 1. Les forces armées d'une Partie à un conflit se composent de toutes les forces, tous les groupes et toutes les unités armés et organisés qui sont placés sous un commandement responsable de la conduite de ses subordonnés devant cette Partie, même si celle-ci est représentée par un gouvernement ou une autorité non reconnus par une Partie adverse. Ces forces armées doivent être soumises à un régime de discipline interne qui assure, notamment, le respect des règles du droit international applicable dans les conflits armés. »

Art. 43, PROTOCOLE ADDITIONNEL AUX CONVENTIONS DE GENÈVE DU 12 AOÛT 1949 RELATIF À LA PROTECTION DES VICTIMES DES CONFLITS ARMÉS INTERNATIONAUX (PROTOCOLE I).

FORCES ARMEES D'UN ETAT [Armed forces of a State]

- « 1. Les groupes armés qui sont distincts des forces armées d'un Etat ne devraient en aucune circonstance enrôler ni utiliser dans les hostilités des personnes âgées de moins de 18 ans. »

Art. 1, Protocole facultatif à la Convention relative aux relative aux droits de l'enfant, concernant l'implication d'enfants dans les conflits armés.

FORCES DU MARCHE [Market forces]

– « Les seules forces du marché ne peuvent garantir la préservation et la promotion de la diversité culturelles, gage de développement humain durable.[...] »

Art. 11, Déclaration universelle sur la diversité culturelle.

GASTRITE, ENTERITE OU COLIQUE CHRONIQUES DURANT PLUS D'UNE ANNEE ET AFFECTANT GRAVEMENT L'ETAT GENERAL [Chronic gastritis, enteritis or colitis, having lasted more than one year and seriously affecting the general condition]

– « *e)* Les affections chroniques graves des organes digestifs, par exemple : ulcère de l'estomac ou du duodénum; suite d'intervention chirurgicale sur l'estomac faite en captivité; gastrite, entérite ou colique chroniques durant plus d'une année et affectant gravement l'état général; cirrhose hépatique; cholécystopathie chronique*; etc. »

Annexe I, 3, Convention de Genève relative au traitement des prisonniers de guerre.

GENOCIDE [Genocide]

– « 28. La Conférence mondiale sur les droits de l'homme se déclare consternée par les violations massives des droits de l'homme, notamment celles qui prennent la forme de génocide, de "nettoyage ethnique" et de viol systématique des femmes en temps de guerre, violations qui sont à l'origine d'exodes massifs de réfugiés et de déplacements de personnes.[...] »

I, Déclaration et Programme d'action de Vienne.

– « 2. Une des violations les plus graves de ce principe est constituée par l'apartheid qui, comme le génocide, est un crime contre l'humanité et qui trouble gravement la paix et la sécurité. »

Art. 4, Déclaration sur la race et les préjugés raciaux.

– « *Considérant* que l'Assemblée générale de l'Organisation des Nations Unies, par sa résolution 96 (I) en date du 11 décembre 1946, a déclaré que le génocide est un crime du droit des gens, en contradiction avec l'esprit et les fins des Nations Unies et que le monde civilisé condamne, »

Pp.1, Convention pour la prévention et la répression du crime de génocide.

– « *Reconnaissant* qu'à toutes les périodes de l'histoire le génocide a infligé de grandes pertes à l'humanité, »

Pp.2, CONVENTION POUR LA PRÉVENTION ET LA RÉPRESSION DU CRIME DE GÉNOCIDE.

– « Dans la présente Convention, le génocide s'entend de l'un quelconque des actes ci-après, commis dans l'intention de détruire, ou tout ou en partie, un groupe national, ethnique, racial ou religieux, comme tel :

a) Meurtre de membres du groupe;

b) Atteinte grave à l'intégrité physique ou mentale de membres du groupe;

c) Soumission intentionnelle du groupe à des conditions d'existence devant entraîner sa destruction physique totale ou partielle;

d) Mesures visant à entraver les naissances au sein du groupe;

e) Transfert forcé d'enfants du groupe à un autre groupe. »

Art. II, CONVENTION POUR LA PRÉVENTION ET LA RÉPRESSION DU CRIME DE GÉNOCIDE.

– « 2. Le génocide s'entend de l'un quelconque des actes ci-après, commis dans l'intention de détruire, en tout ou en partie, un groupe national, ethnique, racial ou religieux, comme tel :

a) Meurtre de membres du groupe ;

b) Atteinte grave à l'intégrité physique ou mentale de membres du groupe ;

c) Soumission intentionnelle du groupe à des conditions d'existence devant entraîner sa destruction physique totale ou partielle ;

d) Mesures vidant à entraver les naissances au sein du groupe ;

e) Transfert forcé d'enfants du groupe à un autre groupe »

Art. 4, STATUT DU TRIBUNAL INTERNATIONAL CHARGÉ DE POURSUIVRE LES PERSONNES PRÉSUMÉES RESPONSABLE DE VIOLATIONS GRAVES DU DROIT INTERNATIONAL HUMANITAIRE COMMISES SUR LE TERITOIRE DE L'EX-YOUGOSLAVIE DEPUIS 1991.

Art. 2, STATUT DU TRIBUNAL PÉNAL INTERNATIONAL CHARGÉ DE JUGER LES PERSONNES PRÉSUMÉES RESPONSABLES D'ACTES DE GÉNOCIDE OU D'AUTRES VIOLATIONS GRAVES DU DROIT INTERNATIONAL HUMANITAIRE COMMIS SUR LE TERRITOIRE DU RWANDA ET LES CITOYENS RWANDAIS PRÉSUMÉS RESPONSABLES DE TELS ACTES OU VIOLATIONS COMMIS SUR LE TERRITOIRE D'ETATS VOISINS ENTRE LE 1ER JANVIER 1994 ET LE 31 DÉCEMBRE 1994.

– « Aux fins du présent Statut, on entend par crime de génocide l'un quelconque des actes ci-après commis dans l'intention de détruire, en tout ou en partie, un groupe national, ethnique, racial ou religieux, comme tel:

a) Meurtre de membres du groupe;

b) Atteinte grave à l'intégrité physique ou mentale de membres du groupe;

c) Soumission intentionnelle du groupe à des conditions d'existence devant entraîner sa destruction physique totale ou partielle;

d) Mesures visant à entraver les naissances au sein du groupe;

e) Transfert forcé d'enfants du groupe à un autre groupe. »

Art. 6, STATUT DE ROME DE LA COUR PENALE INTERNATIONALE.

GENOME HUMAIN [Human Genome]

– « Le génome humain sous-tend l'unité fondamentale de tous les membres de la famille humaine, ainsi que la reconnaissance de leur dignité intrinsèque et de leur diversité. Dans un sens symbolique, il est le patrimoine de l'humanité. »

Art. 1, DÉCLARATION UNIVERSELLE SUR LE GÉNOME HUMAIN ET LES DROITS DE L'HOMME.

– « Le génome humain, par nature évolutif, est sujet à des mutations. Il renferme des potentialités qui s'expriment différemment selon l'environnement naturel et social de chaque individu, en ce qui concerne notamment l'état de santé, les conditions de vie, la nutrition et l'éducation. »

Art. 3, DÉCLARATION UNIVERSELLE SUR LE GÉNOME HUMAIN ET LES DROITS DE L'HOMME.

GENS DE MER [Seafarer]

– « Aux fins de la présente Convention:
[...]

c) L'expression "gens de mer", qui comprend les pêcheurs, désigne les travailleurs migrants employés à bord d'un navire immatriculé dans un Etat dont ils ne sont pas ressortissants; »

Art. 2, § 2, CONVENTION INTERNATIONALE SUR LA PROTECTION DES DROITS DE TOUS LES TRAVAILLEURS MIGRANTS ET DES MEMBRES DE LEUR FAMILLE.

GLAUCOME [Glaucoma]

– « *i)* La cécité des deux yeux ou celle d'un œil lorsque la vue de l'autre œil est moins de 1, malgré l'emploi de verres correcteurs; la diminution de l'acuité visuelle ne pouvant être corrigée à 1/2 pour un œil au moins*; les autres affections oculaires graves, par exemple : glaucome; iritis; chloroïdite; trachome; etc. »

Annexe I, 3, CONVENTION DE GENÈVE RELATIVE AU TRAITEMENT DES PRISONNIERS DE GUERRE.

GROSSESSE ET AFFECTIONS OBSTETRICALES, LORSQUE L'HOSPITALISATION EN PAYS NEUTRE EST IMPOSSIBLE [Normal pregnancy, and obstetrical disorder, where it is impossible to accommodate in a neutral country]

– « *f*) Les affections chroniques graves des organes génito-urinaires, par exemple : maladies chroniques du rein avec troubles consécutifs; néphrectomie pour un rein tuberculeux; pyélite chronique ou cystite chronique; hydro ou pyonéphrose; affections gynécologiques chroniques graves; grossesses et affections obstétricales, lorsque l'hospitalisation en pays neutre est impossible; etc. »

Annexe I, 3, CONVENTION DE GENÈVE RELATIVE AU TRAITEMENT DES PRISONNIERS DE GUERRE.

GROSSESSE FORCEE [Forced pregnancy]

– « *g*) Viol, esclavage sexuel, prostitution forcée, grossesse forcée, stérilisation forcée ou toute autre forme de violence sexuelle de gravité comparable; »

Art. 7, § 1, STATUT DE ROME DE LA COUR PÉNALE INTERNATIONALE.

« 2. Aux fins du paragraphe 1[36]:

---

[36] « 1. Aux fins du présent Statut, on entend par crime contre l'humanité l'un quelconque des actes ci-après lorsqu'il est commis dans le cadre d'une attaque généralisée ou systématique lancée contre toute population civile et en connaissance de cette attaque:
a) Meurtre;
b) Extermination;
c) Réduction en esclavage;
d) Déportation ou transfert forcé de population;
e) Emprisonnement ou autre forme de privation grave de liberté physique en violation des dispositions fondamentales du droit international;
f) Torture;
g) Viol, esclavage sexuel, prostitution forcée, grossesse forcée, stérilisation forcée ou toute autre forme de violence sexuelle de gravité comparable;
h) Persécution de tout groupe ou de toute collectivité identifiable pour des motifs d'ordre politique, racial, national, ethnique, culturel, religieux ou sexiste au sens du paragraphe 3, ou en fonction d'autres critères universellement reconnus comme inadmissibles en droit international, en corrélation avec tout acte visé dans le présent paragraphe ou tout crime relevant de la compétence de la Cour;
i) Disparitions forcées de personnes;
j) Crime d'apartheid;

[...]

f) Par «grossesse forcée», on entend la détention illégale d'une femme mise enceinte de force, dans l'intention de modifier la composition ethnique d'une population ou de commettre d'autres violations graves du droit international. Cette définition ne peut en aucune manière s'interpréter comme ayant une incidence sur les lois nationales relatives à la grossesse; »

Art. 7, STATUT DE ROME DE LA COUR PÉNALE INTERNATIONALE.

GUERRE [War]

- « [...] guerre, qu'il s'agisse des guerres civiles ou des guerres entre Etats,[...] »

8, DÉCLARATION DU MILLÉNAIRE.

HANDICAP [Handicap]

- « 6. [...] Ils ont même permis de définir pour la première fois l'handicap comme une fonction des rapports existant entre les personnes handicapées et leur cadre de vie »

INTRODUCTION, RÈGLES POUR L'ÉGALISTION DES CHANCES DES PERSONNES HANDICAPÉES.

- « 18. Par « handicap », il faut entendre la perte ou la restitution des possibilités de participer à la vie de la collectivité à égalité avec les autres, le mot lui-même désignant implicitement le rapport entre le handicapé et son milieu. On souligne ainsi les inadéquations du milieu physique et des nombreuses activités organisées – information, communication, éducation, etc. – , qui empêchent les handicapés de participer à la vie de la société dans l'égalité. »

INTRODUCTION, RÈGLES POUR L'ÉGALISATION DES CHANCES DES PERSONNES HANDICAPÉES.

- « 20. En 1980, l'Organisation mondiale de la santé a adopté une classification internationale des déficiences, incapacités et handicaps qui a défini une approche à la fois plus précise et relativiste. La Classification internationale des handicapés : déficiences, incapacités et désavantages établit des distinctions claires entre la déficience, l'incapacité et handicap. Elle est couramment utilisée dans les domaines suivants : réadaptation, éducation, statistiques, prise de décisions, législation, démographie,

---

k) Autres actes inhumains de caractère analogue causant intentionnellement de grandes souffrances ou des atteintes graves à l'intégrité physique ou à la santé physique ou mentale. »

sociologie, économie et anthropologie. Selon certains des spécialistes à qui elle s'adresse, il se pourrait que la définition du terme « handicap » qui est donnée revête un caractère trop médicale encore, qu'elle soit indûment centrée sur l'individu, et qu'elle ne précise pas assez clairement la manière dont la situation sociale, les attentes de la collectivité et d'autres préoccupations exprimées par les utilisateurs depuis la publication de la Classification, il y a 12 ans, dans les révisions dont celle-ci doit faire l'objet. »[i]

INTRODUCTION, RÈGLES POUR L'ÉGALISATION DES CHANCES DES PERSONNES HANDICAPÉES.

HANDICAPE [Disabled person]

– « 1. Le terme "handicapé" désigne toute personne dans l'incapacité d'assurer par elle-même tout ou partie des nécessités d'une vie individuelle ou sociale normale, du fait d'une déficience, congénitale ou non, de ses capacités physiques ou mentales. »

DÉCLARATION DES DROITS DES PERSONNES HANDICAPÉES.

HANDICAPES [Persons with disabilities]

– « 1. On trouve des handicapés dans toutes les régions du monde et dans toutes les catégories sociales. Le nombre des handicapés est élevé et augmente encore dans le monde entier. »

INTRODUCTION, RÈGLES POUR L'ÉGALISATION DES CHANCES DES PERSONNES HANDICAPÉES.

– « 26. Les handicapés font partie de la société et ont le droit de rester dans leur collectivité d'origine. Ils doivent recevoir l'assistance dont ils ont besoin dans le cadre des structures ordinaires d'enseignements, de santé, d'emploi et de services sociaux. »

INTRODUCTION, RÈGLES POUR L'ÉGALISATION DES CHANCES DES PERSONNES HANDICAPÉES.

---

[i] "20. In 1980, the World Health Organization adopted an international classification of impairments, disabilities and handicaps, which suggested a more precise and at the same time relativistic approach. The International Classification of Impairments, Disabilities, and Handicaps makes a clear distinction between 'impairment', 'disability' and 'handicap'. It has been extensively used in areas such as rehabilitation, education, statistics, policy, legislation, demography, sociology, economics and anthropology. Some users have expressed concern that the Classification, in its definition of the term 'handicap', may still be considered too medical and too centred on the individual, and may not adequately clarify the interaction between societal conditions or expectations and the abilities of the individual. Those concerns, and others expressed by users during the 12 years since its publication, will be addressed in forthcoming revisions of the Classification."

– « 3. Tous les handicapés, y compris les personnes souffrant d'une incapacité grave ou d'incapacités multiples, qui ont besoin de réadaptation devraient y avoir accès. »

I, Règle 3, RÈGLES POUR L'ÉGALISATION DES CHANCES DES PERSONNES HANDICAPÉES.

HAUT COMMISSAIRE AUX DROITS DE L'HOMME [High commissioner for human rights]

– « 18. La Conférence mondiale sur les droits de l'homme recommande à l'Assemblée générale, lorsqu'elle examinera son rapport, à sa quarante-huitième session, d'étudier en priorité la question de la création d'un haut commissariat aux droits de l'homme pour promouvoir et protéger l'ensemble de ces droits. »

II, DÉCLARATION ET PROGRAMME D'ACTION DE VIENNE.

HOMME [Man]

– « *Convaincue* que l'homme ne peut satisfaire pleinement ses aspirations que dans un ordre social juste [...] »

Pp.5, DÉCLARATION SUR LE PROGRÈS ET LE DÉVELOPPEMENT DANS LE DOMAINE SOCIAL.

HORS DE COMBAT [Hors de combat]

– « 2. Est hors de combat toute personne :

a) qui est au pouvoir d'une Partie adverse,

b) qui exprime clairement son intention de se rendre, ou

c) qui a perdu connaissance ou est autrement en état d'incapacité du fait de blessures ou de maladie et en conséquence incapable de se défendre, à condition que, dans tous les cas, elle s'abstienne de tout acte d'hostilité et ne tente pas de s'évader. »

Art. 41, PROTOCOLE ADDITIONNEL AUX CONVENTIONS DE GENÈVE DU 12 AOÛT 1949 RELATIF À LA PROTECTION DES VICTIMES DES CONFLITS ARMÉS INTERNATIONAUX (PROTOCOLE I).

HYDRARGYRISME [Mercury poisoning]

– « *o)* Les intoxications chroniques graves, par exemple : saturnisme, hydrargyrisme; morphinisme, cocaïnisme, alcoolisme; intoxications par les gaz et par les radiations; etc. »

Annexe I, 3, CONVENTION DE GENÈVE RELATIVE AU TRAITEMENT DES PRISONNIERS DE GUERRE.

HYDRO OU PYONEPHROSE [Hydronephrosis or pyonephrosis]

– « *f)* Les affections chroniques graves des organes génito-urinaires, par exemple : maladies chroniques du rein avec troubles consécutifs; néphrectomie pour un rein tuberculeux; pyélite chronique ou cystite chronique; hydro ou pyonéphrose; affections gynécologiques chroniques graves; grossesses et affections obstétricales, lorsque l'hospitalisation en pays neutre est impossible; etc. »

Annexe I, 3, CONVENTION DE GENÈVE RELATIVE AU TRAITEMENT DES PRISONNIERS DE GUERRE.

IDENTITE D'ORIGINE [Identity of Origin]

– « 3. L'identité d'origine n'affecte en rien la faculté pour les êtres humains de vivre différemment, ni les différences fondées sur la diversité des cultures, du milieu et de l'histoire, ni le droit de maintenir l'identité culturelle. »

Art. 1, DéCLARATION SUR LA RACE ET LES PRÉJUGÉS RACIAUX.

INCAPACITE [Disability]

– « 17. Le mot « incapacité » recouvre à lui seul nombre de limitations fonctionnelles différentes qui peuvent frapper chacun des habitants du globe. L'incapacité peut être d'ordre physique, intellectuel ou ßsensoriel, ou tenir à un état pathologique ou à une maladie mentales. Ces déficiences, états pathologiques ou maladies peuvent être permanentes ou temporaires. »

INTRODUCTION, RÈGLES POUR L'ÉGALISATION DES CHANCES DES PERSONNES HANDICAPÉES.

– « 20. En 1980, l'Organisation mondiale de la santé a adopté une classification internationale des déficiences, incapacités et handicaps qui a défini une approche à la fois plus précise et relativiste. La Classification internationale des handicapés : déficiences, incapacités et désavantages établit des distinctions claires entre la déficience, l'incapacité et handicap. Elle est couramment utilisée dans les domaines suivants : réadaptation, éducation, statistiques, prise de décisions, législation, démographie, sociologie, économie et anthropologie. Selon certains des spécialistes à qui elle s'adresse, il se pourrait que la définition du terme « handicap » qui est donnée revête un caractère trop médicale encore, qu'elle soit indûment centrée sur l'individu, et qu'elle ne précise pas assez clairement la manière dont la situation sociale, les attentes de la collectivité et d'autres pré-

occupations exprimées par les utilisateurs depuis la publication de la Classification, il y a 12 ans, dans les révisions dont celle-ci doit faire l'objet. »[j]
INTRODUCTION, RÈGLES POUR L'ÉGALISATION DES CHANCES DES PERSONNES HANDICAPÉES.

INDIVIDU [Everyone ;Individual]

– « 1. L'individu a des devoirs envers la communauté dans laquelle seul le libre et plein développement de sa personnalité est possible. »
Art. 29, DÉCLARATION UNIVERSELLE DES DROITS DE L'HOMME.

– « Prenant en considération le fait que l'individu a des devoirs envers autrui et envers la collectivité à laquelle il appartient et est tenu de s'efforcer de promouvoir et de respecter les droits reconnus dans le présent Pacte, »
Pp. 5, PACTE INTERNATIONAL RELATIF AUX DROITS ÉCONOMIQUES, SOCIAUX ET CULTURELS.
Pp. 5, PACTE INTERNATIONAL RELATIF AUX DROITS CIVILS ET POLITIQUES.

INDIVIDUS, GROUPES, INSTITUTIONS ET ORGANISATIONS NON GOUVERNEMENTALES [Individuals, groups, institutions and non-governmental organizations]

– « 2. Les individus, groupes, institutions et organisations non gouvernementales ont un rôle important à jouer et une responsabilité à assumer en ce qui concerne la sauvegarde de la démocratie, la promotion des droits de l'homme et des libertés fondamentales ainsi que la promotion et le progrès de sociétés, institutions et processus démocratiques.

3. Les individus, groupes, institutions et organisations non gouvernementales ont également un rôle important à jouer et une responsabilité à assumer pour ce qui est de contribuer, selon qu'il convient, à la promotion du droit de chacun à un ordre social et international grâce auquel les droits et libertés énoncés dans la Déclaration universelle des

---

[j] "20. In 1980, the World Health Organization adopted an international classification of impairments, disabilities and handicaps, which suggested a more precise and at the same time relativistic approach. The International Classification of Impairments, Disabilities, and Handicaps makes a clear distinction between 'impairment', 'disability' and 'handicap'. It has been extensively used in areas such as rehabilitation, education, statistics, policy, legislation, demography, sociology, economics and anthropology. Some users have expressed concern that the Classification, in its definition of the term 'handicap', may still be considered too medical and too centred on the individual, and may not adequately clarify the interaction between societal conditions or expectations and the abilities of the individual. Those concerns, and others expressed by users during the 12 years since its publication, will be addressed in forthcoming revisions of the Classification."

droits de l'homme et les autres instruments relatifs aux droits de l'homme peuvent être réalisés dans leur intégralité. »

Art. 18, DÉCLARATION SUR LE DROIT ET LA RESPONSABILITÉ DES INDIVIDUS, GROUPES ET ORGANES DE LA SOCIÉTÉ DE PROMOUVOIR ET PROTÉGER LES DROITS DE L'HOMME ET LES LIBERTÉS FONDAMENTALES UNIVERSELLEMENT RECONNUS.

INDIVIDUS, ORGANISATIONS NON GOUVERNEMENTALES ET INSTITUTIONS COMPETENTES [Individuals, non-governmental organizations and relevant institutions]

– « Les individus, organisations non gouvernementales et institutions compétentes ont un rôle important à jouer pour ce qui est de sensibiliser davantage le public aux questions relatives à tous les droits de l'homme et à toutes les libertés fondamentales, en particulier dans le cadre d'activités d'éducation, de formation et de recherche dans ces domaines en vue de renforcer encore, notamment, la compréhension, la tolérance, la paix et les relations amicales entre les nations ainsi qu'entre tous les groupes raciaux et religieux, en tenant compte de la diversité des sociétés et des communautés dans lesquelles ils mènent leurs activités. »

Art. 16, DÉCLARATION SUR LE DROIT ET LA RESPONSABILITÉ DES INDIVIDUS, GROUPES ET ORGANES DE LA SOCIÉTÉ DE PROMOUVOIR ET PROTÉGER LES DROITS DE L'HOMME ET LES LIBERTÉS FONDAMENTALES UNIVERSELLEMENT RECONNUS.

INFRACTIONS GRAVES [Grave breaches]

– « Les infractions graves visées à l'article précédent[37] sont celles qui comportent l'un ou l'autre des actes suivants, s'ils sont commis contre des

---

[37] « Les Hautes Parties contractantes s'engagent à prendre toute mesure législative nécessaire pour fixer les sanctions pénales adéquates à appliquer aux personnes ayant commis, ou donné l'ordre de commettre, l'une ou l'autre des infractions graves à la présente Convention définies à l'article suivant.

Chaque Partie contractante aura l'obligation de rechercher les personnes prévenues d'avoir commis, ou d'avoir ordonné de commettre, l'une ou l'autre de ces infractions graves, et elle devra les déférer à ses propres tribunaux, quelle que soit leur nationalité. Elle pourra aussi, si elle le préfère, et selon les conditions prévues par sa propre législation, les remettre pour jugement à une autre Partie contractante intéressée à la poursuite, pour autant que cette Partie contractante ait retenu contre lesdites personnes des charges suffisantes.

Chaque Partie contractante prendra les mesures nécessaires pour faire cesser les actes contraires aux dispositions de la présente Convention, autres que les infractions graves définies à l'article suivant.

En toutes circonstances, les inculpés bénéficieront de garanties de procédure et de libre défense qui ne seront pas inférieures à celles prévues par les articles 105 et suivants de la Convention de Genève relative au traitement des prisonniers de guerre du 12 août 1949. »

personnes ou des biens protégés par la Convention: l'homicide intentionnel, la torture ou les traitements inhumains, y compris les expériences biologiques, le fait de causer intentionnellement de grandes souffrances ou de porter des atteintes graves à l'intégrité physique ou à la santé, la déportation ou le transfert illégaux, la détention illégale, le fait de contraindre une personne protégée à servir dans les forces armées de la Puissance ennemie, ou celui de la priver de son droit d'être jugée régulièrement et impartialement selon les prescriptions de la présente Convention, la prise d'otages, la destruction et l'appropriation de biens non justifiées par des nécessités militaires et exécutées sur une grande échelle de façon illicite et arbitraire. »

Art. 147, CONVENTION DE GENÈVE RELATIVE À LA PROTECTION DES PERSONNES CIVILES EN TEMPS DE GUERRE DU 12 AOÛT 1949.

– « 2. Les actes qualifiés d'infractions graves dans les Conventions constituent des infractions graves au présent Protocole s'ils sont commis contre des personnes au pouvoir d'une Partie adverse protégées par les articles 44[38],

[38] « 1. Tout combattant, au sens de l'article 43, qui tombe au pouvoir d'une Partie adverse est prisonnier de guerre.

2. Bien que tous les combattants soient tenus de respecter les règles du droit international applicable dans les conflits armés, les violations de ces règles ne privent pas un combattant de son droit d'être considéré comme combattant ou, s'il tombe au pouvoir d'une Partie adverse, de son droit d'être considéré comme prisonnier de guerre, sauf dans les cas prévus aux paragraphes 3 et 4.

3. Pour que la protection de la population civile contre les effets des hostilités soit renforcée, les combattants sont tenus de se distinguer de la population civile lorsqu'ils prennent part à une attaque ou à une opération militaire préparatoire d'une attaque. Etant donné, toutefois, qu'il y a des situations dans les conflits armés où, en raison de la nature des hostilités, un combattant armé ne peut se distinguer de la population civile, il conserve son statut de combattant à condition que, dans de telles situations, il porte ses armes ouvertement :

a) pendant chaque engagement militaire; et

b) pendant le temps où il est exposé à la vue de l'adversaire alors qu'il prend part à un déploiement militaire qui précède le lancement d'une attaque à laquelle il doit participer.

Les actes qui répondent aux conditions prévues par le présent paragraphe ne sont pas considérés comme perfides au sens de l'article 37, paragraphe 1 c.

4. Tout combattant qui tombe au pouvoir d'une Partie adverse, alors qu'il ne remplit pas les conditions prévues à la deuxième phrase du paragraphe 3, perd son droit à être considéré comme prisonnier de guerre, mais bénéficie néanmoins de protections équivalentes à tous égards à celles qui sont accordées aux prisonniers de guerre par le IIIe Convention et par le présent Protocole. Cette protection comprend des protections équivalentes à celles qui sont accordées aux prisonniers de guerre par la IIIe Convention dans le cas où une telle personne est jugée et condamnée pour toutes infractions qu'elle aura commises.

45[39] et 73[40] du présent Protocole, ou contre des blessés, des malades ou des naufragés de la Partie adverse protégés par le présent Protocole, ou contre le personnel sanitaire ou religieux, des unités sanitaires ou des moyens de transport sanitaire qui sont sous le contrôle de la Partie adverse et protégés par le présent Protocole.

---

5. Le combattant qui tombe au pouvoir d'une Partie adverse alors qu'il ne participe pas à une attaque ou à une opération militaire préparatoire d'une attaque ne perd pas, en raison de ses activités antérieures, le droit d'être considéré comme combattant et prisonnier de guerre.
6. Le présent article ne prive personne du droit d'être considéré comme prisonnier de guerre aux termes de l'article 4 de la IIIe Convention.
7. La présent article n'a pas pour objet de modifier la pratique des Etats, généralement acceptée, concernant le port de l'uniforme par des combattants affectés aux unités armées régulières en uniforme d'une Partie au conflit;
8. Outre les catégories de personnes visées à l'article 13 des Ire et IIe Conventions, tous les membres des forces armées d'une Partie au conflit, tels qu'ils sont définis à l'article 43 du présent Protocole, ont droit à la protection accordée par lesdites Conventions s'ils sont blessés ou malades, ou dans le cas de la IIe Convention, s'ils sont naufragés en mer ou en d'autres eaux. »

[39] « 1. Une personne qui prend part à des hostilités et tombe au pouvoir d'une Partie adverse est présumée être prisonnier de guerre et par conséquent se trouve protégée par la IIIe Convention lorsqu'elle revendique le statut de prisonnier de guerre, ou qu'il apparaît qu'elle a droit au statut de prisonnier de guerre, ou lorsque la Partie dont elle dépend revendique pour elle ce statut par voie de notification à la Puissance qui la détient ou à la Puissance protectrice. S'il existe un doute quelconque au sujet de son droit au statut de prisonnier de guerre, cette personne continue à bénéficier de ce statut et, par suite, de la protection de la IIIe Convention et du présent Protocole, en attendant que son statut soit déterminé par un tribunal compétent.
2. Si une personne tombée au pouvoir d'une Partie adverse n'est pas détenue comme prisonnier de guerre et doit être jugée par cette Partie pour une infraction liée aux hostilités, elle est habilitée à faire valoir son droit au statut de prisonnier de guerre devant un tribunal judiciaire et à obtenir que cette question soit tranchée. Chaque fois que la procédure applicable le permet, la question doit être tranchée avant qu'il soit statué sur l'infraction. Les représentants de la Puissance protectrice ont le droit d'assister aux débats au cours desquels cette question doit être tranchée, sauf dans le cas exceptionnel où ces débats ont lieu à huis clos dans l'intérêt de la sûreté de l'Etat. Dans ce cas, la Puissance détentrice doit en aviser la Puissance protectrice.
3. Toute personne qui, ayant pris part à des hostilités, n'a pas droit au statut de prisonnier de guerre et ne bénéficie pas d'un traitement plus favorable conformément à la IVe Convention a droit, en tout temps, à la protection de l'article 75 du présent Protocole. En territoire occupé, une telle personne, sauf si elle est détenue pour espionnage, bénéficie également, nonobstant les dispositions de l'article 5 de la IVe Convention, des droits de communication prévus par ladite Convention. »

[40] « Les personnes qui, avant le début des hostilités, sont considérées comme apatrides ou réfugiés au sens des instruments internationaux pertinents acceptés par les Parties intéressées ou de la législation nationale de l'Etat d'accueil ou de résidence, seront, en toutes circonstances et sans aucune distinction de caractère défavorable, des personnes protégées au sens des Titres I et III de la IVe Convention. »

3. Outre les infractions graves définies à l'article 11[41], les actes suivants, lorsqu'ils sont commis intentionnellement, en violation des dispositions pertinentes du présent Protocole, et qu'ils entraînent la mort ou causent des atteintes graves à l'intégrité physique ou à la santé, sont considérés comme des infractions graves au présent Protocole :

a) soumettre la population civile ou des personnes civiles à une attaque;

b) lancer une attaque sans discrimination atteignant la population civile ou des biens de caractère civil, en sachant que cette attaque causera des pertes en vies humaines, des blessures aux personnes

---

[41] « 1. La santé et l'intégrité physiques ou mentales des personnes au pouvoir de la Partie adverse ou internées, détenues ou d'une autre manière privées de liberté en raison d'une situation visée à l'article premier ne doivent être compromises par aucun acte ni par aucune omission injustifiés. En conséquence, il est interdit de soumettre les personnes visées au présent article à un acte médical qui ne serait pas motivé par leur état de santé et qui ne serait pas conforme aux normes médicales généralement reconnues que la Partie responsable de l'acte appliquerait dans des circonstances médicales analogues à ses propres ressortissants jouissant de leur liberté.
2. Il et en particulier interdit de pratiquer sur ces personnes, même avec leur consentement :
a) des mutilations physiques;
b) des expériences médicales ou scientifiques;
c) des prélèvements de tissus ou d'organes pour des transplantations,
sauf si ces actes sont justifiés dans les conditions prévues au paragraphe 1.
3. Il ne peut être dérogé à l'interdiction visée au paragraphe 2 c que lorsqu'il s'agit de dons de sang en vue de transfusion ou de peau destinée à des greffes, à la condition que ces dons soient volontaires et ne résultent pas de mesures de coercition ou de persuasion et qu'ils soient destinés à des fins thérapeutiques dans des conditions compatibles avec les normes médicales généralement reconnues et avec les contrôles effectués dans l'intérêt tant du donneur que du receveur.
4. Tout acte ou omission volontaire qui met gravement en danger la santé ou l'intégrité physiques ou mentales de toute personne au pouvoir d'une Partie autre que celle dont elle dépend et qui, soit contrevient à l'une des interdictions énoncées aux paragraphes 1 et 2, soit ne respecte pas les conditions prescrites au paragraphe 3, constitue une infraction grave au présent Protocole.
5. Les personnes définies au paragraphe 1 ont le droit de refuser toute intervention chirurgicale. En cas de refus, le personnel sanitaire doit s'efforcer d'obtenir une déclaration écrite à cet effet, signée ou reconnue par le patient.
6. Toute Partie au conflit doit tenir un dossier médical pour tout don de sang en vue de transfusion ou de peau destinée à des greffes par les personnes visées au paragraphe 1, si ce don est effectué sous la responsabilité de cette Partie. En outre, toute Partie au conflit doit s'efforcer de tenir un dossier de tous les actes médicaux entrepris à l'égard des personnes internées, détenues ou d'une autre manière privées de liberté en raison d'une situation visée à l'article premier. Ces dossiers doivent en tout temps être à la disposition de la Puissance protectrice aux fins d'inspection. »

civiles ou des dommages aux biens de caractère civil, qui sont excessifs au sens de l'article 57, paragraphe 2 a iii[42];

c) lancer une attaque contre des ouvrages ou installations contenant des forces dangereuses, en sachant que cette attaque causera des pertes en vies humaines, des blessures aux personnes civiles ou des dommages aux biens de caractère civil, qui sont excessifs au sens de l'article 57, paragraphe 2 a iii[43];

d) soumettre à une attaque des localités non défendues et des zones démilitarisées;

e) soumettre une personne à une attaque en la sachant hors de combat;

f) utiliser perfidement, en violation de l'article 37[44], le signe distinctif de la croix rouge, du croissant rouge ou du lion-et-soleil rouge ou d'autres signes protecteurs reconnus par les Conventions ou par le présent Protocole.

4. Outre les infractions graves définies aux paragraphes précédents et dans les Conventions, les actes suivants sont considérés comme des infractions

---

[42] « iii) s'abstenir de lancer une attaque dont on peut attendre qu'elle cause incidemment des pertes en vies humaines dans la population civile, des blessures aux personnes civiles, des dommages aux biens de caractère civil, ou une combinaison de ces pertes et dommages, qui seraient excessifs par rapport à l'avantage militaire concret et direct attendu; »

[43] *Ibid.*

[44] « Il est interdit de tuer, blesser ou capturer un adversaire en recourant à la perfidie. Constituent une perfidie les actes faisant appel, avec l'intention de la tromper, à la bonne foi d'un adversaire pour lui faire croire qu'il a le droit de recevoir ou l'obligation d'accorder la protection prévue par les règles du droit international applicable dans les conflits armés. Les actes suivants sont des exemples de perfidie :
a) feindre l'intention de négocier sous le couvert du pavillon parlementaire, ou feindre la reddition;
b) feindre une incapacité due à des blessures ou à la maladie;
c) feindre d'avoir le statut de civil ou de non-combattant;
d) feindre d'avoir un statut protégé en utilisant des signes emblèmes ou uniformes des Nations Unies, d'Etats neutres ou d'autres Etats non Parties au conflit.
2. Les ruses de guerre ne sont pas interdites. Constituent des ruses de guerre les actes qui ont pour but d'induire un adversaire en erreur ou de lui faire commettre des imprudences, mais qui n'enfreignent aucune règle du droit international applicable dans les conflits armés et qui, ne faisant pas appel à la bonne foi de l'adversaire en ce qui concerne la protection prévue par ce droit, ne sont pas perfides. Les actes suivants sont des exemples de ruses de guerre: l'usage de camouflages, de leurres, d'opérations simulées et de faux renseignements. »

graves au Protocole lorsqu'ils sont commis intentionnellement et en violation des Conventions ou du présent Protocole :

a) le transfert par la Puissance occupante d'une Partie de sa population civile dans le territoire qu'elle occupe, ou la déportation ou le transfert à l'intérieur ou hors du territoire occupé de la totalité ou d'une Partie de la population de ce territoire, en violation de l'article 49 de la IVe Convention[45];

b) tout retard injustifié dans le rapatriement des prisonniers de guerre ou des civils;

c) les pratiques de l'apartheid et les autres pratiques inhumaines et dégradantes, fondées sur la discrimination raciale, qui donnent lieu à des outrages à la dignité personnelle;

d) le fait de diriger des attaques contre les monuments historiques, les oeuvres d'art ou les lieux de culte clairement reconnus qui constituent le patrimoine culturel ou spirituel des peuples et auxquels une protection spéciale a été accordée en vertu d'un arrangement particulier, par exemple dans le cadre d'une organisation internationale compétente, provoquant ainsi leur destruction sur une grande échelle, alors qu'il n'existe aucune preuve de violation par la Partie adverse de l'article 53, alinéa b[46], et que les monuments

---

[45] « Les transferts forcés, en masse ou individuels, ainsi que les déportations de personnes protégées hors du territoire occupé dans le territoire de la Puissance occupante ou dans celui de tout autre Etat, occupé ou non, sont interdits, quel qu'en soit le motif.
Toutefois, la Puissance occupante pourra procéder à l'évacuation totale ou partielle d'une région occupée déterminée, si la sécurité de la population ou d'impérieuses raisons militaires l'exigent. Les évacuations ne pourront entraîner le déplacement de personnes protégées qu'à l'intérieur du territoire occupé, sauf en cas d'impossibilité matérielle. La population ainsi évacuée sera ramenée dans ses foyers aussitôt que les hostilités dans ce secteur auront pris fin.
La Puissance occupante, en procédant à ces transferts ou à ces évacuations, devra faire en sorte, dans toute la mesure du possible, que les personnes protégées soient accueillies dans des installations convenables, que les déplacements soient effectués dans des conditions satisfaisantes de salubrité, d'hygiène, de sécurité et d'alimentation et que les membres d'une même famille ne soient pas séparés les uns des autres.
La Puissance protectrice sera informée des transferts et évacuations dès qu'ils auront eu lieu.
La Puissance occupante ne pourra retenir les personnes protégées dans une région particulièrement exposée aux dangers de la guerre, sauf si la sécurité de la population ou d'impérieuses raisons militaires l'exigent.
La Puissance occupante ne pourra procéder à la déportation ou au transfert d'une partie de sa propre population civile dans le territoire occupé par elle. »

[46] « b) d'utiliser ces biens à l'appui de l'effort militaire; ».

historiques, oeuvres d'art et lieux de culte en question ne sont pas situés à proximité immédiate d'objectifs militaires;

e) le fait de priver une personne protégée par les Conventions ou visée au paragraphe 2 du présent article de son droit d'être jugée régulièrement et impartialement. »

Art. 85, PROTOCOLE ADDITIONNEL AUX CONVENTIONS DE GENÈVE DU 12 AOÛT 1949 RELATIF À LA PROTECTION DES VICTIMES DES CONFLITS ARMÉS INTERNATIONAUX (PROTOCOLE I).

INSTAURATION D'UNE PAIX DURABLE [Establishment of a lasting peace on Earth]

– « *Consciente* que, en cette ère nucléaire, l'instauration d'une paix durable sur la Terre est une condition primordiale de la préservation de la civilisation humaine et de la survie de l'humanité, »

Pp. 5, DÉCLARATION SUR LE DROIT DES PEUPLES À LA PAIX.

INSTITUTITONS NATIONALES [National institutions]

– « 3. Les institutions nationales ont, notamment, les attributions suivantes :

a) Fournir à titre consultatif au gouvernement, au parlement et à tout autre organe compétent, soit à la demande des autorités concernées, soit en usant de sa faculté d'autosaisine, des avis, recommandations, propositions et rapports concernant toutes questions relatives à la promotion et à la protection des droits de l'homme ; les institutions nationales peuvent décider de les rendre publics ; ces avis, recommandations, propositions et rapports ainsi que toute prérogative des institutions nationales se rapportent aux domaines suivants :

i) Les dispositions législatives et administratives et les dispositions relatives à l'organisation judiciaire dont l'objet est de protéger et d'étendre les droits de l'homme ; à cet égard, les institutions nationales examinent la législation et les textes administratifs en vigueur, ainsi que les projets et propositions de lois, et font les recommandations qu'elles estiment appropriées pour que ces textes se conforment aux principes fondamentaux des droits de l'homme ; elles recommandent, si nécessaire, l'adoption d'une nouvelle législation, l'adaptation de la législation de la législation en vigueur, et l'adoption ou la modification des mesures administratives ;

ii) Les cas de violations des droits de l'homme dont elles décideraient de se saisir ;

iii) L'élaboration de rapports sur la situation nationale des droits de l'homme en général, ainsi que sur des questions plus spécifiques ;

iv) Attirer l'attention du gouvernement sur les cas de violations des droits de l'homme où qu'ils surviennent dans le pays, lui proposer toutes initiatives tendant à y mettre fin et, le cas échéant, émettre un avis sur les positions et réactions du gouvernement ;

b) promouvoir et assurer l'harmonisation des lois, des règlements et des pratiques en vigueur sur le plan national avec les instruments internationaux relatifs aux droits de l'homme, auxquels l'Etat est partie, et leur mise en œuvre effective ;

c) Encourager la ratification de ces instruments ou l'adhésion à ces textes, et s'assurer de leur mise en œuvre ;

d) Contribuer aux rapports que les Etats doivent présenter aux organes et comités des Nations Unies, ainsi qu'aux institutions régionales, en application de leurs obligations conventionnelles et, le cas échéant, émettre un avis à ce sujet, dans le respect de leur indépendance ;

e) Coopérer avec l'Organisation des Nations Unies et tout autre organisme des Nations Unies, les institutions régionales et les institutions nationales d'autres pays qui ont compétence dans les domaines de la promotion et de la protection des droits de l'homme ;

f) Coopérer à l'élaboration de programmes concernant l'enseignement et la recherche sur les droits de l'homme et de participer à leur mise en œuvre dans les milieux scolaires, universitaires et professionnels ;

g) Faire connaître les droits de l'homme et la lutte contre toutes les formes de discrimination, notamment la discrimination raciale, en sensibilisant davantage l'opinion publique, notamment par l'information et l'enseignement, et en faisant appel à tous les organes de presse. »

Principes concernant le statut des institutions nationales (Principes de Paris).

INTENTION [Intent]

– « 2. Il y a intention[k] au sens du présent article lorsque:

a) Relativement à un comportement, une personne entend adopter ce comportement;

b) Relativement à une conséquence, une personne entend causer cette conséquence ou est consciente que celle-ci adviendra dans le cours normal des événements. »

ART. 30, STATUT DE ROME DE LA COUR PÉNALE INTERNATIONALE.

INTERET DES ENFANTS [Interest of the children (the)]

– « *b*) [...] l'éducation familiale contribue à faire bien comprendre que la maternité est une fonction sociale et à faire reconnaître la responsabilité commune de l'homme et de la femme dans le soin d'élever leurs enfants et d'assurer leur développement, étant entendu que l'intérêt des l'enfants est la condition primordiale dans tous les cas. »

Art. 5, CONVENTION SUR L'ÉLIMINATION DE TOUTES LES FORMES DE DISCRIMINATION À L'ÉGARD DES FEMMES.

– « Les Etats Parties prennent toutes les mesures appropriées pour éliminer la discrimination à l'égard des femmes dans toutes les questions découlant du mariage et dans les rapports familiaux et, en particulier, en assurent, sur la base de l'égalité de l'homme et de la femme.

[...]

f) Les mêmes droits et responsabilités en matière de tutelle, de curatelle, de garde et d'adoption des enfants, ou d'institutions similaires, lorsque ces concepts existent dans la législation nationale; dans tous les cas, l'intérêt des enfants est la considération primordiale; »

Art. 16, CONVENTION SUR L'ÉLIMINATION DE TOUTES LES FORMES DE DISCRIMINATION À L'ÉGARD DES FEMMES.

---

[k] "2. For the purposes of this article, a person has intent where:
(*a*) In relation to conduct, that person means to engage in the conduct;
(*B*) IN RELATION TO A CONSEQUENCE, THAT PERSON MEANS TO CAUSE THAT CONSEQUENCE OR IS AWARE THAT IT WILL OCCUR IN THE ORDINARY COURSE OF EVENTS."

INTERNEMENT [Internment]

– « [...] l'internement ou l'emprisonnement sera pour de telles infractions la seule mesure privative de liberté [...] »

Art. 68, al. 1, CONVENTION DE GENÈVE RELATIVE À LA PROTECTION DES PERSONNES CIVILES EN TEMPS DE GUERRE DU 12 AOÛT 1949.

INTOLERANCE ET DISCRIMINATION FONDEES SUR LA RELIGION OU LA CONVICTION [Intolerance and discrimination based on religion or belief]

– « 2. Aux fins de la présente Déclaration, on entend par les termes "intolérance et discrimination fondées sur la religion ou la conviction" toute distinction, exclusion, restriction ou préférence fondées sur la religion ou la conviction et ayant pour objet ou pour effet de supprimer ou de limiter la reconnaissance, la jouissance ou l'exercice des droits de l'homme et des libertés fondamentales sur une base d'égalité. »

Art. 2, DÉCLARATION SUR L'ÉLIMINATION DE TOUTES LES FORMES D'INTOLÉRANCE ET DE DISCRIMINATION FONDÉES SUR LA RELIGION OU LA CONVICTION.

INTOXICATIONS PAR LES GAZ ET PAR LES RADIATIONS [Gas or radiation poisoning]

– « *o)* Les intoxications chroniques graves, par exemple : saturnisme, hydrargyrisme; morphinisme, cocaïnisme, alcoolisme; intoxications par les gaz et par les radiations; etc. »

Annexe I, 3, CONVENTION DE GENÈVE RELATIVE AU TRAITEMENT DES PRISONNIERS DE GUERRE.

IRITIS [Iritis]

– « *i)* La cécité des deux yeux ou celle d'un œil lorsque la vue de l'autre œil est moins de 1, malgré l'emploi de verres correcteurs; la diminution de l'acuité visuelle ne pouvant être corrigée à 1/2 pour un œil au moins*; les autres affections oculaires graves, par exemple : glaucome; iritis; chloroïdite; trachome; etc. »

Annexe I, 3, CONVENTION DE GENÈVE RELATIVE AU TRAITEMENT DES PRISONNIERS DE GUERRE.

JEUNES DETENUS [Young prisoners]

– « 2) La catégorie des jeunes détenus doit comprendre en tout cas les mineurs qui relèvent des juridictions pour enfants. En règle générale, ces jeunes délinquants ne devraient pas être condamnés à des peines de prison. »

5, ENSEMBLE DE RÈGLES MINIMA POUR LE TRAITEMENT DES DÉTENUS.

JUGES [Judges]

– « *Considérant* que les juges se prononcent en dernier ressort sur la vie, les libertés, les droits, les devoirs et les biens des citoyens; »

Pp. 7, PRINCIPES FONDAMENTAUX RELATIFS À L'INDÉPENDANCE DE LA MAGISTRATURE.

JUSTICE POUR MINEURS [Juvenile justice]

– « 1.4 La justice pour mineurs fait partie intégrante du processus de développement national de chaque pays, dans le cadre général de la justice sociale pour tous les jeunes, contribuant ainsi, en même temps, à la protection des jeunes et au maintien de la paix et de l'ordre dans la société. »

ENSEMBLE DE RÈGLES MINIMA DES NATIONS UNIES CONCERNANT L'ADMINISTRATION DE LA JUSTICE POUR LES MINEURS (RÈGLES DE BEIJING).

– « [...] L'article 1.4 définit la justice pour mineurs comme faisant partie intégrante de la justice sociale pour les jeunes, [...] »

1.6, *Commentaire*, ENSEMBLE DE RÈGLES MINIMA DES NATIONS UNIES CONCERNANT L'ADMINISTRATION DE LA JUSTICE POUR LES MINEURS (RÈGLES DE BEIJING).

– « L'article 5 concerne deux des objectifs les plus importants de la justice pour mineurs. Le premier est la recherche du bien-être du mineur. C'est l'objectif principal des systèmes juridiques où les cas des délinquants juvéniles sont examinés par les tribunaux pour enfants ou par les autorités administratives, mais il faut insister aussi sur le bien-être du mineur dans les systèmes juridiques où ils relèvent des juridictions de droit commun, pour éviter que ne soient prises des sanctions uniquement punitives. (Voir également l'article 14)[47].

---

[47] « 14. Autorité compétente pour juger

14.1 Si le cas d'un jeune délinquant n'a pas fait l'objet d'une procédure extra-judiciaire (prévue à l'article 11), il est examiné par l'autorité compétente (cour, tribunal, commission, conseil, etc.), conformément aux principes d'un procès juste et équitable.

14.2 La procédure suivie doit tendre à protéger au mieux les intérêts du jeune délinquant et se déroulera dans un climat de compréhension, permettant ainsi à celui-ci d'y participer et de s'exprimer librement.

Commentaire :

Il est difficile de donner de l'organisme compétent ou de la personne compétente une définition qui décrirait de façon universellement acceptable l'autorité juridictionnelle.

Le second objectif est le "principe de proportionnalité". Ce principe bien connu sert à modérer les sanctions punitives, généralement en les rapportant à la gravité du délit. Pour les délinquants juvéniles, il faut tenir compte non seulement de cette gravité mais aussi des circonstances personnelles. Celles-ci (position sociale, situation de famille, dommages causés par le délit ou autres facteurs influant sur les circonstances personnelles) doivent intervenir pour proportionner la décision (par exemple en tenant compte de l'effort du délinquant pour indemniser la victime ou de son désir de revenir à une vie saine et utile). »

ENSEMBLE DE RÈGLES MINIMA DES NATIONS UNIES CONCERNANT L'ADMINISTRATION DE LA JUSTICE POUR LES MINEURS (RÈGLES DE BEIJING).

LEPRE [Leprosy]

– « *s)* Les maladies infectieuses chroniques graves persistant une année après le début, par exemple : paludisme avec altérations organiques prononcées; dysenterie amibienne ou bacillaire avec troubles considérables; syphilis viscérale tertiaire, résistant au traitement; lèpre; etc. »

ANNEXE I, 3, CONVENTION DE GENÈVE RELATIVE AU TRAITEMENT DES PRISONNIERS DE GUERRE.

LIBERTE (LA) [Freedom]

– « 6. Nous estimons que certaines valeurs fondamentales doivent sous-tendre les relations internationales au XXe siècle, à savoir :

La liberté. Les hommes et les femmes ont le droit de vivre et d'élever leurs enfants dans la dignité, à l'abri de la faim et sans craindre la violence, l'oppression ou l'injustice. C'est un mode de gouvernance democratique des affaires publiques, fondé sur la volonté et la participation des populations, qui permet le mieux de garantir ces droits.

L'expression "autorité compétente" est censée comprendre les présidents de cours ou de tribunaux (composés d'un juge unique ou de plusieurs membres), à savoir les magistrats professionnels et non professionnels, ainsi que les commissions administratives (systèmes écossais et scandinave, par exemple) ou d'autres organismes communautaires moins officiels, spécialisés dans la solution des conflits et de caractère juridictionnel.
La procédure suivie pour juger les jeunes délinquants doit en tout état de cause se conformer aux normes minima, assurées presque universellement à tout accusé par le respect des formes légales. Dans ces formes, un procès "juste et équitable" comprend des garanties fondamentales telles que la présomption d'innocence, la comparution et la déposition de témoins, les moyens ordinaires de défense, le droit de garder le silence, le droit de répliquer en dernier à l'audience, le droit de faire appel, etc. (Voir également l'article 7.1.) »

[...]»

Premier note (•), DÉCLARATION DU MILLÉNAIRE.

– « Considérant que la liberté est un droit que tout être humain acquiert à sa naissance,[l] »

Pp. 1, CONVENTION SUPPLÉMENTAIRE RELATIVE À L'ABOLITION DE L'ESCLAVAGE, DE LA TRAITE DES ESCLAVES ET DES INSTITUTIONS ET PRATIQUES ANALOGUES À L'ESCLAVAGE.

LIBERTE DE LA RECHERCHE [Freedom of research]

– « (*b*) La liberté de la recherche, qui est nécessaire au progrès de la connaissance, procède de la liberté de pensée. [...] »

Art. 12, DÉCLARATION UNIVERSELLE SUR LE GÉNOME HUMAIN ET LES DROITS DE L'HOMME.

LIBERTES FONDAMENTALES [Fundamental freedoms]

– « *Reconnaissant et affirmant* que tous les droits de l'homme découlent de la dignité et de la valeur inhérentes à la personne humaine, que la personne humaine est le sujet même des droits de l'homme et des libertés fondamentales et que, par conséquent, elle doit en être le principal bénéficiaire et participer activement à leur réalisation, »

Pp. 2, VIENNA DECLARATION AND PROGRAMME OF ACTION.

– « 1. La Conférence mondiale sur les droits de l'homme réaffirme l'engagement solennel pris par tous les Etats de s'acquitter de l'obligation de promouvoir le respect universel, l'observation et la protection de l'ensemble des droits de l'homme et des libertés fondamentales pour tous, conformément à la Charte des Nations Unies, aux autres instruments relatifs aux droits de l'homme et au droit international. Le caractère universel de ces droits et libertés est incontestable. »

I, DÉCLARATION ET PROGRAMME D'ACTION DE VIENNE.

– « Les droits de l'homme et les libertés fondamentales sont inhérents[m] à tous les êtres humains; leur promotion et leur protection incombent au premier chef aux gouvernements. »

I, 1, al. 3, DÉCLARATION ET PROGRAMME D'ACTION DE VIENNE.

---

[l] " *Considering* that freedom is the birthright of every human being,"

[m] "Human rights and fundamental freedoms are the birthright of all human beings; their protection and promotion is the first responsibility of Governments."

- « 63. La Conférence mondiale sur les droits de l'homme réaffirme que les droits de l'homme et les libertés fondamentales sont tous universels et, de ce fait, s'appliquent sans réserve aucune aux personnes souffrant d'incapacités. »

II, DÉCLARATION ET PROGRAMME D'ACTION DE VIENNE.

- « 2. Tous les droits de l'homme et toutes les libertés fondamentales sont indivisibles et interdépendantes; la réalisation, la promotion et la protection des droits civils, politiques, économiques, sociaux et culturels doivent bénéficier d'une attention égale et être envisagées avec une égale urgence. »

Art. 6, DÉCLARATION SUR LE DROIT AU DÉVELOPPEMENT.

- « *Réaffirmant* que tous les droits de l'homme et toutes les libertés fondamentales sont universels, indivisibles, interdépendants et indissociables, et qu'il faut les promouvoir et les rendre effectifs en toute équité, sans préjudice de leur mise en œuvre individuelle, »

Pp. 6, DÉCLARATION SUR LE DROIT ET LA RESPONSABILITÉ DES INDIVIDUS, GROUPES ET ORGANES DE LA SOCIÉTÉ DE PROMOUVOIR ET PROTÉGER LES DROITS DE L'HOMME ET LES LIBERTÉS FONDAMENTALES UNIVERSELLEMENT RECONNUS.

LOCALITE NON DEFENDUE [Non-defended locality]

- « 2. Les autorités compétentes d'une Partie au conflit pourront déclarer localité non défendue tout lieu habité se trouvant à proximité ou à l'intérieur d'une zone où les forces armées sont en contact et qui est ouvert à l'occupation par une Partie adverse. Une telle localité doit remplir les conditions suivantes :

  a) tous les combattants ainsi que les armes et le matériel militaire mobiles devront avoir été évacués;

  b) il ne doit pas être fait un usage hostile des installations ou des établissements militaires fixes;

  c) les autorités et la population ne commettront pas d'actes d'hostilité;

  d) aucune activité à l'appui d'opérations militaires ne doit être entreprise. »

Art. 59, PROTOCOLE ADDITIONNEL AUX CONVENTIONS DE GENÈVE DU 12 AOÛT 1949 RELATIF À LA PROTECTION DES VICTIMES DES CONFLITS ARMÉS INTERNATIONAUX (PROTOCOLE I).

MAGISTRATS [Judiciary]

– « 2. Les magistrats règlent les affaires dont ils sont saisis impartialement, d'après les faits et conformément à la loi, sans restrictions et sans être l'objet d'influences, incitations, pressions, menaces ou interventions indues, directes ou indirectes, de la part de qui que ce soit ou pour quelque raison que ce soit. »

PRINCIPES FONDAMENTAUX RELATIFS À L'INDÉPENDANCE DE LA MAGISTRATURE.

– « 3. Les magistrats connaissent de toute affaire judiciaire et ont le pouvoir exclusif de décider si une affaire dont ils sont saisis relève de leur compétence telle qu'elle est définie par la loi. »

PRINCIPES FONDAMENTAUX RELATIFS À L'INDÉPENDANCE DE LA MAGISTRATURE.

MAGISTRATS DU PARQUET [Prosecutors]

– « 3. Les magistrats du parquet, en tant qu'agents essentiels de l'administration de la justice, doivent toujours préserver la dignité et l'honneur de leur charge. »

PRINCIPES DIRECTEURS APPLICABLES AU RÔLE DES MAGISTRATS DU PARQUET.

MAINTIEN DU COLONIALISME [Continued existence of colonialism]

– « *Convaincue* que le maintien du colonialisme empêche le développement de la coopération économique internationale, entrave le développement social, culturel et économique des peuples dépendants et va à l'encontre de l'idéal de paix universelle des Nations Unies, »

Pp. 7, DÉCLARATION SUR L'OCTROI DE L'INDÉPENDANCE AUX PAS ET AUX PEUPLES COLONIAUX.

MALADES [Sick]

- « Aux fins du présent Protocole :

  a) les termes "blessés" et "malades" s'entendent des personnes, militaires ou civiles, qui, en raison d'un traumatisme, d'une maladie ou d'autres incapacités ou troubles physiques ou mentaux, ont besoin de soins médicaux et qui s'abstiennent de tout acte d'hostilité. Ces termes visent aussi les femmes en couches, les nouveau-nés, et les autres personnes qui pourraient avoir besoin de soins immédiats, telles que les infirmes et les femmes enceintes, et qui s'abstiennent de tout acte d'hostilité; »

Art. 8, PROTOCOLE ADDITIONNEL AUX CONVENTIONS DE GENÈVE DU 12 AOÛT 1949 RELATIF À LA PROTECTION DES VICTIMES DES CONFLITS ARMÉS INTERNATIONAUX (PROTOCOLE I).

MALADIE MENTALE [Mental illness]

– « 2. La décision de maladie mentale ne doit jamais se fonder sur des considérations politiques, économiques ou de situation sociale, ni d'appartenance à un groupe culturel, racial ou religieux, ni sur aucune autre considération n'ayant pas de rapport direct avec l'état de santé mentale.

  3. Les conflits familiaux ou professionnels, ou la non-conformité aux valeurs morales, sociales, culturelles ou politiques ou aux convictions religieuses prévalant dans la société à laquelle une personne appartient ne doivent jamais être des facteurs déterminants dans le diagnostic de maladie mentale.

  4. Le fait qu'une personne ait été soignée ou hospitalisée dans le passé ne peut en lui- même justifier un diagnostic présent ou futur de maladie mentale. »

Principe 4, PRINCIPES POUR LA PROTECTION DES PERSONNES ATTEINTES DE MALADIE MENTALE ET POUR L'AMÉLIORATION DES SOINS DE SANTÉ MENTALE.

MALADIES CHRONIQUES DU REIN AVEC TROUBLES CONSECUTIFS [Chronic diseases of the kidney with consequent disorders]

– « *f)* Les affections chroniques graves des organes génito-urinaires, par exemple : maladies chroniques du rein avec troubles consécutifs; néphrectomie pour un rein tuberculeux; pyélite chronique ou cystite chronique; hydro ou pyonéphrose; affections gynécologiques chroniques graves; grossesses et affections obstétricales, lorsque l'hospitalisation en pays neutre est impossible; etc. »

Annexe I, 3, CONVENTION DE GENÈVE RELATIVE AU TRAITEMENT DES PRISONNIERS DE GUERRE.

MANDAT SPECIFIQUE QUI A ETE CONFIE A L'UNESCO [Specific mandate which has been entrusted to UNESCO]

– « *Consciente* du mandat spécifique qui a été confié à l'UNESCO, au sein du système des Nations Unies, d'assurer la préservation et la promotion de la féconde diversités culturelles, »

Pp. 10, DÉCLARATION UNIVERSELLE SUR LA DIVERSITÉ CULTURELLE.

MARIAGE [Marriage]

– « 1. Aucun mariage ne pourra être contracté légalement sans le libre et plein consentement des deux parties, ce consentement devant être exprimé par elles en personne, en présence de l'autorité compétente pour célébrer le mariage et de témoins, après une publicité suffisante, conformément aux dispositions de la loi. »

Art. 1, CONVENTION SUR LE CONSENTEMENT AU MARIAGE, L'ÂGE MINIMUM DU MARIAGE ET L'ENREGISTREMENT DES MARIAGES.

MATERIEL [Matériel]

– « Aux fins du présent Protocole :

[…]

d) le terme "matériel" des organismes de protection civile s'entend de l'équipement, des approvisionnements et des moyens de transport que ces organismes utilisent pour accomplir les tâches énumérées à l'alinéa a[48]. »

---

[48] « a) l'expression "protection civile" s'entend de l'accomplissement de toutes les tâches humanitaires, ou de plusieurs d'entre elles, mentionnées ci-après, destinées à protéger la population civile contre les dangers des hostilités ou des catastrophes et à l'aider à surmonter leurs effets immédiats ainsi qu'à assurer les conditions nécessaires à sa survie. Ces tâches sont les suivantes :

i) service de l'alerte;

ii) évacuation;

iii) mise à disposition et organisation d'abris;

iv) mise en oeuvre des mesures d'obscurcissement;

v) sauvetage;

vi) services sanitaires y compris premiers secours et assistance religieuse;

vii) lutte contre le feu;

viii) repérage et signalisation des zones dangereuses;

ix) décontamination et autres mesures de protection analogues;

x) hébergement et approvisionnements d'urgence;

xi) aide en cas d'urgence pour le rétablissement et le maintien de l'ordre dans les zones sinistrées;

Art. 61, PROTOCOLE ADDITIONNEL AUX CONVENTIONS DE GENÈVE DU 12 AOÛT 1949 RELATIF À LA PROTECTION DES VICTIMES DES CONFLITS ARMÉS INTERNATIONAUX (PROTOCOLE I).

MATERNITE [Maternity]

- « *b*) [...] la maternité est une fonction sociale [...][n] »

Art. 5, CONVENTION SUR L'ÉLIMINATION DE TOUTES LES FORMES DE DISCRIMINATION À L'ÉGARD DES FEMMES.

MECONNAISSANCE ET MEPRIS DES DROITS DE L'HOMME [Disregard and contempt for human rights]

- « *Considérant* que la méconnaissance et le mépris des droits de l'homme ont conduit à des actes de barbarie qui révoltent la conscience de l'humanité [...] »

Pp. 2, DÉCLARATION UNIVERSELLE DES DROITS DE L'HOMME.

MEMBRES DE LA FAMILLE [Members of the family]

- « Aux fins de la présente Convention, l'expression "membres de la famille" désigne les personnes mariées aux travailleurs migrants ou ayant avec ceux-ci des relations qui, en vertu de la loi applicable, produisent des effets équivalant au mariage, ainsi que leurs enfants à charge et autres personnes à charge qui sont reconnues comme membres de la famille en vertu de la législation applicable ou d'accords bilatéraux ou multilatéraux applicables entre les Etats intéressés. »

Art. 4, CONVENTION INTERNATIONALE SUR LA PROTECTION DES DROITS DE TOUS LES TRAVAILLEURS MIGRANTS ET DES MEMBRES DE LEUR FAMILLE.

MEMBRES DE LA FAMILLE HUMAINE [Members of the human family]

- « *Considérant* que, conformément aux principes énoncés dans la Charte des Nations Unies, la reconnaissance de la dignité inhérente à tous les membres de la famille humaine et de leurs droits égaux et inaliénables

---

xii) rétablissement d'urgence des services d'utilité publique indispensables;
xiii) services funéraires d'urgence;
xiv) aide à la sauvegarde des biens essentiels à la survie;
xv) activités complémentaires nécessaires à l'accomplissement de l'une quelconque des tâches mentionnées ci-dessus, comprenant la planification et l'organisation mais ne s'y limitant pas; »

[n] "(*b*) [...] maternity as a social function[...]"

constitue le fondement de la liberté, de la justice et de la paix dans le monde, »

Pp. 1, PACTE INTERNATIONAL RELATIF AUX DROITS ÉCONOMIQUES, SOCIAUX ET CULTURELS.
Pp. 1, PACTE INTERNATIONAL RELATIF AUX DROITS CIVILS ET POLITIQUES.

MEMBRES DES FORCES ARMEES [Members of the armed forces]

– « 2. Les membres des forces armées d'une Partie à un conflit (autres que le personnel sanitaire et religieux visé à l'article 33 de la IIIe Convention[49]) sont des combattants, c'est-à-dire ont le droit de participer directement aux hostilités. »

Art. 43, PROTOCOLE ADDITIONNEL AUX CONVENTIONS DE GENÈVE DU 12 AOÛT 1949 RELATIF À LA PROTECTION DES VICTIMES DES CONFLITS ARMÉS INTERNATIONAUX (PROTOCOLE I).

---

[49] « Les membres du personnel sanitaire et religieux retenus au pouvoir de la Puissance détentrice en vue d'assister les prisonniers de guerre, ne seront pas considérés comme prisonniers de guerre. Toutefois, ils bénéficieront au moins de tous les avantages et de la protection de la présente Convention, ainsi que de toutes les facilités nécessaires pour leur permettre d'apporter leurs soins médicaux et leurs secours religieux aux prisonniers de guerre. Ils continueront à exercer, dans le cadre des lois et règlements militaires de la Puissance détentrice, sous l'autorité de ses services compétents et en accord avec leur conscience professionnelle, leurs fonctions médicales ou spirituelles au profit des prisonniers de guerre appartenant de préférence aux forces armées dont ils relèvent. Ils jouiront, en outre, pour l'exercice de leur mission médicale ou spirituelle, des facilités suivantes :

a) Ils seront autorisés à visiter périodiquement les prisonniers de guerre se trouvant dans des détachements de travail ou dans des hôpitaux situés à l'extérieur du camp. L'autorité détentrice mettra à leur disposition, à cet effet, les moyens de transport nécessaires.

b) Dans chaque camp, le médecin militaire le plus ancien dans le grade le plus élevé sera responsable auprès des autorités militaires du camp pour tout ce qui concerne les activités du personnel sanitaire retenu. A cet effet, les Parties au conflit s'entendront dès le début des hostilités au sujet de la correspondance des grades de leur personnel sanitaire, y compris celui des sociétés visées à l'article 26 de la Convention de Genève pour l'amélioration du sort des blessés et des malades dans les forces armées en campagne du 12 août 1949. Pour toutes les questions relevant de leur mission, ce médecin, ainsi d'ailleurs que les aumôniers, auront accès direct auprès des autorités compétentes du camp. Celles-ci leur donneront toutes les facilités nécessaires pour la correspondance ayant trait à ces questions.

c) Bien qu'il soit soumis à la discipline intérieure du camp dans lequel il se trouve, le personnel retenu ne pourra être astreint à aucun travail étranger à sa mission médicale ou religieuse.

Au cours des hostilités, les Parties au conflit s'entendront au sujet d'une relève éventuelle du personnel retenu et en fixeront les modalités.

Aucune des dispositions qui précèdent ne dispense la Puissance détentrice des obligations qui lui incombent à l'égard des prisonniers de guerre dans les domaines sanitaire et spirituel. »

MENACE A LA VIE ET A LA SECURITE DES RESPONSABLES DE L'APPLICATION DES LOIS [Threat to the life and safety of law enforcement officials]

– « *Attendu* qu'une menace à la vie et à la sécurité des responsables de l'application des lois doit être tenue pour une menace à la stabilité de la société dans son ensemble, »

Pp. 2, PRINCIPES DE BASE SUR LE RECOURS À LA FORCE ET L'UTILISATION DES ARMES À FEU PAR LES RESPONSABLES DE L'APPLICATION DES LOIS.

MEPRIS ET LA VIOLATION DES DROITS DE L'HOMME ET DES LIBERTES FONDAMENTALES (LE) [Disregard and infringement of human rights and fundamental freedoms]

– « *Considérant* que le mépris et la violation des droits de l'homme et des libertés fondamentales, en particulier du droit à la liberté de pensée, de conscience, de religion ou de conviction, quelle qu'elle soit, sont directement ou indirectement à l'origine de guerres et de grandes souffrances infligées à l'humanité, spécialement dans les cas où ils servent de moyen d'ingérence étrangère dans les affaires intérieures d'autres Etats et équivalent à attiser la haine entre les peuples et les nations, »

Pp. 3, DÉCLARATION SUR L'ÉLIMINATION DE TOUTES LES FORMES D'INTOLÉRANCE ET DISCRIMINATION FONDÉES SUR LA RELIGION OU LA CONVICTION.

MERCENAIRE [Mercenary]

– « 1. Le terme « mercenaire » s'entend de toute personne :

a) Qui est spécialement recrutée dans le pays ou à l'étranger pour combattre dans un conflit armé ;

b) Qui prend part aux hostilités essentiellement en vue d'obtenir un avantage personnel et à laquelle est effectivement promise, par une partie au conflit ou en son nom, une rémunération matérielle nettement supérieure à celle qui est promise ou payée à des combattants ayant un rang et une fonction analogues dans les forces armées de cette partie ;

c) Qui n'est ni ressortissante d'une partie au conflit, ni résidente du territoire contrôlé par une partie au conflit ;

d) Qui n'est pas membre des forces armées d'une partie au conflit ; et *e*) Qui n'a pas été envoyée par un Etat autre qu'une partie au conflit en mission officielle en tant que membre des forces dudit Etat ; »

2. Le terme « mercenaire » s'entend également[50], dans toute autre situation, de toute personne :

a) Qui est spécialement recrutée dans le pays ou à l'étranger pour prendre part à un acte concerté de violence visant à :

(i)Renverser un gouvernement ou, de quelque autre manière, porter atteinte à l'ordre constitutionnel d'un Etat ; ou

(ii)Porter atteinte à l'atteinte à l'intégrité territoriale d'un Etat ;

b) Qui prend part à un tel acte essentiellement en vue d'obtenir un avantage personnel significatif et est poussée à agir par la promesse le paiement d'une rémunération matérielle ;

c) Qui n'est ni ressortissante ni résidente de l'Etat contre lequel un tel acte est dirigé ;

d) Qui n'a pas été envoyée par un Etat en mission officielle ; et

e) Qui n'est pas membre ßdes forces armées de l'Etat sur le territoire duquel l'acte a eu lieu ;

Art. 1, CONVENTION INTERNATIONALE CONTRE LE RECRUTEMENT, L'UTILISATION, LE FINANCEMENT ET L'INSTRUCTION DE MERCENAIRES.

– « 2. Le terme "mercenaire" s'entend de toute personne :

a) qui est spécialement recrutée dans le pays ou à l'étranger pour combattre dans un conflit armé;

b) qui en fait prend une part directe aux hostilités;

---

[50] « 1. Le terme « mercenaires » s'entend de toute personne :
a) Qui est spécialement recrutée dans le pays ou à l'étranger pour combattre dans un conflit armé ;
b) Qui prend part aux hostilités essentiellement en vue d'obtenir un avantage personnel et à laquelle est effectivement promise, par une partie au conflit ou en son nom, une rémunération matérielle nettement supérieure à celle qui est promise ou payée à des combattants ayant un rang et une fonction analogues dans les forces armées de cette partie ;
c) Qui n'est ni ressortissante d'une partie au conflit, ni résidente du territoire contrôlé par une partie au conflit ;
d) Qui n'est pas membre des forces armées d'une partie au conflit ; et
e) Qui n'a pas été envoyée par un Etat autre qu'une partie au conflit en mission officielle en tant que membre des forces dudit Etat ; »

c) qui prend part aux hostilités essentiellement en vue d'obtenir un avantage personnel et à laquelle est effectivement promise, par une Partie au conflit ou en son nom, une rémunération matérielle nettement supérieure à celle qui est promise ou payée à des combattants ayant un rang et une fonction analogues dans les forces armées de cette Partie;

d) qui n'est ni ressortissant d'une Partie au conflit, ni résident du territoire contrôlé par une Partie au conflit;

e) qui n'est pas membre des forces armées d'une Partie au conflit; et

f) qui n'a pas été envoyée par un Etat autre qu'une Partie au conflit en mission officielle en tant que membre des forces armées dudit Etat. »

ART. 47, PROTOCOLE ADDITIONNEL AUX CONVENTIONS DE GENÈVE DU 12 AOÛT 1949 RELATIF À LA PROTECTION DES VICTIMES DES CONFLITS ARMÉS INTERNATIONAUX (PROTOCOLE I).

MERCENAIRES [Mercenaries]

– « *Sachant* que des mercenaires sont recrutés, utilisés, financés et instruits pour des activités qui violent des principes du droit international tels que ceux de l'égalité souveraine, de l'indépendance politiques et de l'intégrité territoriale des Etats ainsi que de l'autodétermination des peuples.»

Pp. 2, CONVENTION INTERNATIONALE CONTRE LE RECRUTEMENT, L'UTILISATION, LE FINANCEMENT ET L'INSTRUCTION DE MERCENAIRES.

MERES [Mothers]

– « *Consciente* de sa responsabilité en ce qui concerne l'avenir de la jeune génération et le sort des mères, qui jouent un rôle important dans la société, dans la famille et en particulier dans l'éducation des enfants, »

Pp.8, DÉCLARATION SUR LA PROTECTION DES FEMMES ET DES ENFANTS EN PÉRIODE D'URGENCE ET DE CONFLIT ARMÉ.

MESURES DISCRIMINATOIRES [Measures [...] Discriminatory]

– « 2. Les mesures appliquées conformément à la loi et destinées exclusivement à protéger les droits et la condition particulière des femmes, surtout des femmes enceintes et des mères d'enfants en bas âge, des enfants, des adolescents et des personnes âgées, malades ou handicapées ne sont pas réputées être des mesures discriminatoires. La nécessité de ces mesures et leur application pourront toujours faire l'objet d'un examen par une autorité judiciaire ou autre. »

Principe 5, ENSEMBLE DE PRINCIPES POUR LA PROTECTION DE TOUTES LES PERSONNES SOUMISES À UNE FORME QUELCONQUE DE DÉTENTION OU D'EMPRISONNEMENT.

MESURES NON PRIVATIVES DE LIBERTE [Non-custodial measures]

– « 3.8 Les mesures non privatives de liberté ne comportent pas d'expérimentation médicale ou psychologique effectuée sur le délinquant, ni de risque indu de dommage physique ou mental pour celui-ci. »

RÈGLES MINIMA DES NATIONS UNIES POUR L'ÉLABORATION DE MESURES NON-PRIVATIVES DE LIBERTÉ (RÈGLES DE TOKYO).

MESURES NON PRIVATIVES DE LIBERTE (L'ADOPTION, LA DEFINITION ET L'APPLICATION DE) [Non-custodial measures (the introduction, definition and application of)]

– « 3.1 L'adoption, la définition et l'application de mesures non privatives de liberté doivent être prescrites par la loi. »

RÈGLES MINIMA DES NATIONS UNIES POUR L'ÉLABORATION DE MESURES NON PRIVATIVES DE LIBERTÉ (RÈGLES DE TOKYO) .

MEUTRE [Murder]

– « Les Hautes Parties contractantes s'interdisent expressément toute mesure de nature à causer soit des souffrances physiques, soit l'extermination des personnes protégées en leur pouvoir. Cette interdiction vise non seulement le meurtre, la torture, les peines corporelles, les mutilations et les expériences médicales ou scientifiques non necessities par le traitement médical d'une personne protégée, mais également toutes autres brutalités, qu'elles soient le fait d'agents civils ou d'agents militaires. »

Art. 32, Convention de Genève relative à la protection des personnes civiles en temps de guerre du 12 août 1949.

– « *a*) les atteintes portées à la vie, à la santé et au bien-être physique ou mental des personnes, notamment:

  i) le meurtre; »

Art. 75, § 2., Protocole additionnel aux Conventions de Genève du 12 août 1949 relatif à la protection des victimes des conflits armés internationaux (Protocole I).

MIGRATIONS [Migration]

– « *Tenant compte* du fait que, dans de nombreux cas, les migrations sont la source de graves problèmes pour les membres de la famille des travailleurs migrants ainsi que pour les travailleurs migrants eux-mêmes, en particulier du fait de la dispersion de la famille, »

Pp. 12, Convention internationale sur la protection des droits de tous les travailleurs migrants et des membres de leur famille.

MINEUR [Juvenile]

– « 11. Aux fins des présentes Règles, les définitions ci-après sont applicables:

  a) Par mineur, on entend toute personne âgée de moins de 18 ans. L'âge au-dessous duquel il est interdit de priver un enfant de liberté est fixé par la loi; »

Règles des Nations Unies pour la protection des mineurs privés de liberté.

– « 1.2 Les Etats Membres s'efforcent de créer des conditions qui assurent au mineur une vie utile dans la communauté, propre à encourager chez lui pendant la période de sa vie où il est le plus exposé à un comportement déviant, un processus d'épanouissement personnel et d'éducation aussi éloigné que possible de tout contact avec la criminalité et la délinquance. »

Ensemble de règles minima des Nations Unies concernant l'administration de la justice pour les mineurs (Règles de Beijing).

– « 2.2 Aux fins du présent Ensemble de règles, chaque Etat Membre applique les définitions ci-après de manière compatible avec son système et ses concepts juridiques propres :

  a) Un mineur est un enfant ou un jeune qui, au regard du système juridique considéré, peut avoir à répondre d'un délit selon des modalités différentes de celles qui sont appliquées dans le cas d'un adulte; »

ENSEMBLE DE RÈGLES MINIMA DES NATIONS UNIES CONCERNANT L'ADMINISTRATION DE LA JUSTICE POUR LES MINEURS (RÈGLES DE BEIJING).

MISERE [Extreme poverty]

– « [...] la misère, phénomène abject et déshumanisant qui touche actuellement plus d'un milliard de personnes. [...] »[o]

11, DÉCLARATION DU MILLÉNAIRE.

MONDIALISATION [Globalization]

– « 5. Nous sommes convaincus que le principal défi que nous devons relever aujourd'hui est de faire en sorte que la mondialisation devienne une force positive pour l'humanité toute entière. Car si elle offre des possibilités immenses, à l'heure actuelle ses bienfaits sont très inégalement réparties, [...] »

I, DÉCLARATION DU MILLÉNAIRE.

MORPHINISME [Morphinism]

– « *o)* Les intoxications chroniques graves, par exemple : saturnisme, hydrargyrisme; morphinisme, cocaïnisme, alcoolisme; intoxications par les gaz et par les radiations; etc. »

Annexe I, 3, CONVENTION DE GENÈVE RELATIVE AU TRAITEMENT DES PRISONNIERS DE GUERRE.

MOYEN DE TRANSPORT SANITAIRE [Medical transports]

– « Aux fins du présent Protocole :

[...]

g) l'expression "moyen de transport sanitaire" s'entend de tout moyen de transport, militaire ou civil, permanent ou temporaire, affecté exclusivement au transport sanitaire et placé sous la direction d'une autorité compétente d'une Partie au conflit;

Art 8. , PROTOCOLE ADDITIONNEL AUX CONVENTIONS DE GENÈVE DU 12 AOÛT 1949 RELATIF À LA PROTECTION DES VICTIMES DES CONFLITS ARMÉS INTERNATIONAUX (PROTOCOLE I).

---

[o] " [...]dehumanizing conditions of extreme poverty, to which more than a billion of them [men, women and children] are currently subjected. [...]"

MOYENS DE TRANPORT SANITAIRE PERMANENTS [Permanent medical transports]

– « Aux fins du présent Protocole :

[...]

> *k*) sont "permanents" le personnel sanitaire, les unités sanitaires et les moyens de transport sanitaire affectés exclusivement à des fins sanitaires pour une durée indéterminée. Sont "temporaires" le personnel sanitaire, les unités sanitaires et les moyens de transport sanitaire utilisés exclusivement à des fins sanitaires pour des périodes limitées, pendant toute la durée de ces périodes. A moins qu'elles ne soient autrement qualifiées, les expressions "personnel sanitaire", "unité sanitaire" et "moyen de transport sanitaire" couvrent un personnel, des unités ou des moyens de transport qui peuvent être soit permanents soit temporaires; »

Art. 8, PROTOCOLE ADDITIONNEL AUX CONVENTIONS DE GENÈVE DU 12 AOÛT 1949 RELATIF À LA PROTECTION DES VICTIMES DES CONFLITS ARMÉS INTERNATIONAUX (PROTOCOLE I).

MOYENS DE TRANSPORT SANITAIRE TEMPORAIRES [Temporary medical transports]

– « Aux fins du présent protocole :

[...]

> *k*) [...]Sont "temporaires" le personnel sanitaire, les unités sanitaires et les moyens de transport sanitaire utilisés exclusivement à des fins sanitaires pour des périodes limitées, pendant toute la durée de ces périodes. A moins qu'elles ne soient autrement qualifiées, les expressions "personnel sanitaire", "unité sanitaire" et "moyen de transport sanitaire" couvrent un personnel, des unités ou des moyens de transport qui peuvent être soit permanents soit temporaires;]

Art. 8, PROTOCOLE ADDITIONNEL AUX CONVENTIONS DE GENÈVE DU 12 AOÛT 1949 RELATIF À LA PROTECTION DES VICTIMES DES CONFLITS ARMÉS INTERNATIONAUX (PROTOCOLE I).

MUTILATIONS [Mutilation]

– « Les Hautes Parties contractantes s'interdisent expressément toute mesure de nature à causer soit des souffrances physiques, soit l'extermination des personnes protégées en leur pouvoir. Cette interdiction vise non seulement le meurtre, la torture, les peines corporelles, les mutilations et les expériences médicales ou scientifiques non nécessitées par le traitement médical d'une personne protégée, mais également toutes autres brutalités, qu'elles soient le fait d'agents civils ou d'agents militaires. »

Art. 32, Convention de Genève relative à la protection des personnes civiles en temps de guerre du 12 août 1949.

– « *a*) les atteintes portées à la vie, à la santé et au bien-être physique ou mental des personnes, notamment:

[...]

iv) les mutilations; »

Art. 75, § 2., Protocole additionnel aux Conventions de Genève du 12 août 1949 relatif à la protection des victimes des conflits armés internationaux (Protocole I).

NAUFRAGES [Shipwrecked]

– « Aux fins du présent Protocole :

[...]

b) le terme "naufragés" s'entend des personnes, militaires ou civiles, se trouvant dans une situation périlleuse en mer ou en d'autres eaux par suite de l'infortune qui les frappe ou qui frappe le navire ou l'aéronef les transportant, et qui s'abstiennent de tout acte d'hostilité. Ces personnes, à condition qu'elles continuent à s'abstenir de tout acte d'hostilité, continueront d'être considérées comme des naufragés pendant leur sauvetage jusqu'à ce qu'elles aient acquis un autre statut en vertu des Conventions ou du présent Protocole; »

Art. 8, Protocole additionnel aux Conventions de Genève du 12 août 1949 relatif à la protection des victimes des conflits armés internationaux (Protocole I).

NAVIRE [Vessel]

– - « Aux fins du présent Protocole :

[...]

d) Le terme « navire » désigne tout type d'engin aquatique, y compris un engin sans tirant d'eau et un hydravion, utilisé ou capable d'être utilisé comme moyen de transport sur l'eau, à l'exception d'un navire de guerre, d'un navire de guerre auxiliaire ou autre navire appartenant à un gouvernement ou exploité par lui, tant qu'il est utilisé exclusivement pour un service public non commercial. »

Art. 3, Protocole contre le trafic illicite de migrants par terre, air et mer, additionnel à la Convention des Nations Unies contre la criminalité transnationale organisée.

NAVIRE ET EMBARCATION SANITAIRES [Medical ships and craft]

– « Aux fins du présent Protocole :

[...]

i) l'expression "navire et embarcation sanitaires" s'entend de tout moyen de transport sanitaire par eau; »

Art. 8, PROTOCOLE ADDITIONNEL AUX CONVENTIONS DE GENÈVE DU 12 AOÛT 1949 RELATIF À LA PROTECTION DES VICTIMES DES CONFLITS ARMÉS INTERNATIONAUX (PROTOCOLE I).

NEOCOLONIALISME (ELIMINATION DE TOUTES LES FORMES DE) [Neo-colonialism (eradication of all forms of)]

– « *Soulignant* que l'élimination de l'apartheid, de toutes les formes de racisme, de discrimination raciale, de colonialisme, de néocolonialisme, d'agression, d'occupation et domination étrangères et d'ingérence dans les affaires intérieures des Etats est indispensable à la pleine jouissance par l'homme et la femme de leurs droits, »

Pp. 10, CONVENTION SUR L'ÉLIMINATION DE TOUTES LES FORMES DE DISCRIMINATION À L'ÉGARD DES FEMMES.

NEPHRECTOMIE POUR UN REIN TUBERCULEUX [Nephrectomy because of a tubercular kidney]

– « *f)* Les affections chroniques graves des organes génito-urinaires, par exemple : maladies chroniques du rein avec troubles consécutifs; néphrectomie pour un rein tuberculeux; pyélite chronique ou cystite chronique; hydro ou pyonéphrose; affections gynécologiques chroniques graves; grossesses et affections obstétricales, lorsque l'hospitalisation en pays neutre est impossible; etc. »

Annexe I, 3, CONVENTION DE GENÈVE RELATIVE AU TRAITEMENT DES PRISONNIERS DE GUERRE.

NETTOYAGE ETHNIQUE [Ethnic cleansing]

– « 28. La Conférence mondiale sur les droits de l'homme se déclare consternée par les violations massives des droits de l'homme, notamment celles qui prennent la forme de génocide, de "nettoyage ethnique" et de viol systématique des femmes en temps de guerre, violations qui sont à l'origine d'exodes massifs de réfugiés et de déplacements de personnes. [...] »

I, DÉCLARATION ET PROGRAMME D'ACTION DE VIENNE.

NOUVEL ORDRE ECONOMIQUE INTERNATIONAL [New international economic order]

– « *Convaincus* que l'instauration du nouvel ordre économique international fondé sur l'équité et la justice contribuera de façon significative à promouvoir l'égalité entre l'homme et la femme, »

Pp.9, CONVENTION SUR L'ÉLIMINATION DE TOUTES LES FORMES DE DISCRIMINATION À L'ÉGARD DES FEMMES.

OCCUPATION [Occupation]

– « La Convention s'appliquera également dans tous les cas d'occupation de tout ou partie du territoire d'une Haute Partie contractante, même si cette occupation ne rencontre aucune résistance militaire. »

Art. 2, al. 2, CONVENTION DE GENÈVE RELATIVE AU TRAITEMENT DES PRISONNIERS DE GUERRE.
Art. 2, al. 2, CONVENTION DE GENÈVE RELATIVE À LA PROTECTION DES PERSONNES CIVILES EN TEMPS DE GUERRE DU 12 AOÛT 1949.

OPPROBRE, LE SILENCE, LA DISCRIMINATION ET LA DENEGATION AINSI QUE L'ABSENCE DE CONFIDENTIALITE (L') [Stigma, silence, discrimination and denial, as well as a lack of confidentiality]

– « 13. Notant également que l'opprobre, le silence, la discrimination et la dénégation ainsi que l'absence de confidentialité compromettent les efforts de prévention, de soins et de traitement et aggravent les effets de l'épidémie sur les individus, les familles, les communautés et les nations, et qu'il faut également y remédier; »

DÉCLARATION D'ENGAGEMENT SUR LE VIH/SIDA.

ORGANE DE REVISION [Review body (the)]

– « Dans les présents Principes :

[...]

L'expression « organe de révision » désigne l'organe créé en application du Principe 17[1] pour examiner le placement ou le maintien d'office d'un patient dans un service de santé mentale; »

---

[1] « Organe de révision

1. L'organe de révision est un organe judiciaire ou un autre organe indépendant et impartial établi et agissant selon les procédures fixées par la législation nationale. Il prend ses décisions

Al. 3, DEFINITIONS, PRINCIPES POUR LA PROTECTION DES PERSONNES ATTEINTES DE MALADIE MENTALE ET POUR L'AMÉLIORATION DES SOINS DE SANTÉ MENTALE[P].

ORGANISATION [Organisation]

– « Dans la présente convention, le terme organisation signifie toute organisation de travailleurs ou d'employeurs ayant pour but de promouvoir et de défendre les intérêts des travailleurs ou des employeurs. »

Art. 10, CONVENTION SUR LA LIBERTÉ SYNDICALE ET LA PROTECTION DU DROIT SYNDICAL, (N° 87).

ORGANISATION DES NATIONS UNIES [United nations]

– « [...] Etant l'organisation la plus universelle et la plus représentative qui existe dans le monde, l'Organisation des Nations Unies [...] »

6, sixième note (•), DÉCLARATION DU MILLÉNAIRE.

– « 32. Nous réaffirmons solennellement, en cette occasion historique, que l'Organisation des Nations Unies est le lieu de rassembler indispensable de l'humanité tout entière où nous nous efforçons de concrétiser nos

---

avec le concours d'un ou plusieurs praticiens de santé mentale qualifiés et indépendants et tient compte de leur avis.

2. Comme prescrit au paragraphe 2 du Principe 16, l'organe de révision procède à l'examen initial d'une décision de placer ou de garder d'office un patient dès que possible après l'adoption de cette décision et selon des procédures simples et rapides fixées par la législation nationale.

3. L'organe de révision examine périodiquement les cas des patients placés d'office à des intervalles raisonnables fixés par la législation nationale.

4. Tout patient placé d'office peut présenter à l'organe de révision une demande de sortie ou de placement volontaire, à des intervalles raisonnables fixés par la législation nationale.

5. A chaque réexamen, l'organe de révision examine si les conditions du placement d'office énoncées au paragraphe 1 du Principe 16 sont toujours réunies, sinon, il est mis fin au placement d'office du patient.

6. Si, à tout moment, le praticien de santé mentale chargé du cas estime que les conditions pour maintenir une personne en placement d'office ne sont plus réunies, il prescrit qu'il soit mis fin au placement d'office de cette personne.

7. Un patient ou son représentant personnel ou toute autre personne intéressée a le droit de faire appel devant une instance supérieure d'une décision de placement ou de maintien d'office d'un patient dans un service de santé mentale. »

[P] S.p. 8, DEFINITIONS, Principles for the protection of persons with mental illness and the improvement of mental health care.

aspirations universelles à la paix, à la coopération et au développement.
[...] »

DÉCLARATION DU MILLÉNAIRE.

ORGANISMES DE PROTECTION CIVILE [Civil defence organizations]

– « Aux fins du présent Protocole :
[...]

b) l'expression "organismes de protection civile" s'entend des établissements et autres unités qui sont mis sur pied ou autorisés par les autorités compétentes d'une Partie au conflit pour accomplir l'une quelconque des tâches mentionnées à l'alinéa *a*[2] et qui sont exclusivement affectés et utilisés à ces tâches; »

Art. 61, PROTOCOLE ADDITIONNEL AUX CONVENTIONS DE GENÈVE DU 12 AOÛT 1949 RELATIF À LA PROTECTION DES VICTIMES DES CONFLITS ARMÉS INTERNATIONAUX (PROTOCOLE I).

PACTES INTERNATIONAUX RELATIFS AUX DROITS DE L'HOMME [International Covenants on Human Rights]

[2] « *a*) l'expression "protection civile" s'entend de l'accomplissement de toutes les tâches humanitaires, ou de plusieurs d'entre elles, mentionnées ci-après, destinées à protéger la population civile contre les dangers des hostilités ou des catastrophes et à l'aider à surmonter leurs effets immédiats ainsi qu'à assurer les conditions nécessaires à sa survie. Ces tâches sont les suivantes :
i) service de l'alerte;
ii) évacuation;
iii) mise à disposition et organisation d'abris;
iv) mise en œuvre des mesures d'obscurcissement;
v) sauvetage;
vi) services sanitaires y compris premiers secours et assistance religieuse;
vii) lutte contre le feu;
viii) repérage et signalisation des zones dangereuses;
ix) décontamination et autres mesures de protection analogues;
x) hébergement et approvisionnements d'urgence;
xi) aide en cas d'urgence pour le rétablissement et le maintien de l'ordre dans les zones sinistrées;
xii) rétablissement d'urgence des services d'utilité publique indispensables;
xiii) services funéraires d'urgence;
xiv) aide à la sauvegarde des biens essentiels à la survie;
xv) activités complémentaires nécessaires à l'accomplissement de l'une quelconque des tâches mentionnées ci-dessus, comprenant la planification et l'organisation mais ne s'y limitant pas; »

– « *Réaffirmant* également l'importance de la Déclaration universelle des droits de l'homme et des Pactes internationaux relatifs aux droits de l'homme en tant qu'éléments fondamentaux des efforts internationaux visant à promouvoir le respect universel effectif des droits de l'homme et des libertés fondamentales, ainsi que l'importance des autres instruments relatifs aux droits de l'homme adoptés par les organes et organismes des Nations Unies, et de ceux adoptés au niveau régional, »[3]

Pp. 2, DÉCLARATION SUR LE DROIT ET LA RESPONSABILITÉ DES INDIVIDUS, GROUPES ET ORGANES DE LA SOCIÉTÉ DE PROMOUVOIR ET PROTÉGER LES DROITS DE L'HOMME ET LES LIBERTÉS FONDAMENTALES UNIVERSELLEMENT RECONNUS.

PAIX ET SECURITE INTERNATIONALES [International peace and security]

– « *Convaincue* que la paix et la sécurité internationales, d'une part, et le progrès social et le développement économique, d'autre part, sont étroitement interdépendants et s'influencent mutuellement, »

Pp. 6, DÉCLARATION SUR LE PROGRÈS ET LE DÉVELOPPEMENT DANS LE DOMAINE SOCIALE.

– « *Considérant* que la paix et la sécurité internationales sont des éléments essentiels pour la réalisation du droit au développement, »

Pp.11, DÉCLARATION SUR LE DROIT AU DÉVELOPPEMENT.

PALUDISME [Malaria]

– « Que d'ici là [2015], nous aurons arrêté la propagation du VIH/sida, et commencé à inverser la tendance actuelle, et que nous aurons maîtrisé le fléau du paludisme et des autres grandes maladies qui affligent l'humanité. »

19, quatrième note (•), DÉCLARATION DU MILLÉNAIRE.

---

[3] Face à la version papier sur laquelle nous travaillons existe une version electronique dont le texte diffère et dont voici la version : « *Réaffirmant également* l'importance de la Déclaration universelle des droits de l'homme[2] et des Pactes internationaux relatifs aux droits de l'homme Résolution 2200 A (XXI), annexe. en tant qu'éléments fondamentaux des efforts internationaux visant à promouvoir le respect universel et effectif des droits de l'homme et des libertés fondamentales, ainsi que l'importance des autres instruments relatifs aux droits de l'homme adoptés par les organes et organismes des Nations Unies, et de ceux adoptés au niveau regional. »

PALUDISME AVEC ALTERATIONS ORGANIQUES PRONONCEES [Malaria with decided organic impairment]

– « *s)* Les maladies infectieuses chroniques graves persistant une année après le début, par exemple : paludisme avec altérations organiques prononcées; dysenterie amibienne ou bacillaire avec troubles considérables; syphilis viscérale tertiaire, résistant au traitement; lèpre; etc. »

Annexe I, 3, CONVENTION DE GENÈVE RELATIVE AU TRAITEMENT DES PRISONNIERS DE GUERRE.

PARENTS ADOPTIFS [Adoption]

– « 14. [...]le recours à des foyers de substitution (parents nourriciers ou adoptifs) [...] »[q]

PRINCIPES DIRECTEURS DES NATIONS UNIES POUR LA PRÉVENTION DE LA DÉLINQUANCE JUVÉNILE (PRINCIPES DIRECTEURS DE RIYAD).

PARENTS NOURRICIERS [Foster care]

– « 14. [...]le recours à des foyers de substitution (parents nourriciers ou adoptifs) [...] »[r]

PRINCIPES DIRECTEURS DES NATIONS UNIES POUR LA PRÉVENTION DE LA DÉLINQUANCE JUVÉNILE (PRINCIPES DIRECTEURS DE RIYAD).

PARTAGE DES RESPONSABILITES (LE) [Shared responsibility]

– « 6. Nous estimons que certaines valeurs fondamentales doivent sous-tendre les relations internationales au XXe siècle, à savoir :

[...]

> *Le partage des responsabilités.* La responsabilité de la gestion, à l'échelle mondiale, du développent économique et social, ainsi que des menaces qui pèsent sur la paix et la sécurité internationales, doit être partagée entre toutes les nations du monde et devrait être exercée dans un cadre multilatéral. Etant l'organisation la plus universelle et la plus représentative qui existe dans le monde, l'Organisation des Nations Unies a un rôle central à jouer à cet égard. »

Sixième note (•), DÉCLARATION DU MILLÉNAIRE.

[Q] "14. [...] ALTERNATIVE PLACEMENTS INCLUDING FOSTER CARE AND ADOPTION [...]"

[R] "14. [...] ALTERNATIVE PLACEMENTS INCLUDING FOSTER CARE AND ADOPTION [...]"

PARTICIPATION POPULAIRE [Popular participation]

– « 2. Les Etats doivent encourager dans tous les domaines la participation populaire, qui est un facteur important du développement et de la pleine réalisation de tous les droits de l'homme. »

Art. 8, DÉCLARATION SUR LE DROIT AU DÉVELOPPEMENT.

PATIENT [Patient]

– « Dans les présents Principes :

[…]

Le terme « patient » désigne une personne qui reçoit des soins de santé mentale et s'entend de toutes les personnes qui sont admises dans un service de santé mentale; »

Al. 4, DEFINITIONS, PRINCIPES POUR LA PROTECTION DES PERSONNES ATTEINTES DE MALADIE MENTALE ET POUR L'AMÉLIORATION DES SOINS DE SANTÉ MENTALE[s].

PATRIMOINE [Heritage]

– « Chaque création puise aux racines des traditions culturelles, mais s'épanouit au contact des autres cultures. C'est pourquoi le patrimoine, sous toutes ses formes, doit être préservé, mis en valeur et transmis aux générations futures en tant que témoignage de l'expérience et des aspirations humaines, afin de nourrir la créativité dans toute sa diversité et d'inspirer un véritable dialogue entre les cultures. »

Art. 7, DÉCLARATION UNIVERSELLE SUR LA DIVERSITÉ CULTURELLE.

PAUVRETE [Poverty]

– « 11. Estimant que la pauvreté, le sous-développement et l'analphabétisme figurent parmi les principaux facteurs contribuant à la propagation du VIH/sida, et notant avec une vive préoccupation que l'épidémie aggrave la pauvreté et entrave ou enraye désormais le développement dans un grand nombre de pays et qu'il faudrait donc y remédier dans une optique intégrée; »

DÉCLARATION D'ENGAGEMENT SUR LE VIH/SIDA.

---

[s] S.P. 6, DEFINITIONS, Principles for the protection of persons with mental illness and the improvement of mental health care.

PAYS DONT ELLE A LA NATIONALITE (DU) [Country of his nationality (the)]

– « Dans le cas d'une personne qui a plus d'une nationalité, l'expression "du pays dont elle a la nationalité" vise chacun des pays dont cette personne a la nationalité. Ne sera pas considérée comme privée de la protection du pays dont elle a la nationalité toute personne qui, sans raison valable fondée sur une crainte justifiée, ne s'est pas réclamée de la protection de l'un des pays dont elle a la nationalité. »

Art. 1, § 2, al. 2, CONVENTION RELATIVE AU STATUT DES RÉFUGIÉS.

PEINE DE MORT [Death penalty]

– « 1. Il ne sera admis aucune réserve au présent Protocole, en dehors de la réserve formulée lors de la ratification ou de l'adhésion et prévoyant l'application de la peine de mort en temps de guerre à la suite d'une condamnation pour crime de caractère militaire, d'une gravité extrême commis en temps de guerre. »

Art. 2, DEUXIÈME PROTOCOLE FACULTATIF SE RAPPORTANT AU PACTE INTERNATIONAL RELATIF AUX DROITS CIVILS ET POLITIQUES VISANT À ABOLIR LA PEINE DE MORT.

PEINE OU TRAITEMENT CRUEL, INHUMAIN OU DEGRADANT [Cruel, inhuman or degrading treatment or punishment]

– « L'expression "peine ou traitement cruel, inhumain ou dégradant" doit être interprétée de façon à assurer une protection aussi large que possible contre tous sévices, qu'ils aient un caractère physique ou mental, y compris le fait de soumettre une personne détenue ou emprisonnée à des conditions qui la privent temporairement ou en permanence de l'usage de l'un quelconque de ses sens, tels que la vue ou l'ouïe, ou de la conscience du lieu où elle se trouve et du passage du temps. »

Principe 6, ENSEMBLE DE PRINCIPES POUR LA PROTECTION DE TOUTES LES PERSONNES SOUMISES À UNE FORME QUELCONQUE DE DÉTENTION OU D'EMPRISONNEMENT.

– « Aucun responsable de l'application des lois ne peut infliger, susciter ou tolérer un acte de torture ou quelque autre peine ou traitement cruel, inhumain ou dégradant, ni ne peut invoquer un ordre de ses supérieurs ou des circonstances exceptionnelles telles qu'un état de guerre ou une menace de guerre, une menace contre la sécurité nationale, l'instabilité politique intérieure ou tout autre état d'exception pour justifier la torture ou d'autres peines ou traitements cruels, inhumains ou dégradants.

Commentaire:

a) Cette interdiction découle de la Déclaration sur la protection de toutes les personnes contre la torture et autres peines ou traitements cruels, inhumains ou dégradants, adoptée par l'Assemblée générale et aux termes de laquelle:

"[Cet acte constitue] un outrage à la dignité humaine et doit être condamné comme un reniement des buts de la Charte des Nations Unies et comme une violation des droits de l'homme et des libertés fondamentales proclamés dans la Déclaration universelle des droits de l'homme [et d'autres instruments internationaux en matière de droits de l'homme]."

[...]

c) L'expression "peine ou traitement cruel, inhumain ou dégradant" n'a pas été définie par l'Assemblée générale, mais doit être interprétée de façon à assurer une protection aussi large que possible contre tous abus, qu'ils aient un caractère physique ou mental. »

Art. 5, CODE DE CONDUITE POUR LES RESPONSABLE DE L'APPLICATION DES LOIS.

PEINES CORPORELLES [Corporal punishment]

– « Les Hautes Parties contractantes s'interdisent expressément toute mesure de nature à causer soit des souffrances physiques, soit l'extermination des personnes protégées en leur pouvoir. Cette interdiction vise non seulement le meurtre, la torture, les peines corporelles, les mutilations et les expériences médicales ou scientifiques non nécessitées par le traitement médical d'une personne protégée, mais également toutes autres brutalités, qu'elles soient le fait d'agents civils ou d'agents militaires. »

Art. 32, CONVENTION DE GENÈVE RELATIVE À LA PROTECTION DES PERSONNES CIVILES EN TEMPS DE GUERRE DU 12 AOÛT 1949.

– -« *a*) les atteintes portées à la vie, à la santé et au bien-être physique ou mental des personnes, notamment:

[...]

iii) les peines corporelles; [...] »

Art. 75, § 2., PROTOCOLE ADDITIONNEL AUX CONVENTIONS DE GENÈVE DU 12 AOÛT 1949 RELATIF À LA PROTECTION DES VICTIMES DES CONFLITS ARMÉS INTERNATIONAUX (PROTOCOLE I).

PENALEMENT RESPONSABLE [Criminally responsible]

- « 3. Aux termes du présent Statut, une personne est pénalement responsable et peut être punie pour un crime relevant de la compétence de la Cour si:

  a) Elle commet un tel crime, que ce soit individuellement, conjointement avec une autre personne ou par l'intermédiaire d'une autre personne, que cette autre personne soit ou non pénalement responsable;

  b) Elle ordonne, sollicite ou encourage la commission d'un tel crime, dès lors qu'il y a commission ou tentative de commission de ce crime;

  c) En vue de faciliter la commission d'un tel crime, elle apporte son aide, son concours ou toute autre forme d'assistance à la commission ou à la tentative de commission de ce crime, y compris en fournissant les moyens de cette commission;

  d) Elle contribue de toute autre manière à la commission ou à la tentative de commission d'un tel crime par un groupe de personnes agissant de concert. Cette contribution doit être intentionnelle et, selon le cas:

  i) Viser à faciliter l'activité criminelle ou le dessein criminel du groupe, si cette activité ou ce dessein comporte l'exécution d'un crime relevant de la compétence de la Cour; ou

  ii) Être faite en pleine connaissance de l'intention du groupe de commettre ce crime;

  e) S'agissant du crime de génocide, elle incite directement et publiquement autrui à le commettre;

  f) Elle tente de commettre un tel crime par des actes qui, par leur caractère substantiel, constituent un commencement d'exécution mais sans que le crime soit accompli en raison de circonstances indépendantes de sa volonté. Toutefois, la personne qui abandonne l'effort tendant à commettre le crime ou en empêche de quelque autre façon l'achèvement ne peut être punie en vertu du présent Statut pour sa tentative si elle a complètement et volontairement renoncé au dessein criminel. »

Art. 25, Statut de Rome de la Cour pénale internationale.

– « 1. Sauf disposition contraire, nul n'est pénalement responsable et ne peut être puni à raison d'un crime relevant de la compétence de la Cour que si l'élément matériel du crime est commis avec intention et connaissance.

2. Il y a intention au sens du présent article lorsque:

a) Relativement à un comportement, une personne entend adopter ce comportement;

b) Relativement à une conséquence, une personne entend causer cette conséquence ou est consciente que celle-ci adviendra dans le cours normal des événements.

3. Il y a connaissance, au sens du présent article, lorsqu'une personne est consciente qu'une circonstance existe ou qu'une conséquence adviendra dans le cours normal des événements. «Connaître» et «en connaissance de cause» s'interprètent en conséquence. »

Art. 30, Statut de Rome de la Cour pénale internationale.

PERFIDIE [Perfidy]

– « 1. Il est interdit de tuer, blesser ou capturer un adversaire en recourant à la perfidie. Constituent une perfidie les actes faisant appel, avec l'intention de la tromper, à la bonne foi d'un adversaire pour lui faire croire qu'il a le droit de recevoir ou l'obligation d'accorder la protection prévue par les règles du droit international applicable dans les conflits armés. Les actes suivants sont des exemples de perfidie :

a) feindre l'intention de négocier sous le couvert du pavillon parlementaire, ou feindre la reddition;

b) feindre une incapacité due à des blessures ou à la maladie;

c) feindre d'avoir le statut de civil ou de non-combattant;

d) feindre d'avoir un statut protégé en utilisant des signes emblèmes ou uniformes des Nations Unies, d'Etats neutres ou d'autres Etats non Parties au conflit. »

Art. 37, Protocole additionnel aux Conventions de Genève du 12 août 1949 relatif à la protection des victimes des conflits armés internationaux (Protocole I).

PERSECUTIONS [Persecution]

– « 2. Aux fins du paragraphe 1[4]:
[...]

g) Par «persécution», on entend le déni intentionnel et grave de droits fondamentaux en violation du droit international, pour des motifs liés à l'identité du groupe ou de la collectivité qui en fait l'objet; »
Art. 7, STATUT DE ROME DE LA COUR PÉNALE INTERNATIONALE.

PERSONNE (TOUTE) [Everyone]

– « Toute personne, en tant que membre de la société[...] »
Art. 22, DÉCLARATION UNIVERSELLE DES DROITS DE L'HOMME.

PERSONNE ACCUSEE [Accused]

– « 3. Toute personne accusée est présumée innocente jusqu'à ce que sa culpabilité ait été établie conformément aux disposition du présent Statut. »
Art. 21, STATUT DU TRIBUNAL INTERNATIONAL CHARGÉ DE POURSUIVRE LES PERSONNES PRÉSUMÉES RESPONSABLE DE VIOLATIONS GRAVES DU DROIT INTERNATIONAL HUMANITAIRE COMMISES SUR LE TERITOIRE DE L'EX-YOUGOSLAVIE DEPUIS 1991.

---

[4] « 1. Aux fins du présent Statut, on entend par crime contre l'humanité l'un quelconque des actes ci-après lorsqu'il est commis dans le cadre d'une attaque généralisée ou systématique lancée contre toute population civile et en connaissance de cette attaque:
a) Meurtre;
b) Extermination;
c) Réduction en esclavage;
d) Déportation ou transfert forcé de population;
e) Emprisonnement ou autre forme de privation grave de liberté physique en violation des dispositions fondamentales du droit international;
f) Torture;
g) Viol, esclavage sexuel, prostitution forcée, grossesse forcée, stérilisation forcée ou toute autre forme de violence sexuelle de gravité comparable;
h) Persécution de tout groupe ou de toute collectivité identifiable pour des motifs d'ordre politique, racial, national, ethnique, culturel, religieux ou sexiste au sens du paragraphe 3, ou en fonction d'autres critères universellement reconnus comme inadmissibles en droit international, en corrélation avec tout acte visé dans le présent paragraphe ou tout crime relevant de la compétence de la Cour;
i) Disparitions forcées de personnes;
j) Crime d'apartheid;
k) Autres actes inhumains de caractère analogue causant intentionnellement de grandes souffrances ou des atteintes graves à l'intégrité physique ou à la santé physique ou mentale. »

Art. 20, STATUT DU TRIBUNAL PÉNAL INTERNATIONAL CHARGÉ DE JUGER LES PERSONNES PRÉSUMÉES RESPONSABLES D'ACTES DE GÉNOCIDE OU D'AUTRES VIOLATIONS GRAVES DU DROIT INTERNATIONAL HUMANITAIRE COMMIS SUR LE TERRITOIRE DU RWANDA ET LES CITOYENS RWANDAIS PRÉSUMÉS RESPONSABLES DE TELS ACTES OU VIOLATIONS COMMIS SUR LE TERRITOIRE D'ETATS VOISINS ENTRE LE 1ER JANVIER 1994 ET LE 31 DÉCEMBRE 1994.

PERSONNE DE CONDITION SERVILE [Person of servile status (a)]

– « Aux fins de la présente Convention :
  [...]
  > *b*) La «personne de condition servile» est celle qui est placée dans le statut ou la condition qui résulte d'une des institutions ou pratiques visées à l'article premier[5] de la présente Convention; »

Art. 7, CONVENTION SUPPLÉMENTAIRE RELATIVE À L'ABOLITION DE L'ESCLAVAGE, DE LA TRAITE DES ESCLAVES ET DES INSTITUTIONS ET PRATIQUES ANALOGUES À L'ESCLAVAGE.

---

[5] « Chacun des Etats parties à la présente Convention prendra toutes les mesures, législatives et autres, qui seront réalisables et nécessaires pour obtenir progressivement et aussitôt que possible l'abolition complète ou l'abandon des institutions et pratiques suivantes, là où elles subsistent encore, qu'elles rentrent ou non dans la définition de l'esclavage qui figure à l'article premier de la Convention relative à l'esclavage signée à Genève le 25 septembre 1926 :
a) La servitude pour dettes, c'est-à-dire l'état ou la condition résultant du fait qu'un débiteur s'est engagé à fournir en garantie d'une dette ses services personnels ou ceux de quelqu'un sur lequel il a autorité, si la valeur équitable ce ces services n'est pas affectée à la liquidation de la dette ou si la durée de ces services n'est pas limitée ni leur caractère défini;
b) Le servage, c'est-à-dire la condition de quiconque est tenu par la loi, la coutume ou un accord, de vivre et de travailler sur une terre appartenant à une autre personne et de fournir à cette autre personne, contre rémunération ou gratuitement, certains services déterminés, sans pouvoir changer sa condition;
c) Toute institution ou pratique en vertu de laquelle :
i) Une femme est, sans qu'elle ait le droit de refuser, promise ou donnée en mariage moyennant une contrepartie en espèces ou en nature versée à ses parents, à son tuteur, à sa famille ou à toute autre personne ou tout autre groupe de personnes;
ii) Le mari d'une femme, la famille ou le clan de celui-ci ont le droit de la céder à un tiers, à titre onéreux ou autrement;
iii) La femme peut, à la mort de son mari, être transmise par succession à une autre personne;
d) Toute institution ou pratique en vertu de laquelle un enfant ou un adolescent de moins de dix-huit ans est remis, soit par ses parents ou par l'un d'eux, soit par son tuteur, à un tiers, contre paiement ou non, en vue de l'exploitation de la personne, ou du travail dudit enfant ou adolescent. »

PERSONNE DETENUE [Detained person]

– « Aux fins de l'Ensemble de principes:
[…]

b) Le terme "personne détenue" s'entend de toute personne privée de la liberté individuelle sauf à la suite d'une condamnation pour infraction; »

Emploi des termes, ENSEMBLE DE PRINCIPES POUR LA PROTECTION DE TOUTES LES PERSONNES SOUMISES À UNE FORME QUELCONQUE DE DÉTENTION OU D'EMPRISONNEMENT.

PERSONNE EMPRISONNEE [Imprisoned person]

– « Aux fins de l'Ensemble de principes:
[…]

c) Le terme "personne emprisonnée" s'entend de toute personne privée de la liberté individuelle à la suite d'une condamnation pour infraction; »

Emploi des termes, ENSEMBLE DE PRINCIPES POUR LA PROTECTION DE TOUTES LES PERSONNES SOUMISES À UNE FORME QUELCONQUE DE DÉTENTION OU D'EMPRISONNEMENT.

PERSONNE HUMAINE [Human being; Human person]

– « *Reconnaissant* que ces droits découlent de la dignité inhérente à la personne humaine. »

Pp. 2, PACTE INTERNATIONAL RELATIF AUX DROITS ÉCONOMIQUES, SOCIAUX ET CULTURELS.
Pp. 2, PACTE INTERNATIONAL RELATIF AUX DROITS CIVILS ET POLITIQUES.

– « 1. Le droit à la vie est inhérent à la personne humaine. Ce droit doit être protégé par la loi. Nul ne peut être arbitrairement privé de la vie. »

ART. 6, PACTE INTERNATIONAL RELATIF AUX DROITS CIVILS ET POLITIQUES.

– « 1. Toute personne privée de sa liberté est traitée avec humanité et avec le respect de la dignité inhérente à la personne humaine. »

ART. 10, PACTE INTERNATIONAL RELATIF AUX DROITS CIVILS ET POLITIQUES.

– « […] la personne humaine est le sujet même des droits de l'homme et des libertés fondamentales et que, par conséquent, elle doit en être le principal bénéficiaire et participer activement à leur réalisation, »

Pp. 2, DÉCLARATION ET PROGRAMME D'ACTION DE VIENNE.

– « Ainsi qu'il est dit dans la Déclaration sur le droit au développement, la personne humaine est le sujet central du développement.

I, 10, al.2, DÉCLARATION ET PROGRAMME D'ACTION DE VIENNE.

– « Toute personne soumise à une forme quelconque de détention ou d'emprisonnement est traitée avec humanité et avec le respect de la dignité inhérente à la personne humaine. »

Principe 1, ENSEMBLE DE PRINCIPES POUR LA PROTECTION DE TOUTES LES PERSONNES SOUMISES À UNE FORME QUELCONQUE DE DÉTENTION OU D'EMPRISONNEMENT.

– « *Reconnaissant* que ces droits[6] procèdent de la dignité inhérente à la personne humaine, »

Pp.2, CONVENTION CONTRE LA TORTURE ET AUTRES PEINES OU TRAITEMENT CRUELS, INHUMAINS OU DÉGRADANTS.

– « *Rappelant* que, pour les cas non prévus par le droit en vigueur, la personne humaine reste sous la sauvegarde des principes de l'humanité et des exigences de la conscience publique, »

Pp. 4, PROTOCOLE ADDITIONNEL AUX CONVENTION DE GENÈVE DU 12 AOÛT 1949 RELATIF À LA PROTECTION DES VICTIMES DES CONFLITS ARMÉS NON INTERNATIONAUX (PROTOCOLE II).

PERSONNEL [Personnel]

– « Aux fins du présent Protocole :

[...]

c) le terme "personnel" des organismes de protection civile s'entend des personnes qu'une Partie au conflit affecte exclusivement à l'accomplissement des tâches énumérées à l'alinéa *a*[7], y compris le

---

[6] Droits égaux et inaliénables de tous les membres de la famille humaine.

[7] « *a*) l'expression "protection civile" s'entend de l'accomplissement de toutes les tâches humanitaires, ou de plusieurs d'entre elles, mentionnées ci-après, destinées à protéger la population civile contre les dangers des hostilités ou des catastrophes et à l'aider à surmonter leurs effets immédiats ainsi qu'à assurer les conditions nécessaires à sa survie. Ces tâches sont les suivantes :

i) service de l'alerte;

ii) évacuation;

iii) mise à disposition et organisation d'abris;

iv) mise en oeuvre des mesures d'obscurcissement;

v) sauvetage;

vi) services sanitaires y compris premiers secours et assistance religieuse;

vii) lutte contre le feu;

viii) repérage et signalisation des zones dangereuses;

personnel assigné exclusivement à l'administration de ces organismes par l'autorité compétente de cette Partie; »

Art. 61, PROTOCOLE ADDITIONNEL AUX CONVENTIONS DE GENÈVE DU 12 AOÛT 1949 RELATIF À LA PROTECTION DES VICTIMES DES CONFLITS ARMÉS INTERNATIONAUX (PROTOCOLE I).

PERSONNEL RELIGIEUX [Religious personnel]

– « Aux fins du présent Protocole :

[...]

d) l'expression "personnel religieux" s'entend des personnes, militaires ou civiles, telles que les aumôniers, exclusivement vouées à leur ministère et attachées :

i) soit aux forces armées d'une Partie au conflit;

ii) soit aux unités sanitaires ou aux moyens de transport sanitaire d'une Partie au conflit;

iii) soit aux unités sanitaires ou aux moyens de transport sanitaire visés à l'article 9, paragraphe 2[8];

iv) soit aux organismes de protection civile d'une Partie au conflit;

le rattachement du personnel religieux à ces unités peut être permanent ou temporaire et les dispositions pertinentes prévues à l'alinéa k[9] s'appliquent à ce personnel; »

---

ix) décontamination et autres mesures de protection analogues;
x) hébergement et approvisionnements d'urgence;
xi) aide en cas d'urgence pour le rétablissement et le maintien de l'ordre dans les zones sinistrées;
xii) rétablissement d'urgence des services d'utilité publique indispensables;
xiii) services funéraires d'urgence;
xiv) aide à la sauvegarde des biens essentiels à la survie;
xv) activités complémentaires nécessaires à l'accomplissement de l'une quelconque des tâches mentionnées ci-dessus, comprenant la planification et l'organisation mais ne s'y limitant pas; »

[8] « 2. Les dispositions pertinentes des articles 27 et 32 de la Ire Convention s'appliquent aux unités et moyens de transport sanitaires permanents (autres que les navires-hôpitaux, auxquels l'article 25 de la IIe Convention s'applique), ainsi qu'à leur personnel, mis à la disposition d'une Partie au conflit à des fins humanitaires :
a) par un Etat neutre ou un autre Etat non Partie à ce conflit;
b) par une société de secours reconnue et autorisée de cet Etat;
c) par une organisation internationale impartiale de caractère humanitaire. »

[9] « *k*) sont "permanents" le personnel sanitaire, les unités sanitaires et les moyens de transport sanitaire affectés exclusivement à des fins sanitaires pour une durée indéterminée. Sont "temporaires" le personnel sanitaire, les unités sanitaires et les moyens de transport sanitaire

Art. 8, Protocole additionnel aux Conventions de Genève du 12 août 1949 relatif à la protection des victimes des conflits armés internationaux (Protocole I).

PERSONNEL SANITAIRE [Medical personnel]

– « Aux fins du présent Protocole :

[...]

c) l'expression "personnel sanitaire" s'entend des personnes exclusivement affectées par une Partie au conflit soit aux fins sanitaires énumérées à l'alinéa e[10], soit à l'administration d'unités sanitaires, soit encore au fonctionnement ou à l'administration de moyens de transport sanitaire. Ces affectations peuvent être permanentes ou temporaires. L'expression couvre :

i) le personnel sanitaire, militaire ou civil, d'une Partie au conflit, y compris celui qui est mentionné dans les Ire et IIe Conventions, et celui qui est affecté à des organismes de protection civile;

ii) le personnel sanitaire des Sociétés nationales de la Croix-Rouge (Croissant-Rouge, Lion-et-Soleil- Rouge) et autres sociétés nationales de secours volontaires dûment reconnues et autorisées par une Partie au conflit;

iii) le personnel sanitaire des unités ou moyens de transport sanitaire visés à l'article 9, paragraphe 2[11]; »

---

utilisés exclusivement à des fins sanitaires pour des périodes limitées, pendant toute la durée de ces périodes. A moins qu'elles ne soient autrement qualifiées, les expressions "personnel sanitaire", "unité sanitaire" et "moyen de transport sanitaire" couvrent un personnel, des unités ou des moyens de transport qui peuvent être soit permanents soit temporaires; »

[10] « e) l'expression "unités sanitaires" s'entend des établissements et autres formations, militaires ou civils, organisés à des fins sanitaires, à savoir la recherche, l'évacuation, le transport, le diagnostic ou le traitement – y compris les premiers secours – des blessés, des malades et des naufragés, ainsi que la prévention des maladies. Elle couvre entre autres les hôpitaux et autres unités similaires, les centres de transfusion sanguine, les centres et instituts de médecine préventive et les centres d'approvisionnement sanitaire, ainsi que les dépôts de matériel sanitaire et de produits pharmaceutiques de ces unités. Les unités sanitaires peuvent être fixes ou mobiles, permanentes ou temporaires; »

[11] « 2. Les dispositions pertinentes des articles 27 et 32 de la Ire Convention s'appliquent aux unités et moyens de transport sanitaires permanents (autres que les navires-hôpitaux, auxquels l'article 25 de la IIe Convention s'applique), ainsi qu'à leur personnel, mis à la disposition d'une Partie au conflit à des fins humanitaires :

a) par un Etat neutre ou un autre Etat non Partie à ce conflit;

b) par une société de secours reconnue et autorisée de cet Etat;

c) par une organisation internationale impartiale de caractère humanitaire. »

Art. 8, PROTOCOLE ADDITIONNEL AUX CONVENTIONS DE GENÈVE DU 12 AOÛT 1949 RELATIF À LA PROTECTION DES VICTIMES DES CONFLITS ARMÉS INTERNATIONAUX (PROTOCOLE I).

PERSONNEL SANITAIRE PERMANENT [Permanent medical personnel]

– « Aux fins du présent Protocole :
[...]

k) sont "permanents" le personnel sanitaire, les unités sanitaires et les moyens de transport sanitaire affectés exclusivement à des fins sanitaires pour une durée indéterminée. Sont "temporaires" le personnel sanitaire, les unités sanitaires et les moyens de transport sanitaire utilisés exclusivement à des fins sanitaires pour des périodes limitées, pendant toute la durée de ces périodes. A moins qu'elles ne soient autrement qualifiées, les expressions "personnel sanitaire", "unité sanitaire" et "moyen de transport sanitaire" couvrent un personnel, des unités ou des moyens de transport qui peuvent être soit permanents soit temporaires; »

Art. 8, PROTOCOLE ADDITIONNEL AUX CONVENTIONS DE GENÈVE DU 12 AOÛT 1949 RELATIF À LA PROTECTION DES VICTIMES DES CONFLITS ARMÉS INTERNATIONAUX (PROTOCOLE I).

PERSONNEL SANITAIRE TEMPORAIRE [Temporary medical personnel]

– « Aux fins du présent protocole :
[...]

k) [...]Sont "temporaires" le personnel sanitaire, les unités sanitaires et les moyens de transport sanitaire utilisés exclusivement à des fins sanitaires pour des périodes limitées, pendant toute la durée de ces périodes. A moins qu'elles ne soient autrement qualifiées, les expressions "personnel sanitaire", "unité sanitaire" et "moyen de transport sanitaire" couvrent un personnel, des unités ou des moyens de transport qui peuvent être soit permanents soit temporaires;]

Art. 8, PROTOCOLE ADDITIONNEL AUX CONVENTIONS DE GENEVE DU 12 AOUT 1949 RELATIF A LA PROTECTION DES VICTIMES DES CONFLITS ARMES INTERNATIONAUX (PROTOCOLE I).

PERSONNES [Persons]

– « Toutes les personnes sont égales devant la loi et ont droit sans discrimination à une égale protection de la loi. [...] »

Art. 26, PACTE INTERNATIONAL RELATIF AUX DROITS CIVILS ET POLITIQUES.

PERSONNES AGEES [Older persons]

– « *Consciente* de la contribution que les personnes âgées apportent à leurs sociétés respectives, »

Pp. 1, PRINCIPES DES NATIONS UNIES POUR LES PERSONNES ÂGÉES.

– « *Consciente* que l'extrême diversité de la situation des personnes âgées, non seulement d'un pays à l'autre mais encore à l'intérieur d'un même pays et d'une personne à l'autre, appelle des politiques différenciées, »

Pp. 5, PRINCIPES DES NATIONS UNIES POUR LES PERSONNES ÂGÉES.

PERSONNES SOUFFRANT D'INCAPACITES [Persons with disabilities]

– « 63. La Conférence mondiale sur les droits de l'homme réaffirme que les droits de l'homme et les libertés fondamentales sont tous universels et, de ce fait, s'appliquent sans réserve aucune aux personnes souffrant d'incapacités. Tous les êtres humains naissent égaux et ont les mêmes droits à la vie et au bien-être, à l'éducation et au travail, à une vie indépendante et à une participation active à tous les aspects de la vie en société. [...] »

II, DÉCLARATION ET PROGRAMME D'ACTION DE VIENNE.

PEUPLES [Peoples]

– « Tous les peuples ont le droit de disposer d'eux-mêmes. En vertu de ce droit, ils déterminent librement leur statut politique et assurent librement leur développement économique, social et culturel. »[t]

Art. 1, 1, PACTE INTERNATIONAL RELATIF AUX DROITS ÉCONOMIQUES, SOCIAUX ET CULTURELS.
Art. 1, 1, PACTE INTERNATIONAL RELATIF AUX DROITS CIVILS ET POLITIQUES.

– « Tous les peuples ont le droit de disposer d'eux-mêmes. En vertu de ce droit, ils déterminent librement leur statut politique et poursuivent librement leur développement économique, social et culturel.

I, 2, al. 1, DÉCLARATION ET PROGRAMME D'ACTION DE VIENNE.

[t] "All peoples have the right of self-determination. By virtue of that right they freely determine their political status and freely pursue their economic, social and cultural development."

– « 2. Tous les peuples ont le droit de libre détermination ; en vertu de ce droit, ils déterminent librement leur statut politique et poursuivent librement leur développement économique, sociale et culturel. »

DÉCLARATION SUR L'OCTROI DE L'INDÉPENDANCE AUX PAYS ET AUX PEUPLES COLONIAUX.

– « 4. Tous les peuples du monde sont dotés des mêmes facultés leur permettant d'atteindre la plénitude de développement intellectuel, technique, social, économique, culturel et politique. »

Art. 1, DÉCLARATION SUR LA RACE ET LES PRÉJUGÉS RACIAUX.

PEUPLES INDIGENES [Indigenous peoples]

– « 1. La présente convention s'applique:

[...]

b) aux peuples dans les pays indépendants qui sont considérés comme indigènes du fait qu'ils descendent des populations qui habitaient le pays, ou une région géographique à laquelle appartient le pays, à l'époque de la conquête ou de la colonisation ou de l'établissement des frontières actuelles de l'Etat, et qui, quel que soit leur statut juridique, conservent leurs institutions sociales, économiques, culturelles et politiques propres ou certaines d'entre elles.

2. Le sentiment d'appartenance indigène ou tribale doit être considéré comme un critère fondamental pour déterminer les groupes auxquels s'appliquent les dispositions de la présente convention.

3. L'emploi du terme *peuples* dans la présente convention ne peut en aucune manière être interprété comme ayant des implications de quelque nature que ce soit quant aux droits qui peuvent s'attacher à ce terme en vertu du droit international. »

Art. 1, CONVENTION RELATIVE AUX PEUPLES INDIGÈNES ET TRIBAUX (N° 169).

PEUPLES TRIBAUX [Tribal peoples]

– « 1. La présente convention s'applique:

a) aux peuples tribaux dans les pays indépendants qui se distinguent des autres secteurs de la communauté nationale par leurs conditions sociales, culturelles et économiques et qui sont régis totalement ou partiellement par des coutumes ou des traditions qui leur sont propres ou par une législation spéciale; [...]

2. Le sentiment d'appartenance indigène ou tribale doit être considéré comme un critère fondamental pour déterminer les groupes auxquels s'appliquent les dispositions de la présente convention.

3. L'emploi du terme *peuples* dans la présente convention ne peut en aucune manière être interprété comme ayant des implications de quelque nature que ce soit quant aux droits qui peuvent s'attacher à ce terme en vertu du droit international.»

Art. 1, CONVENTION RELATIVE AUX PEUPLES INDIGÈNES ET TRIBAUX, (N° 169).

PIRES FORMES DE TRAVAIL DES ENFANTS (Les) [Worst forms of child labour (The)]

– « Article 3
Aux fins de la présente convention, l'expression "les pires formes de travail des enfants" comprend :

a) Toutes les formes d'esclavage ou pratiques analogues telles que la vente et la traite des enfants, la servitude pour dettes et le servage ainsi que le travail forcé ou obligatoire, y compris le recrutement forcé ou obligatoire des enfants en vue de leur utilisation dans les conflits armés ;

b) L'utilisation, le recrutement ou l'offre d'un enfant à des fins de prostitution, de production de matériel pornographique ou de spectacles pornographiques ;

c) L'utilisation, le recrutement ou l'offre d'un enfant aux fins d'activités illicites, notamment pour la production et le trafic de stupéfiants, tels que les définissent les conventions internationales pertinentes ;

d) Les travaux qui, par leur nature ou les conditions dans lesquelles ils s'exercent, sont susceptibles de nuire à la santé, à la sécurité ou à la moralité de l'enfant. »

ART. 3, CONVENTION SUR LES PIRES FORMES DE TRAVAIL DES ENFANTS (N° 182).

PISTOLETS [Pistols]

– « 3. Ne sera pas considéré non plus comme acte nuisible à l'ennemi le port d'armes légères individuelles par le personnel civil de protection civile, en vue du maintien de l'ordre ou pour sa propre protection. Toutefois, dans les zones où des combats terrestres se déroulent ou semblent devoir se dérouler, les Parties au conflit prendront les dispositions appropriées pour limiter ces armes aux armes de poing, telles que les pistolets ou revolvers, afin de faciliter la distinction entre le personnel de protection civile et les combattants. Même si le personnel de protection civile porte d'autres armes légères individuelles dans ces zones, il doit être respecté et protégé dès qu'il aura été reconnu comme tel. »

ART. 65, PROTOCOLE ADDITIONNEL AUX CONVENTIONS DE GENÈVE DU 12 AOÛT 1949 RELATIF À LA PROTECTION DES VICTIMES DES CONFLITS ARMÉS INTERNATIONAUX (PROTOCOLE I).

PLEINE UTILISATION DES RESSOURCES HUMAINES [Full utilization of human resources]

– « Le progrès et le développement dans le domaine social exigent la pleine utilisation des ressources humaines, ce qui comporte notamment :

  a) L'encouragement des initiatives créatrices dans une opinion publique éclairée;

  b) La diffusion d'informations d'ordre national et international en vue de développer chez les individus la conscience des transformations qui interviennent dans l'ensemble de la société;

  c) La participation active de tous les éléments de la société, individuellement ou par l'intermédiaire d'associations, à la définition et à la réalisation des buts communs du développement dans le plein respect des libertés fondamentales consacrées dans la Déclaration universelle des droits de l'homme;

  d) Le fait d'assurer aux secteurs défavorisés ou marginaux de la population des chances égales de progrès social et économique afin de réaliser une société effectivement intégrée. »

Art. 5, DÉCLARATION SUR LE PROGRÈS ET LE DÉVELOPPEMENT DANS LE DOMAINE SOCIALE.

PLURALISME CULTUREL [Cultural pluralism]

– « Dans nos sociétés de plus en plus diversifiées, il est indispensable d'assurer une interaction harmonieuse et un vouloir vivre ensemble de personnes et de groupes aux identités culturelles à la fois plurielles, variées et dynamiques. Des politiques favorisant l'intégration et la participation de tous les citoyens sont garantes de la cohésion sociale, de la vitalité de la société civile et de la paix. Ainsi défini, le pluralisme culturel constitue la réponse politique au fait de la diversité culturelle. Indissociable d'un cadre démocratique, le pluralisme culturel est propice aux échanges culturels et à l'épanouissement des capacités créatrices qui nourrissent la vie publique. »

Art. 2, DÉCLARATION UNIVERSELLE SUR LA DIVERSITÉ CULTURELLE.

PLUS HAUTE ASPIRATION DE L'HOMME [Highest aspiration of the common people (the)]

– « [...] l'avènement d'un monde où les êtres humains seront libres de parler et de croire, libérés de la terreur et de la misère, a été proclamé comme la plus haute aspiration de l'homme, »

Pp. 2, DÉCLARATION UNIVERSELLE DES DROITS DE L'HOMME.

POLITIQUE ACTUELLEMENT ADOPTEES EN FAVEUR DES HANDICAPES [Present disability policy]

– « 3. Les politiques actuellement adoptées en faveur des handicapés sont le produit des 200 dernières années. A bien des égards, elles reflètent les conditions de vie générales ainsi que les politiques sociéconomiques de diverses époques. Bien des éléments particuliers influent cependant aussi sur les conditions de vie des handicapés. L'ignorance, l'abandon, la superstition et la crainte ont toujours compté parmi les facteurs sociaux qui isolent les handicapés et font obstacle à leur épanouissement. »

INTRODUCTION, RÈGLES POUR L'ÉGALISATION DES CHANCES DES PERSONNES HANDICAPÉES.

POLITIQUES CULTURELLES [Cultural policies]

– « Article 9- Les politiques culturelles, catalyseur de créativité »[u]

DÉCLARATION UNIVERSELLE SUR LA DIVERSITÉ CULTURELLE.

POLYARTHRITE CHRONIQUE EVOLUTIVE PRIMAIRE ET SECONDAIRE [Primary and secondary progressive chronic polyarthritis]

– « *p)* Les affections chroniques des organes locomoteurs avec troubles fonctionnels manifestes, par exemple : arthroses déformantes; polyarthrite chronique évolutive primaire et secondaire; rhumatisme avec manifestations cliniques graves; etc. »

Annexe I, 3, CONVENTION DE GENEVE RELATIVE AU TRAITEMENT DES PRISONNIERS DE GUERRE.

POPULATION CIVILE [Civilian population]

– « 2. La population civile comprend toutes les personnes civiles.

---

[u] « Article 9- Cultural policies as catalysts of creativity »

3. La présence au sein de la population civile de personnes isolées ne répondant pas à la définition de personne civile ne prive pas cette population de sa qualité. »

Art. 50, PROTOCOLE ADDITIONNEL AUX CONVENTIONS DE GENÈVE DU 12 AOÛT 1949 RELATIF À LA PROTECTION DES VICTIMES DES CONFLITS ARMÉS INTERNATIONAUX (PROTOCOLE I).

POPULATIONS DESTABILISEES PAR LES CONFLITS ARMES, LES SITUATIONS D'URGENCE HUMANITAIRE ET LES CATASTROPHES NATURELLES [Populations destabilized by armed conflict, humanitarian emergencies and natural disasters]

– « 75. [...] les populations déstabilisées par les conflits armés, les situations d'urgence humanitaire et les catastrophes naturelles, en particulier les réfugiés et les personnes déplacées, et notamment les femmes et les enfants, sont plus exposées au risque d'infection à VIH; et, s'il y a lieu, intégrer les composantes VIH/sida dans les programmes d'assistance internationaux; »

DÉCLARATION D'ENGAGEMENT SUR LE VIH/SIDA.

PORNOGRAPHIE METTANT EN SCENE DES ENFANTS [Child pornography]

– « *Convaincus* que l'élimination de la vente d'enfants, de la prostitution des enfants et de la pornographie mettant en scène des enfants sera facilitée par l'adoption d'une approche globale tenant compte des facteurs qui contribuent à ces phénomènes, notamment le sous-développement, la pauvreté, les disparités économiques, l'inéquité des structures socioéconomiques, les dysfonctionnement familiaux, le manque d'éducation, l'exode rural, la discrimination fondée sur le sexe, le comportement sexuel irresponsable des adultes, les pratiques traditionnelles préjudiciables, les conflits armées et la traite des enfants, »

Pp. 7, PROTOCOLE FACULTATIF À LA CONVENTION RELATIVE AUX DROITS DE L'ENFANT, CONCERNANT LA VENTE D'ENFANTS, LA PROSTITUTION DES ENFANTS ET LA PORNOGRAPHIE METTANT EN SCÈNE DES ENFANTS.

– « Aux fins du présent Protocole :

[...]

c) On entend par pornographie mettant en scène des enfants toute représentation, par quelques moyen que ce soit, d'un enfant s'adonnant à des activités sexuelles explicites, réelles ou simulées, out toute représentation des organes sexuels d'un enfant, à des enfant, à des fins principalement sexuelles. »

Art. 2, PROTOCOLE FACULTATIF À LA CONVENTION RELATIVE AUX DROITS DE L'ENFANT, CONCERNANT LA VENTE D'ENFANTS, LA PROSTITUTION DES ENFANTS ET LA PORNOGRAPHIE METTANT EN SCÈNE DES ENFANTS.

POSSESSION D'EFFETS PERSONNELS [Possession of personal effects]

– « 35. La possession d'effets personnels est un élément fondamental du droit à la vie privée et est essentielle au bien- être psychologique du mineur. [...] »

RÈGLES DES NATIONS UNIES POUR LA PROTECTION DES MINEURS PRIVÉS DE LIBERTÉ.

POUVOIRS INTERMEDIAIRES ET POUVOIRS LOCAUX [Provincial and local governments]

– « *g*) Une étroite coopération interdisciplinaire entre pouvoir central, pouvoirs intermédiaires (province, Etat, département) et pouvoirs locaux, [...] »[v]

9, PRINCIPES DIRECTEURS DES NATIONS UNIES POUR LA PRÉVENTION DE LA DÉLINQUANCE JUVÉNILE (PRINCIPES DIRECTEURS DE RIYAD).

PRATICIEN DE SANTE MENTALE [Mental health practitioner]

– « Dans les présents Principes :

[...]

> L'expression "praticien de santé mentale" désigne un médecin, un psychologue clinicien, un infirmier (une infirmière), un(e) travailleur(euse) social(e) ou toute autre personne dûment formée et qualifiée, ayant des compétences particulières en matière de soins de santé mentale; »

Al. 5, DEFINITIONS, PRINCIPES POUR LA PROTECTION DES PERSONNES ATTEINTES DE MALADIE MENTALE ET POUR L'AMÉLIORATION DES SOINS DE SANTÉ MENTALE.

PRATIQUES DE L'APARTHEID [Practices of apartheid]

– « *c*) les pratiques de l'apartheid et les autres pratiques inhumaines et dégradantes, fondées sur la discrimination raciale, qui donnent lieu à des outrages à la dignité personnelle; »

---

[v] " (*g*) Close interdisciplinary co-operation between national, State, provincial and local governments,[...]"

Art. 85, § 4., PROTOCOLE ADDITIONNEL AUX CONVENTIONS DE GENÈVE DU 12 AOÛT 1949 RELATIF À LA PROTECTION DES VICTIMES DES CONFLITS ARMÉS INTERNATIONAUX (PROTOCOLE I).

PREJUGE RACIAL [Racial prejudice]

– « 3. Le préjugé racial, historiquement lié aux inégalités de pouvoir, se renforçant en raison des différences économiques et sociales entre les individus et les groupes humains, et visant encore aujourd'hui à justifier de telles inégalités, est totalement injustifié. »

Art. 2, DÉCLARATION SUR LA RACE ET LES PRÉJUGÉS RACIAUX.

PRESUMEE INNOCENTE [Presumed innocent]

– « 1. Toute personne accusée d'un acte délictueux est présumée innocente jusqu'à ce que sa culpabilité ait été légalement établie au cours d'un procés public où toutes les garanties nécessaires à sa défense lui auront été commis. »

ART. 11, DÉCLARATION UNIVERSELLE DES DROITS DE L'HOMME.

– « 2. Toute personne accusée d'une infraction pénale est présumée innocente jusqu'à ce que sa culpabilité ait été légalement établie. »

Art. 14, PACTE INTERNATIONAL RELATIF AUX DROITS CIVILS ET POLITIQUES.

PREVENTION [Prevention]

– « 22. On entend par « prévention » toute action visant à empêcher les déficients physiques, mentales ou sensorielles de survenir (prévention primaire) ou à défaut, d'empêcher que ces déficiences n'entraînent une limitation fonctionnelle permanente ou l'incapacité (prévention secondaire). La prévention peut prendre diverses formes : soins de santé primaires, soins prénatals et postnatals efficaces, éducation en matière de nutrition, campagnes de vaccination contre les maladies transmissibles, mesures de lutte contre les maladies endémiques, règlements et programmes de sûreté ayant pour objet d'éviter les accidents dans différents milieux, notamment adaptation du cadre de travail en vue d'empêcher les incapacités et les maladies professionnelles, prévention des incapacités résultant de la pollution de l'environnement ou de conflit armés. »

INTRODUCTION, RÈGLE POUR L'ÉGALISATION DES CHANCES DES PERSONNES HANDICAPÉES.

PREVENU [Untried prisoners]

– « 84. 1) Tout individu arrêté ou incarcéré en raison d'une infraction à la loi pénale et qui se trouve détenu soit dans des locaux de police soit dans une maison d'arrêt, mais n'a pas encore été jugé, est qualifié de "prévenu" dans les dispositions qui suivent. »

ENSEMBLES DE RÈGLES MINIMA POUR LE TRAITEMENT DES DÉTENUS.

PRINCIPE DE L'EGALITE DE DROITS [Principle of equal rights]

– « 25. Le principe de l'égalité de droits signifie que les besoins de tous on une importance égale, que c'est en fonction de ces besoins que les sociétés doivent être planifiées et que toutes les ressources doivent être employées de façon à garantir à chacun des possibilités de participation dans l'égalité. »

INTRODUCTION, RÈGLES POUR L'ÉGALISATION DES CHANCES DES PERSONNES HANDICAPÉES.

PRINCIPE DE L'EGALITE EN DIGNITE ET EN DROITS [Principle of equality in dignity and rights]

– « 1. Le principe de l'égalité en dignité et en droits de tous les êtres humains et de tous les peuples, quelles que soient leur race, leur couleur et leur origine, est un principe généralement accepté et reconnu en droit international. En conséquence, toute forme de discrimination raciale pratiquée par l'Etat constitue une violation du droit international qui entraîne sa responsabilité internationale. »

Art. 9, DÉCLARATION SUR LA RACE ET LES PRÉJUGÉS RACIAUX.

PRINCIPE DE LA NON-DISCRIMINATION [Principle of the inadmissibility of discrimination]

– « *Notant* que la Déclaration universelle des droits de l'homme affirme le principe de la non-discrimination[w] et proclame que tous les êtres humains naissent libres et égaux en dignité et en droit, et que chacun peut se

---

[w] "*Noting* that the Universal Declaration of Human Rights affirms the principle of the inadmissibility of discrimination and proclaims that all human beings are born free and equal in dignity and rights and that everyone is entitled to all the rights and freedoms set forth therein, without distinction of any kind, including distinction based on sex,"

prévaloir de tous les droits et de toutes les libertés qui y sont énoncés, sans distinction aucune, notamment de sexe, »

Pp.2, CONVENTION SUR L'ÉLIMINATION DE TOUTES LES FORMES DE DISCRIMINATION À L'ÉGARD DES FEMMES.

PRINCIPE DE PROPORTIONNALITE [Principle of proportionality]

– « Le second objectif est le "principe de proportionnalité". Ce principe bien connu sert à modérer les sanctions punitives, généralement en les rapportant à la gravité du délit. Pour les délinquants juvéniles, il faut tenir compte non seulement de cette gravité mais aussi des circonstances personnelles. Celles-ci (position sociale, situation de famille, dommages causés par le délit ou autres facteurs influant sur les circonstances personnelles) doivent intervenir pour proportionner la décision (par exemple en tenant compte de l'effort du délinquant pour indemniser la victime ou de son désir de revenir à une vie saine et utile). »

5, al.2, *Commentaire*, ENSEMBLE DE RÈGLES MINIMA DES NATIONS UNIES CONCERNANT L'ADMINISTRATION DE LA JUSTICE POUR LES MINEURS (RÈGLES DE BEIJING).

PRISONNIERS DE GUERRE [Prisoners of war]

– « A. Sont prisonniers de guerre, au sens de la présente Convention, les personnes qui, appartenant à l'une des catégories suivantes, sont tombées au pouvoir de l'enemi :

1) les membres des forces armées d'une Partie au conflit, de même que les membres des milices et des corps de volontaires faisant partie de ces forces armées;

2) les membres des autres milices et les membres des autres corps de volontaires, y compris ceux des mouvements de résistance organisés, appartenant à une Partie au conflit et agissant en dehors ou à l'intérieur de leur propre territoire, même si ce territoire est occupé, pourvu que ces milices ou corps de volontaires, y compris ces mouvements de résistance organisés, remplissent les conditions suivantes :

a) d'avoir à leur tête une personne responsable pour ses subordonnés;

b) d'avoir un signe distinctif fixe et reconnaissable à distance;

c) de porter ouvertement les armes;

d) de se conformer, dans leurs opérations, aux lois et coutumes de la guerre;

3) les membres des forces armées régulières qui se réclament d'un gouvernement ou d'une autorité non reconnus par la Puissance détentrice;

4) les personnes qui suivent les forces armées sans en faire directement partie, telles que les membres civils d'équipages d'avions militaires, correspondants de guerre, fournisseurs, membres d'unités de travail ou de services chargés du bien-être des militaires, à condition qu'elles en aient reçu l'autorisation des forces armées qu'elles accompagnent, celles-ci étant tenues de leur délivrer à cet effet une carte d'identité semblable au modèle annexé;

5) les membres des équipages, y compris les commandants, pilotes et apprentis, de la marine marchande et les équipages de l'aviation civile des Parties au conflit qui ne bénéficient pas d'un traitement plus favorable en vertu d'autres dispositions du droit international;

6) la population d'un territoire non occupé qui, à l'approche de l'ennemi, prend spontanément les armes pour combattre les troupes d'invasion sans avoir eu le temps de se constituer en forces armées régulières, si elle porte ouvertement les armes et si elle respecte les lois et coutumes de la guerre.

B. Bénéficieront également du traitement réservé par la présente Convention aux prisonniers de guerre :

1) Les personnes appartenant ou ayant appartenu aux forces armées du pays occupé si, en raison de cette appartenance, la Puissance occupante, même si elle les a initialement libérées pendant que les hostilités se poursuivent en dehors du territoire qu'elle occupe, estime nécessaire de procéder à leur internement, notamment après une tentative de ces personnes non couronnée de succès pour rejoindre les forces armées auxquelles elles appartiennent et qui sont engagées dans le combat, ou lorsqu'elles n'obtempèrent pas à une sommation qui leur est faite aux fins d'internement;

2) les personnes appartenant à l'une des catégories énumérées au présent article que des Puissances neutres ou non belligérantes ont reçues sur leur territoire et qu'elles sont tenues d'interner en vertu du droit international, sous réserve de tout traitement plus favorable que ces Puissances

jugeraient bon de leur accorder et exception faite des dispositions des articles 8[12], 10[13], 15[14], 30, cinquième alinéa[15], 58 à 67 inclus[16], 92[17], 126[18] et,

---

[12] « La présente Convention sera appliquée avec le concours et sous le contrôle des Puissances protectrices chargées de sauvegarder les intérêts des Parties au conflit. A cet effet, les Puissances protectrices pourront, en dehors de leur personnel diplomatique ou consulaire, désigner des délégués parmi leurs propres ressortissants ou parmi les ressortissants d'autres Puissances neutres. Ces délégués devront être soumis à l'agrément de la Puissance auprès de laquelle ils exerceront leur mission.
Les Parties au conflit faciliteront, dans la plus large mesure possible, la tâche des représentants ou délégués des Puissances protectrices.
Les représentants ou délégués des Puissances protectrices ne devront en aucun cas dépasser les limites de leur mission, telle qu'elle ressort de la présente Convention; ils devront notamment tenir compte des nécessités impérieuses de sécurité de l'Etat auprès duquel ils exercent leurs fonctions. »

[13] « Les Hautes Parties contractantes pourront, en tout temps, s'entendre pour confier à un organisme présentant toutes garanties d'impartialité et d'efficacité les tâches dévolues par la présente Convention aux Puissances protectrices.
Si des prisonniers de guerre ne bénéficient pas ou ne bénéficient plus, quelle qu'en soit la raison, de l'activité d'une Puissance protectrice ou d'un organisme désigné conformément à l'alinéa premier, la Puissance détentrice devra demander soit à un Etat neutre, soit à un tel organisme, d'assumer les fonctions dévolues par la présente Convention aux Puissances protectrices désignées par les Parties au conflit.
Si une protection ne peut être ainsi assurée, la Puissance détentrice devra demander à un organisme humanitaire, tel que le Comité international de la Croix-Rouge, d'assumer les tâches humanitaires dévolues par la présente Convention aux Puissances protectrices ou devra accepter, sous réserve des dispositions du présent article, les offres de services émanant d'un tel organisme.
Toute Puissance neutre ou tout organisme invité par la Puissance intéressée ou s'offrant aux fins susmentionnées devra, dans son activité, rester conscient de sa responsabilité envers la Partie au conflit dont relèvent les personnes protégées par la présente Convention, et devra fournir des garanties suffisantes de capacité pour assumer les fonctions en question et les remplir avec impartialité.
Il ne pourra être dérogé aux dispositions qui précèdent par accord particulier entre des Puissances dont l'une se trouverait, même temporairement, vis-à-vis de l'autre Puissance ou de ses alliés, limitée dans sa liberté de négociation par suite des événements militaires, notamment en cas d'une occupation de la totalité ou d'une partie importante de son territoire.
Toutes les fois qu'il est fait mention dans la présente Convention de la Puissance protectrice, cette mention désigne également les organismes qui la remplacent au sens du présent article. »

[14] « La Puissance détentrice des prisonniers de guerre sera tenue de pourvoir gratuitement à leur entretien et de leur accorder gratuitement les soins médicaux que nécessite leur état de santé. »

[15] « Les frais de traitement, y compris ceux de tout appareil nécessaire au maintien des prisonniers de guerre en bon état de santé, notamment des prothèses, dentaires ou autres, et des lunettes, seront à la charge de la Puissance détentrice. »

[16] *Art. 58* : « Dès le début des hostilités et en attendant de s'être mise d'accord à ce sujet avec la Puissance protectrice, la Puissance détentrice pourra fixer la somme maximum en espèces ou

sous une forme analogue que les prisonniers de guerre pourront avoir sur eux. Tout excédent légitimement en leur possession, retiré ou retenu, sera, de même que tout dépôt d'argent effectué par eux, porté à leur compte et ne pourra être converti en une autre monnaie sans leur assentiment.
Quand les prisonniers de guerre seront autorisés à faire des achats ou à recevoir des services, contre paiements en espèces à l'extérieur du camp, ces paiements seront effectués par les prisonniers eux-mêmes ou par l'administration du camp, qui portera ces paiements au débit du compte des prisonniers intéressés. La Puissance détentrice édictera les dispositions nécessaires à ce sujet. »
Art. 59 : « Les sommes en monnaie de la Puissance détentrice retirées aux prisonniers de guerre, conformément à l'article 18, au moment où ils sont faits prisonniers, seront portées au crédit du compte de chacun d'eux, conformément aux dispositions de l'article 64 de la présente section.
Seront également portées au crédit de ce compte les sommes en monnaie de la Puissance détentrice qui proviennent de la conversion des sommes en d'autres monnaies, retirées aux prisonniers de guerre à ce même moment. »
Art. 60 : « La Puissance détentrice versera à tous les prisonniers de guerre une avance de solde mensuelle, dont le montant sera fixé par la conversion dans la monnaie de ladite Puissance des sommes suivantes :
Catégorie I : prisonniers de grade inférieur à sergent : huit francs suisses.
Catégorie II : sergents et autres sous-officiers ou prisonniers de grade équivalent : douze francs suisses.
Catégorie III : officiers jusqu'au grade de capitaine ou prisonniers de grade équivalent : cinquante francs suisses.
Catégorie IV : commandants ou majors, lieutenants-colonels, colonels ou prisonniers de grade équivalent : soixante francs suisses.
Catégorie V : officiers généraux ou prisonniers de grade équivalent : soixante-quinze francs suisses.
Toutefois, les Parties au conflit intéressées pourront modifier par accords spéciaux le montant des avances de solde dû aux prisonniers de guerre des différentes catégories énumérées ci-dessus.
En outre, si les montants prévus au premier alinéa ci-dessus étaient trop élevés comparés à la solde payée aux membres des forces armées de la Puissance détentrice ou si, pour toute autre raison, ils devaient causer un embarras sérieux à cette Puissance, celle-ci, en attendant la conclusion d'un accord spécial avec la Puissance dont dépendent les prisonniers de guerre en vue de modifier ces montants :
a) continuera de créditer les comptes des prisonniers de guerre des montants indiqués au premier alinéa;
b) pourra temporairement limiter à des sommes qui sont raisonnables les montants, prélevés sur les avances de solde, qu'elle mettra à la disposition des prisonniers de guerre pour leur usage; toutefois, pour les prisonniers de la catégorie I, ces sommes ne seront jamais inférieures à celles que verse la Puissance détentrice aux membres de ses propres forces armées.
Les raisons d'une telle limitation seront communiquées sans délai à la Puissance protectrice. »
Art. 61 : « La Puissance détentrice acceptera les envois d'argent que la Puissance dont dépendent les prisonniers de guerre leur fera parvenir à titre de supplément de solde, à condition que les montants soient les mêmes pour chaque prisonnier de la même catégorie, qu'ils soient versés à tous les prisonniers de cette catégorie dépendant de cette Puissance, et qu'ils soient portés, dès que possible, au crédit des comptes individuels des prisonniers,

conformément aux dispositions de l'article 64. Ces suppléments de solde ne dispenseront la Puissance détentrice d'aucune des obligations qui lui incombent aux termes de la présente Convention. »

Art. 62 : « Les prisonniers de guerre recevront, directement des autorités détentrices, une indemnité de travail équitable, dont le taux sera fixé par ces autorités, mais qui ne pourra jamais être inférieure à un quart de franc suisse par journée entière de travail. La Puissance détentrice fera connaître aux prisonniers ainsi qu'à la Puissance dont ils dépendent, par l'entremise de la Puissance protectrice, le taux des indemnités de travail journalières qu'elle aura fixé.

Une indemnité de travail sera également versée par les autorités détentrices aux prisonniers de guerre affectés d'une manière permanente à des fonctions ou à un travail artisanal en rapport avec l'administration, l'aménagement intérieur ou l'entretien des camps, ainsi qu'aux prisonniers requis d'exercer des fonctions spirituelles ou médicales au profit de leurs camarades.

L'indemnité de travail de l'homme de confiance, de ses auxiliaires et, éventuellement, de ses conseillers sera prélevée sur le fonds alimenté par les bénéfices de cantine; le taux en sera fixé par l'homme de confiance et approuvé par le commandant du camp. Si ce fonds n'existe pas, les autorités détentrices verseront à ces prisonniers une indemnité de travail équitable. »

Art. 63 : « Les prisonniers de guerre seront autorisés à recevoir les envois d'argent qui leur seront adressés individuellement ou collectivement.

Chaque prisonnier de guerre disposera du solde créditeur de son compte, tel qu'il est prévu à l'article suivant, dans les limites fixées par la Puissance détentrice, qui effectuera les paiements demandés. Sous réserve des restrictions financières ou monétaires qu'elle estime essentielles, les prisonniers de guerre seront autorisés à effectuer des paiements à l'étranger. Dans ce cas, la Puissance détentrice favorisera spécialement les paiements que les prisonniers adressent aux personnes qui sont à leur charge.

En tout état de cause, les prisonniers de guerre pourront, si la Puissance dont ils dépendent y consent, faire exécuter des paiements dans leur propre pays selon la procédure suivante : la Puissance détentrice fera parvenir à ladite Puissance, par l'entremise de la Puissance protectrice, un avis qui comprendra toutes indications utiles sur l'auteur et le bénéficiaire du paiement ainsi que le montant de la somme à payer, exprimé en monnaie de la Puissance détentrice; cet avis sera signé par le prisonnier intéressé et contresigné par le commandant du camp. La Puissance détentrice débitera le compte du prisonnier de ce montant; les sommes ainsi débitées seront portées par elle au crédit de la Puissance dont dépendent les prisonniers.

Pour appliquer les prescriptions qui précèdent, la Puissance détentrice pourra utilement consulter le règlement-type figurant dans l'annexe V de la présente Convention. »

Art. 64 : « La Puissance détentrice tiendra pour chaque prisonnier de guerre un compte qui contiendra au moins les indications suivantes :

1) les montants dus au prisonnier ou reçus par lui à titre d'avance de solde, d'indemnité de travail ou à tout autre titre; les sommes, en monnaie de la Puissance détentrice, retirées au prisonnier; les sommes retirées au prisonnier et converties, sur sa demande, en monnaie de ladite Puissance.

2) les sommes remises au prisonnier en espèces ou sous une forme analogue; les paiements faits pour son compte et à sa demande; les sommes transférées selon le troisième alinéa de l'article précédent. »

Art. 65 : « Toute écriture passée au compte d'un prisonnier de guerre sera contresignée ou paraphée par lui ou par l'homme de confiance agissant en son nom.

Les prisonniers de guerre recevront en tout temps des facilités raisonnables pour consulter leur compte et en recevoir une copie; le compte pourra être vérifié également par les représentants de la Puissance protectrice lors des visites de camp.
Lors du transfert des prisonniers de guerre d'un camp dans un autre, leur compte personnel les suivra. En cas de transfert d'une Puissance détentrice à une autre, les sommes leur appartenant qui ne sont pas dans la monnaie de la Puissance détentrice les suivront; une attestation leur sera délivrée pour toutes les autres sommes qui resteraient au crédit de leur compte.
Les Parties au conflit intéressées pourront s'entendre pour se communiquer, par l'entremise de la Puissance protectrice et à des intervalles déterminés, les relevés des comptes des prisonniers de guerre. »
Art. 66: « Lorsque la captivité du prisonnier de guerre prendra fin, par libération ou rapatriement, la Puissance détentrice lui délivrera une déclaration signée par un officier compétent et attestant le solde créditeur qui lui est dû à la fin de sa captivité. D'autre part, la Puissance détentrice fera parvenir à la Puissance dont dépendent les prisonniers de guerre, par l'entremise de la Puissance protectrice, des listes donnant toutes les indications sur les prisonniers dont la captivité a pris fin par rapatriement, libération, évasion, décès ou toute autre manière, et attestant notamment les soldes créditeurs de leurs comptes. Chaque feuille de ces listes sera authentifiée par un représentant autorisé de la Puissance détentrice.
Les Puissances intéressées pourront, par accord spécial, modifier tout ou partie des dispositions prévues ci-dessus.
La Puissance dont le prisonnier de guerre dépend sera responsable du soin de régler avec lui le solde créditeur lui restant dû par la Puissance détentrice à la fin de sa captivité. »
Art. 67: « Les avances de solde versées aux prisonniers de guerre conformément à l'article 60 seront considérées comme faites au nom de la Puissance dont ils dépendent; ces avances de solde, ainsi que tous les paiements exécutés par ladite Puissance en vertu de l'article 63, troisième alinéa, et de l'article 68, feront l'objet d'arrangements entre les Puissances intéressées, à la fin des hostilités. »

[17] « Un prisonnier de guerre qui tente de s'évader et qui est repris avant d'avoir réussi son évasion, au sens de l'article 91, ne sera passible pour cet acte, même en cas de récidive, que d'une peine disciplinaire.
Le prisonnier repris sera remis aussitôt que possible aux autorités militaires compétentes.
En dérogation à l'article 88, quatrième alinéa, les prisonniers de guerre punis à la suite d'une évasion non réussie pourront être soumis à un régime de surveillance spécial, à condition toutefois que ce régime n'affecte pas leur état de santé, qu'il soit subi dans un camp de prisonniers de guerre et qu'il ne comporte la suppression d'aucune des garanties qui leur sont accordées par la présente Convention. »

[18] « Les représentants ou les délégués des Puissances protectrices seront autorisés à se rendre dans tous les lieux où se trouvent des prisonniers de guerre, notamment dans les lieux d'internement, de détention et de travail; ils auront accès à tous les locaux utilisés par les prisonniers. Ils seront également autorisés à se rendre dans les lieux de départ, de passage ou d'arrivée des prisonniers transférés. Ils pourront s'entretenir sans témoin avec les prisonniers, et en particulier avec leur homme de confiance, par l'entremise d'un interprète si cela est nécessaire.
Toute liberté sera laissée aux représentants et aux délégués des Puissances protectrices quant au choix des endroits qu'ils désirent visiter; la durée et la fréquence de ces visites ne seront pas

lorsque des relations diplomatiques existent entre les Parties au conflit et la Puissance neutre ou non belligérante intéressée, des dispositions qui concernent la Puissance protectrice. Lorsque de telles relations diplomatiques existent, les Parties au conflit dont dépendent ces personnes seront autorisées à exercer à l'égard de celles-ci les fonctions dévolues aux Puissances protectrices par la présente Convention sans préjudice de celles que ces Parties exercent normalement en vertu des usages et des traités diplomatiques et consulaires.

C. Le présent article réserve le statut du personnel médical et religieux tel qu'il est prévu à l'article 33[19] de la présente Convention. »

---

limitées. Elles ne sauraient être interdites qu'en raison d'impérieuses nécessités militaires et seulement à titre exceptionnel et temporaire.
La Puissance détentrice et la Puissance dont dépendent les prisonniers de guerre à visiter pourront s'entendre, le cas échéant, pour que des compatriotes de ces prisonniers soient admis à participer aux visites.
Les délégués du Comité international de la Croix-Rouge bénéficieront des mêmes prérogatives. La désignation de ces délégués sera soumise à l'agrément de la Puissance au pouvoir de laquelle se trouvent les prisonniers de guerre à visiter. »

[19] « Les membres du personnel sanitaire et religieux retenus au pouvoir de la Puissance détentrice en vue d'assister les prisonniers de guerre, ne seront pas considérés comme prisonniers de guerre. Toutefois, ils bénéficieront au moins de tous les avantages et de la protection de la présente Convention, ainsi que de toutes les facilités nécessaires pour leur permettre d'apporter leurs soins médicaux et leurs secours religieux aux prisonniers de guerre.
Ils continueront à exercer, dans le cadre des lois et règlements militaires de la Puissance détentrice, sous l'autorité de ses services compétents et en accord avec leur conscience professionnelle, leurs fonctions médicales ou spirituelles au profit des prisonniers de guerre appartenant de préférence aux forces armées dont ils relèvent. Ils jouiront, en outre, pour l'exercice de leur mission médicale ou spirituelle, des facilités suivantes :
a) Ils seront autorisés à visiter périodiquement les prisonniers de guerre se trouvant dans des détachements de travail ou dans des hôpitaux situés à l'extérieur du camp. L'autorité détentrice mettra à leur disposition, à cet effet, les moyens de transport nécessaires.
b) Dans chaque camp, le médecin militaire le plus ancien dans le grade le plus élevé sera responsable auprès des autorités militaires du camp pour tout ce qui concerne les activités du personnel sanitaire retenu. A cet effet, les Parties au conflit s'entendront dès le début des hostilités au sujet de la correspondance des grades de leur personnel sanitaire, y compris celui des sociétés visées à l'article 26 de la Convention de Genève pour l'amélioration du sort des blessés et des malades dans les forces armées en campagne du 12 août 1949. Pour toutes les questions relevant de leur mission, ce médecin, ainsi d'ailleurs que les aumôniers, auront accès direct auprès des autorités compétentes du camp. Celles-ci leur donneront toutes les facilités nécessaires pour la correspondance ayant trait à ces questions.
c) Bien qu'il soit soumis à la discipline intérieure du camp dans lequel il se trouve, le personnel retenu ne pourra être astreint à aucun travail étranger à sa mission médicale ou religieuse.

Art. 4, CONVENTION DE GENÈVE RELATIVE AU TRAITEMENT DES PRISONNIERS DE GUERRE.

PRIVATION DE LIBERTE [Deprivation of liberty]

– « 11. Aux fins des présentes Règles, les définitions ci-après sont applicables: [...]

> *b*) Par privation de liberté, on entend toute forme de détention, d'emprisonnement ou le placement d'une personne dans un établissement public ou privé dont elle n'est pas autorisée à sortir à son gré, ordonnés par une autorité judiciaire, administrative ou autre. »

RÈGLES DES NATIONS UNIES POUR LA PROTECTION DES MINEURS PRIVÉS DE LIBERTÉ.

PROCES « JUSTE ET EQUITABLE » [Due process of law]

– « La procédure suivie pour juger les jeunes délinquants doit en tout état de cause se conformer aux normes minima, assurées presque universellement à tout accusé par le respect des formes légales. Dans ces formes, un procès "juste et équitable" comprend des garanties fondamentales telles que la présomption d'innocence, la comparution et la déposition de témoins, les moyens ordinaires de défense, le droit de garder le silence, le droit de répliquer en dernier à l'audience, le droit de faire appel, etc. (Voir également l'article 7.1.)[20][x]»

14, *Commentaire*, ENSEMBLE DE RÈGLES MINIMA DES NATIONS UNIES CONCERNANT L'ADMINISTRATION DE LA JUSTICE POUR LES MINEURS (RÈGLES DE BEIJING).

Au cours des hostilités, les Parties au conflit s'entendront au sujet d'une relève éventuelle du personnel retenu et en fixeront les modalités.
Aucune des dispositions qui précèdent ne dispense la Puissance détentrice des obligations qui lui incombent à l'égard des prisonniers de guerre dans les domaines sanitaire et spirituel. »

[20] « 7.1 Les garanties fondamentales de la procédure telles que la présomption d'innocence, le droit à être informé des charges, le droit de garder le silence, le droit à l'assistance d'un conseil, le droit à la présence d'un parent ou tuteur, le droit d'interroger et de confronter les témoins et le droit à un double degré de juridiction sont assurées à tous les stades de la procédure. »

[x] " The procedure for dealing with juvenile offenders shall in any case follow the minimum standards that are applied almost universally for any criminal defendant under the procedure known as "due process of law". In accordance with due process, a "fair and just trial" includes such basic safeguards as the presumption of innocence, the presentation and examination of witnesses, the common legal defences, the right to remain silent, the right to have the last word in a hearing, the right to appeal, etc. (See also rule 7.1.)"

PROCESSUS DE MIGRATION DES TRAVAILLEURS MIGRANTS ET DES MEMBRES DE LEUR FAMILLE [Migration process of migrant workers and members of their families]

– « 2. La présente Convention s'applique à tout le processus de migration des travailleurs migrants et des membres de leur famille, qui comprend les préparatifs de la migration, le départ, le transit et toute la durée du séjour, l'activité rémunérée dans l'Etat d'emploi, ainsi que le retour dans l'Etat d'origine ou dans l'Etat de résidence habituelle. »

Art. 1, CONVENTION INTERNATIONALE SUR LA PROTECTION DES DROITS DE TOUS LES TRAVAILLEURS MIGRANTS ET DES MEMBRES DE LEUR FAMILLE.

PROCESSUS DE MONDIALISATION [Process of globalization]

– « *Considérant* que le processus de mondialisation, facilité par l'évolution rapide des nouvelles technologies de l'information et de la communication, bien que constituant un défi pour la diversité culturelle, crée les conditions d'un dialogue renouvelé entre les cultures et les civilisations, »

Pp. 9, DÉCLARATION UNIVERSELLE SUR LA DIVERSITÉ CULTURELLE.

PROFESSION [Occupation]

– « 3. Aux fins de la présente Convention, les mots "emploi" et "profession" recouvrent l'accès à la formation professionnelle, l'accès à l'emploi et aux différentes professions, ainsi que les conditions d'emploi. »

Art. 1, CONVENTION CONCERNANT LA DISCRIMINATION (EMPLOI ET PROFESSION) (N° 111).

PROGRES SOCIAL [Social progress]

– « *Convaincue* que la paix et la sécurité internationales, d'une part, et le progrès social et le développement économique, d'autre part, sont étroitement interdépendants et s'influencent mutuellement, »

Pp. 6, DÉCLARATION SUR LE PROGRÈS ET LE DÉVELOPPEMENT DANS LE DOMAINE SOCIALE.

– « L'augmentation rapide du revenu national et des richesses et leur répartition équitable entre tous les membres de la société sont à la base de tout progrès social et devraient par conséquent être au premier plan des préoccupations de tous les Etats et de tous les gouvernements. »

Art. 7, Al.1 , DÉCLARATION SUR LE PROGRÈS ET LE DÉVELOPPEMENT DANS LE DOMAINE SOCIALE.

PROMOTION ET PROTECTION DE TOUS LES DROITS DE L'HOMME ET DE TOUTES LES LIBERTES FONDAMENTALES [Promotion and protection of all Human rights and fundamental freedoms]

– « 4. La promotion et la protection de tous les droits de l'homme et de toutes les libertés fondamentales doivent être considérées comme un objectif prioritaire de l'Organisation des Nations Unies conformément à ses buts et principes, eu égard en particulier à l'objectif de coopération internationale. Eu égard à ces buts et principes, la promotion et la protection de tous les droits de l'homme est une préoccupation légitime de la communauté internationale. Les organes et les institutions spécialisées s'occupant des droits de l'homme doivent donc renforcer encore la coordination de leurs activités en se fondant sur l'application uniforme et objective des instruments internationaux en la matière. »

I, DÉCLARATION ET PROGRAMME D'ACTION DE VIENNE.

PROMOTION ET PROTECTION DES DROITS DES PERSONNES APPARTENANT A DES MINORITES NATIONALES OU ETHNIQUES, RELIGIEUSES ET LINGUISTIQUES [Promotion and protection of the rights of persons belonging to national or ethnic, religious and linguistic minorities]

– « *Considérant* que la promotion et la protection des droits des personnes appartenant à des minorités nationales ou ethniques, religieuses et linguistiques contribuent à la stabilité politique et sociale des Etats dans lesquels elles vivent, »

Pp. 5, DÉCLARATION DES DROITS DES PERSONNES APPARTENANT À DES MINORITÉS NATIONALES OU ETHNIQUES, RELIGIEUSES ET LINGUISTIQUES.

PROSTITUTION [Prostitution]

– « *Considérant* que la prostitution et le mal qui l'accompagne, à savoir la traite des êtres humains en vue de la prostitution, sont incompatibles avec la dignité et la valeur de la personne humaine et mettent en danger le bien-être de l'individu, de la famille et de la communauté, »

Pp. 1, CONVENTION POUR LA RÉPRESSION DE LA TRAITE DES ÊTRES HUMAINS ET DE L'EXPLOITATION DE LA PROSTITUTION D'AUTRUI.

PROSTITUTION DES ENFANTS [Child prostitution]

– « *Convaincus* que l'élimination de la vente d'enfants, de la prostitution des enfants et de la pornographie mettant en scène des enfants sera facilitée par l'adoption d'une approche globale tenant compte des facteurs qui contribuent à ces phénomènes, notamment le sous-développement, la pauvreté, les disparités économiques, l'inéquité des structures socioéconomiques, les dysfonctionnement familiaux, le manque d'éducation, l'exode rural, la discrimination fondée sur le sexe, le comportement sexuel irresponsable des adultes, les pratiques traditionnelles préjudiciables, les conflits armées et la traite des enfants, »

Pp. 7, PROTOCOLE FACULTATIF À LA CONVENTION RELATIVE AUX DROITS DE L'ENFANT, CONCERNANT LA VENTE D'ENFANTS, LA PROSTITUTION DES ENFANTS ET LA PORNOGRAPHIE METTANT EN SCÈNE DES ENFANTS.

– « Aux fins du présent Protocole :
[...]

On entend par prostitution des enfants le fait d'utiliser un enfant aux fins d'activités sexuelles contre rémunération ou toute autre forme d'avantage ; »

Art. 2, PROTOCOLE FACULTATIF À LA CONVENTION RELATIVE AUX DROITS DE L'ENFANT, CONCERNANT LA VENTE D'ENFANTS, LA PROSTITUTION DES ENFANTS ET LA PORNOGRAPHIE METTANT EN SCÈNE DES ENFANTS.

PROSTITUTION FORCEE [Enforced prostitution]

– « *g*) Viol, esclavage sexuel, prostitution forcée, grossesse forcée, stérilisation forcée ou toute autre forme de violence sexuelle de gravité comparable; »

Art. 7, STATUT DE ROME DE LA COUR PÉNALE INTERNATIONALE.

– « les atteintes à la dignité de la personne, notamment les traitements humiliants et dégradants, la prostitution forcée et toute forme d'attentat à la pudeur; »

Art. 75, *b*), PROTOCOLE ADDITIONNEL AUX CONVENTIONS DE GENÈVE DU 12 AOÛT 1949 RELATIF À LA PROTECTION DES VICTIMES DES CONFLITS ARMÉS INTERNATIONAUX (PROTOCOLE I).

PROTECTION CIVILE [Civil defence]

– « Aux fins du présent Protocole :

a) l'expression "protection civile" s'entend de l'accomplissement de toutes les tâches humanitaires, ou de plusieurs d'entre elles, mentionnées ci-après, destinées à protéger la population civile contre les dangers des hostilités ou des catastrophes et à l'aider à surmonter leurs effets immédiats ainsi qu'à assurer les conditions nécessaires à sa survie. Ces tâches sont les suivantes :

i) service de l'alerte;

ii) évacuation;

iii) mise à disposition et organisation d'abris;

iv) mise en oeuvre des mesures d'obscurcissement;

v) sauvetage;

vi) services sanitaires y compris premiers secours et assistance religieuse;

vii) lutte contre le feu;

viii) repérage et signalisation des zones dangereuses;

ix) décontamination et autres mesures de protection analogues;

x) hébergement et approvisionnements d'urgence;

xi) aide en cas d'urgence pour le rétablissement et le maintien de l'ordre dans les zones sinistrées;

xii) rétablissement d'urgence des services d'utilité publique indispensables;

xiii) services funéraires d'urgence;

xiv) aide à la sauvegarde des biens essentiels à la survie;

xv) activités complémentaires nécessaires à l'accomplissement de l'une quelconque des tâches mentionnées ci-dessus, comprenant la planification et l'organisation mais ne s'y limitant pas; »

Art. 61, Protocole additionnel aux Conventions de Genève du 12 août 1949 relatif à la protection des victimes des conflits armés internationaux (Protocole I).

PROTECTION CONSTANTE ET LA REALISATION DES DROITS DES PERSONNES APPARTENANT A DES MINORITES NATIONALES OU ETHNIQUES, RELIGIEUSES ET LINGUISTIQUES (LA) [Constant promotion and realization of

the rights of persons belonging to national or ethnic, religious and linguistic minorities]

– « *Soulignant* que la promotion constante et la réalisation des droits des personnes appartenant à des minorités nationales ou ethniques, religieuses et linguistiques, faisant partie intégrante de l'évolution de la société dans son ensemble et s'inscrivant dans un cadre démocratique fondé sur la légalité, contribueraient au renforcement de l'amitié et de la coopération entre les peuples et les Etats, »

Pp. 6, DÉCLARATION DES DROITS DES PERSONNES APPARTENANT À MINORITÉS NATIONALES OU ETHNIQUES, RELIGIEUSES ET LINGUISTIQUES.

PUISSANCE PROTECTRICE [Protecting power]

– « *c*) l'expression "Puissance protectrice" s'entend d'un Etat neutre ou d'un autre Etat non Partie au conflit qui, désigné par une Partie au conflit et accepté par la Partie adverse, est disposé à exercer les fonctions assignées à la Puissance protectrice aux termes des Conventions et du présent Protocole; »

Art. 2, PROTOCOLE ADDITIONNEL AUX CONVENTIONS DE GENÈVE DU 12 AOÛT 1949 RELATIF À LA PROTECTION DES VICTIMES DES CONFLITS ARMÉS INTERNATIONAUX (PROTOCOLE I).

PYELITE CHRONIQUE OU CYSTITE CHRONIQUE [Chronic pyelitis or chronic cystisis]

– « *f*) Les affections chroniques graves des organes génito-urinaires, par exemple : maladies chroniques du rein avec troubles consécutifs; néphrectomie pour un rein tuberculeux; pyélite chronique ou cystite chronique; hydro ou pyonéphrose; affections gynécologiques chroniques graves; grossesses et affections obstétricales, lorsque l'hospitalisation en pays neutre est impossible; etc. »

Annexe I, 3, CONVENTION DE GENÈVE RELATIVE AU TRAITEMENT DES PRISONNIERS DE GUERRE.

RACISME [Racism]

– « *Constatant* avec la préoccupation la plus vive que le racisme, la discrimination raciale, le colonialisme et l'apartheid continuent à sévir dans le monde sous ses formes toujours renouvelées, tant par le maintien de dispositions législatives et de pratiques de gouvernements et d'administration contraires aux principes des droits de l'homme, que la permanence de structures marquées par l'injuste et le mépris de la personne humaine et engendrant l'exclusion, l'humiliation et l'exploitation, ou l'assimilation forcée, des membres de groupes défavorisés, »

Pp. 12, DÉCLARATION SUR LA RACE ET LES PRÉJUGÉES RACIAUX.

– « 2. Le racisme englobe les idéologies racistes, les attitudes fondées sur les préjugés raciaux, les comportements discriminatoires, les dispositions structurelles et les pratiques institutionnalisées qui provoquent l'inégalité raciale, ainsi que l'idée fallacieuse que les relations discriminatoires entre groupes sont moralement et scientifiquement justifiables; il se manifeste par des dispositions législatives ou réglementaires et par des pratiques discriminatoires, ainsi que par des croyances et des actes antisociaux; il entrave le développement de ses victimes, pervertit ceux qui le mettent en pratique, divise les nations au sein d'elles-mêmes, constitue un obstacle à la coopération internationale, et crée des tensions politiques entre les peuples; il est contraire aux principes fondamentaux du droit international et, par conséquent, il trouble gravement la paix et la sécurité internationales. »

Art. 2, DÉCLARATION SUR LA RACE ET LES PRÉJUGÉES RACIAUX.

RACISME (ELIMINATION DE TOUTES LES FORMES DE) [Racism (eradication of all forms)]

– « *Soulignant* que l'élimination de l'apartheid, de toutes les formes de racisme, de discrimination raciale, de colonialisme, de néocolonialisme, d'agression, d'occupation et domination étrangères et d'ingérence dans les affaires intérieures des Etats est indispensable à la pleine jouissance par l'homme et la femme de leurs droits, »

Pp. 10, CONVENTION SUR L'ÉLIMINATION DE TOUTES LES FORMES DE DISCRIMINATION À L'ÉGARD DES FEMMES.

REACTIONS DE LA SOCIETE ET DE LA JUSTICE A LA CRIMINALITE ET A LA DELINQUANCE JUVENILES [Societal and justice responses to juvenile crime and delinquency]

– « [...] Etant donné les modifications rapides et souvent radicales des styles de vie des jeunes et des formes et dimensions de la criminalité juvénile, les réactions de la société et de la justice à la criminalité et à la délinquance juvéniles sont souvent réprimées et inadaptées. »

30, *Commentaire*, ENSEMBLE DE RÈGLES MINIMA DES NATIONS UNIES CONCERNANT L'ADMINISTRATION DE LA JUSTICE POUR LES MINEURS (RÈGLES DE BEIJING).

READAPTATION [Rehabilitation]

– « 23. La « réadaptation » vise à permettre aux handicapés d'atteindre et de préserver un niveau fonctionnel optimal du point de vue physique, sensoriel, intellectuel, psychique ou social et à les doter ainsi des moyens d'acquérir une plus grande indépendance. Elle peut consister à recréer ou à rétablir des fonctions ou à compense la perte ou l'absence de fonctions ou insuffisance fonctionnelle. Le processus de réadaption ne commence pas forcément par des soins médicaux. Il comprend des mesures et des activités très diverses, qui peuvent aller de la réadaptation géénrale à des mesures plus spécialisées, comme la réadaptation professionnelle. »

INTRODUCTION, RÈGLE POUR L'ÉGALISATION DES CHANCES DES PERSONNES HANDICAPÉES.

REALISATION UNIVERSELLE DES DROITS DES PERSONNES ET DES LIBERTES FONDAMENTALES [Realization of human rights and fundamental freedoms for all]

– « La réalisation universelle des droits de la personne et des libertés fondamentales est indispensable si l'on veut réduire la vulnérabilité face au VIH/sida »

DÉCLARATION D'ENGAGEMENT SUR LE VIH/SIDA.

REALISATIONS DE LA SCIENCE ET DE LA TECHNIQUE [Scientific and technological achievements]

– « *Constatant avec inquiétude* que les réalisations de la science et de la technique peuvent être utilisées pour accélérer la course aux armements, réprimer les mouvements de libération nationale et priver les individus et les peuples de leurs droits de l'homme et libertés fondamentales, »

Pp. 3, DÉCLARATION SUR L'UTILISATION DU PROGRÈS DE LA SCIENCE ET DE LA TECHNIQUE DANS L'INTÉRÊT DE LA PAIX ET AU PROFIT DE L'HUMANITÉ.

– « *Constatant également avec inquiétude* que les réalisations de la science et de la technique peuvent présenter des dangers pour les droits civils et politiques de l'individu ou du groupe ainsi que pour la dignité humaine, »

Pp. 4, DÉCLARATION SUR L'UTILISATION DU PROGRÈS DE LA SCIENCE ET DE LA TECHNIQUE DANS L'INTÉRÊT DE LA PAIX ET AU PROFIT DE L'HUMANITÉ.

REALISATIONS DES DIFFERENTS PEUPLES (LES DIFFERENCES ENTRE LES) [Achievements of the different peoples (differences between)]

– « 5. Les différences entre les réalisations des différents peuples s'expliquent entièrement par des facteurs géographiques, historiques, politiques, économiques, sociaux et culturels. Ces différences ne peuvent en aucun cas servir de prétexte à un quelconque classement hiérarchisé des nations et des peuples. »

Art.1, DECLARATION SUR LA RACE ET LES PREJUGES RACIAUX.

RECHERCHES SUR LE GENOME HUMAIN ET LEURS APPLICATIONS [Research on the human genome and the resulting applications]

- « *Reconnaissant* que les recherches sur le génome humain et leurs applications ouvrent d'immenses perspectives d'amélioration de la santé des individus et de l'humanité tout entière, mais soulignant qu'elles doivent en même temps respecter pleinement la dignité, la liberté et les droits de l'homme, ainsi que l'interdiction de toute forme de discrimination fondée sur les caractéristiques génétiques, »

Pp. 6, DÉCLARATION UNIVERSELLE SUR LE GÉNOME HUMAIN ET LES DROITS DE L'HOMME.

REDUCTION EN ESCLAVAGE [Enslavement]

– « 2. Aux fins du paragraphe 1[21]:
[…]

---

[21] « 1. Aux fins du présent Statut, on entend par crime contre l'humanité l'un quelconque des actes ci-après lorsqu'il est commis dans le cadre d'une attaque généralisée ou systématique lancée contre toute population civile et en connaissance de cette attaque:
a) Meurtre;
b) Extermination;
c) Réduction en esclavage;
d) Déportation ou transfert forcé de population;
e) Emprisonnement ou autre forme de privation grave de liberté physique en violation des dispositions fondamentales du droit international;
f) Torture;
g) Viol, esclavage sexuel, prostitution forcée, grossesse forcée, stérilisation forcée ou toute autre forme de violence sexuelle de gravité comparable;
h) Persécution de tout groupe ou de toute collectivité identifiable pour des motifs d'ordre politique, racial, national, ethnique, culturel, religieux ou sexiste au sens du paragraphe 3, ou en fonction d'autres critères universellement reconnus comme inadmissibles en droit international,

c) Par «réduction en esclavage», on entend le fait d'exercer sur une personne l'un quelconque ou l'ensemble des pouvoirs liés au droit de propriété, y compris dans le cadre de la traite des être humains, en particulier des femmes et des enfants; »

Art. 7, STATUT DE ROME DE LA COUR PÉNALE INTERNATIONALE.

REFUGIE [Refugee]

– « A. Aux fins de la présente Convention, le terme "réfugié" s'appliquera à toute personne :

1) Qui a été considérée comme réfugiée en application des Arrangements du 12 mai 1926 et du 30 juin 1928, ou en application des Conventions du 28 octobre 1933 et du 10 février 1938 et du Protocole du 14 septembre 1939 ou encore en application de la Constitution de l'Organisation internationale pour les réfugiés.

Les décisions de non-éligibilité prise par l'Organisation internationale pour les réfugiés pendant la durée de son mandat ne font pas obstacle à ce que la qualité de réfugié soit accordée à des personnes qui remplissent les conditions prévues au paragraphe 2 de la présente section.

2) Qui, par suite d'événements survenus avant le premier janvier 1951 et craignant avec raison d'être persécutée du fait de sa race, de sa religion, de sa nationalité, de son appartenance à un certain groupe social ou de ses opinions politiques, se trouve hors du pays dont elle a la nationalité et qui ne peut ou, du fait de cette crainte, ne veut se réclamer de la protection de ce pays; ou qui, si elle n'a pas de nationalité et se trouve hors du pays dans lequel elle avait sa résidence habituelle à la suite de tels événements, ne peut ou, en raison de ladite crainte, ne veut y retourner.

Dans le cas d'une personne qui a plus d'une nationalité, l'expression "du pays dont elle a la nationalité" vise chacun des pays dont cette personne a la nationalité. Ne sera pas considérée comme privée de la protection du pays dont elle a la nationalité toute personne qui, sans raison valable fondée sur une crainte justifiée, ne s'est pas réclamée de la protection de l'un des pays dont elle a la nationalité.

---

en corrélation avec tout acte visé dans le présent paragraphe ou tout crime relevant de la compétence de la Cour;

i) Disparitions forcées de personnes;

j) Crime d'apartheid;

k) Autres actes inhumains de caractère analogue causant intentionnellement de grandes souffrances ou des atteintes graves à l'intégrité physique ou à la santé physique ou mentale. »

B. 1) Aux fins de la présente Convention, les mots "événements survenus avant le premier janvier 1951" figurant à l'article 1, section A, pourront être compris dans le sens de soit *a*) "événements survenus avant le premier janvier 1951 en Europe", soit *b*) "événements survenus avant le premier janvier 1951 en Europe ou ailleurs"; et chaque Etat contractant fera, au moment de la signature, de la ratification ou de l'adhésion, une déclaration précisant la portée qu'il entend donner à cette expression au point de vue des obligations assumées par lui en vertu de la présente Convention.

2) Tout Etat contractant qui a adopté la formule *a* pourra à tout moment étendre ses obligations en adoptant la formule *b* par notification adressée au Secrétaire général des Nations Unies.

C. Cette Convention cessera, dans les cas ci-après, d'être applicable à toute personne visée par les dispositions de la section A ci-dessus :

1) Si elle s'est volontairement réclamée à nouveau de la protection du pays dont elle a la nationalité; ou

2) Si, ayant perdu sa nationalité, elle l'a volontairement recouvrée; ou

3) Si elle a acquis une nouvelle nationalité et jouit de la protection du pays dont elle a acquis la nationalité; ou

4) Si elle est retournée volontairement s'établir dans le pays qu'elle a quitté ou hors duquel elle est demeurée de crainte d'être persécutée; ou

5) Si, les circonstances à la suite desquelles elle a été reconnue comme réfugiée ayant cessé d'exister, elle ne peut plus continuer à refuser de se réclamer de la protection du pays dont elle a la nationalité;
Etant entendu, toutefois, que les dispositions du présent paragraphe ne s'appliqueront pas à tout réfugié visé au paragraphe 1 de la section A du présent article qui peut invoquer, pour refuser de se réclamer de la protection du pays dont il a la nationalité, des raisons impérieuses tenant à des persécutions antérieures;

6) S'agissant d'une personne qui n'a pas de nationalité, si, les circonstances à la suite desquelles elle a été reconnue comme réfugiée ayant cessé

d'exister, elle est en mesure de retourner dans le pays dans lequel elle avait sa résidence habituelle;
Etant entendu, toutefois, que les dispositions du présent paragraphe ne s'appliqueront pas à tout réfugié visé au paragraphe 1 de la section A du présent article qui peut invoquer, pour refuser de retourner dans le pays dans lequel il avait sa résidence habituelle, des raisons impérieuses tenant à des persécutions antérieures.

D. Cette Convention ne sera pas applicable aux personnes qui bénéficient actuellement d'une protection ou d'une assistance de la part d'un organisme ou d'une institution des Nations Unies autre que le Haut Commissariat des Nations Unies pour les réfugiés.
Lorsque cette protection ou cette assistance aura cessé pour une raison quelconque, sans que le sort de ces personnes ait été définitivement réglé, conformément aux résolutions y relatives adoptées par l'Assemblée générale des Nations Unies, ces personnes bénéficieront de plein droit du régime de cette Convention.

E. Cette Convention ne sera pas applicable à une personne considérée par les autorités compétentes du pays dans lequel cette personne a établi sa résidence comme ayant les droits et les obligations attachés à la possession de la nationalité de ce pays.

F. Les dispositions de cette Convention ne seront pas applicables aux personnes dont on aura des raisons sérieuses de penser :

a) Qu'ellesont commis un crime contre la paix, un crime de guerre ou un Crime contre l'humanité, au sens des instruments internationaux élaborés pour prévoir des dispositions relatives à ces crimes;

b) Qu'elles ont commis un crime grave de droit commun en dehors du pays d'accueil avant d'y être admises comme réfugiés;

c) Qu'elles se sont rendues coupables d'agissements contraires aux buts et aux principes des Nations Unies. »

CONVENTION RELATIVE AU STATUT DES RÉFUGIÉS.

– « 2. Aux fins du présent Protocole, le terme "réfugié", sauf en ce qui concerne l'application du paragraphe 3[22] du présent article, s'entend de

---

[22] « 3. Le présent Protocole sera appliqué par les Etats qui y sont parties sans aucune limitation géographique; toutefois, les déclarations déjà faites en vertu de l'alinéa a du paragraphe 1 de la section B de l'article premier de la Convention par des Etats déjà parties à celle-ci s'appliqueront

toute personne répondant à la définition donnée à l'article premier[23] de la Convention[24] comme si les mots "par suite d'événements survenus avant le 1er janvier 1951 et..." et les mots "... à la suite de tels événements" ne figuraient pas au paragraphe 2 de la section A de l'article premier. »

Art. 1, PROTOCOLE RELATIF AU STATUT DES RÉFUGIÉS.

REGLES [...] CARATERE COUTUMIER AU PLAN INTERNATIONAL [International customary rules]

– « 14. Bien que l'application n'en soit pas obligatoire, les Règles viendront à prendre un caractère coutumier au plan international si un grand nombre d'Etats les appliquent dans l'intention de faire respecter une norme de droit international. [...] »

INTRODUCTION, RÈGLES POUR L'ÉGALISATION DES CHANCES DES PERSONNES HANDICAPÉES.

REGLES DE DROIT INTERNATIONAL APPLICABLE DANS LES CONFLITS ARMES [Rules of international law applicable in armed conflict]

– « *b*) l'expression "règles du droit international applicable dans les conflits armés" s'entend des règles énoncées dans les accords internationaux auxquels participent les Parties au conflit ainsi que des principes et règles du droit international généralement reconnus qui sont applicables aux conflits armés; »

Art. 2, PROTOCOLE ADDITIONNEL AUX CONVENTIONS DE GENÈVE DU 12 AOÛT 1949 RELATIF À LA PROTECTION DES VICTIMES DES CONFLITS ARMÉS INTERNATIONAUX (PROTOCOLE I).

RELIGION [Religion]

– « *Considérant* que la religion ou la conviction constitue pour celui qui la professe un des éléments fondamentaux de sa conception de la vie et que la liberté de religion ou de conviction doit être intégralement respectée et garantie, »

Pp. 4, DÉCLARATION SUR L'ÉLIMINATION DE TOUTES LES FORMES D'INTOLÉRANCE ET DE DISCRIMINATION FONDÉES SUR LA RELIGION OU LA CONVICTION.

---

aussi sous le régime du présent Protocole, à moins que les obligations de l'Etat déclarant n'aient été étendues conformément au paragraphe 2 de la section B de l'article premier de la Convention. »

[23] Voir ci-dessus, même terme.

[24] Convention relative au statut des réfugiés.

REMISE [Surrender]

– « Aux fins du présent Statut:
a) On entend par «remise» le fait pour un État de livrer une personne à la Cour en application du présent Statut. »

Art. 102, STATUT DE ROME DE LA COUR PÉNALE INTERNATIONALE.

REMUNERATION [Remuneration]

– « Aux fins de la présente Convention:

a) Le terme "rémunération" comprend le salaire ou traitement ordinaire, de base ou minimum, et tous autres avantages, payés directement ou indirectement, en espèces ou en nature, par l'employeur au travailleur en raison de l'emploi de ce dernier; »

Art. 1, CONVENTION SUR L'ÉGALITÉ DE RÉMUNÉRATION, (N° 100).

REPARATION [Restitution]

– « 8. Les auteurs d'actes criminels ou les tiers responsables de leur comportement doivent, en tant que de besoin, réparer équitablement le préjudice causé aux victimes, à leur famille ou aux personnes à leur charge. Cette réparation doit inclure la restitution des biens, une indemnité pour le préjudice ou les pertes subis, le remboursement des dépenses engagées en raison de la victimisation, la fourniture de services et le rétablissement des droits. »

DÉCLARATION DES PRINCIPES FONDAMENTAUX DE JUSTICE AUX VICTIMES DE LA CRIMINALITÉ ET AUX VICTIMES D'ABUS DE POUVOIR.

REPRESANTANT PERSONNEL [Personal representative]

– « Dans les présents Principes :
[...]

L'expression « représentant personnel » désigne une personne à qui incombe en droit le devoir de représenter les intérêts d'un patient dans tout domaine déterminé ou d'exercer des droits déterminés en son nom, et s'entend notamment du parent ou du représentant légal d'un mineur, à moins que la législation nationale n'en dispose autrement; »

Al. 6, DEFINITIONS, PRINCIPES POUR LA PROTECTION DES PERSONNES ATTEINTES DE MALADIE MENTALE ET POUR L'AMÉLIORATION DES SOINS DE SANTÉ MENTALE[Y].

RESPECT DE LA DIVERSITE DES CULTURES, LA TOLERANCE, LE DIALOGUE ET LA COOPERATION [Respect for the diversity of cultures, tolerance, dialogue and cooperation]

– « *Affirmant* que le respect de la diversité des cultures, la tolérance, le dialogue et la coopération, dans un climat de confiance et compréhension mutuelles sont un des meilleurs gages de la paix et de la sécurité internationales, »

Pp. 7, DÉCLARATION UNIVERSELLE SUR LA DIVERSITÉ CULTURELLE.

RESPECT DE LA NATURE (LE) [Respect for nature]

– «6. Nous estimons que certaines valeurs fondamentales doivent sous-tendre les relations internationales au XXe siècle, à savoir :

[...]

Le respect de la nature. Il convient de faire preuve de prudence dans la gestion de toutes les espèces vivantes et de toutes les ressources naturelles, conformément aux préceptes du développement durable. C'est à cette condition que les richesses incommensurables que la nature nous offre pourront être préservées et léguées à nos descendants. Les modes de production et de consommation qui ne sont pas viables à l'heure actuelle doivent être modifiés, dans l'intérêt de notre bien-être futur et dans celui de nos descendants.

[...]»

Cinquième note (•), DÉCLARATION DU MILLÉNAIRE.

RESPONSABILITE PENALE [Criminal responsibility]

– « 1. Outre les autres motifs d'exonération de la responsabilité pénale prévus par le présent Statut, une personne n'est pas responsable pénalement si, au moment du comporte ment en cause:

a) Elle souffrait d'une maladie ou d'une déficience mentale qui la privait de la faculté de comprendre le caractère délictueux ou la

[Y] S.P. 7, DEFINITIONS, Principles for the protection of persons with mental illness and the improvement of mental health care.

nature de son comportement, ou de maîtriser celui-ci pour le conformer aux exigences de la loi;

b) Elle était dans un état d'intoxication qui la privait de la faculté de comprendre le caractère délictueux ou la nature de son comportement, ou de maîtriser celui-ci pour le conformer aux exigences de la loi, à moins qu'elle ne se soit volontairement intoxiquée dans des circonstances telles qu'elle savait que, du fait de son intoxication, elle risquait d'adopter un comportement constituant un crime relevant de la compétence de la Cour, ou qu'elle n'ait tenu aucun compte de ce risque;

c) Elle a agi raisonnablement pour se défendre, pour défendre autrui ou, dans le cas des crimes de guerre, pour défendre des biens essentiels à sa survie ou à celle d'autrui ou essentiels à l'accomplissement d'une mission militaire, contre un recours imminent et illicite à la force, d'une manière proportionnée à l'ampleur du danger qu'elle courait ou que couraient l'autre personne ou les biens protégés. Le fait qu'une personne ait participé à une opération défensive menée par des forces armées ne constitue pas en soi un motif d'exonération de la responsabilité pénale au titre du présent alinéa;

d) Le comportement dont il est allégué qu'il constitue un crime relevant de la compétence de la Cour a été adopté sous la contrainte résultant d'une menace de mort imminente ou d'une atteinte grave, continue ou imminente à sa propre intégrité physique ou à celle d'autrui, et si elle a agi par nécessité et de façon raisonnable pour écarter cette menace, à condition qu'elle n'ait pas eu l'intention de causer un dommage plus grand que celui qu'elle cherchait à éviter. Cette menace peut être:

i) Soit exercée par d'autres personnes;

ii) Soit constituée par d'autres circonstances indépendantes de sa volonté.»

Art. 31, Statut de Rome de la Cour pénale internationale.

RESPONSABILITES INHERENTES AUX ACTIVITES DES CHERCHEURS [Responsibilities inherent in the activities of researchers]

– « Les responsabilités inhérentes aux activités des chercheurs, notamment la rigueur, la prudence, l'honnêteté intellectuelle et l'intégrité, dans la conduite de leurs recherches ainsi que dans la présentation et l'utilisation de leurs résultats, devraient faire l'objet d'une attention particulière dans le cadre des recherches sur le génome humain, compte tenu de leurs implications éthiques et sociales. Les décideurs publics et privés en matière de politiques scientifiques ont aussi des responsabilités particulières à cet égard. »

Art. 13, DÉCLARATION UNIVERSELLE SUR LE GÉNOME HUMAIN ET LES DROITS DE L'HOMME.

RESPONSABLE DE L'APPLICATION DES LOIS [Law enforcement officials]

– « D'après le *Commentaire* de l'article premier du Code de conduite pour les responsables de l'application des lois, l'expression "responsable de l'application des lois" englobe tous les représentants de la loi, qu'ils soient désignés ou élus, qui exercent des pouvoirs de police et en particulier des pouvoirs d'arrestation ou de détention. Dans les pays où des pouvoirs de police sont exercés par des autorités militaires, en uniforme ou en civil, ou par des forces de sécurité de l'Etat, la définition des responsables de l'application de la loi s'étend également aux agents de ces services. »

Note de bas de page (*) pp. 1, PRINCIPES DE BASE SUR LE RECOURS À LA FORCE ET L'UTILISATION DES ARMES À FEU PAR LES RESPONSABLES DE L'APPLICATION DES LOIS.

RESPONSABLES DE L'APPLICATION DES LOIS [Law enforcement officials]

– « *a*) L'expression "responsables de l'application des lois" englobe tous les représentants de la loi, qu'ils soient désignés ou élus, qui exercent des pouvoirs de police et en particulier des pouvoirs d'arrestation ou de détention. »

Art. 1, *Commentaire*, CODE DE CONDUITE POUR LES RESPONSABLE DE L'APPLICATION DES LOIS.

RESSOURCES DE LA MER ET DES EAUX INTERIEURES [Marine and inland water resources]

– « 5. Aujourd'hui, plus que jamais, l'utilisation des ressources de la mer et des eaux intérieures est en train de devenir une source importante d'aliments et de bien-être économique. [...] »

DÉCLARATION UNIVERSELLE POUR L'ÉLIMINATION DÉFINITIVE DE LA FAIM ET DE LA MALNUTRITION.

RESTITUTION [Restitution]

– « 10. Dans tous les cas où des dommages graves sont causés à l'environnement, la restitution doit inclure autant que possible la remise en état de l'environnement, la restitution de l'infrastructure, le remplacement des équipements collectifs et le remboursement des dépenses de réinstallation lorsque ces dommages entraînent la dislocation d'une communauté. »

DÉCLARATION DES PRINCIPES FONDAMENTAUX DE JUSTICE AUX VICTIMES DE LA CRIMINALITÉ ET AUX VICTIMES D'ABUS DE POUVOIR.

REVOLTE CONTRE LA TYRANNIE ET L'OPPRESSION [Rebellion against and oppression]

– « *Considérant* qu'il est essentiel que les droits de l'homme soient protégés par un régime de droit pour que l'homme ne soit pas contraint, en suprême recours, à la révolte contre la tyrannie et l'oppression, »

Pp. 3, DÉCLARATION UNIVERSELLE DES DROITS DE L'HOMME.

REVOLVERS [Revolvers]

– « 3. Ne sera pas considéré non plus comme acte nuisible à l'ennemi le port d'armes légères individuelles par le personnel civil de protection civile, en vue du maintien de l'ordre ou pour sa propre protection. Toutefois, dans les zones où des combats terrestres se déroulent ou semblent devoir se dérouler, les Parties au conflit prendront les dispositions appropriées pour limiter ces armes aux armes de poing, telles que les pistolets ou revolvers, afin de faciliter la distinction entre le personnel de protection civile et les combattants. Même si le personnel de protection civile porte d'autres armes légères individuelles dans ces zones, il doit être respecté et protégé dès qu'il aura été reconnu comme tel. »

Art. 65, PROTOCOLE ADDITIONNEL AUX CONVENTIONS DE GENEVE DU 12 AOUT 1949 RELATIF A LA PROTECTION DES VICTIMES DES CONFLITS ARMES INTERNATIONAUX (PROTOCOLE I).

RHUMATISME AVEC MANIFESTATIONS CLINIQUES GRAVES [Rheumatism with serious clinical symptoms]

– «*p)* Les affections chroniques des organes locomoteurs avec troubles fonctionnels manifestes, par exemple : arthroses déformantes; poly-arthrite chronique évolutive primaire et secondaire; rhumatisme avec manifestations cliniques graves; etc. »

Annexe I, 3, CONVENTION DE GENÈVE RELATIVE AU TRAITEMENT DES PRISONNIERS DE GUERRE.

RUSES DE GUERRE [Ruses of war]

– « 2. Les ruses de guerre ne sont pas interdites. Constituent des ruses de guerre les actes qui ont pour but d'induire un adversaire en erreur ou de lui faire commettre des imprudences, mais qui n'enfreignent aucune règle du droit international applicable dans les conflits armés et qui, ne faisant pas appel à la bonne foi de l'adversaire en ce qui concerne la protection prévue par ce droit, ne sont pas perfides. Les actes suivants sont des exemples de ruses de guerre : l'usage de camouflages, de leurres, d'opérations simulées et de faux renseignements. »

Art. 37, PROTOCOLE ADDITIONNEL AUX CONVENTIONS DE GENÈVE DU 12 AOÛT 1949 RELATIF À LA PROTECTION DES VICTIMES DES CONFLITS ARMÉS INTERNATIONAUX (PROTOCOLE I).

SATURNISME [Lead poisoning]

– « *o)* Les intoxications chroniques graves, par exemple : saturnisme, hydrargyrisme; morphinisme, cocaïnisme, alcoolisme; intoxications par les gaz et par les radiations; etc. »

Annexe I, 3, CONVENTION DE GENÈVE RELATIVE AU TRAITEMENT DES PRISONNIERS DE GUERRE.

SECURITE SOCIALE [Social security]

– « *b*) La sécurité sociale (les dispositions légales relatives aux accidents du travail, aux maladies professionnelles, à la maternité, à la maladie, à l'invalidité, à la vieillesse et au décès, au chômage, aux charges de famille, ainsi qu'à tout autre risque qui, conformément à la législation nationale, est couvert par un système de sécurité sociale), [...] »

Art. 24, CONVENTION RELATIVE AU STATUT DES APATRIDES.

Art. 24, CONVENTION RELATIVE AU STATUT DES RÉFUGIÉS.

SERVAGE [Serfdom]

– « Chacun des Etats parties à la présente Convention prendra toutes les mesures, législatives et autres, qui seront réalisables et nécessaires pour obtenir progressivement et aussitôt que possible l'abolition complète ou l'abandon des institutions et pratiques suivantes, là où elles subsistent encore, qu'elles rentrent ou non dans la définition de l'esclavage qui figure à l'article premier de la Convention relative à l'esclavage signée à Genève le 25 septembre 1926:

[...]

> Le servage, c'est-à-dire la condition de quiconque est tenu par la loi, la coutume ou un accord, de vivre et de travailler sur une terre appartenant à une autre personne et de fournir à cette autre personne, contre rémunération ou gratuitement, certains services déterminés, sans pouvoir changer sa condition; »

Art. 1, CONVENTION SUPPLÉMENTAIRE RELATIVE À L'ABOLITION DE L'ESCLAVAGE, DE LA TRAITE DES ESCLAVES ET DES INSTITUTIONS ET PRATIQUES ANALOGUES À L'ESCLAVAGE.

SERVICE DE SANTE MENTALE [Mental health facility]

– « Dans les présents Principes :

[...]

> L'expression « service de santé mentale » désigne tout établissement ou toute unité d'un établissement qui se consacre principalement aux soins de santé mentale; »

Al. 7, DEFINITIONS, PRINCIPES POUR LA PROTECTION DES PERSONNES ATTEINTES DE MALADIE MENTALE ET POUR L'AMÉLIORATION DES SOINS DE SANTÉ MENTALE[z].

SERVITUDE POUR DETTES [Debt bondage]

– « Chacun des Etats parties à la présente Convention prendra toutes les mesures, législatives et autres, qui seront réalisables et nécessaires pour obtenir progressivement et aussitôt que possible l'abolition complète ou l'abandon des institutions et pratiques suivantes, là où elles subsistent encore, qu'elles rentrent ou non dans la définition de l'esclavage qui figure à l'article premier[25] de la Convention relative à l'esclavage signée à Genève le 25 septembre 1926 :

---

[z] S.p. 4, DEFINITIONS, Principles for the protection of persons with mental illness and the improvement of mental health care.

[25] « Aux fins de la présente Convention, il est entendu que :
1 L'esclavage est l'état ou condition d'un individu sur lequel s'exercent les attributs du droit de propriété ou certains d'entre eux;
2 La traite des esclaves comprend tout acte de capture, d'acquisition ou de cession d'un individu en vue de la réduire en esclavage; tout acte d'acquisition d'un esclave en vue de le vendre ou de l'échanger; tout acte de cession par vente ou échange d'un esclave acquis en vue d'être vendu ou échangé, ainsi que, en général, tout acte de commerce ou de transport d'esclaves. »

a) La servitude pour dettes, c'est-à-dire l'état ou la condition résultant du fait qu'un débiteur s'est engagé à fournir en garantie d'une dette ses services personnels ou ceux de quelqu'un sur lequel il a autorité, si la valeur équitable ce ces services n'est pas affectée à la liquidation de la dette ou si la durée de ces services n'est pas limitée ni leur caractère défini; »

ART. 1, CONVENTION SUPPLÉMENTAIRE RELATIVE À L'ABOLITION DE L'ESCLAVAGE, DE LA TRAITE DES ESCLAVES ET DES INSTITUTIONS ET PRATIQUES ANALOGUES À L'ESCLAVAGE.

SEUIL DE RESPONSABILITE PENALE [Minimum age of criminal responsibility]

– « Le seuil de responsabilité pénale varie largement selon les époques et les cultures. L'attitude moderne serait de se demander si un enfant peut supporter les conséquences morales et psychologiques de la responsabilité pénale, c'est-à-dire si un enfant, compte tenu de sa capacité de discernement et de compréhension, peut être tenu responsable d'un comportement essentiellement antisocial. Si l'âge de la responsabilité pénale est fixé trop bas ou s'il n'y a pas d'âge limite du tout, la notion n'a plus de sens. En général, il existe une relation étroite entre la notion de responsabilité pour un comportement délictueux ou criminel et les autres droits et responsabilités sociales (par exemple la situation matrimoniale, la majorité civile, etc.). »

4, *Commentaire*, ENSEMBLE DE RÈGLES MINIMA DES NATIONS UNIES CONCERNANT L'ADMINISTRATION DE LA JUSTICE POUR LES MINEURS (RÈGLES DE BEIJING).

SEXE [Gender]

– « 3. Aux fins du présent Statut, le terme «sexe» s'entend de l'un et l'autre sexes, masculin et féminin, suivant le contexte de la société. Il n'implique aucun autre sens. »

Art. 7, STATUT DE ROME DE LA COUR PÉNALE INTERNATIONALE.

SIGNAL DISTINCTIF [Distinctive signal]

– « Aux fins du présent Protocole :

[...]

m) l'expression "signal distinctif" s'entend de tout moyen de signalisation destiné exclusivement à permettre l'identification des unités et moyens de transport sanitaires, prévu au Chapitre III[26] de l'Annexe I au présent Protocole. »

---

[26] « Chapitre III – Signaux distinctifs
Article 5 – Utilisation facultative
1. Sous réserve des dispositions de l'article 6 du présent Règlement, les signaux définis dans le présent Chapitre pour l'usage exclusif des unités et moyens de transport sanitaires ne doivent pas être utilisés à d'autres fins. L'emploi de tous les signaux visés au présent Chapitre est facultatif.
2. Les aéronefs sanitaires temporaires qui, faute de temps ou en raison de leurs caractéristiques, ne peuvent pas être marqués du signe distinctif, peuvent utiliser les signaux distinctifs autorisés dans le présent Chapitre. Toutefois la méthode de signalisation la plus efficace d'un aéronef sanitaire en vue de son identification et de sa reconnaissance est l'emploi d'un signal visuel, soit le signe distinctif, soit le signal lumineux défini à l'article 6, soit les deux, complété par les autres signaux mentionnés aux articles 7 et 8 du présent Règlement.
Article 6 – Signal lumineux
1. Le signal lumineux, consistant en un feu bleu scintillant, est prévu à l'usage des aéronefs sanitaires pour signaler leur identité. Aucun autre aéronef ne peut utiliser ce signal. La couleur bleue recommandée s'obtient au moyen des coordonnées trichromatiques ci-après :
limite des verts y = 0,065 + 0,805x limite des blancs y = 0,400 - x limite des pourpres x = 0,133 + 0,600y
La fréquence recommandée des éclats lumineux bleus est de 60 à 100 éclats par minute.
2. Les aéronefs sanitaires devraient être équipés des feux nécessaires pour rendre le signal lumineux visible dans toutes les directions possibles.
3. En l'absence d'accord spécial entre les Parties au conflit, réservant l'usage des feux bleus scintillants à l'identification des véhicules et des navires et embarcations sanitaires, l'emploi de ces signaux pour d'autres véhicules ou navires n'est pas interdit.
Article 7 – Signal radio
1. Le signal radio consiste en un message radiotéléphonique ou radiotélégraphique, précédé d'un signal distinctif de priorité, qui doit être défini et approuvé par une Conférence administrative mondiale des radiocommunications de l'Union internationale des télécommunications. Ce signal est émis trois fois avant l'indicatif d'appel du transport sanitaire en cause. Le message est émis en anglais à intervalles appropriés, sur une ou plusieurs fréquences spécifiées comme il est prévu au paragraphe 3. Le signal de priorité est exclusivement réservé aux unités et moyens de transport sanitaires.
2. Le message radio, précédé du signal distinctif de priorité visé au paragraphe 1, contient les éléments suivants :
a) indicatif d'appel du moyen de transport sanitaire;
b) position du moyen de transport sanitaire;
c) nombre et type des moyens de transport sanitaire;
d) itinéraire choisi;
e) durée en route et heure de départ et d'arrivée prévues, selon le cas;
f) autres informations telles que l'altitude de vol, les fréquences radioélectriques veillées, les langages conventionnels, les modes et codes des systèmes de radar secondaires de surveillance.
3. Pour faciliter les communications visées aux paragraphes 1 et 2, ainsi que les communications visées aux articles 22, 23, 25, 26, 27, 28, 29, 30 et 31 du Protocole, les Hautes Parties contractantes, les Parties à un conflit ou l'une des Parties à un conflit, agissant d'un commun accord ou

Art. 8, Protocole additionnel aux Conventions de Genève du 12 août 1949 relatif à la protection des victimes des conflits armés internationaux (Protocole I).

SIGNE DISTINCTIF [Distinctive emblem]

– « Aux fins du présent Protocole :
[…]

l) l'expression "signe distinctif" s'entend du signe distinctif de la croix rouge, du croissant rouge ou du lion-et-soleil rouge, sur fond blanc, quand il est utilisé pour la protection des unités et moyens de transport sanitaires et du personnel sanitaire et religieux et de son matériel; »

Art. 8, Protocole additionnel aux Conventions de Genève du 12 août 1949 relatif à la protection des victimes des conflits armés internationaux (Protocole I).

SITUATION DES PEUPLES QUI SOUFFRENT DE LA FAIM ET DE LA SOUS-ALIMENTATION [Situation of the peoples afflicted by hunger and malnutrition]

– « *c*) La situation des peuples qui souffrent de la faim et de la sous-alimentation a pour origine des circonstances historiques et en particulier les inégalités sociales, ainsi que, souvent, la domination étrangère et coloniale, l'occupation étrangère, la discrimination raciale, l'apartheid et le néocolonialisme sous toutes ses formes, et reste l'un des principaux

---

isolément, peuvent définir, conformément au Tableau de répartition des bandes de fréquences figurant dans le Règlement des radiocommunications annexé à la Convention internationale des télécommunications, et publier les fréquences nationales qu'elles choisissent pour ces communications. Ces fréquences doivent être notifiées à l'Union internationale des télécommunications, conformément à la procédure approuvée par une Conférence administrative mondiale des radiocommunications.

Article 8 – Identification par moyens électroniques

1. Le système de radar secondaire de surveillance (SSR), tel qu'il est spécifié à l'Annexe 10 de la Convention de Chicago du 7 décembre 1944 relative à l'Aviation civile internationale mise à jour périodiquement, peut être utilisé pour identifier et suivre le cheminement d'un aéronef sanitaire. Le mode et le code SSR à réserver à l'usage exclusif des aéronefs sanitaires doivent être définis par les Hautes Parties contractantes, les Parties au conflit ou une des Parties au conflit, agissant d'un commun accord ou isolément, conformément à des procédures à recommander par l'Organisation de l'Aviation civile internationale.

2. Les Parties au conflit peuvent, par accord spécial, adopter pour leur usage entre elles un système électronique analogue pour l'identification des véhicules sanitaires et des navires et embarcations sanitaires. »

obstacles à la pleine émancipation et au progrès des pays en développement et de tous les peuples en cause; »

DÉCLARATION UNIVERSELLE POUR L'ÉLIMINATION DÉFINITIVE DE LA FAIM ET DE LA MALNUTRITION.

SOCIETES NATIONALES DE LA CROIX-ROUGE [National Red Cross societies]

– « *a*) les Sociétés nationales de la Croix-Rouge (du Croissant-Rouge, du Lion et Soleil Rouges) reconnues pourront poursuivre les activités conformes aux principes de la Croix-Rouge tels qu'ils sont définis par les Conférences internationales de la Croix-Rouge. Les autres sociétés de secours devront pouvoir poursuivre leurs activités humanitaires dans des conditions similaires; »

Art. 63, CONVENTION DE GENÈVE RELATIVE À LA PROTECTION DES PERSONNES CIVILES EN TEMPS DE GUERRE DU 12 AOÛT 1949.

– « 1. [...] La population civile et les sociétés de secours, telles que les Sociétés nationales de la Croix-Rouge (Croissant-Rouge, Lion-et-Soleil-Rouge), seront autorisées, même dans les régions envahies ou occupées [...]»

Art. 17, PROTOCOLE ADDITIONNEL AUX CONVENTIONS DE GENÈVE DU 12 AOÛT 1949 RELATIF À LA PROTECTION DES VICTIMES DES CONFLITS ARMÉS INTERNATIONAUX (PROTOCOLE I).

SOINS DE SANTE MENTALE [Mental health care]

– « Dans les présents Principes :

[...]

L'expression « soins de santé mentale » s'entend notamment de l'analyse de l'état mental d'une personne et du diagnostic porté en l'espèce, ainsi que du traitement, des soins et de la réadaptation dispensés en cas de maladie mentale ou de soupçon de maladie mentale. »

Al. 8, DEFINITIONS, PRINCIPES POUR LA PROTECTION DES PERSONNES ATTEINTES DE MALADIE MENTALE ET POUR L'AMÉLIORATION DES SOINS DE SANTÉ MENTALE[AA].

[AA] S.p. 3, DEFINITIONS, Principles for the protection of persons with mental illness and the improvement of mental health care.

SOINS MEDICAUX [Medical attention]

– « *a*) Les "soins médicaux", expression qui désigne les services rendus par le personnel médical, y compris les médecins agréés et le personnel paramédical, doivent être assurés lorsqu'ils sont nécessaires ou demandés. »

Art.6, *Commentaire*, CODE DE CONDUITE POUR LES RESPONSABLE DE L'APPLICATION DES LOIS.

SOLIDARITE (LA) [Solidarity]

– « 6. Nous estimons que certaines valeurs fondamentales doivent sous-tendre les relations internationales au XXe siècle, à savoir :
[…]

La solidarité . Les problèmes mondiaux doivent être gérés multilatéralement et de telle façon que les coûts et les charges soient justement répartis conformément aux principes fondamentaux de l'équité et de la justice sociale. Ceux qui souffrent ou qui sont particulièrement défavorisés méritent une aide de la part des privilégiés.
[…] »

Troisième note (•), DÉCLARATION DU MILLÉNAIRE.

SOUS-DEVELOPPEMENT [Underdevelopment]

– « 11. Estimant que la pauvreté, le sous-développement et l'analphabétisme figurent parmi les principaux facteurs contribuant à la propagation du VIH/sida, et notant avec une vive préoccupation que l'épidémie aggrave la pauvreté et entrave ou enraye désormais le développement dans un grand nombre de pays et qu'il faudrait donc y remédier dans une optique intégrée; »

DÉCLARATION D'ENGAGEMENT SUR LE VIH/SIDA.

STERILISATION FORCEE [Enforced sterilization]

– « *g*) Viol, esclavage sexuel, prostitution forcée, grossesse forcée, stérilisation forcée ou toute autre forme de violence sexuelle de gravité comparable; »

Art. 7, STATUT DE ROME DE LA COUR PÉNALE INTERNATIONALE.

STRUCTURE FAMILIALE [Family group]

– « *Reconnaissant* qu'il importe d'encourager le renforcement de la structure familiale de manière à en faire la cellule fondamentale de la société et que les hommes et les femmes ont, à partir de l'âge nubile, le droit de se marier et de fonder une famille, qu'ils ont des droits égaux au regard du mariage et que le mariage ne peut être conclu qu'avec le libre et plein consentement des futurs époux, conformément aux dispositions de l'article 16[27] de la Déclaration de l'homme, »

Pp. 1, RECOMMANDATION SUR LE CONSENTEMENT AU MARIAGE, L'ÂGE MINIMUM DU MARIAGE ET L'ENREGISTREMENT DES MARIAGES.

SUBSTITUT [Substitute]

– « *d*) l'expression "substitut" s'entend d'une organisation qui remplace la Puissance protectrice conformément à l'article 5[28]. »

---

[27] « 1. A partir de l'âge nubile, l'homme et la femme, sans aucune restriction quant à la race, la nationalité ou la religion, ont le droit de se marier et de fonder une famille. Ils ont des droits égaux au regard du mariage, durant le mariage et lors de sa dissolution.
2. Le mariage ne peut être conclu qu'avec le libre et plein consentement des futurs époux.
3. La famille est l'élément naturel et fondamental de la société et a droit à la protection de la société et de l'Etat. »

[28] « 1. Il est du devoir des Parties à un conflit, dès le début de ce conflit, d'assurer le respect et la mise en œuvre des Conventions et du présent Protocole par l'application du système des Puissances protectrices, y compris notamment la désignation et l'acceptation de ces Puissances conformément aux paragraphes ci- après. Les Puissances protectrices seront chargées de sauvegarder les intérêts des Parties au conflit.
2. Dès le début d'une situation visée à l'article premier, chacune des Parties au conflit désignera sans délai une Puissance protectrice aux fins d'application des Conventions et du présent Protocole et autorisera, également sans délai et aux mêmes fins, l'activité d'une Puissance protectrice que la Partie adverse aura désignée et qu'elle-même aura acceptée comme telle.
3. Si une Puissance protectrice n'a pas été désignée ou acceptée dès le début d'une situation visée à l'article premier, le Comité international de la Croix-Rouge, sans préjudice du droit de toute autre organisation humanitaire impartiale de faire de même, offrira ses bons offices aux Parties au conflit en vue de la désignation sans délai d'une Puissance protectrice agréée par les Parties au conflit. A cet effet, il pourra notamment demander à chaque Partie de lui remettre une liste d'au moins cinq Etats que cette Partie estime acceptables pour agir en son nom en qualité de Puissance protectrice vis-à-vis d'une Partie adverse et demander à chacune des Parties adverses de remettre une liste d'au moins cinq Etats qu'elle accepterait comme Puissance protectrice de l'autre Partie; ces listes devront être communiquées au Comité dans les deux semaines qui suivront la réception de la demande; il les comparera et sollicitera l'accord de tout Etat dont le nom figurera sur les deux listes.
4. Si, en dépit de ce qui précède, il y a défaut de Puissance protectrice, les Parties au conflit devront accepter sans délai l'offre que pourrait faire le Comité international de la Croix-Rouge

Art. 2, PROTOCOLE ADDITIONNEL AUX CONVENTIONS DE GENÈVE DU 12 AOÛT 1949 RELATIF À LA PROTECTION DES VICTIMES DES CONFLITS ARMÉS INTERNATIONAUX (PROTOCOLE I).

SUITE D'INTERVENTION CHIRURGICALE SUR L'ESTOMAC FAITE EN CAPTIVITE [Sequelae of gastric operations performed in captivity]

– « *e)* Les affections chroniques graves des organes digestifs, par exemple : ulcère de l'estomac ou du duodénum; suite d'intervention chirurgicale sur l'estomac faite en captivité; gastrite, entérite ou colique chroniques durant plus d'une année et affectant gravement l'état général; cirrhose hépatique; cholécystopathie chronique; etc. »

Annexe I, 3, CONVENTION DE GENÈVE RELATIVE AU TRAITEMENT DES PRISONNIERS DE GUERRE.

SUJETION DES PEUPLES [Subjection of peoples]

– « 1. La sujétion des peuples à une subjugation, à une domination et à une exploitation étrangères constitue un déni des droits fondamentaux de l'homme, est contraire à la Charte des Nations Unies et compromet la cause de la paix et de la coopération mondiales. »

DÉCLARATION SUR L'OCTROI DE L'INDÉPENDANCE AUX PAYS ET AUX PEUPLES COLONIAUX.

SUPERIORITE/INFERIORITE RACIALE OU ETHNIQUE (THEORIE) [Racial or ethnic superiority/inferiority (theory)]

---

ou toute autre organisation présentant toutes garanties d'impartialité et d'efficacité, après dues consultations avec lesdites Parties et compte tenu des résultats de ces consultations, d'agir en qualité de substitut. L'exercice de ses fonctions par un tel substitut est subordonné au consentement des Parties au conflit; les Parties au conflit mettront tout en oeuvre pour faciliter la tâche du substitut dans l'accomplissement de sa mission conformément aux Conventions et au présent Protocole.

5. Conformément à l'article 4, la désignation et l'acceptation de Puissances protectrices aux fins d'application des Conventions et du présent Protocole n'auront pas d'effet sur le statut juridique des Parties au conflit ni sur celui d'un territoire quelconque, y compris un territoire occupé.

6. Le maintien des relations diplomatiques entre les Parties au conflit ou le fait de confier à un Etat tiers la protection des intérêts d'une Partie et de ceux de ses ressortissants conformément aux règles du droit international concernant les relations diplomatiques ne fait pas obstacle à la désignation de Puissances protectrices aux fins d'application des Conventions et du présent Protocole.

7. Toutes les fois qu'il est fait mention ci-après dans le présent Protocole de la Puissance protectrice, cette mention désigne également le substitut. »

– « 1. Toute théorie faisant état de la supériorité ou de l'infériorité intrinsèque de groupes raciaux ou ethniques qui donnerait aux uns le droit de dominer ou d'éliminer les autres, inférieurs présumés, ou fondant des jugements de valeur sur une différence raciale, est sans fondement scientifique et contraire aux principes moraux et éthiques de l'humanité. »

Art.2, DÉCLARATION SUR LA RACE ET LES PRÉJUGÉS RACIAUX.

SYSTEME DE LA JUSTICE POUR MINEURS [Juvenile justice system]

– « 5.1 Le système de la justice pour mineurs recherche le bien-être du mineur et fait en sorte que les réactions vis-à-vis des délinquants juvéniles soient toujours proportionnées aux circonstances propres aux délinquants et aux délits. »

ENSEMBLE DE RÈGLES MINIMA DES NATIONS UNIES CONCERNANT L'ADMINISTRATION DE LA JUSTICE POUR LES MINEURS (RÈGLES DE BEIJING).

SYPHILIS VISCERALE TERTIAIRE RESISTANT AU TRAITEMENT [Tertiary visceral syphilis resistant to treatment]

– « *s)* Les maladies infectieuses chroniques graves persistant une année après le début, par exemple : paludisme avec altérations organiques prononcées; dysenterie amibienne ou bacillaire avec troubles considérables; syphilis viscérale tertiaire, résistant au traitement; lèpre; etc. »

Annexe I, 3, CONVENTION DE GENÈVE RELATIVE AU TRAITEMENT DES PRISONNIERS DE GUERRE.

TACHE PRIMORDIALE DE TOUS LES ETATS ET DE TOUTES LES ORGANISATIONS INTERNATIONALES [Primary task of all States and international organizations]

– « *Estimant* que la tâche primordiale de tous les Etats et de toutes les organisations internationales est d'éliminer de la société tous les fléaux et tous les obstacles qui s'opposent au progrès social, et notamment l'inégalité, l'exploitation, la guerre, le colonialisme et le racisme, »

Pp. 13 , DÉCLARATION SUR LE PROGRÈS ET LE DÉVELOPPEMENT DANS LE DOMAINE SOCIALE.

TERRES [Lands]

– « 2. L'utilisation du terme *terres* dans les articles 15[29] et 16[30] comprend le concept de territoires, qui recouvre la totalité de l'environnement des régions que les peuples intéressés occupent ou qu'ils utilisent d'une autre manière. »

Art. 13, CONVENTION RELATIVE AUX PEUPLES INDIGÈNES ET TRIBAUX, (N° 169).

TOLERANCE (LA) [Tolerance]

– « 6. Nous estimons que certaines valeurs fondamentales doivent sous-tendre les relations internationales au XXe siècle, à savoir :
[...]

---

[29] « 1. Les droits des peuples intéressés sur les ressources naturelles dont sont dotées leurs terres doivent être spécialement sauvegardés. Ces droits comprennent celui, pour ces peuples, de participer à l'utilisation, à la gestion et à la conservation de ces ressources.
2. Dans les cas où l'Etat conserve la propriété des minéraux ou des ressources du sous-sol ou des droits à d'autres ressources dont sont dotées les terres, les gouvernements doivent établir ou maintenir des procédures pour consulter les peuples intéressés dans le but de déterminer si et dans quelle mesure les intérêts de ces peuples sont menacés avant d'entreprendre ou d'autoriser tout programme de prospection ou d'exploitation des ressources dont sont dotées leurs terres. Les peuples intéressés doivent, chaque fois que c'est possible, participer aux avantages découlant de ces activités et doivent recevoir une indemnisation équitable pour tout dommage qu'ils pourraient subir en raison de telles activités. »

[30] « 1. Sous réserve des paragraphes suivants du présent article, les peuples intéressés ne doivent pas être déplacés des terres qu'ils occupent.
2. Lorsque le déplacement et la réinstallation desdits peuples sont jugés nécessaires à titre exceptionnel, ils ne doivent avoir lieu qu'avec leur consentement, donné librement et en toute connaissance de cause. Lorsque ce consentement ne peut être obtenu, ils ne doivent avoir lieu qu'à l'issue de procédures appropriées établies par la législation nationale et comprenant, s'il y a lieu, des enquêtes publiques où les peuples intéressés aient la possibilité d'être représentés de façon efficace.
3. Chaque fois que possible, ces peuples doivent avoir le droit de retourner sur leurs terres traditionnelles, dès que les raisons qui ont motivé leur déplacement et leur réinstallation cessent d'exister.
4. Dans le cas où un tel retour n'est pas possible, ainsi que déterminé par un accord ou, en l'absence d'un tel accord, au moyen de procédures appropriées, ces peuples doivent recevoir, dans toute la mesure possible, des terres de qualité et de statut juridique au moins égaux à ceux des terres qu'ils occupaient antérieurement et leur permettant de subvenir à leurs besoins du moment et d'assurer leur développement futur. Lorsque les peuples intéressés expriment une préférence pour une indemnisation en espèces ou en nature, ils doivent être ainsi indemnisés, sous réserve des garanties appropriées.
5. Les personnes ainsi déplacées et réinstallées doivent être entièrement indemnisées de toute perte ou de tout dommage subi par elles de ce fait. »

La tolérance. Les êtres humains doivent se respecter mutuellement dans toute la diversité de leurs croyances, de leurs cultures et de leurs langues. Les différences qui existent au sein des sociétés et entre les sociétés ne devraient pas être redoutés ni réprimées, mais vénérées en tant que bien précieux de l'humanité. il faudrait promouvoir activement une culture de paix et le dialogue entre toutes les civilisations.

[...]»

Quatrième note (•), DÉCLARATION DU MILLÉNAIRE.

TORTURE [Torture]

– « 1. Aux fins de la présente Déclaration, le terme "torture" désigne tout acte par lequel une douleur ou des souffrances aiguës, physiques ou mentales, sont délibérément infligées à une personne par des agents de la fonction publique ou à leur instigation, aux fins notamment d'obtenir d'elle ou d'un tiers des renseignements ou des aveux, de la punir d'un acte qu'elle a commis ou qu'elle est soupçonnée d'avoir commis, ou de l'intimider ou d'intimider d'autres personnes. Ce terme ne s'étend pas à la douleur ou aux souffrances résultant uniquement de sanctions légitimes, inhérentes à ces sanctions ou occasionnées par elles, dans une mesure compatible avec l'Ensemble de règles minima pour le traitement des détenus.

2. La torture constitue une forme aggravée et délibérée de peines ou de traitements cruels, inhumains ou dégradants. »

Art. 1, DÉCLARATION SUR LA PROTECTION DE TOUTES LES PERSONNES CONTRE LA TORTURE ET AUTRES PEINES OU TRAITEMENTS CRUELS, INHUMAINS OU DÉGRADANTS.

– « 1. Aux fins de la présente Convention, le terme "torture" désigne tout acte par lequel une douleur ou des souffrances aiguës, physiques ou mentales, sont intentionnellement infligées à une personne aux fins notamment d'obtenir d'elle ou d'une tierce personne des renseignements ou des aveux, de la punir d'un acte qu'elle ou une tierce personne a commis ou est soupçonnée d'avoir commis, de l'intimider ou de faire pression sur elle ou d'intimider ou de faire pression sur une tierce personne, ou pour tout autre motif fondé sur une forme de discrimination quelle qu'elle soit, lorsqu'une telle douleur ou de telles souffrances sont infligées par un agent de la fonction publique ou toute autre personne agissant à titre officiel ou à son instigation ou avec son consentement exprès ou tacite. Ce terme ne s'étend pas à la douleur ou aux souffrances résultant uniquement de sanctions légitimes, inhérentes à ces sanctions ou occasionnées par elles.

2. Cet article est sans préjudice de tout instrument international ou de toute loi nationale qui contient ou peut contenir des dispositions de portée plus large. »

Art. 1, CONVENTION CONTE LA TORTURE ET AUTRES PEINES OU TRAITEMENT CRUELS, INHUMAINS OU DÉGRADANTS.

– « Aucun responsable de l'application des lois ne peut infliger, susciter ou tolérer un acte de torture ou quelque autre peine ou traitement cruel, inhumain ou dégradant, ni ne peut invoquer un ordre de ses supérieurs ou des circonstances exceptionnelles telles qu'un état de guerre ou une menace de guerre, une menace contre la sécurité nationale, l'instabilité politique intérieure ou tout autre état d'exception pour justifier la torture ou d'autres peines ou traitements cruels, inhumains ou dégradants.

Commentaire:

a) Cette interdiction découle de la Déclaration sur la protection de toutes les personnes contre la torture et autres peines ou traitements cruels, inhumains ou dégradants, adoptée par l'Assemblée générale et aux termes de laquelle:

"[Cet acte constitue] un outrage à la dignité humaine et doit être condamné comme un reniement des buts de la Charte des Nations Unies et comme une violation des droits de l'homme et des libertés fondamentales proclamés dans la Déclaration universelle des droits de l'homme [et d'autres instruments internationaux en matière de droits de l'homme]."

b) Dans ladite Déclaration, la torture est définie comme suit:

"Le terme "torture" désigne tout acte par lequel une douleur ou des souffrances aiguës, physiques ou mentales, sont délibérément infligées à une personne par des agents de la fonction publique ou à leur instigation, aux fins notamment d'obtenir d'elle ou d'un tiers des renseignements ou des aveux, de la punir d'un acte qu'elle a commis ou qu'elle est soupçonnée d'avoir commis, ou de l'intimider ou d'intimider d'autres personnes. Ce terme ne s'étend pas à la douleur ou aux souffrances résultant uniquement de sanctions légitimes, inhérentes à ces sanctions ou occasionnées par elles, dans une mesure compatible avec l'Ensemble de règles minima pour le traitement des détenus."

Art.5, CODE DE CONDUITE POUR LES RESPONSABLE DE L'APPLICATION DES LOIS.

– « Aucune torture physique ou morale ni aucune contrainte ne pourra être exercée sur les prisonniers de guerre pour obtenir d'eux des renseignements de quelque sorte que ce soit. Les prisonniers qui refuseront de répondre ne pourront être ni menacés, ni insultés, ni exposés à des désagréments ou désavantages de quelque nature que ce soit. »[ab]

Art. 17, al. 4, CONVENTION DE GENÈVE RELATIVE AU TRAITEMENT DES PRISONNIERS DE GUERRE.

– « 2. Aux fins du paragraphe 1[31]:

[...]

e) Par «torture», on entend le fait d'infliger intentionnellement une douleur ou des souffrances aiguës, physiques ou mentales, à une personne se trouvant sous sa garde ou sous son contrôle; l'acception de ce terme ne s'étend pas à la douleur ou aux souffrances résultant uniquement de sanctions légales, inhérentes à ces sanctions ou occasionnées par elles; »

Art. 7, STATUT DE ROME DE LA COUR PÉNALE INTERNATIONALE.

[AB] " No physical or mental torture, nor any other form of coercion, may be inflicted on prisoners of war to secure from them information of any kind whatever. Prisoners of war who refuse to answer may not be threatened, insulted, or exposed to any unpleasant or disadvantageous treatment of any kind. ."

[31] « 1. Aux fins du présent Statut, on entend par crime contre l'humanité l'un quelconque des actes ci-après lorsqu'il est commis dans le cadre d'une attaque généralisée ou systématique lancée contre toute population civile et en connaissance de cette attaque:

a) Meurtre;

b) Extermination;

c) Réduction en esclavage;

d) Déportation ou transfert forcé de population;

e) Emprisonnement ou autre forme de privation grave de liberté physique en violation des dispositions fondamentales du droit international;

f) Torture;

g) Viol, esclavage sexuel, prostitution forcée, grossesse forcée, stérilisation forcée ou toute autre forme de violence sexuelle de gravité comparable;

h) Persécution de tout groupe ou de toute collectivité identifiable pour des motifs d'ordre politique, racial, national, ethnique, culturel, religieux ou sexiste au sens du paragraphe 3, ou en fonction d'autres critères universellement reconnus comme inadmissibles en droit international, en corrélation avec tout acte visé dans le présent paragraphe ou tout crime relevant de la compétence de la Cour;

i) Disparitions forcées de personnes;

j) Crime d'apartheid;

k) Autres actes inhumains de caractère analogue causant intentionnellement de grandes souffrances ou des atteintes graves à l'intégrité physique ou à la santé physique ou mentale. »

- « Les Hautes Parties contractantes s'interdisent expressément toute mesure de nature à causer soit des souffrances physiques, soit l'extermination des personnes protégées en leur pouvoir. Cette interdiction vise non seulement le meurtre, la torture, les peines corporelles, les mutilations et les expériences médicales ou scientifiques non nécessitées par le traitement médical d'une personne protégée, mais également toutes autres brutalités, qu'elles soient le fait d'agents civils ou d'agents militaires. »

Art. 32, Convention de Genève relative à la protection des personnes civiles en temps de guerre du 12 août 1949.

- « *a*) les atteintes portées à la vie, à la santé et au bien-être physique ou mental des personnes, notamment:
 [...]
 ii) la torture sous toutes ses formes, qu'elle soit physique ou mentale; »

Art. 75, § 2., Protocole additionnel aux Conventions de Genève du 12 août 1949 relatif à la protection des victimes des conflits armés internationaux (Protocole I).

TOURISME SEXUEL [Sex tourism]

- « *Profondément préoccupés* par la pratique répandue et persistante du tourisme sexuel auquel les enfants sont particulièrement exposés, dans la mesure où il favorise directement la vente d'enfants, la prostitution des enfants et la pornographie mettant en scène des enfants, »

Pp. 4, Protocole facultatif à la Convention relative aux droits de l'enfant, concernant la vente d'enfants, la prostitution des enfants et la pornographie mettant en scène des enfants.

TOUTES LES FORMES DE VIOLENCE CONTRE LES FEMMES ET LES FILLES [All forms of violence against women and girls]

- « 61. [...] toutes les formes de violence contre les femmes et les filles, y compris les pratiques traditionnelles et coutumières néfastes, les sévices, le viol et autres formes de violence sexuelle, les voies de fait et la traite des femmes et des filles; »

Déclaration d'engagement sur le VIH/sida.

TRACHOME [Trachoma]

- « *i)* La cécité des deux yeux ou celle d'un œil lorsque la vue de l'autre œil est moins de 1, malgré l'emploi de verres correcteurs; la diminution de l'acuité visuelle ne pouvant être corrigée à 1/2 pour un œil au moins*; les autres affections oculaires graves, par exemple : glaucome; iritis; chloroïdite; trachome; etc. »

Annexe I, 3, CONVENTION DE GENÈVE RELATIVE AU TRAITEMENT DES PRISONNIERS DE GUERRE.

TRAFIC ILLICITE DES MIGRANTS [Smuggling of migrants]

– « Aux fins du présent Protocole :

a) L'expression « trafic illicite de migrants » désigne le fait d'assurer, afin d'en tirer, directement ou indirectement, un avantage financier ou un autre avantage matériel, l'entrée illégale dans un État Partie d'une personne qui n'est ni un ressortissant ni un résident permanent de cet État; »

Art. 3, PROTOCOLE CONTRE LE TRAFIC ILLICITE DE MIGRANTS PAR TERRE, AIR ET MER, ADDITIONNEL À LA CONVENTION DES NATIONS UNIES CONTRE LA CRIMINALITÉ TRANSNATIONALE ORGANISÉE.

TRAITE DES ESCLAVES [Slave trade]

– « Aux fins de la présente Convention , il est entendu que :
[...]

2. La traite des esclaves comprend tout acte de capture, d'acquisition ou de cession d'un individu en vue de la réduire en esclavage; tout acte d'acquisition d'un esclave en vue de le vendre ou de l'échanger; tout acte de cession par vente ou échange d'un esclave acquis en vue d'être vendu ou échangé, ainsi que, en général, tout acte de commerce ou de transport d'esclaves. »

Art. 1, CONVENTION RELATIVE À L'ESCLAVAGE.

– « Aux fins de la présente Convention :
[...]

c) La «traite des esclaves» désigne et comprend tout acte de capture, d'acquisition ou de cession d'une personne en vue de la réduire en esclavage; tout acte d'acquisition d'un esclave en vue de le vendre ou de l'échanger; tout acte de cession par vente ou échange d'une personne acquise en vue d'être vendue ou échangée, ainsi qu'en général tout acte de commerce ou de transport d'esclaves, quel que soit le moyen de transport employé. »

Art. 7, CONVENTION SUPPLÉMENTAIRE RELATIVE À L'ABOLITION DE L'ESCLAVAGE, DE LA TRAITE DES ESCLAVES ET DES INSTITUTIONS ET PRATIQUES ANALOGUES À L'ESCLAVAGE.

TRAITE DES ETRES HUMAINS EN VUE DE LA PROSTITUTION [Traffic in persons for the purpose of prostitution]

– « *Considérant* que la prostitution et le mal qui l'accompagne, à savoir la traite des êtres humains en vue de la prostitution, sont incompatibles avec la dignité et la valeur de la personne humaine et mettent en danger le bien-être de l'individu, de la famille et de la communauté, »

Pp. 1, CONVENTION POUR LA RÉPRESSION DE LA TRAITE DES ÊTRES HUMAINS ET DE L'EXPLOITATION DE LA PROSTITUTION D'AUTRUI.

TRAITE DES ETRES HUMAINS ET DE L'EXPLOITATION DE LA PROSTITUTION D'AUTRUI (LA) [Traffic in persons and the exploitation of prostitution of others (the)]

– « Les Parties à la présente Convention conviennent de punir toute personne qui, pour satisfaire les passions d'autrui :

1) Embauche, entraîne ou détourne en vue de la prostitution une autre personne, même consentante;

2) Exploite la prostitution d'une autre personne, même consentante. »

Art. 1, CONVENTION POUR LA RÉPRESSION DE LA TRAITE DES ÊTRES HUMAINS ET DE L'EXPLOITATION DE LA PROSTITUTION D'AUTRUI.

– « Les Parties à la présente Convention conviennent également de punir toute personne qui :

1) Tient, dirige ou, sciemment, finance ou contribue à financer une maison de prostitution;

2)Donne ou prend sciemment en location, en tout ou en partie, un immeuble ou un autre lieu aux fins de la prostitution d'autrui. »

Art. 2, CONVENTION POUR LA RÉPRESSION DE LA TRAITE DES ÊTRES HUMAINS ET DE L'EXPLOITATION DE LA PROSTITUTION D'AUTRUI.

TRAITE DES PERSONNES [Trafficking in persons]

– « Aux fins du présent Protocole :

a) L'expression « traite des personnes » désigne le recrutement, le transport, le transfert, l'hébergement ou l'accueil de personnes, par la menace de recours ou le recours à la force ou à d'autres formes de contrainte, par enlèvement, fraude, tromperie, abus d'autorité ou d'une situation de vulnérabilité ou par l'offre ou l'acceptation de paiements ou d'avantages pour obtenir le consentement d'une personne ayant autorité sur une autre aux fins d'exploitation. l'exploitation comprend au minimum, l'exploitation sexuelle, le travail ou les services forcés, l'esclavage ou les pratiques analogues à l'esclavage, la servitude ou le prélèvement d'organes ;

b) Le consentement d'une victime de la traite des personnes à l'exploitation envisagée, telle qu'énoncée à l'alinéa *a* du présent article, est indifférent lorsque l'un quelconque des moyens énoncés à l'alinéa *a* a été utilisé ;

c) Le recrutement, le transport, le transfert, l'hébergement ou l'accueil d'un enfant aux fins d'exploitation sont considérés comme une « traite de personnes » même s'ils ne font appel à aucun des moyens énoncés à l'alinéa *a* du présent article ;

*d)*Le termes « enfant » désigne toute personnes âgée de moins de 18 ans. »

Art. 3, Protocole additionnel à la Convention des Nations Unies contre la criminalité transnationale organisée, visant à prévenir, réprimer et punir la traite des personnes en particulier des femmes et des enfants.

TRAITEMENTS HUMILIANTS ET DEGRADANTS [Humiliating and degrading treatment]

– « *c*) les atteintes à la dignité des personnes, notamment les traitements humiliants et dégradants; »

Art.3, § 1, Convention de Genève relative à la protection des personnes civiles en temps de guerre du 12 août 1949.

– « *b*) les atteintes à la dignité de la personne, notamment les traitements humiliants et dégradants, la prostitution forcée et toute forme d'attentat à la pudeur; »

Art. 75, Protocole additionnel aux Conventions de Genève du 12 août 1949 relatif à la protection des victimes des conflits armés internationaux (Protocole I).

– « *e*) les atteintes à la dignité de la personne, notamment les traitements humiliants et dégradants, le viol, la contrainte à la prostitution et tout attentat à la pudeur; »

Art. 4, 2., Protocole additionnel aux Convention de Genève du 12 août 1949 relatif à la protection des victimes des conflits armés non internationaux (Protocole II).

TRANSFERT DE LA SCIENCE ET DE LA TECHNIQUE [Transfer of science and technology]

– « *Consciente* du fait que le transfert de la science et de la technique est l'un des principaux moyens d'accélérer le développement économique des pays en développement, »

Pp. 7, DÉCLARATION SUR L'UTILISATION DU PROGRÈS DE LA SCIENCE ET DE LA TECHNIQUE DANS L'INTÉRÊT DE LA PAIX ET AU PROFIT DE L'HUMANITÉ.

TRANSFERTS FORCES [Forcible transfers]

– « Les transferts forcés, en masse ou individuels, ainsi que les déportations de personnes protégées hors du territoire occupé dans le territoire de la Puissance occupante ou dans celui de tout autre Etat, occupé ou non, sont interdits, quel qu'en soit le motif. »

Art. 49, al. 1, CONVENTION DE GENÈVE RELATIVE À LA PROTECTION DES PERSONNES CIVILES EN TEMPS DE GUERRE DU 12 AOÛT 1949.

TRANSPORT SANITAIRE [Medical transportation]

– « Aux fins du présent Protocole :
[...]

f) l'expression "transport sanitaire" s'entend du transport par terre, par eau ou par air des blessés, des malades et des naufragés, du personnel sanitaire et religieux et du matériel sanitaire protégés par les Conventions et le présent Protocole; »

Art. 8, PROTOCOLE ADDITIONNEL AUX CONVENTIONS DE GENÈVE DU 12 AOÛT 1949 RELATIF À LA PROTECTION DES VICTIMES DES CONFLITS ARMÉS INTERNATIONAUX (PROTOCOLE I).

TRAVAIL [Work ; Labour]

– « 2) Afin de prévenir la discrimination à l'égard des femmes en raison de leur mariage ou de leur maternité et de garantir leur droit effectif au travail, les Etats Parties sengagent à prendre des mesures appropriées ayant pour objet :
[...]

d) D'assurer une protection spéciale aux femmes enceintes dont il est prouvé que le travail est nocif.[ac] »

[ac] "2. In order to prevent discrimination against women on the grounds of marriage or maternity and to ensure their effective right to work, States Parties shall take appropriate measures:

Art. 11, CONVENTION SUR L'ÉLIMINATION DE TOUTES LES FORMES DE DISCRIMINATION À L'ÉGARD DES FEMMES.

– « 67. [...]Le travail doit toujours être considéré comme un instrument d'éducation et un moyen d'inculquer au mineur le respect de soi- même pour le préparer au retour dans sa communauté, et ne doit pas être imposé comme une sanction disciplinaire. [...] »

RÈGLES DES NATIONS UNIES POUR LA PROTECTION DES MINEURS PRIVÉS DE LIBERTÉ.

TRAVAIL DES ENFANTS [Child labour]

– « *Reconnaissant* que le travail des enfants est pour une large part provoqué par la pauvreté et que la solution à long terme réside dans la croissance économique soutenue menant au progrès social, et en particulier à l'atténuation de la pauvreté et à l'éducation universelle ; »

Pp. 5, CONVENTION SUR LES PIRES FORMES DE TRAVAIL DES ENFANTS (N° 182).

TRAVAIL FORCE OU OBLIGATOIRE [Forced or compulsory labour]

– « *c*) N'est pas considéré comme "travail forcé ou obligatoire" au sens du présent paragraphe:

i) Tout travail ou service, non visé à l'alinéa b, normalement requis d'un individu qui est détenu en vertu d'une décision de justice régulière ou qui, ayant fait l'objet d'une telle décision, est libéré conditionnellement;

ii) Tout service de caractère militaire et, dans les pays où l'objection de conscience est admise, tout service national exigé des objecteurs de conscience en vertu de la loi;

iii) Tout service exigé dans les cas de force majeure ou de sinistres qui menacent la vie ou le bien-être de la communauté;

iv) Tout travail ou tout service formant partie des obligations civiques normales. »

Art. 8.3, PACTE INTERNATIONAL RELATIF AUX DROITS CIVILS ET POLITIQUES.

[...]
(*d*) To provide special protection to women during pregnancy in types of work proved to be harmful to them."

– « Les Hautes Parties contractantes reconnaissent que le recours au travail forcé ou obligatoire peut avoir de graves conséquences et s'engagent, chacune en ce qui concerne les territoires soumis à sa souveraineté, juridiction, protection, suzeraineté ou tutelle, à prendre des mesures utiles pour éviter que le travail forcé ou obligatoire n'amène des conditions analogues à l'esclavage.

Il est entendu :

1. Que, sous réserve des dispositions transitoires énoncées au paragraphe 2 ci-dessous, le travail forcé ou obligatoire ne peut être exigé que pour des fins publiques;

2. Que, dans les territoires où le travail forcé ou obligatoire, pour d'autres fins que des fins publiques, existe encore, les Hautes Parties contractantes s'efforceront d'y mettre progressivement fin, aussi rapidement que possible, et que, tant que ce travail forcé ou obligatoire existera, il ne sera employé qu'à titre exceptionnel, contre une rémunération adéquate et à la condition qu'un changement du lieu habituel de résidence ne puisse être imposé;

3. Et que, dans tous les cas, les autorités centrales compétentes du territoire intéressé assumeront la responsabilité du recours au travail forcé ou obligatoire. »

Art. 1, Convention relative à l'esclavage.

– « 1. Aux fins de la présente convention, le terme « travail forcé ou obligatoire » désignera tout travail ou service exigé d'un individu sous la menace d'une peine quelconque et pour lequel ledit individu ne s'est pas offert de plein gré.

2. Toutefois, le terme travail forcé ou obligatoire ne comprendra pas, aux fins de la présente convention:

a) tout travail ou service exigé en vertu des lois sur le service militaire obligatoire et affecté à des travaux d'un caractère purement militaire;

b) tout travail ou service faisant partie des obligations civiques normales des citoyens d'un pays se gouvernant pleinement lui-même;

c) tout travail ou service exigé d'un individu comme conséquence d'une condamnation prononcée par une décision judiciaire, à la condition que ce travail ou service soit exécuté sous la surveillance et le contrôle des autorités publiques et que ledit individu ne soit pas concédé ou mis à la disposition de particuliers, compagnies ou personnes morales privées;

d) tout travail ou service exigé dans les cas de force majeure, c'est-à-dire dans les cas de guerre, de sinistres ou menaces de sinistres tels qu'incendies, inondations, famines, tremblements de terre, épidémies et épizooties violentes, invasions d'animaux, d'insectes ou de parasites végétaux nuisibles, et en général toutes circonstances mettant en danger ou risquant de mettre en danger la vie ou les conditions normales d'existence de l'ensemble ou d'une partie de la population;

e) les menus travaux de village, c'est-à-dire les travaux exécutés dans l'intérêt direct de la collectivité par les membres de celle-ci, travaux qui, de ce chef, peuvent être considérés comme des obligations civiques normales incombant aux membres de la collectivité, à condition que la population elle-même ou ses représentants directs aient le droit de se prononcer sur le bien-fondé de ces travaux. »

Art. 2, CONVENTION SUR LE TRAVAIL FORCÉ (N° 29).

– « 4. N'est pas considéré comme "travail forcé ou obligatoire" au sens du présent article:

a) Tout travail ou service, non visé au paragraphe 3[32] du présent article, normalement requis d'un individu qui est détenu en vertu d'une décision de justice régulière ou qui, ayant fait l'objet d'une telle décision, est libéré conditionnellement;

b) Tout service exigé dans les cas de force majeure ou de sinistres qui menacent la vie ou le bien-être de la communauté;

c) Tout travail ou tout service formant partie des obligations civiques normales dans la mesure où il est également imposé aux nationaux de l'Etat considéré. »

Art. 11, CONVENTION INTERNATIONALE SUR LA PROTECTION DES DROITS DE TOUS LES TRAVAILLEURS MIGRANTS ET DES MEMBRES DE LEUR FAMILLE.

---

[32] « 3. Le paragraphe 2 du présent article ne saurait être interprété comme interdisant, dans les Etats où certains crimes peuvent être punis de détention accompagnée de travaux forcés, l'accomplissement d'une peine de travaux forcés infligée par un tribunal compétent. »

TRAVAILLEURS ADMIS POUR UN EMPLOI SPECIFIQUE [Specified-employment worker]

– « Aux fins de la présente Convention:
[...]

g) L'expression "travailleurs admis pour un emploi spécifique" désigne les travailleurs migrants:

i) Qui ont été envoyés par leur employeur pour un temps limité et déterminé dans un Etat d'emploi pour accomplir une mission ou une tâche spécifique; ou

ii) Qui entreprennent pour un temps limité et déterminé un travail exigeant des compétences professionnelles, commerciales, techniques ou autres hautement spécialisées; ou

iii) Qui, à la demande de leur employeur dans l'Etat d'emploi, entreprennent pour un temps limité et déterminé un travail de caractère provisoire ou de courte durée;

et qui sont tenus de quitter l'Etat d'emploi soit à l'expiration de leur temps de séjour autorisé, soit plus tôt s'ils n'accomplissent plus la mission ou la tâche spécifique, ou s'ils n'exécutent plus le travail initial; »

Art. 2, § 2, CONVENTION INTERNATIONALE SUR LA PROTECTION DES DROITS DE TOUS LES TRAVAILLEURS MIGRANTS ET DES MEMBRES DE LEUR FAMILLE.

TRAVAILLEURS D'UNE INSTALLATION EN MER [Worker on an offshore installation]

– « Aux fins de la présente Convention:
[...]

d) L'expression "travailleurs d'une installation en mer" désigne les travailleurs migrants employés sur une installation en mer qui relève de la juridiction d'un Etat dont ils ne sont pas ressortissants; »

Art. 2, § 2, CONVENTION INTERNATIONALE SUR LA PROTECTION DES DROITS DE TOUS LES TRAVAILLEURS MIGRANTS ET DES MEMBRES DE LEUR FAMILLE.

TRAVAILLEURS EMPLOYES AU TITRE DE PROJET [Project-tied worker]

– « Aux fins de la présente Convention:

[...]

f) L'expression "travailleurs employés au titre de projets" désigne les travailleurs migrants qui ont été admis dans un Etat d'emploi pour un temps déterminé pour travailler uniquement à un projet spécifique exécuté dans cet Etat par leur employeur; »

Art. 2, § 2, CONVENTION INTERNATIONALE SUR LA PROTECTION DES DROITS DE TOUS LES TRAVAILLEURS MIGRANTS ET DES MEMBRES DE LEUR FAMILLE.

TRAVAILLEURS FRONTALIERS [Frontier worker]

– « Aux fins de la présente Convention:

[...]

a) L'expression "travailleurs frontaliers" désigne les travailleurs migrants qui maintiennent leur résidence habituelle dans un Etat voisin auquel ils reviennent en principe chaque jour ou au moins une fois par semaine; »

Art. 2, § 2, CONVENTION INTERNATIONALE SUR LA PROTECTION DES DROITS DE TOUS LES TRAVAILLEURS MIGRANTS ET DES MEMBRES DE LEUR FAMILLE.

TRAVAILLEURS INDEPENDANTS [Self-employed worker]

– « Aux fins de la présente Convention:

[...]

h) L'expression "travailleurs indépendants" désigne les travailleurs migrants qui exercent une activité rémunérée autrement que dans le cadre d'un contrat de travail et qui tirent normalement leur subsistance de cette activité en travaillant seuls ou avec les membres de leur famille, et tous autres travailleurs migrants reconnus comme travailleurs indépendants par la législation applicable de l'Etat d'emploi ou par des accords bilatéraux ou multilatéraux. »

Art. 2, § 2, CONVENTION INTERNATIONALE SUR LA PROTECTION DES DROITS DE TOUS LES TRAVAILLEURS MIGRANTS ET DES MEMBRES DE LEUR FAMILLE.

TRAVAILLEURS ITINERANTS [Itinerant worker]

– « Aux fins de la présente Convention:

[...]

e) L'expression "travailleurs itinérants" désigne les travailleurs migrants qui, ayant leur résidence habituelle dans un Etat, doivent, de par la nature de leur activité, se rendre dans d'autres Etats pour de courtes périodes; »

Art. 2, § 2, CONVENTION INTERNATIONALE SUR LA PROTECTION DES DROITS DE TOUS LES TRAVAILLEURS MIGRANTS ET DES MEMBRES DE LEUR FAMILLE.

TRAVAILLEURS MIGRANTS [Migrant workers]

– « *Considérant* la situation de vulnérabilité dans laquelle se trouvent fréquemment les travailleurs migrants et les membres de leur famille du fait, entre autres, de leur éloignement de l'Etat d'origine et d'éventuelles difficultés tenant à leur présence dans l'Etat d'emploi, »

PP. 10, CONVENTION INTERNATIONAL SUR LA PROTECTION DES DROITS DE TOUS LES TRAVAILLEURS MIGRANTS ET DES MEMBRES DE LEUR FAMILLE.

– - « Aux fins de la présente Convention:

1. L'expression "travailleurs migrants" désigne les personnes qui vont exercer, exercent ou ont exercé une activité rémunérée dans un Etat dont elles ne sont pas ressortissantes; »

Art. 2, CONVENTION INTERNATIONALE SUR LA PROTECTION DES DROITS DE TOUS LES TRAVAILLEURS MIGRANTS ET DES MEMBRES DE LEUR FAMILLE.

TRAVAILLEURS MIGRANTS ET MEMBRES DE LEUR FAMILLE [Migrant workers and members of their families]

– « La présente Convention ne s'applique pas:

a) Aux personnes envoyées ou employées par des organisations et des organismes internationaux ni aux personnes envoyées ou employées par un Etat en dehors de son territoire pour exercer des fonctions officielles, dont l'admission et le statut sont régis par le droit international général ou par des accords internationaux ou des conventions internationales spécifiques;

b) Aux personnes envoyées ou employées par un Etat ou pour le compte de cet Etat en dehors de son territoire qui participent à des programmes de développement et à d'autres programmes de coopération, dont l'admission et le statut sont régis par un accord spécifique conclu avec l'Etat d'emploi et qui, conformément à cet accord, ne sont pas considérées comme des travailleurs migrants;

c) Aux personnes qui deviennent résidentes d'un Etat autre que leur Etat d'origine en qualité d'investisseurs;

d) Aux réfugiés et aux apatrides, sauf disposition contraire de la législation nationale pertinente de l'Etat partie intéressé ou des instruments internationaux en vigueur pour cet Etat;

e) Aux étudiants et aux stagiaires;

f) Aux gens de mer et travailleurs des installations en mer qui n'ont pas été autorisés à résider ou à exercer une activité rémunérée dans l'Etat d'emploi. »

Art. 3, CONVENTION INTERNATIONALE SUR LA PROTECTION DES DROITS DE TOUS LES TRAVAILLEURS MIGRANTS ET DES MEMBRES DE LEUR FAMILLE.

TRAVAILLEURS MIGRANTS ET MEMBRES DE LEUR FAMILLE (DEPOURVUS DE DOCUMENTS OU EN SITUATION IRREGULIERE) [Migrant workers and members of their families (non-documented or in irregular situation)]

– « Aux fins de la présente Convention, les travailleurs migrants et les membres de leur famille:
[...]

b) Sont considérés comme dépourvus de documents ou en situation irrégulière s'ils ne remplissent pas les conditions prévues à l'alinéa *a* du présent article[33]. »

Art. 5 , CONVENTION INTERNATIONALE SUR LA PROTECTION DES DROITS DE TOUS LES TRAVAILLEURS MIGRANTS ET DES MEMBRES DE LEUR FAMILLE.

TRAVAILLEURS MIGRANTS ET MEMBRES DE LEUR FAMILLE (POURVUS DE DOCUMENTS OU EN SITUATION REGULIERE) [Migrant workers and members of their families (documented or in regular situation)]

– « Aux fins de la présente Convention, les travailleurs migrants et les membres de leur famille:

a) Sont considérés comme pourvus de documents ou en situation régulière s'ils sont autorisés à entrer, séjourner et exercer une activité rémunérée dans l'Etat d'emploi conformément à la législation dudit Etat et aux accords internationaux auxquels cet Etat est partie; »

---

[33] « *a*) Sont considérés comme pourvus de documents ou en situation régulière s'ils sont autorisés à entrer, séjourner et exercer une activité rémunérée dans l'Etat d'emploi conformément à la législation dudit Etat et aux accords internationaux auxquels cet Etat est partie; »

Art. 5, CONVENTION INTERNATIONALE SUR LA PROTECTION DES DROITS DE TOUS LES TRAVAILLEURS MIGRANTS ET DES MEMBRES DE LEUR FAMILLE.

TRAVAILLEURS SAISONNIERS [Seasonal worker]

– « Aux fins de la présente Convention:
[...]
b) L'expression "travailleurs saisonniers" désigne les travailleurs migrants dont l'activité, de par sa nature, dépend des conditions saisonnières et ne peut être exercée que pendant une partie de l'année; »

Art. 2, § 2, CONVENTION INTERNATIONALE SUR LA PROTECTION DES DROITS DE TOUS LES TRAVAILLEURS MIGRANTS ET DES MEMBRES DE LEUR FAMILLE.

ULCERE DE L'ESTOMAC OU DU DUODENUM [Gastric or duodenal ulcer]

– « *e)* Les affections chroniques graves des organes digestifs, par exemple : ulcère de l'estomac ou du duodénum; suite d'intervention chirurgicale sur l'estomac faite en captivité; gastrite, entérite ou colique chroniques durant plus d'une année et affectant gravement l'état général; cirrhose hépatique; cholécystopathie chronique*; etc. »

Annexe I, 3, CONVENTION DE GENÈVE RELATIVE AU TRAITEMENT DES PRISONNIERS DE GUERRE.

UNITES SANITAIRES [Medical units]

– « Aux fins du présent Protocole :
[...]
e) l'expression "unités sanitaires" s'entend des établissements et autres formations, militaires ou civils, organisés à des fins sanitaires, à savoir la recherche, l'évacuation, le transport, le diagnostic ou le traitement – y compris les premiers secours – des blessés, des malades et des naufragés, ainsi que la prévention des maladies. Elle couvre entre autres les hôpitaux et autres unités similaires, les centres de transfusion sanguine, les centres et instituts de médecine préventive et les centres d'approvisionnement sanitaire, ainsi que les dépôts de matériel sanitaire et de produits pharmaceutiques de ces unités. Les unités sanitaires peuvent être fixes ou mobiles, permanentes ou temporaires; »

Art. 8, PROTOCOLE ADDITIONNEL AUX CONVENTIONS DE GENÈVE DU 12 AOÛT 1949 RELATIF À LA PROTECTION DES VICTIMES DES CONFLITS ARMÉS INTERNATIONAUX (PROTOCOLE I).

UNITES SANITAIRES PERMANENTES [Permanent medical units]

– « Aux fins du présent Protocole :

[...]

k) sont "permanents" le personnel sanitaire, les unités sanitaires et les moyens de transport sanitaire affectés exclusivement à des fins sanitaires pour une durée indéterminée. Sont "temporaires" le personnel sanitaire, les unités sanitaires et les moyens de transport sanitaire utilisés exclusivement à des fins sanitaires pour des périodes limitées, pendant toute la durée de ces périodes. A moins qu'elles ne soient autrement qualifiées, les expressions "personnel sanitaire", "unité sanitaire" et "moyen de transport sanitaire" couvrent un personnel, des unités ou des moyens de transport qui peuvent être soit permanents soit temporaires; »

Art. 8, PROTOCOLE ADDITIONNEL AUX CONVENTIONS DE GENEVE DU 12 AOUT 1949 RELATIF A LA PROTECTION DES VICTIMES DES CONFLITS ARMES INTERNATIONAUX (PROTOCOLE I).

UNITES SANITAIRES TEMPORAIRES [Temporary medical units]

– « Aux fins du présent protocole :

[...]

k) [...]Sont "temporaires" le personnel sanitaire, les unités sanitaires et les moyens de transport sanitaire utilisés exclusivement à des fins sanitaires pour des périodes limitées, pendant toute la durée de ces périodes. A moins qu'elles ne soient autrement qualifiées, les expressions "personnel sanitaire", "unité sanitaire" et "moyen de transport sanitaire" couvrent un personnel, des unités ou des moyens de transport qui peuvent être soit permanents soit temporaires;]

Art. 8, PROTOCOLE ADDITIONNEL AUX CONVENTIONS DE GENEVE DU 12 AOUT 1949 RELATIF A LA PROTECTION DES VICTIMES DES CONFLITS ARMES INTERNATIONAUX (PROTOCOLE I).

VEHICULE SANITAIRE [Medical vehicles]

– « Aux fins du présent Protocole :

[...]

h) l'expression "véhicule sanitaire" s'entend de tout moyen de transport sanitaire par terre; »

Art. 8, PROTOCOLE ADDITIONNEL AUX CONVENTIONS DE GENÈVE DU 12 AOÛT 1949 RELATIF À LA PROTECTION DES VICTIMES DES CONFLITS ARMÉS INTERNATIONAUX (PROTOCOLE I).

VENTE D'ENFANTS [Sale of children]

– « *Convaincus* que l'élimination de la vente d'enfants, de la prostitution des enfants et de la pornographie mettant en scène des enfants sera facilitée par l'adoption d'une approche globale tenant compte des facteurs qui contribuent à ces phénomènes, notamment le sous-développement, la pauvreté, les disparités économiques, l'inéquité des structures socioéconomiques, les dysfonctionnement familiaux, le manque d'éducation, l'exode rural, la discrimination fondée sur le sexe, le comportement sexuel irresponsable des adultes, les pratiques traditionnelles préjudiciables, les conflits armées et la traite des enfants, »

Pp. 7, PROTOCOLE FACULTATIF À LA CONVENTION RELATIVE AUX DROITS DE L'ENFANT, CONCERNANT LA VENTE D'ENFANTS, LA PROSTITUTION DES ENFANTS ET LA PORNOGRAPHIE METTANT EN SCÈNE DES ENFANTS.

– « Aux fins du présent Protocole :

> On entend par vente d'enfants tout acte ou toute transaction en vertu desquels un enfant est remis par toute personne ou tout groupe de personnes à une autre personne ou un autre groupe de personnes contre rémunération ou tout autre avantage ; »

Art. 2, PROTOCOLE FACULTATIF À LA CONVENTION RELATIVE AUX DROITS DE L'ENFANT, CONCERNANT LA VENTE D'ENFANTS, LA PROSTITUTION DES ENFANTS ET LA PORNOGRAPHIE METTANT EN SCÈNE DES ENFANTS.

VICTIME [Victim]

– « 2. Une personne peut être considérée comme une "victime", dans le cadre de la présente Déclaration, que l'auteur soit ou non identifié, arrêté, poursuivi ou déclaré coupable, et quels que soient ses liens de parenté avec la victime. Le terme "victime" inclut aussi, le cas échéant, la famille proche ou les personnes à la charge de la victime directe et les personnes qui ont subi un préjudice en intervenant pour venir en aide aux victimes en détresse ou pour empêcher la victimisation. »

DÉCLARATION DES PRINCIPES FONDAMENTAUX DE JUSTICE RELATIFS AUX VICTIMES DE LA CRIMINALITÉ ET AUX VICTIMES D'ABUS DE POUVOIR.

VICTIMES [Victims]

– « 1. On entend par "victimes" des personnes qui, individuellement ou collectivement, ont subi un préjudice, notamment une atteinte à leur intégrité physique ou mentale, une souffrance morale, une perte matérielle, ou une atteinte grave à leurs droits fondamentaux, en raison d'actes ou d'omissions qui enfreignent les lois pénales en vigueur dans un Etat Membre, y compris celles qui proscrivent les abus criminels de pouvoir. »

DÉCLARATION DES PRINCIPES FONDAMENTAUX DE JUSTICE RELATIFS AUX VICTIMES DE LA CRIMINALITÉ ET AUX VICTIMES D'ABUS DE POUVOIR.

– « 18. On entend par "victimes" des personnes qui, individuellement ou collectivement, ont subi des préjudices, notamment une atteinte à leur intégrité physique ou mentale, une souffrance morale, une perte matérielle, ou une atteinte grave à leurs droits fondamentaux, en raison d'actes ou d'omissions qui ne constituent pas encore une violation de la législation pénale nationale, mais qui représentent des violations des normes internationalement reconnues en matière de droits de l'homme. »

DÉCLARATION DES PRINCIPES FONDAMENTAUX DE JUSTICE RELATIFS AUX VICTIMES DE LA CRIMINALITÉ ET AUX VICTIMES D'ABUS DE POUVOIR.

VIH/SIDA [HIV/AIDS]

– « Que d'ici là [2015], nous aurons arrêté la propagation du VIH/sida, et commencé à inverser la tendance actuelle, et que nous aurons maîtrisé le fléau du paludisme et des autres grandes maladies qui affligent l'humanité. »

19, quatrième note (•), DÉCLARATION DU MILLÉNAIRE.

– « 2. Profondément préoccupés par le fait que l'épidémie mondiale de VIH/sida, en raison de son ampleur et de son incidence dévastatrices, constitue une crise mondiale et l'un des défis les plus redoutables pour la vie et la dignité humaines ainsi que pour l'exercice effectif des droits de l'homme, compromet le développement social et économique dans le monde entier et affecte la société à tous les niveaux – national, local, familial et individuel; »

DÉCLARATION D'ENGAGEMENT SUR LE VIH/SIDA.

– « 3. Notant avec une profonde préoccupation qu'à la fin de 2000, il y avait dans le monde entier 36,1 millions de personnes atteintes du VIH/sida,

90 p. 100 dans les pays en développement et 75 p. 100 en Afrique subsaharienne; »
DÉCLARATION D'ENGAGEMENT SUR LE VIH/SIDA.

– « 4. Constatant avec une vive préoccupation que chacun, riche ou pauvre, sans distinction d'âge, de sexe ni de race, est touché par l'épidémie de VIH/sida, tout particulièrement dans les pays en développement, et que les femmes, les jeunes et les enfants, surtout les filles, sont les plus vulnérables; »
DÉCLARATION D'ENGAGEMENT SUR LE VIH/SIDA.

VIOL [Rape]

– « *g)* Viol, esclavage sexuel, prostitution forcée, grossesse forcée, stérilisation forcée ou toute autre forme de violence sexuelle de gravité comparable;»
Art. 7, § 1, STATUT DE ROME DE LA COUR PÉNALE INTERNATIONALE.

– « Les femmes seront spécialement protégées contre toute atteinte à leur honneur, et notamment contre le viol, la contrainte à la prostitution et tout attentat à leur pudeur. »
Art. 27, CONVENTION DE GENÈVE RELATIVE À LA PROTECTION DES PERSONNES CIVILES EN TEMPS DE GUERRE DU 12 AOÛT 1949.

– « 1. Les femmes doivent faire l'objet d'un respect particulier et seront protégées, notamment contre le viol, la contrainte à la prostitution et toute autre forme d'attentat à la pudeur. »
Art. 76, PROTOCOLE ADDITIONNEL AUX CONVENTIONS DE GENÈVE DU 12 AOÛT 1949 RELATIF À LA PROTECTION DES VICTIMES DES CONFLITS ARMÉS INTERNATIONAUX (PROTOCOLE I).

– « *e)* les atteintes à la dignité de la personne, notamment les traitements humiliants et dégradants, le viol, la contrainte à la prostitution et tout attentat à la pudeur; »
Art. 4, 2., PROTOCOLE ADDITIONNEL AUX CONVENTION DE GENÈVE DU 12 AOÛT 1949 RELATIF À LA PROTECTION DES VICTIMES DES CONFLITS ARMÉS NON INTERNATIONAUX (PROTOCOLE II).

VIOL SYSTEMATIQUE DES FEMMES EN TEMPS DE GUERRE [Systematic rape of women in war situations]

– « 28. La Conférence mondiale sur les droits de l'homme se déclare consternée par les violations massives des droits de l'homme, notamment celles qui prennent la forme de génocide, de "nettoyage ethnique" et de viol systématique des femmes en temps de guerre, violations qui sont à l'origine d'exodes massifs de réfugiés et de déplacements de personnes. [...] »

I, DÉCLARATION ET PROGRAMME D'ACTION DE VIENNE.

VIOLATION DES LOIS OU COUTUMES DE GUERRE [Violations of the laws or customs of war]

– « *Violations des lois ou des coutumes de la guerre*

Le Tribunal international est compétent pour poursuivre les personnes qui commettent des violations des lois ou coutumes de la guerre. Ces violations comprennent, sans y être limitées ;

a) L'emploi d'armes toxiques ou d'autres armes conçues pour causer des souffrances inutiles ;

b) La destruction sans motif des villes et des villages ou la dévastation que ne justifient pas les exigences militaires ;

c) L'attaque ou le bombardement, par quelque moyen que ce soit, de villes, villages, habitations ou bâtiments non défendus ;

d) La saisie, la destruction ou l'endommagement délibérée d'édifices consacrés à la religion, à la bienfaisance et à l'enseignement, aux arts et aux sciences, à des monuments historiques, à des œuvres d'at et à des œuvres de caractère scientifique ;

e) Le pillage de biens publics ou privés. »

Art. 3, STATUT DU TRIBUNAL INTERNATIONAL CHARGÉ DE POURSUIVRE LES PERSONNES PRÉSUMÉES RESPONSABLE DE VIOLATIONS GRAVES DU DROIT INTERNATIONAL HUMANITAIRE COMMISES SUR LE TERITOIRE DE L'EX-YOUGOSLAVIE DEPUIS 1991.

VIOLENCE [Violence]

– « *Alarmée* de constater que les femmes ont du mal à s'assurer l'égalité juridique, sociale, politique et économique dans la société, en raison notamment de la persistance et du caractère endémique de la violence, »

Pp. 11, DÉCLARATION SUR L'ÉLIMINATION DE LA VIOLENCE À L'ÉGARD DES FEMMES.

VIOLENCE A L'EGARD DES FEMMES [Violence against women]

– « *Reconnaissant* que la violence à l'égard des femmes traduit des rapports de force historiquement inégaux entre hommes et femmes, lesquels ont abouti à la domination et à la discrimination exercées par les premiers et freiné la promotion des secondes, et qu'elle compte parmi les principaux mécanismes sociaux auxquels est due la subordination des femmes aux hommes, »

Pp. 6, DÉCLARATION SUR L'ÉLIMINATION DE LA VIOLENCE À L'ÉGARD DES FEMMES.

– « Aux fins de la présente Déclaration, les termes "violence à l'égard des femmes" désignent tous actes de violence dirigés contre le sexe féminin, et causant ou pouvant causer aux femmes un préjudice ou des souffrances physiques, sexuelles ou psychologiques, y compris la menace de tels actes, la contrainte ou la privation arbitraire de liberté, que ce soit dans la vie publique ou dans la vie privée. »

Art. 1, DÉCLARATION SUR L'ÉLIMINATION DE LA VIOLENCE À L'ÉGARD DES FEMMES.

– « La violence à l'égard des femmes s'entend comme englobant, sans y être limitée, les formes de violence énumérées ci-après :

  a) La violence physique, sexuelle et psychologique exercée au sein de la famille, y compris les coups, les sévices sexuels infligés aux enfants de sexe féminin au foyer, les violences liées à la dot, le viol conjugal, les mutilations génitales et autres pratiques traditionnelles préjudiciables à la femme, la violence non conjugale, et la violence liée à l'exploitation;

  b) La violence physique, sexuelle et psychologique exercée au sein de la collectivité, y compris le viol, les sévices sexuels, le harcèlement sexuel et l'intimidation au travail, dans les établissements d'enseignement et ailleurs, le proxénétisme et la prostitution forcée;

  c) La violence physique, sexuelle et psychologique perpétrée ou tolérée par l'Etat, où qu'elle s'exerce. »

Art. 2, DÉCLARATION SUR L'ÉLIMINATION DE LA VIOLENCE À L'ÉGARD DES FEMMES.

VIOLENCE SEXUELLE [Sexual violence]

– « xxii) Le viol, l'esclavage sexuel, la prostitution forcée, la grossesse forcée, telle que définie à l'article 7, paragraphe 2, alinéa f) [34], la stérilisation forcée ou toute autre forme de violence sexuelle constituant une infraction grave aux Conventions de Genève; »

---

[34] « *f*) Par «grossesse forcée», on entend la détention illégale d'une femme mise enceinte de force, dans l'intention de modifier la composition ethnique d'une population ou de commettre d'autres violations graves du droit international. Cette définition ne peut en aucune manière s'interpréter comme ayant une incidence sur les lois nationales relatives à la grossesse; »

Art. 8, § 2, *b*), STATUT DE ROME DE LA COUR PÉNALE INTERNATIONALE.

ZONE DE CONTACT [Contact zone]

– « 2. L'expression "zone de contact" s'entend de toute zone terrestre où les éléments avancés des forces opposées sont au contact les uns des autres, particulièrement là où ils sont exposés à des tirs directs à partir du sol. »

Art. 26, PROTOCOLE ADDITIONNEL AUX CONVENTIONS DE GENÈVE DU 12 AOÛT 1949 RELATIF À LA PROTECTION DES VICTIMES DES CONFLITS ARMÉS INTERNATIONAUX (PROTOCOLE I).

ZONES DEMILITARISEES [Demilitarized Zones]

– « 3. L'objet d'un tel accord[35] sera normalement une zone remplissant les conditions suivantes :

a) tous les combattants, ainsi que les armes et le matériel militaire mobiles, devront avoir été évacués;

b) il ne sera pas fait un usage hostile des installations ou des établissements militaires fixes;

c) les autorités et la population ne commettront pas d'actes d'hostilité;

d) toute activité liée à l'effort militaire devra avoir cessé.

Les Parties au conflit s'entendront au sujet de l'interprétation à donner à la condition posée à l'alinéa d et au sujet des personnes, autres que celles mentionnées au paragraphe 4[36], à admettre dans la zone démilitarisée. »

Art. 60. – *Zones démilitarisées*, PROTOCOLE ADDITIONNEL AUX CONVENTIONS DE GENÈVE DU 12 AOÛT 1949 RELATIF À LA PROTECTION DES VICTIMES DES CONFLITS ARMÉS INTERNATIONAUX (PROTOCOLE I).

---

[35] Art. 60 « 1. Il est interdit aux Parties au conflit d'étendre leurs opérations militaires aux zones auxquelles elles auront conféré par accord le statut de zone démilitarisée si cette extension est contraire aux dispositions d'un tel accord. »

[36] « 4. La présence, dans cette zone, de personnes spécialement protégées par les Conventions et par le présent Protocole et de forces de police retenues à seule fin de maintenir l'ordre public n'est pas contraire aux conditions posées au paragraphe 3. »

Les sujets des droits de l'homme

Age (personnes âgées)

- Apatride
- Comportement ou la conduite d'un jeune qui n'est pas conforme aux normes et valeurs sociales (le)
- Discriminations
- Enfant
- Mesures discriminatoires
- Personnes âgées
- Seuil de responsabilité pénale
- VIH/sida

Colonialisme (néocolonialisme, colonisation, indépendance, autodétermination)

- Agression d'occupation et de domination étrangères et d'ingérence dans les affaires intérieures des Etats (élimination d')
- Apartheid
- Apartheid (Elimination de l')
- Autorités compétentes
- Colonialisme
- Colonialisme (élimination de toutes les formes de)
- Conditions propices au développement pour une grande partie de l'humanité
- Crime d'apartheid
- Développement et le progrès dans le domaine social (le)
- Discrimination
- Discrimination raciale
- Discrimination raciale (élimination de la)
- Droit des peuples à disposer d'eux-mêmes
- Maintien du colonialisme
- Mercenaires
- Néocolonialisme (élimination de toutes les formes de)
- Peuples indigènes
- Racisme

- Racisme (élimination de toutes les formes de)
- Situation des peuples qui souffrent de la faim et de la sous-alimentation
- Sujétion des peuples
- Tâche primordiale de tous les Etats et de toutes les organisations internationales
- Travail forcé ou obligatoire
-

Corruption
- Document de voyage ou d'identité frauduleux

Crime contre l'humanité
- Apartheid
- Apatride
- Crime d'apartheid
- Crimes contre l'humanité
- Erreur de droit
- Génocide
- Réfugié

Croix rouge
- Comité international de la Croix Rouge
- Conflits armés
- Crimes de guerre
- Infractions graves
- Moyen de transport sanitaire
- Personnel sanitaire
- Prisonniers de guerre
- Signal distinctif
- Signe distinctif
- Sociétés nationales de la croix-rouge
- Substitut

Culture
- Attaque lancée contre une population civile
- Biens et services culturels
- Création
- Crimes de guerre
- Culture
- Culture, la famille, les valeurs morales et la religion (la)
- Défense de la diversité culturelle
- Délinquant juvénile
- Démocratie
- Développement

- Développement et le progrès dans le domaine social (le)
- Dignité
- Discrimination
- Discrimination à l'égard des femmes
- Discrimination raciale
- Discriminations
- Diversité culturelle
- Droit à la liberté d'expression
- Droit des peuples à disposer d'eux-mêmes
- Droits civils, politiques, économiques, sociaux et culturels
- Droits culturels
- Droits de l'homme
- Education de l'enfant
- Famille
- Force du marché
- Identité d'origine
- Infractions graves
- Instauration d'une paix durable
- Justice pour mineurs
- Libertés fondamentales
- Maintien du colonialisme
- Maladie mentale
- Mandat spécifique qui a été confié à l'UNESCO
- Mondialisation
- Patrimoine
- Peuples
- Peuples indigènes
- Peuples tribaux
- Pluralisme culturel
- Politiques culturelles
- Processus de mondialisation
- Réalisations des différents peuples (les différences entre les)
- Réduction en esclavage
- Respect de la diversité des cultures, la tolérance, le dialogue et la coopération
- Tolérance (la)

Démocratie

- Actes, méthodes et pratiques de terrorisme
- Démocratie
- Individus, groupes, institutions et organisations non gouvernementales

Développement

- Afrique
- Afrique subsaharienne
- Analphabétisme
- Bien-être des peuples du monde
- Causes socioéconomiques profondes du trafic illicite de migrants
- Communauté
- Conditions primordiales du progrès et du développement
- Conditions propices aux développement pour une grande partie de l'humanité
- Culture
- Démocratie
- Désarmement
- Développement
- Développement et le progrès dans le domaine social (le)
- Discrimination
- Diversité culturelle
- Droit au développement
- Droit des peuples à disposer d'eux-mêmes
- Egalité (l')
- Epidémie mondiale de VIH/sida
- Etre humain
- Facteurs qui rendent les personnes [...] vulnérables à la traite
- Force du marché
- Justice pour mineurs
- Maintien du colonialisme
- Organisation des Nations Unies
- Paix et sécurité internationales
- Partage des responsabilités (le)
- Participation populaire
- Pauvreté
- Personne humaine
- Peuples
- Pleine utilisation des ressources humaines
- Pornographie mettant en scène des enfants
- Progrès social
- Prostitution des enfants
- Respect de la nature (le)
- Sous-développement
- Transfert de la science et de la technique
- Travail des enfants
- Vente d'enfants
- VIH/sida

Dignité (honneur, décente)

- Acte conduisant à une disparition forcée
- Acte de torture
- Attentat à la pudeur
- Avocats
- Clonage à des fins de reproduction d'êtres humains
- Conflits armés
- Contrainte à la prostitution
- Crimes de guerre
- Culture
- Défense de la diversité culturelle
- Développement et le progrès dans le domaine social (le)
- Dignité
- Discrimination
- Droit qu'a toute personne de jouir de conditions de travail justes et favorables
- Droits de l'homme
- Droits fondamentaux
- Epidémie mondiale de VIH/sida
- Etres humains
- Extrême pauvreté et l'exclusion sociale (l')
- Fondement de la liberté, de la justice et de la paix dans le monde
- Génome humain
- Infractions graves
- Liberté (la)
- Libertés fondamentales
- Magistrats du parquet
- Membres de la famille humaine
- Peine ou traitement cruel, inhumain ou dégradant
- Personne humaine
- Pratique d'apartheid
- Principe de l'égalité en dignité et en droits
- Prostitution
- Prostitution forcée
- Réalisation de la science et de la technique
- Recherches sur le génome humain et leurs applications
- Torture
- Traitements humiliants et dégradants
- VIH/sida
- Viol

Discrimination (apartheid)

- Agression d'occupation et de domination étrangères et d'ingérence dans les affaires intérieures des Etats (élimination d')
- Apartheid
- Apartheid (Elimination de l')
- Attaque lancée contre une population civile
- Barrières raciales
- Colonialisme
- Colonialisme (élimination de toutes les formes de)
- Conditions propices aux développement pour une grande partie de l'humanité
- Crime d'apartheid
- Crimes contre l'humanité
- Déséquilibre existant dans les relations économiques internationales
- Différence entre les taux de rémunération
- Discrimination
- Discrimination à l'égard des femmes
- Discrimination raciale
- Discrimination raciale (élimination de la)
- Distinction de caractère défavorable
- Doctrine de supériorité fondée sur la différenciation entre les races
- Droit qu'à toute personne de jouir de conditions de travail justes et favorables
- Droits fondamentaux
- Egalisation des chances
- Egalité de rémunération entre la main d'œuvre masculine et féminine pour travail de valeur égale
- Femmes
- Génocide
- Infractions graves
- Institutions nationales
- Intérêt des enfants
- Intolérance et discriminations fondées sur la religion ou la conviction
- Néocolonialisme (élimination de toutes les formes de)
- Opprobre, le silence, la discrimination et la dénégation ainsi que l'absence de confidentialité (l')
- Persécutions
- Pornographie mettant en scène des enfants
- Pratique d'apartheid
- Principe de la non-discrimination
- Prostitution des enfants
- Racisme
- Racisme (élimination de toutes les formes de)
- Recherches sur le génome humain et leurs applications

- Réduction en esclavage
- Situation des peuples qui souffrent de la faim et de la sous-alimentation
- Torture
- Travail
- Vente d'enfants
- Violence à l'égard des femmes

Discrimination positive (mesure spéciale)

- Attaques sans discrimination
- Crimes de guerre
- Discrimination raciale
- Discriminations
- Infractions graves
- Mesures discriminatoires

Disparition forcée

- Disparitions forcées de personnes

Economie (pauvreté, misère, finances, contributions)

- Afrique
- Afrique subsaharienne
- Analphabétisme
- Bien-être des peuples du monde
- Biens et services culturels
- Causes socioéconomiques profondes du trafic illicite de migrants
- Communauté
- Conditions primordiales du progrès et du développement
- Crimes contre l'humanité
- Culture
- Déficiences
- Délinquant juvénile
- Démocratie
- Désarmement
- Déséquilibre existant dans les relations économiques internationales
- Développement
- Développement et le progrès dans le domaine social (le)
- Différence entre les taux de rémunération
- Discrimination
- Discrimination à l'égard des femmes
- Discrimination raciale
- Diversité culturelle
- Droit à la liberté de pensée, de conscience, de religion ou de conviction

- Droit de toute personne à un niveau de vie suffisant
- Droit des peuples à disposer d'eux-mêmes
- Droits civils, politiques, économiques, sociaux et culturels
- Droits de l'homme
- Epidémie mondiale de VIH/sida
- Esclavage
- Exercice et renforcement de la souveraineté permanente des Etats sur leurs richesses et ressources naturelles
- Extrême pauvreté et l'exclusion sociale (l')
- Facteurs qui rendent les personnes [...] vulnérables à la traite
- Famille
- Femmes
- Femmes rurales
- Force du marché
- Handicap
- Incapacité
- Justice pour mineurs
- Liberté de la recherche
- Libertés fondamentales
- Maintien du colonialisme
- Maladie mentale
- Misère
- Mondialisation
- Nouvel ordre économique international
- Paix et sécurité internationales
- Partage des responsabilités (le)
- Pauvreté
- Personne de condition servile
- Peuples
- Peuples indigènes
- Peuples tribaux
- Pleine utilisation des ressources humaines
- Plus haute aspiration de l'homme
- Politique actuellement adoptées en faveur des handicapés
- Pornographie mettant en scène des enfants
- Préjugé racial
- Prisonniers de guerre
- Processus de mondialisation
- Progrès social
- Prostitution des enfants
- Réalisations des différents peuples (les différences entre les)
- Respect de la nature (le)

- Ressources de la mer et des eaux intérieures
- Servitude pour dettes
- Solidarité (la)
- Sous-développement
- Terres
- Transfert de la science et de la technique
- Travail des enfants
- Vente d'enfants
- VIH/sida
- Violence

Education (enseignement, ignorance)

- Alcool
- Analphabétisme
- Biens à caractère civil
- Conflits armés
- Crimes de guerre
- Culture
- Déficiences
- Dignité
- Discrimination
- Discriminations
- Droit à la liberté d'expression
- Droit à la liberté de pensée, de conscience et de religion
- Droit à la liberté de pensée, de conscience, de religion ou de conviction
- Education
- Education de l'enfant
- Education familiale
- Enseignement
- Etres humains
- Génome humain
- Handicap
- Handicapés
- Incapacité
- Individus, organisations non gouvernementales et institutions compétentes
- Institutions nationales
- Intérêt des enfants
- Mineur
- Pauvreté
- Personnes souffrant d'incapacités
- Politique actuellement adoptées en faveur des handicapés
- Pornographie mettant en scène des enfants

- Prostitution des enfants
- Racisme
- Sous-développement
- Travail
- Travail des enfants
- Travailleurs migrants et membres de leur famille
- Vente d'enfants
- Violation des lois ou coutumes de guerre
- Violence à l'égard des femmes
-

Egalité

- Culture
- Développement et le progrès dans le domaine social (le)
- Différence entre les taux de rémunération
- Discrimination
- Discrimination à l'égard des femmes
- Discrimination raciale
- Discriminations
- Droit qu'a toute personne de jouir de conditions de travail justes et favorables
- Droits de l'homme
- Education de l'enfant
- Egalisation des chances
- Egalité (l')
- Egalité de rémunération entre la main d'œuvre masculine et féminine pour travail de valeur égale
- Egalité entre les sexes et émancipations des femmes
- Etres humains
- Fondement de la liberté, de la justice et de la paix dans le monde
- Handicap
- Intérêt des enfants
- Intolérance et discrimination fondées sur la religion ou la conviction
- Mercenaires
- Personnes
- Personnes souffrant d'incapacités
- Pleine utilisation des ressources humaines
- Principe de l'égalité de droits
- Principe de l'égalité en dignité et en droits
- Principe de la non-discrimination
- Tâche primordiale de tous les Etats et de toutes les organisations internationales
- Violence

Enfant (mineur, jeune, fillette)

- Accroissement de la délinquance juvénile
- Apatride
- Blessés
- Comportement ou la conduite d'un jeune qui n'est pas conforme aux normes et valeurs sociales (le)
- Crimes contre l'humanité
- Crimes de guerre
- Délinquant juvénile
- Droits de l'enfant
- Droits fondamentaux des femmes et des fillettes
- Education de l'enfant
- Education familiale
- Egalité entre les sexes et émancipations des femmes
- Enfant
- Enfants
- Esclavage
- Eviter de [lui] nuire
- Facteurs qui rendent les personnes [...] vulnérables à la traite
- Famille
- Fillettes
- Forces armées d'un Etat
- Intérêt des enfants
- Jeunes détenus
- Justice pour mineurs
- Liberté (la)
- Malades
- Maternité
- Membres de la famille
- Mères
- Mesures discriminatoires
- Mineur
- Parents adoptifs
- Parents nourriciers
- Personne de condition servile
- Pires formes de travail des enfants (les)
- Populations déstabilisées par les conflits armés, les situations d'urgence humanitaire et les catastrophes naturelles
- Pornographie mettant en scène des enfants
- Possession d'effets personnels
- Principe de proportionnalité
- Procès « juste et équitable »

- Réactions de la société et de la justice à la criminalité et à la délinquance juvéniles
- Réduction en esclavage
- Représentant personnel
- Seuil de responsabilité pénale
- Structure familiale
- Système de la justice pour les mineurs
- Tourisme sexuel
- Toutes les formes de violence contre les femmes et les filles
- Traite des êtres humains et de l'exploitation de la prostitution d'autrui (la)
- Travail des enfants
- Vente d'enfants
- VIH/sida
- Violence à l'égard des femmes

Environnement (nature)

- Catastrophes naturelles
- Conflits armés
- Conflits et catastrophes naturelles
- Crimes contre l'humanité
- Culture
- Diversité culturelle
- Education de l'enfant
- Populations déstabilisées par les conflits armés, les situations d'urgence humanitaire et les catastrophes naturelles
- Prévention
- Respect de la nature (le)
- Ressources de la mer et des eaux intérieures
- Restitution
- Terres

Esclavage (exploitation)

- Attaque lancée contre une population civile
- Contrainte à la prostitution
- Crimes contre l'humanité
- Crimes de guerre
- Déportation ou transfert forcé de population
- Discrimination raciale
- Esclavage
- Esclavage sexuel
- Exploitation
- Facteurs qui rendent les personnes [...] vulnérables à la traite
- Fillettes

- Grossesse forcée
- Personne de condition servile
- Pires formes de travail des enfants (les)
- Prostitution
- Prostitution des enfants
- Prostitution forcée
- Réduction en esclavage
- Servage
- Servitude pour dettes
- Tâche primordiale de tous les Etats et de toutes les organisations internationales
- Torture
- Toutes les formes de violence contre les femmes et les filles
- Traite des esclaves
- Traite des êtres humains en vue de la prostitution
- Traite des êtres humains et de l'exploitation de la prostitution d'autrui (la)
- Travail forcé ou obligatoire
- Vente d'enfants
- Viol
- Violence à l'égard des femmes
- Violence sexuelle

Famille

- Culture, la famille, les valeurs morales et la religion (la)
- Dignité
- Discriminations
- Droit de toute personne à un niveau de vie suffisant
- Droit qu'à toute personne de jouir de conditions de travail justes et favorables
- Education familiale
- Epidémie mondiale de VIH/sida
- Esclavage
- Famille
- Famille élargie
- Femmes rurales
- Infractions graves
- Intérêt des enfants
- Maladie mentale
- Membres de la famille
- Mères
- Migrations
- Opprobre, le silence, la discrimination et la dénégation ainsi que l'absence de confidentialité (l')
- Parents adoptifs

- Parents nourriciers
- Personne de condition servile
- Pornographie mettant en scène des enfants
- Principe de proportionnalité
- Procès « juste et équitable »
- Processus de migration des travailleurs migrants et des membres de leur famille
- Prostitution
- Prostitution des enfants
- Réparation
- Représentant personnel
- Sécurité sociale
- Structure familiale
- Traite des êtres humains en vue de la prostitution
- Travailleurs indépendants
- Travailleurs migrants et membres de leur famille
- Travailleurs migrants et membres de leur famille (dépourvus de documents ou en situation irrégulière)
- Travailleurs migrants et membres de leur famille (pourvus de documents ou en situation régulière)
- Vente d'enfants
- VIH/sida
- Violence à l'égard des femmes

Femme (fillette)

- Affections gynécologiques chroniques graves
- Blessés
- Crimes contre l'humanité
- Discrimination à l'égard des femmes
- Droit qu'à toute personne de jouir de conditions de travail justes et favorables
- Droits fondamentaux des femmes et des fillettes
- Education familiale
- Egalité (l')
- Egalité de rémunération entre la main d'œuvre masculine et féminine pour travail de valeur égale
- Egalité entre les sexes et émancipations des femmes
- Esclavage
- Facteurs qui rendent les personnes [...] vulnérables à la traite
- Femmes
- Femmes rurales
- Fillettes
- Génocide

- Grossesses et affections obstétricales, lorsque l'hospitalisation en pays neutre est impossible
- Grossesse forcée
- Intérêt des enfants
- Malades
- Maternité
- Mères
- Mesures discriminatoires
- Personne de condition servile
- Populations déstabilisées par les conflits armés, les situations d'urgence humanitaire et les catastrophes naturelles
- Réduction en esclavage
- Sexe
- Toutes les formes de violence contre les femmes et les filles
- Travail
- VIH/sida
- Viol
- Viol systématique des femmes en temps de guerre
- Violence
- Violence à l'égard des femmes

Gène

- Clonage à des fins de reproduction d'êtres humains
- Dignité
- Génome humain
- Recherches sur le génome humain et leurs applications
- Responsabilités inhérentes aux activités des chercheurs

Génocide

- Apartheid
- Crimes contre l'humanité
- Crimes politiques
- Droits fondamentaux
- Extermination
- Génocide
- Grossesse forcée
- Méconnaissance et mépris des droits de l'homme
- Nettoyage ethnique
- Pénalement responsable
- Viol systématique des femmes en temps de guerre
- Violence sexuelle

Géographie

- Afrique
- Afrique subsaharienne
- Amérique Latine(région de l')
- Asie et du Pacifique(région de l')
- Autorités compétentes pour prendre une décision
- Caraïbes(région de l')
- Crimes contre l'humanité
- Déportation ou transfert forcé de population
- Europe centrale et Orientale(région de l')
- Handicapés
- Justice pour mineurs
- Peuples indigènes
- Réfugié
- VIH/sida

Guerre (militaire, conflit, force armée, militaire, hostilités)

- Absence de guerre
- Actes nuisibles à l'ennemi (ne sont pas considérés comme)
- Agression d'occupation et de domination étrangères et d'ingérence dans les affaires intérieures des Etats (élimination d')
- Apatride
- Attaque lancée contre une population civile
- Attaques
- Attaques sans discrimination
- Biens à caractère civil
- Blessés
- Comité international de la Croix Rouge
- Conflit armé
- Conflits armés
- Conflits et catastrophes naturelles
- Crime d'agression
- Crimes contre l'humanité
- Crimes de guerre
- Désarmement
- Emeutes
- Enlèvement de mines
- Espionnage
- Evasion
- Expériences médicales ou scientifiques non nécessitées par traitement médical
- Forces armées
- Forces armées d'un Etat

- Génocide
- Guerre
- Hors de combat
- Infractions graves
- Instauration d'une paix durable
- Localité non défendue
- Malades
- Matériel
- Membres des forces armées
- Mépris et la violation des droits de l'homme et des libertés fondamentales (le)
- Mercenaire
- Mercenaires
- Meurtre
- Moyen de transport sanitaire
- Moyens de transport sanitaire permanents
- Moyens de transport sanitaire temporaire
- Mutilations
- Naufrages
- Navire
- Nettoyage ethnique
- Occupation
- Organismes de protection civile
- Peine de mort
- Peine ou traitement cruel, inhumain ou dégradant
- Peines corporelles
- Perfidie
- Personne humaine
- Personnel
- Personnel religieux
- Personnel sanitaire
- Personnel sanitaire permanent
- Personnel sanitaire temporaire
- Pires formes de travail des enfants (les)
- Population civile
- Populations déstabilisées par les conflits armés, les situations d'urgence humanitaire et les catastrophes naturelles
- Pornographie mettant en scène des enfants
- Prévention
- Prisonniers de guerre
- Prostitution des enfants
- Protection civile
- Puissance protectrice

- Réalisation de la science et de la technique
- Réfugié
- Règles de droit international applicable dans les conflits armés
- Responsabilité pénale
- Ruses de guerre
- Sociétés nationales de la croix-rouge
- Substitut
- Tâche primordiale de tous les Etats et de toutes les organisations internationales
- Torture
- Transferts forcés
- Travail forcé ou obligatoire
- Unités sanitaires
- Unités sanitaires permanentes
- Unités sanitaires temporaires
- Véhicule sanitaire
- Vente d'enfants
- Viol systématique des femmes en temps de guerre
- Violation des lois ou coutumes de guerre
- Zone de contact
- Zones démilitarisées

Handicapé

- Autorité indépendante
- Conseil
- Consentement en connaissance de cause
- Déficiences
- Discrimination
- Discriminations
- Egalisation des chances
- Handicap
- Handicapé
- Handicapés
- Incapacité
- Mesures discriminatoires
- Personnes souffrant d'incapacités
- Politique actuellement adoptées en faveur des handicapés
- Réadaptation
- Règles [...]caractère coutumier au plan international

Humain

- Acte conduisant à une disparition forcée
- Acte de torture

- Apartheid
- Clonage à des fins de reproduction d'êtres humains
- Colonialisme
- Communauté
- Culture
- Défense de la diversité culturelle
- Développement et le progrès dans le domaine social (le)
- Dignité
- Discrimination
- Discrimination raciale
- Discrimination raciale (élimination de la)
- Droit à la liberté d'expression
- Droit au développement
- Droits de l'homme
- Droits fondamentaux
- Droits fondamentaux des femmes et des fillettes
- Education
- Egalité (l')
- Enfant
- Epidémie mondiale de VIH/sida
- Esclavage
- Esclave
- Etre humain
- Etres humains
- Expérience médicale ou scientifique
- Extrême pauvreté et l'exclusion sociale (l')
- Facteurs qui rendent les personnes [...] vulnérables à la traite
- Fondement de la liberté, de la justice et de la paix dans le monde
- Génome humain
- Handicap
- Homme
- Incapacité
- Identité d'origine
- Individu
- Individus, groupes, institutions et organisations non gouvernementales
- Individus, organisations non gouvernementales et institutions compétentes
- Liberté (la)
- Libertés fondamentales
- Misère
- Néocolonialisme (élimination de toutes les formes de)
- Peine ou traitement cruel, inhumain ou dégradant
- Personne (toute)

- Personne humaine
- Plus haute aspiration de l'homme
- Principe de l'égalité en dignité et en droits
- Principe de la non-discrimination
- Prostitution
- Racisme
- Racisme (élimination de toutes les formes de)
- Réalisation de la science et de la technique
- Recherches sur le génome humain et leurs applications
- Tolérance (la)
- Torture
- Traite des êtres humains en vue de la prostitution
- Traitements humiliants et dégradants
- VIH/sida

Humanitaire (assistance, sanitaire)

- Comité international de la Croix Rouge
- Conflits armés
- Crimes contre l'humanité
- Droit à la liberté de pensée, de conscience, de religion ou de conviction
- Infractions graves
- Matériel
- Membres des forces armées
- Moyens de transport sanitaire permanents
- Moyens de transport sanitaire temporaires
- Navire et embarcation sanitaires
- Organismes de protection civile
- Personnel
- Personnel religieux
- Personnel sanitaire
- Personnel sanitaire permanent
- Personnel sanitaire temporaire
- Populations déstabilisées par les conflits armés, les situations d'urgence humanitaire et les catastrophes naturelles
- Prisonniers de guerre
- Protection civile
- Signal distinctif
- Signe distinctif
- Sociétés nationales de la croix-rouge
- Substitut
- Transport sanitaire
- Unités sanitaires

- Unités sanitaires permanentes
- Unités sanitaires temporaires
- Véhicule sanitaire

Humanité
- Conditions propices aux développement pour une grande partie de l'humanité
- Culture
- Dignité
- Diversité culturelle
- Etres humains
- Fondement de la liberté, de la justice et de la paix dans le monde
- Génocide
- Génome humain
- Instauration d'une paix durable
- Membres de la famille humaine
- Mépris et la violation des droits de l'homme et des libertés fondamentales (le)
- Mondialisation
- Organisation des Nations Unies
- Paludisme
- Patrimoine
- Personne humaine
- Personnel
- Recherches sur le génome humain et leurs applications
- Supériorité/infériorité raciale ou ethnique
- Tolérance (la)
- VIH/sida

Identité
- Culture
- Dignité
- Diversité culturelle
- Education de l'enfant
- Identité d'origine
- Pluralisme culturel

Intégrité mentale
- Attaque lancée contre une population civile
- Blessés
- Consentement en connaissance de cause
- Crimes contre l'humanité
- Discrimination
- Education de l'enfant

- Erreur de droit
- Erreur de fait
- Génocide
- Handicap
- Handicapé
- Handicapés
- Incapacité
- Infractions graves
- Malades
- Maladie mentale
- Mesures non privatives de liberté
- Mesures non privatives de liberté (l'adoption, la définition et l'application)
- Meurtre
- Mutilations
- Organe de révision
- Patient
- Peine ou traitement cruel, inhumain ou dégradant
- Peines corporelles
- Praticien de santé mentale
- Prévention
- Réadaptation
- Réduction en esclavage
- Responsabilité pénale
- Sécurité sociale
- Service de santé mentale
- Seuil de responsabilité pénale
- Soins de santé mentale
- Torture
- Victimes
- Violence à l'égard des femmes

Intégrité Physique (intégrité corporelle, mutilations)

- Asthme chronique
- Attaque lancée contre une population civile
- Attaques sans discrimination
- Blessés
- Bronchectasie
- Bronchite chronique se prolongeant pendant plus d'une année en captivité
- Conflits armés
- Crimes contre l'humanité
- Crimes de guerre
- Diabète sucré nécessitant un traitement à l'insuline

- Dysenterie amibienne ou bacillaire avec troubles considérables
- Education de l'enfant
- Emphysème pulmonaire grave (avec ou sans bronchite)
- Equivalents à la perte d'une main ou d'un pied
- Expériences médicales ou scientifiques non nécessitées par traitement médical
- Génocide
- Glaucome
- Grossesse forcée
- Handicap
- Handicapé
- Handicapés
- Incapacité
- Infractions graves
- Iritis
- Lèpre
- Malades
- Mesures non privatives de liberté
- Mesures non privatives de liberté (l'adoption, la définition et l'application)
- Meurtre
- Mutilations
- Paludisme avec altérations organiques prononcées
- Peine ou traitement cruel, inhumain ou dégradant
- Peines corporelles
- Prévention
- Réadaptation
- Réduction en esclavage
- Responsabilité pénale
- Sécurité sociale
- Stérilisation forcée
- Syphilis viscérale tertiaire, résistant au traitement
- Torture
- Trachome
- Victimes
- Violence à l'égard des femmes
- Violence sexuelle

Justice (juridique)

- Autorité compétente
- Autorité judiciaire
- Autorité judiciaire ou autre (une)
- Autorités compétentes pour prendre une décision
- Autorités ou instances de contrôle ou de recours compétentes

- Avocats
- But et la justice des peines et mesures privatives de liberté
- Communication de masse
- Connaissance
- Conseil
- Cour pénale internationale
- Crime d'agression
- Crimes politiques
- Crimes contre l'humanité
- Crimes de guerre
- Délinquant juvénile
- Délinquants
- Délit
- Détention
- Détention provisoire
- Développement et le progrès dans le domaine social (le)
- Dignité
- Droits de l'enfant
- Emprisonnement
- Enfant
- Erreur de droit
- Erreur de fait
- Fondement de la liberté, de la justice et de la paix dans le monde
- Infractions graves
- Institutions nationales
- Jeunes détenus
- Juges
- Justice pour mineurs
- Magistrats
- Magistrats du parquet
- Menace à la vie et à la sécurité des responsables de l'application des lois
- Membres de la famille humaine
- Mesures discriminatoires
- Mineur
- Mutilations
- Nouvel ordre économique international
- Organe de révision
- Peine de mort
- Peine ou traitement cruel, inhumain ou dégradant
- Personne accusée
- Personne détenue
- Personne emprisonnée

- Présumée innocente
- Privations de liberté
- Procès « juste et équitable »
- Réactions de la société et de la justice à la criminalité et à la délinquance juvéniles
- Remise
- Responsabilité pénale
- Responsable de l'application des lois
- Responsables de l'application des lois
- Système de la justice pour les mineurs
- Travail forcé ou obligatoire
- Victime
- Victimes
- Violence

Langue

- Consentement en connaissance de cause
- Discrimination
- Discriminations
- Distinction de caractère défavorable
- Droits civils, politiques, économiques, sociaux et culturels
- Education de l'enfant
- Promotion et protection de tous les droits de l'homme et de toutes les libertés fondamentales
- Promotion et protection des droits des personnes appartenant à des minorités nationales ou ethniques, religieuses et linguistiques
- Protection constante et la réalisation des droits des personnes appartenant à des minorités nationales ou ethniques, religieuses et linguistiques (la)
- Tolérance (la)

Liberté

- Consentement en connaissance de cause
- Culture
- Démocratie
- Dignité
- Diversité culturelle
- Droit à la liberté d'expression
- Droit à la liberté de pensée, de conscience et de religion
- Droit à la liberté de pensée, de conscience, de religion ou de conviction
- Droit à la liberté d'opinion et d'expression
- Education de l'enfant
- Etres humains
- Fondement de la liberté, de la justice et de la paix dans le monde

- Juges
- Liberté (la)
- Liberté de la recherche
- Libertés fondamentales
- Membres de la famille humaine
- Mineur
- Personne détenue
- Peuples
- Plus haute aspiration de l'homme
- Principe de la non-discrimination
- Recherches sur le génome humain et leurs applications
- Religion
- Structure familiale

Logement
- Biens à caractère civil
- Droit de toute personne à un niveau de vie suffisant
- Matérie

Mariage
- Certaines coutumes, anciennes lois et pratiques intéressant le mariage et la famille
- Discrimination à l'égard des femmes
- Esclavage
- Famille
- Intérêt des enfants
- Mariage
- Membres de la famille
- Personne de condition servile
- Structure familiale
- Travail

Migrant
- Causes socioéconomiques profondes du trafic illicite de migrants
- Dignité
- Document de voyage ou d'identité frauduleux
- Entrée illégale
- Etat d'emploi
- Etat d'origine
- Etat de transit
- Exploitation
- Famille

- Gens de mer
- Membres de la famille
- Migrations
- Processus de migration des travailleurs migrants et des membres de leur famille
- Trafic illicite des migrants
- Travail forcé ou obligatoire
- Travail d'une installation en mer
- Travailleurs admis pour un emploi spécifique
- Travailleurs employés au titre de projet
- Travailleurs transfrontaliers
- Travailleurs indépendants
- Travailleurs itinérants
- Travailleurs migrants
- Travailleurs migrants et membres de leur famille
- Travailleurs migrants et membres de leur famille (dépourvus de documents ou en situation irrégulière)
- Travailleurs migrants et membres de leur famille (pourvus de documents ou en situation régulière)
- Travailleurs saisonniers
-

Minorité (autochtone, tribu)

- Apartheid
- Apartheid (Elimination de l')
- Colonialisme
- Crimes contre l'humanité
- Défense de la diversité culturelle
- Discrimination
- Discrimination raciale
- Education de l'enfant
- Peuples indigènes
- Promotion et protection de tous les droits de l'homme et de toutes les libertés fondamentales
- Promotion et protection des droits des personnes appartenant à des minorités nationales ou ethniques, religieuses et linguistiques
- Protection constante et la réalisation des droits des personnes appartenant à des minorités nationales ou ethniques, religieuses et linguistiques (la)
- Racisme
- Restitution
- Terres
- Travail forcé ou obligatoire

Nation

- Attaque lancée contre une population civile
- Buts et principes énoncés dans la Charte des Nations Unies
- Conditions primordiales du progrès et du développement
- Conditions propices aux développement pour une grande partie de l'humanité
- Crimes de guerre
- Déclaration universelle des droits de l'homme
- Dignité
- Discrimination
- Droits de l'enfant
- Droits de l'homme
- Education
- Education de l'enfant
- Egalité (l')
- Epidémie mondiale de VIH/sida
- Individus, organisations non gouvernementales et institutions compétentes
- Mépris et la violation des droits de l'homme et des libertés fondamentales (le)
- Opprobre, le silence, la discrimination et la dénégation ainsi que l'absence de confidentialité (l')
- Partage des responsabilités (le)
- Persécutions
- Peuples tribaux
- Promotion et protection de tous les droits de l'homme et de toutes les libertés fondamentales
- Promotion et protection des droits des personnes appartenant à des minorités nationales ou ethniques, religieuses et linguistiques
- Protection constante et la réalisation des droits des personnes appartenant à des minorités nationales ou ethniques, religieuses et linguistiques (la)
- Racisme
- Réalisation de la science et de la technique
- Réalisations des différents peuples (les différences entre les)
- Nationalité (apatride, réfugiés, ascendance nationale, origine nationale)
- Apatride
- Crimes de guerre
- Discrimination
- Discrimination raciale
- Discriminations
- Etranger
- Gens de mer
- Infractions graves
- Pays dont elle a la nationalité (du)
- Persécutions

- Populations déstabilisées par les conflits armés, les situations d'urgence humanitaire et les catastrophes naturelles
- Réduction en esclavage
- Réfugié
- Structure familiale
- Trafic illicite des migrants
- Travail d'une installation en mer
- Travailleurs migrants et membres de leur famille
- Viol systématique des femmes en temps de guerre
- Norme
- Absence de guerre
- Acte de torture
- Autorités compétentes pour prendre une décision
- Buts et principes énoncés dans la Charte des Nations Unies
- Certaines coutumes, anciennes lois et pratiques intéressant le mariage et la famille
- Comportement ou la conduite d'un jeune qui n'est pas conforme aux normes et valeurs sociales (le)
- Conditions primordiales du progrès et du développement
- Conflits armés
- Crime d'agression
- Crimes contre l'humanité
- Crimes de guerre
- Culture
- Culture, la famille, les valeurs morales et la religion (la)
- Déclaration universelle des droits de l'homme
- Défense de la diversité culturelle
- Dignité
- Droits de l'homme
- Droits fondamentaux
- Education de l'enfant
- Enfant
- Esclavage
- Esclave
- Extrême pauvreté et l'exclusion sociale (l')
- Famille
- Femmes rurales
- Fondement de la liberté, de la justice et de la paix dans le monde
- Génocide
- Haut commissaire aux droits de l'homme
- Individu
- Individus, groupes, institutions et organisations non gouvernementales
- Infractions graves

- Libertés fondamentales
- Membres de la famille humaine
- Naufrages
- Nettoyage ethnique
- Pactes internationaux relatifs aux droits de l'homme
- Peine ou traitement cruel, inhumain ou dégradant
- Personne de condition servile
- Personnel sanitaire
- Pleine utilisation des ressources humaines
- Prisonniers de guerre
- Puissance protectrice
- Réduction en esclavage
- Règles [...]caractère coutumier au plan international
- Règles de droit international applicable dans les conflits armés
- Révolte contre la tyrannie et l'oppression
- Servage
- Servitude pour dettes
- Signal distinctif
- Sujétion des peuples
- Torture
- Transport sanitaire
- Travailleurs indépendants
- Violence sexuelle
- Zones démilitarisées

Nourriture

- Afrique
- Afrique subsaharienne
- Bien-être des peuples du monde
- Crimes contre l'humanité
- Droit de toute personne à un niveau de vie suffisant
- Extermination
- Génome humain
- Infractions graves
- Liberté (la)
- Prévention
- Ressources de la mer et des eaux intérieures
- Situation des peuples qui souffrent de la faim et de la sous-alimentation

Organisation des Nations Unies (ONU, organisations internationales)

- Absence de guerre

- Apatride
- Assemblée générale
- Buts et principes énoncés dans la Charte des Nations Unies
- Certaines coutumes, anciennes lois et pratiques intéressant le mariage et la famille
- Conditions primordiales du progrès et du développement
- Conflits armés
- Cour pénale internationale
- Crime d'agression
- Crimes contre l'humanité
- Déclaration universelle des droits de l'homme
- Déficiences
- Développement et le progrès dans le domaine social (le)
- Dignité
- Discriminations
- Droits de l'homme
- Droits fondamentaux
- Education
- Education de l'enfant
- Famille
- Fondement de la liberté, de la justice et de la paix dans le monde
- Génocide
- Handicap
- Haut commissaire aux droits de l'homme
- Incapacité
- Individus, groupes, institutions et organisations non gouvernementales
- Institutions nationales
- Libertés fondamentales
- Maintien du colonialisme
- Mandat spécifique qui a été confié à l'UNESCO
- Membres de la famille humaine
- Organisations des Nations Unies
- Pactes internationaux relatifs aux droits de l'homme
- Partage des responsabilités (le)
- Peine ou traitement cruel, inhumain ou dégradant
- Pleine utilisation des ressources humaines
- Protection constante et la réalisation des droits des personnes appartenant à des minorités nationales ou ethniques, religieuses et linguistiques (la)
- Réfugié
- Sujétion des peuples
- Tâche primordiale de tous les Etats et de toutes les organisations internationales
- Torture
- Travailleurs migrants et membres de leur famille

Paix (sécurité)

- Apartheid
- Apatride
- Conflits armés
- Crimes contre l'humanité
- Crimes de guerre
- Dignité
- Discrimination
- Discriminations
- Education
- Education de l'enfant
- Fondement de la liberté, de la justice et de la paix dans le monde
- Génocide
- Individus, organisations non gouvernementales et institutions compétentes
- Instauration d'une paix durable
- Justice pour mineurs
- Maintien du colonialisme
- Membres de la famille humaine
- Organisation des Nations Unies
- Paix et sécurité internationales
- Partage des responsabilités (le)
- Pluralisme culturel
- Progrès social
- Racisme
- Réfugié
- Respect de la diversité des cultures, la tolérance, le dialogue et la coopération
- Sujétion des peuples
- Tolérance (la)

Pays pauvres

- Afrique
- Afrique subsaharienne
- Bien-être des peuples du monde
- Causes socioéconomiques profondes du trafic illicite de migrants
- Désarmement
- Développement
- Situation des peuples qui souffrent de la faim et de la sous-alimentation
- Sous-développement
- Transfert de la science et de la technique
- VIH/sida
- Pénal
- Accroissement de la délinquance juvénile

- Acte de corruption
- Aide postpénitentiaire (efficace au détenu libéré)
- Arrestation
- Attaque lancée contre une population civile
- But et la justification des peines et mesures privatives de liberté (le)
- Connaissance
- Corruption
- Cour pénale internationale
- Crime
- Crimes politiques
- Crimes contre l'humanité
- Délinquant juvénile
- Délinquants
- Déportation ou transfert forcé de population
- Détention
- Détention provisoire
- Disparitions forcées de personnes
- Document de voyage ou d'identité frauduleux
- Droits fondamentaux
- Emeutes
- Emprisonnement
- Erreur de droit
- Esclavage sexuel
- Eviter de [lui] nuire
- Génocide
- Infractions graves
- Intention
- Jeunes détenus
- Juges
- Justice pour mineurs
- Méconnaissance et mépris des droits de l'homme
- Meurtre
- Mineur
- Peine de mort
- Peines corporelles
- Pénalement responsable
- Persécutions
- Personnes accusée
- Personne détenue
- Personne emprisonnée
- Pornographie mettant en scène des enfants
- Présumée innocente

- Prévenu
- Principe de proportionnalité
- Privations de liberté
- Procès « juste et équitable »
- Réactions de la société et de la justice à la criminalité et à la délinquance juvéniles
- Remise
- Réparation
- Responsable de l'application des lois
- Responsables de l'application des lois
- Seuil de responsabilité pénale
- Système de la justice pour les mineurs
- Torture
- Victimes

Peuple

- Bien-être des peuples du monde
- Buts et principes énoncés dans la Charte des Nations Unies
- Conditions primordiales du progrès et du développement
- Déclaration universelle des droits de l'homme
- Démocratie
- Désarmement
- Développement
- Développement et le progrès dans le domaine social (le)
- Discrimination
- Droit des peuples à disposer d'eux-mêmes
- Education de l'enfant
- Maintien du colonialisme
- Mépris et la violation des droits de l'homme et des libertés fondamentales (le)
- Peuples
- Peuples indigènes
- Peuples tribaux
- Principe de l'égalité en dignité et en droits
- Promotion et protection de tous les droits de l'homme et de toutes les libertés fondamentales
- Racisme
- Réalisations des différents peuples (les différences entre les)
- Responsabilité pénale
- Situation des peuples qui souffrent de la faim et de la sous-alimentation
- Sujétion des peuples
- Terres

Politique

- Afrique
- Afrique subsaharienne
- Attaque lancée contre une population civile
- Bien-être des peuples du monde
- Communauté
- Conditions primordiales du progrès et du développement
- Crimes contre l'humanité
- Crimes politiques
- Démocratie
- Développement
- Développement et le progrès dans le domaine social (le)
- Discrimination
- Discrimination à l'égard des femmes
- Discrimination raciale
- Disparitions forcées de personnes
- Distinction de caractère défavorable
- Droit à la liberté d'opinion et d'expression
- Droit des peuples à disposer d'eux-mêmes
- Droits civils, politiques, économiques, sociaux et culturels
- Droits de l'homme
- Famille
- Maladie mentale
- Mercenaires
- Pactes internationaux relatifs aux droits de l'homme
- Peuples
- Peuples indigènes
- Pluralisme culturel
- Politique actuellement adoptées en faveur des handicapés
- Politiques culturelles

Privation de liberté (Internement, emprisonnement, otage)

- Acte conduisant à une disparition forcée
- Aide postpénitentiaire (efficace au détenu libéré)
- Attaque lancée contre une population civile
- But et la justice des peines et mesures privatives de liberté
- Conflits armés
- Crimes contre l'humanité
- Crimes de guerre
- Déportation ou transfert forcé de population
- Détention
- Détention provisoire

- Dignité
- Disparitions forcées de personnes
- Emprisonnement
- Espionnage
- Etablissements ouverts
- Evasion
- Infractions graves
- Internement
- Jeunes détenus
- Membres des forces armées
- Mineur
- Peine ou traitement cruel, inhumain ou dégradant
- Personne détenue
- Personne emprisonnée
- Personne humaine
- Prévenu
- Prisonniers de guerre
- Privations de liberté
- Réduction en esclavage
- Torture
- Violence à l'égard des femmes

Race (ethnie, couleur, origine)

- Agression d'occupation et de domination étrangères et d'ingérence dans les affaires intérieures des Etats (élimination d')
- Apartheid
- Apartheid (Elimination de l')
- Attaque lancée contre une population civile
- Barrières raciales
- Colonialisme
- Colonialisme (élimination de toutes les formes de)
- Conditions propices aux développement pour une grande partie de l'humanité
- Conflits armés
- Crime d'apartheid
- Crimes contre l'humanité
- Déséquilibre existant dans les relations économiques internationales
- Développement et le progrès dans le domaine social (le)
- Discrimination
- Discrimination raciale
- Discrimination raciale (élimination de la)
- Distinction de caractère défavorable
- Doctrine de supériorité fondée sur la différenciation entre les races

- Droits civils, politiques, économiques, sociaux et culturels
- Education
- Famille
- Génocide
- Individus, organisations non gouvernementales et institutions compétentes
- Institutions nationales
- Maladie mentale
- Néocolonialisme (élimination de toutes les formes de)
- Nettoyage ethnique
- Persécutions
- Pratique d'apartheid
- Préjugé racial
- Principe de l'égalité en dignité et en droits
- Promotion et protection de tous les droits de l'homme et de toutes les libertés fondamentales
- Promotion et protection des droits des personnes appartenant à des minorités nationales ou ethniques, religieuses et linguistiques
- Protection constante et la réalisation des droits des personnes appartenant à des minorités nationales ou ethniques, religieuses et linguistiques (la)
- Racisme
- Racisme (élimination de toutes les formes de)
- Réduction en esclavage
- Réfugié
- Situation des peuples qui souffrent de la faim et de la sous-alimentation
- Structure familiale
- Supériorité/infériorité raciale ou ethnique
- Tâche primordiale de tous les Etats et de toutes les organisations internationales
- VIH/sida
- Viol systématique des femmes en temps de guerre
- Violence sexuelle

Relativisme

- Culture
- Culture, la famille, les valeurs morales et la religion (la)
- Déclaration universelle des droits de l'homme
- Défense de la diversité culturelle
- Délinquant juvénile
- Délit
- Dignité
- Diversité culturelle
- Droits de l'homme
- Enfant

- Famille
- Handicap
- Identité d'origine
- Individus, organisations non gouvernementales et institutions compétentes
- Patrimoine
- Personnes âgées
- Pluralisme culturel
- Réalisations des différents peuples (les différences entre les)
- Seuil de responsabilité pénale
- Sexe
- Tolérance (la)

Santé (Médecine, expérience)

- Aéronefs sanitaires
- Affections gynécologiques chroniques graves
- Alcool
- Alcoolisme
- Amérique Latine(région de l')
- Arthroses déformantes
- Asie et du Pacifique(région de l')
- Asthme chronique
- Blessés
- Bronchectasie
- Bronchite chronique se prolongeant pendant plus d'une année en captivité
- Caraïbes(région de l')
- Cécité des yeux ou celle d'un œil
- Chloroidite
- Cholécystopathie chronique
- Cirrhose hépatique
- Cocaïnisme
- Conflits armés
- Consentement en connaissance de cause
- Crimes contre l'humanité
- Crimes de guerre
- Culture, la famille, les valeurs morales et la religion (la)
- Déficiences
- Diabète sucré nécessitant un traitement à l'insuline
- Droit à la liberté de pensée, de conscience, de religion ou de conviction
- Droit qu'à toute personne de jouir de conditions de travail justes et favorables
- Dysenterie amibienne ou bacillaire avec troubles considérables
- Emphysème pulmonaire grave (avec ou sans bronchite)
- Epidémie mondiale de VIH/sida

- Equivalents à la perte d'une main ou d'un pied
- Europe centrale et Orientale(région de l')
- Expérience médicale ou scientifique
- Expériences médicales ou scientifiques non nécessitées par traitement médical
- Extermination
- Famille
- Gastrite, entérite ou colique chroniques durant plus d'une année et affectant gravement l'état général
- Génome humain
- Glaucome
- Grossesses et affections obstétricales, lorsque l'hospitalisation en pays neutre est impossible
- Handicap
- Handicapé
- Handicapés
- Hors de combat
- Hydrargyrisme
- Hydro ou pyonéphrose
- Incapacité
- Infractions graves
- Intoxications par les gaz et parles radiations
- Iritis
- Lèpre
- Malades
- Maladies chroniques du rein avec troubles consécutifs
- Maladie mentale
- Matériel
- Membres des forces armées
- Mesures discriminatoires
- Mesures non privatives de liberté
- Mesures non privatives de liberté (l'adoption, la définition et l'application)
- Meurtre
- Morphinisme
- Moyens de transport sanitaire permanents
- Moyens de transport sanitaire temporaires
- Mutilations
- Navire et embarcation sanitaires
- Néphrectomie pour un rein tuberculeux
- Opprobre, le silence, la discrimination et la dénégation ainsi que l'absence de confidentialité (l')
- Organe de révision
- Organismes de protection civile
- Paludisme

- Paludisme avec altérations organiques prononcées
- Patient
- Peines corporelles
- Personnel
- Personnel religieux
- Personnel sanitaire
- Personnel sanitaire permanent
- Personnel sanitaire temporaire
- Pires formes de travail des enfants (les)
- Polyarthrite chronique évolutive primaire et secondaire
- Praticien de santé mentale
- Prévention
- Prisonniers de guerre
- Protection civile
- Pyélite chronique ou cystite chronique
- Réadaptation
- Réduction en esclavage
- Responsabilités inhérentes aux activités des chercheurs
- Rhumatisme avec manifestations cliniques graves
- Saturnisme
- Sécurité sociale
- Service de santé mentale
- Signe distinctif
- Soins de santé mentale
- Soins médicaux
- Suite d'intervention chirurgicale sur l'estomac faite en captivité
- Syphilis viscérale tertiaire, résistant au traitement
- Torture
- Trachome
- Transport sanitaire
- Travail forcé ou obligatoire
- Ulcère de l'estomac ou du duodenum
- Unités sanitaires
- Unités sanitaires permanentes
- Unités sanitaires temporaires
- Véhicule sanitaire
- VIH/sida

Sexe (genre)

- Apartheid (Elimination de l')
- Attaque lancée contre une population civile
- Conflits armés

- Crimes contre l'humanité
- Différence entre les taux de rémunération
- Discrimination
- Discrimination à l'égard des femmes
- Distinction de caractère défavorable
- Discriminations
- Droit qu'à toute personne de jouir de conditions de travail justes et favorables
- Droits civils, politiques, économiques, sociaux et culturels
- Education de l'enfant
- Egalité de rémunération entre la main d'œuvre masculine et féminine pour travail de valeur égale
- Egalité entre les sexes et émancipations des femmes
- Néocolonialisme (élimination de toutes les formes de)
- Nouvel ordre économique international
- Persécutions
- Pornographie mettant en scène des enfants
- Principe de la non-discrimination
- Prostitution des enfants
- Sexe
- Vente d'enfants
- VIH/sida
- Violence à l'égard des femmes

Sexe (Violence)

- Attaque lancée contre une population civile
- Attentat à la pudeur
- Conflits armés
- Contrainte à la prostitution
- Crimes contre l'humanité
- Crimes de guerre
- Esclavage sexuel
- Exploitation
- Fillettes
- Génocide
- Grossesse forcée
- Nettoyage ethnique
- Pires formes de travail des enfants (les)
- Pornographie mettant en scène des enfants
- Prostitution
- Prostitution des enfants
- Prostitution forcée
- Réduction en esclavage

- Stérilisation forcée
- Torture
- Tourisme sexuel
- Toutes les formes de violence contre les femmes et les filles
- Traite des êtres humains en vue de la prostitution
- Traite des êtres humains et de l'exploitation de la prostitution d'autrui (la)
- Traitements humiliants et dégradants
- Vente d'enfants
- Viol
- Viol systématique des femmes en temps de guerre
- Violence à l'égard des femmes
- Violence sexuelle

Social

- Afrique
- Afrique subsaharienne
- Causes socioéconomiques profondes du trafic illicite de migrants
- Communauté
- Comportement ou la conduite d'un jeune qui n'est pas conforme aux normes et valeurs sociales (le)
- Conditions primordiales du progrès et du développement
- Culture
- Délinquant juvénile
- Démocratie
- Désarmement
- Développement
- Développement et le progrès dans le domaine social (le)
- Discrimination
- Discrimination à l'égard des femmes
- Discrimination raciale
- Discriminations
- Doctrine de supériorité fondée sur la différenciation entre les races
- Droit des peuples à disposer d'eux-mêmes
- Droits civils, politiques, économiques, sociaux et culturels
- Droits de l'homme
- Education familiale
- Epidémie mondiale de VIH/sida
- Extrême pauvreté et l'exclusion sociale (l')
- Famille
- Génome humain
- Handicapés
- Homme

- Incapacité
- Individus, groupes, institutions et organisations non gouvernementales
- Intérêt des enfants
- Justice pour mineurs
- Libertés fondamentales
- Maintien du colonialisme
- Maladie mentale
- Misère
- Paix et sécurité internationales
- Partage des responsabilités (le)
- Personne (toute)
- Peuples
- Peuples indigènes
- Peuples tribaux
- Pleine utilisation des ressources humaines
- Pluralisme culturel
- Politique actuellement adoptées en faveur des handicapés
- Pornographie mettant en scène des enfants
- Praticien de santé mentale
- Préjugé racial
- Principe de proportionnalité
- Processus de mondialisation
- Progrès social
- Prostitution des enfants
- Réadaptation
- Réalisations des différents peuples (les différences entre les)
- Réfugié
- Responsabilités inhérentes aux activités des chercheurs
- Sécurité sociale
- Seuil de responsabilité pénale
- Situation des peuples qui souffrent de la faim et de la sous-alimentation
- Solidarité (la)
- Tâche primordiale de tous les Etats et de toutes les organisations internationales
- Vente d'enfants
- VIH/sida
- Violence
- Violence à l'égard des femmes

Spirituel

- Attaque lancée contre une population civile
- Conflits armés
- Conviction

- Crimes contre l'humanité
- Crimes de guerre
- Culture
- Culture, la famille, les valeurs morales et la religion (la)
- Discrimination
- Discriminations
- Distinction de caractère défavorable
- Diversité culturelle
- Droit à la liberté de pensée, de conscience et de religion
- Droit à la liberté de pensée, de conscience, de religion ou de conviction
- Droits civils, politiques, économiques, sociaux et culturels
- Droits de l'homme
- Education
- Education de l'enfant
- Famille
- Génocide
- Individus, organisations non gouvernementales et institutions compétentes
- Infractions graves
- Intolérance et discriminations fondées sur la religion ou la conviction
- Maladie mentale
- Matériel
- Membres des forces armées
- Mépris et la violation des droits de l'homme et des libertés fondamentales (le)
- Organismes de protection civile
- Persécutions
- Personnel
- Personnel religieux
- Prisonniers de guerre
- Promotion et protection de tous les droits de l'homme et de toutes les libertés fondamentales
- Promotion et protection des droits des personnes appartenant à des minorités nationales ou ethniques, religieuses et linguistiques
- Protection civile
- Protection constante et la réalisation des droits des personnes appartenant à des minorités nationales ou ethniques, religieuses et linguistiques (la)
- Réduction en esclavage
- Réfugié
- Religion
- Signe distinctif
- Structure familiale
- Tolérance (la)
- Transport sanitaire
- Violation des lois ou coutumes de guerre

Tolérance

- Education
- Education de l'enfant
- Individus, organisations non gouvernementales et institutions compétentes
- Respect de la diversité des cultures, la tolérance, le dialogue et la coopération
- Tolérance (la)

Torture (traitement inhumains et dégradants)

- Acte de torture
- Attaque lancée contre une population civile
- Attentat à la pudeur
- Conflits armés
- Contrainte à la prostitution
- Crimes contre l'humanité
- Crimes de guerre
- Droits fondamentaux
- Expérience médicale ou scientifique
- Expériences médicales ou scientifiques non nécessitées par traitement médical
- Grossesse forcée
- Infractions graves
- Meurtre
- Mutilations
- Peine ou traitement cruel, inhumain ou dégradant
- Peines corporelles
- Prostitution forcée
- Réduction en esclavage
- Torture
- Traitements humiliants et dégradants

Travail (emploi, profession)

- Dignité
- Discrimination
- Discriminations
- Droit à la liberté de pensée, de conscience, de religion ou de conviction
- Droit au travail
- Droit qu'à toute personne de jouir de conditions de travail justes et favorables
- Egalité de rémunération entre la main d'œuvre masculine et féminine pour travail de valeur égale
- Emploi
- Enlèvement de mines
- Esclavage
- Etat d'emploi

– Etat d'origine
– Etat de transit
– Etres humains
– Exploitation
– Femmes
– Femmes rurales
– Gens de mer
– Handicapés
– Maladie mentale
– Membres de la famille
– Organisation
– Personne de condition servile
– Personnes souffrant d'incapacités
– Pires formes de travail des enfants (les)
– Prisonniers de guerre
– Profession
– Réadaptation
– Rémunération
– Sécurité sociale
– Servage
– Travail
– Travail des enfants
– Travail forcé ou obligatoire
– Travail d'une installation en mer
– Travailleurs admis pour un emploi spécifique
– Travailleurs employés au titre de projet
– Travailleurs transfrontaliers
– Travailleurs indépendants
– Travailleurs itinérants
– Travailleurs migrants
– Travailleurs migrants et membres de leur famille
– Travailleurs migrants et membres de leur famille (dépourvus de documents ou en situation irrégulière)
– Travailleurs migrants et membres de leur famille (pourvus de documents ou en situation régulière)
– Travailleurs saisonniers
– Violence à l'égard des femmes

VIH/sida

– Afrique
– Afrique subsaharienne
– Amérique Latine(région de l')

- Analphabétisme
- Asie et du Pacifique(région de l')
- Caraïbes(région de l')
- Catastrophes naturelles
- Conflits armés
- Conflits et catastrophes naturelles
- Culture, la famille, les valeurs morales et la religion (la)
- Egalité entre les sexes et émancipations des femmes
- Epidémie mondiale de VIH/sida
- Europe centrale et Orientale(région de l')
- Famille
- Opprobre, le silence, la discrimination et la dénégation ainsi que l'absence de confidentialité (l')
- Paludisme
- Pauvreté
- Populations déstabilisées par les conflits armés, les situations d'urgence humanitaire et les catastrophes naturelles
- Réalisation universelle des droits des personnes et des libertés fondamentales
- Sous-développement
- Toutes les formes de violence contre les femmes et les filles
- VIH/sida

Les Documents Applicables

Code de conduite pour les responsables de l'application des lois (17 décembre 1979)

Convention concernant la discrimination (emploi et profession) (N° 111, O.I.T.)(25 juin 1958)

Convention concernant la lutte contre la discrimination dans le domaine de l'enseignement (14 décembre 1960)

Convention contre la torture et autres peines ou traitement cruels, inhumains ou dégradants (10 décembre 1984)

Convention de Genève relative à la protection des personnes civiles en temps de guerre du 12 août 1949 (21 avril-12 août 1949)

Convention de Genève relative au traitement des prisonniers de guerre (21 avril-12 août 1949)

Convention internationale contre le recrutement, l'utilisation, le financement et l'instruction de mercenaires (4 décembre 1989)

Convention internationale sur l'élimination de toutes les formes de discrimination raciale (21 décembre 1965)

Convention internationale sur la protection des droits de tous les travailleurs migrants et des membres de leur famille (18 décembre 1990)

Convention pour la prévention et la répression du crime de génocide (9 décembre 1948)

Convention pour la répression de la traite des êtres humains et de l'exploitation de la prostitution d'autrui (2 décembre 1949)

Convention relative à l'esclavage (25 septembre 1926)

Convention relative au statut des apatrides (26 avril 1954)

Convention relative au statut des réfugiés (14 décembre 1950)

Convention relative aux droits de l'enfant (20 novembre 1989)

Convention relative aux peuples indigènes et tribaux (N° 169, O.I.T.) (27 juin 1989)

Convention supplémentaire relative à l'abolition de l'esclavage, de la traite des esclaves et des institutions et pratiques analogues à l'esclavage (7 septembre 1956)

Convention sur l'abolition du travail forcé (N°105, O.I.T.)(25 juin 1957)

Convention sur l'âge minimum (N° 138, O.I.T.) (26 juin 1973)

Convention sur l'égalité de rémunération (N° 100, O.I.T.)(29 juin 1951)

Convention sur l'élimination de toutes les formes de discrimination à l'égard des femmes (18 décembre 1979)

Convention sur l'imprescriptibilité des crimes de guerre et des crimes contre l'humanité (26 novembre 1968)

Convention sur la liberté syndicale et la protection du droit syndical (N° 87, O.I.T.)(9 juillet 1948)

Convention sur la politique de l'emploi (N° 122, O.I.T.)(9 juillet 1964)

Convention sur la réduction des cas d'apatridie (4 décembre 1954)

Convention sur le consentement au mariage, à l'âge minimum du mariage et l'enregistrement des mariages (7 novembre 1962)

Convention sur le droit d'organisation et de négociation collective (N° 98, O.I.T.)(1er juillet 1949)

Convention sur le travail forcée (N° 29, O.I.T.)(28 juin 1930)

Convention sur les pires formes de travail des enfants (N° 182, O.I.T.) (17 juin 1999)

Déclaration d'engagement sur le VIH/SIDA (27 juin 2001)

Déclaration des droits des personnes appartenant à des minorités nationales ou ethniques, religieuses et linguistiques (18 décembre 1992)

Déclaration des droits personnes handicapées (9 décembre 1975)

Déclaration des droits du déficient mental (20 décembre 1971)

Déclaration des principes fondamentaux de justice relatifs aux victimes de la criminalité et aux victimes d'abus de pouvoir (29 novembre 1985)

Déclaration du Millénaire (8 septembre 2000)

Déclaration et Programme d'action de Vienne (25 juin 1993)

Déclaration sur l'élimination de la violence à l'égard des femmes (20 décembre 1993)

Déclaration sur l'élimination de toutes les formes d'intolérance et de discrimination fondées sur la religion ou la conviction(25 novembre 1981)

Déclaration sur l'octroi de l'indépendance aux pays et aux peuples coloniaux (14 décembre 1960)

Déclaration sur l'utilisation du progrès de la science et de la technique dans l'intérêt de la paix et au profit de l'humanité (10 décembre 1975)

Déclaration sur la protection de toutes les personnes contre la torture et autres peines ou traitements cruels, inhumains ou dégradants (9 décembre 1975)

Déclaration sur la protection de toutes les personnes contre les disparitions forcées (18 décembre 1992)

Déclaration sur la protection des femmes et des enfants en période d'urgence et de conflit armé (14 décembre 1974)

Déclaration sur la race et les préjugés raciaux (27 novembre 1978)

Déclaration sur le droit au développement (4 décembre 1986)

Déclaration sur le droit des peuples à la paix (12 novembre 1984)

Déclaration sur le droit et la responsabilité des individus, groupes et organes de la société de promouvoir et protéger les droits de l'homme et les libertés fondamentales universellement reconnus (9 décembre 1998)

Déclaration sur le progrès et le développement dans le domaine social (11 décembre 1969)

Déclaration sur les droits de l'homme des personnes qui ne possèdent pas la nationalité du pays dans lequel elles vivent (13 décembre 1985)

Déclaration universelle des droits de l'homme (10 décembre 1948)

Déclaration universelle pour l'élimination définitive de la faim et de la malnutrition (17 décembre 1974)

Déclaration universelle sur la diversité culturelle (2 novembre 2001)

Déclaration universelle sur le génome humain et les droits de l'homme (9 décembre 1998)

Deuxième Protocole facultatif se rapportant au Pacte international relatif aux droits civils et politiques, visant à abolir la peine de mort (15 décembre 1989)

Directives relatives aux enfants dans le système de justice pénale (21 juillet 1997)

Ensemble de principes pour la protection des toutes les personnes soumises à une forme quelconque de détention ou d'emprisonnement (9 décembre 1988)

Ensemble de règles minima des Nations Unies concernant l'administration de la justice pour mineurs (Règles de Beijing)(29 novembre 1985)

Ensemble de règles minima pour le traitement des détenus (31 juillet 1957, 13 mai 1977)

Garanties pour la protection des droits des personnes passibles de la peine de mort (17 décembre 1979)

Pacte international relatif aux droits civils et politiques (16 décembre 1966)

Pacte international relatif aux droits économiques, sociaux et culturels (16 décembre 1966)

Principes concernant le statut des institutions nationales (Principes de Paris)(20 décembre 1993)

Principes d'éthique médicale applicables au rôle du personnel de santé, en particulier des médecins, dans la protection des prisonniers et des détenus contre la torture et autres peines ou traitements cruels, inhumains ou dégradants (18 décembre 1982)

Principes de base relatifs au rôle du barreau (27 août-7 septembre 1990)

Principes de base sur le recours à la force et l'utilisation des armes à feu par les responsables de l'application des lois (27 août-7 septembre 1990)

Principes de la coopération internationale en ce qui concerne le dépistage, l'arrestation, l'extradition et le châtiment des individus coupables de crimes de guerre et de crimes contre l'humanité (3 décembre 1973)

Principes des Nations Unies pour les personnes âgées (16 décembre 1991)

Principes directeurs applicables au rôle des magistrats du parquet(27 août-7 septembre 1990)

Principes directeurs des Nations Unies pour la prévention de la délinquance juvénile (Principes directeurs de Riyad)(14 décembre 1990)

Principes fondamentaux relatifs à l'indépendance de la magistrature (29 novembre 1985, 13 décembre 1985)

Principes fondamentaux relatifs au traitement des détenus (14 décembre 1990)

Principes pour la protection des personnes atteintes de maladie mentale et pour l'amélioration des soins de santé mentale (17 décembre 1991)

Principes relatifs à la prévention efficace des exécutions extrajudiciaires, arbitraires et sommaires et aux moyens d'enquêter efficacement sur ces exécutions (24 mai 1989)

Principes relatifs aux moyens d'enquêter efficacement sur la torture et autres peines ou traitements cruels, inhumains ou dégradants pour établir la réalité des faits (4 décembre 2000)

Protocole additionnel à la Convention des Nations Unies contre la criminalité transnationale organisée, visant à prévenir, réprimer et punir la traite des personnes, en particulier des femmes et des enfants (15 novembre 2000)

Protocole additionnel aux Conventions de Genève du 12 août 1949 relatif à la protection des victimes des conflits armés internationaux (Protocole I)(8 juin 1977)

Protocole additionnel aux Conventions de Genève du 12 août 1949 relatif à la protection des victimes des conflits armés no internationaux (Protocole II)(8 juin 1977)

Protocole amendant la Convention relative à l'esclavage signée à Genève le 25 septembre 1926 (23 octobre 1953)

Protocole contre le trafic illicite de migrants par terre, air, mer, additionnel à la Convention des Nations Unies contre la criminalité transnationale organisée (15 novembre 2000)

Protocole facultatif à la Convention relative aux droits de l'enfant, concernant l'implication d'enfants dans les conflits armés (25 mai 2000)

Protocole facultatif à la Convention relative aux droits de l'enfant, concernant la vente d'enfants, la prostitution des enfants et la pornographie mettant en scène des enfants (25 mai 2000)

Protocole facultatif à la Convention sur l'élimination de toutes les formes de discrimination à l'égard des femmes (10 décembre 1999)

Protocole facultatif se rapportant à la Convention contre la torture et autres peines ou traitement cruels, inhumains ou dégradants (18 décembre 2002)

Protocole facultatif se rapportant au Pacte international relatif aux droits civils et politiques (16 décembre 1966)

Protocole instituant une Commission de conciliation et de bons offices chargée de rechercher la solution des différends qui naîtraient entre Etats parties à la Convention concernant la lutte contre la discrimination dans le domaine de l'enseignement (10 décembre 1962)

Protocole relatif au statut des réfugiés (18 novembre 1966)

Recommandation sur le consentement au mariage, à l'âge minimum du mariage et l'enregistrement des mariages (1er novembre 1965)

Règles des Nations Unies pour la protection des mineurs privés de liberté (14 décembre 1990)

Règles minima des Nations Unies pour l'élaboration de mesures non privatives de liberté (Règles de Tokyo) (14 décembre 1990)

Règles pour l'égalisation des chances des personnes handicapées (20 décembre 1993)

Résolution 1803 (XVII) de l'Assemblée générale en date du 14 décembre 1962 : « Souveraineté permanente sur les ressources naturelles » (14 décembre 1962)

Statut de Rome de la Cour pénale internationale (17 juillet 1998)

Statut du Tribunal international chargé de poursuivre les personnes présumées responsables de violations graves du droit international humanitaire commises sur le territoire de l'ex-Yougoslavie depuis 1991 (25 mai 1993)

Statut du Tribunal pénal international chargé de juger les personnes présumées responsables d'actes de génocide ou d'autres violations graves du droit international humanitaire commis sur le territoire du Rwanda et les citoyens rwandais présumés responsables de tels actes ou violations commis sur le territoire d'Etats voisins entre le 1er janvier 1994 et le 31 décembre 1994 (8 novembre 1994)